Translated Texts for Historians

This series is designed to meet the needs of students of ancient and medieval history and others who wish to broaden their study by reading source material, but whose knowledge of Latin or Greek is not sufficient to allow them to do so in the original languages. Many important Late Imperial and Dark Age texts are currently unavailable in translation and it is hoped that TTH will help to fill this gap and to complement the secondary literature in English which already exists. The series relates principally to the period 300-800 AD and includes Late Imperial, Greek, Byzantine and Syriac texts as well as source books illustrating a particular period or theme. Each volume is a self-contained scholarly translation with an introductory essay on the text and its author and notes on the text indicating major problems of interpretation, including textual difficulties.

Editorial Committee

Sebastian Brock, Oriental Institute, University of Oxford
Averil Cameron, Keble College, Oxford
Henry Chadwick, Oxford
John Davies, University of Liverpool
Carlotta Dionisotti, King's College London
Peter Heather, University College London
Robert Markus, University of Nottingham
John Matthews, Queen's College, Oxford
Raymond Van Dam, University of Michigan
Michael Whitby, University of Warwick
Ian Wood, University of Leeds

General Editors

Gillian Clark, University of Liverpool
Mary Whitby, Royal Holloway, London

Front cover: Part of base of gold-glass beaker in the British Museum, c. 4th Century AD.

D1336321

A full list of published titles in the Translated Texts for Historians series is available from the publishers.

The following are the most recent published volumes:

The Lives of the Ninth-Century Popes (*Liber Pontificalis*)
Translated with an introduction and commentary by RAYMOND DAVIS
Volume 20: 360pp., 1995, ISBN 0-85323-479-5

Bede: On the Temple
Translated with notes by SEÁN CONNOLLY,
introduction by JENNIFER O'REILLY
Volume 21: 192pp., 1995, ISBN 0-85323-049-8

Pseudo-Dionysius of Tel-Mahre: *Chronicle*, Part III
Translated with notes and introduction by WITOLD WITAKOWSKI
Volume 22: 192pp., 1995, ISBN 0-85323-760-3

Venantius Fortunatus: Personal and Political Poems
translated with notes and introduction by JUDITH GEORGE
Volume 23: 192pp., 1995, ISBN 0-85323-179-6

For full details of Translated Texts for Historians, including prices and ordering information, please write to the following:

All countries, except the USA and Canada: Liverpool University Press, Senate House, Abercromby Square, Liverpool, L69 3BX, UK (*tel* 0151-794 2233, *fax* 0151-708 6502).

USA and Canada: University of Pennsylvania Press, Blockley Hall, 418 Service Drive, Philadelphia, PA 19104-6097, USA (*tel* [215] 898-6264, *fax* [215] 898-0404).

Translated Texts for Historians
Volume 20

The Lives of the Ninth-Century Popes
(Liber Pontificalis)

THE ANCIENT BIOGRAPHIES OF
TEN POPES FROM A.D. 817-891

Translated with an introduction
and commentary by
RAYMOND DAVIS

Liverpool
University
Press

First published 1995 by
Liverpool University Press
Senate House
Abercromby Square
Liverpool
L69 3BX

British Library Cataloguing-in-Publication Data
A British Library CIP Record is available
ISBN 0-85323-479-5

Printed in the European Union by
Page Bros, Norwich, England

CONTENTS

PREFACE

This volume fulfils the promise made in the introduction to my *Lives of the Eighth-Century Popes*. It contains a translation of and commentary on some three-eighths of the *Liber Pontificalis* of the Roman church, from A.D. 817 to the point where what Duchesne called 'l'ancien livre pontifical' finally expires. The precise terminal date is given on the title page as A.D. 891, but the reader should be warned that the text of the life of Hadrian II stops at the end of the year 870, that there is then a gap for the last two years of that pope's life, that the next three popes are omitted entirely, and that the fragment dealing with Stephen V (886-891) breaks off after perhaps no more than the first year or two of his pontificate. No lives were written for the next two centuries. Many manuscripts contain catalogues with little beyond the names and tenures of the popes in this period. These catalogues may be found in Duchesne's edition (and see Piazzoni 1989-90), but are not included here, any more than are the more extended biographies which were resumed from the time of Gregory VII and were continued by various writers down to the fifteenth century.

The format of the present volume is very closely modelled on that covering the eighth century, and the introduction to that volume explains the policies adopted with regard to the numbering of the chapters (Vignoli's system as given in Duchesne's text), the paragraphing (almost entirely Duchesne's), and the rendering of proper names. As before, the text translated is Duchesne's, though his punctuation is not held sacrosanct; attention is drawn in the commentary to a few small variations from his text, and there too will be found suggestions for some of the *loci corrupti* which that great scholar did not attempt to mend. Year-headings are inserted where Geertman's study (*More veterum*) of the building-works and donations in certain of these lives enabled him to establish the year-divisions in the archival documents incorporated in the text; they are likely to be at least approximately correct. For the lengthy life of Leo IV, not analysed by Geertman, I have ventured a chronology (pp. 108-110) but not risked inserting it into the translation; so too for the life of Nicholas (pp. 203-4). In the commentary I have attempted to include whatever material in Duchesne's notes still seems valid and useful.

As before, my debts are many. T. F. X. Noble's *Republic of St Peter* has remained of great benefit for the lives of the earlier part of this century; for the later lives Janet Nelson's works have been invaluable, especially her translation of the *Annals of St-Bertin*, published (1991) in the Manchester series of Ninth-Century Histories.

I have been particularly fortunate in having had the services of Clive Cheesman, who has pondered the entire translation and made large numbers of suggestions for improvement, the great majority of which I have adopted; his influence has been much greater than it has been possible to acknowledge in the commentary. My colleagues in Belfast have also been most helpful: I single out Brian Scott who has so readily shared with me his thoughts on many 'difficult' passages that I submitted to him, and Margaret Mullett and Dion Smyth who have been a mine of information on matters Byzantine; Fred Williams and Brian Campbell have also supplied useful advice. Errors that remain are, of course, my own responsibility. The map of Rome, reproduced from the earlier volume, results from the cartographic skills of Christa Mee. I am most grateful to the Queen's University of Belfast for a grant towards the costs of publication.

It is a great sadness to me that Margaret Gibson, to whose learning, encouragement, common sense, enthusiasm, and practical advice throughout this project I, with all contributors to this series, owe so much, has not lived to see the publication of this volume.

INTRODUCTION

In this volume are given the last ten lives from the ancient, continuous, *Liber Pontificalis* of the Roman Church. The lives differ markedly from each other in character: the broken fragment of life 101 (Eugene II) composed in very simple language; the lengthy high-flown eulogy in life 102 of the ephemeral pope Valentine. Yet (except for 102) all the lives down to 107 (Nicholas) are much taken up with lists of building-works and enrichments for churches at Rome. Life 107, however, has been reworked; as is explained in the introduction to that life (p. 189), the text was taken over by a writer (possibly John Hymmonides the Deacon) who inserted a number of historical passages, some even at the cost of excising parts of an already-prepared text; while life 108, which contains no material on buildings and endowments and is probably the work of the interpolator of life 107, is entirely devoted to 'straight history'.

Life 108 in fact breaks off two years before the death of its subject, albeit with a good finishing flourish. The introduction to that life (pp. 249-50) suggests that the author's political views and the politics of the time would have made it very difficult for him to continue without treading on thin ice. And the next three popes found (it seems) no biographers. Then life 112 (Stephen V), a mere fragment, shows that the task of compilation was again taken up after an interval of some 15 years; the author of this fragment plays safe by incorporating, uniquely, a sermon delivered by the pope against witchcraft and against talking in church. But the fragment was a mere flicker before the LP was finally extinguished.

What caused this cessation? An answer to this question may provide some insight into the very nature of the LP. Undoubtedly the troubles of the Roman church in the next few decades played a part in the failure of papal biographers to continue their task: under the short-lived successors of Formosus, violently quarrelling with each other over their attitude to Formosus, it would have been as difficult for biographers to write as it was for the author of life 108 to finish his task. Even so, had they confined themselves, as the authors of many earlier lives did, to neutral statements about the background and ordination of each pope, and then to listing endowments, the task would not have been impossible. The LP ceased mainly because it had already been taken out of the hands of authors who were prepared to write in this way, and thus the tradition of compilation in the milieu from which earlier lives had emerged had already been broken.

Who, then, were the anonymous biographers who had compiled the

LP decade after decade, and why had they done so? I remain satisfied that Duchesne was right to see in the *vestiarium* at the Lateran the milieu in which generations of compilers lived and worked. The view has been challenged. Caspar thought that Duchesne was right only for the lives down to the middle of the eighth century, after which stage the compilers came from the Lateran *scrinium* (chancery). In an important article Noble (1985) holds that the authors throughout were notaries from the chancery. He stresses the reference to the creation by pope Fabian in the mid-third century of notaries to record martyr-acts (LP 21:2, BP 8); the remark about the death of Ambrose, *primicerius* of the notaries (94:24); and the concentration in life 96 on the career of the *primicerius* Christopher. Yet the statement about Fabian is legendary, if not fiction; the death of Ambrose is an interpolation into the text; and it would hardly have been possible to deal with the pontificate of Stephen III without giving prominence to Christopher. It is more significant that in life 97 (cc. 64, 67) the compiler adds epithets in commendation of Januarius, the *vestiarius* then in post. Nowhere else in the LP is any Lateran bureaucrat praised. The author of this late eighth-century life was surely Januarius's subordinate; and there seems no reason why most of the lives of the ninth century should not come from the same milieu, just as lives before the seventh century had done: note, for instance, the interest shown in the sacking of the *vestiarium* by Maurice and Isaac before the ordination of pope Severinus in 640 (73:1-5, BP 65-6). There may be exceptions: perhaps the history of the fall of the Lombard kingdom which forms the first part of the life of Hadrian I is from elsewhere. But otherwise it seems much more satisfactory to assume that the LP, devoting as it does so much space to church buildings and enrichment, comes from the hands of clerks who worked in the very office where these matters were the prime concern. Perhaps, though, it matters little whether the writers came from one Lateran office or another. It is enough to accept that until Nicholas's time they were not among the ecclesiastical or lay nobility of Rome; they were, relatively, humble clerks.

    Why did they write at all? As explained in my *Book of Pontiffs* (iv-v), the origins of the LP are to be found in the propaganda battles of the schism at the very beginning of the sixth century when Symmachus and Laurentius fought for possession of the Roman see. Once written and consolidated by interested contemporaries down to 530 and then 538, the work was left aside. The quality of the rest of the sixth-century lives does not suggest a contemporary compiler. But from some point in the first half of the seventh century (perhaps under Honorius) the lives become ongoing compilations by contemporary writers; and I can see no reason to suppose that this ever ceased to be so, even in the ninth century (note especially the curious case, already mentioned, of the life of pope Valentine), though naturally one cannot exclude touching up after the death of the subject of each biography. Why, then, from the early seventh century to the late ninth did contemporary clerks compile these biographies? Never to be underestimated is the 'lethargy-factor': a job was to be done because it had 'always' (as compilers would have imagined) been done, much as ceremonies continue to be performed long after their purpose has been forgotten. Nor, in so far as there were more positive purposes, should we conclude that these were necessarily the same in each generation; or that the motives of compilers can necessarily be deduced from the uses to which the finished product was put.

Noble (1985) suggests three motives: the LP was an official version of papal history for the training of young clerics; but, since much of the material was too advanced for use at this level, it was also to be a ready-reference work for veterans; and it was to act as an inventory of archives (presumably, though, the archives of the *vestiarium* rather than those of the chancery). That the LP may have been used at Lucca for the education of clerics (though to what purpose is baffling) tells nothing about the education of clerics at Rome; and I cannot help feeling that if the LP was used as a textbook someone would at some point have done something about the Latin style and syntax. Some Roman clergy may have learnt from it; but I cannot believe it was written to be part of a regular curriculum. The second motive suggested supposes that the record of relations, political or ecclesiastical, with Byzantines, Lombards and Franks is complete enough to be useful. It is not; for the Franks it is sufficient to note the hiatus in the account of Charlemagne's dealings with Hadrian I and Leo III from 774 to 799 and after 800, or the inadequate account given in the life of Gregory IV, which manages not to mention that pope's personal intervention north of the Alps. The third suggested motive depends on what, to us, is self-evident: a record office is useless without an inventory or catalogue of some kind. Yet if the LP was written to provide an archival inventory, it is difficult to see how a researcher would actually be helped by it to find anything. We should not assume that any ancient archive was easy to consult, or that the order of documents was ever more than chronological (if that). Archives were kept as often as not, I suspect, because it seemed wrong to throw documents away, rather than in any expectation that the preserved material would be consulted, or with any plan to make life easy for researchers. The 'lethargy-factor' worked here as well. The archive material which is incorporated in the LP (in a very summary fashion and with no obvious principle of selection) is there because it recorded what was, in the rather narrow outlook of the compilers, the chief way in which each pope had glorified God, St Peter, and the Roman church - the institution with which the authors' loyalty lay. It is this loyalty, not their deliberate purpose, that they reveal. As Noble (1985:356) rightly stresses, by compiling an institutional history of an unprecedented kind the writers succeeded in depicting the 'ceaseless march through time of a seemingly timeless institution'. But I doubt whether that was the conscious motive of any of the successive biographers.

Under Nicholas the compilation was taken over by one or more writers from a higher status in society, whose purpose was closer to what we understand as historiographical, but who soon found that the task of writing both fully and honestly was one that they could not sustain. Compilation ceased because the tradition was cut; except for its brief flicker under Stephen V the candle was snuffed out. Even the last lives that had been compiled seem not to have become widely known, even at Rome. When in the late 930s Flodoard of Rheims visited Rome to find material for the verses he was composing on all the popes back to Peter, he was well received by pope Leo VII, and the finished product shows that he had access to a copy of the LP. But his copy, it is clear, did not extend beyond life 107 (Nicholas); for the next 22 popes, but never earlier, his verses depend on the verse epitaphs on the papal graves at St Peter's, many of which still survive and can be compared with his efforts (his only other source for this period seems to have been the letters exchanged between the popes and the archbishops of Rheims). Even life 108 (Hadrian II) was unavailable to him, let alone the fragment on Stephen V or any other lives if such existed. It is hardly likely that he was denied access to an up-dated LP, or that having made the effort to come to Rome he was too unconcerned to seek it out (Duchesne II. IX-XI).

The manuscript tradition and variant recensions.

The later the life, the fewer the manuscripts. This results from the fact that our surviving MSS are all copies of on-going texts which left Rome at different dates and therefore ended at different points. The earlier the text left Rome, the longer the opportunities for its diffusion. By life 100, with which the present volume begins, there are only five manuscripts of the full text, and the situation deteriorates even further in the ninth century. Lives 109 to 111 are missing entirely (if they were ever written), while the last paragraph of life 112, the last in the series, is known from only one manuscript, itself incomplete.

Apart from normal textual variants, the manuscripts bear witness to different recensions; the text did not have the sacrosanctity of a literary work, and the very fact of its anonymity may even have encouraged interpolations in and modifications to the existing text. In some cases manuscripts show a strong tendency to regularize spelling and grammar to accord with classical norms. In the present volume, the most startling textual variation is in the second half of life 104, where the lost E^5 provided a totally different recension; and political considerations may explain the absence of life 106 from C^4 and the fact that D ends with life 105.

Until the 11th century editorial activity only occasionally took the form of deliberate excision of material. But from the 11th century on, new recensions were produced which treated the ancient text in a much more cavalier fashion. For example, the earliest of these, that of Adhémar of Chabannes, has a text down to life 105 showing many alterations to the text and heavily abbreviating longer lives by excising most of the register-type material on donations and repairs to churches as no longer of interest. The same can be said of other medieval recensions. In the twelfth century Cardinal Pandulf produced what is known as the 'third edition' of the LP (known from the *Codex Dertusensis* and from Petrus Gulielmus' manuscript, *Vaticanus* 3762, see Přerovský's edition), which was itself designed as a preliminary to newly composed lives beginning with Gregory VII. Medieval recensions are not much help for the text of the earlier lives; at the most they reflect the readings of one manuscript of the standard text which was used to produce a new edition. The recensions provide, in Duchesne's view, no help in any of the difficult passages.

THE MANUSCRIPTS OF THE LIBER PONTIFICALIS FOR THE LIVES FROM A.D. 817 ONWARDS.

Group C:

C^4: *Parisinus* 5140, 11th century, has the lives down to 105:109, followed by 107 and 108; earlier parts of the text, which can be compared with other MSS of the group, show that it thoroughly reworks the style and grammar; Duchesne found it difficult to record its readings but gave them where he considered them important.

Group D:

D: *Parisinus* 5516, from Tours, written before mid-871; Duchesne preferred its readings to those of other MSS for lives 98ff. It lacks 102 and ends at 105:66 (a second hand continues to 105:79). For these lives Duchesne gives all its readings other than spelling variants.

Group E:

E^1: *Vaticanus* 3764, from Cava or Farfa, end of 11th century; this is the only manuscript which continues through to the last known paragraph of life 112. Five copies, made in the 16th and 17th centuries, are known, and it was the basis of all the pre-Duchesne editions. Duchesne gives its readings in full, even the very frequent grammatical improvements, and also the corrections made in the MS, which he thinks represent a collation with its original.

E^2: *Parisinus* 5143, 14th century, is much the same as E^1 but, though not derived from it, is less valuable; it stops at 112:18.

E^5 (lost): *Farnesianus*, an uncial 9th century MS; some folios were already missing when the existing collations by Holstein and Bianchini were made; the MS then contained, of the present lives, only part of 104 (in a startlingly different recension, known also to pseudo-Liutprand). Duchesne gives all known details of its readings; from 104:21 he prints its text in a separate column. For earlier lives its text was close to E^{126}; its loss is unfortunate given the late date of MSS of this class, and it is even more unfortunate that before its disappearance so much was already missing, most tantalizingly the last part of 104.

E^6: *Laurentianus* LXVI, 35, 15th century (closest to E^{12} but full of faults, gaps, and arbitrary changes); it stops at 112:15.

Duchesne saw no point in regularly giving the readings of E^{26}. But where all other MSS fail in the last part of 105 and all of 106 and 112, rather than follow E^1 alone he does consider E^{26}, even though all three are members of the same group.

The later recensions are represented by the following MSS.

The recension compiled c. 1030 by Adhémar of Chabannes is represented by:

Alentianus 18, 11th century (has the lives down to 105:84; the manuscript was used by Orderic Vitalis as source for his own brief lives of the popes, appended to Book II of his *Ecclesiastical History*);

Rotomagensis 31, 11th century (probably a copy of the last, but with alterations and abridgments);

Parisinus 5094, 11th century, with a text identical to the *Alentianus*; and

Ottobonianus 2629, 15th century, which has the same text but with some contamination from a different recension, and also has the Scholia on the LP of Peter, bishop of Orvieto in the 14th century.

Parisinus 5145, 15th century, has a similar text, though now down to 104:24 only, and the Scholia.

It seems that Adhémar himself produced an abridgment of his own recension, with a version of life 108 not found elsewhere (see pp. 293-4); it is represented by:

Parisinus 2400, 11th century, which goes down to life 107;

Parisinus 2268, 11th century has the same text, as does

Parisinus 5517, end of 11th century.

The text from which Adhémar worked for these lives seems to have been a MS similar to, but not identical with, D.

Around 1120, Lambert, canon of St Omer, produced his *Liber Floridus* (the original MS survives, *Gandavensis* 92), but for these lives he based himself on the Annals of St Bertin. At least 10 descendants of the surviving MS are known.

The English recension of the time of William of Malmesbury:

Cantabrigiensis 2021 (KK IV 6) has a version of the LP partly abridged and partly with much interpolated material; for these lives it has a list of popes only.

Harleianus 633, 12th century, has a similar arrangement.

From the above listing one can quantify the decline in the number of available MSS as the text proceeds. Excluding the later recensions there are, with all or most of each of lives 100-101 and 103, 5 MSS; for 102, 105, 107-108, 4 MSS; and for 106 and 112 merely 3.

TEXTS AND COMMENTARIES

Le Liber Pontificalis, Texte, introduction et commentaire, ed. L. Duchesne, 2 volumes, 1886-1892; reissued by Cyrille Vogel, 1955-57, with a third volume in part updating the commentary and with useful bibliography and full indexes. The three volumes are cited as Duchesne, I, II and III; the text of lives 100-112 is in Duchesne, II.

Monseigneur Duchesne et son temps, Actes du Colloque organisé par l'école française de Rome (23-25 mai 1973), Collection de l'école française de Rome 23 (Rome, 1975) has various articles including C. Pietri, 'Duchesne et la topographie romaine', 23-48, and C. Vogel, 'Le *Liber Pontificalis* dans l'édition de Louis Duchesne. État de la question', 99-127.

Anastasii abbatis opera omnia : *Patrologia Latina*, volumes 127-8, ed. J.-P. Migne, Paris, 1852. This reprints the Bianchini edition of 1718 with the pre-Duchesne text of the LP, but without commentaries for the lives of this period.

Liber Pontificalis nella recensione di Pietro Guglielmo O.S.B. et del card. Pandolfo, glossato da Pietro Bohler, ed. Ulderico Přerovský, (3 vols., Studia Gratiana 21-23, Rome, 1978), contains the 'Third edition' of the LP, which heavily shortened the texts of these lives; Přerovský prints Duchesne's text for comparison.

The Turin and other medieval catalogues of churches are in C. Hülsen, *Le Chiese di Roma* (Florence, 1927), and R. Valentini & G. Zucchetti, *Codice topografico della città di Roma*, volume 3 (Rome, 1946).

For other primary sources see the lists in Nelson, *AB*, and Reuter, *AF*.

ABBREVIATIONS

Most of these are standard; below are listed those which are particularly frequent or may mystify.

AB   *Les Annales de Saint-Bertin*, ed. F. Grat, J. Vieillard and S. Clémencet (Paris, 1964); translation and commentary by Janet Nelson, *The Annals of St-Bertin*, Ninth-century histories, volume 1 (Manchester, 1991).

AF   *Annales Fuldenses*, ed. F. Kurze, *MGH SSrG* 7 (Hannover, 1891); translation and commentary by Timothy Reuter, *The Annals of Fulda*, Ninth-century histories, volume 2 (Manchester, 1992).

ARF   *Annales Regni Francorum (741-829)*, ed. F. Kurze, *MGH SSrG* 6 (Hannover, 1895); translation by B. W. Scholz and B. Rogers, in *Carolingian Chronicles* (Ann Arbor, 1970), 37-125.

BP   *The Book of Pontiffs (Liber Pontificalis)*, translated with an introduction by Raymond Davis (Liverpool, 1989).

JP   Jaffé, *Regesta Pontificum Romanorum ab condita ecclesia ad a. 1198*, 2ª edit. cur. S. Loewenfeld, F. Kaltenbrunner, P. Wald, 2 vols. (Berlin 1885-88, reprint Graz, 1958).

LECP   *The Lives of the Eighth-Century Popes (Liber Pontificalis)*, translated with an introduction and commentary by Raymond Davis (Liverpool, 1992).

MGH   *Monumenta Germaniae Historica:*
       Cap   *Capitularia regum Francorum*
       Conc   *Concilia aevi karolini*
       DD C III   *Diplomata Caroli III*
       DD O I   *Diplomata Ottonis I*
       Ep   *Epistulae*
       EKA   *Epistulae Merowingici et Karolini Aevi*
       SS   *Scriptores*
       SSrG   *Scriptores rerum Germanicarum in usum scholarum*
       SSrL   *Scriptores rerum Langobardicarum et Italicarum*

100. PASCHAL (817-824).

This life shows the signs, which began with life 99 and become the norm for the next few lives, of slipshod composition, especially in chronological data. The author provides a fairly basic account of Paschal's character and career to his ordination, mentions his concern for captives, and then devotes the rest of the text, except for the concluding formulae, to Paschal's foundations, buildings, donations and associated events. All this is written in a rather convoluted style which can create obscurities, not clarified by a penchant for using plural participles with a singular meaning or by a predilection for the verb *cōmere* (and its adjective *compte*). It is true that Paschal's works in Rome were important. His buildings suggest a continuation of Leo III's attempts to renew the face of Rome according to early Christian models, and the footnotes attempt to draw attention to the architectural features at S. Prassede (cc. 8-10), S. Maria in Domnica (cc. 11-13) and S. Cecilia in Trastevere (cc. 14-21). These churches were provided with remarkable mosaics, many still surviving (including portraits of Paschal: a photograph of that at S. Prassede is in *NCE* 11.1048). This provision suggests Paschal's reaction to the revival of iconoclasm by Leo V (813-820); though our author shows no more awareness of this than he does of the pope's giving refuge to Greek monks fleeing persecution and of his unsuccessful support of Theodore of Studios, the leading iconodule of the time.

But the author's blinkered approach to his task allows him to omit the even more important events connected with the Carolingian empire. The first of these is the agreement in 817 with Louis the Pious known as the *Pactum Ludovicianum* (*MGH Cap* 1.352-5); this is dealt with in *LECP* 231-3, in view of the light it throws on the very similar but less well recorded deal struck between Stephen IV and Louis in 816, which is mentioned in the LP. Soon after his election the new pope sent an embassy to Louis:

'asking that the covenant made with his predecessors should also be solemnly concluded with him. The nomenclator Theodore brought this message and was granted his request'

(*ARF* 817 Scholz 102).

By this renewed pact Louis again confirmed the pope in his possession of territories and of patrimonies further afield (listed in *LECP* 232), committed himself to a policy of not interfering in the papal state unless invited by the pope or anyone who was oppressed, and promised not to intervene in papal elections, though a new pope, after his consecration, was to notify the emperor and renew the pact. In giving these guarantees

to Stephen IV and now to Paschal, Louis went further than Charlemagne
had ever done. Harmony between church and empire generally ensued.
When Louis divided his empire in 817 he had Paschal confirm it.
Around 818 (J2550, *MGH Ep* 5.68 no. 10) Paschal wrote to Louis about
the reverence due to priests and reminded him about the vows he had
shortly before made, in front of relics, his clerics and the faithful, to
defend St Peter's affairs in his own jurisdiction. In 821 Louis received
Paschal's envoys, bishop Peter of Centumcellae and the *nomenclator*
Leo and soon dismissed them. Then Paschal sent his legates Theodore
the *primicerius* (father-in-law of the *nomenclator* Leo) and Florus the
superista, who in October 821 came to Thionville with rich gifts for the
marriage of Louis's son king Lothar I to Irmengard (*ARF* 821 Scholz
108-9; Astronomer, *Vita Hludovici Pii* 34). When Louis chose Ebbo (on
whom see 104:16) to evangelize the Danes, he first sent him to Rome,
late in 822; Paschal commended him and Halitgar bishop of Cambrai,
and appointed the former as his legate in the north (J2553, *MGH Ep*
5.68-9 no. 11).

Meanwhile Paschal ruled the papal state without Frankish
interference. When Lothar was in Italy, dispensing justice on his father's
instructions (this was not new: Lothar and some of his closest advisers
had been in Italy a number of times since 822), Paschal invited him to
Rome and on Easter Sunday, 5 April 823, gave him 'the crown of the
kingdom and the title of Emperor and Augustus', with a ceremony
(added to the ritual used for Charlemagne in 800) by which he presented
the new emperor with a sword to symbolize his duty to suppress evil.
From Rome Lothar returned in June to Pavia where Louis now was
(*ARF* 823; Scholz 112-3; Astronomer, 36). This coronation, which must
have been with Louis's agreement, strengthened the idea that an
emperor owed his title to coronation by the pope (Stephen IV had
crowned Louis at Rheims in 816) but that the ceremony ought better to
occur, as in 800, at Rome.

But there was more than this to Lothar's appearance in Rome. All
was not well, though certainty about what was wrong is unattainable:
the evidence is 'scanty and enigmatic, but it points in a straight line to
turbulence and unsavory behavior' (Noble, 309). It seems that Paschal's
style of government had gained him enemies, especially among the
nobles; and given the strength of papal control, these enemies could turn
nowhere but to the Franks. In Rome, Lothar issued a judgment in favour
of the abbey of Farfa being exempt from papal taxes, a marker, perhaps,
both that Paschal could expect more imperial interference and that his
enemies could expect support from Lothar if they wanted it. The late
ninth-century *Libellus de imperatoria potestate in urbe Roma* (ed.

Zucchetti, *FSI* vol. 55, pp. 197-8) states that at this time all the 'greater men of the city had become adherents of the emperor'. No doubt the pope still had his supporters (certainly those mentioned in the story below who acted as envoys on his behalf, and the bishops, evidently from a wide area, who joined him in his oath of purgation), but that he had enemies and that they had grievances is clear from the remarks, albeit inexplicit, of Paschasius Radbertus (*Vita Walae*, 1.28). Next year the *Constitutio Romana* (*MGH Cap* 1.323, no. 161, cc. 2, 6) would refer to unjust seizures of land, depredations by papal officials, and church possessions seized as if by papal permission. In 962 the *Ottonianum* (*MGH DD O I* 326, no. 235) would refer to unpardonable deeds at this time. Lothar's coronation at Rome would have given Paschal's opponents time and opportunity to put forward their grievances; after all, the *Ludovicianum* had allowed appeals to the emperor by those oppressed within the papal state. It is regrettable that

'only the dim outlines of the problems of these years can be perceived by historians because papal biographers usually supplied few details, and Frankish writers were generally in the dark because Carolingian inquests, of which there were many, repeatedly crashed against walls of silence. Factional squabbles, probably having something to do with land battles and court cases, seem to have been behind all these difficulties. More cannot be said with confidence.'

(Noble, 312)

The climax soon came. In July 823 Louis heard that the already-mentioned Theodore and Leo, the *primicerius* and the *nomenclator*, had been blinded and decapitated in the Lateran,

'and that this fate had befallen them because they had always acted loyally towards the young emperor Lothar. There were also some who said that this had been done on either the order or the advice of Pope Paschal'

(*ARF* 823 Scholz 113; cf. Astronomer, 37). There seem to have been at least two other victims, Floro and Sergius (mentioned in the *Constitutio Romana*). Even if, as Paschal later admitted, it was members of St Peter's *familia* (the farmer soldiers of the rural *domuscultae*) rather than the pope himself who instigated the action, these Lateran officials must have been seen as more loyal to the Franks than to Paschal. Perhaps the victims' friends now appealed to Louis at Aachen; but whether asked to intervene or not, Louis decided to act:

'Adalung, abbot of the monastery of St. Vaast, and Hunfrid, count of Chur, were dispatched with orders to get to the bottom of this matter. But before they departed, envoys of Pope Paschal arrived, Bishop John of Silva Candida and Benedict, archdeacon of the Holy Apostolic See, pleading with the emperor to exonerate the pope from the infamous rumor that he had consented to the murder of the men in question. When the emperor had given a reasonable answer and dismissed them, he ordered his envoys to go to Rome, as previously decided, and to find out the truth'

(*ARF* 823 Scholz 113; cf. Astronomer, 37).

But this commission was never able to carry out the investigation or put anyone on trial. In the presence of the envoys at the Lateran that autumn, copying the action of Leo III in 800, Paschal and many bishops purged themselves on oath of any wrongdoing (cf. Adelson and Baker 1952:35-80). Paschal thus forestalled any attempt by Louis to interfere in the papal state.

'The envoys who went to Rome could not determine exactly what had happened. Pope Paschal, with a large number of bishops (34 bishops, 5 priests and deacons, Thegan, *Gesta Hludowici imperatoris* 30), purged himself by oath from any complicity in this deed. On the other hand, he defended with great vigor the murders of the above-mentioned men because they belonged to the *familia* of St Peter, condemned the dead as guilty of lèse majesté, and proclaimed that they had been justly slain'

(*ARF* 823 Scholz 113-4).

As Noble, 310, observes, if Romans who attacked the pope were committing an offence amounting to treason, this speaks 'eloquently for the independence of the pope's position within the empire'; but we are not told that the imperial side would have accepted this argument, and it is likely that Louis was becoming convinced that closer control over Rome was necessary. Next Paschal

'sent to the emperor Bishop John of Silva Candida and the librarian Sergius, as well as the subdeacon Quirinus and the master of the horse Leo along with the afore-mentioned envoys who had been dispatched to him. When the emperor heard from these men as well as from his own envoys of the pontiff's oath and the vindication of the defendants, he believed that there was nothing else for him to do in this matter and sent Bishop John and his companions back to the pope with a suitable answer'

(*ARF* 823 Scholz 113-4; cf. Astronomer, 37; Thegan, 30). When these envoys returned to Rome, they

'found the pope in bad health and already near death. In fact he died within a few days after their arrival...'

(*ARF* 824 Scholz 115);

a disputed papal election ensued. Thus Paschal did not live to see the closer control over Rome introduced by the *Constitutio Romana*, for which see the introduction to the next life. Events of the kind here ignored by the LP were nothing new (compare the happenings of 767-772, 799, and 815), and would recur, whatever measures were taken by the Carolingians to impose greater control.

100. 1. PASCHAL [I, 25 January 817 - 16 February 824[1]], of Roman origin, son of Bonosus,[2] held the see 7 years [0] months 17 days. From[3] his earliest youth he was bound over to the worship of God, and at the holy church's patriarchate[4] he was imbued with the study of God's saving Scripture; spiritually trained both in psalm-chanting and in the sacred pages of the New and Old Testaments, elegant, and perfect in all goodness, he was made subdeacon and afterwards honourably consecrated priest.[5] He was holy, chaste, godly, innocent, outspoken, devout, fully pure, and he was most cheerful and happy in opportunely distributing all he had as alms to the poor. So he frequently applied himself to talking of the things of God with religious and holy monks as an unremitting duty by day and night, and he humbly and becomingly throve on prayers, vigils and daily fasting.

2. When his predecessor the thrice-blessed lord pope Leo noticed he was so untiring in all this endeavour, and was devout and religious, he entrusted him with the rule of St Stephen the first martyr's monastery, called Major,[6] close to the basilica of St Peter prince of the apostles, for

---

[1] For Paschal's death on 16 February 824 (with Eugene II's ordination on Sunday 21 February) see 101:1 n. 1. For Paschal's tenure, the variants in the LP MSS are (C) 6 years 17 days, (E) 7 years 5 months 16 days; the Montecassino Catalogue has 7 years 16 days. Read 7 years 22 days (xxii for xvii); or accept 7 years 16 days, from Sunday 1 February 817, but the vacancy from 24/25 January in 817 is given as '2 days' (99:5).

[2] Paschal's mother was Theodora *episcopa*, cf. n. 29.

[3] The eulogy that follows (cc. 1-3) is based on 98:1-2 (and its sources, 91:1, 93:1).

[4] Paschal was educated in the Lateran, like popes Gregory II and Leo III (91:1, 98:1).

[5] Very probably, though not certainly, by Leo III. How Paschal was employed before he was made abbot we are not told; perhaps he did spend many years in the papal administration (Kelly, 99; Sullivan, *NCE* 11.1048), but the LP does not say so.

[6] St Stephen Major's is identical with St Stephen's *cata Galla patricia* (cf. 97:53 with n. 90); this follows from a document of 1073-4, the sale of landholdings by Benedict 'archpriest of the venerable monastery St Stephen Major called cata Galla...' (Schiaparelli 1901:490f, no. 26). Paschal was clearly not the first abbot, the 'suitable person' appointed when Hadrian I reformed the congregation here about 775 (97:53); perhaps his appointment was made when Leo III (in 809-10, 98:90) rebuilt the monastery; as pope, Paschal presented gifts (c. 27). The monastery had an oratory, but it is unclear when the surviving basilica (S. Stefano degli Abessini) was built. Its plan is closest to that of S. Prassede (Krautheimer, *Corpus* 4.180-198): 81 Roman feet long, 27 feet wide, with trabeated colonnades each with 8 columns, 2 aisles each 17 feet wide, a continuous transept 22 feet deep and 61½ to 63 feet long, an apse, an annular crypt, overall 130 feet long and 70 feet wide. The lintel of one of the lamp niches in the crypt has an inscription of Leo IV. Because of this the crypt used to be considered later than the church built by Leo III. But crypt and church are of one build, and Krautheimer suggests that all is Leo IV, though LP 105 is silent. That life has other gaps in its account of building works; and Leo IV was involved enough with St Stephen Major to transfer to it jurisdiction over S. Pellegrino (n. 53 below). Yet the likeness to S. Prassede might better imply that it is all Leo III's work, just a few years before S. Prassede was built, and 'included' (so to speak)

it is written: 'No one after lighting a lamp puts it in a cellar or under a bushel, but on a stand, that those who enter may see the light'.[7] So it was that he who amended this temporal life for himself with a view to everlasting gain, soberly and usefully guiding it, zealously set forth for his subjects a fine example of living well and a way of enhancing their piety.[8] He also provided the bounty of hospitality for the pilgrims and disabled who for the love of St Peter the apostle flocked from distant regions to his door, preparing what was necessary for their needs. This he had done quietly, and disbursed it cheerfully. Every day he continued to grow in the work he did for God until his predecessor lord pope Stephen departed this life to eternal bliss. 3. So when fame spread particularly far and wide so many instances of his good activity, and almighty God, consenting to the rule of his church being under the care of godly government, fitly and moderately arranged it, then with one heart and mind and with the intervention of God's will he was raised up to the apostolic see as pontiff by all the *sacerdotes* and dignitaries and all the clergy, also the leaders and whole Roman people, to the praise and glory of almighty God.[9]

He was[10] a most seemly observer of the precepts of the Fathers, the teachings of the pontiffs, the rules of the canons and the enactments of the laws, and from the time of his ordination he was a noble promulgator of the rule of justice for all; slow to anger and quick to have pity, repaying no one evil for evil, nor taking vengeance according to what each one committed, but ever compassionate, he loved and governed with dutiful love all the citizens and the Roman people whom God entrusted to him. He was a devotee, a restorer and in every way a most devout adorner of all God's churches with great endeavour and wisdom for the customary concern of religion.

---

by the LP in its reference to Leo III's rebuilding of the monastery; Leo IV's inscription need not be original.

[7] Luke 11.33.

[8] Krautheimer, *Corpus* 4.180, citing Ferrari, 320 f, plausibly interprets the convoluted Latin to mean that as abbot Paschal reformed the congregation and (next sentence) directed its attention to caring for pilgrims and the lame who come to St Peter's.

[9] *ARF* 817 Scholz 102: 'Meanwhile, Pope Stephen died on (*circiter*) January 25, not three months after his return to Rome. Paschal was elected as his successor. As soon as he had been solemnly consecrated, he sent gifts and an apologetic letter to the emperor (Louis the Pious, 814-840). In the letter he claimed that the papal dignity had been forced on him not only against his will but even against his most violent resistance'. The speed with which Paschal's ordination was carried out, only 2 days (99:5) after Stephen IV's death, may reflect a concern to forestall any interference from Louis, now protector of the Roman church; but Paschal was careful to announce his election to Louis immediately and to stress his unwillingness (Kelly, 99).

[10] For the continuing eulogy, cf. 91:1 and 98:2.

4. This blessed prelate sought out and found many bodies of the saints, whom he carefully and becomingly buried inside the city to God's honour and glory. For his clergy he increased the stipend for priestly functions[11] many times over. And because he laid up all his treasure[12] in the heavenly temple, <he was concerned> most of all for prisoners and exiles, and not only those from overseas regions; he ransomed men and women with gold and silver, and he even searched step by step along the farflung routes of roads, found them whether in the parts of Spain or in any other place, and as a good and true shepherd brought them back home.

[A.D. 817, January - August:]

5. On the holy altar of St Peter prince of the apostles he provided a cloth decorated with wondrous beauty, made of gold and jewels, representing this apostle's release from chains by the angel.[13] In his venerable basilica in front of the entrance leading to his body, at the place *Ferrata*, he set up an altar[14] and in it he also becomingly placed St Xystus the martyr and pontiff's body for veneration, and above it he suitably furnished an arch decorated with mosaic.

Also in St Peter's holy church, close to the entrance leading to St Petronilla's, he splendidly constructed an oratory[15] of enormous size, and he decorated the vaulting over the columns in the square with mosaic and beautiful minerals. In it he buried memorably and honourably the bodies of the martyrs SS Processus and Martinian to almighty God's honour and glory. In its apse he arranged and inserted among the marble constructions a very beautiful silver-gilt image with various representations, weighing 62½ lb; also silver lilies weighing 17 lb 3 oz, and 7 fine gold bowls, weighing in all 13 lb 2 oz. **6.** He provided 3 silver-gilt images in the same venerable place, one of the

---

[11] So the whole phrase (*roga... in presbiterio*) at 98:2; where (n. 6) it is pointed out that by now the expression may refer to gratuities paid on important feastdays.

[12] Cf. Matt. 19.21, Mark 10.21, Luke 18.22; and Matt. 6.19.

[13] Acts 12.7. Paschal's first recorded gift as pope is of a cloth of identical design to the first gift made by Hadrian I, 97:45. The symbolism could suit different political situations. On textiles in general see Lopez 1945, Forbes 1964, Volbach 1969, Reinhold 1970, Muthesius 1984, Oikonomides 1986.

[14] This oratory was just in front (to the east) of the southern part of the entrance screen to the confessio; it was dedicated jointly to SS Xystus II and Fabian (c. 24; and so called in the epitaph of Sergius II, buried in it in 847, see 104:48 with n. 94). In the 12th century Mallius referred to Paschal's 'arch with mosaic' as still surviving.

[15] In the SE corner of the transept (St Petronilla's opened from the southern end of the transept). Mallius added to the LP account that Paschal put the bodies 'in a porphyry shell, as it appears, and to revere them he surrounded the place with bronze railings; down to our own time it was still considered so holy that women were not allowed in'.

Saviour our Lord Jesus Christ, the other two of the martyrs SS Processus and Martinian, weighing in all 36 lb; he also presented another image of fine gold to adorn this oratory, weighing 13 lbs 3 oz. Likewise 8 canisters of fine silver, weighing 43 lb; he also set up there a silver shell for sponges for the night-time *diligentiae*,[16] weighing 7 lb 9 oz. He also rightly decorated in the same venerable place fine gold bejewelled keys in the shape of a cross, weighing .. lb. There too he arranged a cornice, which he overlaid with silver sheets weighing 20 lb; and above it he set up 2 silver arches and 4 chevrons weighing in all 60 lb. For decoration he surrounded the altar's *propitiatorium* with silver sheets, and he nobly furnished round his holy confessio inside and outside, with its grills, weighing in all .. lb. On these holy martyrs' altar he furnished 2 cloths, one of which he wondrously adorned with a gold-studded gold-interwoven cross, the other with fourfold-woven silk; he also adorned 7 great gold-interwoven veils, sewn around with a purple fringe.

7. We think this too should not be passed over in silence, that at that time, with devilish cunning at work, through the carelessness of some men of English race their whole quarter,[17] called *burgus* in their language, was so burnt with an abounding flame of fire, that not even traces of their former dwelling could be found in that place. By its exuberance this fire devastated as kindling almost all the portico which leads to the prince of the apostles' basilica. When the thrice-blessed pontiff realized this at about the twilight hour of the night, for love of St Peter the apostle's church and because of those pilgrims' great devastation, he immediately hastened there on horseback without putting his shoes on. So great was almighty God's mercy at his arrival, that at the place in which this angelic pontiff first stood he allowed the force

---

[16] This is the technical name for a ceremony, as is clear from *Ordo Romanus* 44 (Andrieu, 4.417 ff), a document written 824-7 by a copyist at Ratisbon who had a Roman source but interpolated some Frankish terms. The inscriptional record of Gregory III's synod at St Peter's (92:6 with n. 23) has *diligentiam facere*; the Life of St Amand refers to it as a nightfall ceremony at St Peter's at or before the middle of the 7th century (though the life was written rather later). The *primicerius* used a sponge to wash the inside and outside of the confessio after the removal of the censer from the vertical shaft which led down into the tomb (Andrieu, 4.423); Leo III had provided two of these apostolic thuribles for St Peter's, 98:67-68 with n. 121, and two for St Paul's, 98:68; Leo IV would provide one for SS Quattuor Coronati, 105:45. A similar ceremony seems to have taken place at Montecassino at the tomb of St Benedict (Andrieu, 4.426). It is not clear how often the ceremony was performed; at St Peter's by the 12th century the censer was renewed once a year only and the washing was no longer performed (Andrieu, 4.425). The notion of Barbier Montault (cited by Andrieu) that the *concha* ('shell') was a chamber-pot may be disregarded.

[17] The English borgo, quarter of the Schola Saxonum; for its site cf. 98:19 with n. 49.

of the fire to cross over no further. But he besought God's clemency, and the crowd of the faithful who were there fought the flames, and the fire was by God's mercy extinguished. So it happened that for the space of the whole night until dawn he stood in the same place on watch. So afterwards the thrice-blessed pastor, noticing the need of those pilgrims, which had crept in through the plotting of the devil's trickery, bestowed so many gifts and benefits for their needs, as he was ever accustomed to do; he supplied everything abundantly, gold and silver, clothing for their bodies as well as the rest of the nourishment needed. Also a quantity of trees to provide timber, so that they could restore their homes as required in the same place as they had been before. As for the portico which had been wrecked by the same disaster, he fittingly and solidly restored it better than it had been.

[A.D. 817-818:]
8. In the church of St Peter the prince of the apostles his mentor, this distinguished pontiff provided 46 gold-studded veils for the arches of the *presbyterium*, representing the miracles of the apostles, which the Lord saw fit to work through them.

The church of Christ's martyr St Praxedes,[18] built a long time ago, was now suffering such fatigue[19] from its great age that collapse to its foundations was threatening its ruin; this venerable pontiff anticipating its ruin and applying care to that church, often being on the watch there, shifted and erected it in another place not far away, an improvement on what it had formerly been.[20] He fittingly decorated this church's apse

---

[18] Compare the language at 104:27ff, for which this passage is the source.

[19] Although S. Prassede had been restored *in integro* less than 40 years previously (97:78), it was now abandoned and replaced on a new site. Krautheimer, *Corpus* 3.258, comments that the *titulus* had existed since at least 491; even before Paschal moved it it was called *ecclesia* (so in the list of 807, though *titulus* earlier in life 98), but that might mean no more than a large room inside a *titulus*. There is no certain archaeological evidence for the earlier church. One suggestion is that the left-hand side of the present atrium is the remnant of the nave arcade of the earlier church with reversed orientation, and presumably of fourth- or fifth-century date; the fragment of a half-dome whose original span was some 12 m, found near the SW corner of this atrium, suggests a sizeable building with this vault rising somewhere near the present atrium, but the fragment may have come from another building, below the atrium. Perhaps the most likely suggestion is that the site of the *titulus* (with, then, no purpose-built church) was the *insula* which has partly survived in the houses along the Via di San Martino and higher up below the atrium and façade of Paschal's church, some 8 m above the ancient street level; this would be 'not far from' the new site.

[20] The 9th-century building largely survives, with a few later alterations. Krautheimer, *Corpus* 3.239-259 passim, comments on its fine state of preservation as a perfect example of the Carolingian revival at Rome, showing the continuation of the movement which began under Hadrian I and Leo III, 'striving towards a renascence of Early Christian types and ideas in politics, liturgy and architecture'. With S. Stefano degli Abessini, it is the

adorned with mosaic work in different colours.[21] Likewise he embellished the triumphal arch[22] with the same minerals, carrying it out in a marvellous fashion.
[A.D. 818-819:]

9. This holy and distinguished pontiff sought out, found and collected many bodies of saints[23] lying in destroyed cemeteries, with dutiful

---

only example in Rome of a type common north of the Alps, based on the design of St Peter's, though much smaller in size and with two aisles not four. S. Prassede has a nave 36 m long and 14 m wide with aisles 5½ m wide, 11 columns 5 m high on each side (only 16 are now visible). The present Romanesque porch at street level may include elements of a 9th-century porch; from it a flight of steps leads to an open atrium, on the west side of which are two of the original atrium columns in situ, on a stylobate of 'Servian' blocks, and whose arches are surmounted by Carolingian brickwork. On the north of the atrium is the façade of the basilica, this façade also resting on 'Servian' blocks. The exterior walls of the basilica are Carolingian and the apse brickwork has the usual Carolingian modules. In at least one window 9th-century gypsum gratings have survived. Restorations in 1914 uncovered some plutei from the 9th-century chancel screen, now placed in the transept wing.

[21] S. Prassede has the most important group of 9th-century mosaics in Rome (Oakeshott 1967:204-12; cf. Krautheimer, *Corpus* 3.250). The inner wall of the apse was sheathed with marble plaques, removed in 1730. The apse-vault (Oakeshott 207 and pl. 127) still has Christ standing on the River Jordan, flanked on the right by SS Peter, Pudentiana and Zeno, on the left by SS Paul and Praxedes with Paschal himself wearing a square halo (his portrait thus survives; and his monogram is on the intrados of the apse-arch, *ibid.* and fig. 6); the draperies have areas of coloured decoration; a palm-tree flanks the figures on both sides, that on the left with a phoenix in its foliage. Below is the Lamb of God on a green platform from which the four rivers of Paradise flow, flanked by 12 lambs on a gold background. Below, the inscription (ed. Dümmler, *MGH Poet. Lat. Aevi Kar.* 2.662 no. 1) alludes to the 'bodies', with which Paschal enriched the church. The mosaic is a copy of that at SS Cosma e Damiano (dated 526-30; Oakeshott, 90-94, Duchesne I.280): Praxedes and Pudentiana replace Cosmas and Damian, Paschal and Zeno replace Felix IV and St Theodore; Duchesne thought it a slavish copy in a style of more advanced barbarism. Tastes have changed.

[22] The triumphal arch has the original mosaic (Mauck, 1987; Oakeshott, 206-7, plate 121) showing apostles and martyrs in the Heavenly Jerusalem (Revelation 21) with golden walls. In the centre stands Christ, in a red and gold robe, and on each side is an angel with a green halo; in the city are the 12 apostles, with John the Baptist and the Virgin to the left, Praxedes to the right; on either side of the city are white-robed martyrs approaching, bearing palm-branches, the group on the left, which includes women, marshalled by 3 lay figures in green, red and blue, that on the right by 1 lay and 2 clerical figures in green, red and gold; those on the right are met at the city-gate by St Peter and an archangel. Below the martyrs are confessors, also with palm-branches, but suffering slightly from the destruction of most of the lower part of the springings of the arch in 16th-century alterations. Jerusalem and the martyrs are a further allusion to the relics Paschal placed in the church. The mosaic decoration of the triumphal arch is continued on the transept-wall by a large mosaic outlining the opening of the apse, showing the 24 Elders (some heavily restored) and the Lamb (Rev. 4); the north transept has fresco decoration (well preserved inside the campanile) in a style regarded as somewhat old-fashioned for the 9th century.

[23] A marble inscription against the first column on the right (full text in Duchesne II 64) catalogues the relics. The present plaque was apparently prepared by Cardinal Ludovico Pico della Mirandola during restorations in 1730, but it was intended as a more legible

concern that they should not remain neglected;[24] with great affection and veneration he removed and buried them in the church of Christ's said martyr St Praxedes, which he had wonderfully renewed and constructed, with the assistance of all the Romans, bishops, priests, deacons and clerics chanting psalms of praise to God. And while these inner cares of the holy and angelic prelate's heart were afoot, in his anxiety to gain aid[25] before the Lord almighty by the prayers of those whose holy bodies are buried therein, who beyond the stars[26] are unceasingly pleasing to God, he constructed in that place from its foundations a monastery,[27] which he dedicated in the name of the virgin St Praxedes; in[28] this too he gathered a holy community of Greeks, which he placed therein to carry out carefully by day and night praises to almighty God and his saints resting therein, chanting the psalms in the Greek manner. **10.** On that venerable monastery he conferred many estates and landed properties in the city and the country, and he enriched it profusely and abundantly.

---

version of a 13th-century original, though how reliably this was copied cannot be known (Krautheimer, *Corpus* 3.235-6, citing Grisar 1899:plate V, 2). This inscription was much later than Paschal's time, but may have been based on a 9th-century document. It records that on 20 July of the 10th indiction (817; incorrect on Geertman's chronology here followed) Paschal placed under the altar of S. Prassede: (1) pontiffs, Urban, Stephen, Antheros, Miltiades, Fabian, Julius, Pontian, Siricius, Lucius, Xystus, Felix, Anastasius and Caelestinus; (2) bishops, Stratonicus, Leucius and Optatus; (3) priests and deacons, Nicomedes the archpriest, Justus and Cyrinus, Cyriac the deacon, Nemesius and Iacheus; (4) martyrs, Zoticus, Hereneus, Iacinthus, Amantius, Marius, Audifax, Abbacuc; 800 others; Castulus, Felix, Miles, Gordian, Epimachus, Servilian, Sulpicius, Diogenes, Bastus; 62 others; Marcellian, Mark, Festus; 2 others; Tertullinus, Faustus, Bonosus, Maurus, Calumniosus, John, Exsuperantius, Castus, Cyril; the 7 brothers; Honoratus, Theodosius, Basilius, Crescentius, Largus, Smaragdus, Crescentio, Jason, Maurus, Hippolytus, Pontian, Chrysanthus; 66 others; 1024 others; Maurus, Arthemius, Polio; 62 others; (5) virgins and widows, Praxedes, Pudentiana, Juliana, Symphorosa, Felicula, Marina, Candida, Paulina, Daria, Basilla, Paulina, Memmia, Martha, Emerentiana, Zoe, Tiburtias. On the right of the basilica's entrance where the body of his mother the *episcopa* Theodora lay, he placed: (6) the priest Zeno and 2 others. In the oratory of St John the Baptist on the left of the basilica, which is the *secretarium*: (7) Maurus; 40 martyrs. In the oratory of St Agnes in the monastery above: (8) the martyrs, pope Alexander, priests Eventius and Theodulus. Stated total, 2300; the items (excluding Theodora) add to 2151 (86 are named).

[24] Cf. 95:4, pope Paul's removal of relics from the cemeteries to within the city.

[25] *iuvarentur*; but *iuvaretur* in the parallel passage (104:29) is grammatically better.

[26] The expression *super astra placentium* is suggested by the second line of the inscription on the apse mosaic (*super aethra placentis*).

[27] Paschal seems to have incorporated in his new monastery of St Praxedes the oratory of the monastery of St Agnes *ad Dua Furna*, and the two institutions were henceforth regarded as a single monastery, Ferrari, 4-5. It was to this monastery, rather than to the church, that later gifts of textiles were made (103:29, 105:15). On the older monastery see 98:78 n. 150 (with the further suggestion that the monastery of SS Hadrian and Laurence was also united with it).

[28] The rest of this c. and the 1st sentence of the next are modelled very closely on 95:5.

Also in that church he built an oratory of Christ's martyr St Zeno, and there he also placed his holy body, and fully adorned it with mosaic.[29] In the same church he provided a silver canopy weighing 910 lb;[30] he also wondrously adorned the holy altar's *propitiatorium* with silver sheets. He beautifully embellished and gilded her[31] confessio, with its grills,[32] walling it inside and outside, weighing in all 300 lb. Over her venerable altar he provided a *spanoclist* diadem adorned with deep yellow gold and various stones, weighing 5 lb 2½ oz. On that holy altar he provided a gold-studded cloth, adorned with various representations, of wondrous size and beauty. There too he provided another gold-studded cloth made of gold and jewels, representing the virgins with their lamps alight, wondrously embellished and decorated. And at that virgin's holy body[33] he presented an image with silver sheets in relief,[34]

---

[29] Paschal's mother Theodora had her tomb in this oratory (see the relic catalogue, lines 36-42, cf. n. 23). Despite alterations made (according to Duchesne) in 1223 when the Column of the Scourging was placed here, the oratory still survives with its 9th-century mosaics (these have been partly retouched; on them see Oakeshott, pp. 207-12 with plates XIX, XXI-XXII, 125-7; Mackie, 1989; Wisskirchen, 1991). Krautheimer (*Corpus*, 3.252-5, 259) remarks that the sculptural decoration illustrates the character of 9th-century art in the use both of spoils and of original ornament. The oratory is based closely on the architecture of two Roman mausolea, one pagan (the tomb of the Cercenii), the other presumably Christian (the so-called chapel of St Tiburtius adjoining SS Marcellino e Pietro). It opens off the right aisle in line with the centre of the 8th intercolumniation in the nave arcade. The entrance doorway is flanked by a pair of Ionic columns with black granite shafts, supporting a sculptured cornice with an inscribed couplet naming Paschal (ed. Dümmler, *MGH Poet. Lat. aevi Kar.* 2.662 no. 2), followed by his monogram. The wall above the door (Oakeshott, 207 and plate 125) has, outside, mosaic medallions of Christ, the Apostles, the Virgin and saints. The chapel is a square cross-vaulted chamber, 3.5 x 3.6 m, with barrel-vaulted rectangular exedrae opening on three sides. All the vaults are covered with mosaics. The exedra opposite the door is 2.5 x 1.5 m, and has an altar (the mosaic altar-piece is probably 11th-century, Oakeshott, 207-8 and plate 126). The two side exedrae are 1.7 x 1.3 m. The walls are covered with marble; the floor has an opus sectile pavement, with a large round porphyry plaque in the centre. Mosaics on a gold ground cover the vaulted zone of the chapel; four angels support a bust of Christ on the groin vault (Oakeshott, plates XXI-XXII and 127; cf. p. 210 and plate 128 for its relationship with the 6th-century vault-mosaic in the Archbishops' Chapel at Ravenna); figures of saints (Oakeshott, plate XIX) occupy the lunettes, and smaller groups fill the exedrae lunettes, including Theodora in the left niche, opposite St Zeno's tomb; her portrait is adorned with a square halo, and at the side the words THEOROR(a) EPISCOPA.

[30] Now against the side walls of the chancel are six decorative Roman columns; probably they were used by Paschal in the 9th century, four of them perhaps to bear the canopy (Krautheimer, *Corpus* 3.257, who at n. 5 states that four arches of the canopy, 1.13 x 2.13 m, survive in the right-hand transept).

[31] Or 'its' (the altar's), and similarly below (the text is dealing with the main part of S. Prassede, not the chapel of St Zeno).

[32] Probably double doors are meant (so Krautheimer, *Corpus* 3.234).

[33] In the crypt under the high altar.

[34] *praefiguratis* seems to mean 'in relief'; Krautheimer, *loc. cit.*, paraphrases 'a silver-

weighing 99 lb.

11. This kind prelate provided in the same monastery an oratory of Christ's martyr St Agnes,[35] decorated with wondrous beauty.

As for the church of God's holy mother our lady the ever-virgin Mary, called Domnica,[36] built of old and now close to ruin, this pontiff with skilful vigilance renewed it building it from the foundations bigger and better than it had been before. He wondrously decorated this church's apse with mosaic.[37] There too he presented many gifts[38] - a

---

plated statue or relief'.

[35] This oratory is mentioned in the relic catalogue (cf. n. 23) at line 48 as *sursum*, in the upper part of the monastery. On Agnes's cult here see Duchesne 1907:485.

[36] S. Maria in Domnica is not mentioned before Leo III's time (LP 98:29 with n. 75, and the Einsiedeln Itinerary), but it must have existed, and as a deaconry, since the start of Hadrian I's pontificate. Paschal entirely rebuilt the church after the threat of imminent collapse of an older building; but (Krautheimer, *Corpus* 2.308-321) this does not mean that the older building had been a church in origin. The original deaconry had probably been installed in the precinct-barracks of the Statio Cohortis V Vigilum, located south and west (in the gardens of the Villa Mattei) of the 9th-century church, and the remains under the present church were probably part of it (the ruins of the Castra Peregrinorum below and beside the nearby S. Stefano Rotondo are not related). When it was made a deaconry an oratory will have been provided, but no traces have been found. The core of Paschal's church is well preserved: the façade, aisle-walls, nave-walls and the three apses are all homogeneous, but the portico dates to 1513-14. There are 9 columns each side of the nave; one of the capitals is 9th-century, the others earlier spoils. The nave, aisles, arcade, clerestory and three apses are all 9th-century; the central apse's wall rests on 'Servian' blocks. The original façade is not known, nor whether there was an original portico; the one replaced in the 16th century need not have been 9th-century. Krautheimer remarks that the church is characteristic of the Carolingian revival of Early Christian church planning in Rome, except for the side apses, whose function is obscure (perhaps for offertory rites: no minor altars seem to have existed). Triple apses are of eastern origin, common there from the end of the 5th century, and reached Europe via the Adriatic ports (Salona, Parenzo, S. Apollinare in Classe) in the sixth century; the idea came to Rome at about the same time (S. Giovanni in Porta Latina), but they were not common till generally adopted in North Italy in the 8th and 9th centuries. At Rome they are found at S. Angelo in Pescheria in 755, S. Maria in Cosmedin 772-95. Direct Greek influence at this date need not be invoked. It seems to follow that the triapsidal church of S. Maria delle Grazie at Santa Maria Capua Vetere cannot be Constantinian (LP 34:31, BP 25 with p. xxvi), *pace* M. Pagano & J. Rougetet (cited at BP xlvii).

[37] This mosaic survives (as does that on the triumphal arch, not mentioned in the LP; on both see Oakeshott, 203-4 and plates XX, 114-120). With a design unique in Rome, and a technique like that on the surviving copy of the Triclinium of Leo III, the apse has the Virgin (with the Child on her knee) in a deep-blue robe, seated on a red cushion on a golden throne with a golden carpet in front. Her right hand is extended towards Paschal (square halo, yellow vestment, and pallium), who kneels at her feet, touching her shoe; to either side are angels. Paschal's monogram is on the apse-arch, and along the foot of the mosaic the inscription records his splendid decoration in the Virgin's honour of a once-ruinous church; Krautheimer, *Corpus* 2.316 and fig. 241.

[38] Paschal's gifts in cc. 11-14 allowed Krautheimer, *Corpus* 2.319, to reconstruct the chancel layout: an altar with silver canopy, closed off by four curtains, the altar with a *propitiatorium* of silver plaques. The small window into the confessio was protected by 2 small grills, one outside, one inside, and framed, it seems, by a silver arch resting on

silver canopy weighing 332 lb; he embellished and decorated the holy altar's *propitiatorium* with silver sheets. He also completed and adorned in wondrous manner its confessio, with the grills, inside and outside, weighing 115 lb 3 oz. There too he provided a fine gold bowl, weighing 2 lb 8 oz. Also a silver arch and 2 colonnettes with 2 chevrons, weighing .. lb. **12.** And on the holy altar he provided a gold-studded cloth, representing the birth of our Lord Jesus Christ, adorned with wondrous beauty. There too he provided a beautiful cross-adorned silk cloth with a purple fringe; and another cloth of byzantine purple, with a gold-studded panel with the face of God's holy mother and angels standing as her retinue, with a fringe of cross-adorned silk; also another cloth of cross-adorned silk, with peacocks and in the centre a purple cross. Also 2 fourfold-woven cloths with purple crosses in the centre. There too he provided a gold-woven cloth with a purple fringe; 1 red silk altarcloth. **13.** Round the altar he provided 4 red silk veils with chevrons and a cross of fourfold weave. This venerable prelate provided on the beam in front of the vestibule of the altar 3 tyrian veils and 5 interwoven with gold; on the great arches of that church[39] he provided 20 veils of fourfold weave, and for the arches of the *presbyterium* 4 small cross-adorned silk veils; also, at the entrance to the *presbyterium* 3 tyrian veils. **14.** This kind pontiff provided at that church's entrance a great curtain of fourfold weave with a fringe interwoven with gold.

[A.D. 819-820: St Caecilia]

Now this same pontiff, Lord Christ almighty's servant, had unceasingly and with foresight the greatest care and solicitude for God's churches. And one day when, in his endeavour to pray, he came to the church[40] of God's virgin Christ's martyr St Caecilia, he saw that this

---

2 colonnettes. In front of the (vestibule of the) altar a rood beam extended across the opening of the apse; the 2 sets of curtains for this (3 and 5) perhaps suggest that 4 columns supported the rood. In front of the apse a chancel seems to have projected into the eastern bays of the nave. The 4 small curtains for the arches of the *presbyterium* presumably closed 2 arches in each side of the chancel. At the entrance to the *presbyterium* 3 purple curtains were hung, possibly placed inside 3 arches.

[39] For the nave arcade (*arcus maiores*). There are 22 arches in the nave; but Duchesne and Krautheimer agree that 20 were to be adorned, excluding the last on each side. The column each side nearest the altar is of porphyry, while all the others are granite; the last arch each side was evidently reckoned as part of the *presbyterium*.

[40] The church of S. Cecilia is first referred to in the LP at 61:4 (BP 57), in the year 545, but is certainly at least of fourth-century date. In all that follows it should be remembered that whatever Paschal found, it was not the body of a Roman martyr named Caecilia. There is no early evidence for a martyr so named; Caecilia will have been the foundress of the *titulus*. It is possible that she was later identified with a martyr from somewhere else, as happened to the foundress of the *titulus Anastasiae*, for whom a homonymous martyr was found by coopting Anastasia of Sirmium.

church's walls were now shaken with extreme old age and about to fall to the foundations; they had been weakened for a long time by the infirmity of age; almost broken in ruins, they had long remained damaged. Putting endeavour into the work, he began to construct a new church at that place with magnificent workmanship, and he endeavoured to complete it satisfactorily, an improvement on how it had been.[41]

15. There is another thing which we think should not be omitted.[42] One day when he had made his way to St Peter the prince of the apostles' church to celebrate the customary vigils before St Peter and to stay and sing morning praises in front of his confessio as Sunday dawned, he sank into a sudden sleep and saw standing beside him a girl who had the appearance of a virgin and was adorned with the clothing of an angel. She uttered these words:[43] 'We thank you greatly for

---

[41] The church still survives, disfigured by later restorations. It is unclear whether what Paschal replaced was a true basilica or merely the original *titulus* made up of various buildings from the 1st through to the 4th or 6th centuries. The new church (Krautheimer, *Corpus* 1.104-112 passim) is of normal type for the 9th century: a nave 150 Roman feet long (or excluding the apse 133⅓ feet), its width increasing from 46⅓ to 48⅓ feet (excluding the column widths), its height 44 feet; two aisles 25 feet high, of which the left increases from 13¼ to 13⅔ feet (excluding the column widths), while the right decreases from 15⅓ to 12⅔ feet. The irregularities may be due to the use of older walls as foundations. The nave has 13 arcades; only two columns now survive, at a distance apart of 9 feet, the height being 14⅔ feet (including Ionic base and Corinthian capital); the arches are about 20 feet high from the original floor (some 8 inches below the present). For the apse interior see c. 19 and n. 56. The exterior of the apse has undulating brickwork, visible too on the outside of the right aisle and in the walls of the nave. Above each arch is a window 4 feet 2 inches wide and 10 feet high, with 4 feet 10 inches between each. The original façade had three windows; there is no trace of windows in the aisles. Originally it seems that there were no galleries; the present one is 13th-century. Above the so-called Bath of S. Cecilia is a chapel which may be original; if so it parallels that of St Zeno at S. Prassede. The present atrium, a four-sided portico of columns and arches, may be on 9th-century foundations; the width of the porticoes is 12⅓ feet, much like that of the aisles. All is uniform construction of Paschal's time, and is very typical of Roman 9th-century architecture, cf. S. Marco, S. Anastasia's 3rd phase, S. Prassede, S. Stefano degli Abessini, and S. Martino. All are simple basilicas with a nave, two aisles separated by columns, and an atrium. Not all have a transept, but most have an annular crypt. All are lit by windows above the nave while the aisles are unlit; 9th-century windows are larger than those of the 8th century and have double arches. The columns, whether for an arcade or for an architrave, are close (9-11 feet). The brickwork is regular but undulating. All is closer to Early Christian than to 6th/8th-century work.

[42] There exists a fragment of a letter purportedly written by Paschal on the discovery of St Caecilia's body. It exists in two versions, one published by Bosio (Duchesne cites his *Historia passionis S. Caeciliae*, Rome 1600, 42) from three MSS which differed between themselves in some respects, and one by Baronius (821 §4-6, in ed. Venice 1711 vol. 9 p. 598; J2555 *Cum summae*, Mansi 14.373-4, *PL* 102.1085-8). Baronius took the letter as genuine and as the biographer's source; Duchesne saw that it was a forgery based on the LP, and that of the two versions one derives from the other, the older being much closer to the LP.

[43] The precise meaning of her words is obscure. From what follows it seems that Paschal had been inquiring (pointlessly) where the Lombards were supposed to have taken her

abandoning the struggle you had long undertaken on my part when you lent your ears to the deceptive reports that were spread. It is because you have been so much in my service that we are able to speak to each other with our own voices.' The pontiff was now listening carefully, and began eagerly to inquire who she was who spoke such words to him, and what her name was. To him she replied: 'If you ask my name, I am called Caecilia, Christ's servant.' To her the chief prelate spoke: 'How can I believe this, since for a long time the story has been told that the body of Caecilia, this venerable martyr of Christ, had been stealthily purloined by Aistulf king of the Lombards and by his men, when he was besetting Rome as an enemy.'[44] When the venerable pontiff suggested such things, almighty God's handmaid said to him: 'That the Lombards sought eagerly to find me is certainly true; but I was aided by the assistance of my Lord Jesus Christ and my lady, God's holy mother the ever-virgin Mary, and they were unable either to find me or to take me far away from here as they wished. And so, as you have begun to look for me, you should not stop applying yourself with unceasing effort to find me, because the Lord God for whose love and honour I suffered has been pleased that you should find me and bury me in the church you have newly built.' So saying, she was taken from his sight.

16. Then, when morning praises were over, this venerable pontiff, in view of the sign so clearly and indubitably revealed, painstakingly began to seek here and there where her sacred body might lie buried. As he sought carefully, God granted that he discovered it, clothed in gold vestments, in the cemetery of Praetextatus[45] outside the Appian Gate,

---

body, but had given this up; now the reward for his effort would be to discover it untouched. The variants in the letter (n. 42) are of little help to elucidate the sense (e.g. 'hesitation' in place of 'struggle').

[44] In 756; cf. 94:41.

[45] This raises a problem. Caecilia's traditional tomb is in a different cemetery, that of S. Callisto (or St Xystus), just outside the papal crypt. The third of Bosio's MSS of the forged letter (n. 42) also gave the cemetery as *Praetextati*; of the other two MSS, one gave *Xysti seu Praetextati* as Baronius's version, the other (unless it is Bosio's correction) *sancti Sixti*. The letter has: 'we (Paschal), hastening to the cemetery of St Xystus or Praetextatus sited outside the Porta Appia (as is clearly related in her holy passion), found her with her venerable husband in golden garments among our colleagues the bishops'. The LP omits this reference to the earlier popes, which must indicate the papal crypt in S. Callisto. The Passion of Caecilia (*BHL* 1495), perhaps of late 5th-century date, also puts her 'among the bishops' and is likely to be the source of the letter; no other evidence puts her inside the crypt, but the expression may have been used loosely to mean the tomb just outside it. How is the conflict between the two cemeteries to be resolved? De Rossi (*Roma sotterranea* 2.131-6) argued that *Praetextati* was wrong and was to be corrected to *Xysti* or *Callisti*, to square with what he believed to be reality. But since she was found next to Valerian (her supposed husband, and one of a trio of genuine

with the body of her venerable husband Valerian,[46] and also the linens full of the blood of her martyrdom when, stricken by the ungodly executioner, she was consecrated a martyr of the Lord Christ who reigns for ever. These linens had been used to wipe away the holy martyr's blood; soaked in sacred blood from the executioner's three strokes, they were discovered wrapped at the feet of her body.[47] **17.** Handling all these things himself, he gathered them and with great honour placed that virgin's body with the martyrs her dear husband Valerian and Tiburtius and Maximus, also the pontiffs Urban and Lucius, under the sacred altar

---

Roman martyrs, with Tiburtius and Maximus) and he had certainly been in Praetextatus, he had to believe that Valerian and his companions had been translated before Paschal's time to Callistus to be near her. To support this view, he cited the Hieronymian Martyrology, which has the 3 martyrs both on 14 April in Praetextatus and on 21 April but in Callistus, and suggested that the latter entry referred to such a translation. Duchesne objected that all the 7th-century topographers put the 3 martyrs in Praetextatus, so the supposed record on 21 April would have to be of a later translation; and from the textual history of the Hieronymian this is impossible. In any case Hadrian I had recently restored the basilica of Tiburtius, Valerian and Maximus (LP 97:78 with n. 164), which he would hardly have done if their bodies were no longer there (as Delehaye accepts, *Mart. Hieron.* 14 April). Duchesne concluded that the Hieronymian entry on 21 April was really the Octave of the 3 martyrs, celebrated not at their own tomb but in Callistus where Caecilia, the heroine of their legend, was buried. So the translation of the 3 from Praetextatus to Callistus rests entirely on the forged letter, or rather a contamination of its text from the passion of Caecilia; and this evidence is too weak if there is another explanation of how Paschal found both Caecilia and Valerian in Praetextatus. Duchesne suggested that it was not the 3 who were translated to Callistus, but Caecilia herself to Praetextatus, where Paschal found her. This accords with the LP whose Roman author would not confuse two cemeteries; and Paschal's actions must have been well known at Rome. It also explains how it had come to be believed that the Lombards had taken her body: if it was still at Callistus how could any Roman, let alone a pope, not know it? Her tomb there was surely empty. Perhaps her body was taken from it to Praetextatus during the Lombard invasion; a custodian could have thought it wise to move the relics out of harm's way; if this was done secretly it could have been forgotten. Vogel accepted Duchesne's hypothesis. Meanwhile Franchi de' Cavalieri (1912) rejected *Praetextati* and believed in a translation, but merely from within the papal crypt to just outside it, where Paschal found her. Delehaye objected to both De Rossi and Duchesne (*Comm. in Mart. Hieron.*, 21 April, 22 Nov.); the 3 martyrs were in Praetextatus; in the entry for them in the Hieronymian on 21 April the location 'at Callistus' has slipped forward from the entry for pope Gaius, buried there on 22 April; the day itself might or might not be an octave of their real feast on 14 April. Delehaye did not explain how Caecilia could be in Praetextatus under Paschal. The truth of course is that since Caecilia was not a genuine martyr, a body could have been identified as hers in either cemetery, and the statement in the Passio may not have been the only one current.

[46] That the genuine martyr Valerian was the husband of Caecilia depends solely on the fictitious Passion of Caecilia (*BHL* 1495); cf. n. 45.

[47] The LP does not actually state that the body was incorrupt. The similar story that during restorations at S. Cecilia in 1599 Cardinal Paolo Sfondrati opened the sarcophagus and found it so is well-known; it was given originally by Baronius, 821 § 13ff; and is highly dubious (cf. n. 65). Stefano Maderno's white marble statue of the recumbent Caecilia under the high altar (there is a copy at the tomb in S. Callisto) represents what is reported to have been seen.

in the church dedicated in the name of this holy martyr inside this city of Rome's walls, to almighty God's praise and glory.[48]

For the honour and help of these holy martyrs he built a monastery[49] close to that church at the place called *Colles Jacentes* in honour of the virgins and martyrs SS Agatha and Caecilia; in it he set up a community of monks serving God, to sing the daily praises to the Lord almighty in this *titulus* of St Caecilia day and night. **18.** For[50] the support and fitting up of the lamps and for the monks'[51] needs and remuneration, and out of the love and regard he had towards his predecessor lord pope Leo III of godly memory, he bethought himself of St Peregrinus's hostel,[52] which that predecessor of his had built at St Peter the apostle's at the place called Naumachia; it was being devoured by poverty and want, thanks to the neglect and abandonment of those in charge. So to give godly assistance for the said community of monks in that monastery he confirmed for them by his written charter this hostel with farms, homesteads and estates, tenants and houses, households and everything as is fair and reasonable according to what the laws lay down; the charter covered both what his predecessor donated to the hostel, and what he himself in godly devotion added for the increase of the monastery, in the way of lands, vines, houses and rural households.[53]

---

[48] Dümmler, *MGH Poet. Lat. aevi Kar.* 2.663 no. 3, gives from Baronius, 821 §7, the verse inscription placed before the altar in the confessio, but containing as it does the expression *Paschalis primus* it cannot be original. In one version of the forged letter (n. 42), Caecilia is translated not to S. Cecilia in Trastevere as in the LP but to the monastery of SS Andrew and Gregory on the Caelian (on this church's claims, De Rossi, *Roma sotterranea* 2.136). Perhaps the Caelian claim originated from a corruption of *Collis iacentes*, the location of the monastery near the *titulus* mentioned in this chapter. A mixed text of the letter has Paschal put her in her *titulus*, under an altar of St Andrew, which is then described as in the monastery of SS Andrew, Gregory, Agatha and Caecilia in the place *Collis iacentes*. This name for the monastery clearly doubles up the dedications of the two different monasteries. Bosio knew both versions; two of his MSS gave Trastevere, the third gave the Caelian.

[49] On this monastery, Ferrari, 23-5. Nearly all (including Krautheimer, *Corpus* 1.95-112) agree that it was a new foundation, despite the discovery nearby in 1904 of the tombstone of a 6th-century abbess. The monastery was not immediately adjoining the basilica of St Caecilia, but at a short distance, *ad colles iacentes* (which refers to the hillside near the basilica, the name deriving from some small district or street nearby); but it was near enough for the monks to attend choir in the *titulus* day and night, Ferrari, 25; Armellini-Cecchelli, *Chiese*, 825.

[50] The contorted Latinity of this passage rather obscures the point that Paschal is giving S. Pellegrino with its lands to the monastery of SS Agatha and Caecilia.

[51] Those of SS Agatha and Caecilia in the previous chapter.

[52] Cf. 98:81, 90 and n. 177. The hostel's construction is here explicitly attributed to Leo III, which helps to clarify 98:90.

[53] This arrangement did not last. Under Leo IV the church and hostel of S. Pellegrino with its many goods came under the jurisdiction of St Stephen Major's, a grant known

19. For love of the venerable saints,[54] to decorate this church[55] this holy prelate provided an apse adorned with mosaic[56] and a silver canopy[57] of wondrous size, weighing 600 lb 8 oz. He finished and marvellously embellished the holy altar's *propitiatorium* and the confessio inside and out, and its grills, with silver sheets, weighing in all 154 lb 15 oz[58]. At this virgin's holy body[59] he presented an image of

---

from its confirmation on 24 March 1053 by Leo IX for the 'canons' residing in St Stephen Major, and which provides information about Paschal's arrangements (*PL* 143.717 n. 80; Ferrari, 321, n. 10, and 325; Schiaparelli 1901:473-477 n. 17). S. Pellegrino's properties included 'the island Martana (in Lake Bolsena), the churches of St Stephen and St Valentine with houses... as our predecessor Paschal, who had been rector of that monastery, gave this patrimony... And Paschal himself as pontiff named the monastery of the island St Stephen's after the monastery of St Stephen Major in whose jurisdiction it is ... St Mary's church called 'in Turre' (the gatehouse to St Peter's), which Paschal granted in a privilege to the said monastery with books and vestments, crosses and thuribles of silver, with houses and cells close to it, with the Paradise and the porticoes as far as the Silver Door (the main door of St Peter's) that you may close and open it, with everything contained within them, with the sewer and the greater and lesser steps as far as the piazza called Cortina'.
[54] Agatha and Caecilia.
[55] S. Cecilia in Trastevere (not S. Pellegrino).
[56] The apse is semicircular, with a diameter of 30 Roman feet; its walls probably had marble revetment, and it had four windows (Krautheimer, *Corpus* 1.110). The apse-mosaic survives (Oakeshott, pp. 212-2, plates 129-131, 133, 137), despite damage by water. Oakeshott describes it as one of the most moving for which Paschal was responsible. The principal composition is copied from that at S. Prassede (itself based on SS Cosmas & Damian's), showing, below the Divine Hand, a wide-eyed Christ, standing in heavenly glory, in front of clouds (but almost on a level with his followers, rather than high above them as at S. Prassede), dressed in gold with lines of red, and with a gold halo; he is giving a blessing in the Greek manner (fourth finger to the thumb). On his left and right are Peter and Paul; on Peter's left, Valerian (in unusual garments perhaps intended to mark him out as a layman, a white mantle with gold decoration, above a green scarf) and Caecilia, both with martyrs' crowns; on Paul's left, Agatha is presenting Paschal (depicted as younger and more 'spiritual' than at S. Prassede, with a blue square halo edged with white, and wearing a white dalmatic, gold chasuble, and later-style pallium). The ground is of flowers, with palm-trees on either side, the one next to Paschal containing a phoenix. All the figures are unnaturally tall and thin, and the composition is in general two-dimensional and linear. At the summit of the vault is Paschal's monogram. Below the main design is the usual group of sheep on either side of the Lamb of God, with the cities of Jerusalem and Bethlehem at each end. Below this is the inscription in gold lettering on a deep-blue ground (ed. Dümmler, *MGH Poet. Lat. aevi Kar.* 2.662 no. 4). Duchesne noted that there were also mosaics on the apse-arch, destroyed in 1725; in the springings were the 24 Elders of Revelation; at the top the Virgin seated on a throne with the child Jesus, between 2 angels; on right and left, separated by palmtrees, 10 female saints leaving the mystical cities of Jerusalem and Bethlehem and approaching the Virgin's throne. Except for certain details this composition was copied from the façade-mosaic of S. Maria in Trastevere.
[57] After the mosaic, the LP deals with objects of precious metal and fabrics given at the time of the foundation for the altar, the iconostasis, the body of the church, and the crypt. But the order is not very systematic; the locations below follow Duchesne's suggestions. The canopy of course is over the altar.
[58] The text may be wrong; there were 12, not 16, ounces in a pound.

silver sheets weighing 95 lb. In front of the altar's vestibule he provided a cornice covered in silver sheets and 2 columns, where he placed 1 arch and 2 chevrons, weighing in all 100½ lb. There too[60] he presented 3 silver-gilt images weighing 48½ lb. **20.** For this church's arches[61] this prelate provided 26 great silver chalices weighing in all 109½ lb. There too he presented[62] 2 silver canisters with six wicks, weighing 2 lb 9 oz; a fine gold bowl weighing 3 lb. This pontiff provided 2 silver canisters with nine wicks, weighing 10 lb; 3 silver bowls weighing 5 lb; a silver-gilt thurible weighing 1 lb. For the holy altar[63] this kind prelate provided a cloth of byzantine purple, with a gold-studded panel in the middle representing an angel crowning St Caecilia and Valerian and Tiburtius, with a gold-studded fringe decorated with wondrous beauty. There too he provided a crimson gold-interwoven cloth with a fringe of dyed purple round it. For love of this virgin he provided another purple gold-interwoven cloth, embellished and adorned with a gold-worked cross in the middle. On the same altar he provided a white medallioned cloth with little roses, with a purple cross in the middle, with *psilliae* and a fringe of byzantine purple, beautifully decorated. On the same altar he presented a fourfold-woven cloth. The venerable pontiff provided 4 crimson veils[64] hanging round the altar, with crosses and chevrons of interwoven gold and fourfold weave. On the casket[65]

---

[59] The same expression as in c. 10; like S. Prassede, this church had an accessible annular crypt. The next chapter mentions a casket (*arcella*) for the body, for which the pope offers fabrics. There was certainly no altar inside the crypt. The image will presumably have been of the saint herself.

[60] Still at the iconostasis.

[61] In the body of the church; the 26 chalices are for suspending in the nave arcades. There are in fact 13 arcades each side (Krautheimer, *Corpus* I.110), if those of the esonarthex are included and those of the entrance arcade excluded.

[62] The canisters and bowls in this and the next sentence are lights, presumably for the body of the church.

[63] This and the next few lines list five textiles for the altar, so that with one in use there would be four spares.

[64] Four curtains to hang between the canopy columns round the altar.

[65] *Arcella*: a casket or special reliquary; Duchesne noted that its location is not stated. As altar ornaments have just been mentioned, and the next chapter starts with an *arcella* for the body, he identified the latter as the *arcella* for the head; the diminutive would hardly suit a sarcophagus for the whole body. The words *ad corpus* are omitted in some MSS (the best has simply *arcella*); Duchesne thought that the longer reading, that best attested in the MSS, was to be understood not as meaning 'for' the body but merely as an indication of place - the reliquary 'at the body' in the crypt. This *arcella* was soon replaced by a silver shell-shaped reliquary (c. 28) and it was Caecilia's head which Paschal put in it. In 105:41 it is still the head that is referred to: Leo IV gave it to SS Quattro Coronati; Duchesne refrained from speculating whether this was the same head Paschal had enshrined. A distribution of Caecilia's relics is here attested by a contemporary author who worked from the official records of the papal *vestiarium*, which

wherein he laid that virgin's venerable head, he provided[66] a small tyrian cloth with a purple fringe. There too he presented a green gold-interwoven cloth; another cross-adorned cloth with a fringe of purple dye; there too a cloth of purple with a gold-interwoven fringe. **21.** In the casket at this virgin's body he provided a fourfold-woven cloth with a fourfold-woven fringe, also another cloth, cross-adorned, with a fringe of purple dye. In the same church[67] he provided 25 tyrian veils with a fringe of byzantine purple, and 4 green veils with a fringe of dyed purple. There too he presented 3 crimson veils with a fringe of purple, also 2 small gold-interwoven veils with a purple fringe, and 2 tyrian veils with a gold-interwoven fringe. For this church's arches[68] this venerable and distinguished pontiff provided 12 gold-interwoven veils and 14 of fourfold weave. In the arches[69] of the *presbyterium* he provided 12 small tyrian veils with a fringe of byzantine purple. At this church's entrance[70] this God-protected venerable prelate provided a great fourfold-woven and cross-adorned curtain, beautifully adorned.

[A.D. 820-821:]

22. This pontiff, with his watchful concern for the monasteries constructed all round, stuck to his purpose and inquired what they had. He discovered that SS Sergius and Bacchus's monastery[71] behind the Lateran patriarchate's aqueduct was destitute of everything, so that the community of the Lord's handmaids which existed in it, were, through poverty and want, unable to sing any praises to the almighty Lord and his saints. The venerable pastor was moved to pity by this inquiry. He accomplished it that God's handmaids could exist well and religiously; and he gathered and set up a community of monks in it. He enriched

---

is an excellent reason for suspecting the story of Cardinal Sfondrati's discoveries (n. 47). Franchi de' Cavalieri (1912) argued that the story of this discovery is untrustworthy and that there is no reason why the head could not have been detached from the body and put in a separate reliquary.

[66] The rest of this chapter and the first sentence of the next record six textiles (one in use, five spares) to cover the *arcella* of Caecilia's relics.

[67] We are back in the body of the church.

[68] The arcades in the body of the church.

[69] We are now back at the iconostasis; the 12 small veils are to hang in the arches of the *presbyterium*, the sacred enclosure of the chancel.

[70] Finally back to the body of the church: a large curtain for the main door.

[71] This monastery was situated behind the Claudian aqueduct, on the other side of it in relation to the Lateran Palace, and is to be identified with St Sergius at 98:79 (where see n. 154). Paschal added it to the monasteries already charged with choir service at the Lateran. Duchesne thought there were already three of these, but possibly there were only two: St Pancras's and SS Andrew and Bartholomew's (on both see 97:68 for the choral arrangements); there seems to be no evidence that St Stephen's at the Lateran (98:76) participated, though this is suggested at 98 n. 154.

that monastery and increased it fully and adequately with many sources of revenue in households, farmsteads, vineyards, houses, and places in the city and countryside. He laid down that the resident community, with every necessity provided for, should day and night chant praises and hymns melodiously to the only God and his saints in the Saviour our Lord Jesus Christ's venerable church close to the Lateran.

23. In SS Processus and Martinian the martyrs' oratory, which he himself had constructed, inside the church of St Peter prince of the apostles, he presented a fine gold image with the face of God's holy mother, weighing 10 lb 4 oz. There too he provided a cloth of byzantine purple, with 2 gold-studded panels, with the face of St Peter and of SS Processus and Martinian, and a gold-studded fringe, adorned with great beauty. Also there he presented an all-silk cloth, with a gold-studded panel in the middle with the image[72] of our Lord Jesus Christ's lordly resurrection and a fringe of byzantine purple, beautifully embellished. He also presented to these saints 9 all-silk veils with a fringe of fourfold weave and byzantine purple. There too he provided 6 small tyrian veils, with a gold-interwoven fringe; a silver thurible wondrously gilded, weighing 1 lb.

24. In SS Xystus and Fabian the martyrs' oratory,[73] this pontiff provided 3 silver bowls weighing 5 lb 6 oz. In front of this oratory's image he provided a gold-studded veil, wondrously adorned. On their venerable altar he provided a crimson cloth, with a cross of byzantine purple in the middle and a fringe also of purple. Also in this oratory this pontiff presented an all-silk cloth with 2 gold-studded crosses in the middle and a cross-adorned fringe, decorated with various pearls. There too he provided another gold-interwoven cloth with a purple cross in the middle. To decorate this oratory he provided 4 crimson veils with a fringe of byzantine purple; also 4 all-silk veils with a fringe of fourfold weave and of dyed purple.

25. In SS Cosmas and Damian the martyrs' church[74] on the Via Sacra this kind prelate provided a tyrian cloth, with a gold-studded panel in the middle with the face of our Lord Jesus Christ and the martyrs SS Cosmas and Damian with the three other brothers,[75] with a gold-worked

---

[72] So, it seems, for *vultus*; the face alone could hardly be shown resurrecting.

[73] In St Peter's, like the last-mentioned oratory; cf. c. 5 and n. 14.

[74] Founded by Felix IV (56:2 BP 51); often called 'at the Three Fates', cf. 97 n. 87.

[75] Cosmas and Damian were supposed to have had 3 brothers Anthimus, Leontius and Euprepes, also martyrs; this is the earliest reference to them at Rome, where Cosmas and Damian had been known since at least the early 6th century (LP 53:9 BP 46). The 3 names (with the variant Leon for Leontius) appear with Cosmas and Damian on 27 October as martyrs in Arabia in the *Synaxarium Constantinopolitanum* (ed. Delehaye

cross and an all-silk fringe, beautifully embellished and adorned. On top of their sacred altar he presented a tyrian cloth wondrously adorned. In front of that altar's vestibule he provided 3 tyrian veils with a fringe of byzantine purple.

26. In the Saviour our Lord Jesus Christ's monastery in the territory of Rieti,[76] the venerable pontiff provided a gold-studded cloth representing our Lord Jesus Christ resplendent in heaven with archangels and apostles, decorated with wondrous beauty with various pearls. To decorate the holy altar in the same monastery he presented another gold-interwoven cloth, with crosses of byzantine purple and a gold-studded fringe, wondrously decorated.

[A.D. 821-822:]
In St Mennas the martyr's church he provided a fourfold-woven cloth with a fringe of byzantine purple.

In St Peter the apostle's church at Centumcellae[77] this holy and angelic pontiff presented a silver-gilt chalice and paten weighing 4 lb 3 oz.

27. In the church of St Peter the apostle his mentor he provided a gospel-book with a silver cover weighing 8 lb 8 oz.

In St Stephen the first martyr's monastery,[78] called Major, at St Peter's, the kind prelate provided 4 white all-silk cloths, with gold-worked crosses in the middle, with various pearls and a purple fringe, wondrously adorned. There too this pontiff presented a gold-interwoven

---

144.24), though not on the other dates (1 July, 29 October, 1 November, 9 December) when Cosmas and Damian (the same or supposed homonyms) were honoured in the east. In the west, where Cosmas and Damian were celebrated on 27 September, the extra names are unknown to the *Martyrologium Hieronymianum* in the late 6th century, to Bede in the 8th century, and, in the first half of the 9th century, to the Anonymus Lugdunensis and to Florus; but they soon appeared in Wandelbert's verse martyrology (*MGH Poet. Lat. aevi Kar.* 2.595, vv. 598-600) and in the first edition of Ado (*Le martyrologe d'Adon*, edd. J. Dubois & G. Renaud, 329-331); hence they were adopted by Usuard, and by the Roman Martyrology of the 16th century. The source of Wandelbert and Ado will be one of the unedited passions of Cosmas and Damian (*BHL* 1968, 1971-5), likely to be of little historical value.

[76] Cf. 96:5.

[77] Despite Gregory III's fortifications (92:16) the Saracens had pillaged Centumcellae in 813 (cf. 105:99) and scattered its inhabitants. A church could well have survived. *ARF* 813 Scholz 96 describes how Count Irmingar of Ampurias set an ambush near Majorca for the Moors who were returning from Corsica to Spain with much booty; he captured 8 ships, on which he found more than 500 Corsican prisoners. In revenge the Moors ravaged Centumcellae in Tuscia and Nice in Narbonensis; attacking Sardinia also, they were repelled, defeated in battle by the Sardinians, and turned back after losing many of their men. The city would be refounded by Leo IV on a new site and named Leopolis (105:99-102). See Lauer 1900:147ff; Calisse 1908.

[78] The monastery where Paschal had once been abbot, cf. c. 2.

cloth, with a gold-worked cross in the middle and a gold-studded fringe. In the same monastery this prelate provided a gold-interwoven cloth, with a gold-studded panel in the middle with the face of God's holy mother and the apostles SS Peter and Paul, and a purple fringe. There too he presented 2 cross-adorned cloths, with gold-studded crosses in the middle and a purple fringe. For this oratory's decoration he provided a great fourfold-woven veil, with 4 gold-worked crosses in the middle and a purple fringe.

28. In the holy Archangel's deaconry this pontiff presented a cloth of byzantine purple, with a gold-studded cross in the middle and a gold-studded fringe, beautifully embellished.

In St Caecilia the martyr's church he provided a silver shell, in which he laid that virgin's precious head,[79] weighing 8½ lb.

In St Cyriac the martyr's church *in Thermis*[80] this prelate presented 8 gold-interwoven veils, with a gold-interwoven fringe.

[A.D. 822-823:]

29. In the holy Archangel's oratory,[81] which his predecessor lord pope Leo had once established and constructed, this pontiff, relying on God, provided an all-silk white cloth with a gold-studded panel in the middle representing our Lord Jesus Christ's resurrection, and a gold-studded fringe, wondrously adorned. There too he presented another cloth interwoven with gold, with a fringe of byzantine purple. In the same oratory this pontiff provided another cloth of fourfold weave, sown around, representing God's holy mother, beautifully embellished and adorned.

30. This holy and orthodox pontiff, spurred by God's inspiration, observed that the holy and undefiled virgin Mary our lady's church called *Ad Praesepe* had formerly been constructed in such a way that women standing behind the pontiff's seat for the holy ceremonies of mass were almost next to the pontiff;[82] consequently, if the pontiff

---

[79] See n. 65.

[80] See 97:70 with n. 137.

[81] The oratory of St Michael at the Lateran Palace; cf. 98:92 with n. 179.

[82] All that follows describes alterations to the west end of the 5th-century basilica made long before Nicholas IV in 1295 constructed the present (7 m deep) transept and apse. Corbett's hypothetical drawing of Paschal's arrangements of this part of the basilica is given in Krautheimer, *Corpus* 3.53 fig. 54; apart from the LP, the main source for the arrangements from Paschal's time till 1295 is John the Deacon, *Liber de ecclesia Lateranensi* (written between 1073 and 1159; *PL* 194.1557) c. 14, who states that at St Mary's the throne was under a window in an apse that had 5 windows. The difficulty is to explain the pre-Paschal arrangement. Following De Rossi, Duchesne explained the passage as follows. The throne was too low down and too close to the *matroneum*, so the women could overhear the pope's conversation. The original apse pavement was at nave

wanted to have any conversation with his assistants, he could not do so, given the women's very close crowding, without their intruding; and he observed that there was a broad enough space available so that the seat could be moved from there. Putting endeavour into the task, he began to act unremittingly to raise on high the seat which was set too low down, so that he could pour forth prayers in greater intimacy with the Lord, by arranging that the concourses of people should instead be at a slightly lower level. He fashioned the seat better than it had formerly been, adorned with beautiful marble, and constructed from each side steps by which to reach it. And raising[83] the altar's pavement he covered it with precious marble. **31.** Therein he set up 6 columns[84] of purple colour in front of the holy altar's confessio; on top of these he placed

---

level (Krautheimer, *Corpus* 3.52), and the *matroneum* was behind the apse, no doubt because it could not be set in its usual place at the end of the women's (right-hand) side of the church, the top of the side aisle being a sort of vestibule for the Manger. The apse was supported not by a wall but on columns; further back a concentric semi-circular wall formed the basilica's outer wall. Between this wall and the *presbyterium* was the *matroneum*, from which the *presbyterium* was visible through the arches formed by the columns. Traces of a similar arrangement have been seen at, e.g., SS Cosmas and Damian's, in two churches at Naples, and in Duchesne's time at the basilica of St Demetrius at Salonika where, he stated, it was easy to distinguish the later masonry built to blind the apse arcades and support the apse vault. At St Mary Major the papal throne was in the centre, and it occupied the middle of the 5 arcades; that there were 5 arcades follows from there being 5 windows above (John the Deacon). That the present apse has only 4 windows is irrelevant: it is not even on the same site as the pre-1295 apse. When the throne was still at ground level, the women in the *matroneum* could overhear the pope. Paschal raised it a few steps to stop this. Pesarini (*Studi Romani* I.416) suggested a slightly different explanation: a *presbyterium* like that at St Paul's between the altar and the apse; this also gives 2 concentric semi-circles, but the complete enclosure was the apse itself, open to the women, who were kept from the *presbyterium* and the throne by the inner pierced colonnade; Paschal removed the pierced colonnade and moved the throne to the back of the apse (much as Sixtus V did at St Paul's). But while this was possible at St Paul's with its 22 m deep transept, St Mary's then had no transept; there would be no space for an inner colonnade. But it may be that the explanations of De Rossi, Duchesne and Pesarini are all misconceived. Krautheimer (*Corpus* 3.52) nowhere assumes a double apse, and considers that Paschal's changes are best explained by supposing that the women stood in the aisle, and that the throne was *beside* the high altar but close to the last part of the nave colonnade; so Paschal moved the throne to the apse beneath the middle window (of the 5), where John the Deacon later saw it.

[83] This was to stop the newly-raised throne dominating the altar. In the 17th century Strozzi saw what must have been this 9th-century pavement, some 33 cm above the original nave level (Krautheimer, *Corpus* 3.52). Cf. the activity of Gregory IV at S. Maria in Trastevere (103:31-2), though he had the added problem of housing relics.

[84] The text now describes how after transferring the throne to the apse Paschal installed a pergola (in effect an iconostasis) of six porphyry columns bearing a white marble architrave or lintel ('beam'). Four of the six columns were still there in the 16th century (Krautheimer, *Corpus* 3.52). Duchesne believed that the fine porphyry columns that now carry the baldacchino in St Mary Major's are four of Paschal's set of six. For the lamps and curtains connected with the pergola see cc. 32 and 36.

a beam of white marble; and linking them on right and left[85] with new purple marble,[86] he decorated them with engravings and adorned them very neatly. He repaired this church's *presbyterium* with various marble,[87] an improvement on how it used to be.

He wondrously adorned the holy altar's *propitiatorium* and the confessio inside and out, and its grills, with fine gold weighing 174 lb 6 oz. He also embellished this basilica's altar with silver sheets with various representations, and gilded it;[88] it weighs 385 lb. **32.** There too, the kind and distinguished prelate presented 6 bowls[89] of fine gold with various jewels, weighing 20 lb 6 oz; he laid down that day and night they should always be alight in front of the sacred altar. Relying on God's inspiration he presented in this basilica 8 silver arches with 16 columns,[90] weighing 218 lb 8 oz. In front of the altar's vestibule[91] he provided great silver railings weighing 78 lb. There too he presented 6 chandeliers,[92] weighing 60½ lb. Also, for this church's great arches he provided 42 great hanging chalices of silver,[93] weighing in all 281 lb. There too, for love of our same lady the Virgin, the venerable prelate presented 4 silver crowns weighing 62 lb 3 oz; also 2 silver canisters weighing 13½ lb.[94] He also provided there a silver-gilt image with the

---

[85] 'On right and left': the columns were in two groups of three, with no link in the central gap.

[86] i.e. the columns were linked by a balustrade of porphyry.

[87] John the Deacon (n. 82) states that the apse's mosaic decoration had 'fish among flowers, and animals with birds', but does not say whether the mosaic was on the apse-vault or the pavement; the LP description of variegated marble panels suggests a pavement, so this may be what Paschal installed, Krautheimer, *Corpus* 3.52.

[88] For *compsit* with *deauravit* cf. c. 10; but there and here *deauravit* may be an error for *decoravit*, linked with *compsit* elsewhere in this life.

[89] Lighting fixtures. Krautheimer, *Corpus* 3.53, suggests that they were six bracket-lamps for the six columns of the pergola.

[90] After the altar, the LP deals with the *presbyterium*. 'With' means 'resting on', Krautheimer, who (*Corpus* 3.53) finds the 8 arches and 16 columns more obscure than the pergola, but notes that they are mentioned immediately before the silver main gates at the altar vestibule, and thinks they may have formed a fenced-off area in front of the altar, like the early *scholae cantorum* at S. Marco and S. Pietro in Vincoli, but made of metal rather than masonry. Duchesne's explanation was that the enclosure had 8 arcades each supported by 2 colonnettes; if the iconostasis was at the 2nd nave-column, the enclosure had 7 arcades supported by the 6 porphyry columns, then the 2 intercolumniations of the nave; so, not counting the central arcade (the altar-vestibule, dealt with next), there were 8 openings, hence 8 arches with 16 columns.

[91] The central approach to the *presbyterium* in front of the altar.

[92] Either (Duchesne) one chandelier in front of each of the pergola's 6 porphyry columns, or (Krautheimer) one above each of the columns, on the marble lintel.

[93] Lighting fixtures. There were 42 intercolumniations in the nave; cf. Leo III's 42 veils (98:50). The LP writes 'arches' even though the colonnade had an architrave.

[94] The crowns and canisters are lamps; the figures 4 and 2 suggest that they were

face of God's holy mother Mary, weighing 17 lb 3 oz. **33.** On this basilica's sacred altar,[95] the servant of Christ the Lord almighty presented 2 gold-studded cloths representing our Lord Jesus Christ's nativity, with a fringe, decorated with various jewels and wondrously adorned with pearls. There too he presented another gold-studded cloth representing our Lord Jesus Christ's baptism by John in the Jordan, with a gold-studded fringe, wondrously adorned. There too he embellished a gold-studded cloth representing our Lord Jesus Christ's resurrection, with a gold-studded fringe and decorated with various pearls. **34.** Led by God's love, this holy and venerable pontiff provided there on the same altar another gold-studded cloth representing God's blessed mother's bodily assumption, with a gold-studded fringe and beautifully embellished and adorned with various pearls. There too the kind prelate provided another gold-studded cloth representing our Lord Christ's ascension, fitly adorned. There too, for love of the same virgin, he constructed another gold-studded cloth representing the coming of the Holy Ghost on the apostles, decorated and adorned with various pearls. He also joined to it another gold-studded cloth representing Palm Sunday, modestly embellished and adorned. There too this pontiff embellished another all-silk cloth with a gold-interwoven fringe. Also, for weekdays, he presented 2 gold-interwoven cloths with a fourfold-woven fringe, beautifully decorated. **35.** Spurred by God's inspiration, this holy prelate provided for this church's great arches[96] 14 gold-interwoven veils and 14 of fourfold-weave, also 14 of *imizilum*. For love of our same lady, our Lord Jesus Christ's servant provided for the arches of this church's *presbyterium* 26 gold-studded veils,[97] representing our Lord Jesus Christ and the nativity and assumption of the same undefiled virgin. For the same arches he also presented 24 veils of fourfold weave, sown round with various representations. The almighty Lord Christ's servant presented a wondrously adorned alexandrian tapestry high up in the *aspectus*[98] of the apse. **36.** He also

---

connected with the pergola.

[95] The text moves to the hangings and textiles, beginning with 11 fabrics (1 in use, 10 spare?) for the altar, occupying all of cc. 33-34.

[96] Three sets of 14 veils, for the 42 intercolumniations of the nave.

[97] Duchesne noted that two groups of veils are attributed to the *presbyterium*-arcades, one of 26, one of 24 veils; probably the figures should be the same; 24 is better, as a multiple of 8 (the *presbyterium* had 8 arcades, above). This would provide 3 or 6 sets, depending whether the curtains were draped in pairs or one by one.

[98] *aspectus* is obscure. Perhaps this tapestry was behind the throne in the opening of the central arcade, the place mentioned in 98:95: 'over the perch above the throne'.

presented on that basilica's great beam[99] a great veil of interwoven gold, with 7 gold-studded panels and a fringe of byzantine purple; to decorate the same basilica he provided on that beam 6 fourfold-woven veils and 4 veils of *imizilum*. Close to the vestibule of the altar in the apse[100] this pontiff provided 12 fourfold-woven veils; there too, 6 purple veils. At the entrance[101] to the same basilica this venerable prelate provided a great alexandrian curtain, embellished and adorned with various representations. Also, for weekdays, he presented another wondrously adorned alexandrian curtain. In the same basilica the kind and distinguished pontiff presented 6 white all-silk veils on the great beam, with a gold-interwoven fringe. In this basilica's apse he placed 6 white veils with a gold-interwoven fringe; also 4 white veils with a fringe of byzantine purple.

37. Since this thrice-blessed pastor often bestowed such great concern and watchfulness on the condition of God's holy churches, in the same basilica he also wondrously embellished and adorned the altar of the Manger[102] and the venerable confessio on the farther and the nearer sides with fine gold with various representations, weighing 134 lb 4 oz; onto it he fixed silver-gilt with various representations, weighing 254 lb 4 oz. There too this pontiff presented 3 bowls of fine gold with various jewels, weighing in all 8 lb 10 oz. He also placed there 5 crimson veils with a fringe of byzantine purple.

38. In his heartfelt love this holy bishop provided in Christ's martyr St Caecilia's church a gold-studded cloth representing our Lord Jesus

---

[99] Duchesne located this beam below the triumphal arch, but there was no such arch before 1295; though perhaps there could have been a beam across between the nave architraves in front of the *presbyterium*; the 'great veil' could have been draped from it down to the pavement of the church. Immediately after come 10 veils (6 and 4) arranged 'on the beam ... to decorate the same basilica'. A little lower comes another group of 6 and 4 veils for the same place; Duchesne could not see how to combine these with the great veil. But for Krautheimer, *Corpus* 3.52, the large curtain is for the new pergola's (c. 31) wider central opening; the 10 curtains are also for the pergola, 6 perhaps for the column shafts and 4 for the lateral intercolumniations. The words, half-way through the chapter, 'for weekdays', may cover the rest of the chapter; if so, all the items following are cheaper spare sets of curtains.

[100] Duchesne believed this referred to the lateral arcades of the apse; the central arcade has already been provided for. The veils for the apse are distributed in twelves or sixes, and the figure six recurs a little further on.

[101] Clearly the main door (cf. c. 21 and n. 70); Duchesne remarked that it was still customary to hang door-curtains (*cortinae*) in the open bays of the doors of basilicas.

[102] The *Praesepe* after which S. Maria Maggiore was at this date generally named; cf. 92:8 with n. 30. The Manger altar first occurs at 97:84 (A.D. 785-6). The relic and *memoria* of the Manger were in a separate oratory with its own altar and confessio. It was moved in 1588 to the new Sixtine Chapel within the basilica; a 16th-century plan (Krautheimer's figure 28a in *Corpus* 3) shows its earlier (original?) site.

Christ's resurrection wonderfully embroidered and adorned.
[A.D. 823-824:]
   On the altar of St Peter prince of the apostles, where his holy body lies, this God-protected, venerable and distinguished pontiff provided a *spanoclist* deep yellow gold *propitiatorium*, depicted with various representations and wondrously adorned, weighing 200 lb. For the love of God's same apostle his mentor he presented in the same church for the arches of the *presbyterium* 46 gold-studded veils representing our Lord Jesus Christ's passion and resurrection.
   In the martyrs SS Cosmas and Damian's church on the Via Sacra he provided an all-silk cloth beautifully embellished and adorned.
   39. In God's holy mother the ever-virgin Mary our lady's basilica called *ad Praesepe* this kind prelate provided 6 gold bowls, adorned with various jewels, weighing 6 lb; there too he presented a fine gold apostolic[103] bowl weighing 5 lb; there too he provided 8 silver chandeliers weighing in all 82 lb. For love of our same lady he presented in that basilica 4 columns and 1 arch, weighing in all 60 lb. This pontiff provided on that church's venerable altar a white cloth with a gold-studded cross in the middle, sown round with various jewels and beautifully decorated; he linked with it another cloth of byzantine purple, it too with a gold-studded cross, becomingly decorated with various stones. To adorn that church he also provided for the arches of the *presbyterium* .. gold-studded veils representing our Lord Jesus Christ's passion and resurrection. On that church's great beam he presented 6 other veils with a fourfold-woven fringe. On that church's beams he provided 6 gold-interwoven veils. Round that church's altar he presented 4 white all-silk veils with a fourfold-woven fringe.
   40. In God's blessed mother's church called *Domnica* this venerable prelate provided silver railings[104] weighing 66 lb.
   In God's blessed mother our lady's church at Vescovio[105] in Sabina he provided a gold-interwoven cloth with a fringe of byzantine purple.
   He died when God called him. He was buried in St Peter's.[106] He

---

[103] *apostolatus*; the meaning may be 'a lamp adorned with figures of the apostles' (in a Roman context probably just Peter and Paul).

[104] Or 'grills'; probably for the confessio (so Krautheimer, *Corpus* 3.310). For the building of this church and its other decorations see cc. 11-14.

[105] *Episcopio*, whence the modern form of the place-name. Duchesne (I.188 n. 7) noted that in the 9th century the seat of the bishopric of Sabina was still in its ancient place at Forum Novum, where this church, called S. Maria di Vescovio, survives. It is mentioned in a letter by Hadrian I in 781 (J2433, *CC* p. 219): 'the church of God's mother Mary in the place called Foronovo'.

[106] The compiler fails to mention that the burial was carried out with some difficulty.

performed two ordinations, one in December, the other in March, .. priests, 7 deacons; for various places .. bishops. His bishopric was vacant 4 days in January of the 1st indiction [823].[107]

Thegan, *Gesta Hludowici imperatoris* 30: 'Pope (Paschal) died, and the Roman people did not want his corpse buried in the church of St Peter the apostle, before pope Eugene succeeded him; and he ordered his body to be buried in the place that he, while alive, had constructed'. The tomb was probably in one of the two chapels he had founded, that of SS Processus and Martinian, or that of SS Xystus and Fabian. The epitaph is lost. For the troubles at this date see also *ARF* 824 Scholz 115, and Paschasius Radbertus, *Vita Walae* 1.28 Cabaniss 143; and the discussion in the introduction to life 101. Such a popular uproar suggests that Paschal was detested and had made many enemies as a result of his harsh rule; see the introduction to this life.

[107] The vacancy was 5 days; and the month and year stated (January 823) are false. The year was 824, cf. *ARF* 824 Scholz 115, *Annales Auscienses, MGH SS* 3.171 etc. For the calendar date of Paschal's death (16 February) see 101:1 n. 1, evidence not known to Duchesne, who placed Paschal's death on 11 February 824, a Saturday (it was in fact a Thursday).

101. EUGENE II (824-827).

The author of this life adopts a very simple language and straightforward style, but his text is unfinished and seems to be no more than a preliminary draft, produced with what Duchesne described as a quite peculiar negligence in contrast with the rest of the LP. The faults are due in part to its incompleteness, but it may be doubted if a finished version would have provided much more than the register material on which the compiler had embarked where the text breaks off. Two MSS (CE) attempt to supplement the lack of even the usual formulaic material; they cannot name the pope's father, but they claim that the pope was of Roman origin (true no doubt - he was the candidate of the nobility) and attribute a false length to his tenure of the see. So it is no surprise that we hear nothing, for instance, of Eugene's concern for the pagan Danes. Eugene extended the commendation Paschal had given to Ebbo of Rheims to include Anskar and his companions, and they began their missionary labours in autumn 826 (J2564).

It is far more serious that the very significant political events of this pontificate are alluded to in only the vaguest way (c. 3, return of exiles). That Eugene's election was disputed is asserted categorically by *ARF* 824, though the LP mentions no competition and claims that Eugene was elected by the whole Roman people (c. 2), a notion repeated at 102:4. It is usually thought that the authors of the LP are here disingenuous. But it may be that they are, albeit misleadingly, noting that (thanks to the *Ludovicianum* of 817) the electorate was no longer limited to the clergy as it had been since 769. The actual wording of *ARF* is important:

'In his (Paschal's) place, when two were elected in a popular dispute, yet Eugene archpriest of St Sabina's *titulus*, the faction of the nobles being victorious, was put forward (*subrogatus*) and elected. When the subdeacon Quirinus had brought the news of this to the emperor (Louis), he, at a meeting about 24 June at Compiègne...'

The translation in Scholz, 115, clearly takes *subrogatus* to mean that Eugene was a substitute for the dead Paschal rather than for other candidates, I think wrongly. The difficulties surrounding Eugene's election are confirmed by Paschasius Radbertus, *Vita Walae* 1.28; he records how the monk Wala, adviser to Louis and Lothar, returned to France

'with almost all matters put right and holy Eugene ordained as bishop of the apostolic see; and he (Wala) is said to have put much effort into his ordination (or 'into arranging this' but not, *pace* Cabaniss, 143, 'in administration'), so that somehow things which had been negligently corrupted for a long time by many men might thereafter be put to rights through him (Eugene).'

From these two Frankish accounts it is clear that Wala exercised some influence in securing the election of a candidate from among the nobility, in contrast, therefore, to Paschal, who had been supported by the clerical bureaucracy. So, for example, Duchesne:

'Eugene's accession was a reaction against Paschal's policy which had been rumblingly hostile to the empire in so far as this claimed authority over the city and territory of Rome.'

So it is generally assumed that Eugene defeated a candidate from among Paschal's supporters. This inference is, I believe, false: it does not account for the fact that the name of the competitor is nowhere recorded, and more seriously it does not allow for the use of the word *subrogatus* in *ARF*. The Annals are specific that there was a double election before Eugene was 'substituted'; the words surely mean that the popular faction, itself divided, produced and even elected two candidates, allowing the nobles to substitute Eugenius.

What is more, the events have to be fitted into the newly established chronology (see n. 1 to the life), on which Eugene's election took place on the day of Paschal's death, 16 February, and his ordination five days later. On the old dating Eugene was not elected and ordained until early June and it was assumed that disturbances after Paschal's death lasted several months with the nobility and the clerical bureaucracy each making a rival nomination; eventually Wala somehow pushed through the ordination of the candidate favoured by the nobility and by himself. Eugene immediately notified the Frankish court and swore his oath of loyalty to Louis (on the meaning of this oath see below). The subdeacon Quirinus took the news to Louis some time before a meeting held at Compiègne about 24 June, and in August Louis sent Lothar to Rome.

Some modification of this is required if Eugene's ordination was three months earlier than formerly assumed. The 'disturbances' (in Wala) may refer to events before Paschal's death and possibly continuing after Eugene's election, not merely in the interval between the two events. The double election to which *ARF* refers surely means that the non-noble 'popular' faction was itself split and could not decide between two of its own candidates. And perhaps it was this very fact that gave Wala the opportunity to rush the election and ordination of a third candidate, Eugene, who was 'substituted' before the opposition could unite. Louis may well have heard the news well before 24 June. Since there was no urgency shown between June, when Louis decided to send his son Lothar to Rome, and Lothar's actual departure after mid-August, there is equally no reason to suppose that the council held at Compiègne in late June was held very soon after Quirinus's arrival.

At Compiègne, Louis decided to send Lothar to Rome,

'so that in his stead he might lay down and fix with the new pontiff and the Roman people what the need of the situation demanded... Lothar... was honourably received by the pontiff Eugene. When he had informed him of his instructions, with the benevolent assent of this pontiff he so corrected the state of the Roman people, which had for a long time been corrupted by the perversity of certain prelates [popes, cf. Astronomer below], that all who had been seriously desolated by the seizure of their property were magnificently consoled by the return of their goods which had occurred thanks to his arrival, God granting it' (*ARF* 824).

Astronomer, *Vita Hludovici Pii* 38, is more explicit than the Annals: 'When there was an inquiry into what had happened, that is, why those who had been loyal to the emperor and to himself and to the Franks had been destroyed by a wicked death, and those who survived were held as a laughing-stock to the rest, and why such great quarrels resounded against the pontiffs of the Romans and the judges, it was found that by the ignorance or lack of concern of certain pontiffs [Leo III and Paschal] and by the blind and insatiable cupidity of many judges the estates of many had been unjustly confiscated. And so, for returning what had been unjustly taken away, Lothar created great joy for the Roman people.'

Lothar's *Constitutio* (see below) names three dead victims of the recent troubles; one, Theodore, is clearly the *primicerius* killed in 823; Floro and Sergius are unknown. But in all three cases their families had been ruined, and restitution was now to be made.

The impression from these Frankish documents is confirmed by the brief remark in the LP (c. 3) about the return of exiles (otherwise unrecorded) and restoration of property; the latter is attributed to Eugene, not Lothar, but we may assume the two were in agreement.

Lothar was in Rome on 13 November 824 when in his presence and at his request Eugene conferred the pallium on archbishop Adalram (*MGH Ep* 5.313). It was in the same month, and we must assume that it was again with Eugene's agreement, that Lothar published his *Constitutio Romana* (*MGH Cap* 1, 322-4). By this he fulfilled his father's mandate: the frequent troubles and arbitrary judicial excesses that had marked the pontificates of Leo and Paschal were to be ended and order restored by modifying the relationship between Rome and the empire.

The constitutional issues are fully discussed by Noble, 313-322, to whom the following account is heavily indebted. He sees the agreement as both conservative, safeguarding the position of the papal state, and innovative: while it does not give the western emperor any equivalent to the former Byzantine control over Rome it does go beyond the *Ludovicianum* of 817, establishing an imperial envoy in Rome and so linking the state more closely to the empire.

The *Constitutio* deals firstly (art. 1) with the law of persons, giving immunity to anyone who has procured the pope's or the emperor's special protection; anyone violating this is liable to the death penalty. 'We also decree that they are to observe just obedience in all things to the apostolic lord and his leaders and judges, for bringing about justice'.

Ordinary inhabitants of Rome (art. 5) are to chose once for all whether they wish to live under Roman, Frankish or Lombard law, and this is to be respected, with access to the appropriate courts (this would protect the many non-Romans who lived in the state and preferred Germanic law). All who have suffered injustice are to be compensated (Lothar did not regard papal officials as blameless).

Many articles are intended to control the behaviour of dukes and officials at Rome. They are to obey the pope, and every year the officials must attend on the emperor so that he can advise them on their functions (art. 8), but it is not suggested that they are Louis's appointees or that he could dismiss them. Noble (320-1) sees this as a means to give fuller protection to everyone in the papal state, as a guarantee to the pope against his own officials, and as in no way reducing the pope's privilege as a direct overlord within the empire.

The people are not to attack the pope or each other. Two permanent envoys are to be established, one appointed by the pope, the other by the emperor; these are to report every year to the emperor on how the dukes and judges dispense justice. Complaints against negligence by the dukes and judges are to be addressed by these envoys to the pope, who is to select one of the envoys to put matters right; if the pope fails to do this immediately, the imperial envoy is to tell the emperor, who will send other envoys to settle matters (art. 4). Noble (321) comments that the imperial envoy resembles a referee more than an official placed to challenge the pope's authority. But Benedict, brother of Sergius II, may have owed his power in Rome to his being one of these envoys (see pp. 73-4).

Papal elections are dealt with in article 3; the electorate is to be 'the Romans to whom the privilege had been granted from of old by the constitutions of the holy Fathers'. This included the laity, as had been done already in the pact of 817, when the untraditional decision of Stephen III's synod in 769 reserving the elections to the clergy had been abrogated (cf. n. 64 to 96:20). And sure enough the LP henceforth mentions or implies the role of the laity, often stressing the part played by the nobles: in 827 for Valentine (102:4) and for Gregory IV (103:4); in 844 for Sergius II (104:4); in 847 for Leo IV (105:5); in 855 for Benedict III (106:4); in 858 for Nicholas (107:5-6; the clergy and the nobility gather with 'all the people' in one fairly small basilica); in 867 for Hadrian II (108:4, 6; all the Romans and strangers present, rich and poor, clerical and lay, demand Hadrian, but the election itself is carried out by the bishops, the clergy, the nobles and their 'compliant' people!).

The Carolingians did not attempt to resuscitate the (largely theoretical) right the Byzantine emperors had had to refuse to confirm the candidate elected. The only difference, a rather minor one, from the arrangements of 817 is that in the oath they would have to take to the

two emperors (see below) the Romans would have to swear not to
interfere unjustly and uncanonically in the election, and not to allow the
ordination of the elected candidate to go ahead until the emperor's
envoy had confirmed fair play. Hitherto the emperors had taken no part
at all in the election; the recent disorders in Rome produced this
arrangement by which they could now take punitive action against any
who interfered with the electoral arrangements established in 817. One
effect of the arrangment would be a prolonged interval if the emperor's
envoy were not present.

It also emerges (from the last part of the oath taken by the Romans)
that before being ordained a pope-elect was to take an oath, such as
Eugene had already given in writing, before the imperial legate. This
must have been part of the pact in 824 (there are no reasons to suppose
another pact in 825); and it clearly became the norm, even if we have
no information on what happened when Valentine became pope in 827.
The delay between Gregory IV's election that same year and his
ordination gave time for the legate to arrive to receive the oath (see 103
n. 11). In 844 Sergius II delayed swearing until after his ordination
(104:15); Leo IV's oath in 847 is specifically mentioned in the
Ottonianum of 962 (Sickel 1883:181). This papal oath has been
generally assumed to be one of loyalty sworn by a subject to the
emperor, and as a far greater acknowledgment of imperial sovereignty
than Eugene's predecessors had made. Others have suggested that it was
the oath taken by Eugene ratifying the *Constitutio*, henceforth to be
taken by his successors before their consecration. But the oath to be
sworn is one that Eugene had already sworn (perhaps in Wala's
presence) before the *Constitutio* was issued; and this must be the one he
was required to swear by the *Ludovicianum* of 817 (so, e.g. Bertolini
1956:53ff) - a confirmation of the alliance with the Franks such as
previous popes had made on various occasions (though not at the time
of their election) since 757. The only innovation was that the oath be
sworn before ordination and in the presence of the envoy, to remind the
pope of his reciprocal obligations with the Franks (Noble, 317-18).

There was now, however, an oath which all Romans, apart from the
pope, were to take. We know of it not from the MSS of the *Constitutio*
itself, but from the *Continuatio Romana* of Paul the Deacon's *History
of the Lombards* (*anno* 825, *MGH SSrL* 203).

'In the name of almighty God, on these holy Gospels and on this Cross of our Lord
Jesus Christ, and on the body of the blessed Peter prince of the apostles, I promise that
from this day until my death I will be faithful to our lords the emperors Louis and
Lothar with all my strength without fraud or evil craftiness, saving the faith promised
to our lord the pope. I will prevent with all my power and understanding any election
of a pontiff to the see of Rome taking place other than in conformity with canon law
and justice, and I will not consent to the consecration of the one elected until he takes

the oath in public and in the presence of our lord's delegate, with the oath that lord pope Eugene for the safety of everyone freely put in writing'.

The crucial problem about the two oaths is how far they acknowledged imperial sovereignty and, by changing the status of the pope and his subjects, compromised the existence of the papal state. Traditionally the arrangements of 824 have been seen (except by those who dismiss the oath as a later imperial forgery) as marking 'a revolution in Franco-papal relations' (Halphen), and 'the high point of Frankish control of the papacy' (Kelly). Unlike the oath sworn by the pope, that sworn by the Romans certainly begins as that of a Frankish subject. This was new, but it was not an acceptance of imperial sovereignty since, as Noble has shown, there is a 'safeguard' by which the Romans owed allegiance to the pope first, and only then to the emperor. The reciprocal friendship between the Franks and Romans had since 754 required the Franks to protect the Romans; but it was increasingly protection from each other that they most needed; and Frankish investigations into happenings at Rome were liable to be stalled by papal oaths of purgation. The solution of Louis and Lothar was, indeed, to have the Romans swear the oath of Frankish subjects. But this oath did not require obedience, merely a limited allegiance and an abstention from open disloyalty. Yet a Roman breaking the oath could now be brought to book in a way which had been difficult when the constitutional arrangement was that of an alliance between both sides, as it had been during troubles under Leo III and Paschal. 'The *Constitutio* oath was neither more nor less than an efficacious protection device for the pope and for St Peter's people' (Noble, 317-320). In a nutshell, the papal state retained its constitutional autonomy vis-à-vis the empire but its subjects were now, as Noble puts it, 'justiciable' before the emperor; he notes that there had been some precedent at Ravenna for such a 'regime of vaguely concurrent powers'.

Noble concludes (321-2) that the *Constitutio* was deeply conservative. The permanent imperial envoy in Rome formed a slightly stronger bond between the state and the empire, and justice at Rome was supposed to improve. But there was no change from the spirit of the Franco-papal alliance since 754 and the *Ludovicianum* of 817. The *Constitutio* guaranteed the Romans protection not merely against foreign foes, as Stephen II had wanted in 754, but against each other, which was what Eugene wanted now.

Another fault in the LP life of Eugene is the lack of any reference to iconoclasm, an issue which at this point concerned not merely the pope but the emperors in both east and west. Leo V's policy had already caused Paschal concern. In 824 the next emperors Michael II and Theophilus sent an embassy to Louis, which reached him at Rouen on

17 November; the purpose was to get his help for an approach to Rome
(cf. *ARF* 824 Scholz 116). Michael claimed that the cult of images led
to abuses, and knew that the Franks held images to be permissible but
not to be for adoration; he wanted Louis to persuade Eugene to prohibit
veneration. Louis cooperated, and still in 824 he sent envoys, including
Freculf bishop of Lisieux, to Rome to persuade Eugene to compromise.
But Eugene stoutly maintained that, even if the Franks did not accept
it, the question had been dogmatically settled by the second council of
Nicaea in 787 (cf. *LP* 97:88): images must not be adored, but must be
venerated. So this first Frankish embassy failed, but Louis persevered
and was at length able to get Eugene's agreement (Mansi 15, append.
p. 337, *PL* 98.1347, 104.1317 etc.) that the clergy of his own and
Lothar's kingdom should gather statements from the works of the
Fathers which would help produce a satisfactory definition when the
Greek envoys returned to consult him. Louis's theological synod met at
Paris on 1 November 825 (acts in Mansi 14.463, *PL* 98.1299-1350,
MGH Conc 2.473-551), reported against the Council of 787 (images
were not to be destroyed but were not to be venerated) and lambasted
Eugene for protecting error and superstition. In Eugene's name they
prepared a letter to Michael and Theophilus (J2561). Louis and Lothar
sent a new embassy (Jeremias archbishop of Sens and Jonas bishop of
Orleans) to tell Eugene of the decision and take him the letter for
signing and forwarding by them to Constantinople; and perhaps papal
envoys should come with them. But Louis already saw that Eugene
would not abandon the Council of 787 (*MGH Conc* 2.533). The
iconodule Theodore of Studios had already received support from
Paschal which he valued highly, and Eugene had by now made contact
with him; and, like Paschal, Eugene had received eastern refugees from
iconoclasm. Jeremias and Jonas could not shift Eugene: no letters or
envoys went east from Rome. It may have been the papal embassy
which reached Ingelheim in the summer of 826 (Leo bishop of
Centumcellae, Theophylact the *nomenclator*, and Dominic abbot of
Mount Olivet from beyond the seas; *ARF* 826 Scholz 119), that told
Louis of Eugene's refusal. Louis took the matter no further, whether
from respect for a decision by the pope or because he saw no point in
upsetting the political balance recently achieved at Rome merely to
please Constantinople.

Eugene held a synod of 62 bishops, 17 priests and 6 deacons, in St
Peter's on 14-15 November 826 (*MGH Conc* 2.552-583; Mansi 14.999).
The 38 reforming canons are wide-ranging, and were applied to the
Frankish kingdom as well as Rome: they condemn simony, encourage
clerical education, deal with the bishops' qualifications (they are not to

be consecrated unless asked for by clergy and people), and their duties and revenues (they are not to be absent too long from their churches, not to take the lands of their subjects or church property for their own use, not to dismiss their clergy). They deal too with the number, conduct and duties of priests: the assent of the faithful is required for ordination. Arrangements are made for church buildings and institutions; in accordance with Frankish practice, a proprietor who builds a church is not to lose control of it involuntarily. The discipline of abbots, monks and nuns, is then considered, along with the problem of those forced to become monks unwillingly. Sunday observance is stressed; feast days are not to be violated with dancing, dirty songs and choruses. The laity are not to be present in the chancel during the liturgy. Teachers are to be established for the study of letters and the liberal arts. And questions of divorce, bigamy and illicit marriages are considered.

A text preserved independently by cardinal Deusdedit shows that the council also ratified the rules dealing with papal elections. On the council see also the notes to 105:90-92, Leo IV's council of 8 December 853 which largely repeated the enactments of that held by Eugene.

101. 1. EUGENE [II; 21 February¹ 824 - .. August 827]. He² was a
venerable and distinguished man of great sincerity and humility,
instructed in learning, distinguished in speech, fair of form, and
generous to those with requests. Rejecting the world, he thought day and
night on those things alone which were pleasing to Christ. In the time
of this pontiff no small abundance fell not only on the whole of Rome
but also on nearly all of the world; for he unremittingly assigned to
everyone, not only to orphans and widows but even to the rich,
whatever he reckoned was a just burden for his subjects. **2.** In his days
there was great peace and stillness throughout the whole Roman world;
for since he was the friend of all peace, what else were they about if
they too did not themselves do what he with his honourable character
was doing? He was the archpriest of this holy and universal church; in
which for no small time he ruled his assignment wonderfully.
Afterwards, elected by all³ the Romans thanks to the godly report of his
merits, he was made pontiff after holy lord pope Paschal passed away.
3. In the time of his priesthood he held St Sabina the martyr's church
on the Aventine Hill; by God's dispensation, after the grace of the
pontificate was granted him, he brought it to a higher standard and
decorated it all round with pictures.⁴

---

¹ For this date see MS Vat. Lat. 645 fol. 6r, a 9th-century calendar (photograph in *NCE*
5.625): *XIIII kl <Martias> Sol in Pisces. Paschalis papa obiit et Eugenius successit....
VIIII kl. Eugenius prbr. tit. sce. Savine apostolicus ordinatus est*; 21 February was a
Sunday in 824, as required for episcopal ordinations. The LP (in MS D) gives no
chronological data for Eugene; MSS CE add 'held the see 4 years', to which E adds: '2
months 23 days'. The Montecassino Catalogue gives Eugene 3 years 7 months 22 days.
Since his death was in August 827 (see p. 41), perhaps read 3 years 5 months 22 days,
and suppose that he died about 12 August 827; Valentine's 40 days can then be from, say,
Sunday 19 August 827 to 28 September. Baronius's dates in 824 (15 May for Paschal's
death, 18 June for Eugene's accession) and in 827 (11 August both for Eugene's death
and for Valentine's accession) rest on no good authority. The old view (Jaffé 1885:320,
retained e.g. by Noble, 316, and by Kelly, 101) was that Eugene was not elected and
consecrated until early June 824. This was based on 1) the length of Eugene's pontificate
as given in MS E, emended and printed in the text of Vignoli's edition as '3 years 2
months 23 days'; 2) Eugene died in August 827; 3) the news of Eugene's election reached
Compiègne before about 24 June 824; and 4) a synod held at Mantua on 6 June 827 is
dated as in Eugene's fourth year, Mansi 14.493. The newly established date satisfies all
these conditions if MS E is differently emended.
² MSS CE insert the usual formula 'of Roman origin son of' (with no name). His father's
name is given as Bonemund (i.e. Bohemund) in an insertion in one MS of the LP's 'third
edition'.
³ Untrue if it means that the election was unanimous; but it may refer merely to the
involvement of the laity as well as the clergy; see p. 31.
⁴ None of Eugene's work at S. Sabina now survives, though the mosaics of the apse-arch
escaped Sixtus V's restorations long enough to be published by Ciampini (*Vetera*

In his days the Roman judges who were held captive in France returned;[5] he allowed them to enter onto their parents' property and gave them no small amount from the Lateran patriarchate, because they were destitute of almost all their revenues.

In the same church of St Sabina the martyr he provided a fine silver canopy weighing .. lb.[6] There too this venerable prelate presented .....[7]

Monumenta (1690) I.188 pl. 47; Krautheimer, *Corpus* 4.75), who stated that traces of Eugene's pictures could still be seen on the epistyles of the columns. The design consisted of a series of medallions arranged in a semicircle round the curvature of the arch. On top was the Saviour; on each side the busts of 7 (originally 8) men; and the two mystical cities, Jerusalem and Bethlehem. De Rossi noticed the close resemblance of this design to that in St Zeno's oratory at S. Prassede, and the likelihood that the work was done by the same mosaicists. An obstacle is the word *picturis* in this life; the LP, especially in the 9th century, distinguishes paintings and mosaics; the latter are *musivum*, a word not appearing in this life. Yet in this scrap of a life there is no reason to expect the LP's normal standards of accuracy; so Duchesne attributed the mosaic to Eugene, and Krautheimer seems to accept this.

[5] For the context and significance of this see the introduction to this life and to 100. *ARF* and Astronomer do not mention exiles and attribute the restoration of property to Lothar, not Eugene. Relevant is the first chapter of the *Constitutio* of 824, referring to abuses of the judicial system, and showing concern about the property of the widows and orphans of those killed.

[6] Darsy 1961:29 wrongly cites '102 lb' as from Duchesne's text at this point.

[7] The text breaks off leaving the rest of Eugene's gifts unrecorded. This is the last literary reference to S. Sabina's until 1222; Eugene's changes and decorations (on which, Darsy 1961:29; Krautheimer, *Corpus* 4.75) are the only ones recorded or suspected before the 13th century. The iconostasis, some five metres forward from the *presbyterium*, consisted of columns surmounted by a high stone frieze. The gifts included a bronze gate or railings which in the 16th century still enclosed the choir; Pompeio Ugonio (*Historia delle stazioni di Roma*, 1588), c. 10, read on them ('in large letters') the inscription *Eugenius Secundus Papa Romanus*. Another inscription in 4 couplets is still visible at the end of the right aisle: it mentions a pope Eugene who brought to S. Sabina's the bodies of SS Alexander (identified as the 2nd-century pope), Theodulus and Eventius, and placed them close to Sabina and Seraphia in the building which Peter the priest had provided in the time of pope Caelestinus. The verses are leonine, so the inscription is likely to be of the 10th or 11th century, though no doubt Eugene II is referred to (Krautheimer; Berthier 1910:289; photograph in Darsy, 113, fig. 29). Sabina, really the foundress of the *titulus*, was first regarded as a saint from the end of the fifth century, and the legend of her martyrdom (*Aa SS* Augusti VI.496-504) will be later still. Seraphia (Amore 1975:305) is supposed to have been the person who converted Sabina to Christianity; when Sabina was martyred she was buried on 29 August 'in the town of the Vendinenses' (a village near Terni) 'at the arch of Faustinus', where Seraphia was already buried. In 1586-7 the revetment of the apse-wall was reused to pave the apse; the 9th-century chancel enclosure (plaques, inscribed bronze doors, colonnettes and architrave) was dismantled, as was the old altar supported by four columns in the apse (Krautheimer, *Corpus* 4.98).

102. VALENTINE (827).

Next to nothing is known from outside the LP about Valentine or any action he performed during his ephemeral pontificate. *ARF* 827 offers:

'Pope Eugene died in August, in whose place the deacon Valentine was elected and ordained by the Romans; he completed barely one month in the pontificate.'

To this the other annals have nothing to add. From the LP we infer that he was of upper-class family (n. 2); his advance from the subdiaconate (he was ordained by Paschal) to the papacy in ten years at the outside suggests that he was both privileged and youthful. Unanimity is claimed for his election (c. 6); the electorate included the laity (and specifically the dignitaries), a requirement reiterated (from the *Ludovicianum* of 817) in Lothar's *Constitutio* of 824, and ratified at Eugene's Council of November 826. There is no reference to Valentine taking the oath required, but he cannot have failed to fulfil that part of the arrangements; the lack of delay before ordination suggests that the imperial envoy was available at Rome.

The life is composed in an attempt at high style, and the praise for the pope's virtues sounds vapid. Its greatest interest is what it shows about the composition of the LP. A full-scale account of the pope's character, career and ordination was produced at an early moment after he became pope, and tacked on to the incomplete life of Eugene; the compiler clearly had no knowledge that the new pontificate would last a mere 40 days.

* * * * *

102. **1.** VALENTINE [about September 827], of Roman origin, son of Leontius,[1] from the region Via Lata,[2] held the see 40 days. He was a man filled with great holiness and blessedness, and continued overflowing with the grace of the Holy Ghost. He was born of aristocratic and godly parents in this city of Rome (which by God's authority holds the dignity of the highest sacerdotal office and of royal supremacy), and was handed over to an expert master for elementary studies; then he explored the sacred pinnacles of God's law with fully capacious sensibility and retained them in the memory with which he was endowed. In the manner of the nobility he avoided the vain and shameful games of children; his mouth uttered no inappropriate or unsuitable stories, and he engaged in no forbidden works and activities. **2.** Instead, from the earliest flowering of childhood he was given to

---

[1] Son of Peter in MS E (and later versions).

[2] See 97:1 and n. 1. This implies that Valentine was of upper-class family.

godly modesty and sobriety, and, full of the distinguished nectar of God's inspiration, he kept his lips embellished with the trappings of speech and wisdom among all men. With his particular plentifulness of vocabulary and with the resplendent merits of his works, he displayed the elegant mind in his breast, particularly when he presented himself in triumph and affection to all men 'without offence', to use the fine words of the teacher of the gentiles;[3] for, putting a stumbling-block or hindrance in no one's way,[4] he took care with steadfast mind to expend the due of perfect love on his neighbours; and according to the precept spoken by the Lord, he kept his loins girded with chastity and his lamps burning in his hands,[5] that is to say, he shone splendidly in word and deed and was resplendent in the task of teaching through the magnificent token of his praiseworthy example.

3. Aided by the power of God on high, when he had already entered on adulthood, the favour of his goodness and shrewdness was wafted far and wide like sweet-smelling incense, and by the true-spoken account of the faithful it rang loud and clear in the ears of lord Paschal; and when this blessed prelate of godly memory had truly learnt from the people's uniting in his praise that he would be illustrious and distinguished in all things, he advanced him through the ecclesiastical grades to the office of the subdiaconate, and bade him be at his service in the Lateran Palace. And recognizing his life and manner of behaviour and patience, he greatly loved him beyond others. And by the favour of the grace of God from above, to whom he had vowed himself with total devotion of mind and his whole power, this man shone full of the light of truth and wisdom. He was affable in word, lucid in teaching, and conspicuous in countenance; among his brethren he was modest with godly devotion; to his neighbours he was loyal; and relying on his shrewd understanding he embroiled himself in no dealings whereby anyone might, however trivially, be saddened. **4.** Moreover when that pontiff observed that he was elegant and was adorned with so many good things, with works of such great merit and with a noteworthy physical presence, he consecrated him as a deacon of his apostolic see. On account of his merit, wherewith he gleamed brightly and was held in affection and love by all the people of the church and the distinguished assembly of the Romans, he bounteously conferred many gifts and benefits on him, and afterwards made him archdeacon.[6] Now

---

[3] 1 Cor. 10.32.

[4] Rom. 14.13.

[5] Luke 12.35.

[6] This is important, as it implies (unless the mortality of the other deacons was unusually

when this prelate at Christ's bidding climbed to the heights of heaven, Eugene was raised up by all[7] to the pontifical office and set in the apostolic see. He recognized that he was splendidly adorned with all the good things we have mentioned, and all the time he lived he retained him in the place of his dearly beloved; with a keen heart he rejoiced like a father in his own son, and yearned for him to stand unceasingly in his sight.

5. But when the term of this prelate's transient light was accomplished and divinely completed, the whole assembly[8] of the Romans besought the Lord with frequent fasting and prayer about the rule of the pinnacles of the holy see, that he might see fit to reveal to their senses who was worthy of the office of so great a see. But when God's majesty was placated, who was it among the sacerdotal catalogue that he should manifest to them by the arcane will of his power for election, but him whom he had adorned from his mother's breast with so many above-mentioned abundances of virtues and with most beautiful flowering of teaching? and whom should he grant as ruler of the most holy see but him whom he had groomed as a pupil to be entirely constant and faithful to him? **6.** So when the venerable bishops and glorious dignitaries of the Romans and all the people[9] of the widespread City were gathered together in the Lateran Palace, so that they might resound with the single voice of many men what all in their hearts held equally as already revealed from heaven, with the consent of one will[10] there was a loud acclamation: 'Valentine the most holy archdeacon is worthy of the apostolic see! Valentine must be adorned with the badge of the supreme pontificate!' So this was uttered in unison, and then, all of them remaining in peaceful harmony, the sacred [gathering][11] of the clergy and the dignitaries of the Romans with the people as well hurried to the church of God's holy mother the ever-virgin Mary our lady, and found him rendering in his usual manner manifold thanks and praises to the Lord. And straightaway, though he much and long resisted and proclaimed with steadfast voice that he would be unsuited to so great a rule, he was elected by the joyful voices of the beloved people and of

---

quick) that the archidiaconate was held by direct appointment and not simply by the deacon who was senior by date of ordination; cf. 'archpriest' at 104:4.

[7] See 101: n. 3, and p. 31.

[8] Specified in c. 6 to include the laity; cf. introduction to the life.

[9] Cf. *ibid.*

[10] That there was unanimity may be true here, even if the LP's twice repeated claim about the election of 824 is false.

[11] After *sacer* supply some such noun as *coetus*.

both the militias of the Romans;[12] then with praises worthy of his glory and with the fullness of honour they took him to the Lateran patriarchate and set him on the pontifical throne. **7.** His feet were triumphantly kissed by all the senate[13] of the Romans, everything which needed doing was lawfully and reverently carried out, and great was the sobriety, great the joy that endured among men and women of all ages.

And when light dawned on the fair day of his consecration, all the Romans together brought this bishop from the palace to the church of St Peter prince of the apostles, and with the aid of the Majesty enthroned on high they consecrated him supreme pontiff. **8.** Then he ascended the pinnacles of the bountiful see of St Peter, the apostle and the keybearer of the heavenly kingdom; divine praises and sacrifices were piously offered to God, and he returned to the palace with the full and magnificent assembly of the Romans with enormous joy. He splendidly enriched the holy people[14] and the senate and people of Rome with many and various gifts and very loving presents, with the most joyous stewardry and outlay.[15]

He was noteworthy for his stewardry, distinguished for his activity, clear in speech, a neighbour to all in showing pity, and instantly provided timely comfort for those enduring want.

Adorned for heaven with these manifold good things, when Christ called, he was oppressed by bodily trouble and passed away with a precious departure.[16] With the desirable fruit of his most blessed work he joyously went up into the sight of the supreme Majesty, and he reigns and rejoices with the Lord for ever.

---

[12] The meaning seems to be clergy (as *militia Christi*) and laity (the *scholae*).

[13] There is of course no reason to suppose that the Roman senate still existed; the term is a literary variant to describe leading members of the Roman nobility; cf. Toubert 1973:965-6.

[14] The *sacra plebs* is the clergy. At one time it would have meant the laity: cf. *nos servi tui sed et plebs tua sancta* in the Canon of the Roman mass. It equally clearly means the clergy at 104:19 and 105:12.

[15] Such is the meaning of this expression (*dapibus, sumptis*) at 97:92; but in the context of the ordination ceremonies of a pope the reference may be more specifically to a banquet.

[16] Ps. 115 (116.15): 'Precious in the sight of the Lord is the death of his saints'.

103. GREGORY IV (828-844).

The compiler treats (cc. 1-4) of Gregory's early career and election, but then abandons all political history in favour of heavily abridged versions of the registers on buildings and enrichment of churches. The only exception - apparent rather than real, as it does concern building - is the account in cc. 38-40 of the rebuilding of Ostia as 'Gregoriopolis'. A powerful fortress was needed to defend Rome and central Italy from the threat posed by the Saracens, who had landed in Sicily in 827 (see n. 89).

This reflects perhaps the methodology of the compiler rather than any deliberate attempt to suppress the none too successful policies of Gregory. And it is true that at Rome Gregory's pontificate did see much money spent on building and decorating churches; in the apse-mosaic at S. Marco, constructed in 829-831, Gregory's portrait in mosaic survives (photograph in *NCE* 6. 771). His other works included the rebuilding of the ruined Sabbatina aqueduct (c. 19), whose water was needed to operate the mills on the Janiculum.

Gregory's ordination was delayed until the imperial envoy was present and the oath now required could be taken before him (cf. nn. 1, 11), and the link with the Carolingians remained firm as long as that family remained united. Thus about April 828 Gregory sent envoys, the *primicerius*
Quirinus and *nomenclator* Theophylact, to Louis (*ARF* 828; Astronomer, *Vita Hludovici Pii* 42). But the relationship was not necessarily to Rome's advantage: envoys from Louis (bishop Joseph and count Leo) came to Rome in January 829, and at the Lateran in Gregory's presence they delivered a judgment about property rights in favour of the abbey of Farfa and against the Roman church (*Regesto di Farfa* 2.221; Paschal had granted this abbey a tax-exempt status on 1 February 817, *ibid.* 2.186); if Gregory appealed to the emperors he was unsuccessful.

But there ensued dynastic strife between Louis and his sons Lothar, Pepin and Louis the German, which served to loosen the bonds tying Rome to the empire. The sons first revolted in 830: the empress Judith was placed in a convent at Poitiers. The pope and other bishops required Louis to take her back, and a council at Aachen on 2 February 831 did restore Judith to him (Thegan, *Gesta Hludowici imperatoris* 37).

In 833 the three sons again rebelled; Lothar was to supplant his father as emperor. And, as many saw it, the rebels managed to win Gregory to their side: his authority would certainly have been seen as bolstering their plans, in effect as legitimizing Lothar's rebellion (the importance of Gregory's role is controversial; cf. Ganz 1990:546-7; Fried 1990:267-73). Gregory at least claimed that his involvement was in the interests of peace (Thegan, 42), and intended to help restore the unity of the empire and preserve the original agreement about the succession.

Gregory came with Lothar across the Pennine Alps into France. He wrote from Lothar's camp about Easter 833 to archbishop Agobard of Lyons and abbot Wala of Corbie to help him bring concord to the imperial family. Agobard was asked to fast and pray God for the success of Gregory's efforts to obtain from Louis peace and harmony in the imperial family and realm. Wala was adjured to come to the pope's assistance for the achievement of reconciliation between Louis and his sons and nobility, for the unity of the people and for the safety of the empire. But since Louis's supporters looked on Gregory's intervention as partisan, they and the Frankish bishops loyal to Louis received him with open hostility, and threatened him with excommunication if he did not keep his oath to Louis.

Gregory was startled at this, but was very much encouraged by the responses of Agobard and Wala, who sent him earlier papal and patristic writings dealing with the authority the pope had from God and St Peter to spread truth and the gospel, to secure the peace of the churches in order to do this, and reassuring him that as successor of Peter he could be judged by no one. The reluctance of the imperial bishops to meet him Gregory regarded as insolence; he lambasted his critics, scorned their threats, attacked them for attempting to block his embassy of peace, and justified his involvement with the arguments advanced by Wala: as successor of St Peter he had the care of all men's souls, and it was therefore his concern to encourage peace and unity in an empire over which he had superior authority (*MGH Ep* 5.228-232).

From Worms, Louis sent envoys to Gregory in May or June, to ask why he was avoiding meeting him, if he was really present in pursuance of the precedents his predecessors had set. In June Louis and all his forces confronted his three sons with their immense army. The two sides set up opposing camps in Alsace northwest of Colmar at Rotfeld (called, according to a gloss in one MS of *AB*, Nelson 26 n. 1, the Campus Mentitus, 'Field of Lies'; now Sigolsheim). Gregory with his entire Roman entourage was in the sons' camp. On 24 June with battle about to be joined, the sons persuaded Gregory to go to negotiate with their father. Louis received Gregory that day. The pope made it very clear that he had undertaken such a long journey only because it was said that Louis's discord with his sons was irremediable, and he wanted to sow peace on both sides. For some days he stayed with Louis who then sent him to his sons to construct a mutual peace. But in the meantime Lothar and his brothers made use of bribery to bring about defections from Louis, and on the night of his return Gregory found Lothar had tricked him. Most of Louis's supporters had deserted; and Gregory was prevented from fulfilling Louis's orders to return to him. On 30 June Louis had to surrender unconditionally, and was deposed. His wife was taken from him and sent into exile in Lombardy, while Louis and his son Charles were kept under close guard. Gregory had to acquiesce in Lothar's treacherous seizure of power, and Lothar allowed him to return to Rome. He made the journey in July, slower than he would have wished, in great pain, and without the honour that was his due. He must have regretted his involvement (Thegan, 42; Astronomer, 48; *Annales Xantenses* 833; *AB* 833 Nelson 26-7; Paschasius Radbertus, *Vita Walae* 2.14-18; Nithard, *Hist.* 1.4 Scholz 133).

On 1 March 834 Louis was restored as emperor. Lothar meanwhile occupied himself with harassing church property in Italy, and Louis, to make his peace with the pope, censured his son and in 837 sent his legate, abbot Adrebald, to Rome for consultations: Louis's stated object was to make a pilgrimage to Rome, but he really wanted to detach Gregory from Lothar. Adrebald arrived to find Gregory ill, but the pope leapt at the chance of rapprochement and despatched an embassy (Peter bishop of Centumcellae and bishop George, *regionarius* of Rome) to return with Adrebald and a letter to express his gratitude to Louis. At Bologna the embassy was intercepted by Lothar, but Gregory's letters to Louis were got through secretly (Astronomer, 55-56).

After Louis's death on 20 June 840, his sons could not remain in harmony, and Gregory tried, rather more circumspectly than in 833, to achieve peace between Lothar and his brothers. He sent George archbishop of Ravenna as his legate to negotiate; but Lothar detained George and would not let him continue his mission. The bloody conflict at Fontenoy ensued on 25 June 841, in which Lothar was defeated by Charles and Louis. George was taken prisoner in the battle and then sent home with due honour. Gregory's efforts for peace had been ineffectual (*AB* 841 Nelson 50; Agnellus, *Lib. pont. Raven.* (cc. 173, 175, pp. 389-391) is less sympathetic to George's actions).

Continuing the interest shown by Paschal and Eugene II, in 831/2 Gregory received Anskar who since 826 had been evangelizing Denmark and had now been consecrated bishop of Hamburg by Drogo of Metz. On the petition of Ratold bishop of Soissons, Bernold bishop of Strasbourg and count Gerold, Gregory gave Anskar the pallium as archbishop ('of the Nordalbingi'). To him and his successor archbishops Gregory granted the office of legate and papal representative, and the authority to evangelize among the nations of

'Dani, Sueoni, Norvehi, Farrie, Gronlondan, Halsingalondan, Islandan, Scridevindun, the Slavs, and all northern and eastern nations however named.'

Until there were enough native bishops the emperor should arrange for the consecration of Anskar's successors (J2574; Curschmann 1909:13-15).

Significant of the times is the willingness of the Franks to ensure the greater Romanization of their liturgy; significant too is Gregory's cooperation with this. In 831 Gregory received Amalarius of Metz and assigned him to the archdeacon for advice on Roman usages (Amalarius, *De ordine antiphonarii*, prologue). In 835 it was on Gregory's encouragement that Louis extended the observance of All Saints day to all the Frankish realms (*Chron. Sigeberti* 835, *PL* 160.159).

Remarkably little else is recorded of Gregory's pontificate. For the years 838-840 Jaffé gave only two spurious documents, and for 835-6 and 842-3 nothing at all. No doubt this is largely because of the deficiency of the sources. But the pain Gregory was in while returning to Rome in 833, and the fact that he was ill in 837 yet lived on seven years, may suggest that he was unable to be very active. Hrabanus, abbot of Fulda (later archbishop of Mainz) sent to Rome a poem which he dedicated to Gregory (*PL* 107.133-294; cf. *AF* 844 Reuter 23); but when it arrived in 844 the pope was dead.

The author of this life can produce abysmal Latin (cf. particularly cc. 25-27). A stylistic quirk of his is the word *indifferenter* (four times in this life, cc. 23, 35, 38, 40: 'indiscriminately' or 'without distinction'; it is not previously used in the LP, though it recurs at 105:39 and 108:20). The author even produces the word *indiffluenter* (c. 19), unique in the LP.

103. **1.** GREGORY [IV; 29 March[1] 828 to early 844],[2] of Roman origin, son of John, held the see 16 years .. months .. days. A man of stamina, he was kind, filled with holiness and piety, adorned with knowledge, felicitous in expression, modest, beyond all men steadfast to his word, catholic in faith, righteous in works, and a most expert searcher of divine writings. A tireless visitor of holy churches, a father to the poor and a sustainer of all widows, he sought nothing of this earth, was desirous of nothing that passes away, and, abandoning the worldly gains of this present life, by his worthy deserts he gained himself everlasting rewards in heaven.

2. This blessed pontiff was of noteworthy birth[3] but more noteworthy holiness, fair of form, fairer in faith. All these proclamations of praise did not shine only in the time of his pontificate, but even when he was still in the vigour of youthful years he was always unfailingly busy at doing such things. This did not long continue hidden from all the Romans, as it is written: 'No one after lighting a lamp puts it under a bushel, but that it gives light to all in the house'[4], his holy activity from day to day began fully to resound through the whole city of Rome, as the word of the gospel teaches: 'Nothing is covered that may not be revealed or hidden that may not be known'[5]. Thanks to these countless good things, pope Paschal, the holy lord of this sacred see, made him not only subdeacon but also *sacerdos*.[6] **3.** Established in the habit of his

---

[1] For the delay between his election, presumably in 827, and his ordination see n. 11. The date, 29 March (Palm Sunday in that year), for the latter event (accepted by Kelly) is cited in Duchesne III from the 'Ottobonian Martyrology'. But note that the Tallaght Martyrology has on 29 March: *ordinatio Grigorii Nazareni in Armenia*, where Gregory of Nazianzus is evidently meant. Delehaye (*Mart. Hieron.*, 166) did not know the origin of this entry. The MS of Tallaght is the 'Book of Leinster', written after the middle of the 12th century but containing a compilation probably of the early 9th century (Delehaye, *op. cit.*, xii). Gregory of Nazianzus was ordained priest at Christmas 361, as the first bishop of Sasima on an unknown day in 372, and was elected to Constantinople in May 381. Right or wrong, 29 March may refer to this Gregory's ordination to Sasima and have nothing to do with Gregory IV. *ARF*, even though it is the source for the delay of the ordination until the imperial legate had approved the election, might be taken to imply that the ordination was in 827.

[2] The precise dates of Gregory's death and of his successor's ordination are nowhere recorded; 25 January 844 often given for the former is a guess; *AF* Reuter 22 even gives the year as 843. The round 16 years for Gregory's tenure, and the uncertainty about the date of his ordination (last note), make the precise date unascertainable.

[3] He was aristocratic, and was the candidate of the lay nobility who from 817 took part in papal elections.

[4] Luke 11.33 mixed with Matthew 5.15.

[5] Matthew 10.26, where (even in the Vulgate) the two verbs are in the future tense.

[6] His titular church was S. Marco, in the aristocratic quarter, cf. c. 8 and n. 17.

sacerdotal office he continued in chastity and purity, recalling what holy Scripture brings to mind with the words: 'My *sacerdotes* are to devote themselves to nothing other than prayer, reading and fasting.'[7] And while he was concentrating intently on these things, the same lord pontiff Paschal was in the way of mankind taken from this life and Eugene the God-elected bishop gained the dignity of the high pinnacle, continuing therein a short time. After him Valentine was allotted the pinnacle of the prelacy to feed the flocks,[8] but was most speedily taken from this present life.

4. Then the Romans all began to think closely not only on the pontiffs so suddenly lost but also on the next one, and how they could recognize one who was bathed in the grace of the Holy Ghost, under whose teaching and rule the whole nobility of the senators could lawfully live. 'The stronghold in time of trouble'[9], God the creator of all, enflamed the hearts of all these dignitaries with his holy unquenchable light and turned their minds to the godly deeds of blessed pope Gregory IV; and they all agreed with single mind and heart. Elected by them he was conducted to the Lateran patriarchate - they having forcibly removed him from SS Cosmas and Damian the martyrs' basilica,[10] for he was protesting his unsuitability for such a ministry. But as he could not resist such a great multitude, they led him to the said place with hymns and spiritual chants.[11]

5. Now since we cannot in a speedy account trace everything he did, we should albeit briefly bring to the notice of all what he

---

[7] The quotation is not scriptural. The old editors therefore read: *Sacerdotes [mei induantur iustitiam, hoc est,] non in aliis...*, to produce a quotation from Psalm 131 (132).9: 'Let thy priests be clothed with righteousness...'. But cf. similar words in the LP life of St Peter, 1:5 (BP 2), in a speech attributed to the apostle; this could have been regarded as quasi-scriptural, especially by continuators of the LP.

[8] No doubt an allusion to John 21.15-17.

[9] Psalm 9.10.

[10] This was not his titular church, which was S. Marco (see n. 17). Was he somehow assigned to SS Cosmas and Damian's? Not being a titular church this must have had special arrangements for its services; it is usually assumed clergy would be sent there from the Lateran as required; yet S. Marco is considerably closer. But if so it is surprising that this basilica received only one small gift from him as pope (c. 12).

[11] The author stops at the election; Gregory's ordination is merely alluded to in passing in c. 5 (cf. n. 1 above). *ARF* 827: 'When (Valentine) was dead, Gregory priest of St Mark's *titulus* was elected, but was not ordained until the emperor's legate came to Rome and examined the people's election, what kind of man he was.' Gregory will have been required by the *Constitutio* of 824 to take an oath as Eugene II had done, before the emperor's envoy and the people (see introduction to life 101). For Gregory's oath, Noble, 315, cites, apart from *ARF* 827, Astronomer, *Vita Hlodowici* 44, Benedict, *Chronicon* (ed. Zucchetti, 144). In Noble's view a later letter of Gregory refers to his having sworn an oath (*apud* Agobard, *Ep.* 17, *MGH Ep* 5.230).

wholeheartedly and in godly devotion presented to the sacred and venerable places.

[A.D. 828:]

After his election and consecration[12] to the prelacy he began to employ the greatest endeavour for the saints and their churches, to bring them back quickly, with the Lord's protection, to their ancient condition with a new standard; and this he did. St Saturninus the martyr's church outside the Salarian Gate had collapsed to its foundations through its great age and antiquity; he then began to construct it with new building and he adorned it with various pictures; there too, he presented 1 gold-interwoven cloth.

[A.D. 828-9:]

6. After completing what is related above, his pontifical heart then began to attend earnestly to other works of the saints. As he was inflamed with the fire of divine love he took the body of St Gregory, the prelate of this universal church through whom the grace of the Holy Ghost had imparted a gift of unquenchable wisdom to all the earth, from the place where it had formerly been buried, and brought it not far from there to another place newly constructed within St Peter the apostle's church,[13] and he decorated his silver altar on all sides with silver panels, dedicated an oratory to his holy name and depicted his apse above with gilded mosaic. To this oratory he brought the bodies of the martyrs SS Sebastian,[14] Gorgonius and Tiburtius[15] from the cemeteries in which they

---

[12] The phraseology neither implies nor excludes the closeness of the two events.

[13] St Gregory's tomb had earlier been venerated (cf. 98:35) in its original place in the exterior portico *ante secretarium*; there was an altar near or above it (98:68, 84). Gregory IV had the sarcophagus brought inside the basilica, *ante novellum secretarium* as John the Deacon puts it (*Vita Greg.* 4. 80); this was a new chapel built onto St Peter's with an entrance from a spot near the eastern end of the southernmost aisle; see Andrieu 1936:61-101.

[14] Gregory IV put St Sebastian's head in a silver vessel with feet and a lid, of perhaps 6th-century workmanship, still preserved in the Vatican Museum. At the bottom is Gregory IV's inscription in honour of St Sebastian's head. Reliquary and relic were given by Leo IV to SS Quattro Coronati, cf. 105: n. 67; Liebaert 1913:479f; Styger 1935:I,139-148 and plate in vol. II. Sebastian's body (the rest of it, evidently) had been taken (from the Catacomb on the Via Appia) to France: *ARF* 826: 'Hilduin, abbot of... St Denis, sent to Rome, and Eugene... consented to his prayers; he received the bones of Christ's martyr St Sebastian and placed them in St Medard's basilica at Soissons' (there follows an account of miracles at the Soissons sanctuary). Cf. Ado, *Chron.* 840 (after mentioning the death of Louis the Pious): 'In this emperor's time part of St Sebastian's body was taken to Soissons'. A century later the story of this translation was given with many more details by Odilo, a monk of St Medard (Mabillon, *Acta SS OSB*, IV i, p. 383 f).

[15] St Gorgonius's body had been taken to Metz by bishop Chrodegang in the time of Pepin the Short. As for St Tiburtius, soon after Gregory's election in 827 a priest from Soissons, sent by Hilduin, had tried but failed to take him from his tomb (Einhard, *Translatio SS Marcellini et Petri* 8, 10), then four Frankish monks acted for Einhard.

previously lay and placed each of them in separate altars.[16] **7.** For them he decreed in the time of his pontificate that the monks who are established to perform the office in St Peter the apostle's church should not cease to chant praises there to the Lord almighty every day. In the same oratory he presented 18 silk veils large or small, 3 cloths over the altar under which the body of pope St Gregory rests, one gold-studded with a representation; and on each of the altars of those martyrs 1 gold-interwoven cloth; 3 images silvered on top and swathed in gold, representing the Lord's face, and pictures of those whose particular bodies interred there are distinguished by miracles and mighty works. *[A.D. 829-831:]*

8. These works completed, the venerable pontiff immediately turned heart and mind to others. St Mark the confessor and pontiff's church, of which he had undertaken the rule in the time of his sacerdotal office and which had remained in his *ius* and *dicio* until he came to the grace of the pontificate, seemed likely soon to collapse on account of its great age. With the assistance of the Lord almighty he first removed it to its foundations and later with new building he brought it all to a better standard and beauty,[17] and to the delight of all he depicted this basilica's

---

They entered St Tiburtius's basilica (really a kind of annex to that of SS Marcellinus and Peter) on the via Labicana 3 miles from Rome, and first tried to see if they could open Tiburtius's tomb, and then the tombs of Marcellinus and Peter in a crypt contiguous to that basilica. Three days later they returned to St Tiburtius's basilica and attempted to open the altar under which Tiburtius's body was believed to lie, but their equipment was inadequate to deal with the solid marble monument. So they removed Marcellinus instead, and some nights later Peter as well. All this suggests that the basilica was not well guarded, and the loss of Marcellinus and Peter doubtless inspired Gregory IV to remove the other two known saints, Gorgonius and Tiburtius, to a safer spot. The relics of the IV Coronati, originally also in this basilica, were perhaps not known at this time; they were rediscovered by Leo IV (105:41, though the text does not state that it was here that they were found).

[16] The LP implies three separate altars, but Benedict's *Ordo* has only two (other than that of Gregory): one for Sebastian, one for Tiburtius. De Rossi (*Inscr.* II p. 228), no doubt rightly, thought Gorgonius was kept together with Tiburtius: they both came from the same cemetery *ad duas lauros Via Labicana.*

[17] Gregory's rebuilding of his own former *titulus* produced the third church on the site; for what follows see Krautheimer, *Corpus* 2.216-247. Its foundations are immediately on top of the column-footings of the second church. The original church founded by pope Mark (LP 35.3-4 BP 27) was burnt down and rebuilt in the 5th or 6th century on the original foundations, but with the floor about 1 m higher (because of floods?). In 794 this second church was thought to be the original; Hadrian in a letter to Charlemagne (*MGH Ep* 5.49) mentioned it (with those of popes Silvester and Julius) as one of the still surviving large churches with sacred mosaics and other representations and with images. The third church is on the same foundations, but 1¼ m above the floor level of the second church, so 2¼ m above the 4th-century church. The fresh layer of foundation required to raise the level of the third church was provided by a single layer of 'Servian' blocks. The columns were spoils from the earlier church. The orientation was reversed from that of

apse with gold colours on the overlaid mosaic.[18] He built all the roofing anew, and for anything he had previously found in it to be cheap he substituted what was expensive.[19] **9.** So with all this finished, for the remedy and future reward of his soul he presented in this church the following, to remain to future times: 1 gold crown which with most excellent jewels hangs to this day over the altar, and has in its centre a gold cross also with precious jewels; 2 silver chased bowls, hanging before the same altar; 12 other bowls fashioned with English

the second church, so that the entrance was now at the south, as it had been in the first church. An annular crypt (discovered in 1843 and well preserved beneath the apse floor) was built of very poor masonry, but planned at the same time as the apse. A niche below the altar had (when found; it has now faded) a fresco decoration: the head of Christ on its back wall, and the lower limbs of two standing figures on the side walls; this niche was presumably for relics. Substantially it is Gregory's church which survives today, but the nave columns were replaced in the 18th century, and the only obvious 9th-century features are the apse-mosaic with its inscription, the annular crypt, and, on the exterior, the clerestory walls. In the portico are preserved a few *cancelli* with 9th-century interlace patterns, and a small capital, perhaps from an altar canopy, which resembles those flanking the chapel of St Zeno at S. Prassede, built by Paschal. The apse formerly had windows, as can be seen in its depiction in the apse-mosaic; the exterior of the apse is now embedded in the Palazzo Venezia. The foundation walls and clerestory are characteristic of Carolingian Rome, and the church is another example of the 9th-century renascence of Early Christian types (S. Anastasia, S. Cecilia, S. Maria Nova, S. Prassede, SS Nereo e Achilleo, S. Maria in Domnica, S. Martino ai monti).

[18] Gregory's mosaics (with his own portrait; see photograph in, e.g., *NCE* 6.771) still survive on the triumphal arch and in the apse itself, and are particularly important as the last known examples of mosaic-work at Rome for nearly three centuries; see Oakeshott 1967:213-216 with plates XXIII, 132, 134-6. They were long regarded as utterly barbarous (so Duchesne); Oakeshott concedes barbarity only in the lettering that identifies the figures depicted in the apse, and regards the mosaic as having 'an austere dignity which may be found immensely impressive', the work of an artist who 'evolved a highly individual and original style'. The mosaics are very closely related in layout and many details to those at S. Cecilia a dozen years earlier, yet there is a remarkable change in range of colour, technique and artistic purpose. The whole colour scheme is of deep brown, ochre and white; the extensive use of white in much of the clothing of the figures is remarkable. On the triumphal arch are five roundels with the bust of Christ and the four symbolic animals from Ezekiel, representing the evangelists, and on the two sides SS Peter and Paul in white garments. In the apse are seven figures all standing on mats inscribed with their names. In the middle against a gold background is Christ in a purple robe (his 'name' written as Alpha and Omega), giving a blessing in the Greek style, and with a book in his left hand showing the words 'I am the light, I am the life, I am the resurrection'. On his left are St Mark (with a pallium and a deep red chasuble), SS Agapitus and Agnes (the latter in a gold dress and holding a martyr's crown); on his right are SS Felicissimus and Mark the evangelist; Mark is presenting to Christ pope Gregory IV (shown with square halo, pallium and gold chasuble, and holding a model of his basilica). Below Christ is a dove with a halo, perching on the edge of a fountain. In the lower register is the Lamb of God being approached by the usual troup of sheep, with Bethlehem and (presumably) Jerusalem depicted at the far ends. Below this is the dedicatory inscription (ed. Dümmler, *MGH Poet. Lat. aevi Kar.* 2.663 no. 5).

[19] Perhaps this implies the use of spoils where possible.

workmanship;[20] 5 other chased bowls with their feet. There too he presented 3 censers bathed in gold colour; 12 silver canisters; 8 silver crowns, large and small; 3 silver crosses each of 1 lb; 4 candlesticks silvered on top. He provided a fine silver canopy to the praise and honour of the said confessor, weighing 1000 lb. He also decorated his altar with silver panels. **10.** There too, wishing by the practice of temporal things to obtain the everlasting rewards of heaven, this venerable pontiff presented 1 gold-interwoven cloth with swords round it; he provided 1 other dyed purple cloth with eagles. The same prelate presented 1 dyed purple cloth with jewels and gold apples in the middle and round it a gold-studded belt. The holy prelate presented a dyed purple cloth with griffins and unicorns; another cloth with gold-studding round it, with the resurrection of our Lord Jesus Christ in the middle. In the same church this venerable pope presented a cloth with griffins and gold-studding round it, with the birth of our Lord Jesus Christ in the middle; another cloth with gold-studding, with 4 gold-studded wheels and the birth and baptism of our Lord Jesus Christ in the middle. **11.** The same pontiff presented another cloth with lions, with the Lord's resurrection in gold-studding; 8 small gold-interwoven cloths which are placed on the altars reckoned to be around this church;[21] 4 white silk veils, one with tyrian on all sides and a cross and gold-studded chevrons in the middle, one of cross-adorned silk, with a cross of dyed purple and chevrons of tyrian in the middle, the third and fourth the same; 4 veils of rhodian which surround the holy altar, one of which has a gold-studded cross; 26 gold-interwoven veils and also linen ones which hang in the church's arches;[22] alexandrian veils hanging before the great doors, with men and horses; 1 alexandrian curtain; 4 other veils with gold-interwoven swords; 1 veil of eightfold weave; 8 other gold-interwoven veils with a purple fringe around; and 6 other veils with eagles, with a fringe of tyrian around; 5 other gold-interwoven veils with lions and a fringe of tyrian; other alexandrian veils, one of them with wheels and roses in the middle, the other with trees and wheels, hanging before the doors of this church; a small veil of dyed purple, with a man and a horse in the middle; 14 spanish veils with silver; there too, 10 small veils of dyed purple, each of them with ducks. Protected by God's inspiration he presented in the same basilica 1 silver hand-basin.

---

[20] Read *anglorum* with D, the best MS, for *angelorum* printed by Duchesne (which might imply a design featuring angels); cf. the saxon bowls elsewhere.

[21] A clear (the first?) reference to side altars in a *titulus*.

[22] Two sets, perhaps, of 26 for the nave arcades.

[A.D. 829-830:]

12. In SS Cosmas and Damian the martyrs' church he provided 1 gold-interwoven cloth representing these saints, with gold-studding in the middle. In the church of St Abbacyrus and the Archangel *ad Elephantum*[23] he provided another gold-interwoven cloth with a representation embroidered in the middle, with gold-studding.

[A.D. 830-831:]

This God-elected and distinguished bishop presented in St Eustace the martyr's basilica[24] one gold-interwoven cloth with a gold-studded representation in the middle. The same prelate provided 1 other gold-interwoven cloth in SS Sergius and Bacchus the martyrs' church. He provided another gold-interwoven cloth in St Silvester's church on Mount Soracte.[25]

[A.D. 831-32 and 832-33:]

13. When all this was finished and carefully achieved, he provided in St Peter the apostle's church 14 veils with gold-studding, with various representations of the gospels and the passions of SS Peter and Paul and of the apostle Andrew, which hang down before the images bathed in gold and silver, on the beam that is silvered above in front of which you may approach the sacred confessio, very attractive and noteworthy for men to look at.

14. In Christ's martyr St George's church[26] the magnificent prelate

---

[23] This is the only clear mention of a church so named; it was presumably a recent building replacing St Abbacyrus's altar in the Holy Archangel's deaconry (98:108), and was evidently somewhere near the *Elephas herbarius* (in Regio VIII, near the Forum Olitorium, cf. 97:13). Benedict of Mount Soracte (*MGH SS* 3.715) refers, in the context of the year 921, to a church of the Holy Angel near the Tiber, in which is a church of St Abbacyrus and John and St Barbara. There is no certain trace of the church later, though Bosio identified it with ruins on a site which would correspond to the present church of S. Lorenzo de Mondezariis (Hülsen, *Chiese*, 162-3). Abbacyrus (really Abba Cyrus) is the martyr after whom Abukir in Egypt is named.

[24] Cf. 94 n. 6. At this date the 'basilica' may have been no more than an oratory; the first real church on the site is possibly datable from the fact that the year 991 is carved on two of the columns. Nothing now surviving otherwise is earlier than the rebuilding of 1196, and it was again rebuilt in 1701 (Krautheimer, *Corpus* 1.217).

[25] This church here first occurs in the LP; it (and its monastery, 112:17) are first mentioned by Gregory I, *Dial.* 1.7, recording its *praepositus* Nonnosus, but not the dedication to Silvester. The legend was that Silvester had been in exile here: LP 34:2 (BP 14). Gregory II leased to it a farm from the Tuscan patrimony of the church (J2207; this may be the earliest reference to the dedication to Silvester). It was here that king Carloman (son of Charles Martel) became a monk, and in 747 pope Zacharias issued to him a charter about it (J2280). Pope Paul granted it to king Pepin (J2372); in 761-2 he granted it, along with its three subordinate monasteries, to St Silvester's in Rome (J2349 = *CC* 12). In the 10th century under abbot Leo it was restored by Alberic; and it was ultimately united to St Paul's monastery at Rome.

[26] Though the compiler curiously understates it, Gregory's work on the deaconry of S.

provided porticoes on each side[27] and he decorated them with various paintings for this basilica's adornment. With the Lord's help he embellished this deaconry's apse from the foundations with total endeavour. When this God-beloved pontiff carefully saw that this venerable deaconry's *secretarium* was decaying from its great antiquity, in his love for him[28] and to gain the favour of others he newly set it up to better honour. There too the holy pope presented these gifts: 1 gold-interwoven cloth, and another with gold-studding, with an image of the Saviour and of the martyrs Sebastian and Gregory[29]; 2 large gold-interwoven veils, 17 small ones.[30] In this basilica's confessio he provided silver railings swathed in gold.

15. The roofing of St Hadrian the martyr's basilica on the Via Sacra[31] had decayed from great old age, and he newly restored it.

Giorgio in Velabro seems to have amounted to an almost total reconstruction. The deaconry had originally been built in 682-3 (if an interpolation made not earlier than the 10th century into the life of Leo II may be trusted, LP 82:5 BP 79), and it certainly existed before pope Zacharias translated to it from the Lateran the head of St George (93:24 with n. 90), while by 799 it was 'ancient tradition' that warning should be given on St George's feastday and in his church of the litany to be held two days later on 25 April (98:11). It seems (Krautheimer, *Corpus* 1.263-5) that Gregory rebuilt the church on a larger scale, presumably replacing a single-nave chapel by a basilica. The masonry resembles that of S. Maria Nova and S. Martino ai monti, both of the 9th century; even the badly constructed segmental relieving arches above the aisle windows recall S. Maria Nova. The upper windows at S. Giorgio are rectangular, but their dimensions are similar to those of S. Maria Nova and S. Prassede. Rectangular windows in the clerestory and the aisles are not found in other early Christian basilicas in Rome, but are characteristic of Roman secular architecture from late antiquity until the middle ages; the idea may have been 'taken over' when the 9th-century church was built to replace the preceding deaconry building of secular origin. The irregularity of plan (though determined by preexisting buildings) is like that of S. Maria Nova with its aisles of apparently different length. And the majority of the choir screens, with their interlace decoration, resemble those of S. Sabina and S. Maria in Trastevere, both of the 9th century. The apse revetments, including 6th-century capitals, may, like some fragments of earlier choir screens perhaps of the 5th or 6th century, have come from an earlier building, not necessarily on the same site.

[27] 'Porticoes on each side' here probably means the aisles each side of the nave; but Krautheimer, *Corpus* 1.264, overstates the situation by claiming that *porticus* in the LP usually means 'aisles'.

[28] St George, presumably.

[29] One MS (C, given to amending the text) has 'George', which is surely true but not what the author wrote. The full dedication of the deaconry was to SS Sebastian and George (LP 82:5, BP 79); as late as the 13th century, the apse-fresco reflects the double dedication (Krautheimer, *Corpus* 1.264); but St George alone prevailed.

[30] The figure should perhaps be 18 (and MS E has it), reflecting the 9 arcades still on each side of the nave; the two larger curtains were presumably for the apse (Krautheimer, *Corpus* 1.264).

[31] The name Via Sacra here refers to that road's prolongation on the NE side of the Forum, just as the name 'at the Three Fates' which belongs only to one point on this street had been extended to the Via Sacra itself (97 n. 87; cf. 96 n. 25 for the statues of the Fates; and 97 n. 83 for St Hadrian's).

In the Lateran patriarchate he built a *triclinium*[32] decorated with wondrous size, with an apse of mosaic; and two other apses, on the right and left in the cellars, painted with various representations.
[A.D. 831-832:]
In St Clement the confessor's church[33] the holy pope provided a gold-interwoven cloth with lions and a fringe of eightfold weave. In St Theodore the martyr's deaconry, a gold-interwoven cloth adorned with lions, with a fringe of eightfold weave. **16.** In Christ's martyr St Laurence's church outside the walls he provided a gold-studded cloth representing Zacchaeus[34]. He provided another gold-interwoven cloth with griffins, in honour of God's holy mother *ad martyres*. In St Stephen the first martyr's basilica on the Caelian Hill, a cloth of interwoven gold with chevrons. In the deaconry of God's mother St Mary on the Via Lata he provided a cross-adorned silk cloth with a purple fringe.

In the church of God's holy mother the ever-virgin Mary our lady *ad Praesepe* he provided a gold-woven cloth with the birth, baptism, presentation and resurrection, with, at the top of that representation, 380 pearls,[35] 50 jacinths, 22 prases, and round it *albaverae* with the name of lord pope Gregory IV inscribed.

17. At St Hadrian the martyr's deaconry at the Three Fates[36] he provided a gold-interwoven cloth.
[A.D. 832-833:]
In the Apostles' church *ad vincula*[37] the same prelate provided a gold-interwoven cloth with lions and griffins. In St Martin the confessor and pontiff's church, he provided another gold-interwoven cloth with lions and trees. In St Eusebius the martyr's basilica[38] he provided a cloth of

---

[32] Evidently to be distinguished from Leo III's famous *triclinium*. Cf. Rohault de Fleury 1877:78, 386 and pl. IV, for its possible site.

[33] The LP first mentions this church in passing at 94:14, and has repairs at 97:64; its origin is certainly fourth-century, perhaps even earlier, Hülsen, *Chiese*, 238.

[34] Luke 19.2-10. The church will be the tomb-chapel (the present choir of S. Lorenzo), not the *basilica maior* by now dedicated to St Mary, see 105:26 n. 42.

[35] Literally, 'white jewels'.

[36] Cf. n. 31.

[37] The only closely dated reference to S. Pietro in vincoli between 817 and 1448.

[38] Cf. 93 n. 101; 93:27; 97:74. The present building (of 1711-1750) shows nothing earlier than the 12th century (Krautheimer, *Corpus* 1.210); and in the 9th century it may not yet have been strictly a basilica. To the south of the transept, and east behind the apse, are the remains of a late 2nd-century house, whose rooms were from the 4th and 5th centuries progressively transformed through to the middle ages; some of the brickwork suggests 8th-century work (cf. LP on restorations by Zacharias, 93:27, and Hadrian I, 97:74), in part with 'Servian' blocks, and one of these rooms may even have contained an altar on the

purple dye, with eagles and a fringe of fourfold weave. The same
prelate presented in God's mother St Mary's basilica in Trastevere a
tyrian cloth, representing the birth and resurrection of our Lord Jesus
Christ. In the deaconry called *in Aquiro* he presented a cloth of
interwoven gold. In St Mary's deaconry on the Via Lata he also
presented a cloth of interwoven-gold.

[A.D. 833-835:]

18. In the church of St Mark, Christ's confessor and pontiff, this
distinguished and venerable pontiff, relying on God's inspiration,
provided a gilded octagonal paten with an image of our Lord God in the
middle and on the two sides an image of St Mark and of the prelate
himself, weighing 5 lb; and he also presented there a gold-rimmed
octagonal chalice, gilded with leaves, weighing 6 lb; he also took care
to present there a silver *scyphus* weighing 6 lb. There too this pontiff
presented 2 canisters with 9 wicks, together weighing 14 lb.

In the church of St Paul the apostle, teacher of the gentiles, this
pontiff presented a gold-studded cloth representing our Lord God and,
in his retinue on right and left, the 'praiseworthy number'[39] of
archangels and apostles, of wondrous size and beauty, decorated with
various stones and pearls, and beautifully woven.

19. This kind and distinguished pontiff, when as a good and true
shepherd he was showing the greatest care and vigilance on all sides for
the state of God's holy church, considered the need of the Romans that
when they wanted to grind wheat for eating they could never do so: the
aqueduct called Sabbatina[40] was now for very many years broken and
disrupted. The farsighted bishop, relying on God's help, and putting
effort into the work, built and constructed it afresh just as it had been
built from ancient times, so that it now runs to St Peter the apostle's
and the Janiculum with its flow uninterrupted as it used to.

[A.D. 833-834:]

20. In the ever-virgin St Mary's deaconry *in Cosmedin* he provided
a tyrian cloth representing the birth and resurrection of the Lord Christ
our true God. To the honour and glory of God's virgin St Susanna the
holy prelate presented in her church a gold-interwoven cloth with a
fringe of tyrian. In St Cyriac the martyr and deacon's church[41] he

---

precise site of the altar in the present basilica.

[39] Quoted from the *Te Deum*, where however it refers to the prophets; 'goodly fellowship'
in Cranmer's free rendering.

[40] See 97:59, 81, with nn. 109, 171.

[41] Probably not St Cyriac's on the Via Ostiensis (cf. 106:25) but his *titulus in Thermis*
(cf. 100:28), since the other churches in this chapter and the next are inside Rome.

provided a gold-interwoven cloth with a fringe of cross-adorned silk. In St Pudentiana the virgin's church, a gold-interwoven cloth with a fringe of fourfold weave. To St Vitalis the martyr he presented a gold-interwoven cloth, with eagles and a fringe of fourfold weave. **21.** In St Anastasia the martyr's church[42] the same pontiff provided a gold-interwoven cloth with eagles and a fringe of purple dye. In St Lucy the martyr's basilica called Orphea[43] the same prelate presented a gold-interwoven cloth with a fringe of eightfold weave. In St Chrysogonus the martyr's *titulus*[44] the holy pontiff provided a tyrian cloth representing Daniel, with a cross-adorned silk fringe.

[A.D. 834-835:]
In Pammachius's *titulus*[45] the holy pope presented a cloth of cross-adorned silk with a fringe of fourfold weave. In St Caecilia the martyr's church[46] he provided a gold-interwoven cloth with eagles and griffins, with a fringe of purple dye. **22.** In Aemiliana's *titulus* he presented a gold-interwoven cloth with eagles and a fringe of byzantine purple. In St Xystus the martyr and pontiff's church he provided a tyrian cloth representing Daniel, with a fringe of purple dye. In St Balbina the martyr's church[47] he provided a gold-interwoven cloth with a fringe of purple dye. In Damasus's *titulus* he provided a cross-adorned silk cloth with a fringe of byzantine purple. In the church of the apostles James

---

[42] This is the earliest literary reference to the dedicatee of this church as a martyr: the identification of the foundress with the homonymous martyr of Sirmium was now complete. Little of the rebuilding of S. Anastasia by Leo III (98:4) is easily visible after the major alterations of 1721-2. The earliest reference to the church is that Damasus adorned it with pictures (De Rossi, *Inscr. Christ.* II, i p. 150), and its priests signed at the Council of 499. Architecturally, the first, 4th-century, stage of the church was very unusual for its date: it was cruciform, with transept, single nave and apse. In the second stage, possibly 6th century, aisles were added. The third stage, that of Leo III, was a church with a larger nave, aisles, transept, apse and portico; it was provided with small double-arched windows widely spaced in the upper walls, and with columns between the aisles: 10 columns each side and two for the triumphal arch, with a pergola of 6 columns for the chancel. The nave walls and brickwork, the windows with their small proportions and undulating brickwork, and the thickness of the cement, date it to the late 8th or early 9th century, i. e. Leo III. The work is very like that of Leo at S. Maria in Domnica, SS Nereo e Achilleo and S. Stefano degli Abessini, and that of Paschal at S. Prassede and S. Cecilia (Krautheimer, *Corpus* 1.61ff).

[43] This establishment of Honorius (LP 72:6, BP 65) was a deaconry by Leo III's time; from before 1118/9 (as 'S. Lucia in selce') it was a *titulus* (so till 1586), yet till the late 16th century it was merely a small upstairs oratory in a late antique building.

[44] Cf. 92 n. 31.

[45] SS Giovanni e Paolo. First mentioned in the LP at Symmachus, 53:5 (BP 44), but it was at least 100 years older than his time. See Krautheimer, *Corpus* 1.267-303.

[46] The last reference to S. Cecilia's before 1060.

[47] Cf. 98 n. 128.

and Philip he provided a gold-interwoven cloth. In St Marcellus the confessor and pontiff's church he provided a gold-interwoven cloth. In St Laurence's basilica *in Lucina*[48] he provided a cross-adorned silk cloth. In St Valentine's church he provided a gold-interwoven cloth with chevrons of eightfold weave.
[A.D. 835-837:]
23. When all that can be read in what is included above had been liberally finished and accomplished with God's favour by Gregory IV, pope of this undefiled see, wishing not to be slothful he began, without prejudice to his concern for his flocks, to deal with the care of and improvements to the venerable places, so that in his time they might be strengthened and reformed to a new standard. At the intercession of Peter prince of the apostles it was done as he prayed and desired. When the prelate turned such things over in his mind and thought indecisively, suddenly it came to his memory that it was not right for God's holy mother's church, which by the habit of the ancients is even now called Callistus's Trastevere,[49] to continue further without the office of monks, particulary since no small wonders and signs and various mighty works take place in it. **24.** Then with his heart spurred on by God, strengthened by and relying on almighty God's help, he established from its foundations a monastery[50] alongside this basilica and adorned it with new buildings. In it he gathered canonical monks[51] to perform

---

[48] Cf. 97:73. The early 5th-century basilica was built by Xystus III (LP 46:6 BP 36, cf. p. xxx) to replace earlier buildings which had come into Christian hands at least by 366 when Damasus was elected pope there, and there is a 4th-century epitaph, found at St Valentine's, of a priest of the *titulus Lucinae*. Xystus's basilica was typical of its time; its proportions are identical to those of S. Vitale (built under Innocentius, LP 42:3-6 BP 31-2), with a nave 150 Roman feet long and 50 feet wide; but its apse was of an unusual 'stilted' design. In the late 8th century a small apse was added to the side-room on the west of the main apse (the church is orientated to the north); this may be one of the changes recorded as made by Hadrian I (97:73). The basilica was largely rebuilt in the early 12th century, but apart from the narthex and campanile most of what is now visible is Renaissance or baroque, Krautheimer, *Corpus* 2.159-184.

[49] S. Maria in Trastevere, on which see further n. 71.

[50] Known, like the church, as S. Maria in Trastevere. Its full name is given in c. 37: SS Mary, Cornelius & Callistus Trastevere. On the monastery, Ferrari 228-9: it seems to be new, as the LP states, though Ferrari cites Morin, *Revue Bénédictine* 4 (1887), 352, for the view that Gregory IV was restoring an abandoned monastery.

[51] This meaning of *monachos canonicos* was that understood by Mabillon (*Annales O.S.B.* 2.603), 'monks living by a rule, i.e. regular', with *canonicus* being a graecism for *regularis*. But Duchesne thought that the expression meant 'canons', i.e. regular canons living under a rule (*regula*); if so it would be the earliest appearance at Rome of this mixture of clerical life and monastic rule; he stated that it had been introduced in France in the previous century by Chrodegang bishop of Metz; at the council of Aachen in 817 Louis the Pious had reforming rules adopted which did much to spread this institution, by rigidly distinguishing the canonical life from the regular life of those who followed the

the office therein and chant thanks and praises every day and each ensuing night to almighty God with the heart's inmost breath; and, as we see at present, the noteworthy pastor increased and thoroughly consolidated this work with great effort and great endeavour. For where there was previously no special provision, now by God's dispensation there are fair dwellings for monks, and in places which recently seemed to men to be full of brambles and filth cells have now been constructed; and in them, after the offices of praise, Christ's sheep dwell together and sleep most bountifully with all that they need.

25. So[52] at that time this same church was broken down by reason of its great age in certain places around;[53] but he restored it with solid reinforcements[54] on all sides. In it he provided a Manger,[55] a copy of the Manger in God's holy mother's [church] called Major, which he decorated with gold and silver sheets. In it, for the remedy and pardon of sins, he presented these gifts: a gold image[56] representing our lady, with various precious jewels, 13 large jacinths, 10 prases, 29 large

---

rule of St Benedict. Niermeyer, *canonicus* 4, cites this passage: 'enrolled on the list of clerks (belonging to the officially recognized clergy)'; the *canon* would be the list of clergy. This dispute leads Ferrari on to his chapter 'Roman Monastic Observance', pp. 379-407, where, especially at p. 383, he urges that Duchesne was wrong; following Hertling 1930:335-59, Ferrari argues that the LP fits into a long tradition of describing monks who lived as they should be doing as living according to a rule. It does not imply that they lived by any particular rule, whether the Benedictine or any other; compare 97:68 where Hadrian I restored the monastery of Honorius and installed an abbot and monks to live there according to a rule. At Rome, with its usual conservatism, it was only in the 10th century that many monks adopted the Benedictine rule, thanks to Alberic calling in Odo of Cluny to reform the Roman monasteries about 936; only after that could the word 'canon' be used for those who, while living a common life, were not Benedictines and could no longer be described as monks.

[52] cc. 25-27 contain abominable Latinity even by the standards of the LP; whoever made the original entries in the *vestiarium* registers for this year may be to blame. The text may be corrupt in places. For the rarer technical terms see the glossary.

[53] The meaning is probably 'around its outer circuit wall or perimeter'.

[54] Possibly 'buttresses'; but *munitionibus* is probably not so technical.

[55] The 12th-century S. Maria in Trastevere still has a Chapel of the Manger, opening from the middle of the left aisle, but it is entirely modernized. In the 9th century it may have been on the same site but at the lower level (Krautheimer, *Corpus* 3.69).

[56] The 7th-century list of Roman basilicas (*Istae vero ecclesiae* appended to the *Epitome de locis sanctis*, *CChr* 175 p. 321 lines 177-8) contains: 'The Basilica called S. Maria Trastevere; an image of St Mary which was made by itself is there.' From the date of this list it should follow that the image mentioned is different from this one in the LP. But Krautheimer, *Corpus* 3.66, believes the passage is a 9th/10th-century insertion into the *De locis*, citing Bertelli 1961:18ff; it may thus refer to the icon in the LP; that the LP does not call the icon miraculous is no reason to suppose it did not later come to be thought so. Unfortunately the *CChr* editors think that both parts of the *De locis* date to c. 635-645; and the supposed insertion occurs in the oldest MS (Vindobonensis 795, 8th century); if this is right, Krautheimer's explanation must be rejected. Gregory presented another image of the Virgin, cherishing himself, in c. 33.

pearls, 20 large *alabandinae*, .. small pearls, and with various crowns uniform in design around the head; 2 pairs *cercelli* with precious jewels, 18 pearls, 8 prases, 4 jacinths. **26.** In the same place an image with 2 precious necklaces[57] of prases, one of which has 11 pendants; also a gold three-thread necklace with various jewels, 73 pearls and 33 *buticulae*; a necklace on which hang 13 jacinth-jewels; 9 gold *digitiae* hanging on a gold thread; also a threaded necklace, including 14 hanging jacinth-jewels adorned with crosses, with 2 *buticellae* and 3 small ones; all the necklaces with their *petinantes*; 3 fine gold bowls, chased, uniform in design, adorned with crosses, hanging on 3 chains, with lily and hook, with the inscription: 'From the gifts of God and St Mary called Praesepe Trastevere' and 'Lord pope Gregory IV presented this with pure heart'; a Saxon bowl adorned with crosses with a representation like a lion's mane, with various fine gold works, hanging on 4 chains and 1 hook; a gilded Saxon bowl, having [a representation] like 4 lions,[58] with various representations of serpents and in the middle a standing pine-cone and 4 little lioncubs, hanging on 3 chains and 1 hook; also 4 Saxon bowls,[59] each of which includes gilded works, hanging on 3 chains and hooks, 1 of which has 2 glass jewels; this too the lord pontiff Gregory IV presented with willing heart.

27. In the church of St Paul the apostle, teacher of the gentiles, this prelate presented a gold-interwoven curtain, hanging on the triumphal arch, with the annunciation and birth of our Lord Jesus Christ in the middle; 1 dyed purple veil, hanging on the cornice beneath the silver image, and representing the emperor. There too he provided 2 other small gold-interwoven veils, which hang round the altar outside, with[60] [*lora*] 16 in number; 5 veils hanging round the altar inside, with 25 *lora*; 24 veils which hang in the *presbyterium*; 40 gold-interwoven veils which hang in the great arches. On this church's canopy he provided 4 veils.

In Christ's martyr St George's church he provided 6 gold-interwoven veils, with chevrons of eightfold weave around them.

---

[57] *morenae*; some kind of necklaces; see the glossary for this and other technical words in this obscure section.

[58] For *leones IIII* Bianchini had *Leonis IV*, thus attributing prescience to Gregory IV!

[59] The figure '4' seems to belong (in sense) here; 3 chains do not need 4 hooks.

[60] A noun is missing for the 16 objects; parallelism with the next clause ('outside', 'inside'), and the arithmetic (16 for 2 veils, 25 *lora* for 5 veils) suggests *lora*, for the meaning of which see the glossary.

[A.D. 835-836:]
28. In St Saba's monastery[61] this God-protected and distinguished pontiff provided 1 cloth of dyed purple with lions and with a fringe of eightfold weave. In St Anastasius the martyr's monastery[62] he provided 1 cross-adorned silk cloth with a fringe of fourfold weave. In St Andrew's monastery[63] in Clivus Scauri, he provided 1 cross-adorned silk cloth with a fringe of eightfold weave. In St Agatha the martyr's monastery[64] above the Subura he provided 1 cloth of dyed purple with a fringe of eightfold weave. In St Erasmus's monastery[65] he provided 1 cross-adorned silk cloth with a fringe of eightfold weave.

[A.D. 836-837:]
29. In St Lucy's deaconry[66] in Septem Vias he provided 1 cloth of dyed purple with a fringe of eightfold weave. In St Lucy's oratory in Renatus's monastery[67] he provided a cloth of dyed purple with lions and with a fringe of eightfold weave. In St Silvester's monastery[68] he provided 1 cloth of dyed purple with a fringe of eightfold weave; there too he provided another gold-interwoven cloth with griffins and with a purple fringe. In St Praxedes's monastery[69] he provided 1 cloth of dyed purple with a cross-adorned silk fringe.

[A.D. 837-838:]
30. In the basilica of the apostle St Paul the world's teacher, this God-protected and distinguished pontiff provided 22 gold-studded veils for the arches of the *presbyterium*, representing St Paul the apostle himself, and an edging with gold around.

In the church of God's mother the ever-virgin St Mary our lady called Callistus and Cornelius's, this God-elected and distinguished

---

[61] See 96 n. 29.

[62] See 97 n. 189.

[63] See 96 n. 28.

[64] Possibly the monastery founded by Gregory II (91:10, n. 37; cf. 98:56, n. 110). This is the last reference to S. Agata de' Goti before 1461-1496. The original church with nave and two aisles (7 arches each side, with 6 columns and 2 end pilasters) is in the style of the second half of the 5th century: the measurements are probably in byzantine feet because it was built as an Arian church (so Krautheimer, *Corpus* 1.3).

[65] See 98 n. 32.

[66] For the location see 98 n. 86; it was a deaconry in Leo III's time also (98:38, 75); but its context here might suggest it was regarded as a monastery (if so Geertman's year-divisions break down; a monastery should not head the list for a year).

[67] See 98 n. 84.

[68] See 95 nn. 9, 11. This is the last donation to the oratory within the monastery; henceforth it and S Dionysius's basilica (now S. Silvestro in capite) are taken as a single entity; cf. 106:23 for the separate identity of the oratory and the basilica.

[69] See 100:9-11 with notes thereto.

bishop presented 2 silver crowns, with 12 dolphins for each of them, weighing 12 lb. In Christ's martyr St George's deaconry he provided 1 silver crown with 12 dolphins, weighing 6 lb.

[A.D. 838-839:]

31. In the basilica of God's mother the ever-virgin St Mary our lady called Callistus and Cornelius's, this God-protected and distinguished pontiff provided 4 silver canisters, with an inscription of God's holy mother and of lord pope Gregory, weighing 24 lb; and on its altar silver panels weighing 113 lb.

There too in that holy place within the circuit[70] of that church, the venerable pope provided an elaborate and beautiful reconstruction. The altar[71] had previously been sited in a low place, almost in the middle of the nave; the people of both sexes congregated round it, and the pontiff celebrated the sacred mysteries while the people intermingled in disorderly fashion with the clergy. **32.** Furthermore, SS Callistus, Cornelius and Calepodius's holy bodies[72] were entombed in the church's

---

[70] *ambitus* seems to mean the *presbyterium*, including the semi-circular apse; cf. *ambitu abside* in the next chapter, and 104:19 (with n. 34).

[71] The problem for Gregory was like that facing Paschal at S. Maria Maggiore (100:30); his solution was in part the same, but he had the additional problem of housing relics. The present S. Maria in Trastevere is a total reconstruction undertaken 1131-1181 (in part with spoils from the Baths of Caracalla), which entirely altered its condition. There were some excavations by De Rossi in 1865-69, who (Krautheimer, *Corpus* 3.71) mentioned finding, in addition to some earlier elements, a chancel, perhaps that of Gregory IV, two pulpits, the raised level and steps to the 9th-century apse (below the triumphal arch of the 12th-century reconstruction, which added a transept and an apse further back), and the substructure of the 9th-century apse-level. Parts of the chancel screens and ciboria found are now mounted in the narthex and the passage to the right aisle (Krautheimer, 3.69, who thinks they may well be of 9th-century date). De Rossi's discoveries helped Duchesne interpret the present passage. It seems that before Gregory's time there was no *presbyterium* in front of the altar and that the altar ('almost in the middle of the nave') was so close to the people that they 'intermingled with the clergy', especially since the sanctuary was at the same level as the nave ('in a low place'); the Roman Council of 826 had barred the people from the *presbyterium* during the liturgy. Gregory heaped up soil in the apse and inserted in the middle a crypt in which he put the bodies of the three saints whose tomb had hitherto been in the 'southern aisle' (the left, on entering). The altar was then set above this crypt, which was provided with an opening turned towards the nave ('a confessio facing east'); on each side of this confessio steps gave access to the level of the new floor in the apse. The *presbyterium* and its enclosure were extended forward outside the apse; to the north of the *presbyterium* was the *matroneum*.

[72] Duchesne noted that the translation of Callistus and Calepodius from their original burial place in the cemetery on the Via Aurelia is unrecorded (see Duchesne I.142, n. 6), but whenever it happened no church was more suited to receive them than this *titulus* of Callistus. Cornelius had been translated by Hadrian I (97:69) to the church of the *domusculta Capracorum*. The Abbey of Compiègne later claimed to have his body, along with (thanks to Charles the Bald) the relics of Cyprian. Ado's martyrology (14 September) mentions Cyprian's translation there but not that of Cornelius, and if Cornelius was ever taken to Compiègne it was later than Gregory IV's time. But the account of his translation

southern aisle, lying behind the people's backs, and were not worthily honoured. The religious pope did not bear this lightly, but set himself to the task with expert endeavour and very painstakingly, and, embarking on a wondrous work, he finished it excellently. He excavated a crypt,[73] and lifting up these holy bodies with extreme reverence he deposited and buried them honourably at the church's western side, that is, within the circuit of the apse.[74] Round this he accumulated as large a mound as possible, and erected and decorated á *tribunal* which he embellished with wondrous stones.[75] And furthermore[76] he fitted up a confessio facing east, and decorated it by attaching ceilings of breathtaking wonder, inside[77] the altar's risings, i.e. its supports; and this[78] he embellished conspicuously with silver in a quantity wondrous for its amount and adornment, in honour of God's mother the ever-virgin St Mary; he removed the old one of course, and erected steps of beautiful workmanship between the risings. In front of it he constructed from the foundation a *presbyterium* of ample compass and elaborate work, and to this he joined on the northern aisle a *matroneum* fenced round with stone. **33.** Also, adding beauty to the altar and rightly honouring the Lord's mother with gifts, he provided there a gold-studded cloth with byzantine purple, representing our Lord Jesus Christ's birth and resurrection, and also an image of God's mother St Mary cherishing an image of its presenter.

This God-protected and distinguished pontiff provided 6 silver *amae* which go in procession to all the *stationes*, each weighing 13 lb; 2 *scyphi* each weighing 10 lb; 8 *gemelliones* each weighing 2 lb. *[A.D. 839-840:]*

34. After this pontiff had by God's favour completed all this fittingly, he restored to its ancient condition and standard what was damaged through old age at St Peter the apostle's church outside the walls:[79] to

---

published by Lebeuf (*PL* 129.1376) is of very little value.

[73] If Duchesne was right, this was a new crypt hollowed out to make a shrine in the mound of material Gregory had placed in the apse; see n. 71.

[74] Was the unintended effect of this and the later works the undermining of the apse itself? Leo IV (105:60) had to restore the apse, but because of its ruined state Benedict III (106:30) had to rebuild it entirely. Gregory's 'mound and pile' may have been ineffectually intended to repair damage he realized he had caused.

[75] The *tribunal* would now be the floor of the apse, but it is unclear whether the 'wondrous stones' were for the pavement or revetment of the apse.

[76] *supra* cannot mean 'above': the confessio was below the floor of the new chancel.

[77] Or 'below' (*infra* being ambiguous, as often at this date).

[78] The altar, apparently.

[79] Krautheimer, *Corpus* 5.176 and 268, shows that cc. 34-5 list the main components of

beautify the basilica he newly dedicated almost the whole portico[80] over God's mother St Mary's oratory called Mediana with beams and other wood. He also completed with new work and to a noteworthy standard the other portico in front of the silver doors.[81] On the main[82] front of this church's Paradise, on the mosaic, he decreed a very speedy painting and restoration of all that had been damaged from times of old on that wall. **35.** He also renewed this church's portico[83] which is conspicuous above its steps up which the people without distinction have to climb for prayer. Close to the Needle[84] he built a hospice, small yet becomingly constructed, for the pontiff to rest in when after morning prayers or the offices of mass his limbs are liable to fatigue, and he decorated it with noteworthy pictures.

Amongst other instances of good activity he also provided, for the pontiff's requirement and use, in the Lateran patriarchate close to Christ's martyr St Laurence's oratory, a quite suitable dwelling;[85] there

---

the atrium as still known in 16th-century records: a) the oratory on the upper floor of the gatehouse (S. Maria *in Mediana, in Turri, ad Grada,* or *in Gradibus*; from the 12th century also *inter Turres*; see index in Duchesne III.327ff); b) the narthex in front of the basilica's main doors ('portico in front of the silver doors'); c) the façade of the basilica with its decaying mosaic ('main front of this church's Paradise'); d) the portico of the gatehouse above the steps up from the piazza ('this church's portico above its steps'). The only difference from the 16th-century situation was that the atrium was not yet at the level of the narthex and gatehouse-floor but 45 or 90 cm lower; but cf. LP on pope Donus, 80:1 (BP 73), contrast Hadrian I, 97:57; the undated raising of the atrium was after 795 (so Krautheimer); Symmachus's *cantharus* (the *pigna*) will have once stood on a platform which was then buried nearly to its top.

[80] Duchesne III.123 is certainly wrong to identify S. Maria Mediana with the oratory built by Gregory III near the triumphal arch and therefore to suggest that here and immediately below 'portico' seems to have a special sense (since the oratory cannot have had a portico other than the chancel which enclosed it). S. Maria Mediana was not inside the basilica; it was the gatehouse (the *Turris*) at the eastern end of the atrium. Nevertheless the meaning of 'portico' is unusual; Krautheimer, *Corpus* 5.175, suggests it may mean the wooden ceiling or roof in the oratory of S. Maria on the upper floor of the gatehouse, rather than portico in the ordinary sense.

[81] This 'portico' is the entire narthex in front of the basilica itself, Krautheimer, *Corpus* 5.175; despite Duchesne III there is no reason why the word should not cover the whole stretch, not merely the section immediately outside the main (silver) doors.

[82] *principali* is here taken with *fronte*; if it belongs with *musibo* it makes little difference. The mosaic concerned is that on the church's main façade, above the narthex just mentioned; not (*pace* Duchesne) that on the façade of the atrium where Giotto's mosaic later stood. But Duchesne is right to note that the confused text here does not wholly clarify whether new mosaics, replacements, or restorations are meant.

[83] This is the portico of the gatehouse above the steps leading up from the piazza (Krautheimer, *Corpus* 5.175), and through which one entered the atrium of St Peter's.

[84] Cf. 98:27; the obelisk, then to the south of the basilica.

[85] Rohault de Fleury (cf. n. 32) made conjectures about the apartment mentioned here and the buildings in the next chapter. St Laurence's oratory is here implied to be the pope's private chapel. It is first mentioned at 96:4, and survives as the Sancta Sanctorum, at the

too the stillness is excellent, and the pontiff can emerge from it with his clerics and perform the praises due to the Lord almighty.

[A.D. 840-841:]

36. After the building of all this which can be read above, this holy pope Gregory set up and arranged from their foundations to a new standard of workmanship some of the buildings which had been constructed within the palace by the Fathers of old but were now destroyed and almost on the point of collapse from great age. As for the stairs facing the cellar, up or down which men used previously to climb as if it were night, he newly remodelled them so that no darkness could thenceforth impede those passing along them. From this place to St Laurence's oratory he restored all that was old and added other things new, amongst which he ordered the building of 3 parlours. **37.** As for the bath located close to the cellar, he also renewed this throughout from its foundations and adorned it with marble and other pleasing works. It was previously about to collapse from its age, if the foresight and excellent endeavour of this great pontiff had not decreed its restoring to its earlier condition.

In the Saviour's church called Constantinian he provided a gold-woven cloth representing the Palms and the Lord's Supper.[86]

In the venerable monastery[87] of God's mother the ever-virgin St Mary and of SS Cornelius and Callistus, called Trastevere, he provided 6 canisters weighing in all 18 lb; 1 *scyphus* weighing 8 lb 3 oz; an incense-boat[88] with a censer weighing 3 lb; 1 necklace weighing 3 lb; 2 candlesticks weighing .. lb.

[A.D. 841-842:]

38. So all these things were completed and exactly accomplished. Now his holy, venerable and memorable singlemindedness, and the same devoted service that he ever had to almighty God, was as has often been said also solicitous without distinction for the people's future well-being and the deliverance of the fatherland, to prevent the enemy capturing them if God would grant it otherwise. In this holy father and pope's time the ungodly, wicked and God-hated race of the Agareni were rising up from their own territory and compassing nearly every island and

---

top of the Scala Santa; the latter was moved to its present position from St Silvester's oratory in the 16th century, Hülsen, *Chiese*, 291.

[86] The events of Palm Sunday (Christ's entry into Jerusalem) and Maundy Thursday (the Last Supper).

[87] Cf. c. 24 for the foundation of this monastery, here given its full name.

[88] Duchesne prints *cantara* ('chandelier') with the best MS, D; but the context requires *cantra* (so MSS C and E), if as elsewhere this means 'incense-boat'.

mainland district, and atrociously causing - and are still to the present day never ceasing to cause - the looting of men and the devastation of places. So, in view of these unaccustomed and alarming perils, the merciful prelate was much afraid that the people committed to him by God and St Peter dwelling in the cities of Porto and Ostia would feel the detriment of trouble and looting at the hands of the wicked Saracens; and he drew sighs from his inmost heart and wisely began to find out how he could assist and deliver the city of Ostia.[89] **39.** Straightway almighty God put this scheme into his heart: if he wanted to save the people, he had to construct the city there anew from its foundations, since what had been built aforetime was now shaken by old age and wholly destroyed. In pursuit of what God had inspired in him he built from the ground at this city of Ostia a second very solid city; he fortified it all round with higher walls, and with gates and crenellations and trap-doors, and on top he arranged catapults with noble artfulness to fight off the enemy if necessary. On the outside, not far from these walls, he encircled the city with a deeper ditch, to stop the enemy reaching the walls too easily.

40. When the work of new construction on this city was due to start, the holy pope resided there many days himself and with his men he erected no small part of the walls from their foundations, practically taking his allotted turn. From then on, without distinction, he endured in his sacred breast much effort and struggle, until with God prospering it this city was brought to the correct completion of all its building. For this newly constructed city he laid down this name that should endure for ever - Gregoriopolis; all men whether of Roman or of other birth should call it this after his own name Gregory. And it truly deserved to take this title from its founder's name; for with almighty God's help and strengthened by his power he did what we read that no other pontiff has done: he built and designed this work with wondrous beauty and

---

[89] On Gregory IV's work at Ostia see Meiggs 1960:100-103, Broccoli 1982. In view of the place the foundation of Gregoriopolis occupies in the life Duchesne put it near the end of the pontificate after the death of Louis (840) and the Battle of Fontenoy (841), when Rome began to realize that the Franks could hardly be relied on for defence; on Geertman's chronology, adopted here, it will be in 841-2. Since the end of Charlemagne's reign Saracen pirates from Africa had infested the islands of the Tyrrhenian Sea and the Roman coastline. Landing in Sicily in 827, they took Palermo in 831, from where they quickly spread to the mainland, intruding into the quarrels of the Lombard princes of Benevento and Salerno and ravaging the barely-defended coast. Though the name Gregoriopolis did not outlast Gregory, his small enclosure survived and was often repaired: it is the nucleus of modern Ostia. 'There one finds in the midst of hovels a rustic bishopric with a small chapel dedicated to St Aurea which marks the site of the Christian cemetery of ancient Ostia'; so Duchesne; things are tidier today. On St Aurea's see 105:51 and n. 83.

construction for the deliverance of the people and of the fatherland.

41. So while they remained at their stations, this angelic and noteworthy prelate provided in the Saviour our Lord Jesus Christ's basilica close to the Lateran patriarchate 1 gold-studded cloth, representing, on the front of the altar, SS John the Baptist and John the Evangelist; and round the altar, cohering in one body as it were,[90] veils which are also gold-studded, some with embroideries in the manner of griffins, with horns embroidered on their foreheads.

In Christ's martyr St Laurence's monastery[91] called in Pallacinis he provided 6 silver canisters and 2 candlesticks with silver overlaid;[92] 1 silver *scyphus* and 1 silver *ama*. In pope St Gregory's oratory inside St Peter the apostle's church, 4 silver colonnettes with 40 lb of silver.

[A.D. 842-843:]

42. After this this venerable pontiff decreed that a suitably worthy house surrounded on all sides with porticoes and galleries be newly built from the ground in the manor[93] surnamed Draco's; in this, both he and also future pontiffs with all their retinues will be able to stay in residence as long as they are pleased to do so. In another manor[94] called Galeria he built another house, large and spacious and suitably distinguished, for the need and requirement of pontiffs where they may spaciously lodge with all their servants whenever convenient.

43. In God's mother the undefiled virgin our lady St Mary's basilica called *ad martyres*, this beloved and distinguished pontiff, burning with love from on high, provided a fine silver canopy weighing 400 lb; 1 fine silver crown weighing 10½ lb. In St Marcellus the confessor and pontiff's basilica he provided 3 fine silver crowns[95] weighing .. lb. In St George the martyr's deaconry he provided an alexandrian veil with

---

[90] If this is the meaning, *quasi* is oddly placed. Dr Cheesman suggests '<cloths> like veils'. But perhaps read *quattuor*; 'four veils cohering in one body' will be the *tetravela* draped round altars, as elsewhere.

[91] See 97 n. 139.

[92] *desuper inductas*; perhaps more technically 'with silver fused on top'.

[93] Tomassetti 1896:111, locates this *curtis* on a crag overhanging the the Tiber for some 40 metres; Meiggs 1960:264 and map, 112, has Dragone, on the left bank of the Tiber, 6 km upstream as the crow flies, and Dragoncello, a bit further upstream. There are other variants of the name. Duchesne cites *fundus Draconis* in a bull of Gregory VII, and modern properties named Dragone, Le Dragare, La Dragoncella.

[94] The *curtis Galeria* may be part or all of the *domusculta Galeria* founded by Hadrian I on the Via Portuensis at Ponte di Galera (97:55 and n. 98). The two villas in this chapter seem to have been opposite each other on each side of the Tiber.

[95] Reading *coronas* (with MS C) for *coronam* printed by Duchesne from MSS DE; just before, where the singular is required and D has it, both C and E give the plural.

12 pheasants, and 1 feathered[96] linen veil in front of the doors.
[A.D. 843-844:]
44. This blessed pontiff after he ruled the Roman and apostolic see
gloriously for 16 years was taken from this life and went to everlasting
rest. He performed 5 ordinations in March, September and December,
.. priests, .. deacons; for various places 185 bishops. He was buried in
St Peter's.[97] His bishopric was vacant 15 days.

---

[96] Presumably 'depicting feathers', not made of them; cf. usages like *leonatus*.
[97] His epitaph is lost; no author mentions his tomb. For the date see n. 1. The vacancy
of 15 days may or may not be reliable.

104. SERGIUS II (844-847).

This life gives an unusual insight into the process of composition. The first stage was the compilation of the account of Sergius's accession, cc. 1 - 18, and this is given in all of the MSS. The rest of the life exists in two recensions, both of which are, I think, modifications of an earlier version which does not survive. For the earlier surviving recension (given below in curly brackets) there existed only one MS (E^5, the lost *Farnesianus*); the other MSS (and there are not many) give the later recension (in italics below). But pseudo-Liutprand, in his summary of Sergius's life, was clearly following the text of the Farnesi recension. Both recensions give substantially the same material in cc. 19-39, but there are some differences in arrangement, and signs that the later recension has modified misleading expressions in the earlier surviving (and presumably the lost original) recension. After c. 39 the later recension merely gives the concluding formulae of the life; but the earlier surviving recension continued with a blistering attack on Sergius and his brother, followed by divine retribution in the form of the Saracen attack on Rome in 846; the conclusion of this, unfortunately, is lost. Though in the earlier surviving recension, this material cannot have been in the lost original version; otherwise we would have to suppose that the later surviving recension chose to suppress it. To suggest that an attempt was made to deny that the invasion had ever taken place would be implausible: there are back references to the event in later lives. We should suppose then that (after c. 18) a continuator produced a version of cc. 19 - 39, surviving for us in the two later recensions; after c. 39 the author of the earlier of these gave the additional material, but the compiler of the later recension chose merely to conclude with the ordinary formulae.

Despite the efforts of the Roman people (electors, since 817) to have a deacon John (known only from the LP) made pope, and his enthronement in the Lateran Palace, the aristocracy chose the aristocratic (he was closely related to Stephen IV), if elderly and gout-ridden, Sergius as pope. They ejected John from the Lateran, crushed all opposition and had Sergius ordained without waiting for imperial approval as required by the *Constitutio* of 824. Such a claim to independence might be justified by the need to prevent a recurrence of popular opposition (at the next papal election, in 847, a more plausible excuse for the same disregard of the emperor would be at hand). Sergius prevented some of his supporters killing John and had him confined in a monastery; John's later life is unrecorded.

The emperor was angry at this flouting of the *Constitutio*. The consequences are related in cc. 8 - 18 (an important parallel account is given in *AB* 844 Nelson 57, see n. 22 below). Lothar intended to punish the Roman nobles for their action, and in June 844 his son the young Louis II (who would later be sole emperor but was now king of Italy) came from Pavia with an army and with his great-uncle Drogo, archbishop of Metz, the leading Frankish churchman. The LP describes the punitive pillaging of papal territory.

Hoping, perhaps, to forestall an attack on Rome itself, Sergius agreed to receive Louis with due ceremony. There then followed at a synod of some 20 Italian bishops held in St Peter's an inquiry into Sergius's right to the papacy. This was conceded, but he and the citizens of Rome were required to swear an oath to Lothar as emperor as required by the *Constitutio* (Delogu 1968:142-3) and to keep to that document's rules in regard to papal elections. On 15 June 844 Sergius crowned Louis king of the Lombards, anointed him and girded him with a sword. The LP regards as a success for Sergius the fact that he refused the demand of Drogo that the Romans swear an oath of allegiance to Louis as well; that was more than the letter of the *Constitutio* required and would have conceded that the papal state was part of the kingdom of Italy. In relating (c. 16) Sergius's refusal to reinstate archbishops Ebbo and Bartholomew (deposed in 835 for their involvement in the deposition of Louis the Pious), the writer loses an opportunity to point out that Sergius was going against Drogo's proposal; but it may be significant that he fails to mention Sergius's granting to Drogo the status of papal vicar north of the Alps, as Lothar desired (n. 23). The saga of Ebbo's status and his dispute with his successor at Rheims, Hincmar, would drag on long after Ebbo himself died. That Sergius was already involved is known not merely from the LP but from other documents. In 846 Sergius ordered Charles the Bald to send Guntbold archbishop of Rouen and other bishops to meet the pope's envoys at Trier to discuss the quarrel between Hincmar and Ebbo, and to make Hincmar come to the synod; Sergius let Guntbold himself know that after Easter that year (18 April) he would send his envoys to Lothar, and he ordered him to convene with bishops at Trier to resolve the quarrel; Hincmar also was ordered to appear at Trier (J2589-91, Mansi 15.776-7).

Another episcopal dispute was a concern to Sergius, that between Andrew patriarch of Aquileia (at Fréjus) and his rival patriarch Venerius (at Grado). Sergius summoned Andrew to appear at Rome on 11 November with Venerius, but it then occurred to him that the dispute ought not to be resolved without the authority and consent of the emperor. He asked Lothar to grant him licence to convoke a general synod, since the scandals of the church were open knowledge; he promised the parties involved that when he received a reply he would let them know (J2592-3). Sergius's death probably ended this initiative, but his willingness to involve the emperor is significant.

Age and gout perhaps caused what Aherne (1967) describes as Sergius's allegedly tetchy disposition; they certainly seem to have caused him to allow himself to be dominated by his unscrupulous and power-crazed brother Benedict, who obtained, by bribery it was alleged, the bishopric of Albano. In the Farnesi recension the LP lays most of the blame for the faults of Sergius's administration on Benedict: simony in obtaining church appointments was rife; and the LP alludes to other methods of financing the building projects of the time, such as the enlargement of St John Lateran on Sergius's own plan, the rebuilding of S. Martino ai monti, and the repair of the Aqua Jovia (c. 21). To assist his nefarious and lecherous ambitions Benedict even bribed the emperor to have himself granted what is described (c. 41) as 'the primacy and lordship at (of?) Rome', 'the monarchy at (of?) Rome'. There is some obscurity about what is meant by these terms, and whether they represent any change in the delicate constitutional relationship between Rome and the empire as it had existed since 824. The author of the Farnesi recension was not concerned with such niceties.

Down to this point there has been no suggestion that officials in Rome were appointed by the emperor. The *Constitutio* of 824 had devised a means for the emperor to check their good behaviour, but he could not dismiss them and the pope clearly retained the right of appointment (see p. 34). It is possible, firstly, that Sergius was (or was claimed by Benedict to be) so incapacitated that Lothar thought it right to appoint Benedict as a stop-gap until the next papal election: Benedict was, after all, bishop of a suburbicarian see. It would also be possible to suppose that Lothar saw the situation as an excellent opportunity to assert a greater level of imperial power at Rome than had hitherto been feasible. Perhaps he was interfering beyond his rights: after the disputed papal election in 844 the Romans were in no position to object. Yet in the outcome of that election the emperor had not had everything his own way. The regular oath had been sworn to Lothar, but Drogo had failed to get Louis included in the oath; nor could Drogo get Sergius to do what he wanted about Ebbo.

There is, however, another explanation, preferred by Duchesne, and in keeping with the fact that no later holder of such a 'lordship' is recorded. Lothar's *Constitutio* had set up two envoys, one to be appointed by the pope, the other by the emperor. That this arrangement was not a dead letter is clear from the judicial session held by imperial envoys at the Lateran in 829 (see p. 45). Now the *Libellus de imperatoria potestate in urbe Roma* (*MGH SS* 3.721) tells us that Louis II 'in consultation with the chief Romans, established in the city of Rome a certain bishop Arsenius who was adorned with holiness and knowledge and was *apocrisiarius* of the Roman see, and gave him as an assistant John, the deacon and archchancellor and his own secretary, who was later made bishop of Rieti, the place from where he had now been chosen.' Duchesne believed that these two men held the posts created in 824; one came from the papal clergy, was bishop of Orte in Roman territory, and already had the office of papal *apocrisiarius*; the other was a cleric from the duchy of Spoleto and was the imperial archchancellor. Yet despite the latter's status at court, he is only the helper to the papal envoy. In effect, the emperor had somehow achieved a situation in which Arsenius, though appointed 'from the side of the pope', is described by the *Libellus* as appointed by himself - the emperor had in fact made both the envoys into his own agents and confidants. Perhaps this had come about through the practical impossibility of the pope's appointing anyone unacceptable to the emperor. The LP (107:63) and other texts describe Arsenius as both *apocrisiarius* and envoy, and successors are known down to 885 with the same double title (J3015, 3109, 3401). Now Arsenius held the post by 848/9 (*Life of St Conwoïon*, Mabillon, *AaSS OSB* VI.184); Benedict may well have been his predecessor as envoy appointed 'from the side of the pope', in practice on the advice (at the very least) of the emperor. That he abused his powers and that his nomination had been largely due to the emperor changes nothing essential in the constitutional relationship between Rome and the empire.

In August 846 Saracen pirates landed near Ostia, sacked it (and its new fortress Gregoriopolis) and Porto, and plundered the two great shrines outside the Aurelianic walls - St Peter's and St Paul's. To the compiler of the LP (and others) this was divine vengeance for the state to which Sergius and his brother had reduced the church.

A possible gap in the life is on restorations to the monastery of SS Silvester, Stephen & Dionysius, perhaps in 844; but the bull of Sergius II recording this is regarded as spurious (Ferrari, 303, though Kehr 1906:82 n. 4 defended it).

104. **1.** SERGIUS [II; early 844 to 27 January 847],[1] of Roman origin, son of Sergius, of the 4th region, held the see 3 years. He was sprung from an illustrious mother,[2] and she began with great endeavour to educate him on chaste provender, so that no one could hear from him or see in him anything lewd or wanton. He had no little contempt for childish amusements, and so in the eyes of all he was accomplished in godly deeds; he began to shine with the character of his noble ancestors, strengthened and schooled by his mother's pure devices. So every day his mother rejoiced and readily gave thanks to almighty God who granted her such offspring along with help from on high.[3] In the 12th year of his age his mother died and went to the Lord. Orphaned of his mother, his father having long since closed his eyes, he dwelt in his parents' house with his brothers. **2.** Leo III was then ruling the primatial church of Rome, a pope kind and distinguished. Mindful of this notable child's high birth and recalling his parents' nobility, in great love he bade him be brought to his presence. When he had been brought, he began to observe him with a cheerful countenance and an untroubled mind, and his spirit was exceedingly pleased by him. Then the prelate gave him over to the Schola Cantorum[4] to learn general literature and be taught the sweet melodies of chant. This remarkable and adept boy quickly took in the whole scheme of literary learning so that he excelled all the children of that Schola. **3.** When he heard this, the excellent pontiff was daily filled with insatiable joy at the pleasing progress of his childhood. Then he appointed him acolyte in the holy Roman church. But when in the 20th year of his pontificate he completed his service, Stephen took on the sacerdotal office of the Roman church. He too loved him with abundant affection of heart, and when he observed him nobly and perseveringly nimble in God's Scriptures, he straightaway granted him the office of the subdiaconate. In a brief time the rule of his episcopate was accomplished and Paschal took on the reins of the church. He consecrated him as priest of St

---

[1] The terminal date is given in *AB* 847 Nelson 64.

[2] Cf. 99:1 and n. 1; 108:1 and n. 1.

[3] The statement that God gave her a child with help from on high is decidedly curious and reflects on the compiler's contorted style; he may mean that God gave her both the child and the help to rear it.

[4] Otherwise the Orphanage (*Orphanotropheum*), which was therefore, as Noble, 229, points out, not limited to boys from a poor background. Basically it was a school to train youths to chant in the papal liturgy, not a minor seminary; cf. Leclercq 1950:1008-1013; Andrieu 1923:235-274. See further n. 46 to c. 24.

Silvester the confessor and pontiff's *titulus*,[5] a man thoroughly wise, an ornament of life, learning and character. He outshone everyone in compassion, endeavour, vigilance and all excellent principles. **4.** On Paschal's death Eugene received the prelacy's pinnacle, and when Eugene had lasted 3 years in the pontificate, Valentine was consecrated pontiff of this see; on whose demise Gregory took on the church's height. As he loved Sergius attentively, he ordained him archpriest[6] in the holy church; and when he had expertly governed the church 16 years he was brought to his end and died.

So when the dignitaries and leaders of the city of Rome and all the church's people came together to elect a pontiff, and as usually then happens they all acclaimed different candidates, by God's foresight they were suddenly spurred by God's will and began attentively to discuss the archpriest Sergius's religious quality, so that they all acclaimed him and said: 'He is worthy to gain the rule of the pontificate!' And with their intention fixed on this man they all went their own ways. **5.** Suddenly[7] a deacon of this church, a certain John, burst out in such derangement and madness that he won over some naive and rustic folk, gathered a group of rioters and rebels, and entered the patriarchate by force, smashing the doors with weapons of war and overstepping the tradition of law and order. At this deed everyone inside the patriarchate's walls was filled with amazement and fear. When this low gathering of people had stuck with him for the space of an hour, it took fright, abandoned him, and was nowhere to be seen.

After this all the princes of the Roman citizens were indignant, and with a single purpose in mind they all hurried, many of them on horseback, and gathered at St Martin the confessor and pontiff's basilica. From the church they dragged out the archpriest Sergius whom we have been dealing with above, a man approved in all virtue. With great honour, amidst a large escorting assemblage of people and the resounding of abundant acclamations of praise, with hymns and spiritual chants he was elected and brought into the Lateran patriarchate. That same day there was such a heavy snowfall over the city that everyone beheld it white; many were saying this was a token of joy and brightness. **6.** As for the deacon John, the princes of this city of Rome expelled him from the patriarchate in great disgrace and instructed that

---

[5] S. Martino ai monti.

[6] This shows that the archpriest by now was not merely the senior by date of ordination; cf. 102:4 and n. 6 on the archidiaconate.

[7] The wording of the story of John's attempt on the papacy is modelled closely on Rufinus, *HE* 2.10, the account of Ursinus's competition against Damasus in 366.

he be put in strict and secure confinement, to deal with that unholy and dire presumption of utter rashness that this deacon John had dared to perpetrate.[8] The princes' preference was that he should be condemned and deprived of his office in a council of bishops. Indeed some wanted to use swords to tear him limb from limb and finish him off; but the kind and expert prelate Sergius forbade this action, unwilling, as the gospel puts it, to repay anyone evil for evil. **7.** At last, with all the *sacerdotes*, dignitaries and leading men and all the church's people rejoicing, this holy man was ordained and consecrated pontiff in St Peter's sacred apostolic see.

He was remarkable for his birth, his purity of faith, his liberality in preaching, his humility before God and his distinction before men; keen in appearance he was yet keener in mind; a governor of churches, a champion of the peoples, a mentor of the poor, a shelter and comforter of widows, a giver to those in need, a gatherer of the scattered, a preserver of the gathered; he spurned vain and worldly affairs; wisdom's riches alone did he covet and love. **8.** When the news of his holy consecration reached the ears of the unconquered Augustus emperor Lothar, he sent to Rome Drogo,[9] archbishop of the church of Metz, his son His Excellency Louis, and a great army of the Franks; and he bade archbishops and many bishops, abbots and counts to accompany their journey.[10] These, from the moment they entered the limits of the city of Bologna[11] with their armed troops, perpetrated such slaughter and butchery on the people that those who were in the cities and the countryside were terrified by the tyrannical cruelty, abandoned their own places, and concealed themselves in secret hide-outs. While they were wreaking this with savage wickedness in every place and all the cities, by-ways and fields, they reached Fons Capellae.[12] So calm was the weather that no one could see a cloud or sign of rain anywhere in the sky; but suddenly enormously thick black clouds appeared, and while they were surrounded by storms, tempests and flashes, some of Drogo's chief counsellors were smitten and struck down by a bolt of lightning.

---

[8] The language is very close to 96:16, on the imprisonment of the antipope Constantine II.

[9] On Drogo, who was son of Charlemagne, see below cc. 10, 14, and Nelson *AB* 32 n.1, 49 n. 3, 59 n. 23.

[10] The purpose of the mission is the negotiations recounted in cc. 14ff., and, more briefly, in *AB* (quoted in n. 22); and see introduction to this life.

[11] Duchesne noted that for travellers from Pavia through Emilia the territory of Bologna was the beginning of the papal State.

[12] Unidentified. Note that for *Fontem Capellae* in MS D and printed by Duchesne, MSS C and E have *Pontem Capellae*.

Great was the terror that seized all the Franks when they saw this awesome sight. Even so they would not lay aside their ferocious purpose, and with atrocious intent they made their way speedily to the City.   9. When[13] the blessed pope Sergius realized they were coming close, he sent all the judges to meet His Excellency king Louis at some 9 miles from this city of Rome. They welcomed him with standards and with great praises resounding.[14] And when he was only a mile or so away from the City, he sent all the *scholae*[15] of the militia, along with the *patroni*[16], all chanting praises worthy of the noble king, and with the other most learned Greeks of the *militia*,[17] chanting the imperial praises; with these sweet sounds of praise they gloriously welcomed the king. His Holiness despatched venerable crosses, that is standards, to meet him, just as is normal when greeting an emperor or king, and so he had him welcomed most honourably.   10. King Louis, the moment he noticed those holy crosses and standards coming to meet him, became cheerful and mightily glad. Then with his whole people he eagerly made his way to St Peter's with all the Roman judges and *scholae* going before him. On the Sunday[18] after Pentecost the bountiful pontiff with his clergy awaited the king on the steps to the apostle's hall.

When the king arrived, climbing all the steps leading up to St Peter's holy church he approached the pontiff where he was waiting in the atrium at the top of the steps, close to the church doors,[19] with the whole clergy and Roman people. They embraced each other, king Louis held the pontiff's right hand, they entered inside the atrium and came to the silver doors. It was in the atrium that one of the troops, in the

---

[13] From this point through to c. 11, the language is closely modelled on 97:37-38, Hadrian I's reception of Charlemagne in 774. A similar procession came to meet him again before his coronation in 800, *ARF* 800 Scholz 80, cf. LP 98:21.

[14] The *laudes*, a technical phrase, twice in this chapter, and in c. 11; see 98 n. 61, citing Kantorowicz 1946; at 71 and 76-84 he discusses the role of *laudes* in Frankish rulership; see too McCormick 1966:362-383; also *AF* 896 Reuter 133 on the coronation of Arnulf; and perhaps LP 108:25 (praise of Basil I).

[15] The companies of the exercitus Romanus; perhaps also the four *scholae peregrinorum* of the Vatican; cf. 97:35 with n. 54.

[16] Cf. the same note.

[17] The *schola Graecorum*.

[18] 8 June 844. Not until the 14th century would this day be celebrated at Rome as Trinity Sunday.

[19] It is clear that the atrium refers here to the platform at the top of the steps and in front of the gatehouse (the 'church doors', S. Maria *in Turri*) of St Peter's; they then entered through this into the colonnaded area (confusingly also called an atrium, cf. 103 n. 80) and came across this to the silver doors of the basilica itself.

sight of all the Franks, was seized by a demon and much troubled. **11.** Then the bountiful prelate had all St Peter's doors shut and ordered them to be bolted; on the admonishment of the Holy Ghost he thus addressed the king: 'If you have come here with pure purpose and sincere intent and for the safety of the State and of the whole City and of this church, enter these doors at my bidding. But if you have not, these doors will be opened to you neither by me nor by my licence.' The king immediately replied, telling him he had come with no evil purpose or any perverseness or bad intention. Then at the prelate's bidding, with hands held out they opened the doors and in this way they entered St Peter's venerable hall. The whole clergy and all God's servants the monks chanted praise to God and His Excellency, loudly acclaiming: 'Blessed is he who comes in the name of the Lord' etc.[20] And so the king, all the bishops, abbots and judges, and all the Franks who had accompanied him, came with the pontiff close to St Peter's confessio. There they prostrated themselves and gave thanks to our God almighty and to the prince of the apostles. The pontiff gave out the prayer over the people, and they all returned from the church.

12. But afterwards on each of the days following they oppressed all the suburbs with pestilential devastation and they fell on the fields, crops and meadows like a thunderbolt. Meanwhile the God-protected pontiff heard from certain men that they wanted to come inside this world-renowned city for hospitality's sake, but he had the gates barred and bolted, and refused to allow it.

13. The following Sunday,[21] all the archbishops, bishops and abbots, and all the Franks who had come with him, again gathered in the prince of the apostle's basilica along with all the noble and distinguished Romans. Then the bountiful pontiff with his own hands anointed the emperor's son Louis with holy oil, crowned him with a royal and precious crown and made him king of the Lombards. He gave him a royal sword and bade him gird it on himself. When the celebration of mass was done they all returned from the church in gladness with the king.

14. But thereafter,[22] Drogo,[23] archbishop of the church of Metz, whom

---

[20] Ps. 117 (118) 26; Mt 21.9, 23.39; Mk 11.9-10; Lk 13.35, 19.38; Jn 12.13.

[21] If the LP is right about the date this will be 15 June 844; but the LP is wrong about the order of events, cf. n. 22, where are quoted the accounts in *AB* and in Pseudo-Liutprand. Some of the language of the present chapter is borrowed from 98:22-24, the account of Charlemagne's coronation by Leo III.

[22] The account of these negotiations in the LP is composed with what Duchesne described as great reserve: we are told it was lively and Sergius won it, but not what it was about. The order of events in the LP is: crowning of Louis, discussions, swearing of oath to

we have mentioned above, was each day stirring up conflict and serious contention against the holy prelate, all the bishops and all our leading men and dignitaries, and not only Drogo but all the archbishops and bishops who, without any licence or summons from a metropolitan, had joined with him against this universal church, the head of all the churches, namely: the archbishops George of Ravenna and Angilbert of Milan, the bishops[24] Joseph of Ivrea, Aginus of Bergamo, Amalric of Como, Nortcaud of Vercelli, Sigifrid of Reggio, Toringar of Concordia, Odelbert of Acqui, Ambrose of Lucca, John of Pisa, Peter of Volterra, Gausprand of Pistoia, Cantio of Siena, Lupus of Teate[25], Sisimund of Aprutium[26], Picco of Ascoli, Fratellus of Camerino, Gisus of Fermo, Racipert of Nocera, Amadeus of Penne, Donatus of Fiésole and others; and with them in the contest were the counts Boso,[27] Adalgis,[28] John,

---

Lothar. But *AB* 844 Nelson 57 puts the discussions before the crowning: 'Lothar sent his son Louis to Rome with Drogo bishop of Metz: they were to take measures to prevent any future pope being consecrated there, on his predecessor's death, except on Lothar's orders and in the presence of his representatives. They reached Rome and were received with due honour by the pope, who, when the negotiations had been concluded, consecrated Louis king by anointing him, and invested him with a sword.' And Ps.-Liutprand (*PL* 129.1244) also disagrees with the order of events in the LP, giving the oath of loyalty to Lothar, discussions, crowning of Louis: '(Louis and Drogo) after bringing much loss onto the Romans made them swear loyalty to the emperor, and after many conflicts *they at length confirmed Sergius in the see*, and he anointed the emperor's son as king of the Lombards'. This is the only explicit statement that the discussions were an inquiry into Sergius's election. But Pseudo-Liutprand's testimony should not, in my view, be rated too highly; he was summarizing the LP itself, and perhaps over-hastily. The LP is vague about the pope's victory, but it must be talking about this debate, and the conciliar trappings with which it surrounds the affair confirm this: there was no need of a council for the other points at issue. Louis's crowning must have followed the discussions which confirmed the pope in office; the LP has altered the order of events.

[23] At some stage in a letter (*MGH Ep* 5.583, J2586) to the transalpine bishops Sergius granted an enlarged metropolitan status ('his vicar in charge of all the provinces beyond the Alps') to Drogo; he granted him the power to convene general synods; whatever was decided in a provincial synod held by Drogo must be brought to the pope's notice without delay; anyone needing to appeal to the holy see must first submit himself to a hearing by Drogo; anyone not following this advice would never be rashly absolved by the pope unless the case had been first aired in a provincial synod and then in a general hearing by Drogo; and he exhorted the bishops to concord. Cf. introduction to this life and *AB* 844 Nelson 57: 'Bishop Drogo was designated papal vicar in the regions of the Gauls and Germanies'; the vicariate may reflect the ambitions of Lothar to intervene in the church affairs of his brothers' kingdoms, but little came of it (Nelson, citing Devisse 1975:35-52).

[24] The bishops, none of whose sees was then in the papal State, are listed in roughly geographical order: northern Italy (Ivrea to Acqui), Tuscany (Lucca to Siena, with Fiésole misplaced), and the duchy of Spoleto (Chieti to Penne).

[25] Chieti.

[26] Téramo (in the Abruzzi).

[27] See 107:48 with n. 101 for Boso's identity; he is generally assumed to be the father of the Boso there mentioned.

[28] Scarcely the Adalgis who was later duke of Benevento (*AB* 871 Nelson 176 n. 14);

Vuldo, Bernard,[29] Wifrid and Maurinus, and others too. But God's grace inspired this bountiful pontiff and they could not overcome his words and wisdom; so great a strength was in him from on high that there was no argument they could use to trap him or force him to submit. Defeated by him they gave way, full of shame and confusion. Seeing this, they entirely laid aside all the anger and ferocity they were harbouring in their minds.

15. When this was over, they asked the pontiff that all the leading Romans should promise loyalty to king Louis under oath. This the wise prelate refused to grant, but thus addressed them: 'If you want them to take this oath to the great emperor lord Lothar alone, I agree and allow it; but neither I nor any of the Roman nobles agree to this being done for his son Louis'. Then at length, when they were all seated in that church, the blessed pontiff,[30] the great king and all the archbishops and bishops, with the rest of the *sacerdotes* and the leading Romans and Franks in attendance, promised loyalty to the great emperor Lothar, ever Augustus.

16. Next a certain Ebbo and Bartholomew,[31] archbishops who had

---

perhaps the one who was count of Parma by the 830s (Wickham 1981:57).

[29] Probably the same as the Frankish count Bernard much involved in life 106:8-20; not the Bernard killed at Poitou in 844 (see Nelson, *AB* 58 n. 7, 122 n. 3, 151 n. 21).

[30] Duchesne noted that at this point the pope completes the formality of the oath to the emperor, no doubt omitted at the moment of his installation. But see n. 22.

[31] Ebbo (c. 775-851) was archbishop of Rheims, Bartholomew of Narbonne. Ebbo had been chosen by Louis to evangelize the Danes, and had visited Rome in 822 (see p. 2); Paschal had commissioned him and appointed him papal legate for the north. Both archbishops had been implicated in Lothar's revolt and the deposition of Louis. On Louis's reinstatement, Ebbo, at Metz, acknowledged his involvement and that the reinstatement of Louis was right; then in a council at Thionville Ebbo confessed to capital crime and gave his resignation in writing (*AB* 835 Nelson 32-3); Bartholomew was also removed, but neither prelate was immediately replaced. No doubt it was true, as later alleged, that the depositions were on Louis's orders, but canonical procedures had been followed (Nelson 33 n. 3). It was later claimed, very dubiously, that Gregory IV (J2585; Mansi 15.794, letter to pope Nicholas; cf. Hincmar's letters to Anastasius, Egilo and Nicholas) confirmed Ebbo as bishop of Hildesheim; but this is hardly consistent with Sergius now receiving him and Bartholomew into lay communion only. Both Rheims and Narbonne were now in Charles the Bald's kingdom; for Lothar to secure from Sergius the reinstatement of the archbishops would have been a great coup for him. But Drogo, now present, had presided at Thionville and was unlikely to support that council's ruling being overturned; and Sergius may have regarded the request as inopportune so soon after the sons of Louis had reached a peace agreement. By 846 Ebbo was competing for his former see with Hincmar (J2589-90, letters of Hincmar, Mansi 15.776-7), whose ambitions were not such that he could easily brook competition; and by 849 Lothar had reopened the issue of Ebbo's deposition to embarrass Charles (*AB* 849 Nelson 67 n. 1). Even after his death, Ebbo's irregular situation produced doubts about the validity of the ordinations he conducted after his deposition; Hincmar would not acknowledge these and in a synod he deposed all the priests, deacons and subdeacons concerned (*AB* 853 Nelson 76). Benedict

been deprived of office and expelled from the church for their crimes, asked the holy pontiff to see fit to reconcile them and grant them the *pallium*. The prelate pronounced them unworthy to receive communion among the clerics; they might have leave only to communicate among the ordinary people.

17. While king Louis was then living at Rome, Siconulf[32] prince of the Beneventans came to Rome with a great army.[33] The king received him with honour, and he then declared to him everything for which he had come. With joyous spirit the king granted and allowed him everything he had asked for. Since the Franks, Lombards and Beneventans had all gathered together, the crowd of people became so huge that Rome was surrounded on every side: their great numbers destroyed all the crops. Siconulf's heart was burning with desire to see the distinguished pontiff and receive his blessing. The prelate received him, and prostrate on the ground he kissed his precious feet in humility. Receiving his blessing he cheerfully retired from his sight, giving thanks to God.

18. When all this was completed, His Excellency king Louis returned in great gladness to Pavia, from which capital he ruled since the start of his princedom. Then all the senate and people of Rome with their wives and children, glad at their deliverance from the enormous plague and yoke of tyrannical frightfulness, revered the holy prelate Sergius as the

---

III and Nicholas both confirmed this (*AB* 866 Nelson 132). The issue came to a head when one of the clerics, Wulfad, was a candidate for the archbishopric of Bourges. For the sequel see pp. 195-7.

[32] I adopt this spelling as in the MSS and in Erchampert, not Siginulf as in *AB*.

[33] On the death of Sicard (840), the last Lombard prince who had governed the whole duchy of Benevento, his successor Radelgis had to fight a competitor Siconulf, who founded at Salerno a principality to rival Benevento, and then tried to reunite the ancient duchy under himself. Lothar and Louis regarded Siconulf as a usurper. Erchampert (*Historia Langobardorum Beneventanorum* 17-18) states that after taking from Radelgis all the towns and fortresses except Sipontum, he laid siege to Benevento and meanwhile asked his kinsman Guy duke of Spoleto for help. Guy sided with Radelgis and told Siconulf to abandon the siege, which the latter did; out of avarice Guy offered to change sides, but Radelgis prevented this with 70,000 gold coins; 'After this Guy persuaded Siconulf to give him 50,000 gold nummi for the unification of the Beneventan province, and said 'I will make you obtain it on all sides; you may measure it as in your palm'. Then, consenting to his plan, he went to Rome, gave over the gold coins, exchanged oaths, achieved nothing and came away empty-handed'. War continued between Siconulf and Radelgis, providing excellent opportunities for the Saracens near Benevento. Erchampert does not mention any involvement between Siconulf and Lothar or Louis. But *AB* 844 (Nelson 57-58) recounts the same affair with a different slant: 'Siginulf, Duke of the Beneventans, made his submission to Lothar along with all his men, and as a self-imposed penalty gave him 100,000 gold pieces. The Beneventans, who had previously bestowed their loyalties elsewhere, when they found out about this accepted Siginulf and applied themselves to driving the remnants of the Saracens out of their territory.'

author of their salvation and the restorer of peace. But he attributed what had happened to no power of his own but to the gift of God.

19. Now since language does not suffice to arrange a full account of all he achieved, let us pass on to what he presented to the holy places, and begin to outline it.

[A.D. 844:]

At the very start of his pontificate, burning with love from on high, he completed a work of wondrous beauty in the Saviour's basilica called Constantinian. For the circuit[34] of the holy altar therein had formerly been constructed narrowly; with his own hand he traced it out wider and he finished it from the foundations and splendidly adorned it with beautiful columns with carved marble round them on top; and there the holy people have space to stand in while the sacred office is directed. This completed, to adorn and decorate this conspicuous work this bountiful pontiff presented in the same basilica 20 white all-silk veils, decorated around with interwoven gold, and 20 other most excellent gold-interwoven ones decorated around with purple. There too[35] with Christ's cooperation he constructed a wondrous confessio and resplendently embellished it with silver panels and with swathing in gold; with his own hands he consecrated it and put the relics in place. He performed another excellent work outside the doors of this venerable church:[36] the holy thresholds were formerly hidden from the people, and

---

[34] *Ambitus* is probably technical, as in 103:31-2 (with n. 70). As far as we know the arrangement changed by Sergius had subsisted since Constantine built the basilica; the circuit of the *presbyterium* where the 'holy people' (the clergy; see 102 n. 14) found themselves too restricted was now enlarged and rearranged to Sergius's own design (Krautheimer, *Corpus* 5.10). The usual arrangement was a colonnade surmounted by an entablature ('columns with marble on top round them'); the 20 pairs of veils were hung in the intercolumniations. These works will not have outlasted the construction of a transept at the end of the 13th century, if they survived that long.

[35] Sergius next excavated a confessio in front of and beneath the altar, consecrating it by depositing relics as was now usual. Like all ancient cathedrals, the Lateran will almost certainly have had no relics in its altar before this time. Sergius's confessio seems to be represented by the confessio below the present altar.

[36] Krautheimer, *Corpus* 5.85, remarks that this passage is obscure. Some kind of construction, which hid the doors, seems to have risen in front of the church to the east, and Sergius replaced it with some sort of arcade. The text does not mention an atrium. Krautheimer cites Alexander 1970:281ff, especially 284ff, for the valid point that there is proof neither of the presence nor of the absence of a Constantinian atrium at the Lateran; this leaves Duchesne's suggestion that the basilica's doors had previously opened into a colonnaded portico uncertain. There is a reference to an atrium at 97:70, but Krautheimer thinks the LP may there be referring to colonnades and atria at the palace rather than at the basilica; since, however, they are mentioned between the basilica and the baptistery this seems to me unlikely, though not impossible. The construction need not be Constantinian but I accept that there was an atrium by the 9th century. After Sergius II's time, about 960, a chapel of St Thomas was built into the southern end of the narthex:

with great endeavour he rendered them visible to all when he constructed there from the foundations beautifully adorned arches; and these he magnificently adorned with various pictures.

20. For the cure and future reward of his soul this God-protected and distinguished pontiff magnificently and conspicuously decorated the vault of our Lord Jesus Christ's Manger,[37] which is connected to God's holy mother our lady's basilica which everyone calls Major,[38] with silver and gilded panels representing the Lord's incarnation and God's blessed mother Mary's birth;[39] for a period of many years none of the pontiffs had thought to bring it to the appearance[40] of such great beauty.

{**21.**[41] This[42] holy prelate, realizing like a kind and dutiful pastor that the aqueduct Jovia had lain demolished for a period of years and was fully ruined, restored it afresh; and there gushed forth a great abundance of water which satisfied almost the whole city.}

[A.D. 844-45:]

{**22.** In his time[43] the river called Tiber left its channel and spread over the plains. It swelled in great spate on 22 November in the 8th

---

it included, on the east, an earlier triple arcade on piers and columns which has been taken to be the remains of a Constantinian atrium. The north wall of St Thomas's chapel was in line with the south colonnade of the nave and seems originally to have carried the springing of groin vaults and to have had a matching wall further north. Though all is mysterious, Krautheimer suggests there was a vaulted propylon, open to the east (i.e. with arched entrances through its wall), fronting and sheltering the *sacra limina*, the actual doors into the basilica. There were three doors into the basilica's nave (and none into the four aisles), and all three could have been behind such a propylon. A propylon of this kind could have been incorporated into the colonnade of an atrium if or when one was built, but Sergius now removed it and completed the colonnade in front of the doors, making the doors more visible than before. St Thomas's chapel survived the rebuilding of the rest of the portico (1159-1181) by Nicolaus Angeli, but with Angeli's portico it was demolished to make way for the present (1732) façade by Galilei.

[37] On this chapel see 100:37.

[38] The first use of this name in the LP, though only in a casual mention; the LP's medieval continuations first use it in the life of Gregory VII. Unofficially it goes back to the *Epitome de locis sanctis* (*CChr* 175, 321.172: 'the Basilica which is called S. Maria Maior') at the same time as the designation *Ad Praesepe*; cf. 92:8 with n. 30.

[39] This ought to mean the Virgin's own birth, but after the mention of the incarnation Christ's birth from the Virgin must be meant.

[40] Elsewhere (98:31) *species* in such contexts seems to mean value.

[41] From here on Duchesne distributes his text into 2 columns, the left with the text of the Farnesi MS (E⁵), the right with that of the other MSS. In what follows, curly brackets enclose what is in the earlier Farnesi text only, italics are used for what is in the later text only, and ordinary type is used for what is common to both. On the insight this textual tradition gives into the compilation of the LP see p. 71.

[42] The language of this chapter is closely based on 97:65, dealing with Hadrian I's repairs to the Aqua Virgo. On the Aqua Jovia see 97:61 with n. 117.

[43] This chapter is closely modelled on 91:6 and (its derivative) 97:94-5.

indiction [844], a Saturday, the birthday of St Caecilia the martyr. It entered the Roman city by the postern[44] called St Agatha's at the first hour of the day. Meanwhile in some places it even overlapped the city walls and it reached St Laurence's church called Lucina's. From there it entered God's holy ever-virgin mother's on the Via Lata and then crossed to St Mark's. It extended itself through the streets, desolated fields, uprooting trees. That night-time removed the water and the river returned to its own channel.}

23. As this prelate was careful in his anxiety for all the churches,[45] he completed from its foundations, more expansive than it had formerly been, the holy Archangel's basilica established on the summit of Monte Fagano; he bade it be brightly painted with radiant pictures, and he freshly restored its roofing; there he presented {these gifts}: 4 cloths of *ymizinum*; also 4 veils.

24. The Schola Cantorum formerly called the Orphanage[46] through its

---

[44] Cf. LP 54:3, BP 47 where the postern is unnamed, though possibly St Agatha's is intended. It was located in the city-wall along the Tiber close to the Mausoleum of Augustus. Duchesne here summarizes Corvisieri's discussion of this postern. It recurs under the same name in accounts of floods under Benedict III (106:23) and Nicholas (107:15); also in a bull of Agapitus II in 955; and one of John XII in 962 calls it 'the ancient postern which was once styled that of St Agatha'. Another bull of John XII in 956 mentions 'the postern of St Martin', apparently the same as St Agatha's; the change of name came from a nearby church of St Martin not otherwise mentioned till 1026; then a donation in 1045 mentions this as St Martin's church near the 'postern of William', evidently yet another name for the same postern. Cencius calls this church St Martin *de pila*; it also appears as 'of (or close to) the river', but usually, as in the Turin Catalogue, as 'of the postern'. Destroyed in the 16th century and rebuilt with the double dedication to SS Roche and Martin, it is the present S. Rocco a Ripetta (cf. Hülsen, *Chiese*, 385-6). The other posterns mentioned in the LP, the Holy Angel's and the Saxons' (105:73), were gates in the wall of the Leonine City, not that of Rome.

[45] 2 Cor. 11.28.

[46] *Orphanotropheum*; mentioned as the Schola Cantorum in c. 2 above; it recurs as the *Orphanotropheum* at 112:17. The *Liber Diurnus*, ed. Foerster, 176f, 262f, 410f (V97 = C91 = A86), has a *Privilegium*-formula dealing with the recovery of lands wrongly taken from the *Orfanotrofium*; it includes the remark: 'and when defeated by want the place was in straits, the children ceased to frequent it as provision of their expenses was missing; therefore in case the order of singers should be lacking and God's church suffer insult from this...' This confirms the implication in the LP that the Orphanage was or had become a choir-school; cf. *Registrum Sublacense* n. 112 p. 159, a charter of 919, mentioning John, subdeacon of the Roman church and *primicerius* of the Schola Cantorum called the *Orphanotrophium*. The Schola is mentioned in a letter of pope Paul to Pepin (J2371, CC 41, MGH Ep 3.553), and in the various 8th- and 9th-century *Ordines*. John the Deacon (*Vita Greg.* 2.6) attributes its foundation to Gregory I, but this may be no more than a 9th-century inference from the supposed origin of Gregorian chant. As the LP says, the Schola had a chapel to St Stephen; this is still mentioned in Cencius's *Ordo* at the end of the 12th century (Hülsen, *Chiese*, 479). The Schola was suppressed in 1370 (so Hülsen). The Turin Catalogue notes that its chapel was destroyed, but locates it between the churches of St Matthew and St Bartholomew, both in the Via Merulana. Though the site of the latter of these churches is unknown, the statement is enough to

great age {had now decayed and} was almost in ruin and broken {for a long time}; this bountiful and blessed pope, God's clemency willing it, freshly restored it from its foundations, an improvement on what it had been. {Also, in St Stephen the first martyr's oratory in that Schola, he provided 1 gold-interwoven veil with a tyrian fringe; there too he provided a fine silver paten and chalice which together weigh 2 lb 2 oz.}

25. St Romanus the martyr's basilica[47] not far from the City outside the Salarian Gate {for a long time had grown old and was almost on the point of collapse; by his loving effort he constucted it in opus Signinum} *he completed it* from the foundations. He decreed it to be a paroecia[48] of SS Silvester and Martin's titulus {and there he placed 1 gold-interwoven cloth with a purple fringe}.

[A.D. 845-46:]

In the Lateran patriarchate in St Caesarius the martyr's oratory[49] situated in the vestiarium, this God-protected, venerable and distinguished pontiff provided 5 silk veils, one of purple, decorated around with fourfold weave, two of fourfold weave decorated with tyrian, and two of tyrian decorated with byzantine purple.

He[50] built St Theodore the martyr's basilica in the territory of Cora 30 miles from Rome, and he splendidly adorned it with bright pictures.

{**26.** Bathed in the Holy Ghost's enlightenment, this holy prelate

---

indicate that the Schola was in the 'papal quarter' of Rome, and close to the Lateran. Further references to the Schola and its *primicerius* in Kehr 1906:I.17-18.

[47] No such basilica is mentioned in the 7th-century itineraries or in the 12th- to 15th-century catalogues; outside the LP, it occurs only in Bosio's text of the saint's acts; but the acts derive from the *Passio Laurenti*, whose ordinary text merely says that the saint was beheaded outside the Salarian Gate, and says nothing of a church there. The only martyr Romanus in the itineraries is one in the *De locis sanctis*, the *Itin. Malm.* and the *Notitia Ecclesiarum*; he was buried at or near S. Lorenzo on the Via Tiburtina, and the *Notitia* puts him 'at a distance in a cave below'. If this was an underground chapel, it may be to it that the LP refers; if so, Via Salaria is a slip. Or if Salaria is correct, the dedication is an error for one of the many groups of martyrs buried outside the Salarian Gate.

[48] Since at least the 5th century the cemeterial basilicas had been juridically attached to the city *tituli*, which provided clergy for services (cf. LP 42:7 BP 33, S. Agnese assigned to the *titulus Vestinae*). But it is doubtful if the same connexion is meant here, as by now the cemeteries were no longer used for burials; Duchesne suggested that a real rural 'parish' centred on St Romanus's church was meant, juridically attached to and managed by SS Martin and Silvester, but with its own clergy (as is implied by the term *paroecia*). Later, similar parishes would be formed round small churches within Rome, and attached to the ancient *tituli* or even to deaconries; but this division inside the city does not seem to date as far back as the 9th century.

[49] Previously mentioned in the LP at 86:2 (BP 83) and 96:9, and earlier by Gregory I, *Ep.* 13.1. The location is uncertain.

[50] The earlier recension has St Theodore's at Cora (otherwise unknown) in c. 30.

provided on the high altar in the basilica of his mentor St Peter prince of the apostles a gold-studded cloth representing the Saviour our Lord Jesus Christ sitting on a throne and around him angels standing with the apostles.}

(30.) In[51] St Peter the apostle's basilica he provided a gold-studded cloth representing the Saviour in the middle and on his right and left glittering figures of all the holy apostles, and he decorated it with very precious jewels, prases and jacinths.

{27. In God's mother St Mary's church in Arranum[52] this distinguished prelate provided a fine silver-gilt paten and chalice, weighing together 2 lb 1½ oz.}

{Christ's confessor[53] and pontiff St Martin's church, built a long time ago, was now suffering fatigue from its great age so that collapse to its foundations was threatening its ruin; this venerable pontiff anticipating its ruin and applying care to that church, often being on the watch there, shifted and erected it in another place[54] not far away, an improvement on what it had formerly been.[55]   28. This[56] holy and distinguished

---

[51] This is the later recension's version of c. 26.

[52] Unless this is an unknown church at an unidentifiable place, read *in Narrano* for *in Arrano*; for St Mary's 'at Moreno called Narrano' see 105:62 and n. 92.

[53] cc. 27b - 29 of the Farnesi recension are equivalent to cc. 31-32 in the later version. The whole passage (down to 'pleasing to God' in c. 29) is lifted from 100:8-9, Paschal's rebuilding of S. Prassede. The later recension rewrote it, probably because the reference to a change of site was false (though see next note). Both versions give the 'official' view, whereas c. 41 claims that the church was destroyed merely to allow Sergius's brother Benedict to enrich himself. Under Leo III the church had been (for a short time) a deaconry (98:45 with n. 100), but was a *titulus* again by the time Paschal made the future Sergius II its priest, c. 3 above; cf. Hülsen, *Chiese*, 282-3.

[54] The claim that the site was moved is not in the later recension, and this may affect any estimate of the relative value of the two recensions. The problem is that nothing is known of the size or shape of Symmachus's church below it or of the *titulus Equitii* below that (the 6-bay hall to the west is not the *titulus Equitii*, but it may have been the *titulus Silvestri*); Krautheimer, *Corpus* 3.124, remarks that, if there is any truth in the change of site, Sergius's church may have had a slightly different axis from Symmachus's church. Older writers were wrong to believe that Sergius merely modified the previous church; it is certain that Sergius's structure was new (Silvagni 1913:384-8; Kirsch 1918:41-45; Vielliard 1931; and next note).

[55] Krautheimer, *Corpus* 3.93-124, comments that much of the 9th-century exterior of S. Martino is still visible: the apse with the north wall, the east clerestory wall, and the lower courses of the side wall of the east aisle. Inside there is much baroque overlay, but the original structure essentially survives: the shafts and capitals of 12 columns each side of the nave, and almost all their bases. The present crypt probably replaced an annular crypt-passage (like that at S. Marco), and the relic-chamber survives. The basilica is on an artificial platform with 'Servian' foundations; the interior is 26.40 m wide and 41 m long (the apse, projecting to the north, a further 12½ m). The nave has a clear width of 13.50 m; the aisles, including column-widths, exactly half that. Before the floor was lowered 60 cm in the 17th century, the nave was 15.40 m high. The external walls of the aisles, and the clerestory walls, are 0.65 m thick. The 24 Corinthian columns have 20 Corinthian and

pontiff sought out, found and collected many bodies of saints lying in destroyed cemeteries, with that dutiful concern that they should not remain in neglect; with great affection and veneration he removed and buried them in the church of Christ's confessor and pontiff St Martin, which he had wonderfully renewed and constructed, with the assistance of all the Romans, priests, deacons and clerics, chanting psalms of praise to God. **29.** And while these inner cares of the holy and angelic prelate's heart were afoot, in his anxiety to gain aid before the Lord almighty by the prayers of those whose holy bodies were buried therein,[57] who beyond the stars are unceasingly pleasing to God, in the same venerable church he provided windows in the apse, which he adorned with glass and various colours;[58] and he decorated the presbyterium with carved marble.[59] In the same church he provided a fine silver canopy with four porphyry columns, weighing 810 lb.[60]}

{**30.** The venerable and distinguished pontiff built St Theodore the martyr's basilica in the territory of Cora about 30 miles from Rome and he splendidly adorned it with bright pictures; and there he provided 1 gold-interwoven cloth.}

31. These[61] things thoroughly finished, this God-protected and blessed pope, anxious in godly devotion to gain the desirable love of SS Silvester and Martin, completed from its foundations, God's clemency

---

4 composite capitals; they are monoliths with various shafts: 2 cipollino, 5 pavonazzetto, 6 of a dark grey, heavily-veined marble, probably from Teos, and 11 of Thasos marble; all are 4.70 m high, 0.60 m in diameter; capitals and columns are ancient spoils, from more than one building. There was once a square atrium, built on 'Servian' blocks. The church is a perfect example of the latter part of the Carolingian Renaissance in Rome. Entablature over the columns, an atrium, and (probably) an annular crypt, are also found at SS Quattro Coronati, rebuilt at just this date; and they still recall S. Prassede and S. Stefano degli Abessini at the start of the renascence. Technical characteristics (double window-voussoirs, size and spacing of windows, undulating brick courses) are exactly parallel to the other Roman churches of the period, S. Prassede, SS Nereo e Achilleo, S. Maria Nova, and the Carolingian parts of SS Quattro Coronati.

[56] The earlier recension has lifted the language of this chapter and the beginning of the next almost entirely from 100:9, Paschal's burial of relics at S. Prassede.

[57] 'therein' translates *ibidem* from the source passage 100:9, which is better sense than *quidem* here.

[58] i. e. stained-glass windows (Krautheimer).

[59] These works were in the apse rather than the *presbyterium* according to the later recension. The decorations were only completed under Leo IV (see 105:98), whose inscription (n. 72 below) claims that Sergius had died before he could confer any decor on the church, and (despite c. 39) that Leo founded the monastery.

[60] The altar still had four columns in Ugonio's time (1588), but they were 'mischio'; either they were later replacements for those of the 9th century or the LP uses 'porphyry' loosely (Krautheimer).

[61] cc. 31 - 32 are the second recension's version of cc. 27b - 29.

willing it, the church which had been consecrated to their holy name, improving its condition and its beauty; from the start of his sacerdotal office he had strenuously governed it until he was brought to the pinnacle of the pontificate; it had from ancient times given way and decayed from age, and damaged a long time ago it stayed broken in ruins. With great love he depicted its apse in gold colours on the overlaid mosaic. 32. For almighty God's honour, he dedicated and placed under the holy altar[62] *all these: the same prelate St Silvester's body with the martyrs and pontiffs SS Fabian, Stephen and Soter; the martyr Asterius with his holy daughter, and SS Cyriac, Maurus, Largus and Smaragdus; the pontiffs Anastasius and Innocentius; the bishops SS Quirinus and Leo; the martyrs Artemius, Sisianus, Pollio, Theodore, Nicander, Crescentianus and with them the virgin martyrs SS Soteris, Paulina, Memmia, Juliana, Quirilla, Theopiste, Sophia; the widow St Cyriaca; with many others whose names are known to God alone.*[63]

{33. In SS Silvester and Martin the confessors and pontiffs' church he presented:} *When this was wondrously finished, with joyful spirit and concerned intention he presented in this church these things to stay there for ever:* a very precious gold crown with jewels, prases, jacinths and pearls, which is still seen hanging over the altar, with a fine gold cross in the middle, also with precious jewels; also 4 fine silver bowls swathed in gold, hanging before the holy altar's vestibule,[64] and 2 chased gilded bowls with pommels[65]; 2 gold crosses with most excellent jewels, and one other silver cross. In the same basilica he presented 3 censers overlaid with gold colour; 2 patens of fine silver and gilded; 1 silver cullender,[66] gilded, used in the sacred office; 1 {fine} silver crown with bells, with in the middle a cross with a dove.

34. There too, burning with love from on high this blessed pope

---

[62] The relic-chamber is still preserved, a small room 2.9 by 2.5 m, 1.6 m external height, with a barred opening on the north side, and lined with slabs carved with typically 9th-century interlaced ornament (Krautheimer, *Corpus* 3.111).

[63] Even if this list is of no genuine martyrological value it does show what relics 9th-century contemporaries believed were deposited. The LP text is the origin of a 17th-century inscription listing relics (copied from one of the 13th century), now fixed to the wall of the crypt in S. Martino (Krautheimer, *Corpus* 3.91; cf. Armellini-Cecchelli I.267ff).

[64] Krautheimer thinks that 'vestibule' means the space enclosed by the pergola (which bordered the chancel); from Peruzzi's pre-baroque drawing of 1550 it appears that it was three-sided and made up of six columns; of the six, four spanned the nave and two stood behind at the sides.

[65] Perhaps the pommels (*bullae*) on these lighting-fixtures are solid handles of some kind.

[66] *colatorium*; evidently the provision of wine by the communicants at the offertory was still a living ceremony at this date; the wine needed straining.

presented silver handbasins, 3 pairs; *2* {3 fine} silver pint-pots[67]; *4 great silver crowns, with dolphins, weighing .. lb;* 2 chalices of {fine} silver and gilded; {1} great silver paten swathed in gold, with a representation of our Lord Jesus Christ in the middle; *3 pairs candlesticks silvered on top; 3 silver canisters; 1 silver paten with chalice; 1 silver scyphus weighing .. lb.*

For the honour of this venerable basilica he presented 12 brass chandeliers; 6 pairs railings, also of brass.

For the glory and honour of the holy confessors we have mentioned above, this distinguished and venerable prelate provided a fine silver canopy weighing .. lb. He magnificently decorated the holy altar's confessio with silver panels swathed in gold, weighing .. lb, so that he might by their holy intercessions possess the joys of the ethereal kingdom. There too this merciful and kind bishop presented 3 images of silver and swathed in gold, one of them with the representation of our Lord Jesus Christ, the other two with that of SS Silvester and Martin, set over the holy altar's vestibule.[68]

35. In the same basilica he presented a gold-studded cloth, representing the resurrection of our Lord Jesus Christ, with jewels, prases, jacinths and pearls. He provided another very precious gold-studded gold-interwoven cloth with a representation of the Saviour our Lord Jesus Christ in the middle and on his right and left representations of SS Silvester and Martin, also with jewels, prases, jacinths and pearls. The holy prelate also offered 3 alexandrian {crowns} *curtains*[69] woven with most precious work; 24 gold-interwoven veils, decorated round with {byzantine} purple, which hang in this basilica's arches;[70] 15 other gold-interwoven veils with a purple fringe; 4 white all-silk veils surrounding the altar,[71] one of them with a cross in the middle and gold-studded chevrons, the others decorated round with {byzantine} purple.

{36. There too he provided another all-silk gold-studded cloth, with roses, representing the resurrection of our Lord Jesus Christ; and 1 other red cloth with a white winged horse, with a gold-studded fringe, 4 chevrons and a gold-studded cross. In the same church this holy prelate

---

[67] *sextaria*: cf. *sextarium* at 112:19 and the glossary s.v. 'pint'.

[68] Krautheimer thinks that these were reliefs, and that they seem to have been over the entablature surmounting the pergola ('vestibule', cf. n. 64).

[69] The later recension was no doubt right to emend 'crowns' to 'curtains'. Crowns (lights) can hardly have been woven, and 'alexandrian' is an adjective for textiles.

[70] Two further sets of 24 curtains occur in c. 36. There were 13, not 12, intercolumniations each side, and Krautheimer (*Corpus* 3.119) suggests that for liturgical purposes those nearest the altar were left uncurtained.

[71] i. e. for the altar-canopy mentioned in c. 29A = 34B.

provided 3 images of fine silver-gilt, one with the face of the Lord
Saviour, the other two with the faces of the confessors SS Silvester and
Martin, set over the holy altar's vestibule. There too he provided 24
great gold-interwoven veils, and 24 linen ones. **37.** At this church's
entrance the venerable prelate provided a great alexandrian curtain
embellished and adorned with various representations. There too he
provided silver candlesticks, 3 pairs; 4 fine silver crowns; and 1 fine
silver canister. In the same church he provided a red veil with various
fledglings and a fringe of byzantine purple; and 3 coverings of purple
silk over the icons. **38.** In St Martin the confessor's basilica this blessed
pope provided a confessio of fine silver-gilt, with an image of St Mary
with 10 virgins; in the confessio a gospel-book of fine silver-gilt; also
in the confessio 1 pair railings; and in front of this confessio a fine
silver cornice with 2 fine silver columns.}[72]
39. Close to the side of that basilica this noteworthy and holy pope,
protected by God's inspiration, for the Creator's praise constructed from
the foundations a monastery[73] in honour of SS Peter and Paul, Sergius
and Bacchus and Silvester and Martin; in it he established a community
of God's servants the monks for daily praises, praying to the Lord our

---

[72] Though the compiler does not mention it, it seems that Sergius also provided two
pulpits, one of which had his name inscribed (the other had a couplet copied from
Pelagius II's ambo in St Peter's) (De Rossi, *Inscr. Christ.* II.437, Krautheimer, *Corpus*
3.120-1). The apse-mosaic, which disappeared long ago (presumably there was also a
mosaic in the apse half-dome, but it is unknown), was accompanied by an inscription in
12 hexameters (ed. Dümmler, *MGH Poet. Lat. aevi Kar.* 2.663 no. 7), which attributed
the monastery's foundation (despite the LP) to Leo IV, while crediting Sergius with the
building of the *aula*. The decoration, at least, continued under Leo IV (see 105:98; Ferrari,
299ff; Vielliard 1931:90f; Krautheimer, *Corpus* 3.91).
[73] For the monastery see Ferrari 299-301 (he is much concerned to rebut the idea that the
foundation was for Greek monks). Traces of 'Servian' foundations (Krautheimer, *Corpus*
3.112,121) to the west of the church may belong to the monastery, which was built above
the Roman 6-bay hall; it was totally rebuilt in 1930, but the buildings then destroyed seem
to have been romanesque, or even survivals of the original Roman building, rather than
of the 9th century. 'Constructed from the foundations' in the LP should not be trusted! -
as Vielliard 1931:88 observed for this very church; Vielliard (plans I and II) gives
detailed plans of the ancient monastery. He concluded, after examining the building, that
the 9th-century work was just the bolstering of the ancient titular house and the
embellishing of the walls with frescoes. He discovered a small choir chapel, presumably
for office recitation in the winter months, on the second floor of the monastery, and
mentioned as parallel examples the second-floor chapels in S. Silvestro in capite and S.
Prassede (*idem*, 99). The few frescoes remaining today suggest that the monastery was
very richly decorated and quite spacious. The saints depicted are ones usual in Rome:
Agnes, Peter and Paul, Processus and Martinian, John the Evangelist and John the Baptist,
Xystus and Silvester, the Virgin flanked by SS Agape and Irene (*idem*, 93-8). There is no
further information before the year 1000. The 14th-century Turin Catalogue says it was
the *titulus* of a cardinal priest, and served by 15 Carmelites. A copy of an inscription from
the monastery, perhaps from its library, is preserved (De Rossi, *Inscr.* II, 438 note 2).

God in the said church night and day.

{**40.** Now as this pontiff's limbs were weak from a gouty humour, he had lost the power to walk on his feet and had almost lost the use of his hands; but he was rancorous, uncontrolled in speech and given to wrangling, unstable in deed and words, treating everything lightly. That was why the leaders of the Romans set him at nought. Then there was that pontiff's brother, one Benedict by name,[74] very stupid and dull, who because of the pontiff's infirmity had undeservedly usurped the care of church and state. He was a boor and given to unrefined pursuits, so he began to expend all the care of the church and the needs of the state on the construction of walls and various buildings, so much so that he failed neither day nor night to cause incessant trouble and vexation. **41.** This man even went to the lord emperor with large quantities of gifts and sought from him the primacy and lordship[75] at Rome, and bragged that it was granted him. After his return he broke out into great obstinacy and madness, overstepping everyone, to get the monarchy at Rome. Thenceforth he would let no one pay or be paid, be harmed or be helped, except on his say-so. And as he was of uncouth morals, lecherous and always chasing strumpets, he was not afraid to usurp the bishopric of Albano so he could fight for the devil more recklessly.}

{At the start of his supremacy he had destroyed the already-mentioned church of St Martin which had been constructed with the wondrous work of antiquity, so he could use the pretext of its demolition and rebuilding for more readily despoiling the churches and the people. **42.** So the result was that in three years there remained no monastery,[76] whether in Rome or outside, which did not lose its property. Indeed there was hardly a man inside or outside Rome whom he did not despoil by chance or by design. And with imperial permits and instructions he thoroughly strove to extort all this, or actually did so,[77] from both monasteries and people. From of old it was unheard of that anyone for such a length of time could, merely by his own

---

[74] Duchesne noted (after De Rossi, *Inscr.* II, p. 437) that Benedict's name is perhaps decipherable in a monogram occurring in an inscription at S. Martino.

[75] On Benedict's status and its implications for the constitutional position of pope Sergius vis-à-vis the emperor Lothar see the introduction to this life.

[76] This concern for monasteries suggested to Duchesne that the author was a monk.

[77] The text of the last words in this sentence is corrupt; for *aut molibus aut rebus exterus*, I suggest and translate *aut moliebatur aut revera extraxit* (Cicero twice has *extraxit* with *radicitus*, as here). Dr Cheesman neatly suggests participles (*molitus, extrahens*), but prefers to amend *aut mobilibus aut rebus externis*, 'both for movable and for external property'. The reference to imperial permits raises the constitutional questions discussed on pp. 73-4.

machinations and cunning, lay waste and ransack this world-famous city and all the cities subject to it, their fortresses, coastlines and borders.}

{**43.** There flourished in this pontiff's and his brother's time, that is for the three years, the wicked heresy of simony; so much did it flourish that bishoprics were sold in public, and he who paid most got the bishopric. To such avarice were they brought that a bishopric was sold for 2000 mancuses[78] and more still if the buyers could find the funds. No incumbency in the church was granted by them except at a price. When this and the other things mentioned were raging in the church and resounding far and wide among the people, and there was none of the orthodox bishops nor any of the churchmen who would show zeal for God and put themselves forward or treat with the emperor or the king[79] to snuff out such evil, or give themselves over voluntarily to death, as it had been better to die happily than to live unhappily; so when the Lord saw the church, redeemed by his blood, undergoing shipwreck and there was no christian competent to correct such great criminality or recall the authors and abetters of this evil to repentance, so God decided that his church should not endure such a reproach: God sent pagans to avenge what christians had failed to amend.}

{**44.** While this was going on in this pontiff's time, count Adalbert, an active man who was margrave[80] and guardian of the island of Corsica,[81] realizing the need the state was in, sent a letter to Rome with

---

[78] Cf. 97:77 with n. 161, citing Grierson 1954; see further, Keynes & Lapidge 1983:237 n. 37.

[79] Duchesne noted that Louis II was still only king of Italy, so the precise distinction suggests the author of the Farnesi recension was contemporary. But as Louis is called king in earlier chapters of the life (9, 10 twice, 13 crowned king of the Lombards, 15 twice, 17, 18), which the compiler will have read, the inference may not be safe.

[80] *marcensis*, equivalent to *marchio* or *praefectus marcae*. Adalbert was *marchio* of Tuscany 834-886; he is mentioned also in the *Indiculus eorum qui sacramentum fidelitatis iuraverunt* (ed. Boretius, who acceptes Pertz's date 828-9, *MGH Cap* 1.378 line 15), and also in Lothar's capitulary *pro edificatione novae Romae* (ed. Boretius, *MGH Cap* 2.68 no. 203), among the counts charged with the expedition against the Saracens decided on after these events. For his involvement in the attempt in 855 make Anastasius pope see 106:8-20; his attacks (with Lambert his brother-in-law) on papal territory in the 870s would infuriate John VIII (*AB* 878 Nelson 207 with n. 6), who excommunicated him, Lambert, the future pope Formosus, and the *nomenclator* Gregory.

[81] Adalbert seems to have been given some kind of oversight of Corsica. Corsica's status was peculiar: it was part of the papal state but under a special patronage of the Frankish sovereigns (cf. 97:42 and *LECP* 115-6 n. 13; the letter from Leo III to Charlemagne in 808 there cited contains the words: 'About the island of Corsica ... we commit it to your *arbitrium* and *dispositum*'). In 807 Corsica had been defended by the *comes stabuli* Burchard against a Moorish attack from Spain: *ARF* 807 Scholz 87: Charlemagne 'sent his marshal Burchard with a fleet to Corsica to defend the island against the Moors, who in past years used to come there and pillage. The Moors embarked, as usual, from Spain and went ashore first in Sardinia, where they waged a battle with the Sardinians and lost

the message that a multitude of the Saracen race up to 11,000 strong were on their way and coming with 73 ships, on board which were 500 horses, and were saying they were making for Rome;[82] they should try to rescue the treasures of the churches of St Peter the apostle and St Paul, and if possible bring these apostles' bodies inside Rome,[83] so that the wretched breed of pagans could not rejoice over so great a source of succour to us.[84] This was sent on the 10th day of August. Thanks to the fickle and ineffectual power of the above-mentioned men, they received it lightly and as reckoning it of little account, since everyone thought so surprising an event was incredible. Yet the more prudent of the Romans entered on a plan and despatched messengers and letters, along with the letter Adalbert had sent, to the outlying cities and their environs, so that everyone should hasten and come under arms to guard the seashore. They spurned the orders and refused to come, except a very few from some of the cities who came just to investigate.}

{45. A period of twelve days passed and on the 23rd day of August, a Monday, in the 9th indiction [846], the wicked Saracens reached the Roman shoreline close to the city of Ostia.[85] Disembarking, they came

---

many men - three thousand are said to have died there. Then they came by a direct route to Corsica. Here they again engaged in battle with the fleet under Burchard's command, in a harbor of this island. They were defeated and put to flight with thirteen ships lost and most of their men killed'.

[82] On the origins of this expedition, *AB* 846 merely says that in August the Saracens and Moors came to Rome by the Tiber. John the Deacon, *Gesta epp. Neap.* 60 (*MGH SSrL* 432.40-433), has more: 'At that time, with Theophilus dead and his son Michael now emperor, the ships of many Saracens who wanted to commit robberies in Italy landed on Ponza. Then Sergius, the *consularis*, along with the men of Amalfi, Gaeta and Sorrento, putting his trust not in the number of his people but in the Lord's mercy and the prayers of this bishop (John), started out on a war with them. With the Lord's protection he quickly triumphed by defeating them. Equally, he achieved victory over those Ishmaelites who were lying in wait on Licosa. Therefore a great army of those from Palermo came and captured the fortress of Miseno; and thence the Africans, desiring with a mighty arm to devastate all this region, came down on Rome...'. That they had come from Africa is confirmed by 105:7.

[83] Following Grisar 1907:457, Kirschbaum 1959:162 surmised that Adalbert's advice was in part acted on, and that this was the occasion when the heads of the apostles were removed and placed in the ciborium over the altar in the Lateran basilica, where they were venerated by the end of the 11th century; or alternatively that the heads were rescued and moved after the Saracen attack. Such theories lack all foundation.

[84] *ne de tanta salute tra gens* ... is corrupt. The simplest emendation is that suggested to me by Professor Scott and adopted in this translation: for *tra* read *nostra* (written *nra*); or read *ista*, with much the same meaning. Dr Cheesman suggests *tetra* ('the foul breed...'). The problem may be nothing more than a misprint from the only manuscript (now lost). But if the corruption is deeper, I am tempted to suggest: *ne de tanta strage gens* ('over so great a catastrophe'), or even *ne de tanta velut strage gens* ... If the author was capable of irony he might even have written *ne de tanta salutifera strage gens*.

[85] Thanks to the garrison's cowardice Gregory IV's fortress merely served as a redoubt

to that city - its inhabitants had shut it up and fled - and captured it. Then their scouts and others of them began to wheel round and attack anything they could find. Reaching the nearby city of Porto, they found it abandoned by its inhabitants; and purloining supplies and anything they thought they needed from there, on Monday and Tuesday they returned to Ostia.}

{46. When the Romans knew of this, the plan they decided on was to send to Porto the Saxons, the Frisians and the Schola called that of the Franks.[86] These got there on Monday and spent that night there on watch. Next day, Tuesday, some of these Saracens came after plunder. They were captured in flight but escaped across a bridge. They killed twelve of them but the rest escaped on a boat.[87] Once the Romans realized this, they kept a most wearisome watch over the gates of the city of Rome. At last, when no one sent to help them arrived[88] and there was no one to aid them in so great a need, trusting in the help of God and the apostles, they came out that Tuesday with those they had with them, and equipped in military fashion they came to the city of Porto in which there were many Saracen raiders. They killed seven of them, but the others were able to flee across that same wretched bridge and escape. Then all day, around that city and inside it, on horseback and wheeling round, they strove to join battle. When they saw their large numbers and their own small numbers, they decided it would be risky to spend that night there. Regrouping the Saxons, the Frisians and the rest, they set them to guard and watch over the city on account of the raiders, and returned to Rome.}

{47. Next day, Wednesday, when these guards were recklessly sitting down to a meal, the Saracens suddenly fell on them and surrounded and slaughtered them, so that few survived. Those who had escaped they pursued as far as Galeria.[89] Taking to their ships, their footmen and horsemen started hurrying to Rome. All day they journeyed with their ships, and at twilight they came to the locations they had decided on;

---

for the invaders. The name Gregoriopolis (103:40) has already been dropped.

[86] On the *scholae* see 98:19 with n. 49. In Rome they were virtually 'foreigners' compounds', see Krautheimer 1980:82.

[87] *navigio*; it need not have been one of the ships of the invasion fleet.

[88] The translation dodges the issue whether any definite *destinati* are meant (none have been mentioned). If there were none, the following words seem a little redundant; if there were some, translate 'when those sent to help them did not arrive' (more literally, 'they did not receive those sent to help them'). The only possible evidence for auxiliaries being sent would seem to be 'Lothar's commanders', mentioned by *AB* (cf. n. 92), who did arrive later on, but it seems unlikely that these would have been despatched so soon.

[89] Ponte di Galera; cf. 103:42 and n. 94 on Gregory IV's *curtis Galeria*.

and there the horsemen swarmed from the ships, and made a surprise attack on St Peter the prince of the apostles' church with unspeakable iniquities.[90] Then all the companies of Romans, left leaderless, came out to the Campus Neronis[91] to face the armed men....}[92]

---

[90] It is generally accepted that this was the occasion when the shrine of the apostle suffered the severe damage noticed by the excavators. What was taken from the central tomb space, which was ransacked, can never be known; the sources do not mention it, the authorities at the time would scarcely have broadcast it even if they knew. See Toynbee & Ward Perkins 1956:227-8, Kirschbaum 1959:162. Texts from the time show the shock caused by the event: *AB* 846 Nelson 63: 'the Saracens and Moors... laid waste the basilica of St Peter..., and along with the very altar which had been placed over his tomb, they carried off all the ornaments and treasures.' *AF* 846 Reuter 25: 'The Moors... after they had failed to break into the city they destroyed the church of St Peter'. See too *Ann. Xant.*; *Ann. Weissemburg.* 846 (ed. Pertz, *MGH SS* 1.111): 'The church of St Peter the apostle was captured and despoiled by pagans, and when they meant to return home with these spoils a worthy judgment of God fell on them and they all perished at sea'; and Lauer 1899:307. The result was Lothar's decision to order a major campaign against the Saracens and also the fortification of St Peter's; his capitulary *pro edificatione novae Romae* (*MGH Cap* 2.65 no. 203, 2) explains his feelings: 'No one doubts that it is because our sins and iniquities deserve it that so great an ill has befallen Christ's church that even the very Roman church which is the head of christendom has fallen into the hands of infidels and throughout all the borders of our realm and that of our brothers the people of the pagans has prevailed. Therefore we have firmly judged it necessary that with the help of God's mercy we emend everything in which we know he is particularly offended by us and that by making fitting satisfaction we may endeavour to placate the divine justice, so that we can have him placated whom we realize to be angry'; and cf. 105 n. 105. For the date, Zielinski 1991:37-49; c. 7 of the capitulary refers to the attack on St Peter's as 'in this year', and c. 11 requires Louis to reach Pavia by 25 January.

[91] Cf. n. 66 to 91:22.

[92] The LP text breaks off at the most interesting point, though the disaster the Saracens later suffered at sea is mentioned in the next life (105:7). Ps.-Liutprand (*PL* 129.1243-4), who summarizes this version of the LP life of Sergius, abridges what is now lost in a few words, describing great slaughters, captures of towns, booty, and fires; the Saracens defeated the king (Louis) and put him to flight; they departed with enormous booty. More explicit details are given in *AB* 846 Nelson 63, John the Deacon (*Gesta epp. Neap.* 60-61, *MGH SSrL* 433.1-25; continued from n. 82), the *Chronicon S. Benedicti Casinensis* cc. 6 and 12 (*MGH SSrL* 472, edited c. 870 and cited below as *CB*), and Benedict of Mt Soracte (c. 26; *MGH SS* 3.712-3; cited as *BMS*), whose account, written over 100 years later, is an extraordinary farrago and muddle (the pope is 'Gregory', the Leonine City already exists, etc.) and has to be taken with a large grain of salt; yet it may preserve some genuine memory of the events. A reasonably coherent though doubtless incomplete account of what happened can be reconstructed; it is not necessary (as Duchesne supposed) to presume that *AB* inverted the order of the last two events it mentions: the Saracen horde was not monolithic and there can be little doubt that different parties split in different directions. First, events near Rome. Following the sack of St Peter's, there was an attempt by the Romans to resist the Saracens. The LP was about to deal with this when it breaks off. *BMS* mentions an engagement between the Saracens and the 'emperor' Louis II who had come down from Monte Mario; Louis was defeated. It is clear from *AB* that Louis was at Rome fairly early in these events (he 'returned' there after a later defeat; though Duchesne, citing Böhmer-Mühlbacher, *Reg. imp.*, 1094, held that Louis must then still have been in France with his father Lothar); and it is unlikely that the different chroniclers were recording different engagements in the Campus Neronis; no doubt his forces were inadequate, and, as Ps.-Liutprand records, he was put to flight. *BMS* also

48. *This*[93] *blessed pontiff, after he had gloriously ruled the Roman and apostolic see 3 years, was taken from this life and went to everlasting rest. He performed one ordination in March, 8 priests, 3 deacons; for various places 23 bishops. He was buried in St Peter's.*[94]

---

states that Guy, margrave of Spoleto, came to answer the pope's appeal and with Roman help he defeated the enemy and pursued them to Civitavecchia; if this is true it may refer to some skirmishing party, and can be most economically applied to the group mentioned in *AB*: 'Another enemy force reached the church of the blessed Apostle Paul, but they were crushed by the people of the Campagna and all of them were slain...'. The chronological relationship of this with the remaining events is unclear. *CB* mentions the sacking of both basilicas, the killing there of many Saxons (*pace* Duchesne this need not refer to the earlier massacre of Saxons at Porto mentioned in LP c. 47), and of very many others; the Saracens then captured Fondi, and in September decamped to Gaeta (they will have been fearful of having their communications cut, and their fleet will have followed along the coast). John mentions the devastation of both churches and other areas, and the taking of captives, and states that Lothar sent fierce men who chased the Saracens to Gaeta (and from a later remark of his it emerges that at about this time Caesarius the son of duke Sergius was coming with ships from Naples and Amalfi, evidently expecting to take on the Saracen fleet). *AB* states that the Saracens then 'took up a position on a mountain 100 miles from the city, an extremely well-defended site' (this must be Gaeta, about 100 miles along the Via Appia). John writes that at Gaeta they set an ambush; the Franks, unaware, attacked, but their standard-bearer was killed, and the rest were slaughtered. *AB* refers to this defeat: 'Lothar's commanders mercilessly attacked them and were killed'. *CB* states that the Frankish army arrived, was defeated on 10 November, and fled; the Saracens pursued and captured all their property (c. 12 says that Berthar, the next abbot of Montecassino (from 856), fought well at this battle). *AB* says: 'Louis, Lothar's son, king of Italy, joined battle with the Saracens but was defeated and only got back to Rome with difficulty.' John then states that Caesarius prevented the pursuit of the Frankish survivors by bringing about a battle on the seashore; the Saracens tried to capture Gaeta; but with his own and Amalfitan ships Caesarius occupied and defended it. In other words, the fleet of Naples and Amalfi had been cruising near Gaeta and landed troops who arrived to stop the victors, but its leader Caesarius had too few forces to take the offensive and could merely defend Gaeta. *CB*, which not surprisingly is well informed about events in the area of Montecassino, continues that (one group of?) the Saracens burned the cella of S. Andrew; at the cella of S. Apollinaris called Albianum they could see Montecassino, but the late hour prevented their immediate arrival; the weather was calm and dry, the river very low and easily fordable. The monks expected death and prayed for the Lord's mercy; barefoot and with ash on their heads they held litanies to St Benedict. Abbot Bassacius saw a vision of his predecessor Apollinaris who told them to hold litanies and masses, and they would be safe. Rain and storms followed and the Garigliano flooded, so that next day the Saracens could not reach its banks; like barbarians they bit away their fingers and gnashed their teeth, scurrying around in fury. They burned the cellae of SS Stephen and George, and by way of Duo Leones returned to camp; some days later they hamstrung their horses and set sail. John merely states that there was a storm; the Saracens asked for a truce with Caesarius, to beach their ships and depart when the weather would allow; Sergius agreed to their taking an oath to this effect, for fear that if they were stranded they would occupy the country. Then the weather improved and they sailed away.

[93] Though only in the later recension, this passage will also have concluded the earlier recension after the end of the Saracen invasion. Ps.-Liutprand summarizes the invasion (last note), then gives the ordinations (though with 25 bishops, not 23).

[94] Sergius's tomb was in pope Paschal's chapel of SS Xystus and Fabian (100:5), perhaps even in their altar, as is stated in a note in the manuscript which preserves his 14-line

His bishopric was vacant 2 months 15 days.

---

epitaph (ed. Dümmler, *MGH Poet. Lat. aevi Kar.* 2.663; De Rossi, *Inscr. Christ.* II, 213). Sergius is there described as a lover of the people who shepherded the sheep well, the hope of the fatherland, the glory of the world, an excellent governor, eager to carry out God's commands, nurturing the chiefs of the Romans not only with spiritual words but with human necessities; he is compared with St Leo and pope Damasus for his teaching of the flock, his zeal to refresh those in need; and it is implied that he deserved his burial with the remains of his martyred predecessors Fabian and Xystus. The author of the Farnesi recension saw him differently.

105. LEO IV (847-855).

This is the longest life in the LP save that of Leo III (though it is only slightly longer than that of Hadrian I), composed by an author who liked to think that his style was brief (c. 82) and who is concerned to emphasize how 'praiseworthy' Leo was (he uses *laudabilis* seven times). The wording at the end of c. 74 and in c. 84 (so too probably c. 92, and perhaps 'current indiction' in c. 47) implies that Leo was still alive at least when some parts of the life were being composed. The source of the 'we' passage in c. 54 may have been a papal letter (cf. n. 76); but it is at least equally likely that the compiler of that part of the life was a man very high up in the papal administration who was in a position to act as, in effect, the mouthpiece of Leo IV. We are moving away from lives compiled by lowly clerks to those written from a much higher standpoint, as will be seen in the interpolations made in life 107 and in the whole draft of life 108.

Much of the life is devoted to Leo's restoration of and gifts to churches in Rome and its territory. Making good the damage done by the Saracens at St Peter's was a major task for Leo; so too, we are told, at St Paul's, but the only specific detail is that given in c. 96. The attention paid to the monastery of St Martin's by St Peter's, where Leo had been brought up, is only to be expected, though it too may have suffered from the Saracens. His activities at S. Clemente (the lower basilica) extended, though the LP does not mention it, to decorative frescoes in one of which his portrait still survives (photograph in, e.g., *NCE* 8.641). Despite the great length of this life there is one certain omission: the building of S. Maria Nova to replace S. Maria Antiqua. Leo's part in this is mentioned twice in later LP lives, 106:22, 107:37. Another omission may be the building of S. Stefano Maggiore (degli Abessini) near St Peter's, where there is an inscription of Leo IV; but see n. 6 to life 100.

But the life contains a great deal more than the restoring and enriching of churches. The see was now in the hands of an incumbent far more energetic than Gregory IV, and determined to reform the scabrous regime inherited from Sergius II and the latter's brother Benedict; Leo was able to restore papal prestige and prepare the way for the pontificates of his important successors. The disaster of 846 had shown that defence from the Saracens was crucial. The LP provides most of what is known about Leo's efforts to defend Roman territory: the restoration of the walls of Rome in 848-9 (cc. 38-40); the construction of the Leonine City from 848 to 852 (cc. 68-74) which would both protect St Peter's and provide a stronghold for the pope; Leo's organizing of the fleets of Naples, Amalfi and Gaeta, and defeat of the Saracens off Ostia in 849 (cc. 47-54); the settlement of Corsicans as a garrison at Porto (cc. 77-81); and the rebuilding of Centumcellae at Leopolis (cc. 99-105). Leo's concern for reform is most in evidence at the council held at St Peter's on 8 December 853 (cc. 90-92), at which the canons of the council of 826 were renewed and reinforced, and at which Anastasius (see below) was deposed.

We are fortunate that our knowledge of Leo's activities can be supplemented from the 45 letters extracted from his register and preserved in a codex in the British Library. Regrettably some of the letters are mere fragments, sometimes with no known context, and the texts are all given without their dates. They can be only a fraction of Leo's total output, but no very consistent principle of selection is apparent, and we may assume that, with documents known from elsewhere, they provide a typical glimpse into Leo's activities and attitudes.

From this material Leo emerges as one who cared for reform and the restoration of church discipline, and was much involved in the tricky relations between his own state and the Carolingian empire, and between his church and the powerful prelates of that empire.

The LP is surprisingly reticent about Leo's relations with the Frankish emperors Lothar and, increasingly after 850, Louis II. Imperial involvement with Rome is presented as peripheral. We are told that (c. 69) Leo planned to construct the Leonine City in consultation with Lothar, who with his brothers sent much silver for it; that (c. 33) Leo's picture in the shrine of St Peter was accompanied by that of his spiritual son Lothar, that (c. 80) Lothar and Louis were somehow involved in the charter that allowed the Corsicans to settle at Porto, and that (c. 90) the council of 853 was held on the advice of the two emperors. In Leo's last months of life, one papal official, Daniel, accused another, Gratian, of pro-Greek sympathies: this caused Louis to arrive unexpectedly in Rome. Leo greeted him and 'appeased' him. Evidently Leo assumed Louis would think there was no smoke without fire - and Louis would almost certainly have been right. A trial was held, apparently with Leo and Louis as co-judges; Gratian was acquitted, and Louis left Rome just before Leo's death (cc. 110-113). As for Leo's ordination, carried out without waiting for imperial consent as required by the *Constitutio* of 824, the LP (c. 8) assures us that the threat of the Saracens (whose fleet had just sunk) was the excuse, and that no disloyalty to Lothar was meant. But with an eye to what would happen on his own death, Leo wrote at some point in the last four years of his life to both emperors

(J2652, *MGH Ep* 5.604) acknowledging the terms of the *Constitutio*. Late in 853 Leo wrote (J2643, *Ep* 5.601) to Lothar that the imperial *capitula* and the precepts both of Lothar and of previous popes were to be maintained uninfringed. Anyone who told Lothar otherwise was a liar; he added that the wicked claim and unjust activity of one Christopher was well vouched for: so many knew of it that it would be almost impossible to collect all their names. We do not know who this Christopher was, but it looks as if he may have been saying too much, like, perhaps, Daniel. Other men were involved at various points in incidents which for lack of detailed evidence cannot be fully interpreted. Thus, before 850 (J2602, *Ep* 5.607-8) Leo twice asked Louis not to send Peter and Hadrian to him; if he did send them, they would be in danger of their lives. Early in 852 Leo sent his legate Ragibert to Lothar, but Ragibert was killed on his journey in a plot which Leo, writing to Lothar (J2611, *Ep* 5.596), blamed on George, Hadrian and Peter. He added that previous popes, like emperors and kings, had been able to send envoys even to barbarians without such a deed being perpetrated. George, Peter and Hadrian were condemned by Leo for the murder in accordance with Roman law and in the presence of Lothar's envoys (those established by the *Consitutio* of 824). But Lothar ordered Leo to have them retried. Late in 853 Leo wrote to Lothar (J2638, *Ep* 5.600,608) urging him to punish those who attacked the teaching of ancient laws; those three criminals had been properly convicted; the only reason why the death sentence they merited had not been implemented was that this was not allowed at Eastertide, and Roman law should remain in force as it had always done. Presumably the executions were carried out after Whitsun. In a letter of about 853, whose precise context and reference is obscure, Leo wrote (J2646, *Ep* 5.607) to Louis apologizing if any of his actions had been incompetent or if he had not acted with justice for his subjects, and expressing willingness to emend everything by Louis's judgement and that of Louis's envoys. Leo asked him to send envoys to inquire into the matter (whatever it was), just as if Louis were present in person, so that whether the matters were small or great they would leave nothing uninvestigated. Leo could be stern against his enemies; but equally he was concerned for the plight of those whom the emperors imprisoned. About 852 (J2622, *Ep* 5.586) Leo explained to Lothar that popes had always interceded for men who had committed any fault against their princes, and that princes, obeying the Roman see, had restored them to honour and favour; so he too was begging God and human powers on behalf of those who had fallen and were in chains. The context is unknown, but the men sound like political prisoners whom Leo regarded as his own supporters. After all, as he wrote once to Louis (J2630, *Ep* 5.589), the purpose of his own acceptance of the pinnacle of the pontificate was so that he could recall the discordant to concord and emend evil.

For all their obscurity, these incidents are highly suggestive of the tensions that existed, and go a long way to explain why Louis would be so keen to have his own man, Anastasius, on the papal throne. Leo was walking a tightrope. How could he and his state remain loyal to the Franks without being fully integrated into the western empire? In the last resort, Rome depended on the Franks for defence, as Leo well knew. Constantinople could not be depended on for protection against the Saracens in Italy: late in 853 (J2642, *Ep* 5.601) Leo exhorted the army of Franks to fight manfully against the enemies of the faith; he reminded them of the valour and victories of their parents, and held out the promise of heaven to those who died in this war.

The most surprising omission in the life is that of Leo's reception of Louis II at Rome in 850 and anointing of him as emperor (cf. n. 120). It was probably while Louis was in Rome on this occasion that a council was held in his presence at St Peter's to deal with a quarrel between Peter bishop of Arezzo and Cantius bishop of Siena about churches in the county of Siena. After twelve days had been allowed for the production of documents, the decision went in Cantius's favour. But Leo might have preferred to deal with such a matter without Louis. He tried both to be scrupulously correct yet also not to fail in asserting papal authority within the empire. In 853 (J2626, *Ep* 5.588) Leo sent to both emperors the customary branches of victory, as a distinction and honour at Easter. When he wanted Roliand, bishop of Arles, to visit Rome, he asked Lothar to allow it (J2621, *Ep* 5.585). When he granted the pallium to Alteus bishop of Autun, he carefully apologized to Lothar (J2603, *Ep* 5.604) for what seemed uncanonical. In 851 (J2613, *Ep* 5.597) Leo asked the permission of both emperors to consecrate a deacon Colonus as bishop of Rieti, offering to make him bishop of Ascoli instead if they would prefer it. Leo received the reply he wanted, and Colonus was made bishop of Rieti (J2615, *Ep* 5.598). The sovereigns, though, must accept papal judgments. To Charles the Bald Leo wrote in 852 or 853 (J2625, *Ep* 5.606): 'If perhaps, though we cannot believe it, you regard us as useless, the church over which we preside is not useless but is rightly called by all the head and origin of all.' Such deference was typical. Yet Leo's only other surviving letter to Charles, in 853 (J2641, *Ep* 5.601), sharply reminded him that it was uncanonical for a layman to depose priests from the churches for which they had been ordained or into which they had been inducted. It was a difficult balancing-act.

It is at least partly in the context of relations with the empire that we must see Leo's concern to curb those he regarded as turbulent priests. His greatest problem was to be Anastasius, cardinal priest of S. Marcello in Rome itself, who first appears in c. 92 of this life and will recur in lives 106 and 108. But there were others whom Leo had to deal with, most notably John of Ravenna and Hincmar of Rheims. Though not mentioned in this life, they would create problems for Leo's successors, especially Nicholas (life 107). They are worthy of consideration here, partly to explain the background to Nicholas's actions, partly to illustrate Leo's authoritarian approach.

In 853 (J2628, *Ep* 5.588) Leo reprimanded John, archbishop of Ravenna (850-861), that he had done what no priest should do, and also transgressed his oath to the pope, by illegally seizing the properties and fields of Romans. Leo menacingly stated that he would never allow Romans and subjects to be injured by him, and if he continued to misbehave, Leo would personally avenge them and would furiously, boldly and cruelly seize all John's property; and by apostolic authority he abrogated a promise which one Hilarius had been forced to make to John. On John see further 107:21-35.

In 847 Leo granted Hincmar, successor to Ebbo (see p. 72) in the see of Rheims (845-882), the use of the pallium on certain days, then, early in 851 (J2607-8, *Ep* 5.590-1) Leo acceded to a request from Lothar and increased the number of occasions on which Hincmar might wear it, stressing to Hincmar what a unique privilege this was; but he absolutely refused Lothar's request to give him a papal vicariate to give canonical judgment over other archbishops, bishops and abbots in that region, on the grounds that Lothar had already secured from Sergius this position for Drogo of Metz throughout France, Gaul and Germany. But Hincmar acted in matters which went beyond the powers Leo had given him. Later in 851 (J2614, *Ep* 5.598-9) Leo reproached him for excommunicating Falcaric, an (imperial) vassal. He came with letters from Lothar and his brother Louis, claiming that he had been wrongfully excommunicated for putting his concubine in a convent and marrying a wife. Leo wrote that he grieved at Falcaric's anxiety and lamented his excommunication; he threatened Hincmar with the consequences if he did not receive him back into the church.

Perhaps in 852 (J2618-19, *Ep* 5.604-5) Leo stated his objections against Hincmar to all the bishops of Gaul: he had dissolved the vow of a Benedictine monk, had in the lifetime of archbishop Ebbo usurped the bishopric of Rheims, and had now in his pride hurled an anathema against an emperor (Lothar) who had been hallowed by pope Paschal along with his brother king Charles and his wife and sons. Leo wrote to Lothar about this, stating that he was forbidding Hincmar ever imposing an anathema on him or causing him any other injury.

Leo's greatest opportunity to call Hincmar to heel came when Hincmar held a council at Soissons (23 April 853) to annul the ordinations carried out by his predecessor Ebbo after the latter had been deposed. Hearing of this, Leo wrote to Hincmar that he could not yet ratify the council since he had not received its acts, his own legates had not been present at it, no report on it had been received from the emperor, and those whose orders had been annulled were appealing to Rome. Soon after, it seems, Leo followed this up with what amounted to a refusal to recognize the synod. He sent Hincmar an order (J2632, *Ep* 5.589-90), that those who had then been deposed without a fair hearing and were now appealing should have their cases dealt with at a new council, and if, as he said he hoped would not happen, they refused to obey his judgment, no one was to prevent them coming to the apostolic see; he was sending Peter bishop of Spoleto to reconvene the council in his own place; and he ordered that Hincmar should either come to Rome with those bishops who wanted to be heard by the Roman see, or should send his legate. Hincmar later denied receiving this letter. The affair of Ebbo's ordinations would rumble on (p. 165); and Hincmar would cause pope Nicholas some anxiety (107:58).

The chequered career of Anastasius, successively cardinal priest, antipope, papal secretary, and librarian of the holy see, first comes to our attention in c. 92 of this life. Of other sources for his career, *AB* 868 Nelson 145-150 is particularly valuable. He was ordained priest by Leo in 847 for St Marcellus's *titulus*, but in 848 for reasons which remain obscure he left Rome without Leo's permission and stayed outside Roman territory, mainly in the province of Aquileia. Twice Leo proposed holding a council and sent envoys and letters to Anastasius requiring his attendance. Anastasius did not appear, and after he had been absent for two years, Leo took sterner measures: at a council held in Rome on 16 December 850, attended by the archbishops of Ravenna and Milan and 75 bishops, he excommunicated him pending his return. Anastasius stayed away. When he had been absent five years, Leo resolved to journey to Ravenna, and left strict instructions (n. 159) that the business of church and state at Rome should continue as normal. At Ravenna Leo met Louis. At S. Vitale on 29 May 853, he anathematized Anastasius. Returning to Rome, he had a copy of the two sentences against Anastasius (850 and 853) fixed on the door of St Peter's; and on 19 June he held a council of 65 bishops at St Peter's at which the anathema against Anastasius was confirmed. And the anathema was extended to 'all those who wanted to offer him any assistance or comfort in - God forbid - his election to the honour of the pontificate': which at last hints at what Leo's objection to Anastasius was. Leo wrote to all the hierarchy, clerics and laity, to inform them that Anastasius, already excommunicated once (in 850) had now been excommunicated at Ravenna on 29 May and Rome on 19 June. Meanwhile Anastasius moved to Chiusi; the pope had him summoned by three bishops (c. 92), who met him without difficulty and delivered the papal letter they were carrying, inviting him to present himself at Rome on 15 November. He did not comply. At Leo's urging, Louis kept promising to make him appear; but Louis tricked Leo: he claimed he could not find Anastasius and right down to Leo's death he never produced him. In view of Louis's efforts to have Anastasius made pope in 855, there can be little doubt that Anastasius was already leader of an imperial party in Rome, and that Leo's objections to him throughout had been based on Leo's desire to oppose any increase in imperial influence, particularly in papal elections; but even Louis could not protect him from excommunication by Leo. The council scheduled for 15 November was delayed slightly and the 67 bishops met on 8 December 853. They confirmed and added to the 38 canons of Eugene II's council of 826, and then yet again dealt with Anastasius's case. Apart from the LP's account of this council (cc. 90-92), we have the council acts, the text of the summons sent by the three bishops, the pope's speech, and the sentence. Anastasius had now a third and fourth time been summoned by letters from the pope, but as he had not come to two councils of bishops the decree was that he be totally removed from the sacerdotal ministry and never find his place restored. Even the emperor Lothar subscribed to this council. Afterwards Leo wrote to Lothar (J2644, *Ep* 5.602) that the council had been planned for other purposes, but that it was the council itself which had insisted on dealing with Anastasius's abandonment of his church. A copy of the decision, like those of the two earlier councils, was fixed to the door of St Peter's; the three copies were later attached by Hadrian II to a new sentence incurred by Anastasius, and all the material was then inserted by Hincmar into *AB* 868. The story of Anastasius continues with his bid for the papacy in 855; see life 106.

On relations between Leo and Constantinople the LP has nothing, which is the more unfortunate because strains with that patriarchate were being renewed which would cause many problems under Nicholas and Hadrian II. The patriarch Ignatius (whose motives for all this are unknown; cf. Nicetas, *Vita Ignatii*, *PG* 105.511-2) summoned a council and without consulting Rome deposed the bishop of Syracuse, Gregory Asbestas, and some other bishops, Eulampius and Peter. Gregory had fled to Constantinople from the Saracen invasions in 843. To Leo Ignatius's act was aggression, as he saw Sicily as in his own province. When Ignatius wrote to Leo asking for the deprivation to be confirmed, Leo in 853 (J2629, *Ep* 5.589) protested that Ignatius's action was unprecedented (his predecessors had always brought such matters speedily to Rome), and refused to give the confirmation requested since the action had been performed without his legates being present and without his own permission. Ignatius tried offering Leo a pallium; whatever his motive, Leo regarded it as dangerous, as it was a papal prerogative to bestow the pallium throughout Europe (a term including Constantinople!), and sent it back, begging Ignatius not to take this badly (J2647, *Ep* 5.607). This was followed up by another letter from Leo in which Ignatius was ordered to send an envoy to explain the grounds for anathematizing the three bishops (J2654, Mansi 16.427). Ignatius, it seems, ignored this and again asked for confirmation of his decision. Leo refused, and summoned both sides to Rome (J2661, Mansi 15.228, 229). But within months Leo was dead; the next pope would receive an envoy on the matter (106:33).

The life emphasizes (cc. 18, 26) Leo's preaching (an activity in which St Peter was significantly depicted as engaging, c. 55). For us the contents of this can be recovered only from those of Leo's letters that show his concern for moral reform. Thus in 849 he replied to the bishops of Brittany (J2599 *Ep* 5.593) who had enquired about a number of matters. Those guilty of simony could not help themselves by any penance; but bishops accused of this or any other crime had to be judged canonically by a tribunal of 12 bishops or for facts sworn to by 72 witnesses, and had the right of appeal to Rome. The organization of parishes and their clergy is to be subject to a bishop. The casting of lots is no better than witchcraft. Marriages are indissoluble unless they were not freely entered into or, with the consent of both parties, for one to be free for God, though neither may remarry. Church goods may not be alienated to the laity: those who do this gain from it, but the recipients incur a fault. A cleric may not have more than one titular church, though he may have others in commendation. Tithes are due to churches where baptisms are carried out. No meat may be eaten on Wednesays or Fridays and preferably not on Saturdays. Judgments may only be made from the correct canonical sources, councils and the papal decretals (cf. 107 n. 87). Simony was an ongoing problem. Also in 849 (J2600, *Ep* 5.597-8), when consulted by Nominoë duke of Brittany on what was to be done with simoniacs, Leo replied by sending a copy of the relevant canons and exhorting Nominoë not to continue defending Gislard, the intruder into the church of Nantes; Leo still regarded Actard as bishop.

In 853 Leo wrote (J2640, *Ep* 5.600) to Galerius bishop of Tripolis, urging on him the need to uphold the traditional penitential discipline. Leo had heard that in Galerius's territories Christians were avoiding it, with the claim that it unreasonably meant giving up sex within marriage. Leo stated that they were wrong: every Christian was bound to undertake penance for everything illicit. Lawful marriages were not dissolved by it, and Galerius must preach this.

For further enlightenment on the breadth of papal concerns it is worth considering Leo's involvement with Sardinia (for pope Nicholas's concerns there see 107:56). Early in 851 Leo wrote two letters to the Judge of the island. In the first (J2611, *Ep* 5.596) he asked him to send Sardinians, boys, adults and young men under arms, who could fulfil his daily orders. He also asked that if any of the sea-wool called *pinninum* was discovered anywhere he should purchase it, however high the price, and send it to Leo, since it was essential for the vestments that Leo and his chief men wore on solemn festivals. The Judge had sent Leo envoys to inquire about the position of clergy whose promotion had been irregular; Leo replied that they could perform their functions, citing pope Anastasius (II): 'Evil men, by ministering good things, harm not others but only themselves.' In his second letter to the Judge (J2612, *Ep* 596-7), Leo replied to his uncertainty about what to do with criminals who took refuge in a church: Leo replied that the christian emperors had considered the question carefully, and had been accustomed to pardon them, except in a few cases where the crime had been against religion. So the Judge should obey the pope in this, and should grant those who fled to a church their lives and the integrity of their limbs; after all, if they had managed to take refuge with men they would have surely been safe, so their love of God should save them. If the Judge followed this policy God would forgive him his own sins. About two years later the Judge wrote to Leo with some request which Leo regarded as uncanonical; Leo therefore replied, refusing to do what was asked (J2648, *Ep* 5.609). Life in Sardinia, and Leo's concerns, are also illustrated by two letters to John bishop of Cagliari. In one (J2649, *Ep* 5.602-3) he ordered him to destroy the altar in a church of St Michael on the Lustrensis estate, since the church had been consecrated by a heretical archbishop Arsenius, and to build and consecrate a new one. John wrote to Leo to ask why it was that the popes insisted on churchmen being judged apart from laymen, though this did not seem to tally with St Paul's views; Leo replied (J2650, *Ep* 5.611-12) that church rules were to be changed according to the changing of the times.

For Leo's interests we may note, finally, his concern about church music, appropriate enough for one who had been brought up in St Martin's monastery which provided choral services for St Peter's. To abbot Honoratus Leo wrote (J2651, *Ep* 5.603) expressing his regrets that Honoratus hated Gregory's tradition and chose to dissent from everyone else who used Latin to praise God. He explained how Gregory's labour and skill had produced the music to be sung everywhere, so that it would bring even the ignorant and hard-minded to the churches. Honoratus was to use Gregorian chant or be excommunicated. The LP (c. 26), reflecting Leo's interest in liturgy, credits him with instituting the Octave of the Assumption.

CHRONOLOGY AND SUMMARY

Duchesne II p. V commented on the chronological order of the material in this life (but note that the end of c. 84 seems to be filling in material omitted from the beginning of the pontificate).

Geertman 1975:81, however, believes that the register-material, while chronological, is not annalistic: the data were entered at brief intervals, before they were arranged in registers under each indiction-year. This life thus gives a better picture than any other of the day to day records of the *vestiarium*, but the material does not lend itself to being grouped in annual sections. The repetition almost annually of gifts to SS IV Coronati, where Leo had been priest, may, Geertman concedes, give some clue to the year divisions. The references to that church in cc. 41-42 and 44 are both 'enclosed' by material belonging to 848/9; and this is enough to show that, contrary to the practice in earlier lives, a church can now appear twice in the same indiction-year. In fact SS IV Coronati is mentioned 12 times in this life, and Leo's pontificate lasted only 9 indiction-years. Yet there may have been some chronological grouping in the material: the compiler may have used a system of regnal years alongside the indictions. At cc. 18 and 70 he certainly reckons in the former; elsewhere he uses the latter. The solution may be that each indiction year (September to August) was divided in the registers approximately into two halves at the anniversary of Leo's ordination in April; Leo's pontificate would occupy 17 half-years. The remaining problem is that St Peter's is mentioned at least 27 times, and there is no way this can be accommodated to any scheme.

In the following summary of the life, dates stated in the text are given, those known from elsewhere are in brackets; the whole is then divided into half-years on the principle that SS IV Coronati should not be mentioned twice in the same period. The result should give an approximately accurate chronology.

1-4: character, education, career. 5-6: election. 7: fate of the Saracens

(c. Feb./Mar. 847?). 8: ordination (10 April 847).
9: St Peter's. 10: IV Coronati (possibly before Leo's ordination).
[indiction X summer, 847:]
11: S. Maria in vico Sardorum; patriarchate. 12: decree on liturgy at St
Paul's (30 June 847?); earthquake dated 846/7 (July/August 847?);
decree excluding the laity from the *presbyterium*. 13: St Peter's; 14: IV
Coronati; St Peter's. 15: St Andrew's; St Anastasius's; St Praxedes's.
16-17: palace; gold cross. 18: character. 18-19: story of the serpent
(dated 15 August 847). 20: fire in the vicus Saxonum.
[indiction XI winter, 847-848:]
21: St Peter's; St Martin's. 22: IV Coronati;
[indiction XI summer, 848:]
St Peter's. 23: Soracte; St Peter's. 24: St Peter's. 25: monasterium
Corsarum. 26: preaching and actions; institutes Octave of Assumption
(22 August 848?). 27: St Mary's at S. Lorenzo; St Stephen's; St Leo's
oratory. 28: monasterium Corsarum; processional cross. 29: Porto; Silva
Candida. 30: SS Stephen & Cassian; 31: St Leo's shrine at St Peter's.
32-34: St Peter's shrine (33 has Lothar as emperor, evidently without
Louis, so before Easter 850). 35: St Peter's; St Leo's oratory; St
Caesarius's; St Agatha's.
[indiction XII winter, 848-849:]
36: oratories at St Peter's. 37: oratories at St Peter's; Frascati; St
Peter's. 38-40: restoration of walls of Rome dated 848/9. 41-42: IV
Coronati. 43: St Stephen's;
[indiction XII summer, 849:]
St Peter's. 44-5: IV Coronati. 46: Subiaco; St Peter's. 47-54: Saracen
attack dated 848/9.
[indiction XIII winter, 849-850:]
55: St Peter's etc. 56: St Mary's at S. Lorenzo; IV Coronati; St
Stephen's;
[indiction XIII summmer, 850:]
St Peter's. 57: St Laurence's; IV Coronati. 58: his own house made into
monastery of SS Symmetrius & Caesarius. 59: St Mary's at S. Lorenzo;
St Laurence's. 60: S Maria in Trastevere;
[indiction XIV winter, 850-851:]
St Peter's; Frascati. 61: St Peter's. 62: St Silvester's oratory at Lateran
palace; Jerusalem church; St Mary's in Aquiro; Frascati; Moreno;
Maruli. 63: St Mary's at S. Lorenzo; Silva Candida.
[indiction XIV summer, 851:]
64: St Peter's; Sessorian. 65: Subiaco; Fondi; Terracina;
[indiction XV winter, 851-852:]
St Peter's. 66: Silva Candida; St Clement's;

[indiction XV summer, 852:]
St Peter's; Terracina. 67 Porto; St Peter's. 68-74: Leonine city (70: years 2-6; 74: dedicated 27 June 852, which may govern the position of the whole account). 75: Blera; IV Coronati; St Mary's at S Lorenzo. 76: St Clement's; Porto; Anagni. 77-81: defence of Porto with exiled Corsicans. 82: Amélia and Orte.

[indiction I winter, 852-853:]
83: IV Coronati; St Mary's in vico Sardorum.

[indiction I summer, 853:]
84-85: St Peter's (but see above on date of c. 84). 85: St Mary's at S. Lorenzo. 86: St Mary's in vico Sardorum; St Martin's at St Peter's; IV Coronati; St Petronilla's; St Mary's in schola Saxonum.

[indiction II winter, 853-854:]
87-89: St Peter's. 89 St Andrew's; IV Coronati. 90-92: Council (on 8 December 853). 93: St Peter's etc. 94 St Peter's; Frascati.

[indiction II summer, 854:]
95: St Peter's. 96: St Paul's; St Peter's. 97: Balnearola; St Laurence's; St Clement's. 98: Aurelia; SS Silvester & Martin. 99-105: (99 is 40 years after 813, cf. n. 145) Leopolis dedicated 15 August 854; gifts. 105-107: St Peter's. 108: St Martin's (may be connected with a bull of 10 August 854); IV Coronati;

[indiction III winter: 854-855:]
St Peter's. 109: Leopolis; St Mary's vico Sardorum;

[indiction III summer, 855:]
St Peter's. 110-112: receives Louis and holds court with him. 113: soon after Louis's departure Leo dies on 17 July (855).

105. **1.** LEO [IV; 10 April 847 - 17 July 855],[1] of Roman origin, son of Raduald,[2] held the see 8 years 3 months 6 days. This man, so catholic and apostolic, had much patience and much humility; bountiful, dutiful, innocent and kind, a lover of justice and a most ardent governor of the people, he was also an untiring searcher of the Scriptures and was ever intent on watching and prayer; in his sacred breast there dwelt what we read of in the holy gospel, the cunning of a serpent and the innocence of a dove.[3] Filled with the beauty of all holiness, he was a lover of religious men and of those who serve God assiduously in all things; he was a mentor of the poor, a despiser of himself.

2. First of all for the study of letters he was freely given over by his parents to Christ's confessor St Martin's monastery,[4] located outside this city of Rome's walls close to St Peter the apostle's church, until he fully learnt the sacred letters. And there he not merely learnt letters but kept avidly at the study of holy behaviour, not as the boy he then was but like a perfect monk. At the example of his godly behaviour others who lived under the same monastic usage served the Lord almighty more devoutly, and he was with them as one of them. **3.** And since 'a city set on a hill cannot be hid',[5] so too this holy man's reputation could not long stay secret. His fame and the esteem of his holiness were broadcast hither and thither clearer than light, and on the report of many of the faithful were then speedily relayed to the ears of Gregory [IV], the former pontiff, blessed father and pope. When the mastery of such great chastity and worthy behaviour was told him, he straightaway bade

---

[1] The date of death is from c. 113; *AB* 855 Nelson 80 merely states that in August (*sic*) Leo died and Benedict succeeded; neither *AF* nor *AX* mention Leo's accession. For the tenure, MS Paris 5140 agrees with the LP; the Montecassino MS adds an extra day; evidently the ordination was 10 April 847 (Easter Sunday); the preceding vacancy of 2½ months tallies with Sergius's death, 27 January. Older writers had Leo ordained the day Sergius died, or the next day, but this does not fit these data. Leo's election may have followed Sergius's death immediately (c. 6, but see n. 6). Cf. 104 n. 1.

[2] The name suggests a family of Lombard origin.

[3] Matthew 10.16 where the Vulgate has *prudentes* (wise) not *astuti* (cunning); the word may be a reminiscence of its use at 2 Cor. 11.3 (the serpent that seduced Eve).

[4] See 98 n. 138; Ferrari, 235 n. 12, speculates that Leo entered a kind of choir school, possibly under the direction of the monks of St Martin's. John, who was sent to England c. 680, was both abbot of St Martin's and archcantor of St Peter's (on John's activities cf. Andrieu, *Ordines Romani*, 2.xxvii). Certainly this and the other monasteries provided the choirs for St Peter's. The later notion that Leo IV was brought up as a Benedictine is mistaken; no Roman monastery can be truly called Benedictine at this date. The monastery later received Leo's benefactions (cc. 21, 93), was rebuilt by him (c. 108), and granted a charter confirming its properties (n. 156).

[5] Matthew 5.14.

him come forth from the monastery where he was piously living and brought him to the bosom of holy mother church; so that he might ever remain in his household service, he ordered him to be in the Lateran patriarchate; and for the fame of his praiseworthy life he also made him a subdeacon. But though he changed his place and order, yet he even more than before constrained his life and character according to a rule, and improved them by good works, in the service of our supreme Creator. **4.** On the death of Gregory, pope of this holy see, Sergius the archpriest of the holy Roman church was then made prelate; this holy pope made him of whom we have recounted some information above, Leo that is to say, a priest, and bestowed on him the *titulus* of the SS Quattuor Coronati. And while he was there, being effective in good character and ministering what they needed to the poor, and reviving pilgrims, the needy and the deprived, not only by word but also by bodily sustenance, the then prelate Sergius, bishop of the Roman see, was taken from this present life.

In his time the churches of the blessed princes Peter and Paul were thoroughly plundered by the Saracens. **5.** At this distress and wretchedness all the vigour of the Romans melted away and was broken. When this happened, because of the two occurrences and perils, that is, the pontiff's sudden death and the plundering that had taken place in the holy churches and the territories of all the Romans, the whole gathering of the Romans said that there was no way for them to escape the danger of death. With equal devotion and common consultation all the Roman dignitaries thought about who would be the next pontiff, who there might be that could rule and govern so holy and inviolable a place in the fear of almighty God; suddenly the fame of the blessed prelate and also his value was manifested to all, broadcast through the whole city. **6.** The late-departed pontiff had not yet been taken to his proper burial, and lo! everyone from last to first with one voice and one heart, demanded[6] the venerable priest Leo as their pontiff to be, and with many protestations and much clamour they said they would have none other over them as prelate but him whom we have frequently mentioned. We believe it was nothing other than God's love and the clemency of God's power that inflamed and united all their hearts unhesitatingly to demand him. Then they all made their way with

---

[6] On Leo's election *AB* has no more than is quoted in n. 8. The LP implies that Leo was elected the very day of Sergius's death; but perhaps the compiler protests too much: the election may not have been so unanimous. Some gap between election and ordination is implied by the placing of c. 7. Leo's ordination was carried out without Lothar's approval (c. 8, cf. *AB*); why then any delay? Admittedly, if the excuse about the Saracen peril (c. 8) was genuine, Rome may have become tired of waiting.

the joy and gladness of great eagerness to the church of the SS Quattuor Coronati where, as is recorded above, he was living. They took him from there by force and against his will, and with hymns and distinguished acclamations of praise conducted him to the Lateran patriarchate; and in keeping with ancient custom they all kissed his feet. No man can tell in brief how great was the concord and unanimity at his pontifical election.

7. It is not unfitting or blameworthy if as a fearful warning and a record for time to come we note in this present account what at the time of his election[7] God's power, through the support of the apostles and through his own prayers of intercession, did to those Saracens who committed such a wicked crime.[8] For when after perpetrating their wicked and devastating crime they all wanted to return to the African region whence they had come, as we know from a sure report, God allowed them to be overwhelmed in the empty vastness of the sea by the force of winds and storms; and lo! the prayer of the apostles was worthy to achieve anew that ancient miracle over the Egyptians.[9]

8. The Romans too, as we have said, rejoiced in the new pontiff's election, but began to be dismayed again in no small way, in that

---

[7] This may mean 'while he was pope-elect', not at the time of his actual election.

[8] The placing of the incident at this point suggests it is to be dated in February or March 847; *AB* 847 Nelson 64-5 also puts it after Leo's election, but does not mention the ordination: 'The Saracens, their ships loaded down with the vast quantity of treasures they had taken from St-Peter's basilica, were on their way home, when during the sea-voyage they blasphemed with their foul mouths against God and our Lord Jesus Christ and his apostles. Suddenly there arose a terrible storm from which they could not escape, their ships were dashed against each other, and all were lost. The sea tossed up some of the corpses of the drowned Saracens on the shore, still clutching treasures to their breasts. When these treasures were found, they were taken back to the tomb (*memoria*) of the Blessed Apostle Peter.' John, *Gesta epp. Neap.* 60-61 (cf. 104 n. 92) has: 'They set off but while they were furrowing the empty vastness the Lord raised up the south wind which scattered and overwhelmed them, and very few of them returned to their homes'. Cf. the legend in the *Chronica S. Benedicti Casinensis* 6 (cf. same note; *MGH SSrL* 472.37-473.6): 'They set sail. When they were now so close to their province that they could even see the mountains near at hand they came out with a sailor's cheer as is their wont. Then a boat appeared among them with two men on board, one of whom looked like a cleric, the other was dressed as a monk. These said to them: 'Where have you come from and where are you going to?' They replied: 'We come back from Peter in Rome, where we have laid waste his entire shrine (*oratorium*) and despoiled the people and the region. We have defeated the Franks and burnt down Benedict's cells. But tell us who you are.' They told them: 'You will soon see who we are'. Straightway there was a strong tempest and a mighty storm, so all the ships were smashed and all the enemy perished. Not one of them remained to tell the tale to others. And so afterwards the venerable pope Leo surrounded the shrine of St Peter with firm and lofty walls to stop any occurrence like this ever happening at Rome again.' This story seems to put the disaster off the African coast; *AB* perhaps implies that it was off Italy or Sicily.

[9] i.e. the Exodus and the drowning of Pharaoh's host in the Red Sea.

without the emperor's warrant[10] they dared not consecrate the pontiff to be; they feared particularly that the city of Rome was again in danger, just as it had been laid under siege by another enemy previously.[11] Frightened by this fear and future risk, they hallowed him as prelate without the prince's permission, while keeping their loyalty and honour to him, after God, through and in all things.

9. Now as no human assessor is capable of calculating, and no human tongue is able to report, how great this blessed pontiff's goodness and piety was, let us return to what he presented, relying on the love of the saints, to churches, and tell it from the very start of his pontificate.

This noteworthy and distinguished bishop, boiling with love from on high, presented to St Peter the apostle's basilica 1 fine silver crown weighing 24 lb; 2 chased bowls weighing 2 lb; 7 veils, 2 of them of interwoven gold, 2 of cross-adorned silk and 3 of spanish.[12] There he presented for the brightness and glory of that venerable basilica 1 alexandrian curtain of wondrous beauty representing peacocks carrying men on top, and another representation of eagles and wheels and birds with trees.

10. In the basilica of the SS Quattuor Coronati, in which he had skilfully performed his sacerdotal office, this outstanding and wise pope presented 3 fine silver canisters, weighing .. lb, fine silver handbasin 1 pair, weighing .. lb; an incense-boat with 1 censer, weighing .. lb; 12 gold-interwoven veils which to its splendour hang in the church's arches; and 34 white silk veils. In the same basilica for the brightness of the holy altar[13] he provided an all-silk cloth with a gold-studded fringe and another white cloth with roses, with 7 wheels and in the middle a gold-studded panel with the effigy of a man wearing 5 jewels,

---

[10] Required by the *Constitutio* of 824, on which see the introduction to life 101. Eugene's oath then and Leo's now are mentioned in the *Privilegium Ottonis* of 962 (Sickel 1883:181, cf. 158 f): '... according to the contents of the pact, constitution and signed promise of the pontiff Eugene and his successors, i.e. that all the clergy and nobility of the whole Roman people, on account of various needs and to repress the unreasonable asperities of the pontiffs towards the people subject to them, must bind themselves by oath as far as the understanding of each of them extends that the election of pontiffs must in future take place canonically and justly; and that no one will consent to him who is elected to this holy and apostolic rule being consecrated pontiff until in the presence of our envoys or of our son or the whole commonalty he make a promise for the satisfaction of all and the future safety, such as our lord and venerable spiritual father Leo is known freely to have done.'

[11] Given that the Saracen fleet had just sunk, this excuse seems disingenuous, but there may have been other bands of Saracens on the loose. No further attack is reported until 848-9 (cc. 48-54).

[12] See 103:11 and the glossary.

[13] The preceding items were evidently for the body of the church.

prases, on his head; and a white gold-studded cloth with 6 wheels. In the same basilica for the holy altar's honour and glory he provided 4 veils[14] with gold-studded crosses and chevrons; 17 silk veils with wheels, 4 of them with gold-studded chevrons, and with 33 jewels and golden pommels; 1 needlework veil with the effigy of a man sitting on a peacock; 3 veils representing God's holy mother; 14 other gold-interwoven veils; and 2 other purple veils.

11. In God's holy mother's basilica in what is called the Vicus Sardorum,[15] this notable and blessed pope presented a gold-interwoven cloth representing God's holy mother in gold-studding, with the prophets.

This God-beloved and wise pope constructed *sedilia* of marble at the entrance to the patriarchate, which none of the pontiffs had thought to accomplish. As for the veranda[16] which pope Leo III of blessed memory had constructed, its beams were broken from its great age and it was seen to be overwhelmed in ruins, so he newly restored it more beautifully with an improved appearance.

12. In St Paul the apostle's basilica this noteworthy and godly bishop, relying on love from on high, laid down that vespers[17] were to be publicly chanted by all the clergy and the *schola* on his feastday.

In this blessed prelate's time an earthquake occurred in Rome in the 10th indiction [846-847], so that everyone saw all the elements shaken.

The same skilful pontiff, following ancient custom, decreed and laid down with canonical authority that while the holy ceremonies of mass were being celebrated none of the laity should presume to stand, sit or enter in the *presbyterium*, but only the holy people[18] who are established for ministering in the holy office.

13. After the slaughter and plunder which the savage race of the

---

[14] i.e. one for each side of the altar (*tetravela*); textiles in this life are frequently in groups of four, four times for this church (here, c. 22, and c. 42 twice), and for many other churches (e.g. five times in c. 62 alone).

[15] This Vicus Sardorum was 30 miles from Rome (see c. 86), but it is not known where; it is not the Vicus Sardorum within Rome where there was the monastery *de Sardas*, whose oratory was dedicated to St Vitus (98:78).

[16] Cf. 98:92.

[17] The monks of the two monasteries attached to St Paul's (St Caesarius's and St Stephen's) will have chanted their own daily vespers, quite probably in the basilica. Leo IV now instituted a stational vespers such as was celebrated in St Peter's during Easter week. The Roman clergy and the *schola cantorum* would be expected take part as they did at those vespers (and at stational masses on many occasions in the year). If the notice is placed chronologically, Leo's rule may have been made on St Paul's feast (30 June) in 847: an event of the 10th indiction (ending August 847) is mentioned just below, and cc. 18-19 are dated 15 August 847.

[18] *sacra plebs* means the clergy; cf. 102 n. 14.

Agareni carried out in the holy apostles' churches,[19] this blessed pontiff every day stretched his mind to their restoration, that he might replace all that their ungodly hands had stolen, hoping to enjoy an eternal reward in recompense. So in St Peter the apostle's basilica he presented a fine silver cluster, with silver bowls hanging on 7 chains. For the lighting of this basilica he provided a bronze net with 17 silver canisters. He replaced a light of wondrous size for the brightness and glory of the same church. In it he also presented a fine silver crown weighing .. lb; 25 gold-interwoven veils, beautiful ones which hang in the area around the holy altar; 10 veils representing lions, which can be seen hanging in front of the vestibule of the sacred confessio; 46 other gold-interwoven veils which gleam between this venerable basilica's columns to right and left; 33 gold-interwoven veils which hang in the arches for the decoration and adornment of the *presbyterium*; and 18 other gold-interwoven veils which this bountiful pope arranged to hang in various parts of this basilica; and 3 other veils which hang in front of the sacred basilica's doors.

14. In the basilica of the martyrs SS Quattuor Coronati this noteworthy and wise prelate, relying on love from on high, provided a gold-studded cloth representing our lord Jesus Christ's resurrection, with effigies of these martyrs and of the bountiful prelate himself.

The mind of this vigilant[20] prelate shone so greatly with God's love that with willing breast he wanted to restore anew in his distinguished time all the uncountable goods which ungodly hands had formerly stolen from St Peter the apostle's church. So for this church's beauty and honour he provided 2 fine silver crowns, crafted with wondrous work, hanging on silver chains, with jewels and gilt pommels, 1 weighing 132 lb, the other 130, 1 with 37 silver *clamasterii* hanging beneath it, the other with 40. **15.** He who was ever bedecked with God's gift and endeavoured to have worthy care and anxiety for everything, happily provided in St Andrew the apostle's oratory[21] at St Peter's 2 great gold-interwoven veils and 5 other small ones, decorated around with purple.

This God-protected, venerable and distinguished pontiff, for the

---

[19] Nothing is in fact said about Leo IV's restorations at St Paul's until c. 96, though, surprisingly, c. 12 has just referred to minor liturgical arrangements.

[20] *gregorii* (so MS D, almost contemporary with the original), a remarkable use of the word in its etymological sense, not understood by the copyists of MSS CE who substituted *egregii*. Duchesne acutely spotted the same use in Bili the deacon, *Vita Maglorii*, prol., who dedicated his work to his 'vigilant' bishop, Ratuili of Alet, c. 870.

[21] This is the basilica founded by pope Symmachus (LP 53:6, BP 45) in the 2nd- or 3rd-century mausoleum immediately southeast of the transept of St Peter's; it was demolished in 1590 (Hülsen, *Chiese*, 190).

eternal redemption of his soul, provided in St Anastasius's monastery[22] 1 gold-interwoven silk cloth representing eagles; also 2 gold-interwoven veils embellished round with purple. Also he provided in St Praxedes's monastery[23] 1 gold-interwoven cloth.

16. As for the old and ancient rites and ordinances of the sacred palace, various customs which in the time of the pontiffs his predecessors had been broken and abolished, this prelate, from the day when, relying on God's power, he ascended with all kindness Peter the apostle's holy see, therefore keenly and with willing mind tried to restore them all, or to improve their recent condition, as a memorial to his holiness. Lord pope Leo III of good memory had constructed from the ground a dining room[24] and had equipped it with all its adornments, but then because of great age and the unawareness of his predecessor pontiffs these had been removed, and on the day of the Nativity of our Lord Jesus Christ according to the flesh neither lord Gregory nor lord Sergius of holy memory had ever dined there. This blessed and supreme prelate Leo IV with joy and great delight newly replaced all the adornments and dining equipment which had been removed from there and magnificently recalled it to its ancient use. **17.** What is more, Charles of godly memory, emperor of the Franks and Romans, had in the time of lord pope Leo III of holy memory presented in the Saviour our Lord Jesus Christ's basilica called Constantinian a fine gold cross[25] adorned with jewels; the custom was that in litanies it went in front of the holy pontiff, and so it continued till the time of lord pope Paschal, when at the devil's suggestion and instigation evil men carried it off and thieves stealthily took it away from there at night, and thereafter none of his predecessor pontiffs, not lord Paschal nor lord Eugene nor lord Valentine nor lord Gregory nor lord Sergius, thought to restore and replace it for the use of God's holy Roman church. But this magnificent prelate made it of fine gold and adorned it as necessary with pearls and jewels, jacinths and prases, of wondrous size, and replaced it magnificently for the ancient use of God's holy Roman church.

18. This[26] distinguished and noteworthy prelate was a most approved

---

[22] Cf. 97 n. 189.

[23] See 100:9-11.

[24] Duchesne identified this *accubitus* with the *triclinium* with 11 apses in 98:39 (with n. 89). It could as well be Leo's other, better-known, *triclinium* (98:10 with n. 21).

[25] Cf. 98:25 again, with n. 65. Two crosses were required to precede the pope at the Major Litany on 25 April; Andrieu, *Ordines Romani*, 3.248, Ordo 21.10 (cf. 3.236, Ordo 20.7). For the other cross see c. 28.

[26] Note the repetition of the eulogy before the account of Leo's works is continued; cf. lives 106 and 107.

preacher of God's scriptures with knowledge and learning. He shone with such great blessedness and holiness that he wrought wonders in the sight of the whole people of this church founded on Christ. In the first year of his pontificate, close to St Lucy the martyr's basilica[27] in Orphea, in some noisome and hidden caverns arose a serpent of dire sort called *basilisk* in Greek and *regulus*[28] in Latin; by its breath and glance it speedily overwhelmed all who went into those caves and gave them over to danger of death, so that amazement and terror attacked all who gazed on the serpent's might and penetrating power. **19.** This blessed and distinguished pontiff heard how the people were overwhelmed and destroyed, and turned himself to prayer. Unceasingly he besought the Lord with fasting to deliver all men from destruction of this kind. While this was happening, the distinguished and notable day arrived on which God's blessed mother the ever-virgin Mary's assumption is celebrated. Then this universal pope made his way on foot with the clergy from the patriarchate to St Hadrian the martyr's basilica, as is the custom,[29] with hymns and spiritual chants, going ahead of the holy icon. Returning thence with the whole gathering of the faithful he made his way to our Lord and God Jesus Christ's holy mother's called *Praesepe*, with God's praises, and a great assemblage of people accompanying him. When he reached the place where the savage basilisk lay, in noisome caverns as we have already said above, he ordered all the clergy and people to halt,

---

[27] On this 'basilica' see 103:21 with n. 43.

[28] Leo's exorcism of a basilisk has been described as 'legendary', an epithet which does not fit well with a contemporary account. The LP does not state that anyone who saw the creature lived to tell the tale. The escape of methane from the mounds of rubbish which underlay many of the habitations of 9th-century Rome might have caused the phenomena mentioned. For ancient ideas on the βασιλίσκος cf. Heliodorus 3.8 (Everyman, pp. 76-7): 'you have doubtless heard how the serpent called 'the basilisk' by its mere breath and glance will shrivel and cripple whatever comes in its way'; cf. Pliny, *NH* 8.21. Speculation about such a creature is pointless.

[29] The processions on the Marian feastdays (2 February, 25 March, 15 August, 8 September) had been instituted by Sergius I (86:14, BP 87). The custom of carrying the *sancta icona*, the Lateran *acheiropoieta* image, must have been introduced soon after: in 752 (94.11) it was carried in a procession to St Mary Major. The present occasion is 15 August 847; by the 12th century the icon was carried only in the procession on that day. This may already have been the case in the 9th century, though Duchesne's argument that this was so in 752-3 is not convincing. He noted another peculiarity of the procession on 15 August, its celebration at night before matins, while the others were held in the morning before the stational mass; and here Leo IV arrives at St Mary Major 'to display God's praises (*laudes*)', an expression suggesting the office (lauds) rather than mass; if so the peculiarities of the procession on 15 August were earlier than 847, and not instituted to commemorate the occurrence here dealt with. A short poem 'On the Assumption of St Mary, on the night when the *tabula* is carried' was written under Otto III (ed. Di Costanzo 1797:422). Abuses that crept into this nocturnal ceremony induced Pius V to abolish it.

we have already said above, he ordered all the clergy and people to halt, and making his way close to these caverns, he halted fearlessly over the cleft from which the breath of that plague-bearing serpent emerged. Raising eyes and hands to heaven, with abundant tears he besought Christ who is God above all to put to flight by his power the dire kind of serpent from that place. And giving out the prayer over the people he set out to the basilica we have mentioned above to display God's praises.[30] But from that very day the death-dealing basilisk was put to flight and expelled from those caves so that there appeared no further trace of its damage in those places.

20. This bountiful pope performed another wonder; let us begin to tell it briefly. At the very start of his pontificate which we have recorded above, a mighty fire attacked the *vicus* of the Saxons, which by the power of its flames began to burn everything mightily; many rows of people gathered there, wanting to quench the fire's flames. But the breath of the winds made the fire reach high into the sky, burning and reducing everything so that it came to near St Peter the apostle's basilica, consuming and wrecking the homes of the Saxons and Lombards[31] and the portico. Hearing this, the blessed pontiff set out thither in speed and haste, put himself in the path of the fire's force, and began to beseech the Lord to quench the fire's flames. When he made the sign of the cross with his own fingers, the fire could spread its flames no further; unable to endure the blessed pontiff's power, it was quenched and reduced its flames to ash.[32]

21. In St Peter the apostle's basilica this God-beloved and wise pope provided 45 gold-interwoven veils, surrounded with purple. In St Martin's monastery[33] attached to St Peter the apostle's basilica, for the praise and glory of St Martin's shrine this outstanding pontiff provided a cloth representing that saint lying on a bier, with the effigy of the Saviour our Lord Jesus Christ, also the effigy of St Agatha the martyr with the effigy of this bountiful pontiff at its feet, with 17 jacinth jewels. In the same oratory he provided 4 veils, and one[34] with 3 gold-studded roses.

22. In the holy Four Brethren's basilica[35] he provided 1 gold-interwoven cloth representing these holy martyrs and the effigy of the

---

[30] This may mean 'to celebrate lauds (matins)'; see last note.

[31] Cf. n. 49 to 98:19.

[32] Some chemical theory about the nature of flame may be implied.

[33] Cf. cc. 2-3.

[34] Perhaps one of the four, though possibly a fifth is meant.

[35] SS Quattro Coronati, reckoned to be brothers; for their names see n. 62.

great prelate himself, with 12 jewels; also 4 gold-interwoven veils.

In St Peter the apostle his mentor's basilica, this venerable and distinguished pontiff provided chased fine silver canisters weighing .. lb. There too he presented fine silver crowns weighing .. lb. Relying on love from on high, this blessed and distinguished pope presented to St Peter the apostle for the splendour and glory of this sacred basilica a fine silver lantern with two wicks, weighing 45 lb; there too, after the Saracens' savage looting, he provided in this basilica fine silver railings weighing 57 lb.

23. In St Silvester the confessor and pontiff's church[36] on Mount Soracte this blessed prelate provided 1 gold-interwoven cloth with 4 corners, 2 of tyrian and 2 of interwoven gold.

In St Peter the prince of the apostle's church this holy and blessed prelate provided 18 gold-worked veils, representing St Peter, which hang in the arches of the *presbyterium*. Also in St Leo the confessor and pontiff's oratory[37] within this church, 1 gold-interwoven cloth representing eagles. There too he presented 1 silver crown weighing .. lb; he also provided the 20 gold-interwoven veils, decorated on each side with purple. **24.** To St Peter the apostle he presented 16 silver chalices, which are set above the surround of the altar, weighing .. lb; also a hanging chalice with chains and dolphins, weighing .. lb. So after the Saracens' looting of this church this holy and angelic prelate also provided 3 silver images, all of them gilded, at St Peter the apostle's body: one of them with an effigy in the middle of the Saviour our Lord Jesus Christ, decorated on the head in the form of a cross with jewels, jacinths and prases; another, placed on the Saviour's right side, with the face of St Peter the apostle and of St Petronilla; the other, on the left side, depicting the face of St Andrew the apostle and the face of this supreme prelate, weighing 104 lb. There too he provided 12 bronze lights which are set over the holy altar's vestibule.

25. Often this blessed pope greatly yearned to rebuild all the locations of the saints which had been destroyed. As for the monastery *Corsarum*,[38] which is close to St Xystus the martyr and pontiff's

---

[36] On this church and its monastery see 103:12 with n. 25.

[37] See c. 31 and n. 53.

[38] 'Locations of saints' should refer to cemeteries. The connexion in thought may be that relics were transferred from cemeteries to within the city. The monastery may have been seen as virtually an annexe of S. Sisto Vecchio, and it does seem that in the 9th century (or later) relics of Xystus II and some other 3rd-century popes were transferred to S. Sisto: an undated and now lost inscription referred to this (Zucchi 1938:I.330; Krautheimer, *Corpus 4.165*); another inscription listed relics under the high altar. On the monastery see 98:79 and nn. 158-9; n. 88 below; Ferrari, 96-102.

basilica, it had been abandoned through the works of evil men[39] and reduced to a secular dwelling; for his soul's salvation and future reward he restored it perfectly, and in it he established a congregation of God's handmaids to fulfil daily praises to almighty God, increased it with gifts, adorned it with riches, and, restoring by his holy commands all that had been stolen from it, he fully confirmed it all with his sacred hand.

26. This oft-mentioned blessed pope brought many to the knowledge of the truth by his addresses and preaching,[40] and daily displayed wholesome activities to all. The octave day of God's blessed mother's assumption[41] had never before been kept at Rome; he ordered it to be celebrated, spending the night in sacred vigils and in morning praises with all the clergy, in the same ever-virgin our lady's basilica outside the walls close to St Laurence the martyr's basilica.[42] In it there gathered a great multitude of the people, yearning to celebrate the new festivity's ceremony. When this magnanimous bishop saw it, he dispensed silver in full to all who were present at this celebration. **27.**

---

[39] Perhaps this is merely a stock expression, though Ferrari, 98 n. 5, suspects that it masks 'interesting circumstances'.

[40] Duchesne noted the possible relevance to this passage of a sermon on priests' duties (J2659; Mansi 14.889; *PL* 96.1375, 115.675; *Neues Archiv*. VI p. 192, 652) which in some collections bears the name 'pope Leo' or even 'Leo IV'. But he doubted whether it was of papal origin; it shows no traces of Roman usages; it supposes a diocese divided into many rural parishes; the bishop calls himself vicar of the apostles, not vicar of St Peter, etc. Its genuineness was accepted however by Jaffé-Ewald.

[41] The feast itself had been celebrated at Rome since at least the late 7th century (as the 'Dormition', 86:14 BP 87), but was by no means universal in the west (*AB* 862 Nelson 101-2 records that it had not hitherto been celebrated in the diocese of Thérouanne, even though the metropolitan church at Rheims was dedicated to the Virgin); the Gregorian music is mainly borrowed from other feasts (e.g. the introit belongs to St Agatha) and the prayers tend to vary in different manuscripts of the Roman rite, both signs of late acceptance. Leo's purpose in instituting an Octave (22 August) may have been to commemorate the incident in cc. 19ff.

[42] Cf. 97 n. 77. St Laurence's here is the surviving building of Pelagius II (LP 65, BP 61) above the martyr's tomb, which now forms the choir at the east of the basilica whose nave is of the early 13th century; Duchesne, believing that this nave dated to the 5th century, identified it with St Mary's mentioned here. In fact St Mary's was the name acquired (in the LP, first at 97:64) by the huge Constantinian basilica just south of Pelagius's church, whose foundations were still undiscovered in Duchesne's time. In St Mary's were the three oratories named in c. 27. It is mentioned several times in life 105 but not later; clearly little importance was afterwards attached to it. Fire damage seen in the excavations may be of this date (Krautheimer, *Corpus* 2.138). Krautheimer believes that the dedication to St Mary was made in the late 8th century to give the basilica a function; following Josi, he notes an entry in the Reichenau MS (Zürich, Kantonsbibl., Hist. 28) of the *Martyrologium Hieronymianum* (*Aa SS Nov.* II.i.101, 417): '5 August, dedication of the basilica of St Mary, Justin and Crescentia'; Justin and Crescentia were martyrs venerated in this very basilica. But 5 August is the dedication of St Mary Major, and the MS entry probably results from a confusion.

At the same God's mother the ever-virgin Mary's this blessed man provided 1 gold-interwoven cloth; and he provided 45 veils[43] there. Inside[44] this church in the oratory called St Barbara's he presented 1 gold-interwoven cloth. In the same church's oratory of St Nicholas he donated 1 gold-interwoven cloth. In St Eugenia's oratory[45] this God-distinguished bishop provided 1 gold-interwoven cloth. In St Stephen the first martyr's church[46] outside the wall close to St Laurence the martyr's church, with God's help this skilful, holy, totally distinctive and distinguished man with great spirit and pure intention donated 1 gold-interwoven cloth; within this church's walls, in St Leo the martyr's oratory, he provided 1 gold-interwoven cloth.

28. In God's mother the ever-virgin our lady St Mary's church within the said monastery *Corsarum*, this mild pontiff, keen on all good things, presented 1 gold-interwoven cloth; there too, in St Caesarius's oratory he presented 1 gold-interwoven cloth.

This kind man newly provided a gold cross;[47] the cross, as was the custom of old, was carried in the hands of the subdeacons in front of the horse of the pontiffs his predecessors, and, God willing it, he replaced it better in gold, silver and jewels.

29. In the church of St Nympha the martyr[48] in the city of Porto he

---

[43] Krautheimer (*Corpus* 2.138 n. 3) wants to read '65', in view of Hadrian's sets of 65 curtains for the same basilica (97:64). He argues (2.119) that the nave had 24 columns each side (so, with the end piers, 50 intercolumniations); the semicircular inner-apse rested probably on 6 columns with 7 intercolumniations; and the façade had either 3 or 5 arches. 65 curtains would provide for all these with a few to spare.

[44] Or 'below' (*infra*). The location of St Barbara's is not known well enough to resolve this ambiguity. *infra* at the end of the chapter must surely mean 'within'.

[45] The context suggests that this was another oratory in the same basilica.

[46] On this church see 97:75 with n. 151.

[47] This is the second of the two crosses required at the Major Litany, cf. c. 17.

[48] St Nympha's at Porto, first mentioned here, recurs in a charter of Benedict VIII on 1 August 1018 confirming the privileges and properties of the bishopric of Porto (J4024); this shows it was on the seashore near Fiumicino (*focem Miccina*); the same words recur in a grant of Leo IX on 22 April 1049 (J4163). There is no ancient evidence for a St Nympha; she is a personification of the place name *ad Nymphas*, between the Via Cornelia and the Via Portuensis. Her Passion (*BHL* 6254-6) is therefore historically valueless, but it mentions Porto, a place close to Buccina, a crypt near a tall pine-tree, and the church built there. Baronius noted that *ad Nymphas* was commonly called Sancta Nympha, and that traces of the ancient church could be seen there. At it were some fine underground conduits, and he suggested that the place took its name from the abundance of water; he visited it, found the place deserted and the shore abandoned. In 1703 C. B. Piazza (*La Gerarchia cardinalizia*, 59) wrote that the saint was still remembered in the woods not far from Porto, with a church to her, restored from its ruins by Cardinal Francesco Barberini, and a marble statue of her. The origins of the cult are unknown. Her head was said to have been taken by the Saracens to Syria when they looted Porto, and brought back by an ex-Jew in 896. Her body is said to have been taken to S. Maria in

provided 1 gold-interwoven cloth. In SS Cosmas and Damian the martyrs' church[49] at Silva Candida he provided 1 gold-interwoven cloth; there too he provided 4 gold-interwoven veils, decorated around with purple.

This blessed pope used to visit the tombs of the holy martyrs devoutly and with assiduously burning breast; and he prayed to them in vigils and sacred prayers for all the people of the orthodox faith. 30. One day, when he had come to St Laurence the martyr's tomb and had completed the prayer in the usual way, he began to inquire diligently and to say: 'How many monks are there here who render praises to almighty God every day?' Then all those present mentioned to the blessed pontiff that two monasteries[50] had been constructed there by some pontiffs but had been reduced to abandonment by great want and poverty. Then this bountiful pontiff, spurred by the Will from on high, restored the monastery now called that of SS Stephen and Cassian[51] and decorated it opulently with gifts and riches. In it he established many monks of Greek race[52] and of holy behaviour, who might fulfil day and night the praises to almighty God and that martyr.

31. Inside St Peter the apostle's basilica this God-protected and venerable prelate constructed a shrine[53] of wondrous beauty and supreme comeliness. Surrounding it with beautiful marble he splendidly embellished it, and he gloriously adorned its apse in mosaic with gold colour overlaid. In it he buried St Leo the confessor and pontiff's body, constructed a holy altar above, and relying on this love he completed a canopy with gilded crosses to the praise and glory of Christ's name, so he might acquire himself a worthy place in heaven.

Montecellis in 1098 (in the presence of Anselm archbishop of Canterbury), though this church was only consecrated between 1099 and 1118 (Duchesne, *LP* II.305). Her relics appeared elsewhere in the early 12th century. Her head was taken to Palermo in 1593. Her body is said to have been placed at S. Spirito in Sassia. See Delehaye, *AaSS Nov.* IV, 327-328.

[49] This church is mentioned in Leo IV's bull of 854, on which see n. 156.

[50] On these monasteries see 98:77 with nn. 143-144.

[51] Apparently Leo united the two monasteries into one, hence the double dedication, Krautheimer, *Corpus* 2.12, Ferrari 182-3, 187.

[52] Still visible embedded in one of the ambos at St Laurence's is a reused Greek inscription from the second half of the ninth century (*CIG* 8832): +ΕΠ... ΣΕΝΙΟΣ ΗΓΟΥΜΕΝΟΣ ΕΚ ΝΕΑΣ ΕΠΟΙΗΣΑ ΤΟ ΠΡΕΣΒΥΤΕΡΙΟΝ ΤΟΝ...: 'Under ..., I, Arsenius *hegumenus*, renewed the *presbyterium*'; see Ferrari 183, 187.

[53] The text suggests a foundation, but the oratory already existed (cf. c. 23 above, 95:6, 98:84, 87), nor is there any reason to suppose that Leo IV moved its location. Leo had been the first pope to be buried in the exterior narthex of St Peter's; Sergius I had moved his body to a new shrine inside the basilica on 28 June 688 as is known from 86:12 BP 86, and a still extant inscription (text in Duchesne I, 379 n. 35).

32. Once all these works whose details have now been individually written or recorded above were achieved and completed, straightaway this outstanding shepherd and father, though he bore advantageous care and worthy anxiety for all God's churches[54] and was more than anyone intent on every good work, drew deep sighs from his inmost heart, since every day he beheld St Peter the prince of the apostles' sacred altar violated and reduced to such dishonour and vileness by the infidel Saracens, God's enemies, and also because, as we tell in sorrow and mourning, the christian people who on all sides headed for the said prince's sacred home for the sake of prayer or grace were for this reason not as fully zealous to fulfil their vows as they used to be. So, relying on the almighty Lord's help and strengthened by his counsel and power, he very fittingly and honourably decorated with gold and silver panels not only the holy confessio but also the front of that altar, as the present work dedicated there proves in every way clearer than light. **33.** For this reason he encompassed all of the altar's distinguished front with panels freshly dedicated in excellent gold,[55] and with a great number of excellent and precious jewels: he improved the condition and beauty it had previously had. On these panels, which as has been said are of gold, not only does a depiction of the form of our Redeemer shine forth but also his venerable resurrection and the sign of his holy and saving cross, and likewise the faces of Peter and Paul and of Andrew gleam and glisten on the same panels; among them are depicted the venerable persons, dear to God for ever and ever, of the holy prelate Leo IV and of his spiritual son the lord emperor Lothar, for their memorial and reward in time to come. **34.** These worked panels weigh 216 lb of refined gold. In the same way with all the devotion of his mind he brought this altar's confessio to its ancient glory and condition with panels prepared in fine silver; on them we see the Saviour sitting on a throne with precious jewels on his head, on his right are depicted the Cherubim and on his left the faces of the apostles and of others. The railings of the holy confessio are also constructed of silver, with the faces of SS Peter and Paul, all weighing 208 lb. **35.** In St Peter the apostle's basilica this God-beloved and wise pontiff provided 11 gold-worked veils of purple, hanging in all the arches around. In St Leo the

---

[54] Cf. 2 Cor. 11.28.
[55] In the 12th century, the canon Romanus, interpolator of Mallius (De Rossi, *Inscr. christ.* II p. 202), stated that this part of the decoration was still to be seen: 'He had a tablet of gold and enamel made, weighing 216 lb of gold, on which is contained the old and new testament; and he set it on the front of the altar; this too we also saw'. The last words may imply that the gold panelling had disappeared before he wrote.

pontiff's oratory inside St Peter the apostle's church he provided 1 white silk cloth, medallioned, with chevrons and a fringe of purple; also 2 large white veils and 8 small ones.

In the monastery of St Caesarius in Palatio[56] he provided 1 gold-interwoven cloth and 8 veils.

In St Agatha the martyr's cemetery[57] outside St Pancras the martyr's Gate, this God-protected and venerable pontiff for the reward and recompense of his soul presented 1 gold-interwoven cloth and 8 veils.

36. Who can say, who is capable of telling, how many gifts this God-protected and skilful pope devoutly presented to the holy places? In the oratory called that of pope Paul he presented 1 cloth of wondrous beauty, representing eagles, with a gold-studded cross and chevrons. In the oratory of SS Processus and Martinian he presented 1 cloth of no little splendour, with wheels and men and a representation of the cross also of gold-studding and chevrons; in St Petronilla's basilica he achieved 1 other cloth of bright aspect, with wheels and eagles with a gold-studded cross and chevrons. **37.** In God's mother the ever-virgin our lady St Mary's oratory, established at Mediana, he presented 1 cloth, also with wheels and eagles with a gold-studded cross and chevrons. In St Hadrian's oratory[58] he provided 1 cloth with wheels, effigies of men, also with a gold-studded cross and chevrons.

---

[56] Dedications at Rome of monasteries and oratories to St Caesarius have caused confusion. Hitherto the style is used in connexion with two monasteries, that at St Paul's (98:77), and the oratory in that known as *de Corsas* (98:79, 105:28). Also dedicated to St Caesarius, though neither occurs in the donation list of 807, were an oratory in the Lateran patriarchate (96:9, 104:25) and an oratory in the imperial palace on the Palatine (86:2 BP 83). It seems that the latter (presumably after 807) became the nucleus of a Greek monastery (Ferrari, 88-91). Einhard relates (*Translatio bb. Marcellini et Petri, PL* 104.542) that his notary, sent to Rome in 828, conferred with one Basil, a monk who had come from Constantinople to Rome two years earlier 'and had his dwelling there on the Palatine hill with his four disciples among the Greeks who were of the same profession'; Einhard does not mention the name of the monastery; it is first called St Caesarius's here in the LP. About 866 a monk Blasius of Amorium, representing Bulgarian interests in Rome, was received by the superior (Eustratus) and spent 18 years at the λαύρα τοῦ ἐνδόξου καισαρίου. St Caesarius's on the Palatine was where St Sabas the Younger died at the end of the 10th century. There was other Greek settlement nearby (cf. the churches of S. Maria Antiqua, St. Theodore's, St George in Velabro, S. Maria in Cosmedin). The precise location is uncertain; Ferrari, 90-91 prefers the identification of Bartoli who discovered some Byzantine frescoes under the western wing of the Villa Mills; Hülsen, *Chiese*, 232, placed the monastery in the centre of Domitian's stadium; Armellini-Cecchelli, *Chiese*, 1276, follows Bartoli; Krautheimer, *Corpus* 1.113, suspends judgment.

[57] Symmachus's foundation (LP 53:8 BP 45), a cemeterial basilica on the Via Aurelia at the farm Lardarius.

[58] This is the chapel in which Hadrian I was buried. Romanus (cf. n. 55) interpolated Mallius's text to give this oratory, as in the LP, a dedication to St Hadrian. The explanation could be that some time after pope Hadrian's death in 795 an altar was built at his tomb in honour of the homonymous martyr.

effigies of men, also with a gold-studded cross and chevrons.

In St Sebastian the martyr's basilica at Frascati[59] this oft-mentioned and blessed pope presented 1 cloth of precious brightness, also with a gold-studded cloth and chevrons.

In St Peter the apostle's basilica this supreme and distinctive prelate provided 1 all-silk curtain with many representations of immeasurable brightness, for this holy basilica's beauty and glory.

38. When the blessed man and prelate Leo IV had, with God's comfort and with the grace of love and desire, perfectly conferred these and the other things above-written on the various localities of the godly saints, he then began with the consultation of the Lord Jesus Christ to treat of the condition of the city of Rome and the restoration of the walls which by long old age were broken to age and utterly destroyed, in case, if it stayed for long in this neglect and forgetfulness, they could easily with the Lord permitting it be captured or perhaps stormed by an enemy. So, in case this evil should occur in time to come, he took care with all the mind of alacrity to renew to their former standard and beauty all the walls of this city of Rome in the 12th [848-849] and the present indiction. And he ordered not only the walls we have mentioned to be made with speed and agility, but for fear of enemies he also bade that the gates with which the whole city is often closed be quickly rebuilt to a new standard and with very strong timbers. **39.** So that all these things might be brought to completion and rendered beautiful, this apostolic man bustled about with his loyal men without discrimination, not simply staying at ground level but even going on his own feet along the walls and gates, so that in their restoration there might arise no hesitation or delay. So, as has been said, the venerable pontiff had amongst other things the greatest care and anxiety for the city of Rome, and on all sides he brought it to a new and better standard: he ordered 15 towers which he found utterly destroyed round the circuit of the city to be restored from the ground with fresh building. The venerable prelate arranged that two of these be built close to the Portuensis Gate by the very shore of the Tiber, that is close to the river bank, so wisely

---

explanation could be that some time after pope Hadrian's death in 795 an altar was built at his tomb in honour of the homonymous martyr.

[59] This is the first mention anywhere of the name Frascati. The place was in the territory of Tusculum. The local bishopric was Labicum Quintanenses at the 15th mile of the Via Labicana: the bishop attended the Roman Council in 313. In the 7th century the bishops began instead to use the title Tusculum, which was in their territory. When Tusculum was destroyed in 1191 they moved to Frascati, whose real importance dates from that time (Lanzoni, 126). St Sebastian's was the cathedral of Frascati until 1708 and, now dedicated to St Roche, it is known as the *duomo vecchio*.

and prudently as no one previously could think or consider doing. Beforehand not only ships but men as well easily entered by this place, but now small boats will hardly ever be able to come in by it. This was done because of the coming danger of the Saracens and for the city of Rome's safety. **40.** So he took care to strengthen this tower not only with stones but with iron as well so that, should the need occur, no ship could cross through this place. This freshly constructed work provides both defence for the city of Rome and for viewers no small wonder but a large one, as it was done with great prudence, subtle wisdom and honour.

41. For almighty God's honour this God-protected and blessed pope with supreme endeavour and supreme affection of heart wonderfully assembled inside this beloved city's walls many bodies of the saints which had long lain unvenerated. With skilful care he sought and found[60] the bodies of the martyrs the SS Quattuor Coronati. The basilica which had been consecrated to the name of the saints, and which until he was brought to the summit of the pontificate he ruled with wise government, was shaken through the long courses of time by the failing of age and, almost broken into ruins, was seen to be convulsed for a long time past; for their desirable love, by the will of the Clemency of the Power on high, he brought it from the ground to a more splendid and more beautiful state, for almighty God's praise.[61] As for their holy bodies - with[62] Claudius, Nicostratus, Simphronianus and Castorius, and

[60] The text does not say where he found them; cf. 103:6. That they were once venerated at SS Marcellinus and Peter on the Via Labicana is clear from the Itineraries. But they may have been brought to the basilica on the Caelian Hill before the 9th century; Delehaye, *Mart. Hieron.*, *Aa SS Nov.* II.ii.231.

[61] The ancient building was a 4th-century aisleless apsed hall, perhaps, in view of LP 72:4 BP 64, not made into a church until the time of pope Honorius (who was possibly replacing an earlier *titulus*-building elsewhere). This was supplanted, evidently now in view of the present passage, by a Carolingian aisled basilica with a trabeated colonnade, atrium and gate tower (Krautheimer, *Corpus* 4.33-4). This church was destroyed by Robert Guiscard, then rebuilt from 1099 and rededicated by Paschal II on 20 January 1116, *LP* Duchesne II. 305 lines 34-5. A bull of 24 May 1116 refers to the church's reduction in size (Krautheimer, *Corpus* 4.3), though it had probably been intended to be as large as Leo IV's church. Hence the smaller present church with its double courtyard, the inner one occupying the site of part of Leo IV's building.

[62] The translation here follows, as usual, Duchesne's text, at this point in effect MS D (Parisinus 5516, copied before mid-861). 'With' in D (if it is not just loose writing) presumes that the five names following are *not* those of the Four Coronati; D then continues with four other names (Severus to Victorinus) which it claims were the Four. The older tradition, by which the Four Coronati were Pannonian sculptors, gave as their names the first four on this list, and claimed that one Simplicius (the fifth on the list) was martyred with them. A later tradition tried to make them into Romans and substitute the next four names. This might suggest that the compiler of the LP followed the later tradition. However, Duchesne's apparatus records an important set of variants from MS

Simplicius, also Severus, Severianus, Carpophorus and Victorinus the 4 Brethren, also Marius, Audifax and Abbacuc, Felicissimus and Agapitus, Hippolytus with his 18 servants, Aquila and Prisca,[63] Arseus, Aquinus, Narcissus and Marcellinus, Felix and Symmetrius, Candida and Paulina, Anastasius and Felix, Apollio and Benedict, Venantius and Felix, Diogenes and Liberalis, Festus and Marcellus, and Exsuperantius, Pudentiana and Benedict, Felix and Venantus,[64] also the head[65] of St Protus, of St Caecilia,[66] of St Alexander, of St Xystus, of St Sebastian[67] and of the holy virgin Praxedes - he placed them together and buried them under the holy altar; and many others whose names are known to God.[68] **42.** Over it also, to the Creator's glory, [he provided] a fine silver canopy of wondrous workmanship and wondrous size, overlaid

---

C (Parisinus 5140, 11th century) which would modify the translation as follows: 'As for their sacred bodies - *scil.* of Claudius, Nicostratus, Simphronianus and Castorius, and of Simplicius, with Severus, Severianus, Carpophorus and Victorinus the 4 Brethren...'. The effect of this is to follow the older tradition (even though the Roman names are still described as those of Four Brethren). As Delehaye shows, this is greatly preferable on historical grounds (and note that c. 57 below does presume that Claudius and Nicostratus were among the four). It is at least possible that the text of MS C is, despite its later date, original, and that the copyist of D attempted to show that the five Pannonian names were not the IV Coronati, but then neglected to delete the Roman names. The origin of the four Roman names is a group of martyrs at Albano on the Via Appia, culted on 8 August: Secundus, Carpophorus, Victorinus and Severianus (*Depositio Martyrum* in the Chronographer of 354). See Delehaye, *AaSS Nov.* III, especially p. 755.

[63] It is noteworthy that these relics were not given to Prisca's *titulus*. The only references to this church in the LP (lives 97 and 98) are to gifts so small that it is likely that the church was insignificant. Krautheimer, *Corpus* 3.75, suggests that the *titulus* had been installed in some Roman structure, and that the large building which finally replaced it and is the core of the present church dates only from c. 1100. It is not even certain that this is on precisely the same site as the original *titulus*.

[64] A second Venantius? The inscription (n. 68) here substitutes a second Benedict.

[65] Heads? The inscription has the plural.

[66] See 100 n. 65.

[67] Vogel (Duchesne III) notes that this relic was found in 1624 under the high altar; since then it has been kept in the church of SS IV Coronati. See 103 n. 14.

[68] At SS Quattro Coronati there are still two inscriptions, once fixed to the altar but now on the left-hand wall by the sacristy door, concerning the relics under the altar. The two texts are best given in P. A. Galletti, *Inscriptiones romanae infimi aevi Romae exstantes* I, xxvi, and Delehaye, *AaSS Nov.* III 755-6. The right-hand text records Paschal II's renewal of the martyrs' crypt in 1111; it states that in excavating the altar he discovered two shells, one of porphyry, the other of proconnesian marble, containing relics; *pace* Delehaye, there is no reason why an eye-witness should not have seen these shells, and we need not suppose that they come from martyr acts. The left-hand text is probably of about the same date. It gives a list of saints very like that in the LP; hence Erbes and Duchesne thought it was copied from the LP. Delehaye thought that though the present inscription is 12th-century, both it and the LP text could have been copied from an original of Leo IV's time; he noted that the inscription did not conflict with his view that the reading of LP MS C is superior to that of MS D. See also Duchesne 1911:239, and Delehaye 1936:64-73.

with gold colour, with jewels, prases and jacinths, weighing 313½ lb; there too in this church he presented 4 red veils which hang round the altar; and under that holy [altar?][69]... [the holy] prelate provided in the oratory of the same St Barbara located in[70] the church of the SS Quattuor Coronati a silver crown weighing 12 lb; in the same oratory he presented 10 silver bowls weighing .. lb; in the same oratory he provided 4 gold-interwoven cloths, with crosses and chevrons in the middle; and 12 veils.

43. In St Stephen the pontiff's[71] basilica at the 3rd mile on the Via Latina, this venerable pontiff provided 1 gold-interwoven cloth with a cross in the middle; and 6 veils. There too he presented a holy paten and chalice, small, of silver, weighing 1½ lb.

In St Peter the prince of the apostles' church the blessed prelate presented a silver-gilt apostolated thurible, inscribed with the name of lord pope Leo IV, weighing 4 lb. There too, in St Gregory the confessor and pontiff's oratory he provided 1 gold-interwoven cloth, with silver-worked chevrons and a cross. There too, in St Pastor the martyr's oratory,[72] he provided 1 cloth. In God's holy mother's oratory at the ambo[73] he also provided 1 cloth. In the oratory of the Holy and Exalted Cross he also provided 1 cloth. In the oratory at the font he also provided 1 cloth and 10 veils of fourfold weave.

---

[69] A lacuna in the text of MS D, as is clear from the anacoluthon and the need for a reference to St Barbara's oratory to precede the reference to the oratory of 'the same' St Barbara (this cannot refer back to c. 27, where St Barbara's oratory is in a different church). MSS CE attempt to mend the text, neither satisfactorily. The fault was due to haplography between two occurrences of *sanctissimo/us*; the adjective will the first time surely have referred to the altar, beneath which was something, just as what was above it has just been described. There might perhaps have been a reference to the reliquaries, the two shells of porphyry and proconnesian, seen in 1111 (n. 68). Or there might merely have been a reference to railings in the confessio.

[70] So perhaps rather than 'below' (the same problem as at c. 27, n. 44), though the oratory's location is unknown; there is no later record of it (Hülsen, *Chiese*, 205).

[71] The church was really that of the deacon and protomartyr, not that of the pope who died in 257; for its foundation by Demetrias see LP Leo I, 47:1 BP 37.

[72] Just outside the transept at the end of the northern colonnade of the nave; the organ would later be above it. The 8th-century writer who described St Peter's (*Notitia ecclesiarum* 39, *CChr* 175.311 lines 189-90) still knew that St Pastor, the holy shepherd, was St Peter himself: 'then to an altar of the same holy apostle called by the name of the shepherd, where they say a *mansionarius* who fell was saved from ruin by St Peter' (this alludes to a story in Gregory I, *Dial.* 3.24). The LP's reference to St Pastor as a martyr may reflect a confusion common by this date. Even in the 6th century, the Leonine Sacramentary has a St Pastor on 25 December (so too *Mart. Hieron.*); and cf. LP 11.1 BP 5 where the 2nd-century pope Pius is said to be brother of Pastor (a confusion with the title of the work written by Pius's brother Hermas).

[73] This is Gregory III's oratory, just outside the transept at the end of the southern colonnade of the nave, opposite the last-mentioned oratory; cf. 92:6.

44. In the church of the SS Quattuor Coronati, over the high altar, this venerable and distinguished pontiff provided 1 gold-interwoven cloth with a cross in the middle and chevrons and gold-interwoven edging round it. There too in St Barbara's oratory he provided 1 gold-interwoven cloth; in St Xystus's oratory he provided 1 cloth; in St Nicholas's oratory he provided 1 cloth, with eagles on it. In this church he also provided 1 linen curtain with crosses in the middle and gold-interwoven edging round it, of wondrous size. This pope, adorned with godly character and holy works, presented in the oft-mentioned hall, which relying on love he had founded, a fine silver paten overlaid with gold colour, with the trophy of the Cross and the effigy of the Saviour, of God's holy mother and of the holy apostles, adorned to a beautiful pattern, weighing 7 lb; also a holy chalice swathed in gold, with images of the evangelists and a cross, weighing 4 lb. **45.** Also a fine silver-gilt chandelier on which is seen the sign of the cross incised in a circle, with effigies of the prophets and an image of St Stephen the first martyr; also 1 fine silver apostolic[74] thurible; 4 gilded bowls for the splendour of this venerable basilica, weighing 2½ lb. When all this was done, he adorned the confessio with the sacred altar with silver panels weighing 93 lb, and decorated them with effigies of the saints, on top of which he also presented a fine silver diadem with precious jewels and with a cross in the middle, which even now can be seen hanging over that altar; there too he presented 42 gold-interwoven veils and 13 brass chandeliers.

46. Inflamed with love from on high, this same pontiff presented in the monastery[75] of SS Silvester, Benedict and Scholastica, called

---

[74] For the hanging of an 'apostolic' thurible in the shaft down to St Peter's grave see 100:6 with n. 16. Presumably at SS IV Coronati the thurible was suspended into the relic chamber. It may have acquired its name from its being incised with an effigy of the apostles, or by analogy with the censers used at the tombs of the apostles.

[75] This is the earliest certainly authentic literary reference to St Scholastica's monastery at Subiaco. A villa is said to have been built by Nero (a sarcophagus and capitals from it are in the monastery) on the banks of three artificial lakes (the biggest gave way in 1305 and flooded Subiaco). The site is regarded as the cradle of the Benedictine order, where Benedict was a hermit before he made for Montecassino. It is sometimes stated that the monastery was destroyed by the Lombards under Agilulf in 601 and that the monks fled to Rome, to the monastery of St Erasmus on the Caelian; but this is legend, first appearing in the 17th-century *Chronicon Sublacense* (Muratori, *R. It. SS.* 24.929-930); there was no connexion between Subiaco and St Erasmus's before 938, when Leo VII granted St Erasmus's to the abbot of Subiaco (J3608, Ferrari, 123-4). It was restored, supposedly after 104 years, and again destroyed, this time by the Saracens, in 846; this, if little earlier, may be historical, since Leo VII in a charter of 11 July 936 making Subiaco immediately subject to the pope, following its enrichment by himself and by Alberic, remarked that the Saracens destroyed the monastery's ancient cloisters (J3597). The whole early history of Subiaco is vitiated by spurious documents and privileges: e.g. one of Gregory I appeared in time to support a privilege granted in 997, and one of pope

Subiaco, 3 gold-interwoven cloths and also 7 gold-interwoven veils.

In St Peter the apostle's church after the Saracens' looting this blessed prelate provided a crucifix constructed of wondrous size, with jacinth jewels, of fine silver-gilt, weighing 77 lb, and 1 other large pearl.

47. These things, then, amongst others, were wondrously done and achieved in the current 12th indiction [848-9] with the Lord's help through the assiduous prayers and tears of the holy prelate, and it is not superfluous if we endeavour to include them clearer than light in this work, for the sake of his eternal memory, so that men of the present and of time to come may more readily acknowledge how great was this man's sanctity amidst this dismal life. Then[76] after the wicked,[77] lamentable and utterly wretched looting that the Saracens accomplished with the devil's encouragement on the first head of all the churches, that is, the holy Roman church, those sons of Satan again meant to inflict similar loss as before on Roman territory and on St Peter the apostle's church and then head back victorious to the places whence they had come. But the supreme shepherd's care and endeavour shone forth and

---

Zacharias was available for inspection during a legal dispute in April 983 (Kehr 1907:II.90, n. 22), when another privilege, just possibly a genuine one of Gregory IV, was also cited. Leo IV is supposed to have visited Subiaco c. 853, to have dedicated in the cave two altars, one in honour of SS Benedict and Scholastica, one in honour of pope Silvester, to have presented one silver bowl and two gold-interwoven curtains of the kind called *fresatae*, and to have confirmed there all these enrichments (*Chron. Sublac.*, Muratori, *loc. cit.*). St Silvester is supposed to have been the original title of the monastery, with the names of Benedict and Scholastica added later, and that of Silvester subsequently dropped. When the cave began to attract hermits a separate monastery sprang up here, as St Benedict's, c. 1200, and from c. 1400 the old abbey is called St Scholastica's simply. Excavations in 1962 below the present church revealed an oratory, 15 m x 4 m, supposed to be 6th-century and to be Benedict's church to Silvester; and close to it a much larger 9th-century church (whose narthex is thought to survive as the lower part of the bell-tower); both sites are within a third, Romanesque, church. A 12th-(or ?16th-) century inscription records Benedict VII's consecration of this church on '4 December' in a year which may be 979. It was in turn replaced by the present (1769) building; St Scholastica's Abbey (tourist guide), ed. Lozzi, Rome, 1971; Egidi 1904. See c. 65 for another church at Subiaco.

[76] This Saracen incursion is recorded nowhere else. Note that near the end of the story (c. 54) the writer speaks in a way which really suits the pope himself: 'we ordered that some should live... our hope - we have it in God... in case they might live among us.... we ordered that... at the wall which we were beginning'; possibly the author was using a papal letter dealing with a rout of the Saracens. In a fragment of a letter of Leo IV to Louis II (J2620, *MGH Ep* 5.585 no. 1) it is said that when news came that the Saracens were about to land secretly at Porto Leo gathered his forces, decided to head with them for the coast, and left Rome. But the text calls Louis emperor and can therefore be no earlier than 850; the *MGH* editor, A. de Hirsch-Gereuth, dates it September 852. It must refer to an occasion later than the present.

[77] Duchesne compares these expressions with those in the prose inscription from one of the gates of the Leonine City (the last quoted in n. 108).

was vigilant, and they were totally unable to achieve it. **48.** But so that those faithful to the Lord might rightly be yet more faithful and not doubt that his signs and wonders from of old freshly spring forth, there must now be an abridgment from the beginning of what God's mercy venerably achieved for them at that time, and in what great wretchedness and disasters that plague-bearing race were justly crushed and dissolved. So, remembering their former profit and the plunder they had had, they cruelly decided to come again to storm the city of Rome during the 12th indiction with a teeming band of perverse men and with many ships. For many days they lingered at a place called Totarum[78] close to the island of Sardinia. Leaving thence, they essayed to depart to the Port of Rome, with no help from God. **49.** Their hostile and wicked arrival frightened the Romans in no small way. But because almighty God has always kept his church inviolate and afterwards does not stop doing so, he then stirred up the hearts of all the men of Naples, Amalfi[79] and Gaeta amongst others, that they too, along with the Romans, had to rise up and contend mightily against them: then they left their own localities, came with their ships ahead of the unwanted[80] Saracens, suddenly informed the blessed pontiff Leo IV of their arrival, and professed that they had come for no other reason than to win a victory with the Lord's help over the pagans.

50. Then the venerable pontiff bade some of them come on ahead to him in Rome, as he particularly wanted to know from them whether their arrival was peaceful or not; and so it happened. Among them then was one who had been appointed over the army, Caesarius by name, the son of Sergius master of the soldiers.[81] Giving them a kind reception at the Lateran palace, he inquired the motive for their arrival. They swore they had come for no other purpose than that which can be read set down above. The godly *Apostolicus* believed their account, then made his way to the city of Ostia with a great retinue of armed men, and welcomed all the Neapolitans with grand and notable devotion. **51.** When they saw the supreme pontiff they prostrated themselves on the ground at his feet, kissed them reverently, and gave thanks to the

---

[78] Unknown; probably one of the small islands on the east coast of Sardinia.

[79] Meiggs 1960:103: 'Ostia may also [*sc.* as it did to Florence, and later to Orvieto and renaissance Rome] have provided material for the cathedral of Amalfi, for the Amalfi fleet helped to defeat the Saracens near the Tiber mouth, and an Ostian inscription can still be seen in the font of a near-by church' (*CIL* 14.430).

[80] *inutiles* seems to apply to the enemy, and not to be a carping remark against the Roman allies.

[81] Sergius was Duke of Naples. His son Caesarius had already been involved in earlier struggles against the Saracens: see 104 n. 92.

Almighty throned on high, who had decided to send such a bishop to strengthen them. That they might better be the victors over the sons of Belial[82], they begged him earnestly that they might deserve to receive the Lord's body from his sacred hands. With his own lips he chanted mass for them in St Aurea's church,[83] and from his hands, as has been said, they all took communion. Before this happened, with Christ's help he made his way to that church with the Neapolitans, accompanied by hymns, litanies and distinguished chants. In it he knelt and besought the Highest that by his prayers he might see fit to hand over the enemies of christians into the hands of the defenders. His prayer was:[84] 'O God, whose right hand raised up St Peter the apostle lest he sink when walking on the water, and delivered from the depths of the sea his fellow-apostle Paul when three times shipwrecked, graciously hear us and grant that, by the merits of them both, the limbs of these thy faithful, contending against the enemies of thy holy church, may be fortified by thy almighty right hand and gain strength; that by their gaining triumph thy holy name may be seen glorious among all races; through [our Lord Jesus Christ]'.

52. Next day, after the venerable prelate had returned from that city, those allies of and consorters with evil men appeared with many ships close to the seashore of Ostia. The Neapolitans launched an attack on them, meaning to contend mightily, and even wounded some of them - and they would have been triumphant, had it not been for one hindrance that speedily occurred. This was, that while they were contending earnestly with each other a very mighty and overpowering wind was suddenly stirred up, such as no one in these times can remember, and it immediately scattered both fleets, but that of the Saracens more so. So they came to the seashore; then, with the wind blowing and the sea billowing in the storms, they were scattered, and after a time they retreated with their strength broken. Almighty God, as we truly believe, had 'brought forth this wind from his storehouse',[85] and it would not let

---

[82] 1 Sam. 1.16, 2.12, 2 Sam. 16.7, 1 Kings 21.10, 2 Cor. 6.15.

[83] Mentioned at 98:50, and in the late 7th century as repaired by Sergius I (LP 86:13 BP 86, cf. BP xxxv), St Aurea's was in the ancient cemetery of Ostia, but within the 9th-century fortifications of Gregoriopolis, and at some point it became the cathedral, presumably replacing the still undiscovered Constantinian basilica. The present building is late 15th-century. Cf. Broccoli 1982.

[84] As far as 'of them both' this prayer is the collect for the Octave of the Apostles (6 July) in the Gelasian Sacramentary (ed. L. C. Mohlberg et al., 1960, formula V946), *Gregorian Sacramentary* (ed. H. A. Wilson, 1915, 89), Triplex Sacramentary (formula 2117), etc. The original concludes: 'we may gain the glory of eternal life'.

[85] Psalm 134 (135).7.

them sally forth to cause harm. **53.** For these new and mystical wonders which in our times our true God has seen fit to display and manifest for us, though we deserve it not, his clemency is to be glorified and praised for ever, in that he let them behold the place they desired and yet the force of his power drove them far away to prevent their capturing it, and later, through the intercession and merits of SS Peter and Paul princes of the apostles, many of them were all the while extinguished not only by the depth of the sea but by hunger and the sword. Many of them were killed by our men while they endured hunger and want on certain of our islands, while others were taken alive and, to witness to the truth of the event, brought living to Rome. **54.** In case their number might appear too large, the Roman dignitaries ordered that many be hanged on trees near our Port of Rome. We ordered that some should live, bound in iron, but for one reason only, so that they could know clearer than light both our hope, which we have in God, and his ineffable piety, and also their own tyranny. After this, to stop them living among us idly or without distress, we were bidding them carry out everything, sometimes at the wall which we were beginning round St Peter the apostle's church,[86] sometimes at various manufacturers' tasks, whatever seemed necessary. **55.** These, then, as has now been told, were the advantages for which we kept them.

In St Peter the prince of the apostles' basilica after the looting by the savage race of the Agareni, he presented 13 fine silver arches; two of these, which he placed on the right and left side in the *presbyterium*, are of wondrous size, weighing .. lb. In St Peter the apostle's church this blessed prelate provided 1 gold-worked cloth, representing how St Peter preached to the holy Roman church, with 6 white jewels, i. e. pearls, and with 11 prases and 27 jacinths. In St Andrew the apostle's church he provided a marble canopy over the altar, also a silver chalice with 12 crowns hanging on that canopy, weighing .. lb. There too he built a bell-tower and installed a bell with a bronze clapper and a gilded cross. Also in St Peter the apostle's church he presented a fine gold thurible decorated with various jewels.

56. In God's mother the ever-virgin our lady St Mary's church at St Laurence's outside the wall he provided 1 cloth representing our Lord Jesus Christ's resurrection and with an image of this bountiful prelate. In the church of the SS Quattuor Coronati he provided 11 silver canisters weighing 23 lb. In St Stephen the first martyr's church[87] he

---

[86] Cf. cc. 68ff.
[87] Presumably S. Stefano Rotondo on the Caelian, not the basilica on the Via Latina.

presented a gold-worked cloth with 4 jacinth jewels.

In St Peter the apostle's church he presented a fine gold cross with various jewels, jacinths, pearls and emeralds, decorated on a wondrous scale, which stands on the right side close to the high altar; therein too he freshly renewed and silvered the rod on which this cross is held, the silver weighing 11½ lb, with an inscription of the name of lord pope Leo IV.

57. In Christ's martyr St Laurence's church outside the city of Rome's wall this bountiful and supreme prelate, led by his exceeding love and influenced by his good character, provided a fine silk cloth with eagles and with 4 gold-worked panels on each side, with a depiction of this martyr's martyrdom and the image of this prelate.

In the church of the martyrs SS Quattuor Coronati he provided 3 silver-gilt images, one with the Saviour's face, the other 2 with the faces of SS Claudius and Nicostratus, weighing 52½ lb. In the same church he presented 1 silver crown weighing 25 lb; on this church's pergola in front of the high altar he suspended a silver lily with crystal melons and a buttercup. There too he provided 7 silver canisters weighing 12 lb.

58. At his own mansion,[88] whose building from the ground up he had designed and which accrued to him from his parents' ownership, he provided a monastery for God's handmaids in honour of SS Symmetrius and Caesarius; and there he bestowed gifts, a silver-gilt holy paten and chalice with various jewels, weighing .. lb. There too he presented 1 censer with an incense-boat, weighing .. lb. In the same monastery this bountiful pontiff presented 3 fine silver canisters and 1 Saxon bowl, weighing in all 12½ lb. There too, for his soul's reward and recompense, he provided 3 gold-interwoven cloths, one of them with an inlaid needlework panel. There too he provided a fine gold diadem with jewels, prases and jacinths, which hang over the altar, weighing .. lb.

59. In God's mother the ever-virgin St Mary our lady's basilica outside this city of Rome's walls close to St Laurence's this God-protected and venerable pontiff, burning with love from on high,

---

[88] This is the monastery *de Corsas* mentioned as *Corsarum* in cc. 25, 28. The LP takes up again the account of this restoration before listing the pope's gifts. There were originally two separate monasteries (c. 25; and 98:79-80 with nn. 158-159), that *de Corsas* with its oratory of St Caesarius, and that of St Symmetrius. Comparing this passage with cc. 25, 28, we see that Leo IV united the two and installed nuns: a single community may have occupied a split site. The reference to his parents' mansion may apply strictly to St Symmetrius's only; so Duchesne, and Ferrari, 98, concurs (citing other opinions). Zucchi 1938:297-302 locates the monastery *de Corsas* across the Via Appia from S. Sisto Vecchio; the exact site of St Symmetrius's is not known.

presented 1 gold-interwoven cloth, with a gilt panel in the middle with an effigy of our Lord Jesus Christ's nativity and of this bountiful pontiff. In St Laurence the martyr's church outside the walls he presented a silver-gilt thurible with its cover, with chains and pommels round it, weighing 6 lb.

60. In God's mother the ever-virgin St Mary our lady's church in Trastevere the apse through its great age was on the point of collapse;[89] this prelate then restored it.

In St Peter the prince of the apostles' church, for that church's honour and status, he provided a fine silver cluster which hangs in the *presbyterium* in front of the high altar, weighing 138 lb.

In St Sebastian the martyr's church at Frascati he provided a fine silver canister with six lights, weighing 2 lb, with an inscription of the bountiful prelate's name and that of St Sebastian.

61. These things then were fittingly carried out and completed after the Saracens' doleful and wicked looting, and the catholic and totally praiseworthy prelate, for the splendour and praise of the church of Peter the apostle and prince of the apostles, provided a canopy of wondrous size and beauty over its venerable altar, and presented fine-silver gilt columns and lilies, weighing 1606 lb. For this canopy he presented 4 crowns with 16 chalices, of fine gold weighing .. lb, and of silver as above. For the honour and glory of this canopy he provided 46 chalices and crowns, weighing 22 lb 7 oz. Over this canopy's columns to add to their beauty he provided 4 fine silver baskets weighing 42 lb. There too, in front of the altar's circuit, he provided 12 white all-silk medallioned veils with gold-interwoven edging. Therein he presented 14 other linen veils with edging around of white medallioned silk. There too he provided 2 fine silver arches weighing 50 lb.

62. In St Silvester's oratory within the Lateran palace he provided 1 gold-interwoven cloth, with a small gold-studded panel in the middle, and 4 gold-interwoven veils. In the Jerusalem church[90] he provided 1 gold-interwoven cloth and also 4 gold-interwoven veils. In St Mary the virgin's venerable deaconry called *Aquiro* he provided a silver diadem, encircled inside with gold pommels.

In God's mother the ever-virgin St Mary our lady's church[91] at Frascati he presented 1 gold-interwoven cloth, with a small gilt inlaid panel in the middle, and 4 gold-interwoven veils. In God's mother

---

[89] It had been damaged, perhaps, by Gregory IV's remodelling of its interior, 103:31-2; but the next pope had to rebuild it entirely, 106:30.

[90] Sta Croce in Gerusalemme; so too, as 'the Sessorian', in c. 64.

[91] Vanished, and unlocatable.

Mary's church at Moreno, called Narrano,[92] he provided 1 gold-interwoven cloth and also 4 gold-interwoven veils. In St Peter the apostle's church at Marulis[93] he also offered 1 gold-interwoven cloth, with a small gilt inlaid panel in the middle, and 4 gold-interwoven veils.

63. In God's mother the ever-virgin St Mary our lady's basilica at St Laurence's outside the wall, this God-protected and venerable pontiff provided 1 linen curtain with gold-interwoven edging round it and also gold-interwoven crosses in the middle.

In SS Cosmas and Damian's church[94] at Silva Candida he presented 1 red cloth with silver edging round it and crosses in the middle, and 4 veils with eagles.

64. In St Peter the prince of the apostles' church he presented a silver crown encircled with representations outside and gilded, weighing 7 lb. In St Peter the apostle's basilica in front of the confessio of the sacred altar to right and left, this God-protected and blessed pope, relying on love from on high, presented for this basilica's beauty 6 fine silver angels weighing 64 lb.

In[95] the Sessorian he provided a canopy of olive[96] which hangs[97] round the altar, with 4 panels, gilded; also 4 chevrons. There too he provided 4 fine silver arches weighing 100 lb, which stand in the *presbyterium*.

65. In SS Cosmas and Damian's church[98] at the place called Subiaco[99] at about the 40th mile from Rome this blessed pontiff presented 1 gold-interwoven cloth and also 3 gold-interwoven veils.

In the church of Christ's martyr St Gervasius and Protasius in the city

---

[92] Cf. 104:27 with n. 52. The place would be about the 10th mile on the Via Latina. A *corte de Moreni* is mentioned here in a diploma of Agapitus II in 955 (Marini, *Papiri*, 40). The church seems to have acquired the name St Marina's: in 1116 a bull of Paschal II mentions it as such at a farm *Morene* (Duchesne I.193 n. 54).

[93] Cf. 97:76 with n. 158.

[94] See c. 29.

[95] The reference to the Sessorian in Duchesne's text depends on MS D alone; MSS CE corrupt it out of existence into *superscripto*.

[96] Apparently a canopy made of olive-wood, rather than of olive colour; cf. c. 96.

[97] The Latin verb is plural.

[98] For 'church', MSS CE have 'monastery'.

[99] The *Chronicon Sublacense* (Muratori, *R. It. SS.* 24.929; cf. n. 75) distinguishes this church from that of SS Benedict & Scholastica: 'The second abbot after St Benedict was his disciple Honoratus... At that time there had been constructed for the meeting of the community a church in honour of SS Cosmas & Damian; but later a bigger church was constructed and enlarged in honour of St Benedict and of the virgin St Scholastica.' In any case this passage of the LP should be seen in conjunction with Leo IV's other involvement at Subiaco, c. 46.

called Fondi[100] this prelate provided 1 gold-interwoven cloth with a gold-worked cross in the middle, and 1 gold-interwoven veil. In Christ's martyr St Caesarius's church[101] in the city called Terracina the same prelate presented 1 gold-interwoven cloth with a cross in the middle and chevrons and a purple fringe inscribed with the name of lord pope Leo IV, and also 5 gold-interwoven veils.

In St Peter the apostle's basilica he presented 4 fine silver arches weighing 74 lb.

66. In St Rufina the martyr's basilica at Silva Candida he provided a gold-interwoven cloth with a cross in the middle, with a fringe and purple all round, with an inscription of the name of lord pope Leo IV.

In St Clement the martyr and pontiff's church this blessed and clement prelate provided 6 fine silver bowls, three [of them] uniform in design, adorned with crosses, two with the likeness of palms, and one chased, or Saxon, weighing in all 4 lb.

In St Peter the apostle's church this blessed and distinguished pontiff provided 3 fine silver arches with columns and lilies, weighing in all 102 lb.

In St Caesarius's basilica at Terracina this venerable pontiff provided a cloth decorated with fourfold weave and with purple around it, with a gold-studded cross in the middle, with an inscription of the name of lord pope Leo IV.

In St Peter the apostle's basilica he provided 3 fine silver arches, with

---

[100] This was the basilica founded about 403 by St Paulinus of Nola on the site of a small and ruinous church (which Lanzoni, 162, suggests was of early 4th-century date and was the earliest church at Fondi). Paulinus endowed it with relics of SS Gervasius and Protasius, Nazarius and the apostles Andrew and Luke, as his verses state (*Ep.* 32.17, *CSEL* 19.291). Now known as S. Maria, it is the cathedral of Fondi.

[101] The present cathedral of Terracina. This passage is the earliest mention of it (Kehr, 1907:II.117), but the bishopric existed as early as 313, while there is a Christian inscription from the city dated to 345 (*CIL* 10.i.6419-21; 10.ii.8412-13). The Hieronymian Martyrology has Caesarius as a martyr at Terracina on 1 November (and on 21 April, but this may be a dedication to him at Rome). A 5th- or 6th-century Passion (*BHL* 1511-16) has Caesarius as a deacon of African origin, martyred under Nero with the priests Julian and Felix and a monk Eusebius, at Terracina on 1 November, after the martyrdom of the virgins Theodora and Euphrosyna. The story was compiled, perhaps by an African refugee, using names all occurring in the Hieronymian early in November and St John Chrysostom's story of the martyr Julian of Anazarbus (*BHG*[2] 967; *PG* 50.665-676). But the Passion does say that Caesarius was buried on the Via Appia (just before reaching Terracina when coming from Rome), and it was the basilica built on this site (probably long before the 9th century) which became the cathedral. A second cathedral, of St Silvanus, was located at the foot of Mte Leano on the left of the Via Appia when coming from Rome, a mile from Terracina; there is a ruined church there, on the site of a temple. The Hieronymian (10 February) has a confessor named Silvanus at Terracina (Lanzoni, 147-155).

columns and lilies, weighing 60 lb.[102]

67. In God's mother St Mary's church[103] in the city of Porto he provided 1 cloth of spanish, decorated around with gold-interweave, and a silver cross in the middle; also 3 veils of spanish, decorated around with gold-interweave.

In St Peter the apostle's church after the Saracens' looting this God-protected pontiff provided fine silver railings weighing 800 lb, which are in front of his confessio; and 4 silver-gilt panels which are on the steps in front of St Peter the apostle's confessio, and 2 lambs, which weigh altogether 44 lb. There too he presented crowns in porphyry of wondrous size, decorated in fine gold with 12 dolphins, with an inscription of the name of this bountiful prelate, the actual gold weighing 3½ lb; also 10 fine silver arches which altogether weigh 181 lb; and 48 linen veils which hang in the arches there, decorated around with gold-interweave.

68. After all that has been written above it is pleasing now to tell and unravel for an everlasting record in this present account the nature and extent of what the greatest and venerable prelate, spurred on as he was with God's zeal, with skilful and godly endeavour honourably and nobly dedicated[104] for the defence of the whole of mother church in but a short space of time. Thus it was that while all the nobility of the Romans were lamenting exceedingly over what the wicked and malevolent Saracens had just recently inflicted in their looting, for fear they might subsequently cause worse damage if St Peter the apostle's church were not speedily fortified with walls on all sides, this lovable pontiff began to have great distress for all the Romans, and anxiously to think precisely how he could remove so much sickness and fear from their hearts. 69. And when he was frequently slaving at these daily labours, by God's revelation he straightway adopted a plan of this kind:[105] to

---

[102] The repeated gifts of silver arches to St Peter's (three times in two chapters) show the undigested state of the *vestiarium* registers when they were used by our compiler. They need not be variant records of the same gift.

[103] Mentioned in the same charter of 1018 that mentions St Nympha's at Porto, c. 29.

[104] This word will have seemed appropriate because the Leonine City was dedicated on its completion (c. 73). On the city see S. Gibson and B. Ward-Perkins 1979, 1983.

[105] This is disingenuous. The idea, indeed the order, came from Lothar before the end of 846 while Sergius was still alive, though it could just be that Sergius's death delayed the matter and Leo had to intervene to get it restarted. For the date of Lothar's capitulary see 104 n. 90, where c. 2 is quoted; at a later point the text has (*MGH Cap* 2.66.30-67.2): '7. Because for our sins and offences St Peter's church has this year been laid waste and despoiled, with every desire and the greatest urgency we wish to achieve a way by which the church may be restored to prevent the pagans having access to it in future. So we decree and order this to the *Apostolicus* by our letters and envoys, that a very strong wall

elucidate this particular matter very clearly to his beloved spiritual son lord Lothar Augustus and, in this way, through his help and counsel and with the Lord willing it, [to complete] that city which his predecessor pope Leo III had begun to build over against the said apostle's church (in many places he had laid the foundations, but after his passing some men had removed them so that where this wall had previously merited its beginning not even an opening could be seen); this was the work he desired, and, if life should be his companion, with Christ comforting him, he would be willing to bring it to completion. Then the godly and serene Caesar heard about it, and he was straightaway filled with great gladness and rejoicing; he eagerly begged this prelate, who was in every way his spiritual father, to complete the building of so great a work as fast as possible with earnest effort. He and his brothers sent many pounds of silver for it, so that, as has been said, so advantageous a work should in no way remain undelivered. 70. On receiving the very message he hoped for, the distinguished prelate became extremely cheerful.

From then on he began to be mightily anxious about this business. Summoning all the faithful of God's holy church, he personally asked them for advice on how he could finish such a great construction of walls quickly; then they all decided that he should get men in general to turn up in shifts from the individual cities and all the estates, whether public or belonging to monasteries; and so it was done.[106] So in the

---

be built round St Peter's church. But we wish money for this work to be contributed from our whole kingdom, so that so great a work, pertaining to the glory of all, may be completed with the help of all. 8. The bishops will have to be admonished through the whole of lord emperor Lothar's kingdom to preach in their churches and cities, to persuade those who have no benefices yet have possessions and money, by exhorting and urging that, just as those who possess benefices are going to do, so they too should contribute from their money, for the making of a wall round St Peter the apostle's church at Rome, since it is particularly fitting for children to honour their mother and, as far as they can, guard and defend her.' *AB* 851 Nelson 73 ignores Lothar and gives Leo all the credit: 'The Saracens held Benevento and other *civitates*... undistinguished... Leo, fearing an attack of the Saracens, fortified the church of St Peter all around with a wall and continued this wall right up to the city, thus linking the church to the city of Rome.'

[106] The LP explains that the workforce was was conscripted: cities, public estates (*massae*), and monasteries all supply contingents. The public estates seem to be both the papal *domuscultae* (cf. *LECP* 31-34), and former imperial Byzantine lands in the Roman duchy, which may by now have been indistinguishable from *domuscultae*. The farmworkers were the *familia* of St Peter, organized into military units, and administered by their own officials, not under the jurisdiction of neighbouring cities. The monasteries mentioned are those whose property was otherwise juridically exempt; they are probably the three named in the *Libellus de imperatoria potestate in urbe Roma, MGH SS* 3.720, as 'fiscal patrimonies in Roman territory for imperial use': St Saviour's (Rieti), St Mary's (Farfa), and St Andrew's near Mount Soracte. Two inscriptions survive to show that different sections of the work were assigned to gangs from particular places (both now

second year of his prelacy this city began to be built; and in the sixth
year of his consecration, with all its great and wonderful constructions
the whole city was finished on every side.[107] And since by the blessed
prelate's many labours and struggles all the work on the walls had been
completed and delivered as he desired, he began to give manifold and
uncounted thanks to almighty God who saw fit to hear and fulfil his
daily prayers for the new building of the walls. **71.** No man's tongue
could briefly tell the extent and nature of the care, endeavour and
anxiety that the dutiful and praiseworthy shepherd had every day and
night while the construction was proceeding. And because he was doing
nothing else after the necessary duties of the sacred commandments
except what is set down above, truly neither cold nor blasts of wind nor
rain nor any disturbance of the air, great or small, could slow his day-
to-day movement in any way; but now here, now there, watchful and
anxious, he bustled about the various constructions of the walls, so that
our almighty Redeemer might through the godly intercession of the
apostles Peter and Paul decree the speediest fulfilment of his good plan
and desire. And now we can all see it.

72. Then at last, with all the works of the new city finished and
completed as we have frequently related, the blessed pope, who is
through and in all things praiseworthy, in order that this city (which is
called Leonine from its founder's own name) might stand strong and
firm for ever, ordered with the devotion of a great spirit and in joy of
heart that all the bishops, *sacerdotes*, deacons and all the orders of the
clergy of the holy catholic and apostolic Roman church, should, after
litanies and the chanting of the psalter, with hymns and spiritual chants,
go with him round the whole circuit of the walls, barefoot and with ash
on their heads.[108] Among other things he enjoined that the cardinal

---

mounted on the arch through which the Via di Porta Angelica passes; Duchesne I.518 n.
52, III.106). One states that a tower and stretch of wall (*pagina*) were built by the *militia
Capracorum* (a *domusculta*) under the supervision of one Agatho in Leo IV's time; the
other attributes a stretch and two towers to the *militia Saltisine*, an estate or another
domusculta, otherwise unknown.

[107] The work began in 848 and finished in 852. It must have been well advanced by 850,
as the three inscriptions (next note) mention only Lothar as emperor.

[108] The dedication procession stopped at each of the new city's three gates, the Porta S.
Peregrini (Porta Viridaria), the Posterula Castelli (the postern near Castel S. Angelo), and
finally at the postern facing the Saxon quarter. The first two of these opened onto the
Campus Neronis; one linked this with St Peter's, the other linked it with Rome by way
of the Porta S. Petri and Ponte S. Angelo. The third opened onto the road linking the
Vatican with Trastevere, the present Lungotevere Gianicolense and Via Lungara.
Inscriptions on the gates survived long enough to be copied: texts in Duchesne, or De
Rossi (*Inscr. christ.*, 2.324-6, 347; the first two, in elegiacs, also in Dümmler, *MGH Poet.
Lat. aevi Kar.* 2.663 nos. 8-9): 'Traveller who come and go, notice this beauty that Leo

bishops[109] should bless water, so that during the offices of the prayers they might be zealous in casting that water in every direction to hallow the wall as they crossed it. **73.** They humbly fulfilled what he had ordered. The venerable pontiff himself pronounced three prayers over this wall, with much weeping and sighing, asking and beseeching that this city might both be preserved for ever by Christ's aid and endure safe and unshaken from every incursion of its enemies by the guardianship of all the saints and angels. The first prayer, over the gate which looks towards St Peregrinus, begins and ends as follows:[110] 'O God, who didst confer on thy apostle Peter the keys of the kingdom of heaven and didst grant him the pontificate of binding and loosing, grant that by the help of his intercession we may be delivered from the bonds of our sins; and cause that this city which we have newly founded with thy assistance may ever remain safe from thy wrath and have new and manifold triumphs over the enemy on whose account it has been constructed; through [our Lord Jesus Christ].' This dutiful pope gave out the second prayer over the postern[111] where in wondrous fashion it overlooks the Castle called S. Angelo. Here is its text: 'O God who from the very beginning of this world hast vouchsafed to guard and

---

IV has now willingly built. These fair summits shine with shaped marble, made by men's hands and pleasing for their beauty. This triumphant prelate carried out this great work that you see in the time of unconquered Caesar Lothar. I believe that the wars of evil-minded men will never harm you, nor will your enemies triumph further. Rome, head of the world, splendour, hope, golden Rome, o nurse, behold how your prelate's effort is on display! This City is called Leonine from its founder's name.' 'Sing worthy songs, Roman, Frank and Lombard traveller, and all who notice this new work that good bishop Leo IV has rightly done for the salvation, lo, of his fatherland and people. Rejoicing and triumphing for years with the high prince, he completed that whose high honour is resplendent. May almighty God bear to heaven's citadel those whom venerable faith has overcome with such great love. It is called the Leonine City.' 'When the evil-minded race of Saracens again wished to stir up wars and cause depredations as before, God allowed a storm at sea to overwhelm some of them, while Roman soldiers took others alive and, to gain praise and everlasting memory, compelled many bound in iron to carry out various tasks in this so honourable work. Thus has the Lord performed this new wonder in the time of holy pope Leo IV and unconquered lord emperor Lothar ever Augustus.'

[109] The seven suburbicarian bishops, in practice the pope's assistants at Rome; cf. Kuttner 1945. Their sees were Ostia, Porto, Silva Candida (SS Rufina & Secunda), Albano, Labicum (later at Tusculum, then at Frascati), Palestrina, and Sabina (at Vescovio, the ancient Forum Novum, ultimately at Magliano).

[110] The original of this prayer (as far as 'bonds of our sins') was the collect on 29 June for St Peter alone in the Gelasian Sacramentary (formula V918) and for vespers that day in the Gregorian Sacramentary (88); Triplex Sacramentary formulas 540, 2087.

[111] See 97 n. 129 for Hadrian's mausoleum still being called *Hadrianium* in the eighth century. Ado's Martyrology claims that a church of St Michael was dedicated on top of the rotunda by a pope Boniface, generally taken to be Boniface IV; but there is no secure evidence for its origin. Liutprand of Cremona, 3.12, refers to such a church, Hülsen, *Chiese*, 196, Armellini-Cecchelli, *Chiese*, 956-7.

preserve this holy catholic and apostolic Roman church from enemies, forgive and cleanse the bond[112] of our iniquity, and permit this city, which we have newly dedicated in thy holy name by the intercession of thy apostles Peter and Paul, to remain ever safe and unshaken from all the snares of its enemies; through [our Lord Jesus Christ].' He chanted the third prayer over the other postern, which looks towards the Schola Saxonum and is, from their name, called the Postern of the Saxons. This prayer has this particularized[113] text:[114] 'Grant, we beseech thee, almighty and merciful God, that we who cry to thee with all our hearts may, by the intercession of St Peter thy apostle, gain forgiveness from thy piety; and for this city which I thy servant bishop Leo IV have by thy assistance dedicated with new work and which from my name is called Leonine, grant it continually to call on the clemency of thy majesty so that it may remain ever unharmed and secure; through [our Lord Jesus Christ].'

74. In this same city and on the day of the supreme solemnity, to fulfil his desire and the promise he had vowed to God, he distributed a great dispensation of money both to the Romans and to the various races, then with the rest, as has been said, of the *sacerdotes* and all the dignitaries of the Romans he headed for St Peter the apostle's church with prayers and praises of God, and he honourably sang a mass for the Safety of the People[115] in the perpetual security and stability of the city. When these sacred offices were finished, he honoured and enriched all the nobles of Rome with manifold gifts not only of gold and silver but also of silk textiles. That day there was great joy for all; it was the 27th day of June, the day before the vigils of SS Peter and Paul the apostles. And throughout the whole city of Rome there were celebrations of unbounded gladness and unmeasured rejoicing. Because of this, it is the more meet and fitting that we should continually implore the Lord almighty with our whole hearts and pure minds for such a great prelate and shepherd, through whom we know that such an admirable and honourable work had, with the comfort of Christ's power, been accomplished and completed by swift exertion for the safety of all

---

[112] *chirographum*; cf. Col. 2.14.

[113] Or 'personalized', 'specific'; the same word and sense recur in c. 80. The grammar of Leo's particular, personal or specific addition is shaky.

[114] The original of this prayer (as far as 'from thy piety') is assigned in the Gregorian Sacramentary (70) to the Major Litany on 25 April, to be said when the procession reached the atrium of St Peter's; so too Triplex Sacramentary, formula 1615; it is not in the Gelasian Sacramentary (which does not have the Major Litany).

[115] The name is semi-technical, since the proper texts of the mass for that intention began with an introit starting with the words *Salus populi*.

Christians, and also in our prayers that he may enjoy long life[116] and then, for his uncounted efforts and labours, deservedly possess eternal rewards with all the saints for ever.

75. In St Synzygius's church in the city of Blera[117] this blessed pope provided 1 gold-interwoven cloth with gold-studded panels in the middle with an effigy of the Saviour, with 3 prase jewels on his head, and of St Synzygius and of the blessed prelate; and 4 gold-interwoven veils.

In the church of the SS Quattuor Coronati he provided silver candlesticks, 1 pair, weighing 5 lb 6 oz; and 4 silver bowls weighing .. lb. In God's mother St Mary's church at St Laurence's outside the wall, he provided 27 gold-interwoven veils. **76.** In St Clement the martyr and pontiff's church this prelate provided a fine gold carved diadem, without jewels, which hangs over the high altar, with a gold cross in the middle with 5 glass jewels fixed into that cross, and 4, again of glass, which hang loose, weighing 50 *exagia*.

In St Hippolytus the martyr's church on the island called Arsis[118] at Porto, he presented 1 gold-interwoven cloth with silver-worked

---

[116] Another sign of composition while Leo IV was alive; see introduction to this life.

[117] Synzygius ('yoke-fellow', 'team-mate') as the name of a saint at Blera was explained by De Rossi as a hellenized form produced in the Byzantine period of a genuine local saint Sentias (now called St Senzia): the Hieronymian Martyrology has on 25 May 'on an island of Tuscia at the city of Blera' a group of names of which the first is Sentias (many variant readings in MSS) and another is 'Vincentius'. Delehaye (*Mart. Hieron.*) reported that municipal statutes in the archive of the commune, compiled about 1550, state that his relics were preserved in Blera's ancient cathedral, the church of St Nicholas, along with the relics of St 'Viventius'. St Nicholas could be a later dedication of the church mentioned in the LP. St Viventius's is said to be the old name of St Mary's church at Blera, which also claimed the relics of this saint, a bishop whose feast is celebrated on 11 December; as often in the Hieronymian, one local saint has attracted another away from his original day. Blera is not on an island, but the Hieronymian's reference is explicable from the saint's legend (*BHL* 7581): Sentias brought the body of St Mamilianus to the island of Egilium (Giglio), made for Blera, baptized many, and died in peace on 25 May. Nothing certain is known of the saint; Lanzoni, 522-526 (cf. 1096), thought, improbably, that a martyr had been turned into a confessor. Another version (*BHL* 7582) has Sentias go to Spoleto and die there, and the Spoletines build a basilica over his body; this is supposed to be the basilica of S. Salvatore not far from Spoleto.

[118] LP (Silvester) 34:28 BP 24 has an island called Assis between Porto and Ostia; MS E¹ there spells it Arsis as here; the form Assis is found nowhere else. The name must refer to an island in the Tiber delta near its estuary, and the church concerned is located on the present Isola Sacra (cf. 98 n. 92). Nibby (*Dintorni* 2.135) linked the name with the forest mentioned in Livy 2.7.2, where the common reading was Arsis, but the form Arsia, from one MS, confirmed by Valerius Maximus 1.8.5, is now preferred; Plutarch gives Οὖρσον ἄλσος; Dionysius of Halicarnassus has a spelling which suggests an attempt to link the name with the Horatii; Ogilvie 1965:249-250 and 413 suggests a connexion with the unique cognomen Harsa which a later tradition assigned to the early Roman tribune C. Terentilius; some Livian MSS spell the name Arsa, probably influenced by 1 Kings 16.9. Livy's locality is unknown and is unlikely to be an island in the Tiber.

chevrons; 4 gold-interwoven veils. In God's mother the ever-virgin our lady St Mary's church[119] in the city called Anagni he presented 1 gold-interwoven cloth with 4 chevrons; and 4 gold-interwoven veils.

77. In case even now, after what has been elucidated and collected above as true testimony and in clear outlines, we pass over other things in an unbecoming silence, it is pleasing to indicate step by step, briefly indeed, yet clearer than light, the blessed pope's works, as has been promised, with the aid of Jesus Christ's clemency. So when the supreme bishop's mind and spirit were ceaselessly slaving on good works worthy of God, he began to have great solicitude for the city of Porto, precisely how it could stay secure and free from enemies and the sons of Satan both in his own time and for the future. And while he was long and silently taking counsel in his pontifical heart, the almighty Father on high, who never ceases to help his faithful in righteous and godly thoughts, stirred up the minds of the Corsicans (in fear of the Saracens these were in exile from their own territory, and in their fright they were wandering hither and thither with no land of their own), that they ought to come as quickly as they could to the Roman see for refuge and safety; and so it happened. 78. Coming to the sacred home of the prince of the apostles, they were straightaway presented to our thrice-blessed lord pope Leo IV. When he and his dignitaries very sensibly interrogated them on the nature of the current need that threatened them and had caused them to come, as with one voice they declared before him in order, their needs, calamities and distress, and that they would dwell all their days in his and his successor pontiffs' retinue and service. Learning this, the benevolent prelate was immediately greatly elated with joy and gladness, and gave thanks to God who conveyed him such men, who could dwell for ever in the city of Porto. 79. So having heard their many promises, the distinguished pope together with his dignitaries replied to them clearly: 'If you will take care to carry out in fact the words you have told us, we have some very good places in which you can dwell, with the single proviso that you will be good and faithful to us and the pontiffs our successors. The city we shall give you is very strong and fortified; with our Redeemer's protecting help we have recalled it to its former condition with new gates and buildings where required. If as we have said you want to stay there, we shall grant you vineyards and lands and meadows so that you lack nothing; and we also give you what you and your women and children will be able to live on in plenty, until you get it from your own labour; also

---

[119] Anagni cathedral.

oxen, cows and other animals, as we have already stated, if you will do everything in good spirit.' **80.** Then, hearing such promises, the Corsican people were even happier, and they immediately asked the godly pontiff for envoys who could show them the city and district specifically; and so it was done. They found everything pleased them and with good will they all gave this undertaking: 'if our pope and lord sees fit to grant all that we have toured around, we will with every enthusiasm come with all our households and furnishings into the service of St Peter and of him and his successors.' When they had toured the city and all the properties, they returned with these envoys to the venerable pontiff. These envoys, as was said, came and reported the joyful and beneficial news to him, and that the race of the Corsicans had fully undertaken to live and die in these places. So all of them were summoned so that they too[120] could testify in accordance with the unanimous statements of the envoys, and he issued them a pontifical charter in accordance with the charter he had promised, to gain reward and everlasting memory both for the serene Lothar and Louis, the great emperors,[121] and for himself. The tenor and purport of the preamble were that it was to remain intact and unchanged as long as they were totally obedient and faithful to the prelates of the holy see and to the Roman people; and if, perish the idea, they did not keep the whole contents of the charter inviolably, it was laid down that it was to be null and void. **81.** The places given them and assigned by the pontifical envoys, both from the proper ownership of the church and from that of venerable monasteries, also those individuals who were their neighbours,[122] are written and can be read in the pontifical privilege granted them specifically. Lo! the oft-mentioned prelate's mercy, how

---

[120] Reading *ut ipsi* for *et ipse* printed by Duchesne.

[121] *maiores* does not seem to have a comparative force. From here on (852/3) the LP calls Louis emperor; hitherto (life 104) Lothar has been emperor, Louis merely king. Louis's anointing had been performed by Leo in 850, almost certainly on Easter Sunday, 6 April; cf. *AB* 850 Nelson 69. He is often called 'Emperor of Italy' in dating formulae and in Frankish sources such as *AB* and *AF*. Consciously or otherwise this seems to exclude rule over all the Franks. On the other hand it could be thought of as emphasizing his role within Italy and strengthening his hand when he involved himself in affairs at Rome, such as his attempt to make Anastasius pope in 855, and his presence at Nicholas's ordination in 858; cf. Schlesinger 1965:1.799; Zimmermann 1974:379-399; Nelson, *AB*, 69; Reuter, *AF*, 45.

[122] If the genitive *singulorum hominum* is to be taken seriously, this could refer to those neighbours from whom property was taken. But it had been the custom of census officials since at least the 3rd century to identify properties on the ground by mentioning neighbouring landholders, Ulpian in *Digest* 50.15.4. The practice was common sense, and can be illustrated from, e.g., the alimentary inscriptions of Veleia and Ligures Baebiani in the time of Trajan (*CIL* 11.1147; 9.1455).

great and how resplendent it was! In defending the city he not only loved his Roman dignitaries, but he invited men from wherever he could to assemble for their help and comfort: he loved the defence of the fatherland and the safety of the people entrusted to him more than temporal and transitory gain, for which, as we now recall, many have continually lost their lives along with the possessions in which they delighted.

82. After all that has been knit together above in summary fashion, the holy and venerable prelate most triumphantly accomplished other works of much the same kind. The walls and gates of the most ancient cities of Orte and Amélia had fallen to the ground through great old age and lay utterly destroyed; both thieves and robbers were easily gaining access into them, with the entrances wide open and no guard to resist them. This very skilful prelate, seeing how unconcerned the citizens of these cities were, by his encouragement and endeavour restored to their former place and condition the cities we have named, strengthening them by God's grace with walls and new gates not unlike their old ones. In these cities just mentioned, the citizens dwell more secure from the snares of their enemies; also, with the walls and gates closed, the thieves and robbers spoken of will henceforth not be able to cause any loss or theft either by night or day.

83. When these things above mentioned were diligently completed, he provided in the church of the SS Quattuor Coronati 1 fine gold diadem, hanging over the high altar, with chains also of gold, carved with a gold cross in the middle with 14 jewels, five of which are fixed in that cross, while the other nine hang loose there, of which six are pearls and three are jacinths, weighing in all 1 lb ½ oz.

In God's mother St Mary our lady's basilica in the Vicus Sardorum[123] he presented a silver-gilt chalice and paten, 1 pair, with an inscription of the name of lord pope Leo IV, altogether weighing 4 lb 5 oz.

84. When he had completed uncounted works of supreme beauty in the Keybearer of heaven's basilica, this noteworthy and distinguished prelate set up the doors which the wicked Saracen brood had destroyed and stripped of their silver; and he adorned them with many silver panels carved with brilliant and wholesome representations, and repaired them to a condition more beautiful than before; so that all who come to enter this basilica give praises to almighty God and to his holy prelacy, and pray that the many revolving years of life be extended for him who, by a work of such great splendour and such a great weight of beauty,

---

[123] Duchesne prints *Sardonum*, but it is presumably the same as the Vicus Sardorum in c. 11 (*q.v.*) and c. 86; and MS C has *Sardorum* here.

has decorated God's hall with silver weighing 70 lb. At the beginning of his pontificate, since the porticoes on the left side[124] of St Peter's basilica had fallen through extreme age, this supreme God-beloved pontiff renewed them more distinctively with speedy endeavour; and he brilliantly renewed the roofing of this distinguished church with great beams raised up with defiant craftsmanship. **85.** As he saw that the portico adjoining St Andrew's church was about to collapse, he freshly restored and improved it. Relying on unbounded love, he renewed and decorated the vault which is seen in front of the said hall's silver doors.[125] And he performed many kinds of godly activity in that church; if we were fain to put them in writing, the tongue would not suffice to tell nor the joints of the writers' fingers have strength to endure.

So when he was accomplishing many notable works in various of God's churches, this blessed pontiff renewed to a greater beauty and strength the portico[126] in front of God's holy mother's basilica close to St Laurence's basilica outside the walls.

86. In God's holy mother's church at Vicus Sardorum at the 30th mile from Rome he presented 4 catholic books: the Gospels, the Kingdoms,[127] the Psalter, and the Homilies.

In St Martin the confessor and pontiff's church outside St Peter the apostle's gate, 1 silver canister with chains, weighing 4 lb 2 oz. In the church of the SS Quattuor Coronati he provided 2 fine silver censers weighing 2 lb 1 oz. In St Petronilla's church he provided 3 gold-interwoven cloths and 12 veils, 4 of them gold-interwoven, 3 of spanish and 5 of linen. In God's mother St Mary's church which this blessed pontiff newly constructed from the ground over the Schola Saxonum, he presented 3 gold-interwoven cloths, also 4 gold-interwoven veils.

87. In St Peter the apostle's basilica this blessed pontiff provided 27 silvered candles, which stand in the *presbyterium*, weighing in all 40 lb. At the entrance and in the middle of the *presbyterium* he coated the

---

[124] Krautheimer, *Corpus* 5.175, suggests that left here means north. More naturally, one approaches St Peter's from the east, and left means south. At the beginning of the next chapter the portico at St Andrew's is certainly on the south side of St Peter's. Porticoes may refer to the roofing of the aisle or to buildings attached outside.

[125] The portico immediately outside St Peter's.

[126] Krautheimer, *Corpus* 2.138, remarks that, given the site of the *basilica maior* on the Verano (there was no entrance portico, as the people entered through doors in the apse), this passage might refer to the portico which came from the city at the Porta Tiburtina and finished in front of the apse. The earliest references to this are 91:12 and 97:74 (Gregory II and Hadrian I rebuilt it), but it may have been of the same 5th-century date as the porticoes leading to St Peter's and St Paul's (*id.* 2.12).

[127] 'Kingdoms' is the name in the Septuagint of the four books (called 'Kings' in the Vulgate) generally known as 1 and 2 Samuel, 1 and 2 Kings.

beams with fine silver weighing 67 lb 3 oz. While he was inflamed with enthusiasm for the heavenly fatherland and was decorating Christ's churches in order with precious metals and ornaments, he next provided many other things in St Peter the apostle and prince's hall: 1 fine silver crown with 4 silver chains, with 42 dolphins, weighing in all 13 lb. Ever relying on Christ's help and inspired by God, this pontiff provided round St Peter the apostle's altar 4 green silk veils with gold-studded panels, with an effigy of the Saviour and of the apostles Peter and Paul and of the bountiful prelate himself, and in the middle gold-studded crosses and chevrons with roundels in which are images of the apostles adorned with wondrous beauty; on feast days they are hung there to give splendour. **88.** There too he provided other white all-silk veils with roses, wondrously adorned with lattice-work, overshadowing the Easter ceremonies. He presented another small crown there with 4 chains and 10 dolphins, with a lily and a hook, weighing 2 lb. This blessed prelate's mind being ever devoted as a lion,[128] he endeavoured with enormous love to adorn Jesus Christ's churches with precious ornaments, to gain salvation and everlasting life. He did what none of his predecessor pontiffs had thought to do: no doubt fervent with and compelled by the Holy Ghost, he decreed the making of fine gold crowns, resplendent with the noble faces of Christ and the saints, for Peter the prince of the apostles' church, close to the altar under which his sacred body rests; he decreed that two of them be made, to hang on right and left, adorned with gold chains and pommels and prase jewels, with 60 dolphins in all, and weighing 20 lb. **89.** In the same church he provided a silver crucifix, depicted with wondrous work, which shines with great beauty and is placed on the left side when going in,[129] between the great columns, weighing 62½ lb. In St Andrew the apostle's oratory which adjoins St Peter's church this blessed pontiff of the supreme see provided 1 silk cloth representing eagles, with in the middle a gold-studded panel on which there shine images depicting Christ and his disciples on right and left, and the bountiful prelate himself.

After similarly completing all the work with beautiful adornments in

---

[128] A play on words with the pope's name.

[129] Or 'of the entrance'. But the eastern end of the Constantinian nave near the entrance was not demolished until 1605, and the cross here mentioned seems to be one that was rescued from the western part demolished by Julius II nearly a century earlier. The cross is mentioned by various 16th-century authors. It was nearly 3 metres high and 2½ metres wide; only the figure on it was silver, and was almost life-size (1.54 m). It escaped the pillaging of Charles V's army in 1527, but the canons had it melted down in 1550 (see Duchesne, and Cascioli as cited in Duchesne III.124).

the church of the SS Quattuor Coronati, he provided a cloth of the same silk with a gold-studded panel, representing the miracle which the Lord Christ worked to satisfy abundantly 5000 men with sustenance from 5 loaves and 2 fishes.[130]

90. Amidst all these things written above, the oft-named holy prelate began frequently to have especial care and anxiety about the individual rulers of churches, that is bishops, priests, deacons and all the militia of christians. So he wished, as in fact happened, to set before them with Christ's help a new norm from the ancient authorities,[131] on how each of them should lead a chaste and sober life and should in every way please God, to whom we owe it to present an ever blameless service. Then, with the Holy Ghost's grace revealing it to him, and on the advice of the serene emperors Lothar and Louis, in the 30th and in the 5th year of their emperorship and the 7th year of this prelate's pontificate, on the 8th day of December in the 2nd indiction [853],[132] he assembled a holy and venerable synod in St Peter the apostle's church. 91. At it, this catholic and apostolic man and another 67 bishops[133] were in session with him, four of whom were sent by the emperors, Joseph of Ivrea, Nottingus of Brescia, Peter of Spoleto and another Peter of Arezzo. With them in session also was Paul, deacon of the holy church of Ravenna, taking the place of his archbishop John, not counting the priests, deacons and clergy of holy mother church. Then he ordered that the deacons[134] of the holy and universal apostolic see should read before them all 42 chapters which are acknowledged as surely pertaining to the salvation and gain of all christian men. He bade that these chapters be written into the holy canons after the other decrees of the pontiffs, as to be kept inviolate by all in time to come, so that all bishops would have the example of this authority before their eyes and could better instruct and educate their subjects. 92. Then after other matters at this synod Anastasius,[135] cardinal priest of St Marcellus's *titulus*, was canonically

---

[130] Matthew 14.13-21, Mark 6.32-44, Luke 9.10-17, John 6.1-15.

[131] Mainly, it seems, pope Eugene II who held a council in 826; see the introduction to life 101. The council of 8 December 853 issued 42 canons (Mansi 14.1009-1016), 38 of which were repeated with slight additions from the earlier council (14.999-1009).

[132] The dating formulae here given were copied from the Acts of the council, though these rightly give '37th' for '30th' as Lothar's regnal year. But both the Acts and the LP give Louis II's regnal year as 5th; it should be '4th' (cf. n. 120). *AB* also garbles the regnal years as the '42nd' of both emperors (Nelson 147).

[133] The Acts have 67 bishops' signatures, if those of the pope and of the representatives of absentees are counted. The five persons named here head the list. One of the priests present was the next pope, Benedict III (cf. 106:2 n. 3).

[134] Named in the acts as Benedict and Nicholas; the latter would be pope in 858.

[135] Mansi 14.1017-21. On his career to this point see the introduction to this life.

deposed by them all because he had deserted his *paroecia* for 5 years against what the canons lay down, and is even today[136] dwelling in foreign parts. He had been unwilling to come to two councils assembled for his case, neither when summoned by apostolic letters nor when summoned by three bishops, Nicholas, Petronacius and John,[137] so the holy synod unanimously and deservedly deposed him and deprived him of sacerdotal office in accordance with what the sacred canons contain concerning such matters, in the year, month, day and indiction above noted.

93. After this council's excellent sentence, this prelate's blessed mind, ever inflamed with the fire of heavenly love, again began to have great endeavour for the restoration of the adornments of all the equipment of God's churches. In the church of St Peter the kingdom of heaven's keybearer he provided 1 fine silver lantern with 2 wicks, weighing 16 lb. In St Martin's monastery which adjoins this church of the prince of the apostles, he provided another lantern cast in silver and with 2 wicks, weighing 27½ lb; and in SS John and Paul's monastery[138] he provided another silver lantern like the above ones, weighing 22½ lb; these stand close to the lectern on Sundays and feastdays and shine with very bright light for reading the sacred lessons. **94.** This holy pope provided railings cast in silver with lattice-work at the entrance to the *presbyterium* and in front of the confessio of his beloved St Peter the apostle; radiant with beautiful splendour they provoke admiration in the minds of men; two of them weigh 642 lb, the other two 630 lb.

And in St Vincent's church at Frascati[139] he presented 1 gold-interwoven cloth.

95. But as we have often said this serene prelate's mind was filled

---

[136] Perhaps another sign of composition while Leo IV was alive; the words imply that Anastasius had not yet returned and made his attempt to become pope. But the LP may merely be paraphrasing Leo's speech at the council (Mansi 14.1007). Leo uses *paroechiae* for Anastasius's current location (Aquileia), not for his *titulus* in Rome.

[137] Leo also names these three bishops without specifying their sees. Present at the council (Mansi 14.1018) were Nicholas of Anagni, Petronacius (or Petronax) of Albano, and seven bishops named John. If the three are named in the same order of precedence as at the council, the choice for John's see is reduced from seven to three; and if he was from near Rome he will have been bishop of Falerii (Città Castellana).

[138] On this monastery (at St Peter's) see 98 n. 137.

[139] Otherwise unknown, but the LP's phrase is the same as that used in this life to describe two other churches at Frascati (St Sebastian's, cc. 37, 60, and St Mary's, c. 62). Hence Duchesne rejected the notion that this church was the chapel of St Vincent immediately north of St Peter's, which Maffeo Vegio in the 15th century styled 'the temple of St Vincent called by the ancients by the name of Frascati'. Vegio's 'ancients' are unidentified; if he had read the present text he might have wrongly assumed that St Vincent's was close to St Peter's which has just been mentioned.

with great love for St Peter the blessed prelate and apostle, prince of the apostles, and he ever desired to carry out many adornments of his supreme church, whose throne by God's dispensing power he ruled. Thus he provided over his holy altar a gold-studded cloth representing in the middle the Saviour, amidst angels with shining faces, giving the keys of the kingdom to Peter the apostle, and resplendent on right and left with the glorious passion of Peter and Paul; between them is depicted this prelate presenting the city which at Peter's intercession he had ordered to be built, glistening with a cross in gold and jewels; and around and above the altar there are textiles, silk on top, worked with a precious representation of eagles, two of which are gilded. There too he presented 4 veils with gold-studding, on which the prelate himself is depicted, with the Saviour's image shining among angels' faces, presenting the city he had completed from the ground up.

96. As we have albeit briefly now fully described the adornments this pontiff presented to St Peter's church, let us now for an everlasting record endeavour to give a summary notification of what he wrought in the church of St Paul the apostle, teacher of the gentiles, after the ungodly looting of the Agareni.[140] Over his holy body he provided a canopy of wondrous beauty with a huge weight of silver, embellished with silver columns, weighing 946 lb.

But although the pontiff with kind intention bestowed various ornaments with enormous desire, both before and subsequently, on the generality of churches, he was always concerned to present to St Peter something excellent and more beautiful; so he presented him with three olive *masoricae* of admirable beauty, worked in silk and colourfully embroidered, which on feast days hang around the high altar.

97. In St Marcian's church in the *domucella*[141] called Balnearola he provided 1 gold-interwoven cloth and 2 spanish veils.

In Christ's martyr the deacon St Laurence's church he presented 24 gold-interwoven veils which hang in the arches between the great columns.[142]

In St Clement the martyr and pontiff's church he provided a silver

---

[140] Something is at last said to fulfil the promise made in c. 13; yet the compiler reverts to St Peter's almost immediately, and repairs to St Paul's shrine itself had to wait, it seems, until the next pontificate (106:22).

[141] *domucella* seems to be a variant for *domusculta*. Lanzoni, 529, thought that this church might be St Marcian's at Bracciano, dated archaeologically to the 8th or 9th century, and with the oldest campanile near Rome; there is also an ancient cemetery there. Identifying the St Marcian concerned is an insoluble problem.

[142] The columns on either side of what is now the choir at S. Lorenzo fuori le mura (rather than of the Constantinian basilica which by this date was called St Mary's).

handbasin, 1 pair, with, engraved in them, the likeness of a man's head with a vine, and another representation, weighing 3 lb.

98. In God's mother St Mary's church[143] at Aurelia, called 'on the Via Aurelia', this blessed and bountiful prelate presented 1 gold-interwoven cloth. There too, in St Stephen's church he presented 1 other gold-interwoven cloth.

Protected by the right hand on high and ever devoted to God's service, and persevering with sincere mind after many good actions, this distinguished and bountiful prelate adorned and painted in beautiful colours SS Silvester and Martin's church[144] which his predecessor lord Sergius had newly built from its lowest walls; even today its great beauty provokes admiration in human eyes. He coated and adorned its venerable holy altar with fine silver weighing 116 lb.

99. So after the magnificent prelate accomplished with all his mind's devotion the beautiful and praiseworthy works of God's various churches, [he was concerned] in case the christian people in the *castrum* of Centumcellae should continue to perish at the hands of the enemy as was often wont to occur. For 40 years[145] the *castrum* had remained with its walls destroyed and abandoned by its occupants. These had left their own residences for fear of the Saracens until the present, and the people they had left behind, in the manner of beasts, set up their dwellings in woodland glades and untracked mountains; even there, for fear of their enemies day and night, they continued to have no sleep for their eyes nor any bit of rest in the normal human way. **100.** When this so dutiful and praiseworthy prelate was daily grieving for their burden and their quite intolerable, immeasurable and unbelievable distress, with many tears and uncounted prayers he assiduously besought the Lord, the creator of all things, to see fit by the gift of his grace to show him where the city of Centumcellae could be moved to for the safety and deliverance of this christian people. He made his way to it, and with diligent care and endeavour he saw and inspected the areas which adjoined and bordered it. But when a suitable place was seen for building a city, it had a shortage of water, which for men is always very necessary. After traversing all the areas, as we have said, he came at

---

[143] Duchesne thought that this church and the next must have been on an estate in the *domusculta Galeria* (cf. 97:55 with n. 98). They are probably those listed in a bull of John XIX (J4076, December 1026; Marini, *Papiri,* 75) among the churches of the see of Silva Candida: *titulum s. Stephani in Matera, titulum s. Marie in Matera.*

[144] Cf. 104:39 and n. 73. This is the last literary record of the church before 1201.

[145] The figure seems exact. Cf. *ARF* 813 (cited at 100 n. 77); the new city was dedicated on 15 August 854 (c. 103).

length, by the favour of God's mercy, to a place that was excellent and mightily protected, over which his heart was greatly widened,[146] because it provided a supply of water to comfort the people, and other human needs, and water-mills grinding at full capacity. **101.** For the venerable pontiff's memory and praise it is worthwhile that all people should truly believe and know exactly how it was that God's clemency showed him this work which he long investigated and brought to a conclusion through God's counsel and consultation.

One night, when the distinguished bishop lay as usual on his bed and was as normal thinking of God's works, he was transported in his dreams to a place foreseen and pre-ordained, at the 12th mile[147] from Centumcellae; and to a certain Peter, master of the soldiers, as if he were physically present in the actual vision, he indicated one by one the several places where with the pontiff's help he was to found and construct the churches and the gates, and showed him that, thanks to the narrowness of the place, only two gates had to be constructed there. In this secret vision he drew its design with his own fingers. **102.** When day came, he began to have great solicitude about the dream he had seen, and immediately ordered this Peter to come to his presence. He related to him everything he had seen in his dreams and provided him with many mancuses[148] in silver so he could speedily achieve the taking of the people there, by going with them to the replacement for the city of Centumcellae.

By God's favour everything was built and is now resplendent, just as the praiseworthy pope designed it with his own hand in his dream; from his own name he gave it the name Leopolis. After they had begun the building, he came to it with a triumphant multitude of his faithful to see and contemplate the construction. When he saw the gates and churches in those precise areas just as he had shown them, and that his own

---

[146] For the expression *animus dilatatus* cf. perhaps 2 Cor. 6.11.

[147] The place concerned is now Cencelle, on the north of the road from Civitavécchia to Tarquinia. As at the Leonine City, inscriptions were placed over the gates; one survives (Marucchi, *Nuovo Bull.*, VI, 1900, 202), with the monogram of Leo and four lines of verse: 'Though this city is founded within a small wall, none of men's wars shall be able to harm it; now let the savage warrior desist from it, let the enemy desist, so that no one can violate this city.' In 889 when security was restored, the inhabitants returned to their old site but left the old city name at the newer site (the name Leopolis seems to have had no more success than the name Gregoriopolis at Ostia); they referred to the old, reoccupied, site as Civitas Vetula, whence Civitavécchia. At the abandoned site, traces of the towers, walls, buildings and roads have been made out (Guglielmotti 1896:I.57; Lauer 1900:147 and plan).

[148] A mancuse is a gold coin (cf. 97:77 with n. 161 and 104:43 with n. 78). The text may mean that Leo provided the equivalent in silver.

desire was fulfilled by Christ's protection, he therefore gave boundless thanks to the almighty Lord, who had seen fit to show him such a place where the people might be safe and where there was an abundant supply of water, and who had even bestowed stones and sand so that the newly constructed buildings could achieve greater size without labour by the workmen. **103.** Gladdened by all this, the pontiff toured round the city of Leopolis on his own feet with litanies and prayers; with three prayers, representing the Trinity, he consecrated it for ever, and he solemnly performed the office of mass as was customary, and bade that blessed water be cast around the walls. Through the greatness of his love he distributed with his own hands no small dispensation of money to all the people; he commended to the Lord almighty the people and the city that God had shown, that the enemy may never capture or occupy it. With all this achieved, he returned to his residence with great joy and alacrity, now that the entire circuit of the walls had been completed and accomplished by Christ's help in the eighth month and on the fifteenth day, in the eighth year of his prelacy and in the second indiction [854].

104. In the churches he built there he presented many gifts: in St Peter's church,[149] 7 large and small bowls cast in silver, weighing in all 16 lb 1 oz; 1 gilded chandelier; 3 gilded beakers; 5 large and small clasped garments; 1 silver-gilt cross with 1 jewel; 1 other gold cross with a *monocossis* in the middle; and another silver cross with 40 jewels; 1 gold gilt[150] thurible; 1 Saxon *dextra*; 12 gold crowns; 1 bowl and 2 ostrich-eggs.[151] In the same church in this city he provided 2 silk cloths, one of which has a gold-studded panel in the middle and the other has a cross and 4 roundels, with chevrons, in the middle; and 18 gold-interwoven veils; a fine silver crucifix weighing 7 lb.

105. There too, in St Leo's church he presented 1 gilt paten, 1 silver chalice, 2 cloths, one of which is gold-interwoven, decorated around with all-silk, with in the middle a gold-studded wheel and chevrons, and the other is of spanish. Also 7 codices of catholic [books]: the Histories, a Solomon,[152] an Antiphonary and a Psalter, a Sacramentary, the Acts[153]

---

[149] This was the dedication of the only church recorded at the old site of Centumcellae (100:26).

[150] *aureum exauratum*; perhaps an error for *argentum exauratum*.

[151] Perhaps, as in Coptic churches, a symbol or rebirth and resurrection, an ostrich being more easily obtained than a phoenix.

[152] The various 'wisdom' literature of the Old Testament and Apocrypha.

[153] Of saints, not the Acts of the Apostles.

and the Homilies, and a Gospel with silver panels[154].
He adorned God's sacred altar over St Peter the apostle's holy body
with silver and gilded sheets on right and left with the miracles of that
prince of the apostles; they now glisten with great beauty like the stars
of heaven, and weigh in all 84 lb 5 oz.

106. After this holy pope, inspired by the divine clemency of the
everlasting God, had done in various places for the safety of Christians
such noteworthy deeds and immeasurable activity, for his great love of
the heavenly fatherland he took care every day to adorn the holy Roman
church, which is, as the Lord said, founded on a firm rock and is
gloriously resplendent from the holy name of St Peter the prince of the
apostles, with precious decoration of every metal. There too[155] he
completed a silver lectern engraved with exquisite craftsmanship and
standing on four feet; at the top of it there gleams the head of a lion;
and it weighs 31 lb 11 oz. As for the 4 wooden candles which used for
a long time to be set up on feastdays in the sacred middle of the
pontiffs' *presbyterium*, he wisely decided to coat them with fine silver
and established that they stay set up there permanently; no predecessor
of his had thought of doing this; they weigh 55 lb in all. **107.** There
too he provided great silver candlesticks, 1 pair, weighing 48 lb 10 oz,
on which are set fine silver lanterns with 2 wicks, shining close to the
high altar, weighing in all 49 lb; and 7 other silvered candlesticks,
weighing 25 lb 3 oz; he also provided 7 other dark iron candlesticks
with silver on top, weighing 21 lb 3 oz. On the altar itself he provided
a gold-worked cloth, shining all over with white pearls, with jewelled
panels on right and left, with gold roundels around it, on which this
prelate's noteworthy name is inscribed.

108. St Martin's monastery was about to collapse through long old
age; he restored it with wondrous buildings of houses, and he
thoroughly adorned it to better honour than it was before.[156] In it [he

---

[154] How this adds to 7 is not clear. The Acts and Homilies are more likely to have been
separate volumes than the Psalter and Antiphonary.

[155] In St Peter's presumably.

[156] This in spite of the fact that Leo III is claimed to have virtually rebuilt it, 98:90;
perhaps it had suffered when the Saracens attacked St Peter's in 846. But there is further
evidence that Leo IV showered privileges on St Martin's, his own former monastery. On
10 August 854 (very close to the presumed date of the present chapter) he issued a bull
confirming its very extensive possessions (J2653; Marini, *Papiri*, 14-15; Schiaparelli
1901:432-6 no. 2; Ferrari, 232, no. 12, with 236). Leo describes St Martin's as behind the
apse at an entrance into St Peter's (there was an entrance to the choir of St Peter's beside
the apse, in front of St Martin's). He confirms its right to the following: St Saviour's
church for the burial of all pilgrims, the churches (St Mary's, St Michael's and St Justin's)
of the three *Scholae* of Saxons, Frisians and Lombards, St Zeno's church (Hülsen, *Chiese*

presented] a white roseate cloth, with roses and the Saviour with the apostles and the Virgin, inscribed with the name of lord Leo IV; also 5 white roseate veils, one of them with 13 small jewels; 3 silver-gilt almonds. In the church of the SS Quattuor Coronati he provided 1 gold-interwoven cloth.

Also, in St Peter the prince of the apostles' basilica this supreme and orthodox pontiff, prompted by God's inspiration, provided 83 fine silver chalices which hang beneath the main arch and between the great columns on right and left, weighing in all 441 lb. There in front of the vestibule of the sacred altar he built a beam of wondrous beauty which, after the dire race's wicked looting, he adorned with fine silver; on it are set God's holy and venerable images, weighing 60 lb.

109. In St Peter the apostle's church in the city of Leopolis he presented 1 silver-gilt thurible. In God's mother St Mary's church in the Vicus Sardorum, a silver-gilt bowl with a canister, weighing .. lb.

In the venerable Jerusalem monastery[157] close to St Peter the apostle's church he provided a gold-interwoven cloth with roundels, and decorated around with gold-studded edging and 2 *mizine* veils and 3 gold-interwoven ones. This God-protected, venerable and distinguished pontiff provided the *propitiatorium* for St Peter the prince of the apostles' sacred altar where his holy body rests, *spanoclist*, with 72 lb silver and 80 lb gold.

110. In his time[158] one Daniel, master of the soldiers, blinded with a heap of iniquity and stupidity, made his way to the serene footsteps of the emperor lord Louis, and had no hesitation in saying many false, unnecessary and utterly incredible words about Gratian,[159] the eminent

---

502) with houses, etc., 'in this our new Leonine City'; various holdings outside the Porta S. Petri on the Via Clodia at the 4th and 5th mile; lands on the Via Aurelia outside the same gate; St Sebastian's monastery and its property in the city of Centumcellae; lands on the Via Appia in the territory of Velletri; others on the Via Clodia at the 5th mile; others with St Valentine's oratory at Orvieto at the 25th mile; two hospices near St Peter's, and three oratories in the basilica, those of St Xystus *iuxta ferrata*, of St Leo, and of St Hadrian. Ferrari, 236, comments: 'Without doubt this bull represents the high point of the monastery's history, when its influence and wealth were matched by few others.'

[157] See 98 n. 164.

[158] There is no other source for these events. But there are many other traces of political tensions between Leo and Louis II; see the introduction to this life.

[159] In a letter to Louis in September 852, Leo reported on the behaviour of a man of this name (J2620, *MGH Ep* 5.585 no. 1): 'Gratian has not feared to kill many men with steel, water and clubs, and, what is worse, has bound many men with oaths of loyalty to himself, a thing which as you well know it is permitted to none but the emperor or the pope to do'. This is probably not the same man; if he is the same, his relations with the pope must have changed or he would not now be *superista*. At 106:11 his title is expanded to '*superista* of the sacred patriarchate', i.e. chief of the pope's military guard

master of the soldiers and outstanding *superista* and counsellor. He persistently accused him out of envy and falsehood; he told the emperor: 'Gratian, *superista* of the city of Rome, whom you believe loyal to you, said to me privately when I was alone in his house and he was murmuring a lot about the Franks, that the Franks do no good for us and give us no help, but instead they violently steal what is ours. Why do we not call on the Greeks, strike a peace treaty with them and expel the king and race of the Franks from our kingdom and lordship?' Hearing this, the said emperor was inflamed with unbounded fury, and without even sending letters to the Roman pontiff and senate he took care to come speedily to Rome. As is customary, when he came, lord pope Leo was seated at the top of the great steps of St Peter the apostle's. He received him honourably and began to appease[160] him with sweet words of preaching.

111. One day, the emperor and the holy pontiff Leo were in session with all the Roman dignitaries and the noble Franks, in the house[161] which pope Leo III of blessed memory had built close to St Peter the apostle's church, and he held a law sitting about that accusation. Then Daniel, putting on a wicked front and imbued with false thought, publicly stated: 'This Gratian asked my advice about stealing this land of Rome from your power and handing it over to the Greeks.' Straightaway not only Gratian but all the Romans said before the emperor: 'You liar! There is no word of truth in what you say'. **112.** The emperor and all the nobility of the Romans and Franks realized that this Daniel had uttered such a charge against Gratian out of falsehood and envy, and immediately the clement emperor, unwilling to contravene what had been laid down by the Roman emperors of old, laid down that they should try him under Roman law. In this trial Daniel himself was trapped by the words of many and he showed by his own speech that what he had stated about him was false. So he was publicly handed over to Gratian, so that he could have power to do with

---

at the Lateran, by now the centre of government. Lay and clerical judges held courts there, as is shown, e.g., by Leo's letter written when he was leaving for Ravenna about May 853 (J2633, *MGH Ep* 5.599 no. 23): 'We order that in our absence neither the order of the church nor that of the palace should stop, but on the set days all the nobles are to attend at the Lateran palace just as if we were here, and see to law and justice for those who ask and require it'. The *Libellus de imperatoria potestate* (*MGH SS* 3.720) also speaks of a 'place of judgment in the Lateran, where a particular place is named At the Wolf called the mother of the Romans' (the bronze wolf now on the Capitol was kept in a room in the Lateran).

[160] This implies that in Leo's mind Louis would assume not merely the truth of Gratian's alleged disloyalty but also that Gratian had Leo's support.

[161] Cf. 98:27 and n. 68.

him whatever he wished. But when Daniel had already been handed over, the emperor asked Gratian for him with much humble supplication. Gratian immediately gave him over freely, full favour was restored to him, and he was in this way delivered from the peril of death.[162]

113. These things accomplished, the emperor departed; and not many days later holy lord pope Leo IV fell asleep in the Lord, 17 July. He was buried in St Peter's.[163] He performed two ordinations, one in December, the other in March, 19 priests, 8 deacons; for various places 63 bishops.[164]

---

[162] Daniel, having failed to secure the Gratian's conviction, had been subjected under Roman law to a counter-charge of *calumnia* (malicious prosecution) from Gratian; he was convicted, but saved from Gratian's vengeance by Louis, who wanted to protect his over-loyal supporter, and thereby, no doubt, to encourage the reporting of any treasonable activity.

[163] Cf. n. 201 to 98:113.

[164] One of these bishops was Athanasius of Naples, ordained at the altar of St Gregory on 15 March (presumably in 851, when it was a Sunday), *Vita Athanasii* 3, *MGH SSrL* 442.

106. BENEDICT III (855-858).

The anonymous author of this life began his work, it seems, almost as soon as Benedict was ordained; the same writer would be responsible for the first draft of life 107. Both lives follow the method of the author of 105 of repeating a eulogy of the pope after dealing with his ordination and before excerpting the register material (105:18, 106:20, 107:10). But unlike the author of 105, the new author, for all his execrable grammar, makes an attempt at Latin style, partly through the use of favourite words (such as *parvipendere*, four times), but especially through the use of inversion, which is carried out to a point at which maladroit phrasing can destroy the sense of what he is writing. He had interesting events to record. After a summary of Benedict's early career (cc. 1-3), he gives a detailed account of the challenge launched against Benedict by Anastasius who was elected pope at Orte, the conflict between the Roman clergy and Louis II's envoys who supported Anastasius's claim, and the victory and ordination of Benedict (cc. 4-20). For all its bias against Anastasius, the story is quite well treated except for the failure to give either the details of the negotiations on the future of Benedict, Anastasius and others in c. 19 (see n. 45), or the dates of any of the events. In the former case details may have been concealed lest the wrong impression about Benedict be given. The latter case is simply negligence, and it makes precision over Benedict's dates impossible (see n. 1).

What is remarkable is that this compromising account of Anastasius's actions has survived at all. After Benedict's death Anastasius returned to papal favour and influence as secretary to Nicholas and librarian under Hadrian II. The explanation can only be that the account was written while Benedict was alive and the author was free, and that his work was disseminated widely as soon as it was written, as papal lives seem to have been, so that its destruction after 858 was no longer feasible. Yet an attempt at suppression may have been made. Of the four manuscripts which have the full text of the lives of Leo IV's successors, C^4, the oldest, omits all from 105:109 to the end of this life, and in another, E^6, the episode of Anastasius has been suppressed by the omission of everything from the last five words of c. 5 through to 'the elected one, blessed Benedict' in c. 18; these lacunae cannot be fortuitous.

The rest of the life, cc. 21-35, is almost entirely devoted to details of the restorations of churches and the gifts of vessels, lights, images, books and textiles: much was done in a short pontificate. St Paul's, neglected under Leo IV, at last got the attention it required after the Saracen incursion of 846 (cc. 22, 26-28, 31). Otherwise c. 23 recounts the flood of the Tiber in January 856, and cc. 33-34 mention gifts sent by the emperor Michael and those presented by Æthelwulf king of Wessex. Finally c. 36 mentions Benedict's decree on clerical funerals, the ordinations he conducted, and his burial. Geertman suggests a chronology for cc. 21-35; this should not be extended beyond c. 32 (see below). Annual headings are inserted at the appropriate places.

The account of Benedict's pontificate after his ordination is inadequate, and few details are known from elsewhere. In the next life, c.4, we are told that in his administration Benedict had relied heavily on his successor Nicholas (who had been a deacon in the service of the Lateran since the time of Leo IV). There is some exaggeration here; when policies were similar (as they clearly were in some matters, for example, marriage discipline and the case of Engeltrude), and when Nicholas appeared more energetic than his predecessor, it could later be assumed by a eulogist for Nicholas that he had already been the policy-maker. That the same impression of continuity is current today is partly because much of what we know about Benedict's policies is reconstructed from Nicholas's writings, and Nicholas would have tended to gloss over differences from his predecessor's policies and emphasize similarities. Quite certainly the policy towards Anastasius did not remain the same.

Nicholas's life also contains further details about the circumstances of Benedict's death: Louis II had just left Rome, and returned there when the news reached him. But on relations between the Carolingians and Benedict after his ordination the present life is silent. The death of Lothar on what was (probably) the very day of Benedict III's ordination made little difference at Rome, since for some years the old emperor had left Italian affairs to Louis II. Yet just as Louis had just tried to interfere in the papal succession, so Benedict now had an opportunity in the interests of peace to intervene in the disposition of the empire, and with, at least temporarily, rather more success. Louis had been dissatisfied with the arrangements his father Lothar had made, and from early 856 he complained to his uncles Louis the German and Charles the Bald. It may have been Louis who invited papal involvement. His brother Lothar II agreed to meet him, and brought with him the old emperor's third son Charles (of Provence) to a meeting at Orbe in Valais (canton Lausanne) in early October 856. Louis II and Lothar II nearly came to blows, but an accord was signed with the succession being regulated between the three brothers in a compromise which Benedict expressly claims to have been his own work (though we are in the dark exactly how Benedict achieved it): 'the peace which we established between Caesar Louis ever-Augustus and his glorious brothers'(J2669, *MGH Ep* 5.612-4). Charles got Provence and Lyonnais, Lothar II the rest of Cisalpina, and Louis II had to remain satisfied with no more than Italy, which was exactly what Lothar I had arranged.

King Lothar II had been married since 855 to Theutberga, daughter of Boso, and sister of the subdeacon Hubert, whose career was advanced by his sister's marriage: his brother-in-law gave him a duchy in the Jura, where his behaviour attracted the intervention of Benedict. Hubert, after all, was a cleric as well as a noble, and his licentiousness needed curbing. Benedict wrote (*ibid.*) to all the archbishops and bishops in Charles's kingdom, making it clear that he saw Hubert's covetousness as having, 'to the destruction and endangering of many christians', broken the peace he himself had arranged. Apart from various other crimes, Hubert had appropriated St Maurice's monastery at Agaune in Valais by expelling bishop Aimonius, and had defiled St Peter's monastery at Luxeuil by living there with women of easy virtue: he was to appear at Rome within 30 days under pain of excommunication. His breaking of the peace, it has been conjectured, could have been through some kind of interference in Louis's Italian domains: Hubert was at the time an ally of Lothar II who had given him his duchy. But as soon as Lothar started to repudiate his wife, Hubert's sister Theutberga, and to accuse Hubert and Theutberga of incest, Hubert became Lothar's enemy; in the months before Benedict's own death, Hubert successfully resisted Lothar's attacks on his duchy. Benedict's threat of excommunication had not stopped Hubert's scandalous life with concubines or his violent adventures with mercenaries. After Benedict's death, Nicholas also wanted to intervene, and Hubert tried to justify himself (May 863), but was finally killed at Orbe in 864.

Hubert and Theutberga had a brother, the Milanese count Boso (his father's namesake), who had married Engeltrude, daughter of count Matfrid and a kinswoman of Lothar II. After giving him two daughters, Engeltrude, about 856, abandoned her husband, and in the company of one of his vassals, 'as an adulteress with an adulterer', took refuge in Lothar's kingdom (eventually she reached the diocese of Cologne). As the king had now abandoned Theutberga and was living with his concubine Waldrada he could hardly object to the arrangement. Boso said he would forgive Engeltrude if she returned; he then approached Benedict who wrote to Louis II, Lothar, the royal princes, the bishops and all the faithful, asking them to have the fugitive arrested and sent back to Boso (cf. letters of Nicholas *MGH Ep* 6.295, 340, nos. 29 and 53). Benedict's efforts so shortly before his own death had no success;

Lothar protected Engeltrude, and the matter would come to the attention of church councils and of pope Nicholas (cf. 107:48). A letter of Nicholas in 868 hints that Benedict had also been already involved in the thorny question of Lothar II's charges against his wife Theutberga and his attempt to gain a divorce (cf. 107:44-50).

The one known issue which caused difficulties between Rome and Constantinople under Benedict III was that in which Leo IV had already become embroiled (see p. 106): Ignatius's deposition of Gregory of Syracuse and other Sicilian bishops. Benedict showed himself no less firm than Leo in upholding Rome's jurisdiction in the question. Ignatius wanted confirmation of the sentence, Gregory wanted its annulment, and Leo ordered the case to be heard by himself. Gregory sent an envoy named Zacharias to Rome (Nicholas, *Ep.* 90, *MGH Ep* 6.500.9); Ignatius's envoy was Lazarus, certainly the man mentioned in the LP (c. 33). Lazarus probably left Constantinople before it was known that Benedict had succeeded Leo. See c. 33, and n. 81, especially for Stylian's inaccurate account.

Benedict wrote to Ignatius that he was refusing to confirm the deposition; he summoned both parties to Rome so that he could judge the case. Ignatius should either come in person with Zacharias, or he should conduct his business through *apocrisiarii* whom the emperor might send. Meanwhile Benedict was required by the canons to prohibit the bishops from exercising any of their functions until the case was heard (so Nicholas, *MGH Ep* 6.488, 512, nos. 90-91). Hadrian II (*Ep.* 39, *MGH Ep* 6.750-4) later remarked on Ignatius's unwillingness to receive this letter from Benedict. Ignatius himself later stated that he had received Benedict's letter in July (858), and that he himself was deposed some days later (in fact on 23 November 858); but in any case when Ignatius received the letter Benedict was already dead. Gregory knew from his envoy in Rome that Benedict was not supporting Ignatius, and his own attitude to Ignatius became more insolent than ever (or so Nicholas claimed, *Ep.* 90, *MGH Ep* 6.500.9ff). But Benedict's death delayed any decision of the matter, and Ignatius's deposition and repacement by Photius later that year removed the need for a decision. In the longer term these events under Leo and Benedict could be seen as preliminaries to Nicholas's struggle with Photius: they contributed to a growing rift between Rome and the Greek church (Baix 1935:22).

The placing of these events in the LP (c. 33) is out of chronological order: Lazarus's arrival in Rome can hardly be later than 855 or 856. There is a similar dislocation in the case of the next chapter (34), dealing with the arrival of the king of Wessex. It seems that both chapters were added by the compiler as a kind of appendix after he had finished excerpting register material for the pontificate; consequently the chronological place of c. 35, further donations to St Peter's, is obscure.

In Brittany, Leo IV had tried (p. 107) but failed to uphold Actard rather than Gislard as the rightful bishop of Nantes. In 857 the new duke Salomon presented the pope with a request to regularize the situation of the Breton episcopate; other bishops had also been ejected and replaced. Benedict's reply is lost, but cited in a letter from Nicholas to Salomon in 862 (J2708, *Ep.* 107; *MGH Ep* 6.621.6-10); from this it is clear that Benedict kept to Leo's line. No bishop could be deposed without the judgment of twelve bishops, and certainly not by laymen. He excommunicated Gislard, but Gislard still kept control of half the diocese. The schism continued until 1199.

Also inherited from Leo IV was the problem of Hincmar (pp. 103-4). The great archbishop wanted Benedict to reverse Leo IV's refusal to ratify the council of Soissons (853) which had accepted the legitimacy of Hincmar's position as archbishop and had annulled the ordinations carried out by Ebbo after his deposition. Benedict agreed to change Leo's policy, but only if the account of the council Hincmar had sent him was correct (J2664, Mansi 15.110, *PL* 115.689). He also confirmed the metropolitan status of Hincmar's see, subject to the rights of the pope. The change from Leo's policy was remarkable: Hincmar (*Ep.* 11) later had to deny a charge from Nicholas that he had forged this letter himself. The effect of Benedict's acceptance of Soissons was that Rome supported the prohibition on those whom Ebbo had ordained from exercising church functions; the pope had stored up trouble for his successor.

Like Leo (p. 107) Benedict was concerned about questions of penitential discipline. Two of his letters, to Rathold bishop of Strasbourg and Salomon bishop of Constance, deal with those cases which were to be referred to Rome, and show Benedict inflicting canonical penalties outside the ecclesiastical province of Rome on those who committed crimes as serious as parricide and fratricide (Baix 1935:24-5; see J. v. Pflugk-Harttung, *Acta pontificum romanorum inedita* III (Stuttgart 1886), p. 3-4, n. 3 and 4).

Little else is recorded of Benedict except his issuing and confirming of privileges: for example, on 11 May 857 (J2666, Mansi 15.120, *PL* 115.689) he guaranteed to the monastery of St Denis its properties in England. Rather earlier, on 7 October 855, he confirmed in its properties and privileges the monastery of SS Peter, Paul and Stephen at Corbie in the diocese of Amiens; this is worthy of mention here for the reason that the original papyrus of this grant survives at Amiens (see

Baix 1935:24; J2663; *PL* 115.693-701).

Worthy of mention too is a letter to Benedict from Lupus abbot of Ferrières in the diocese of Sens (*Ep.* 103, cf. also 101 and 102, *MGH Ep* 6.89-91). Lupus had visited Rome in 849; now he wanted books, and knowing about the papal library he sent two monks to make copies and also to get instruction on Roman customs, since Lupus believed that in religion and morals variations engendered doubt. The books he wanted were Cicero's *De oratore*, Quintilian's *Institutiones* ('12 books in a not very large volume') (of both these works he had only part), Donatus's *Commentary on Terence*, and Jerome's *Commentary on Jeremiah* from book 7 on (he will have known from Cassiodorus, *De institutione divinarum litterarum* 3, *PL* 70.114, that the work consisted of 20 books, and he had only six of them). It does not follow that these books were available in the papal library; indeed in the case of Jerome's *Commentary on Jeremiah* Lupus will probably have been unlucky: all MSS now surviving are incomplete, and it may be that the author never completed it (Kelly, *Jerome* 317, 327). But the request does show what resources an educated Frank might expect to find available in 9th-century Rome.

Benedict's last dated act was on 30 March 858 when he granted the use of the pallium to Vitalis, patriarch of Grado (J2672), just as he had received it from Leo IV, to be used when celebrating mass for the rest of his life. On the same day Louis II issued at Rome a diploma for the abbey of Nonantola. The next LP life shows that when Benedict died (10 April) Louis had already left Rome and had to return urgently. Although neither the LP nor *AB* mentions it, Bertolini 1966:336 supposes that there must have been a final solemn meeting between Benedict and Louis at St Peter's, given that Easter fell on 3 April. One of the deacons who carried Benedict's remains from the Lateran to St Peter's was Nicholas, his main friend and confidant, and his successor. Though his pontificate lasted only 30 months (which a later tradition would reduce to find space after Leo IV for Pope Joan), the surviving evidence is enough to show that it was no mere interregnum between the pontificates of Leo IV and Nicholas.

106. **1.** BENEDICT [III; 29 September 855 - 10 April 858], of Roman origin, son of Peter, held the see 2 years 6 months 10 days.[1] This blessed man, sprung from loving flesh and blood, was fortified with astral dew; and growing speedily in the study of divine letters, he was given over to his father's discretion to be trained. As a sponge quickly soaks in water, so he learnt the lessons of the sacred volumes; he understood, grasped and set the rudiments in the foundation of his mind, and propagated them on unseen roots. His fame becoming celebrated and widespread, he was brought to the Lateran patriarchate and placed among the clergy. He was prudent in speech, distinguished in doctrine, sober in behaviour, peaceful in conversation, sympathetic to all, accommodating to everyone, and very kind. **2.** When bountiful pope Gregory [IV] saw that he was an expert and useful teacher, he made him a subdeacon in the holy Roman church; and in this order he entered upon many struggles in the holy life: for he overcame the flesh, and the prince of the world and all his wicked arguments.[2] So the prelate Gregory died and departed to the Lord; Sergius [II] took on the government of the Roman church as bishop; and on his death Leo [IV] took on the apostolic see. This pope loved him exceedingly for his most happy acts, and spurred by the Will from on high he consecrated him with great honour as priest for Callistus's *titulus*.[3] **3.** His blessedness shone and flowered forth far and wide, so much so that he was reckoned most blessed in all he said and did. In him God's wisdom was acknowledged to dwell openly, because he warmed everyone and

---

[1] The tenure is one day shorter in E[6], one day longer in the Montecassino catalogue, 2 years 7 months 6 days in Paris 5140. Benedict III's dates are not totally certain; his letters run from 7 October 855 to 30 March 858. It seems there was a vacancy of at least two months after 17 July 855; the possibilities for his ordination are 22 or 29 September or 6 October. His successor was ordained 24 April 858 (though 1 May is not quite impossible). Vogel (in Duchesne III) insists that Benedict's dates were 6 October 855 to 17 April 858, against Duchesne's dates (given in the text) which Bertolini 1966:332 accepts. For what it is worth, E[6] gives a vacancy of 15 days in 858; if this is not a late medieval calculation, it supports Duchesne's chronology.

[2] A similar eulogy recurs in c. 20 (for similar 'doubled' eulogies see 105:18 and 107:10). The laudatory view of Benedict is confirmed, perhaps, by Photius (*Liber de Spiritus Sancti mystagogia* 88, *PG* 102.377-8 ('he was gentle and meek, famed for his ascetic struggles'). Photius could see Benedict as an ally, as Benedict did not accept Ignatius's deposition of Gregory of Syracuse; he also believed that Leo IV initiated, and Benedict III continued, the recitation of the Byzantine creed in Greek at Rome, but that it was stopped by a later pope. Photius approved of Benedict; but it is incredible that he would need inspiration, or be willing to borrow ideas, from a work like the LP to express his (rather conventional) view, as Baix 1935:17 thought.

[3] Benedict signed as priest of St Callistus's *titulus* at the council of 853, when Anastasius was finally deposed (105:92; Mansi 14.1021).

adorned them clearer than light with his bounteous and pure affections; he spurned the delights of this failing and transitory world and to the poor and needy he disbursed whatever they could use. He continued valiant in fasting and assiduous in prayer; every day he remained vigilant in God's praises.

4. The prelate Leo was taken from this world and died. Then all the clergy of this God-protected Roman see and all the dignitaries and the whole senate and people gathered to implore the Lord's clemency, that he would see fit to point out to them all a beatific shepherd who could rule the pinnacle of the apostolate with serenity; they were then inflamed by God's ethereal light and with one consent and effort they promulgated his election as pontiff because of the great sacred works in which he was accomplished.[4] 5. Immediately with keen and general endeavour the plebs and the assembly of the people made their way to Callistus's *titulus* and found him pouring forth prayer, as was his wont, to God almighty. He rose, saw the dense throngs of people, and realized and grasped the situation in his mind. At this he knelt weeping greatly, and with tear-choked voice he implored them all, saying: 'I beg you not to take me away from my church, because I am not capable of sustaining and bearing the load of so great a pinnacle'. But they refused to agree; instead they took him forcibly from that *titulus* with hymns and spiritual chants, and with full rejoicing and ineffable gladness brought him to the Lateran patriarchate and placed him on the pontifical throne as is the usage of the pontiffs and as hoary custom points out. Moreover[5] the city is glad, the church leaps for joy, the elderly rejoice, virgins in triumph sing God's praises, the poor are enriched, the needy prosper, captives are comforted, the maimed rise up, and the sick are healed and gather swift of foot, because the sadness that was widespread

---

[4] According to 108:3 the electorate's first choice was the priest of St Mark's, the future Hadrian II. In view of what follows in cc. 6ff it is unlikely that there was unanimity in favour of Benedict: it is admitted in c. 9 that Anastasius had significant support, and it is certain that he, not Hadrian, was the main challenger. Hadrian and another future pope, Nicholas, may well have been influential at this stage; Hadrian had been a priest since 842 and so was senior to the more recently ordained Benedict. Nicholas had only recently reached the diaconate; Nicholas's father Theodore was a *regionarius*, and Hadrian's family had already produced two popes, Stephen IV and Sergius II. If Hadrian's life is right to claim he had support, could he perhaps have stepped down in favour not of Benedict but of Anastasius? And could he have done so knowing whom Louis II wanted as pope? Bertolini (1966) thinks he would have known of this; though he also believes that the city clergy (presumably with Hadrian among them) were loyal to Benedict. Perhaps so, but there were certainly priests (one even named Hadrian) whom Leo had deposed who sided with Anastasius (see c. 14 and n. 30). On relations between Hadrian and Anastasius see also life 108.

[5] Very similar expressions recur at 107:7, no doubt from the same author.

among them was observed confounded, and flourishing calm was seen raised up.

6. This done, the clergy and all the dignitaries composed the decree, signed it by their own hands and, as ancient custom requires,[6] despatched it to the emperors Lothar and Louis.[7] The envoys who took this decree, Nicholas bishop of Anagni and Mercurius the master of the soldiers,[8] met bishop Arsenius[9] at Gubbio[10] and they engaged in

---

[6] In 844 Lothar had insisted on the terms of the *Constitutio* of 824 being recognized (104 n. 22): an imperial warrant was needed before the pope could be ordained, and the ceremony was to take place in the presence of the imperial envoys. Leo IV had accepted this (see p. 101). The oath of loyalty to Benedict (mentioned in c. 9; and cf. p. 36) will have been taken at this point; the envoys would break it by going over to Anastasius. 'Ancient custom' here must reflect a feeling that the sending of an electoral announcement to the western emperors was a continuity of practice with the Byzantine period; which is why this passage was quoted by Guy of Osnabrück, *Liber de controversia inter Hildebrandum et Heinricum imperatorem* (*MGH libelli de lite imperatorum et pontificum saec. XI et XII conscripti* I.465.15-18).

[7] The election decree will have been composed in the latter part of July, and was therefore addressed to both emperors. Lothar died 29 September 855 (the same day, it seems, as Benedict's ordination) at the monastery of Prüm in the Ardennes, to which he had gone when he abdicated on 23 September. Even when he wrote the first chapters of this life the writer is not yet likely to have known of these events.

[8] Nicholas and Mercurius represent the clerical and lay aristocracy respectively; Nicholas signed at the council of 853 (Mansi 14.1020).

[9] Arsenius, bishop of Orte 855-868, had been very important at Rome since the time of Leo IV (see p. 74) as the imperial envoy and able to dispose of Louis II's favour and influence. Cf. 107:63; 108:43 (his death in 868); and Schieffer 1980:1054-5. He was either the father or the uncle of Anastasius. Bertolini 1966:331, Arnaldi 1961:25, and Petrucci 1962:339, maintain the common view that Arsenius was Anastasius's maternal uncle; so too Kelly, Nelson. This view depends entirely on a letter of late 867 by Anastasius to Ado archbishop of Vienne in which Anastasius apparently so describes himself, *MGH Ep* 7.401.17ff. Bertolini holds that Arsenius was father of Anastasius; so too Lapôtre 1885:29 and Baix 1935:15. At least one word is missing in the text of Anastasius's letter to Ado; Bertolini restores: *Pendet autem anima eius* (Hadrian II) *ex anima avunculi mei, vestri vero <aequivoci, et> Arsenii.* Bertolini's text makes the uncle of Anastasius not Arsenius but a homonym of archbishop Ado; and this Ado will be the 'priest named Ado, a kinsman of his' mentioned at the Roman Council of 12 October 868, held by Hadrian II against Anastasius (*AB* 868 Nelson 149). Lapôtre, already seeing that the text of the letter was at fault, read: *avunculi vestri, mei vero patris Arsenii,* which would make Anastasius a relative of Ado of Vienne. Arnaldi, agreeing that the priest Ado related to Anastasius was not the archbishop, but holding the view that Anastasius was nephew of Arsenius, also made him the half-brother rather than full-brother of Eleutherius: Arsenius would then be Anastasius's stepfather as well as his uncle. This seems to get the best of both worlds. But Hincmar (*AB* 868 Nelson 145) describes Eleutherius as son of Arsenius and as brother of Anastasius. This is surely conclusive; there is no need to posit half-relationships.

[10] Despite the use of the ablative for the locative (usual enough at this date) and the inversion of the names of the place and the bishop (typical of the author's style), Gubbio is where Arsenius met the Roman envoys, not (*pace DHGE* 4.752) his episcopal see; cf. next chapter, and Lapôtre 1885:62. Deusdedit (I.208), basing his comments about these events on the LP, was right to state that Arsenius was bishop of Orte. At the council of

discussion with each other. He buttered them with cunning words, their hearts began to soften and they veered from their loyalty to the elected blessed Benedict. With them he endeavoured to firm up a plot for them to adorn Anastasius with the badge of the pontificate, a man deposed and anathematized, something God's clemency would never tolerate.[11]

7. So they went and gave the decree to the kind Caesar Louis, and returned to Rome with the duplicitous intention that they had in mind. Reporting that the imperial envoys[12] would be arriving, they presented the letters containing the emperor's reply to the remarkable man elected. In their dreadful scheming, in their desire to achieve the plot which, as we have mentioned, they had entered into with Arsenius at Gubbio, they said to all the clergy and to the State's assemblies: 'You must all endeavour to go out along with us to meet the imperial envoys so you can be obedient to the emperor's mandates.'

8. Some days later the envoys whose arrival they had heralded made their way to Orte, 40 miles from Rome. Among them were counts Adalbert[13] and Bernard; they entered it, and, impelled by bishop Arsenius, joined themselves to that priest named Anastasius, the one previously condemned:[14] in the holy synod under the presidency of prelate Leo of blessed memory, he had been, in accordance with the promulgations of the sacred canons, lawfully excommunicated, deposed and bound by an anathema. Not having God before their eyes, like bloodstained tyrants they wanted to confound his commandments, and were considering how to raise up this ejected and anathematized Anastasius to the apostolic pinnacle, contrary to the tradition and enactments of all the prelates and beloved men. 9. The envoys too - those we mentioned above, bishop Nicholas and Mercurius the master of the soldiers, who had delivered our decree about the election of the kind Benedict to the emperor - with the plan drawn up and thought out in their minds, left Rome with some other nobles, Gregory and Christopher masters of the soldiers, and set out as if to meet the emperor's envoys. They made their way to the city of Orte, and, making

---

8 December 853 one Erfo was bishop of Gubbio (Mansi 14.1020, with Ioannes in the margin).
[11] For Anastasius's earlier career see pp. 104-6. After his deposition he had found protection with Louis II. Nicholas, Mercurius and Arsenius represent an important faction, whose opportunity to substitute Anastasius arises from the fact that Benedict, though elected, could not be ordained until imperial approval arrived.
[12] In their presence it would be permissible to ordain the new pope.
[13] Despite Duchesne's caution this must be the same man as count Adalbert, *marcensis et tutor* in 846, 104:44 with n. 80.
[14] Cf. 105:92.

little of and forgetting the oath of loyalty they had taken to the bounteous elected Benedict, they joined themselves to the condemned and deposed priest. Given this opportunity, many others from the City rose up and did the same, as that utterance of the prophet has it, 'devising mischief that could not succeed'. Leaving the city of Orte they arrived close to St Leucius the martyr's basilica,[15] behaving insolently and glorying in the weapons and power of men; with them were Radoald bishop of Porto and Agatho bishop of the city of Todi.[16] These had left Rome secretly, enmeshed themselves in black gloom, and joined the one who was anathematized, with their senses, minds and souls darkened.

10. When God's servant the elected Benedict heard this, he endeavoured to despatch George and Maio,[17] bishops who were venerable, wise and full of all knowledge, with some letters to the imperial envoys. On the advice of the anathematized priest Anastasius they arrested them, tied them up and put them under guard, an action against envoys unheard of even among barbarian races and peoples. Afterwards Christ's minister the elected Benedict sent the remarkable Hadrian, *secundicerius* of the holy apostolic see, and the duke Gregory, to meet them. **11.** Next day, employing a falsehood,[18] they ordered all the clergy, the entire senate and the whole people, 'on the emperor's mandates'[19] to go over the Milvian Bridge to meet them. All the Romans then went along with this, ignorant of the trick and deceit, and leaving the City with one accord they crossed the Milvian Bridge.

As they made their way to the above-mentioned martyr's basilica, the envoys we have already mentioned above, with that deposed and anathematized Anastasius, met the bishops and clergy and dignitaries of the Roman people, and together with them they made their way on horseback by the Campus Neronis[20] to the walls of the City, and also brought Hadrian, the remarkable *secundicerius* we have mentioned above, hedged round with guards.[21] Arresting Gratian, the *superista* of

---

[15] At Tor di Quinto, not far from the Milvian Bridge, cf. 97:77 with n. 160.

[16] Both these bishops signed at the council of 853 (Mansi 14.1020). On Radoald see Lapôtre 1885:74f.

[17] George was bishop of Bomarzo, Maio of Priverno (between Frosinone and Terracina); both signed at the council of 853 (Mansi 14.1020).

[18] The 'falsehood' is what they pretended was in the emperor's mandates.

[19] The expression is a quasi-quotation, in view of 'not ordered in a mandate' below.

[20] Cf. 104:47.

[21] Hadrian's companion duke Gregory is not mentioned; Bertolini 1966:331 plausibly supposes that he had gone over to Anastasius's side.

the sacred patriarchate,[22] and Theodore the *scriniarius*, they held them bound, with spears drawn. This was something the emperors had certainly not ordered in a mandate, nor had they expressed it as their intention; it was the unhappy presumption of the deposed priest that brought it about. **12.** With Caesar's envoys this priest entered the Leonine city[23] by force and, making little of God's will, he suddenly and boldly intruded into the prince of the apostles' basilica, which he ought not to have entered. The extent and nature of the evil and hapless activities he carried out were such as even the Saracen horde had not presumed or thought to carry out therein: he broke the images and burnt them with fire, he destroyed the painting of the synod which pope Leo of blessed memory had had made above the sanctuary's doors, and with a hatchet he hurled down to the ground the icon of our Lord Jesus Christ and his ever-virgin mother.[24] This he should not have done; at that detestable action all the devotees of the orthodox faith[25] wept and groaned, and were filled with sadness and sorrow.[26]

13. This done, the deposed priest entered Rome as an enemy[27] and with his wicked followers swiftly made his way to the Lateran patriarchate; and like a bloodstained tyrant he opened its doors with worldly force and many kinds of weapons, and so entering by this door he sat on the throne which his hands should not even have touched. He

---

[22] On Gratian see 105:110-112 with n. 159 on his post as *superista*.

[23] Completed three years previously, 105:68-74.

[24] What was destroyed was an image of Christ and the Virgin amidst a series of inscriptions recording the sentences pronounced against Anastasius on 16 December 850, 29 May and 19 June 853, and 8 December 853, above the main door of St Peter's. Leo IV had certainly given great prominence to his condemnation of Anastasius. The latter's apparent iconoclasm was not for theological motives. In destroying the pictorial and textual record of his own condemnation he may well have caused more damage than was necessary, and the LP naturally presents this in the worst possible light. In view of what the Saracens had recently done to the tomb of St Peter itself, to describe Anastasius's behaviour as worse than that of the Saracens is hyperbolic.

[25] A reminiscence, though perhaps unconscious, of *orthodoxis... fidei cultoribus* in the Canon of the Roman Mass.

[26] Cf. *AB* 868 Nelson 148 (Hadrian II's version of these events): After Leo's death 'Anastasius, anathematized and deposed, returned with the backing of worldly power' (i.e. with Louis II's help), 'from the secret places in which like a thief he had been skulking. Seduced by diabolical trickery and caught in a fog, in the manner of a brigand he invaded this church which he ought not to have entered at all, and like a savage and a barbarian, to the perdition of his own soul and the danger of this venerable synod, along with his most villainous accomplices and followers he destroyed and threw down that picture in the dust. The most blessed and distinguished Pope Benedict restored and decorated it with colours flowing with light.'

[27] Or 'with a hostile force', though this would merely anticipate the reference to his supporters in the next words.

gave orders to the bishop of Bagnorégio, whose name, inappropriately, was Romanus,[28] whom he saw to be clouded with a bestial mentality, to eject blessed Benedict, whom as we have related the whole Roman people had elected, from the pontifical throne on which he sat. Like a barbarian[29] he took him and stripped him of the pontifical vestments he was wearing, and sated him with many injuries and blows. **14.** Then the deposed Anastasius, acting for man, not God, endeavoured to give this kind elected Benedict over to guards who would strictly confine him, that is, to the former priests John and Hadrian whom the prelate Leo had condemned for their crimes and deposed from every sacerdotal office.[30] Then the entire people were filled with wailing and plentiful weeping, and lay quivering and groaning deeply. Immediately all the bishops and clergy and God's people entered the holy of holies,[31] beating their breasts with copious tears, and lay prostrate on the ground between the vestibule and the altar,[32] begging God's greatness to deliver them by his victorious right hand[33] from the gloom of their great error. Saturday was then taking its course.[34]

15. Next day[35] these bishops with all the clergy and people gathered in Aemiliana's *titulus*,[36] at which those envoys of the emperor had

---

[28] He cannot have been bishop long; the council of 8 December 853 was attended by bishop Leo of Balnorégio. The signatures of the 20 priests then present included two named Romanus (one was the archpriest, at St Pudentiana's, the other priest of SS John and Paul; Mansi 14.1020-1); one of these was perhaps the new bishop.

[29] As opposed to a Roman.

[30] At the council of 853 were two priests named John (of St Chrysogonus's; and of St Prisca's) and two named Hadrian (of St Mark's, the future Hadrian II; and of St Vitalis's) (Mansi 14.1021); if any of these are to be identified with those mentioned here, their depositions must have occurred in the 19 months following the council. The future Hadrian II can be safely excluded; even if his sympathy lay with the imperial party (cf. n. 4), we would certainly have heard of it if he had been deposed.

[31] As a scriptural and liturgical expression, 'Holy of Holies' must be taken figuratively (so too 'between the vestibule and the altar' just below), and not as a reference to the oratory of St Laurence in the Lateran Palace (the later *Sancta Sanctorum* at the top of the *Scala Sancta*). This was too small to hold an assembly of the size implied, and it is likely that Benedict's partisans had been ejected from the whole Lateran complex. They might however have gathered in the adjacent basilica, to which as the cathedral of Rome the term 'Holy of Holies' might be appropriate.

[32] Joel 2.17; cf. previous note.

[33] Cf. perhaps Wisdom 10.20 (the introit for Easter Thursday).

[34] Eight days before Benedict's consecration, so probably 21 September.

[35] i.e. on Sunday. Adalbert and Bernard are anxious in cc. 15-16 to bring the matter to a conclusion by having Anastasius accepted as pope and ordained on the only day the ceremony could by custom take place (for this, 108:9).

[36] SS Quattro Coronati, situated not far from the Lateran; cf. 98:73 with n. 129. This is the last reference to the church under its ancient name; but see Krautheimer, *Corpus* 4.32-3 for the lingering doubt that even at this date there might have been a *titulus Aemilianae*

arrived, roaring and swollen with pride. Launching an attack like savage lions they sprang up to the apse where the bishops sat chanting with the clergy, and they attempted to shatter them with staves raised aloft and to injure them with swords, saying: 'Agree and give your consent to Anastasius's taking over the pinnacle of the pontificate'. But they, filled with the Holy Ghost, asserted: 'We can never agree to one who has been deposed and bound by an anathema by a holy prelate and a blessed synod - we cast him out utterly and exclude him from God's assemblies'. Then in fury they said they would punish them with blows and torments; but almighty God's blessed bishops and those with them made little of their terrors and threats and remained unmoved. **16.** These Franks[37] saw they were steadfast, and filled with anger departed from them and went into some chamber in that basilica. There they considered various plots; and into it they also brought under compulsion the bishops of Ostia and Albano,[38] whom they strove to reduce by mild language and persuasive flattery and later enveloped with threats of violence. They even said to them in sharp tones: 'There is no way for you to keep your lives - you will be subject to a capital penalty unless you give Anastasius the grace of consecration'. But they affirmed they would give themselves over to die and to be torn limb from limb sooner than bestow the blessing of consecration on one who was deposed and condemned by an anathema. They convinced those envoys and proved all their replies from holy scripture, that there was no way they could set that deposed man in the order they were demanding. Straightaway they held a secret discussion in their own tongue; and the fury that overflowed in them began to wane and seemed removed from their minds.

17. When Tuesday dawned,[39] all the bishops with the clergy and

---

surviving separately from SS Quattro.

[37] By describing the envoys as Franks (and then by remarking on 'their own language' in this chapter) the compiler is persisting with the idea implied by his mention of Anastasius's partisan Romanus being un-Roman (Bertolini 1966:332); Anastasius's behaviour, too, has been described as barbarous (c. 13). In the LP account the violence is blamed on Anastasius and on the imperial envoys, but never on Louis himself. Yet the envoys cannot have been pursuing a policy unwanted by Louis who, at a politically difficult time, with his father about to abdicate and with his own rule in practice confined to Italy, will have wanted a pope he could trust, Anastasius, and not Benedict, linked as the latter was with Leo IV who had deposed Anastasius.

[38] The bishops of Ostia, Porto and Albano were the usual consecrators of the pope (cf. 108:9 with n. 22); since Radoald of Porto was already on Anastasius's side it remained to bring round his two colleagues, Megistus of Ostia (so named at the council of 853, Mansi 14.1020) and Petronacius of Albano.

[39] This chapter seems to describe what was in effect a fresh election, in which Benedict was again the victor. Whatever might be said about the regularity of the previous election,

people gathered in the Saviour's basilica called Constantinian, in which all the plebs and the multitude of the people shouted aloud: 'We want the blessed Benedict as pope - it is he we insist on!' The envoys heard this and were surprised.[40] Seeing that no ingenuity would make Christ's unity and beloved concord turn to Anastasius, they summoned the bishops and the other *sacerdotes* with the clergy to one of the chambers in the patriarchate, and they endeavoured to sort out the whole conflict with them. But with plausible words and teaching they overcame the audacity of these envoys, so that the hapless thought in their minds was obviously broken and confused. Realizing this, they said to the venerable bishops: 'Take the one you have elected and bring him to any basilica you wish; then we will cast Anastasius, whom you call deposed, out of this patriarchate; and let us for three days solemnize a fast with prayer, and then let whatever is indicated by the Clemency from on high be fulfilled'. But the bountiful bishops cried: 'Let the intruder, the deposed Anastasius, be cast out of our presence and expelled from this patriarchate, and then we will do what you suggest'.

18. Immediately Anastasius was cast out and expelled from the patriarchate in much disgrace, so that all the devotees of the orthodox faith[41] fulfilled their manifold thanks to our Lord Jesus Christ. The bishops with all the clergy and people took and brought the elected[42] one, blessed Benedict, from the basilica[43] in which the clerics were staying, the same place where the savage Anastasius had put him under guard. With every enthusiasm and rejoicing they went down with him to the Saviour's basilica, called Constantinian. Going out from there, in triumph they set him on the horse on which the prelate Leo used to sit. With a great band of the people going before him they brought him to God's mother's basilica called *Praesepe*; and in it they gave themselves over for three days and nights to fasting and prayer, beseeching the Lord's majesty with many tears.

19. When the fasting was over, all[44] who had joined themselves to the anathematized and deposed one, spurred by God's will and inflamed by

---

the imperial envoys would now witness an election whose regularity they could not doubt. Perhaps the envoys allowed this to cover their own surrender?

[40] The compiler presents this popular demand as the turning point, cf. n. 45.

[41] Again (as in c. 12, cf. n. 25) the phraseology reflects the liturgy.

[42] Reading (so too Vogel in Duchesne III) *electum* for *eiectum*.

[43] Duchesne took this to be one of the inner basilicas of the Lateran Palace, probably the present *Sancta Sanctorum*, cf. n. 31; and Baix 1935:16 stated it as fact. But we are not told where the ex-priests John and Hadrian (c. 14) had confined Benedict; it may not even have been in the Lateran.

[44] Except Radoald, see below.

God's favour, came with one accord to the same basilica in which, as we have said, the elected blessed Benedict was residing, and falling down they began to kiss his footprints. And they said to him: 'We have strayed and departed from you with unsure step, but like a holy shepherd receive the flocks of sheep that stray through the meadows, gather the tired lambs to your bosom, and overshadow us with your wings'. Straightaway the God-protected Benedict thirsted to embrace them all with outstretched arms, pure mind and kind heart, and he adorned them with kisses. He said to them: 'Rejoice, dearly beloved, and be yet more glad, because Christ God's Son has seen fit by his power to unite the Church that was torn'. He said and preached these and like things, and even the imperial envoys gathered there as well, for they were holding secret discussions in wholesome and milder language with the one elected.[45] **20.** But suddenly all the bishops and the whole clergy and the countless multitude of the Roman people took him from that basilica. With hymns and spiritual chants they brought him to the Lateran patriarchate and set him on the pontifical throne from which he had been removed. Then the whole church rejoiced and all the people resoundingly expressed their gladness.

So when Sunday dawned, he was brought by all the bishops, clergy and dignitaries to St Peter the apostle's basilica, and in the sight of all, with the imperial envoys looking on, he was consecrated and ordained

---

[45] The compiler is silent on the details of the envoys' negotiations with Benedict. On the one hand it was now clear both to Benedict and the envoys that Benedict had support from a majority of clergy and people who would not brook Anastasius as pope. The envoys would have to accept this, however grudgingly, and let Benedict's ordination proceed. On the other hand they could not give in too easily; they would have to explain themselves to Louis. Anastasius was ejected from the Lateran. That was inevitable. Benedict also restored the painting and inscriptions at St Peter's (*AB*, quoted in n. 26). In all other respects he showed a surprising leniency, which can only be explained as part of a deal he struck with the envoys who would otherwise still not have accepted him as pope (Bertolini 1966:333). Hincmar alone (and he was no friend of Benedict's) records Hadrian II's statement when deposing Anastasius in 868 that Benedict made Anastasius appear at a council (perhaps on or soon after the day of his ordination), upheld his deposition and stripped him of the sacerdotal vestments he had uncanonically assumed, but readmitted him to lay communion (*AB* 868 Nelson 148). So Anastasius's attempt at the papacy had left him with a lesser penalty than his existing excommunication. As a layman he could be a monk (he was for a time confined to the monastery of S. Maria Trastevere) and his lay state would not prevent him becoming an abbot. Furthermore Benedict had to accept what must have been particularly galling: oversight by Arsenius, Anastasius's father (or uncle) and staunchest supporter, as imperial envoy (he reappears at 107:63), and, still, as bishop of Orte. Another supporter, Radoald, remained bishop of Porto, even if (c. 20) he did not take his usual place in the ordination ceremony. So while the deal presented to Louis was a superficial reverse it was not a total climbdown; Benedict would be compelled to toe the imperial line as much as Anastasius would have done. The compiler's reticence on all this may be due to ignorance, or discretion, or hostility to Anastasius: he may have preferred to omit Benedict's bargain as unsatisfactory.

pontiff for the apostolic see, as is the custom and as ancient tradition requires. But the bishop of Porto[46] was excluded from the church, and he never poured forth the prayer on him which he ought to have done, because he had joined himself to the anathematized one, and had fallen into perjury's abyss and was still there. Then the sacred ceremonies of mass were celebrated, and, ordained, he returned in glory to the pontifical Lateran patriarchate.

He was[47] gentle, and adorned with every sacred work, fair of face and bright of mind, sweet in conversation and kind-hearted in his teaching. But as we are not capable of giving an orderly account of everything, let us endeavour to make our pen stretch to what he presented to the various places of the saints.

[October A.D. 855:]

21. At the very start of his pontificate, boiling with love from on high, in the Saviour's basilica called Constantinian he provided an icon of wondrous beauty of the Redeemer our Lord Jesus Christ himself, trampling the lion and the serpent under foot, of fine silver swathed in gold, weighing 16½lb. In God's holy mother the ever-virgin our lady's basilica called *Praesepe* he presented 1 gold and most precious crown, weighing 4 lb. In this basilica the baptistery[48] had remained roofless for a long time; with swift endeavour, hoping for future reward from the Lord, he restored it and saw to its being brought to its ancient condition. **22.** In St Peter the apostle's basilica this remarkable and blessed pope presented a chased incense-boat of fine silver and swathed in gold, in which incense is put; there too he presented 7 candelabra[49] with horns, of fine silver resplendent with golden colour, weighing 40 lb. In the world's teacher St Paul the apostle's basilica, he decorated the tomb, which had been destroyed by the Saracens, with silver panels weighing 104 lb. In God's holy mother's basilica Trastevere he presented 1 cloth with all-silk decoration round it, with a gold-studded cross in the

---

[46] Radoald (named in c. 9) is presented as disqualified through his adherence to Anastasius. The LP may be disingenuous; there seems no reason why, in view of the deal struck (previous note), he should have been disqualified. He may have refused to take part. Later he would be involved in further misdeeds (cf. life 107).

[47] For the repeated eulogy cf. c. 1 with n. 2.

[48] The first reference since the 5th century to this baptistery, which dated from the building of the basilica under Xystus III (432-440): LP 46:3 (BP 36) records that pope's gift of a silver water-pouring stag at the font and all the sacred silver vessels for baptism, and, 46:7 (BP 37), 'he built the font of the Baptistery at St Mary's and adorned it with porphyry columns'. The exact location of the baptistery is not known.

[49] '7' seems to be the number of candelabra, not the number of 'horns' (i.e. not a single 7-branched candlestick); 'horns' are evidently the projections which earlier compilers would have described as 'dolphins' and which held the wicks.

middle. In God's holy mother's basilica called *Antiqua*,[50] which pope Leo had constructed[51] close to the Via Sacra from its foundations, he

---

[50] The word *Antiqua* may confuse; the building is that now known as S. Maria Nova, or more commonly S. Francesca Romana. As is clear from c. 24 this is on a different site from the ruin now known as S. Maria Antiqua. This was discovered in 1900 in the so-called Library of Augustus on the south side of the Forum (Rushforth 1902:1-123); when it was abandoned, perhaps as a result of the earthquake of 847, its name (Antiqua), privileges, properties, and icon, were transferred to the new building, which was legally the same entity. The name Antiqua was not intended to contrast it with Leo IV's building; it had been in use since at least 640 (its use for a church then less than 100 years old (c. 565-578) is puzzling: Krautheimer, *Corpus* 2.266, thinks that the term may once have referred to the icon). Not surprisingly, Leo's building came to be called Nova as well as Antiqua (107:37), then Nova only, and finally S. Francesca Romana. But though the church took its name from a building on another site, it may not have been the first church on the new site, which may have been that of pope Paul's church of SS Peter & Paul on the Via Sacra near the Temple of Rome, where the apostolic kneeprint-stone is now to be seen. The stone was on the Via Sacra at least from the 6th century; by 1375 it was in front of S. Maria Nova, later inside it. No church of Peter and Paul near here is known in any document after the 8th century, not even in the list of 807 (the church of St Peter in the Einsiedeln Itinerary, between the Palatium Neronis and the Arch of Titus, will be S. Pietro in Vincoli). If it nevertheless survived into the 9th century it may have been destroyed by the earthquake of 847, and Leo IV may have used the site for a replacement of S. Maria Antiqua. Lanciani, Hülsen and Prandi offered various views connecting SS Peter & Paul with parts of the site, and even parts of the structure, of S. Maria Nova. The competing suggestion for the location of SS Peter & Paul's is based on the discovery, when the Basilica of Constantine was cleared in the early 19th century, of the remnants of some Christian murals and of an altar in the apse; De Rossi therefore located SS Peter & Paul's in this apse. The virtual destruction of the Basilica of Constantine in the earthquake of 1349 would then be the occasion when the kneeprint-stone was placed outside S. Maria Nova. See Krautheimer, *Corpus* 1.222.

[51] It is surprising that Leo IV's new building is not mentioned in his own life, but the LP again credits him with the work at 107:37. The surviving medieval church has much in the aisles and nave walls that dates from Leo's building: the following summary is based on Krautheimer, *Corpus* 1.228-243. The church was built so that the western half of the nave overlay the Via Sacra, while the apse, to the east, intrudes into the double podium of the Temple of Venus & Rome. Most of the features recall the basilicas of Leo III and Paschal: the plan has characteristic carelessness: the aisles differ in width, and the sum of the aisle-widths does not equal the nave-width; there is no clear ratio between the height and width of the aisles or nave to each other. The distances between columns and between windows, and the measurement of the windows, vary arbitrarily. The brickwork of the walls is irregular. The brickwork of the clerestory with its small windows recalls S. Cecilia, S. Prassede and S. Martino, which all also have the double arches over the windows, typical of 9th-century Rome. The architrave, instead of an arcade, here, at S. Prassede, and at S. Stefano degli Abessini, is also common in the 9th century, as is the use of 'Servian' blocks in the foundations of the south-west corner of the façade and the south of the nave. The shortening of the south aisle is influenced by the location of the church in the Forum, but it would not have occurred earlier, even though, as it is a deaconry, anomalies can be tolerated (cf. S. Giorgio in Velabro). Construction-technique is consistent with a completion date under Leo IV. The masonry has many more marble fragments than at SS Nereo e Achilleo or S. Prassede, and even than the recent S. Martino; the north aisle is of more careless masonry than the nave, and, apparently, than the short south aisle: a different crew of masons may have built it slightly later. All these irregularities show that it is a latecomer in the 9th-century revival of the early Christian basilica.

provided 13 gold-interwoven veils[52] with a purple fringe. In St Laurence the martyr's basilica outside the city's walls he presented and granted golden keys.

[January A.D. 856:]
23. So in the 5th month[53] after this distinguished pontiff's consecration, i. e. in January, on the ..th day, the river called Tiber left its channel and spread over the plains; it swelled in great spate and entered the city of Rome by the postern-gate called St Agatha's, at the ..th hour of the day. Meanwhile in some places it even lapped over,[54] and entered the church of St Silvester,[55] so that of the steps which go up to St Dionysius's basilica[56] none except the topmost was visible

---

[52] Without manuscript support Krautheimer has 14 veils, and observes that there were probably seven columns each side of the nave (*Corpus* 1.223, 235).

[53] The month stated is a problem; for the date of Benedict's ordination see n. 1; the fifth month should begin 29 January 856 (or 6 February 856); yet the flood was on 6 January. Vogel therefore corrected to 'in the 4th month'. But if 29 September is correct for Benedict's ordination and the reckoning is in full calendar months, September is the first and January is, as required, the fifth. Or perhaps the compiler meant to write 'in the fifth month of the indiction-year'. Alternatively the figure '5th' may have originated as the (missing) day of the month in the next line, if the flood began the day before Epiphany (mentioned below). On the whole this passage supports 29 September rather than 6 October for Benedict's ordination.

[54] 91:6 (the source of this passage) adds 'the city walls'; the compiler was careless.

[55] The text may be at fault here; Duchesne would substitute 'monastery' for 'church'. Cf. 107:15, which is based on this passage. Perhaps expand here to read, as there, 'and entered St Laurence's church called Lucina's; from there it extended itself and entered St Silvester's monastery'. Either solution will considerably ease the following problem (cf. Krautheimer, *Corpus* 4.150,160; Duchesne 1900:317). SS Stephen & Silvester's monastery (now S. Silvestro in Capite) was founded by pope Paul (95:5), whose life clearly distinguishes two separate sanctuaries, an upper oratory with the relics of popes Stephen and Silvester, and a church of great beauty within the monastery. At 98:38 the 'larger basilica' and 'the oratory' are also distinguished. At 107:14 the 'larger church' is again mentioned, and as dedicated to St Dionysius. The present passage is the first to mention St Dionysius's at this complex. The text here as it stands suggests that St Silvester's was the lower church and that from it steps led up to the oratory of St Dionysius. But it would be extraordinary if the church which did not contain St Silvester's body was the one which bore his name; and St Dionysius's must have been a spacious and easily accessible building, since there was a large gathering in it to elect pope Nicholas (107:6). Also it would be odd to measure the height of a flood by a chapel hidden away inside a monastery: the steps of St Dionysius's surely rose from the street itself. St Dionysius's must have been the name, at least by Benedict III's time, of the present S. Silvestro in capite, and the oratory on the monastery's upper floor must be St Silvester's (and/or St Stephen's). Nothing is known about the form or the precise location of the latter, or when the relics of Stephen and Silvester were deposited in it.

[56] The present S. Silvestro in capite (see previous note). The shift of the main basilica's dedication from Dionysius to Silvester occurred about the 11th century; the term *De Capite* is first used in 1194, because the reputed skull of St John the Baptist was brought from Constantinople to this monastery under Innocent II (1130-1143). The earlier dedication was to Dionysius, the pope who died 26 December 267. Loenertz 1948:118ff identified the patron correctly; that it was Denis of Paris was based, as he showed, on the

because of the flooding;[57] from there it expanded over the street called
Via Lata and entered God's mother St Mary's basilica there, and the
water swelled so much that this church's doors could not even be seen
because of the flooding.[58] Then it went up through the streets and by-
ways as far as the Clivus Argentarius.[59] From there it turned a right
angle and entered by the portico[60] in front of St Mark's church, on the
6th day of the same month, the Apparition of our Lord Jesus Christ
according to the flesh, i. e. God's Epiphany. Then it made a rush and

---

imagination of Hilduin, abbot of St Denis, who claimed, c. 835, that Stephen II (Paul's
brother) had brought relics from France in 754; by c. 1000 Benedict of Soracte could state
that Stephen II founded the church to St Denis (with SS Eleutherius and Rusticus)
(Hülsen, *Chiese*, 466; Krautheimer, *Corpus* 4.161). Pope Dionysius's remains were taken
from S. Callisto by Paul, and it is his feastday, 27 December, that is on the inscription at
S. Silvestro (which does not name Denis of Paris; that it does not have Stephen or
Silvester either will be because their relics were in the oratory, not this basilica). The
present 16th/17th-century church has few visible remains of the 8th-century church of St
Dionysius. This (Krautheimer, *Corpus* 4.151-161) was a simple basilica, with a nave about
10 m wide, aisles about 5 m wide, and some 33 m long. The excavation of a new open
confessio in 1906-8 revealed portions of the older church, including the foundation walls
of the nave colonnades, the northern end-walls of both aisles, and the outer wall of the
east aisle; in 1962 'Servian' blocks were found in the foundations of the south-east corner.

[57] In the 8th century the door-lintel of St Mary's deaconry in Via Lata, which the flood
also reached (next note), was c. 2.50 m below the present street. But the original
pavement of S. Silvestro was only 0.90 to 1 m below the present nave and street level.
So the top of the steps mentioned here in the LP would have been 1.4 to 1.5 m below this
level. It follows that the steps mentioned did not reach the church itself, but only came
to an intermediate level somewhere between the nave and the travertine pavement which
marks the ancient street level, buried 4.00 m below the Piazza S. Silvestro. And such an
intermediate level is known: a stretch of marble pavement was seen in front of the
forecourt at a depth of 2.4 m, i.e. 1.6 m above the ancient pavement and exactly at the
level of the door-lintel at S. Maria in Via Lata. This pavement was 3.20 m wide, and may
have been a porch or a landing; there would have been 10 or 11 steps up to it from the
original pavement, then 9 or 10 steps up to the atrium and the church (Krautheimer,
Corpus 4.137-8). The LP's 'topmost step' must refer to this landing.

[58] That both now and (107:15) on 30 October 860 the floods were deep enough to
submerge the doorway of S. Maria in Via Lata proves that this building was much lower
than the present church, built 1491-1506 to replace one constructed in 1049. The church
before that date is to be identified with the remains of a group of six vaulted chambers
under the present church. See 98:45 with n. 102.

[59] This is the earliest occurrence of this name, found in other medieval documents for the
road which corresponded closely with the Via di Marforio until this was swallowed up by
the north-western end of the Via dei Fori Imperiali. Under the Republic the street seems
to have been called Lautumiae, but Platner & Ashby, 121-2, suggested that the name
Clivus Argentarius was in use under the Empire, and derived from the shops of the
argentarii (see further Platner & Ashby, 76, Basilica Argentaria). The street was the only
link between the Forum and the Campus Martius before the imperial fora were built. It
left the Forum between the Curia (S. Adriano) and the Carcer, and ran along the eastern
slope of the Capitoline Hill.

[60] Or the 'narthex' of St Mark's (Krautheimer, *Corpus* 2.217). But the passage seems to
be based on the account of the flood in 791 which spread beyond St Mark's after turning
a right angle by the Portico named Pallacinis (97:94).

began to run down into the sewer close to the monastery[61] of St Silvester and of St Laurence the martyr's called Pallacinis. From that day and thereafter the water gradually began to diminish, and after doing much damage the river returned to its channel: it overturned houses, desolated fields, sweeping crops away and uprooting trees. *[A.D. 855-6:]*

24. This done, the same blessed pope, constrained by great love, provided on the high altar in God's mother the ever-virgin St Mary our lady's church in Trastevere 1 gold-studded cloth, representing God's mother's assumption. In Christ's martyr St Anastasius's monastery[62] called Aqua Salvia he presented 1 Saxon bowl of fine silver weighing 3 lb. In God's holy mother's basilica formerly called Antiqua but now[63] located close to the Via Sacra he provided 1 gold-studded cloth representing the birth of our Lord Jesus Christ according to the flesh. In St Vitus the martyr's monastery[64] he provided 2 six-light canisters of fine silver weighing 4½lb. **25.** In St Cyriac the martyr's church[65] on the Via Ostiensis the venerable and distinguished pontiff provided 1 gold-interwoven cloth. In St Felix the martyr's church[66] *in Pincis* he provided 1 gold-interwoven cloth with griffins. In St Chrysogonus the martyr's

---

[61] If one monastery is meant (rather than both St Silvester's and St Laurence's), 'Silvester' may be an error for 'Stephen' (so Duchesne): St Laurence's had been united with St Stephen Vagauda (97:71). However, the title SS Stephen & Laurence is not used elsewhere for this monastery, Ferrari, 94.

[62] Cf. 103:28, and especially 97:91 with n. 189.

[63] Cf. c. 22 and nn. 50-1. When S. Maria Nova was still thought to be on the same site as S. Maria Antiqua, Duchesne 1897:27-30 wanted to insert *nova dicitur quae* (cf. 107:37). But once the original S. Maria Antiqua was found in 1900, the implication of the manuscript text that there was a move was confirmed. The LP is asserting the legal identity of the church on the new site with that on the old. Even after 1900 some still thought there were two churches of the same name simultaneously during part of the 9th century, and that the definite transfer of the title of the church from S. Maria Antiqua to S. Maria Nova occurred only in the 10th century (cf. Krautheimer, *Corpus* 1.223). This is as unnecessary as it is improbable.

[64] On the problems of identifying the various locations dedicated to St Vitus in Rome see 98:78 with n. 151. Duchesne (I.481) was probably wrong to identify the monastery with the deaconry described as *in Macello* or on the Esquiline. The monastery was that called *de Sardas*, with an oratory dedicated to St Vitus; it may not have been far from the deaconry. Vitus himself was a genuine martyr in Lucania whose cult spread to Rome at least by the 7th century (Gelasian Sacramentary). It is possible that one at least (but which?) of the institutions dedicated to him in Rome was earlier than this. Gregory I (*Ep.* 1.46; ed. *MGH* I.72), writing to Theodorus duke of Sardinia mentions a monastery of St Vitus which one Vitula had founded; and writing (*Ep.* 14.16; *MGH* II.435) to Leo bishop of Catana he mentions a monastery of St Vitus set on Mt Etna. Is the first of these in Rome? Or does Gregory refer twice to the latter?

[65] Cf. 98:109 with n. 195.

[66] Cf. 97:50 with n. 80.

titulus[67] the noteworthy prelate provided 5 fine silver chalices, weighing in all 2 lb ½ oz. In Callistus's *titulus* he provided 1 fine silver *ama* weighing 11 lb; there too he provided 4 bowls weighing 9½ lb; also 9 canisters weighing in all 11 lb. For this church's praise and glory he provided 1 gospel-book sheathed in silver and gold, weighing 15 lb; there too he provided 1 crown, 1 canister, a fine silver arch with 2 chevrons, weighing in all 40 lb. In St Balbina the martyr's[68] church he presented a fine silver gospel-book. **26.** In the world's teacher St Paul the apostle's basilica he provided 1 gold-studded cloth, beautifully adorned on a wondrous scale. In St Peter the prince of the apostles his mentor's church, burning with great love he provided a fine gold cover weighing 3 lb, to cover the navel[69] of the confessio. In the monastery[70] of Christ's martyrs SS Sergius and Bacchus called Callinicum he provided 2 fine silver chalices and 1 paten, 1 colander, 1 incense-boat, 1 censer, weighing in all 4 lb.

[A.D. 856-7:]

This remarkable and blessed pontiff, setting the gaze of his mind on a lofty footing and loving nothing whose end was earthly, delighted only in spiritual and wholesome works, and every day he kept his distinguished glance fixed on everything that brought salvation. **27.** Adorned with these sacred benefits, he presented to the prince of the apostles and the doorkeeper of heaven 1 cloth of wondrous beauty, of gold-wrought work and shining splendour, with the bountiful representation of the annunciation, and the *hypapante*, and how God's only-begotten Son himself entered the temple and sat among the teachers.[71] In St Paul the noteworthy preacher and apostle's basilica this blessed prelate, inflamed with great love and relying on God's support, provided a *spanoclist* crown of fine gold with its chains, with a gold cross in the middle; also a *spaniscus* which hangs permanently over his altar, weighing 2 lb 1 oz; in the same basilica he presented 1 fine silver incense-boat weighing 9 oz.

---

[67] This is the last reference to the old basilica of St Chrysogonus; the next reference is to the new basilica in 1123, on a much higher level, as at present; cf. 92:8.

[68] The last reference to this church until 1489. Balbina was not in fact a martyr but the founder of the *titulus* (cf. 98:73 with n. 128).

[69] The Latin *billicum* is for *umbilicum* and refers to the vertical shaft connecting the confessio with the underground tomb-chamber. The shaft is that in which the 'apostolic thuribles' were suspended, cf. 100 n. 16 etc.

[70] Not the same monastery as SS Sergius & Bacchus's at the Lateran; cf. 98:78 with n. 149.

[71] The three representations are from Luke 1.26-38 (the annunciation), Luke 2.22-39 (the presentation or purification; Candlemas), and Luke 2.47, respectively.

28. This remarkable and blessed pope provided 7 silver crosses;[72] from ancient times they customarily went in procession through all the catholic churches, and had been broken owing to their great age; this distinguished and holy prelate restored them afresh and again raised them up to their ancient condition; they weigh in all 51½ lb.

In Christ's martyr St Sebastian's basilica at Frascati this noteworthy father presented 1 gold-interwoven cloth with a cross with chevrons of fourfold weave in the middle. In[73] St Paul the noteworthy preacher and apostle's basilica he provided 1 rhodian red cloth with gold studding. In St Cyriac the martyr's *titulus*[74] he provided 1 gold-interwoven cloth. **29.** In St Peter the apostle his mentor's basilica this blessed pontiff, boiling with love, provided 1 silver light of wondrous size, weighing .. lb .. oz. In St Laurence the deacon's church outside the walls of this city of Rome, this blessed pontiff, filled by God's inspiration, provided 1 gold-interwoven cloth with gold studding, adorned with wondrous beauty.

Shining with light, he renewed the roofing of St Peter the apostle his mentor's distinguished church, that is the great vault[75] and the other vault which is over his body, by inserting 7 great beams, raised up with defiant ingenuity.

In St Cyriac the martyr's *titulus* he presented 1 gospel-book of fine silver, to that church's praise and glory.

---

[72] These are the seven stational crosses which served to indicate the starting point and then as standards for the Roman people when they came from each of the seven regions to *stationes* or other solemn gatherings. They are mentioned in the *Ordines Romani* from the late 8th century on: *Ordo* 15 § 12 (Andrieu 3.97) begins an account of the papal mass: 'Firstly the seven crosses proceed with psalm-singing and they come to the church where the *statio* has been announced'. This section of *Ordo* 15 is based on *Ordo* 1 § 24, but the seven crosses are not in the earlier text as such; this does however refer (in its longer recension) to 'the others who carry crosses' (Andrieu 2.74). See also Andrieu 3.70-72 n. 2. Other *ordines* of the ninth century mention the seven crosses. In describing the Major Litany on 25 April, *Ordo* 21 § 10 (Andrieu 3.248) states 'the poor come from the *xenodochium* with a wooden painted cross, crying *Kyrie eleison*... and after them come forth the seven stational crosses, carried by *staurophori*, with three lighted candles on each; then follow the bishops, priests, subdeacons, then the pontiff'. Also at Candlemas on 2 February, according to *Ordo* 20 § 7 (Andrieu 3.236), 'there come forth the seven stational crosses, (each) carried by a *staurophorus*, then the priests...'. These crosses or their predecessors may have been those borne in front of exarchs and emperors visiting Rome (97:36-37; 104:9). They were usually kept in St Anastasia's church (Duchesne 1887:402, 411). In the 12th century there were 12 crosses for 12 regions.

[73] MS E⁶ omits all from this point to the end of c. 30, but after c. 32 it inserts an expanded version of the end of c. 30; see n. 79.

[74] Not the church mentioned in c. 25, but, as at 100:28, the *titulus* in Rome.

[75] For this use of *navis* cf. 98:3. The great vault is the ceiling of the nave; at St Peter's this was significantly higher than that of the transept over the confessio.

[A.D. 857-8:]

30. This done, the same blessed pope, constrained by great love, in God's mother the ever-virgin St Mary our lady's church in Trastevere, raised up this church's great apse which was in ruins to a better condition, freshly building it and from its foundations;[76] he decorated the windows[77] with coloured glass and adorned it with a depiction in mosaic; and he freshly renewed the portico and baptistery[78] with the *secretarium*, all of them and the roofing in every case. St Mark the confessor and pontiff's cemetery outside the Appian Gate was then in ruins; he entirely restored it. At SS Peter and Marcellinus the martyrs' church[79] the roof was ancient and close to ruin; he newly restored the roof itself by taking down the most ancient beams and substituting others, and also renewed all the surrounding porticoes.

31. In the oft-mentioned world's noteworthy teacher St Paul the apostle's basilica, this holy bishop the prelate Benedict with great love

---

[76] See the comment in n. 89 on 105:60.

[77] It is unclear whether the windows are those of the apse or of the church (Krautheimer, *Corpus* 3.66).

[78] This is the earliest reference to a baptistery at this church.

[79] MS E[6] (cf. n. 73) has the following corresponding to the end of c. 30:
Since I am bringing this blessed prelate's sacred acts to mind, I am renewed with eagerness and the more compelled to tell his remarkable and happy solicitudes; he worked with the cares of God and with dutiful concern. For when, relying on the gaze from on high, he was continually touring round the saints' churches and beatific cemeteries while chanting songs in which he poured out prayers with copious tears to almighty God for the flock entrusted to him from heaven, that cleansed from all guilt it might remain signed by the holy name, he made his way to SS Peter and Marcellinus the martyrs' basilica in Merulana. He found this weakened with age and broken in ruin, covered in brambles and filled with thorns, so that no entry was available into it. Renewing its foundations with very solid construction, he restored it, improving on its former condition; now the people make their way into it and the full complement converges to praise God's name. Meanwhile he was led by the Holy Ghost to St Mark the confessor and pontiff's cemetery, reckoned as located between the Via Appia and the Via Ardeatina, and he discovered it damaged and broken in many ruins. With great solicitude he rescued it and wonderfully constructed and adorned it; he instituted and restored the mystery of God's worship which had departed from it for long periods of time.
   If this is trustworthy, the basilica of Marcellinus and Peter in the main text is that on the Via Merulana within Rome, not the Constantinian cemeterial-basilica on the Via Labicana. Deichmann and Tschira 1957:80 note that the latter had lost most of its relics in and since 827 (cf. 103 n. 14, 105 n. 60). It was certainly not well guarded, and the transfer of relics suggests that it was gradually abandoned; at some later date a medieval cemetery was established among the nave foundations, Krautheimer, *Corpus* 2.203. So it is unlikely that Benedict III would have bothered to restore it. Krautheimer, *Corpus* 2.194, infers that Deichmann and Tschira assume the present passage relates to the Via Merulana church, and he too (2.203) thinks that 'surrounding porticoes' would better fit this church, whether the expression means the aisles and narthex enveloping the nave, or aisles and ambulatory, or even the porticoes of an enclosure.

ordered the making of a net of beautiful splendour, of wondrous workmanship, all with jewels and *albaverae* and gold pommels, and containing enclosed enamelled pieces of gold, that is 21 large ones and the same number of small ones, and also 11 gold almonds and 10 hanging gold-studded jewels; he presented it, and ordered it to hang permanently over the most holy altar in the apostle's honour.

32. As a capable servant of Christ and as one who with pure heart unceasingly bore the great care of the holy church, he was spurred on by the ethereal Will; he saw that the holy church had suffered the theft or loss of the cover of that volume in which the readings of Paul the apostle's true preaching, and the epistles of the other apostles and of the prophets, are set out in order, readings which the subdeacons, aloft at the ambo, regularly read at all the *stationes* of the churches. Great concern seized him firmly, and he endeavoured to prepare another such volume similarly worthy of it; and he ordered that there be added in it the Greek and Latin readings[80] which the subdeacons regularly read on the Holy Saturday of Easter and on the Saturday of Pentecost. Decorating it with silver panels of wondrous workmanship, he freely presented it to the holy Roman church.

33. In his time Michael,[81] emperor of the city of Constantinople, son

---

[80] The Roman sacramentaries and lectionaries preserve no trace of Greek lessons on these days. But for the Easter Vigil *Ordo Romanus* 23 § 26 (Andrieu III.272, MS of 9th century) implies at least one lesson in Greek, and *Ordo* 30B §§ 39, 41 (Andrieu III.472, late 8th-century MS) assumes that all the lessons, chants and prayers were read first in Greek and then in Latin. The appendix to *Ordo* 28 (Andrieu III.412-13, MS of 2nd half of 9th century) has the same instruction for all four lessons and chants. Andrieu III.272 n. 26 thinks the practice was introduced in the Byzantine period. Perhaps Benedict was attempting to resuscitate a largely moribund custom.

[81] Michael III was nominally emperor from 30 January 842 when his father Theophilus died; he reached his majority in 854. This sending of gifts is connected with the patriarch Ignatius's deposition of the Sicilian bishops Gregory, Eulampius and Peter; for the involvement of Leo IV see p. 108, for that of Benedict p. 164. The present passage is the only allusion to the affair in the LP. Thirty years later Stylian, metropolitan of Neocaesarea, wrote to Stephen V that after his deposition and the anathema Ignatius pronounced against him, Gregory Asbestas sent letters and messages to pope Leo asking for help. Leo wrote to Ignatius requiring him to send an envoy to Rome, through whom Leo might judge the cause of the schismatics. Ignatius immediately sent the monk and confessor Lazarus who knew all about Gregory's case and explained it very carefully to the pope, who confirmed Ignatius's sentence against the schismatics. Then after Leo's death, these again importuned pope Benedict who followed his predecessor and kept to Ignatius's judgment against them (Mansi 16.427-8). Stylian was Ignatius's contemporary, but also a devoted partisan, and his version is none too accurate; but he at least confirms that the envoy sent by Ignatius in response to Leo's request was Lazarus. The LP is likely to be right that it was to Benedict that Lazarus presented Michael's gifts, even if it fails to mention the real reason why Lazarus had been sent to Rome; Stylian is wrong to state that Leo confirmed the sentence (nor did Benedict do this), but he may be right to imply that Lazarus was at any rate given his mission before Leo's death and Benedict's

of the emperor Theophilus, for love of the apostles sent a gift to St Peter the apostle by the hand of the monk Lazarus - he was very well trained in the painter's skill, though he was a Khazar by race. The gift was 1 fine gold gospel-book, with various precious stones; a chalice of gold, surrounded with stones; a hanging net adorned with wondrous beauty with precious jewels, pearls; 2 all-silk veils with all-silk crosses and also gold-studded edging as[82] small covers for that chalice, as is the custom of the Greeks; 1 cloth of fine imperial purple, over the high altar, with representation all over it, lattice-work and roses of gold-studding, decorated with great beauty; also 1 cross-adorned silk veil, with a gold-studded cross; and gold Greek letters.[83]

34. In his time the king of the Saxons named ...[84] came for the sake of prayer; he left all that he had, lost[85] his own kingdom, and made his

---

accession were known at Constantinople.

[82] The veils seem to be the covers, rather than separate items.

[83] I punctuate the last clause differently from Duchesne since Bertolini 1966:335 takes the passage to mean, surely rightly, that Lazarus brought from Michael a letter in Greek, made out in gold.

[84] The West Saxon king whose name caused our compiler problems was Æthelwulf (839-858); his visit was important for relations beween England and the papacy, not least in financial terms. He had originally planned to go to Rome in 839 (Nelson *AB* p. 42 with n. 4), but it was only in the time of Leo IV that he left England, passed through France and was welcomed honourably by Charles the Bald (*AB* 855 Nelson 80, placed before Benedict's succession to Leo), and, accompanied by his son Alfred (the Great), reached Rome. If Asser is to be believed, Æthelwulf had already sent Alfred to Rome in 853 when only five years old, and Leo IV had treated him as a king's son and made him a Roman consul (but see the comments in Keynes & Lapidge 1983:234 n.24). Æthelwulf now spent an entire year in Rome (Asser c. 11, in Keynes & Lapidge 69-70). Unless this is a slip and refers to the whole time the king was actually away from Britain, a year in Rome will have included the death of Leo and the accession of Benedict. The king's return through France is datable from the fact that in July 856 he was betrothed to Charles's daughter Judith. On 1 October 856 at the palace of Verberie he married her; Hincmar of Rheims crowned her, and Æthelwulf formally gave her the title of queen; he then sailed back with his bride to his kingdom in Britain (*AB* 856 Nelson 83). It is clear, at any rate, that the king's visit to Rome did not take place late in Benedict's pontificate as the LP seems to imply. Equally the LP is wrong to state (end of c. 34) that Æthelwulf died a few days after his return, though, curiously, this event did occur in the same year that Benedict's pontificate ended. *AB* 858 Nelson 86 has the death of Æthelwulf and Judith's marriage to his son, her step-son, Æthelbald. Asser c. 16 (Keynes & Lapidge 72) has Æthelwulf live two years after his return from Rome; he died 13 January 858 ('Florence' of Worcester), and was buried at Steyning in Sussex prior to reinterment at Winchester (Keynes & Lapidge 237 n. 38). So the chronological place of this chapter in the LP is odd. It may be governed by the end of the chapter, the reference to the king's death; or maybe the LP's date is influenced by the fact that Rome profited from Æthelwulf's *will*? The compiler was probably as ill-informed on the chronology of Æthelwulf's travels as he was on his name; and this chapter, like c. 33, may be an afterthought placed by the compiler at the end of the register extracts.

[85] *amisit*; as it stands this is apparently false. Keynes & Lapidge 1983:235 n. 26, think that it is a garbled reference to measures taken by Æthelwulf before he left England, or

way to the homes of Peter and Paul the apostles in Rome with a multitude of people. To St Peter the apostle he presented[86] a fine gold crown weighing 4 lb; 2 fine gold beakers weighing .. lb; 1 sword, bound with fine gold; 2 small images of fine gold; 4 silver-gilt Saxon bowls; 1 all-silk tunic with gold-studding; 1 all-silk white shirt with roundels, with gold-studding; 2 large gold-interwoven veils. When the holy lord pope Benedict requested this king of the Saxons to make[87] a public dispensation of money in St Peter the apostle's church from the weight of gold or silver pounds, he gave gold to the bishops, priests, deacons and all the clergy and the leading men of Rome, while to the people he gave a small amount[88] of silver. Afterwards, when the prayer for which he had come was finished, he returned to his own kingdom. A few days later his life came to an end and he went to the Lord.[89]

35. Much concerning himself with all God's churches, and ever rejoicing with his mind's dutiful affection and endeavour at their repair, he provided and renewed with wondrous work, in the basilica of the kingdom of heaven's keybearer his mentor, the silver chandelier previously stolen by the Saracens; it rests on four legs, and in it on feastdays and Sundays a lantern and a candle are placed together, close to the lectern, for that basilica's splendour, and it weighs .. lb.

Indeed, he was always intent on loving God's worship, he loved peace, and with a pure character he was a devotee of all heavenly

---

to developments while he was absent and after he returned. Before his departure (*id.* 235 n. 27) he seems to have divided his realm between his two eldest surviving sons Æthelbald and Æthelbert (Asser calls the former king; the latter signs as king and the Anglo-Saxon Chronicle reckons his reign from 855). When Æthelwulf returned from Rome, Æthelbald tried to stop him regaining his kingdom (Asser c. 12). On Æthelwulf and his kingdom cf. Stafford 1990:149-150.

[86] The terms for some of the gifts are unusual; see glossary on beaker, tunic, shirt.

[87] *facias*, either in error for *faciat*, or a reflexion of direct speech.

[88] Or perhaps 'a mite of silver', with *minutum* as a coin, as in Vulgate Luke 12.59. This was not the end of Æthelwulf's contributions. Not only did he complete the repair of the Schola Saxonum, destroyed by fire in 847 (cf. 105:20), but he was asked by Benedict to institute a fixed contribution charged to his kingdom's treasury in favour of the Roman church. Asser c. 16 (Keynes & Lapidge, 73) states that before dying Æthelwulf laid down, for his soul's sake, that every year there should be sent to Rome 300 mancuses (see 104 n. 78), to be divided three ways: 'in honour of St Peter, especially for the purchase of oil with which all the lamps in that apostolic church were to be filled on Easter eve, and likewise at cockcrow... in honour of St Paul, on the same terms, for the purchase of oil for filling the lamps in the church of St Paul the Apostle on Easter eve and at cockcrow...' and for the pope himself. Ina of Wessex (689-726) and Offa of Mercia (in 794; 365 mancuses) had already set precedents for Peter's Pence, but Keynes & Lapidge, 237 n. 37 and 268 n. 206, deny that even Æthelwulf's arrangement was the origin of this system; they suggest that it began under Alfred in 886/7.

[89] For the chronological problem see n. 84.

works. **36.** He laid down that when a bishop, priest or deacon died, the pontiff, with all the bishops, priests, deacons and other clerics should come together to bury his body and commend his soul; they should do the same when the pontiff departed this life; and he not only taught this but did it. His successor followed his tracks and from his piety towards him he imitated him like a devoted heir, just as in other matters as well. He performed one December ordination, 6 priests, 1 deacon; for various places 66 bishops. He was buried before the doors of St Peter's.[90]

---

[90] The location was in the narthex, immediately to the right of the central door. The epitaph was copied by Mallius (De Rossi, *Inscr.*, II p. 214), and alludes to the tomb's location very close to the main door: 'You whoever hasten hither begging Christ for pardon, I pray you, learn how this place is worthy of tears; lo, in this cold and quiet place the prelate Benedict III encloses the limbs which the earth gave him; and as the roof preserves the doors beneath a covering of stone, he decided that he was unworthy to be in the company of the godly'.

107. NICHOLAS (858-867).

This life is a curious patchwork. It seems that it was first compiled by a writer who followed his predecessors' habits of describing the background and ordination of the new pontiff (cc. 1-10) and then resorting to the registers of donations and restorations to provide material for the rest of the life. The result would have been very similar to life 106: indeed, strong resemblances between the first sections of lives 106 and 107 suggest a common author. But the text was then taken over by a writer more concerned with political history. He interpolated supplements into the lists of restorations and donations, at times even sacrificing the earlier text (see c. 43); how much has been excised we cannot know. The shifts of style are blatant, though the first insertion (c. 19) begins with what might at first sight be taken for register material. To the new compiler belong: cc. 19-20, 21-35, 38-42, part of 43, 44-50, 55-57, 58-63, 64, 68-76, perhaps 77-78, and, probably, part of 83. What is left of the earlier text appears in 1-18, 36-37, part of 43, 51-54, 65-67, 79-82, and parts of 83. The additions (including 77-78) make up about 60% of the extant text, and are marked off in the translation by rows of asterisks.

Stylistic considerations strongly suggest that the additions are from the hand that composed the following life, that of Hadrian II, the author of which may be John the Deacon. Whoever the author, he displays first-hand knowledge of events and was clearly well placed to use important documentary material. The register of Nicholas's correspondence is specifically cited at c. 57; letters are referred to there and at c. 77; and in a number of other places there are similarities between the compiler's phraseology and the wording used by Nicholas in what now survives of his letters or the wording of conciliar material likely to have been kept in the archive (cf. nn. 42, 59, 61, 63, 75-79, 82, 89, 94-5, 97-8, 102, 104, 129). It is fair to judge that the author has used his material competently, yet his account of the history even from a Roman perspective is incomplete. There is one glaring, and significant, omission. Not a word is said about the emperor Louis II's expedition to Rome in the early months of 864 to avenge the deposition of the archbishops of Cologne and Trier (who had supported king Lothar's divorce). This has in turn caused the omission of all the subsequent story of the archbishops' relations with Rome and, with it, all further reference to the king's divorce. The reason may be easily suspected: the author is careful nowhere to offend Louis II. All fault must lie at the door of the archbishops and of their allies Hagano bishop of Bergamo, John archbishop of Ravenna, and the latter's brother Gregory.

We have much information on contemporary events from outside the LP, most notably from the *Annals of St Bertin*, and the many surviving letters from Nicholas's own pen: these, including fragments but excluding dubious and spurious items, are 153 in number and occupy 400 pages in the text edited by Perels for *MGH Ep* 6 (*EKA* 4). Such an abundance of material can be used to flesh out the information in the LP. It is the purpose of this introduction and of the notes to the translation to do this.

Nicholas was a young man when he became pope; born hardly earlier than 820 (n. 4), he was still under fifty when he died. Undoubtedly his election was assisted by the influence of Louis II. The setback to imperial influence caused by Anastasius's failure to obtain the papacy in 855 was now removed, and Anastasius himself was rehabilitated, to become the pope's secretary, and his father Arsenius played a significant part in papal diplomacy. How far Anastasius helped in policy decisions is unknowable, but Nicholas was his own man and was to prove no mere tool of Carolingian interests. He inherited and extended a high view of his office; he was St Peter's vicar and held power over the whole church. Synods were to execute his own decisions. The secular power had a duty to protect the church but no right to interfere in it; yet the church had a duty to influence the state. It followed that archbishops could not deny him the right to overrule their decisions, that kings were not free to adapt the moral law to suit themselves, and that the Byzantine emperor was not to decide for himself, with or without a synod, the succession to the see of Constantinople. His enforcement of these principles earned him respect, sometimes grudging, from his contemporaries, but seldom affection.

These principles involved him in three important areas: relations with the Carolingians (especially the affair of Lothar's divorce, cc. 44-50); conflict with bishops and church councils in the west, not merely in connexion with Lothar's divorce, but even in Italy (cc. 21-35, 43, 64); and relations with the eastern church, especially over the questions of the missions to Bulgaria and Photius's right to the patriarchate of Constantinople (cc. 18-20, 38-42, 68-76).

His belief both in the indissolubility of marriage and in his right to judge cases involving princes brought Nicholas into conflict with Lothar II. Lothar, in 860, divorced queen Theutberga; he had already taken a mistress, Waldrada, and a synod at Aachen in 862 authorized him to marry her. Theutberga had fled to her brother Hubert's protection, and appealed to Nicholas who willingly intervened. His legates attended a synod at Metz in June 863. This recognized Lothar's new marriage: Nicholas suspected that his legates had been bribed, and it is likely enough. When archbishops Theutgaud of Trier and Gunther of Cologne brought the synod's decision to Rome, Nicholas reacted by holding a synod on 30 October to quash the synod of Metz and depose the two archbishops and bishop Hagano who was also implicated.

Such a sentence against his archbishops offended Lothar, who provoked the emperor Louis II into action, on the grounds that the archbishops had gone to Rome under Louis's guarantee; a punitive expedition against Rome, which the LP ignores, was the result. Nicholas was to be bludgeoned into reinstating Theutgaud and Gunther. Details are given by Nicholas (*Ep.* 53, J2886), and there are some points in Erchampert's *History of the Lombards of Benevento*, c. 37 (*MGH SSrL* 248, in the context of Louis II's death in 875), and in the *Libellus de imperatoria potestate*. But the best account by far is *AB* 864 Nelson 112-121. Louis II travelled with his wife Engelberga and with the archbishops. Hearing this, the pope proclaimed a fast and litanies. Louis arrived, and while he was close to St Peter's his men laid into the litany procession, broke its crosses and standards, and put it to flight ('in this tumult the wondrous and venerable cross, constructed most fittingly by Helena of holy memory... was broken and thrown into the mud'). Nicholas was at the Lateran; to avoid being taken prisoner he escaped by boat on the Tiber to St Peter's where he stayed two days fasting. Louis caught fever, but sent his wife to Nicholas to give him a safe-conduct. Nicholas came to Louis, and after discussions he returned to the Lateran; Louis sent the archbishops back to France.

Gunther sent Nicholas, by his brother Hilduin, a letter he had already sent to the bishops in Lothar's realm; if Nicholas would not receive it, Hilduin was to lay it on St Peter's tomb. *AB* 864 Nelson 113-116 then presents this manifesto, in which Gunther and Theutgaud give their version of the events of the previous autumn (*AF* gives a less complete but slightly better text, including the attribution of Nicholas's anger to Anastasius's criminal teaching, cf. Nelson 113 n. 8, 114 n. 10). They state that they had left Rome and had now been called back; they want the other bishops to encourage Louis the German's potential sympathy to Lothar's divorce. They had been sent by fellow bishops to Nicholas, and had presented their document, expecting a reply. But after three weeks they had been given nothing in writing, though Nicholas had once said that their document implied they were excusable and innocent. When called before Nicholas they had been condemned by a mob, not a synod, so they had rejected this sentence, and hold Nicholas excommunicated for his uncanonical and unprecedented behaviour. They know they have supporters against Nicholas; Waldrada's marriage to Lothar is valid. Nicholas refused to receive this statement. Hilduin and his men were impeded by the guards at St Peter's, one of whom was killed in the fracas, but they did put the document on St Peter's tomb, and returned to Gunther. A few days later Louis II left Rome, after much pillage, and celebrated Easter (2 April) at Ravenna. On Good Friday (31 March) Gunther reached Cologne and officiated liturgically in spite of the papal ban (which Theutgaud obeyed).

Fragments survive of Nicholas's letters at this time; in *Ep.* 24, J2766 Nicholas wrote (before he knew of Gunther's celebration of Easter) to drum up support from all the archbishops and bishops of the Gauls: 'if you are unanimous who can resist you? our fathers also resisted kings'; the deposed bishops may communicate as laity, but not excite crowds, stir up scandal, or function as bishops. That was what he had decreed with the synod. On 30 March 864 Nicholas wrote (*Ep.* 25, J2755) to Ado of Vienne urging him to recall Lothar to the right path. In May (*Ep.* 66, J2756) Nicholas ordered Hincmar to shun communion with Gunther who had dared to celebrate liturgically. In the summer Nicholas replied to Louis the German (*Ep.* 26, J2758); he rebuked the king: true, he had not consented to Lothar's union with Waldrada, but he had failed to condemn it; the pope wanted it made clear to all that Louis did not agree with it; he was to avoid communion with Gunther, who had usurped a banned ministry, and Theutgaud, and to order his men to do the same. Nicholas said he would follow Gregory IV's footsteps, and let the bishop of Bremen be archbishop over the Danes and Swedes - though the bishop should never have asked this from Gunther who had no power to grant it.

In an attempt to conciliate Nicholas and to disavow the actions of Hilduin in Rome, Lothar now deposed Gunther from Cologne, but without consulting Nicholas he gave the see to his cousin Hugh. On Nicholas's orders, Gunther came to Rome (with the remnants of the Cologne cathedral treasure); he wanted to explain Lothar's case, and his own, to Nicholas. Bishops from Lothar's kingdom sent envoys to Nicholas, with statements that they had erred about Waldrada. Lothar had already sent Nicholas his own excuses for his conduct and expressed his willingness to correct it (*MGH Ep* 6.217-19). But Nicholas did not give in over the two archbishops. He sent further letters to all the bishops in Gaul to confirm their deposition. In another letter (*Ep.* 29, J2764 of mid-864) Nicholas explained to Rodulf archbishop of Bourges and his suffragans why and on what authority Theutgaud and Gunther had been condemned; under pain of excommunication they were not to communicate with them, and they were to send legates to Rome about

1 November for a further council at which the archbishops could be again condemned.

Nicholas sent letters of forgiveness to the other bishops of Lothar's realm who had agreed to Waldrada but had now admitted their mistake. Two such letters survive: in *Ep.* 30, J2767, of 17 September 864, Nicholas accepted the excuses of Franco bishop of Tongres for attending 'the council of emptiness' (Metz), and forgave him; he praised him for fleeing communion with Gunther, who was usurping a forbidden ministry, and Theutgaud; he urged him to cure Lothar's wound by his advice, until he took back his wife, even if unwillingly. And in *Ep.* 31, J2768, of the same date, Nicholas forgave Adventius bishop of Metz (whose letter of excuse survives, *MGH Ep* 6.219-222, cf. Staubach 1982:196-7). We know also that at this time Nicholas wrote to Charles the Bald and Louis the German to have them send their archbishops or representative bishops to attend the forthcoming council in Rome; Nicholas advised them to tell the bishops of Lothar's kingdom about the synod.

This synod met early in November to confirm the depositions and to deal with the case of Lothar (and that of Ignatius). Gunther and Theutgaud came to the synod, thinking that Louis II's intervention would gain their reinstatement. If *AF* 864 Reuter 51-2 is to be believed, Gunther was repentant for his illicit liturgical activity, and, apparently twice, came to Rome but failed to persuade Nicholas to forgive and reinstate him. Nicholas sent Arsenius to Louis II to ask him to allow Nicholas to send legates to Charles on church affairs. Louis refused, thinking that Nicholas wanted to send legates to France with secret plans against himself. On the death of her brother abbot Hubert, Theutberga came to Charles for protection and was given the convent of Avenay hear Rheims.

So despite his threats and his intervention at Rome, by the end of 864 Louis was forced to give way to Nicholas and let the sentence on the archbishops stand. In February 865 Louis summoned a synod at Pavia, which asked Nicholas to forgive the archbishops; Louis's tone was very different from the one he had used a year earlier (Nelson, *AB*, 123 n. 5; Fuhrmann 1958:4-6; Hartmann 1989:284-5). But before pursuing relations between Nicholas and the the Carolingians further there are examples to be considered of Nicholas's assertion of papal authority over prelates other than Theutgaud and Gunther, and over church councils other than that of Metz.

Nicholas had to assert his authority even in Italy. At Capua, bishop Landulf deposed a deacon Pepo without due process (c. 43); the pope had Pepo reinstated. At Piacenza (c. 64) a deacon Paul had usurped the bishopric from Seufred; Nicholas had Seufred restored and banned Paul ever holding that bishopric. Far more difficult was the situation at Ravenna, where the archbishops had long behaved with a measure of independence that Nicholas could not tolerate. Archbishop John VIII was particularly obnoxious, and had already clashed with Leo IV in 853; his brother Gregory was Duke at a time when Ravenna had become a virtually independent state. John made life difficult for his suffragan bishops and interfered with Roman agents and property. To make matters worse he refused to obey the pope's summons to Rome. Nicholas's victory over him, his deposition and excommunication in March 861, and his submission, oath of loyalty, and restoration the following November, are fully covered by the LP (cc. 21-35). The effect of John's two defeats in one year was greatly to weaken his authority over his suffragans and to strengthen their dependence on Rome (cf. Ewig 1969:144).

In the Frankish kingdoms Nicholas rightly saw Hincmar of Rheims (845-882) as the most powerful archbishop and the one most likely to resent interference from Rome. Here the LP provides adequate information on one aspect only (cc. 58-63), the affair of Rothad II, deposed from his bishopric of Soissons by Hincmar and his suffragans at a council in 862, and his appeal to Rome. Nicholas was particularly concerned about his own right to review cases of deposed clergy who appealed. He ordered the case to be reopened. In January 865 Rothad was cleared, and Arsenius was sent to reinstate him (and dissolve Lothar's marriage). It was in the course of this incident that Nicholas became the first pope to invoke the False Decretals, see n. 128. In its account of the affair the LP introduces Hincmar at c. 58 with a phrase which, as Duchesne remarked, shows a peculiar disdain. Hincmar was well known at Rome, as were his see's importance, his personal worth, and his influence with king Charles and the bishops of the kingdom. But the affair of Rothad caused tense relations between Hincmar and Nicholas; the LP, breathing the same spirit as the pope's letters, reflects this. By a fortunate chance we have an account of the affair from the other side in *AB*, penned at this stage by Hincmar himself.

There is more to be said about Hincmar's dealings with Nicholas. Relations could be merely intrusive, as when (*Ep.* 133, J2837) the pope ordered Hincmar to tell his suffragan Hilmerad bishop of Amiens that Nicholas had imposed penance on a man who had killed a priest and monk. But even before the Rothad affair they had clashed. We know from a letter of Hincmar (*Ep.* 169, *MGH Ep* 8.144) to the pope that Nicholas, about September 863, had threatened to excommunicate him if he were to find that Charles the Bald would fulfil his promise to the papal envoys (Radoald and John) but then fail to receive Charles's daughter Judith and present her to her parents. At about the same date Nicholas (*Ep.* 111, J2746) had attacked Hincmar for his attitude to Robert bishop of Le Mans and for turning Charles's mind against Robert.

A separate issue between Nicholas and Lothar in which Nicholas supported Hincmar's rights was the case of Hilduin, the already-mentioned brother of archbishop Gunther, and a cleric in the diocese of Rheims (cf. Nelson, *AB*, 113 n. 7). In May 863 (*Ep.* 13, J2730) Nicholas ordered the bishops in Lothar's kingdom to persuade the king to remove Hilduin from the see of Cambrai, which Lothar had conferred on him when it had been without a bishop for ten months, and to let the clergy and people elect a bishop canonically. Hilduin himself was ordered (*Ep.* 14, J2732) under pain of anathema to abandon the see and restore what he had stolen. And in *Ep.* 15, J2731, Nicholas blamed Lothar for ignoring Hincmar's jurisdiction by installing Hilduin at Cambrai; he threatened penalties if Hilduin was not ejected and Hincmar's privileges were not respected.

Even after the Rothad affair, Nicholas and Hincmar were found on opposite sides in another incident not mentioned in the LP, and this is worth consideration for the light it throws on their relationship and for its revival of the thorny problem of Ebbo's ordinations (see 104:16). A clerk named Wulfad, a favourite of Charles the Bald from the 850s, was Charles's choice for the see of Bourges in 866 on the death of Rodulf, archbishop since 845. Bourges had to be in safe hands if Charles was to control Aquitaine. Wulfad was elected, an election whose validity, at this date, depended on his being a cleric and not a layman (cf. the case of Photius). But, as *AB* (i.e. Hincmar) explains, Wulfad had been ordained by Ebbo after Ebbo's deposition from the see now held by Hincmar. So Hincmar had a personal interest: if Ebbo's ordinations were valid, his own position at Rheims was in doubt; and at Soissons in 853 he had deposed Wulfad and others ordained by Ebbo (*AB* 866, Nelson 132-4 with nn. 14, 16, 19; *AB* 867 Nelson 138 with n. 3, 140 with n. 11, 141)

For his part, Nicholas had found Rodulf of Bourges obedient and loyal to Rome; in 864 Nicholas had replied to his detailed inquiries on matters of discipline and liturgy (*Ep.* 117 (864), J2765), and he would no doubt wish to see the archbishopric stay in safe hands rather than those of a man indebted to Hincmar; the pope's interest therefore coincided with the king's. However, as the *AB* does not fail to mention, Benedict III had upheld the council of Soissons which had deposed Wulfad (Perels prints Benedict's letter, J2664, in *MGH Ep* 6 as Nicholas

Ep. 59a). What was more, Nicholas himself had at Hincmar's request confirmed the same synod (28 April 863, *Ep.* 59, J2720), at the same time confirming Hincmar's primacy, his pallium and other privileges for the rest of his life, provided he never departed from the precepts of the apostolic see.

By 3 April 866 (*Ep.* 74, J2802) Nicholas was urging Hincmar to restore Wulfad and the others, or at least to convene at Soissons on 18 August with other archbishops and bishops, to deal with the case in a new synod. Of course, if the clerics were to appeal to Rome against the synod, Nicholas reserved judgment to himself; again we see him unhappy at giving a church council the final say. On the same day (*Ep.* 75-6, J2803-4) Nicholas wrote to the archbishops of Tours and Vienne and bade them attend at Soissons; and he apprised Wulfad of the situation. Charles attended the synod in person; and it agreed that Wulfad was validly ordained (canons of the councils of Nicaea (325) and of Carthage (418) were cited), but that Nicholas would need to change the sentence that he himself had confirmed. For fear of schism, the synod decided to defer the question, merely sending letters (Mansi 15.728) to Nicholas. But Charles saw this outcome as unsatisfactory; he requested Nicholas to let Wulfad be consecrated. On 29 August Nicholas (*Ep.* 77, J2811) replied that he could not allow this until he received the synod's acts. Charles went to meet Lothar at Attigny, and Theutberga was summoned there; she had permission to go to Rome. They decided to send a joint embassy to Nicholas to deal with various matters. Without waiting for a reply from Rome Charles had his son Carloman install Wulfad at Bourges, illegally, as the *AB* states, and this muddled the situation further.

Because of his personal interest Hincmar arranged for Charles's envoy, Eigil (who had presided at the recent council), to deal with Nicholas when in Rome, and to take a letter with him (*MGH Ep* 8 nos. 185-8). Eigil delivered the letter to Nicholas, and on 6 December the pope replied at length (*Ep.* 79, J2822). He recounted the whole story of the deposed clerics at Rheims; he attacked Hincmar as guilty of various faults. He praised the synod's agreement to restore the clerics, but blamed them for sending him only the letter and not the complete acts; these he ordered to be sent. The clerics were to be reinstated if no real objection could be alleged against them, though Hincmar was to have a year to appeal about this to the apostolic see; even so, Wulfad should not have been made a bishop in such haste. Nicholas wrote (*Ep.* 80, J2823) to Hincmar on the same date, blaming him for not sending a legate, but merely a letter, and that unsigned; he charged him with misuse of evidence and canon law; and he took the opportunity to attack him on other counts, such as his use of the pallium too frequently. The same day, Nicholas (*Ep.* 78, J2824) also thanked Charles for his zeal in restoring the clerics and mentioned his letters to Hincmar. Yet another letter (*Ep.* 81, J2825) contained Nicholas's congratulations to Wulfad and his restored colleagues - but they must treat Hincmar with due honour and obedience.

Eigil returned to France with the letters from Rome, and on 20 May 867 was received by Charles at Samoussy. The letter to Hincmar must have reached Rheims at much the same time; in Hincmar's view the pope had attributed false statements to him (his rebuttals of Nicholas's charges are *MGH Ep* 8 nos. 198-199). Acting on Nicholas's authority, Charles gave notice of a synod to be held at Troyes on 25 October 867 (Mansi 15.791-6). At this, some bishops wanted to curry favour with Charles and, so *AB* claims, they worked for Wulfad against Hincmar. Hincmar opposed their efforts and (according to Hincmar) the majority prevailed, and sent Nicholas a letter in Hincmar's support. But the messenger handed the letter to Charles, who prepared a letter to Nicholas against Hincmar, and both letters were sent to Rome. When the envoys reached Rome they found Nicholas dying, but able to reply that he would give Hincmar satisfaction on every point. With his need to secure a united western front against the Greeks, Nicholas had no choice but to accept a reconciliation with Hincmar, but face was saved since Hincmar could no longer refuse to accept Wulfad's consecration as archbishop of Bourges as Nicholas and Charles required, while Hincmar kept enough influence to see that problems over the clerics ordained by Ebbo remained, and thereby asserted the legitimacy of his position in Ebbo's bishopric (cf. Nelson, *AB*, 140 n. 11, 141 nn. 3, 14).

Nicholas's opposition to Hincmar then was in support of Charles; but it is necessary to backtrack nearly three years and pursue other matters concerning Nicholas and the Carolingians. *AB* 865 Nelson 122 reports that Lothar had said he himself would go to Rome; but his uncles Charles and Louis the German ordered him first to set his marriage right. Lothar suspected that in his absence they would seize his kingdom, so he asked his brother Louis II to get Nicholas to write to Charles and Louis the German to keep the peace and not harm his interests; Louis II persuaded Nicholas to do this.

In the early spring of 865 Nicholas sent Arsenius to Gaul; his tasks were to achieve peace between the four kings, to deal with the matter of Lothar's divorce and the two deposed archbishops, to reinstate Rothad of Soissons, to take a reply to the archbishop of Besançon on questions of marriage and clerical discipline (*Ep.* 123, J2787), and also to deal with the case of Engeltrude (see c. 48 with n. 100; on Arsenius's mission, Dümmler 1887-8:3.6; *AF* 865 Reuter 53-4). *AB* Nelson 123 comments on Nicholas's threatening tone in his letters to Louis the German and to Charles. The surviving relevant letters of Nicholas carried by Arsenius are: *Ep.* 33, J2773, to Charles on the need for peace between Louis II and Lothar. *Ep.* 34, J2774, to the episcopate in Charles's kingdom: they were to warn Charles to keep out of Louis's kingdom and remind him of the broken treaty with his brothers, so that Louis II, who had his imperial crown from the pope, could govern his hereditary realms, confirmed by the apostolic see (there were similar letters to Louis the German and his bishops). *Ep.* 35, J2776, to the archbishops in Lothar's kingdom, blamed their sloth and their failure to write; they were to persuade Lothar to cast off Waldrada, and he would be excommunicated if he did not obey. *Ep.* 36, J2777 (fragment), to Lothar, complained how the papal legates at Metz in 863 had been corrupted to oppose rather than execute the mission they had been given. *Ep.* 37, J2778, to Lothar, warned him of the excommunication if he did not repent and obey before Arsenius had returned; Nicholas had deferred the penalty only out of love for his brother Louis II (copies of these letters were sent to Charles).

Charles and Louis the German were on such bad terms with Louis II by now that they claimed to Nicholas that they could not let their bishops go to a council at Rome to deal with Lothar's marriage since Louis II would not grant them safe-conduct; Charles was even claiming that bishops were too busy guarding against pirates (Reuter, *AF* 54 n. 7, Dümmler, 1887-8, 2.114-115.) In a letter dated about 22 April 865 (*Ep.* 38, J2788) Nicholas praised Louis the German and Charles for their alliance, but rebuked them for not sending bishops to the Roman synod; they had said they had given Lothar a warning about his marriage, but Nicholas was annoyed that they had not sent him a copy. They had told Nicholas that Lothar intended coming to Rome (and Lothar had sent legates to announce this himself), but Nicholas prohibited Lothar coming; they intended to warn Lothar again about midsummer; Nicholas approved of this, insisting that Lothar must take Theutberga back. He was sending them copies of the letters Arsenius was bringing them so they could check whether these had been tampered with. In a letter of 9 June 865 (*Ep.* 39, J2790) Nicholas explained to Ado of Vienne why the intended Roman synod had not been held; he told him about Arsenius's mission and scotched a rumour that Theutgaud and Gunther had persuaded him to restore them.

Meanwhile Arsenius reached Gaul. In June he was honourably received by Louis the German at Frankfurt, and delivered the letters. With Louis's leave he continued to Gondreville to take Nicholas's letters to Lothar, and threatened him with excommunication if he did not take Theutberga back by the time he reported home. In July Arsenius reached Charles at Attigny and delivered the letters (and Rothad). Then he brought Theutberga, as Nicholas had instructed him, from Charles's kingdom to Lothar at Douzy, and ordered Waldrada to be taken to Italy. He made twelve leading men swear on Lothar's behalf and in Theutberga's presence an oath that Lothar would henceforth treat Theutberga as his true wife and as queen (*AB* 865 Nelson 123-4 with *AF* 865 Reuter 53-4; *AB* gives the text of this oath, dated 3 August 865). Nelson notes (*AB*, 125 n. 11) that one of the bishops present was Ado of Vienne, which suggests both papal and imperial pressure on Lothar: Ado had many contacts in the Carolingian world and was closely linked to Rome. The same day Arsenius restored Theutberga to Lothar (he was to accept her as his wife under threat of hell-fire), but Lothar was unrepentant.

Lothar made his peace with Charles and came to him at Attigny. Arsenius came back there and read out a letter of Nicholas which cursed those who some years before had looted much treasure from Arsenius if they did not restore it. Thanks to Charles, Arsenius was also able to receive back on St Peter's behalf the villa Vendeuvre which Louis the Pious had given to St Peter but which had fallen into the hands of one Wito (Guy). Theutberga then went to Gondreville, followed by Arsenius and Lothar. A few days later Waldrada was brought there; Arsenius celebrated the Assummption with Lothar and Theutberga, with ceremonial designed to demonstrate her regained status, and then took Waldrada to Orbe, where Louis II was expected to meet Lothar. From there Arsenius travelled around Alemannia and Bavaria to receive St Peter's properties in the surrounding districts, and returned to Rome (*AB* 865 Nelson 126).

So officially the year 865 saw Lothar and Theutberga reconciled. The reality was rather different. At the end of the year Lothar ignored his own promise and his magnates' oath, recalled Waldrada from Italy and secretly renewed the liaison. This was too much for Nicholas: Waldrada had failed to visit Rome, had returned to her province with royal status, and was laying snares against Theutberga. On 2 February 866 Nicholas excommunicated Waldrada and all who supported her or communicated with her, until she made satisfaction through penance, and sent letters broadcasting this decision (cf. *Chronicon* of Regino 866; one such letter survives, *Ep.* 42, J2808, 13 June 866; it orders copies to be sent through the neighbouring regions). The deposition of the two archbishops remained a problem. Gunther had been replaced at Cologne by Hugh. But *AB* 866 Nelson 130-1 records that Lothar ('some say at the instance of his brother Louis II'), took the see back and, bribed, gave it to Gunther's brother Hilduin, though in non-sacramental matters Gunther kept control; both Cologne and Trier lacked bishops a long time.

By early 867 Nicholas received a letter from Theutberga saying that of her own freewill she wanted to be stripped of her royal dignity and that Waldrada was Lothar's royal wife. Nicholas did not believe a word of this, and in a letter dated 24 January 867 (*Ep.* 45, J2870) he accused her of lying; Nicholas urged her to be steadfast and forbade her to come to Rome unless Waldrada was sent there first; if she wanted a divorce out of love of purity she should realize that she could not have it unless her husband wanted it as well. The following day, since Lothar's bishops had refused to accept Nicholas's earlier letters on Waldrada's excommunication, Nicholas wrote (*Ep.* 47, J2871) to them to give them that information; he ordered them under threat of excommunication both to make that sentence known and to tell him by letters and legates about Lothar's life with Theutberga. The same day Nicholas wrote (*Ep.* 48, J2872) to Charles that an incredible rumour had reached him that Charles had joined forces with Lothar against Theutberga; he objected to Lothar's plan to prove Theutberga's adultery by single-combat; he asked Charles to see that his letter to Lothar and his bishops was delivered and to tell him of any who refused to receive it. This letter to Lothar also survives (*Ep.* 46, J2873). In it Nicholas wrote that he had found out that Theutberga's letter to him had not been written voluntarily but extorted by force; he explained his views on divorce (as in *Ep.* 45), and ordered that Waldrada's excommunication continue (cf. *AB* 867 Nelson 138-9). On 7 March 867 (*Ep.* 49, J2874) Nicholas asked Louis the German to urge Lothar to show love to Theutberga (and to force Engeltrude to return to her husband Boso).

Lothar had decided to go to Rome and to send Waldrada there ahead of him, but, suspicious of what Charles would do in his absence, he went to see Louis the German at Frankfurt. He committed his whole kingdom to him except for Alsace which he gave to Hugh, his son by Waldrada (*AB* 867 Nelson 139). Replying to a letter from Lothar, Nicholas (*Ep.* 50, J2878, 7 October 867) warned him to order the clergy of Cologne and Trier to gather and elect themselves bishops: the new bishops must be seen to have been elected canonically and not through the favour of Waldrada, Theutgaud or Gunther. They could then be consecrated, and the papal legates would give them the pallium. Nicholas had now decided that such was the gravity of the offences committed by the two former archbishops that all possibility of their restoration had to be permanently excluded (cf. *AF* 868 Reuter 57). On 30 October he wrote (*Ep.* 42, J2885) to Louis the German asking him to stop pestering him to restore them. The same day he wrote (*Ep.* 53, J2886) to the bishops in Louis's kingdom urging them to stop asking him to restore the archbishops. He listed their crimes, recounting the whole story from the beginning (it is to this letter that we owe Nicholas's account of Louis II's intervention in Rome early in 864). In another letter to Louis on the same day (*Ep.* 51, J2884) the pope thanked him for sending a bishop to ask Lothar to fulfil his orders; Lothar must not come to Rome until he had sent Waldrada to Nicholas, had acknowledged Theutberga as queen, and had allowed bishops to be canonically provided at Cologne and Trier; the pope added that he expected Louis's help when papal legates came to collect St Peter's revenue in his kingdom the following May.

So, a fortnight before his own death Nicholas had consistently kept to his stand on the question of Lothar's marriage, yet still felt he needed proof that Lothar had taken Theutberga back.

Nicholas was actively interested in the affairs of the eastern church; the coverage of this in the LP is good though far from impartial (cc. 18-20, 38-42, 68-76). This concern involved him both in the mission to Bulgaria and in the question whether Photius (858-867, 878-886) or Ignatius (847-858, 867-877) was the rightful patriarch of Constantinople; and his interest in Bulgaria itself had repercussions on the relationship with Constantinople, over which he was concerned to assert Roman primacy.

Nicholas clearly hoped to reestablish Rome's erstwhile jurisdiction in Illyricum, an issue which becomes very prominent in the next life. Hence, in part, his interest in the Bulgarian mission, for part of Bulgaria was in the ancient Illyricum. It would be unreasonable to suppose that Nicholas was uninterested in missionary work for its own sake. We have seen evidence of his concern already (p. 192) for the Danes and Swedes. (In another document (J2759, 31 May 864) whose genuineness has been questioned, Nicholas is said to have granted Ansgar archbishop of Hamburg, at the request of Salomon bishop of Constance and legate of Louis the German, the use of the pallium and public authority to evangelize all the nations around, Swedes, Danes, Slavs and others wherever in those areas God has opened the gate to them; to reduce the power of the archbishops of Cologne, he ordered the bishopric of Bremen to be added to the archiepiscopal province of Hamburg.) In another letter of mid-864 (*Ep.* 27, J2761), Nicholas thanked the Danish king Horic for gifts sent through Salomon, expressed his pleasure at the faith the king already had, even before his baptism, and urged him to stop worshipping idols and serving demons. Nicholas was interested also in the missions to Moravia conducted successfully from 863 by the

Byzantine evangelists Cyril and Methodius; in 867 he invited them to Rome (*Translatio S. Clementis* 8; *Vita Methodii* 6). What the LP totally fails to reveal about the Bulgarian mission is that, as in Moravia, Byzantine missionaries were there first. In 866 Nicholas responded to an appeal from king Boris, and sent him missionary bishops, including the later pope Formosus; as Formosus was already bishop of Porto, Nicholas refused to name him archbishop in Bulgaria.

Late in 858 the Byzantine patriarch Ignatius had been forced to abdicate; the layman Photius was chosen to succeed him, and as patriarch he sent letters to Nicholas. Nicholas complained to the emperor Michael III and on 25 September 860 sent envoys to investigate; meanwhile he would not recognize Photius (c. 20). At a synod at Constantinople in 861 the envoys did recognize him (c. 40); when they reported this to Nicholas, the pope disowned them, and on 18 March 862 insisted on the question being judged at Rome (c. 41). Ignatius's supporters presented a biassed view of the case, and at a Roman synod in 863 (c. 42, cf. n. 81), Nicholas rejected the synod of Constantinople, and deposed and excommunicated Photius. Michael protested violently; on 28 September 865 Nicholas defended his actions in a very sharp letter, and expatiated on the rights of the Roman church, though by calling Photius or his representatives to Rome he did not slam the door on a re-examination of the case.

The effect, however, of his sending a mission to Bulgaria and a harsh letter to Photius (both on 13 November 866) was, not surprisingly, that Nicholas infuriated Photius. His missionaries seemed to Photius to be intruding into the work of the Greeks. And the detailed instructions on moral and legal matters that Nicholas supplied to his missionaries was anti-byzantine in spirit. And part of Bulgaria was not in ancient Illyricum at all but within the jurisdiction of Constantinople. The Roman envoys were stopped at the border and went home (c. 72). Photius denounced the Roman interference to the other eastern patriarchs and convoked a synod at Constantinople in the summer of 867, which excommunicated and deposed Nicholas. But Nicholas died before he could know of this and the sequel. In one of his last letters Nicholas bitterly bemoaned the Greek attitude to the Roman church; but the need for a united western front against Constantinople at least brought about a reconciliation with Hincmar. Such was the formal beginning of the Photian schism, which, even when solved, left a bitter memory and played its part in the permanent division between the eastern and western churches.

Had Nicholas lived a few weeks longer he would have seen himself victorious in the east, as he was in the west. But even in Italy there was opposition to him, and the new pope's stance towards his memory would be crucial; in fact Hadrian II advised the bishops attending the synod of Troyes (8 May 868) to have Nicholas's name included in prayers at mass, though not even at Rome did any cult develop around his memory. But events in the east soon showed that Ignatius would not prove a mere tool of Rome; the Bulgarians looked to Constantinople; when Ignatius died he was succeeded by Photius.

CHRONOLOGY OF LIFE 107

For what remains of the account of buildings and donations from the hand of the original compiler, the chronology in Geertman's view (*More veterum*, 211) can be largely reconstructed (though he does not attempt to do it), but, given the way the text was then treated by the second compiler, this gives no guarantee for the chronology of the historical insertions. However, the chronology of these presents little problem, despite some debate about cc. 21-35; see n. 39.

Reckoning the first six months to September 858 as the first indiction-year of Nicholas, but excluding September to November 869, there are 10 indiction-years in the pontificate. St Peter's is the most frequent recipient of attention from Nicholas or others; excluding c. 18 which is part of a historical insertion there are nine references (cc. 13, 14, 17, 36, 43b, 54, 66, 79-80, 81b); so one indiction-year is missing from the record. The second donation (c. 14) is stated to be in the first year of the pontificate, a dating which, if it is reckoned from April 858, does not exclude part of the second indiction-year (indiction VII). The floods in c. 15 are specified as in indiction IX (860-61), and if they are not a later historical insertion (they do not seem to be: the flood of January 856 was included in life 106), they provide another fixed point. It follows that the missing indiction-year is indiction VIII (September 859 - August 860).

The following arrangement of the donations (with the historical insertions starred) may be tentatively proposed:
1-10 Early career, character; ordination in the presence of Louis II.
11-13 donations: indiction VI, April 858 (or even September 857) - August 858.
14 donations (year 1 mentioned, ending April 859): indiction VII, September 858 - August 859.
15 floods of Tiber, 30 October 860, and 27 December (indiction IX).
16-17 donations: indiction IX, September 860 - August 861.
*18-20 eastern affairs: gifts and embassy from Michael III (no later than September 860, so earlier than c. 15, but perhaps in the same

indiction year). Nicholas sends envoys to Constantinople to decide on images and report back about Ignatius.

*21-35 the affair of John of Ravenna, down to 18 November 861.

36-37 donations: indiction X, September 861 - August 862.

*38-42 eastern affairs: misbehaviour of the papal envoys, deposition of Zacharias, March 862 to winter 862-3:

*43a the case of Pepo and Landulf.

43b donations (mainly excised): indiction XI, September 862 - August 863.

*44-50 the case of Lothar's divorce, November 862 - late 863: council of Metz (June 863); Lateran council (30 October 863).

51 Nicholas's scheme to feed the poor.

52-54 donations: indiction XII, September 863 - August 864.

*55-57 consultations of Nicholas, especially on marriages.

*58-63 the case of Rothad and Hincmar (mid-864 to January 865).

*64 the case of Seufred of Piacenza and his deacon Paul.

65-66 Nicholas's sympathy for the lame and blind; he restores St Peter's aqueduct: indiction XIII, September 864 - August 865.

67 Nicholas rebuilds and garrisons Ostia.

*68-76 eastern affairs: Bulgaria and Constantinople, August 866 to November 867 (assassination of Michael III).

*77-78 Nicholas's guidance, letters, character.

79-81a donations: indiction XIV, September 865 - August 866.

81b-82 donations: indiction XV, September 866 - August 867 (donations in indiction I, September - November 867, may have been reserved for the next life, but the material was never used).

83 Ordinations, death, burial, 13 November 867.

107. **1.** NICHOLAS [I; 24 April 858 - 13 November 867], of Roman origin, son of the regionary Theodore,[1] held the see 9 years 2 months 20 days.[2] From his earliest childhood this blessed man's acts shone forth clearly to everyone, and were famed for their incorrupt character. His holy actions distinguished him so beautifully that he took no dishonourable delight in any game or anything else that children are wont to do. He devoted himself to patience and sobriety, glowing with humility and an outstanding degree of purity. His father, as a lover of the liberal arts and well able to kindle the most noble qualities in him, imbued him with chaste nourishment and bountiful habits, and adorned him with studies of literature in his retentive mind,[3] so that there remained no kind of sacred learning that he had not conceived in his interior depths and transmitted to his understanding. He grew in physique and he grew in wisdom, famed, relying on modesty, adorned with knowledge. If he spied anywhere men of commendable character, his interest was aroused, he was eager to associate with them, and he rejoiced with them abundantly. **2.** When with his wise father he used to frequent a particular holy man who used to preach much to the faithful by the enlightenment of the Holy Ghost, this man strongly affirmed that he would climb to the top; for he noticed how great was his inner beauty and how his mind's sweetness glistened. On his

---

[1] There was a Theodore, notary and *scriniarius*, at the council of 853, but Duchesne thought that at this date 'regionary' should refer to one of the defensores in the city administration. Formed into a *schola* by Gregory I, the seven regional defensores, normally clerics, 'formed the elite corps of a body of officials who were ubiquitous in the papal patrimonies, and later in the Republic generally' (Noble, 222-3).

[2] Read '9 years 6 months 20 days' (*vi* for *ii*); Duchesne's apparatus has no variants, MSS C[4] and E[6] attribute '9 years 7 months 19 days' to the vacancy after Nicholas's death. As Nicholas died 13 November 867 (c. 83), the reckoning will be from Sunday 24 April 858. But note that the Montecassino Catalogue has 9 years 6 months 13 days (and Paris 5140 has 9 years 9 months 13 days); Nicholas' ordination could just have been a week later (1 May 858). Cf. 106 n. 1.

[3] Duchesne here prints his own emendation *in optimatis (mentibus)*, no doubt inspired by *nobilissimum* earlier in the sentence, and perhaps supposed to mean 'suited to the mentality of an aristocrat'. But it seems irrelevant to bring in the idea of aristocratic mentality here (unless a contrast is intended with the kind of education given in the *schola cantorum*); and would a ninth-century writer have used *optimas* in the singular? The context suggests meanings such as 'insatiable, retentive, compliant, well-disposed'. Whatever he wrote, it seems likely that the copyists did not understand it. Of the MSS, CE[12] have *inoptinatis*, E[6] has *inopmatis* (Bianchini §577 printed *et optimis artibus*, a desperate emendation). I propose *inopinatis mentibus*: the sense intended may have been 'unopinionated, unprejudiced', or (from *opinatus* as a participle meaning 'filled with images') 'not yet full of images, therefore receptive'. If the compiler had read Ovid, *Heroides* 15.139 *mentis inops* ('frenzied', 'out of my mind'), he may have thought the poet was referring to a mind waiting to be filled.

encouragement he was taken into the order of the clergy, so that what he had sensed by the Will of God might be fulfilled in time to come. Moreover when the prelate Sergius [II] heard that he was rising to the summits of supreme activity, he took him from his parents' house, placed him in the patriarchate, and with the grace of blessing established him in the rank of the subdiaconate.[4] In this he was ever observed to live wonderfully and was fired with heavenly ardour. 3. Pope Sergius was taken from this corruptible life, and the prelate Leo [IV] took on the reins of the Roman church. He very often saw the fruits of the perseverance he achieved, and with enormous love he consecrated him deacon. While he served in this order, so much grace was granted him from above, that he was seen by all to shine with the perfections of supreme activity. By the clergy he was loved, by the nobles praised, by the people magnified.

4. When pope Leo was dead, Benedict [III], a man of wondrous blessedness and a holy pontiff protected from on high, received preferment to the Roman see, and he joined him to his administration, because he loved him more than those close to him by blood relationship, so that he delighted in not being without him for a moment of time.[5] It was with him that he handed down and promulgated a decision on whatever they saw to be suited to the needs of church affairs; he observed how wise was the help his judgment provided and how famous was the power of his mind; for he always used to do by his own effort the more needful things that they each noticed. Brought to the end of his life, he drank the cup of a precious death. And, as he was still a deacon, he bore him on his shoulders[6] with the other deacons to St Peter the apostle's basilica, and with his own hands placed him in the tomb, evincing the meed of affection that he had for him and the integrity of his love.

5. At that time the unconquered Caesar Louis had departed from Rome.[7] When he learnt of his passing he returned there saddened and troubled. The Romans, on losing so great a shepherd, were shedding sad tears of mourning. When the clergy,[8] the dignitaries and the group of

---

[4] Ordination as subdeacon by Sergius (844-7) suggests that Nicholas is unlikely to have been born earlier than about 820.

[5] In other words, Nicholas served in the curia; but for the exaggeration here see p. 162. Note, too, the presumption here that nepotism was to be expected of a pope.

[6] Cf. 106:36.

[7] Louis II was still at Rome 1 April 858 when he dated a privilege for the abbey of Nonantola; Benedict died, probably, 9 days later. Louis returned to influence the election, cf. next note.

[8] Cf. *AB* 858 Nelson 87: 'Nicholas took (Benedict's) place, more through the presence

leading men gathered together, they occupied themselves in fasting, prayer and watching. They besought the Lord with unceasing effort that he might see fit to show them a man such as they had lost, whom they might raise up to the pinnacle of the pontificate. **6.** While this was being done, they gathered with all the people in St Dionysius the confessor and pontiff's basilica.[9] In it they held discussions for some space of hours and inflamed with light from the stars with one accord[10] they enacted that he be prelate of the apostolic see, and at a swift pace they immediately made their way to Peter the prince of the apostles' hall, to which he had fled and where he was lying low: for he said he was unworthy to take on the helm of so great a rule. But those who were present made a rush and took him by force from that basilica. They brought him into the Lateran patriarchate with holy acclamations, and put him on the apostolic throne. **7.** Afterwards he was taken by the groups of nobles and by all the people to St Peter the apostle's basilica, and in Caesar's presence he was consecrated, elevated to the apostolic see and made pontiff; and he celebrated the ceremonies of mass beatifically over the apostle's sacred body. He was taken back to the Lateran patriarchate by thick ranks of leading men and of people with hymns and spiritual chants. Then is the city crowned,[11] the clergy rejoice, the senate are glad and the fullness of people magnificently rejoice.

On the third day from his consecration he dined with the emperor; he was resplendent with sophistic speech, and full of brightness he

---

and favour of King (*sic*) Louis and his magnates than through election by clergy.' Louis's presence at Nicholas's ordination (c. 7) was a clear sign that he approved the election, and it is very likely that he influenced the outcome (he was in Rome), though the LP avoids stating that he took part in it (he was not one of the electorate). The view of the election taken by *AB* is confirmed by the fact that supporters and agents of Louis, such as Radoald of Porto, Arsenius of Orte, and even Anastasius (whom Louis had tried to make pope in 855), though compromised under Benedict, returned to favour under Nicholas and now played major roles. Nelson, *AB* 87 n. 10, comments that members of Nicholas's entourage also attempted to bolster imperial ideology; cf. Delogu 1968:161.

[9] Now S. Silvestro in capite, cf. 106 n. 56; *confessor* is a surprisingly accurate reminiscence that the 3rd-century pope Dionysius was not a martyr, and shows that the mistaken notion that Dionysius was the Parisian martyr had not yet taken root.

[10] According to 108:3 they first attempted to elect the priest of St Mark's (the future Hadrian II), but he refused, as had done in 855. On both occasions he perhaps wished not to impede the imperial candidate (cf. 106 n. 4).

[11] A very similar set of phrases occurs at 106:5, at much the same point of the life. The city is 'crowned' (decorated with garlands). Duchesne noted that with the punctuation of the earlier editions ('He is crowned, the city rejoices...') this passage gave rise to the idea that this was the first papal coronation. It was assumed that Louis II granted this right to Nicholas out of affection and deference; this was taken to be the origin of the first of the crowns eventually comprising the triple tiara.

banqueted in Christ. When the magnificence of the feast was finished he rose, and, kissing Caesar as his spiritual and dearest son, he encompassed him with love unbounded. **8.** These things thus completed, the serene emperor departed from the city and took up residence at the place called Quintus.[12] Hearing this, the blessed prelate, compelled by the fullness of his delight and love, made his way there with the dignitaries and leading men of the Roman name. When His Excellency the emperor saw him, he came to meet him as he arrived; and Caesar took the bridle of the pontiff's horse in his hands and led it on foot the distance of an arrowshot. With him he entered the imperial pavilion, and together they enjoyed wholesome conversations. **9.** And when the tables were decked with banquets, together they took food with spiritual keenness. When they had had their fill and the tables had been removed, the serene Caesar conferred many gifts on the blessed prelate. He received them, mounted his horse and essayed to return whence he had departed. Filled with love for him, the emperor mounted the saddle of the imperial horse and went with him with triumphant resolution. When they reached a certain very open spot on the journey, the emperor dismounted from his horse and again led the pontiff's horse in the way we mentioned above; and decking each other with sweet kisses they radiantly rejoiced. **10.** Caesar returned to his pavilion and continued the journey he had begun. The prelate, hemmed in by the groups of nobles that had sheltered him, entered Rome and was magnified for his bountiful behaviour.

He was[13] handsome in appearance, fair of form, learned in speech, humble in conversation, distinguished in action, intent on fasting and the worship of God, generous to the poor, a protector of orphans, a patron to widows, and the defender of the whole people. But since we cannot set down all the holy works he did in this writing,[14] let us return to what he presented to the holy places.

11. This blessed prelate, filled with God's inspiration, provided in God's mother St Mary our lady's deaconry called *Cosmedin*[15] 1 all-silk cross-adorned cloth, representing 2 large lions. There too he provided

---

[12] At St Leucius's (Tor di Quinto), cf. 106:9.

[13] Compare 106:20, for very similar wording. In both lives 106 and 107 the compiler concludes his account of the election with a resumé of the pope's character before embarking on his excerpts from register material (cf. also 105:18).

[14] Fortunately the interpolator followed a different policy; see p. 189.

[15] Note not merely that this deaconry is placed first but that it recurs twice in this life (cc. 36, 52); this is surprising in a life which (as the text now stands) mentions relatively few churches (only nine, apart from the major basilicas, even fewer if we exclude those beyond the walls).

1 white veil with roses, decorated around with tyrian, of wondrous size. In that deaconry he also presented 1 fine silver Saxon bowl, gilded, they weigh 2 lb 4 oz. **12.** In the Saviour's basilica which has taken its name from that of Caesar,[16] he provided fine silver crosses which hang before the figure of the substance of our Lord Jesus Christ's flesh;[17] on them to his praise and glory is a wax figure on the usual feastdays, weighing 4½ lb. In the ever-virgin Mary our lady's basilica called *Praesepe* he provided 1 fine silver squat chandelier weighing 8 lb 4 oz. **13.** This God-protected and blessed pontiff, filled with favour from on high, presented in St Peter the apostle his mentor's basilica 1 fine gold bowl with precious jewels, weighing 3 lb 9 oz. In this holy basilica's confessio he provided 1 fine gold *iugulum* weighing 2 lb. In the same church he provided 11 fine silver crosses, weighing together 13 lb 5 oz. So too, in St Paul the apostle and teacher of the gentiles' basilica, 2 fine silver crosses, weighing together 4 lb. In St Laurence the martyr's basilica outside the walls he provided 2 fine silver crosses, weighing together 4 lb.

14. In the first year of his pontificate there was brought to his Beatitude a gold crown embellished with precious jewels, with a weight of 8 lb 4 oz; in great love he raised it up on gold chains above the most holy altar for that[18] basilica's glory.

In the same church of St Peter the apostle his mentor, 9 fine silver bowls, weighing in all 12½ lb. In SS Stephen and Silvester's monastery,[19] which former pope Paul of holy memory had newly founded, in the larger church called St Dionysius's, this God-protected, venerable and distinguished pontiff provided 4 cross-adorned silk veils for the holy altar's honour and glory.

15. In this distinguished pontiff's [time],[20] i. e. on the 30th day of October in the 9th indiction [860], the river called Tiber left its channel and spread over the plains; it swelled in great spate and entered the city of Rome by the postern-gate called St Agatha's, at the 10th hour of the day. Meanwhile in some places it even lapped over, and entered St

---

[16] Constantine's basilica (the Lateran).

[17] This odd expression might refer either to a figured crucifix or to an image of the incarnation (perhaps a nativity scene). The expression is not likely to refer to the reserved Sacrament, in spite of the phraseology of the early version of the Roman Eucharistic Prayer given by Ambrose, *de Sacramentis* 5.21 (*CSEL* 73.55): *oblationem... quod est figura corporis et sanguinis...*

[18] In view of the next sentence this may refer to St Peter's, not St. Laurence's.

[19] Cf. 95 nn. 9, 11; 103 n. 68; on the larger church, 106 nn. 55-6.

[20] The expression has been ungrammatically shortened from the source passage, 106:23; for the details see the notes to that chapter.

Laurence's church called Lucina's; from there it extended itself and entered St Silvester's monastery,[21] so that of the steps which go up to St Dionysius's basilica none except the topmost was visible because of the flooding; from there it expanded itself through[22] the street called Via Lata and entered God's mother St Mary's basilica there,[23] and the water swelled so much that this church's doors could not even be seen because of the flooding. Then it went up through the streets and lanes as far as the Clivus Argentarius. From there it turned a right angle and entered by the portico[24] in front of St Mark's church. Then it made a rush and began to run down into the sewer close to the monastery of[25] St Laurence the martyr's called Pallacinis. From that day and thereafter the water gradually began to diminish, and after doing much damage the river returned to its channel: it overturned houses and walls, desolated fields, sweeping crops away and uprooting trees.

In the same way, on the 27th day of December, the feastday of St John the Evangelist, in the same indiction, the river called Tiber again entered, it left its channel... *as above*, in the city of Rome... *all as above*.[26]

16. In the same way this distinguished and blessed pontiff provided in St Valentine's monastery in the territory of Narni, located close to Terni,[27] 1 gold-interwoven cloth representing lions, and *mizinum* around it.

As for the aqueduct called Iocia,[28] which for unrolled periods of years

---

[21] Note that the reference to St Silvester's monastery does not cause the same problems as occur in the MS text of the source passage.

[22] For 'itself through' (*se per*) the source passage 106:23 has 'over' (*super*).

[23] See 106 n. 58 for the level of this church before the 11th century.

[24] Perhaps 'narthex'; see 106 n. 60.

[25] 'of St Silvester and of...' in the source passage.

[26] For this second flood within two months the compiler could not even be bothered to recopy the formulas; hence the references to what precedes.

[27] This monastic church is mentioned at 93:7, 10. Though at the gates of Terni (8 miles from Narni), it is stated to be in the territory of Narni. This is the result of Gregory I (*Ep.* 9.72) having annexed the bishopric of Terni to that of Narni (the bishopric was only reinstated by Honorius III in 1218); Terni was thereby deemed to have lost municipal status.

[28] So the aqueduct's name is spelt in the MSS. Probably the *forma Iobia* or Aqua Iovia (Marcia) is meant; so Duchesne, and Platner & Ashby, 27. This passes over the Arch of Drusus near the Appian Gate (Porta S. Sebastiano), and is often mentioned in the 8th and 9th centuries (cf. 97:61 with n. 117, 104:21, and the Einsiedeln Itinerary: 'the porta Appia: there is the aqueduct Iobia which comes from the Marcia and runs to the river-bank'). After heading towards the Circus Maximus it emptied into the Tiber near the *Schola Graeca* (S. Maria in Cosmedin). There may have been some connexion between its repair and the foundation of a hospice at the same spot recorded in the next sentence. Duchesne noted how the false reading (Tocia) in earlier editions of the LP gave rise to

was much broken - by it used to run the water through a water-pipe[29] into the city of Rome - the venerable and distinguished pontiff made preparations for this aqueduct's building and restoration from the foundations.

At the church of our Lord and God Jesus Christ's same mother called *Cosmedin* he provided a broad, spacious and distinguished hospice for the purposes and need of pontiffs, where they could be fully accommodated with all who were in their service, whenever it was opportune.

17. Also, in St Peter the prince of the apostles his mentor's church he presented 40 veils with gold-studding, representing the figures of lions, in the arch of the *presbyterium*. On the same [church] he conferred a fine silver chain made with nimble workmanship, weighing 4 lb. In the oratory of the Holy Cross, established inside St Peter the apostle's basilica, he provided 1 silver bowl weighing 2 lb. In St Paul the apostle and teacher of the nations' basilica this most holy pontiff provided 1 silver candelabrum weighing 2 lb 6 oz. In St Eusebius the confessor's *titulus* he provided above the canopy a fine silver cross with a melon.

* * * * *

18. In his time Michael, emperor of the city of Constantinople, son of the emperor Theophilus, for love of the apostles sent gifts to St Peter the apostle through bishops named Methodius the metropolitan and bishop Samuel and two others deposed from the episcopal office, Zacharias and a different Theophilus, and another imperial layman named Arsabir, the *protospatharius*:[30] i.e. a fine gold paten with various precious stones, pearls, prases and jacinths; a gold chalice surrounded with stones and with jacinths hanging round it on gold wire, and 2

---

a theory that the name was derived from the *Ptochium Lateranense*, a hospice (πτωχεῖον) known from a bull of Honorius II, 7 May 1128, but not called *ptochium* in any earlier or later documents; and the Aqua Claudia alone was more than sufficient to supply the Lateran district.

[29] Cf. 97:59 with n. 111.

[30] From c. 38 it seems that Arsabir was leader of this embassy. Methodius's see was Gangra. Nicholas (J2819, *Ep.* 91 *MGH Ep* 6.513.15, 13 November 866) wrote: 'suddenly some bishops, one of whom was the metropolitan of Gangra, with the glorious *spatharius* Arsabir, came on an imperial embassy with a royal letter to the apostolic see'. Nicetas (*Vita S. Ignatii*, Mansi 16.236B), who names only bishops Samuel and Theophilus on this embassy, states that Samuel was bishop of Chonae and that Photius had made him an archbishop in despite of the metropolitan of Laodicea. The other two bishops, Zacharias and Theophilus of Amorium, had been deposed by Ignatius and appear in the acts of the 4th session of the council of 869-70 as unyielding supporters of Photius.

repida modelled on peacocks, with a shield[31] and various precious stones, jacinths and pearls, weighing in all .. lb. Also a gold-studded cloth with jewels, pearls, representing the Saviour and SS Peter and Paul and the other apostles with trees and roses, on both sides of the altar, with an inscription of the emperor's name, of wondrous size and beautiful splendour. And handing over many other gifts to the pontiff, they straightaway pronounced the embassy's words enjoined on them.[32] **19.** Now the[33] emperor of the Greeks, having found an opportunity through the removers of the sacred images,[34] requested by his said envoys that the apostolic see send its envoys to Constantinople, intent as he was on the matter of patriarch Ignatius and of Photius the intruder into the church of Constantinople. In this way he wanted - cunningly and jealously as it later appeared - this Ignatius to be condemned by the judgment of the apostolic see, and to replace him in that church with the neophyte Photius. **20.** Then the supreme pontiff,[35] as yet unaware of the emperor's awful idea, sent there two bishops, Radoald and Zacharias,[36] with orders to decide in a synod[37] on whatever the dispute about sacred

---

[31] Sense unclear (and not helped by the mysterious *repida*, for which see the glossary); it can hardly mean 'escutcheon', 'coat of arms', at this date. Note the shields on which copies of the Creed were written, 98:84-5.

[32] The date must be earlier than the date on the letters Nicholas sent with the Roman envoys who accompanied this embassy on its return east, 25 September 860. In the 4th session of the council of 869-70 Hadrian II's envoy, the Roman deacon and future pope Marinus, spoke of the reception the easterners were given at Rome in 860: 'At the time I was a subdeacon of the Roman church; I had been consecrated by the holy Roman pope Leo and serving in the Roman church from my twelfth year of age. When these came to Rome with Arsabir, I was serving in the Roman church of God's holy mother called *Praesepe*. It was there that holy pope Nicholas received them through the satisfaction of a document and an oath, and he did not confer on them communion among the bishops.'

[33] *factus* in Duchesne's text appears as *fatus* in his lemma. I assume the latter.

[34] Nicholas's *Ep.* 82 to Michael, borne by the papal envoys and read at the council in May 861, defends the cult of images, and the council did in fact deal with that topic as well as with the question of Photius (*Ep.* 85; see n. 81 below).

[35] Grégoire 1966:112-3 links Nicholas's attitude to Photius with his anxiety to convert the Bulgarians within Latin jurisdiction; cf. Ullmann 1972:105-6. Important sources are Nicholas *Ep.* 91, recounting the earlier stages of the affair; and the preface of Anastasius to his translation of the council of 869-70 (*PL* 129.9-24, Mansi 16.1-13).

[36] The envoys were the bishops of Porto and Anagni; for Radoald, cf. 106:9, 20.

[37] This council met at Constantinople in May 861 (c. 40). On the embassy from Rome, see Dvornik 1948:74-91 and 1966[a]:450-4; Grégoire 1966:109. The letters they took to Michael and Photius, dated 25 September 860 (*Epp.* 82-83, J2682-3) are preserved in a later letter by Nicholas (*Ep.* 98, J2821, sent in 866 to the patriarchs and bishops of the East, by means of the envoys mentioned in c. 71). Both letters contain Nicholas's complaints. In *Ep.* 82, which was read at the council of May 861, Nicholas praised Michael's concern for concord between the churches, but blamed him for allowing a council to be held at Constantinople without the permission of the Roman see and for allowing Ignatius to be uncanonically deposed and replaced by the layman Photius; he had

images produced, and formally to inquire, only, into the matter of patriarch Ignatius and the neophyte Photius and report back to him. I shall skim briefly below through the nature and extent of their senseless achievements, as they made little of the holy pontiff's injunctions and were bribed with money there, just like Vitalis and Misenus.[38]

21. Meanwhile[39] many of the Ravennates, who were enduring trouble from that city's bishop John over the possessions and property they owned, came to this blessed pope for rescue from such great oppressions. Dutifully heeding their clamours, he frequently warned the archbishop by his legates and in writing[40] to desist from such acts. But

---

sent Radoald and Zacharias to investigate the case; he defended the cult of images, and ordered the archbishop of Thessalonica to be regarded, according to ancient custom, as vicar of the Roman see 'throughout Epirus Vetus, Epirus Nova, Illyricum, Macedonia, Thessaly, Achaia, Dacia Ripensis, Dacia Mediterranea, Moesia, Dardania and Praevalis'. He also asked for the return of the Roman patrimony of Calabria and Sicily, and of the right to consecrate the archbishop of Syracuse (a pointed reference to the deposed Gregory). In *Ep.* 83 Nicholas praised Photius's written profession of faith, but regretted his being made patriarch when only a layman; he deferred confirming him as such until his legates reported back to him.

[38] Cf. c. 42. The text continues with eastern affairs at c. 38.

[39] On the affair of John of Ravenna see Herbers 1991. Chapters 21-35 give rise to a chronological problem. Two councils at Rome are mentioned, one in c. 23, and one in c. 24 scheduled for 1 November; the council described in cc. 29-35 should be the latter. Other sources give the following possibly relevant councils: (a) the 'council of seven canons' which excommunicated John of Ravenna, undated (Muratori, *R. It. SS.* II.ii.127; Mansi 15.658; *PL* 119.794); (b) the Roman council of 70 bishops held on 18 November 861, cf. n. 61; (c) a council to do with John of Ravenna, attended by Athanasius of Naples, cf. n. 49; this cannot be identical with (b) as Athanasius is not among the 70 bishops listed; (d) Nicholas's *Ep.* 154 (J2693, possibly spurious), written to Ado of Vienne, accompanied a copy of the decrees of a council held in Rome in March, year unstated. Different reconciliations of this material have been given, but Duchesne's arrangement is correct and now universally followed. The council of c. 23 is (a), held in 861, in March if it is identified with (d), and attended by Athanasius if it is identified with (c). The council of cc. 24, 29-35 is (b), the Roman council of 70 bishops (without Athanasius), held on 18 November 861 though originally scheduled for 1 November. Duchesne argued cogently that the chronological place of the whole episode in the LP is determined by the event with which it ends, the council (cc. 29-32) at which John appeared and made his submission; if this is 18 November 861, it fits before the next securely datable events in the text, Nicholas's letters of March 862 (c. 42). The acts of the council (see n. 61) correspond verbally with cc. 33-34. The date of *Ep.* 105, in which Nicholas delivers the bishops of Emilia from John's oppressions, clearly after the council of cc. 29-35, is November of indiction 10 (861). It was probably the failure to include this letter that misled Jaffé and Ewald (*Regesta Pontificum*) and others. Ewald agreed that the council of c. 23 was (a), but put it in 862; he put (b) at an earlier stage, corresponding to nothing in the LP; the council of cc. 29-35 is neither (a) nor (b) but one which began on the scheduled date, 1 November (862), and is identical with (c), attended by Athanasius. In favour of this it must be conceded that if Nicholas valued Athanasius's views about John so highly, it would have been surprising that he did not attend the council of cc. 29-35. Nevertheless this is a small point and does not wreck Duchesne's chronology.

[40] Nicholas's warnings do not survive. John's misdeeds and those of his brother duke

he in mental confusion concealed the dutiful father's warnings and had no fear in adding to the former things even worse ones. The more the supreme prelate's kind consideration advised him to come back to his senses, the more he turned himself over to what was worse and he ceased not to add wickedness upon wickedness.[41] **22.** For some he rashly excommunicated, some he turned aside from their visitation to the apostolic see,[42] and the possessions of some he seized without legal judgment. He stole many of the holy Roman church's estates, scorned her envoys and 'emptied the glory'[43] of St Peter the apostle as far as in him lay. If he found charters of St Peter's right[44] in anyone's possession he tore them up and transferred them to St Apollinaris's right. Without canonical judgment he deposed priests and deacons, not only those subject to himself, but those in Emilia[45] who belonged to the apostolic see; some he had confined in prison, some in filthy workhouses, and others he forced to make written confession of a crime they had not committed. **23.** He also suppressed the church's constitutions with no consent from the apostolic see, and when summoned to Rome by the supreme pontiff he boasted he had no need to turn up to a synod.[46] No wonder he did these things afterwards, since at the beginning of his consecration, just like his predecessor Felix,[47] he falsified the bonds and tokens which are normally made by archbishops of Ravenna in the

---

Gregory had already produced protests from Leo IV in 853 (J2627-8). Leo wrote to Gregory that he was not prepared to let his own people suffer at the latter's hands but would personally avenge them. He reminded John that he had broken his oath to the pope and behaved in a manner unprecedented for a priest by seizing the Roman church's property; he threatened that if John continued he would avenge this in person, and he annulled some kind of promise that John had extracted from one Hilarius. A confused memory of the events is detectable in the *Libellus de imperatoria potestate in urbe Roma* (*MGH SS* 3.719-22). Also relevant to relations between Nicholas and John are: *Ep.* 135 (J2841), undated, in which Nicholas tells John that the catechizing of those to be baptized can be done by the *sacerdotes* of every church, as happens at Rome; and *Ep.* 137 (J2843), undated, Nicholas's reply to the archbishop of Ravenna on the case of a senator's adulterous wife who had become a nun.

[41] Ps. 68.28 (69.27).

[42] Nicholas, *Ep.* 105, p. 615.22 ff, reports the complaint of the bishops of Emilia that John had released clerics from their submission to the bishops whenever he saw a personal advantage in doing so, and had prevented the bishops making the customary visits their predecessors had made to the thresholds of the apostles.

[43] 1 Cor. 9.15, 2 Cor. 3.7.

[44] Cf. canon 6 of the council text, quoted in n. 61.

[45] Since clerics in Emilia would normally depend on their own bishops, who were subject to the archbishop of Ravenna, Duchesne suggested that those referred to here were appointed from Rome to serve the estates of the Roman church in the area.

[46] For further details of the complaints about John see c. 32.

[47] LP (Constantine) 90:2, BP 89-90.

church office, and compiled writings that were barbarous when they were not false. Then this pope issued three written summonses[48] to him to attend a synod; and, as he scorned to come, he was deprived of communion by a holy synod.[49] Going to Pavia, he put vexation into Caesar Louis's ears and sought worldly comfort. **24.** Then the emperor provided him with distinguished envoys and, puffed up with pride, he came with them to Rome. But the bountiful pontiff in kindly fashion rebutted these envoys, because against the rules of the canons they communicated with an excommunicate. As they wept for what they had done, the pope - may God preserve him! - imposed on the archbishop that he should attend on 1 November at the synod[50] by which he had been excommunicated, demonstrate full satisfaction and put an end to such great transgression. But he refused and went back home instead.

25. And lo! the men of Emilia and the senators of the city of Ravenna made their way with countless people to this blessed prelate's footsteps in Rome and asked him to imitate our Lord Jesus Christ and not disdain to set out for Ravenna for their recovery, so that he might consider everything[51] and lead them to total freedom. So the blessed pope set out on his own for Ravenna, and when archbishop John knew

---

[48] Not surviving.

[49] This is the Roman 'Council of the Seven Canons'. The first of its canons deals with the archbishop of Ravenna: though accused of heresy both orally and in a document sent to Nicholas by Nandecisus bishop of Pola, he has refused to come to the council or purge himself of the charge; therefore according to the 19th chapter of the Council of Carthage he is excluded from mass and communion and is excommunicated by the synod until he presents himself in Rome and proves he has purged himself; and any who communicate with him are excommunicated. The other canons are as follows: 2) the council teaches that Christ suffered on the cross only as man; 3) it anathematizes those who say that Christ suffered on the cross as God, and also 4) those who assert that original sin is not washed away in baptism (these three canons clarify the heresies of which John was accused: he was stating that Christ had suffered in his divinity and that baptism is not equally efficacious for all recipients); 5) the council confirms what was laid down by Leo IV's council but violated after the death of Benedict III; 6) it anathematizes anyone who denies that the election of the pope is a matter for the *sacerdotes, primates*, nobles and all the clergy of the Roman church as laid down in the council of Stephen (IV); 7) it anathematizes anyone who strikes or injures a bishop. For the possibly spurious letter in which Nicholas sent Ado of Vienne a copy of the decrees of, perhaps, this council, cf. n. 39. Duchesne believed it was this council that Athanasius attended: Nicholas particularly summoned the archbishop of Naples to the synod against John of Ravenna, gave him the third place of honour and gave him John's *cautiones* to read (*Vita S. Athanasii ep. Neapolitani* 4, *MGH SSrL* 444.20 ff).

[50] Between the council of c. 23 and November 861 belong the events of cc. 25-28. John evidently made his refusal to attend known long before the 1st November, not merely between then and 18 November when the council in fact took place. The LP here regards the November council as being that of c. 23 reconvened.

[51] Or (less probably) 'consider them all'.

he would arrive, he straightaway undertook a journey to Pavia to vex the emperor's ears again. **26.** But the splendid prelate mercifully restored to all the people of Ravenna, Emilia and the Pentapolis, what they had lost by the seizures of archbishop John and his brother Gregory, and confirmed what he had returned to them by his preceptive decree.[52]

When the archbishop, as has been said, reached Pavia, and when that city's fellow-citizens together with their bishop Liutard,[53] who had been consecrated by the Roman pontiff, heard that the archbishop had been excommunicated by the supreme pontiff, they gave themselves to so much caution and vigilance that they would not receive him in their homes nor allow the sale of anything to his men, in case by such trafficking they might share even in conversation with them and thereby incur the mark of excommunication. Instead, when they saw any of the archbishop's retinue walking in the streets they shouted: **27.** 'Those are some of the excommunicated; we must not mix with them!' Then the archbishop, seeing he could not in this way achieve the machinations he wanted, repeatedly demanded help from the emperor. At this the emperor gave him an order through a go-between, saying: 'Let him go, put aside his overweening arrogance, and humble himself before the great pontiff to whom we and the church as a whole abase ourselves and bow our necks in obedience and subjection - there is no other way for him to get what he wants'. **28.** When the archbishop heard this, he began to be uneasy and, again asking with importunate prayers for imperial envoys, he came to Rome.

The blessed pope, knowing this and despising all his pride as mere spiders' webs, remained opposed to him and could not be moved from his previous decision. But the holy pope addressed the same imperial envoys, treating them with this kind of great gentleness: 'If our beloved son the lord emperor really knew this archbishop John's actions and character, not only would he never make requests of us on his behalf, but he would send him to us, even if he was unwilling, for his punishment'. **29.** When, as this noteworthy pope had decreed, many bishops[54] of the provinces had met together, he bound the archbishop to come into their presence, to demonstrate full satisfaction concerning

---

[52] Not surviving.

[53] Liutard, one of Louis II's chief counsellors, was, as bishop of Pavia-Ticinum, exempt from the jurisdiction of the archbishop of Milan and directly subject to the pope, cf. LP 90:9 (BP 92).

[54] This is the Roman council of 18 November 861 (for details see n. 61), though the bishops may have begun to convene on the date for which it was scheduled, 1 November. The preliminaries in this chapter may well have occupied over two weeks.

himself and to make adequate amends for his transgression. Hearing this, the archbishop was terrified and, seeing he could expect help from no one, he betook himself to lamenting his distress and complaining about his great trouble, and he tearfully implored those he could, saying: 'Have pity on me, have pity on me, and beg the supreme prelate's clemency to have pity on me, for lo! I am ready to fulfil all he has laid on me'. Many who saw and heard this related it to the supreme bishop, and they clearly expressed what he intimated and promised, uttering it in a tone of lamentation.

30. Then the compassionate pope, imitating the Lord who desires not the death of a sinner, was moved to mercy and decreed the reception of the archbishop, now that he was at length converted to the path of humility. Then he straightaway took the paper, his written promise and oath that at the time of his consecration he had filled with incomplete and confused expressions, as could be seen in them; and writing in his own hand he composed it according to the custom of his predecessors. He went up to the house called Leonine,[55] in which the blessed prelate was in session with many bishops, priests, dignitaries and leading men in attendance,[56] and he placed these writings he had produced on our Lord Jesus Christ's lifegiving cross, on his sandals[57] and on the sacred book of the four holy gospels; and holding these in his hand, he freely swore in a clear voice to the countless audience who had gathered, that all the days of his life he would entirely heed, hold and fulfil what was included and could be read in those written promises of his above-mentioned; and he read them with his own voice in the sight of all and handed them over to the supreme prelate.

31. This done, the remarkable and distinguished pontiff went down next day to the Saviour's basilica called Constantinian with all the bishops and the whole clergy, where at the supreme pontiff's bidding the archbishop was present, and he purged himself of the crime of heresy[58] on which he was arraigned. The pope restored him to communion and kindly conceded him licence to celebrate the ceremonies of holy mass.

Next day, with the supreme and universal pope presiding in the

---

[55] Cf. 98:39 with n. 89.

[56] The acts were signed by 70 bishops, not counting the pope and the archbishop of Ravenna; after them signed 5 Roman priests (one titled *viceagens Romanae ecclesiae*), the archdeacon, 3 other deacons, 12 subdeacons, an *oblationarius* and a *primiscrinius*.

[57] According to the Description of the Lateran attributed to John the Deacon (*PL* 194.1556), this was one of the relics said to be kept in the *Sancta Sanctorum* chapel.

[58] For his heresies see n. 49.

Leonine House, and with the holy college of *sacerdotes* and fellow-bishops in session as usual, the archbishop was present and took his seat at the supreme prelate's bidding. **32.** Then the bishops of Emilia stood up and produced their complaint about this archbishop John[59] in accusatory documents, stating they were enduring many prejudgments and additional impositions at the archbishop's hands. Some of those from Ravenna and Emilia said the same, as anyone can discover if he looks into the acts deposited in the library. Hearing this, the God-protected pontiff, with the holy synod,[60] pronounced such things to be contrary to the norm of the church's rule; and for the correction of these transgressions, as this was how the holy synod acclaimed it should happen, he laid down in a pleasant pronouncement that the Lord's flock, entrusted primarily to him, was not through inaction to be left to be torn by the teeth of wolves. **33.** 'Nevertheless, Archbishop John,' said the noteworthy prelate, 'in order that everything stated can hereafter be more easily put right by a special amendment, we enjoin on you[61] that,

---

[59] The complaints against John are detailed in Nicholas's letter to Peter (see unknown) and the other bishops of Emilia (*Ep.* 105), written to announce their freedom from John's oppression by sending them the *capitula* of this council. This letter specifies (p. 614.19ff) how they had made their complaints in John's presence (he is described as *sanctissimus!*) before the synod, attended by numerous bishops from Campania, Tuscia, the Pentapolis and other regions. Their first complaint had been that once every two years John would tour their bishoprics with some 500 men on horseback and stay so long in each district that their great number consumed everything set aside for the bishop's needs, for the maintenance of the clergy and the poor, the reception of travellers, and the restoration of basilicas and of the bishopric, and would not leave until the local bishop had paid him 200 mancuses and given large gifts to his retinue. He had also made them, despite their unwillingness, take on the continuous care of three or four horses, and every year without a break dig farms *(curtes)* and trench vineyards as if they were bailiffs. He had also alienated from their government and subjected to himself the *plebes, tituli, curtes* and monasteries belonging to their bishoprics. Nicholas then mentions the 'tricesimal' custom, n. 65, and John's prevention of bishops visiting Rome, n. 42.

[60] Nicholas (*Ep.* 105 p. 615.27ff) continues that the bishops in the council had listened to the complaints and unparalleled statements and had all exclaimed that the behaviour was uncanonical and humbly begged Nicholas to forbid it. Nicholas grieved at the way pernicious burdens and evil custom had tyrannically spread in God's church, especially as they had been rashly and uncanonically adopted only in the metropolis of Ravenna, and, in case such things continued as a precedent to infect God's churches by showing metropolitans how they could misbehave, he decreed with the council that the bishops, their successors and their churches were to be relieved of their difficulties. So in the presence of the council he laid a formal and openly published prohibition on John and his successors ever behaving in this way again. He was keeping a copy of the *capitula* and sending them copies to keep for ever.

[61] The canons of the Roman council held by Nicholas against John of Ravenna are known from two MSS in Modena, in which they precede Nicholas's *Ep.* 105, the inferior one (Cod. Mut. capituli A. 6. XIX) given in Mansi 15.598, *PL* 106.787 and Duchesne, the better one (Cod. Mut. capituli O. II. 2) in Perels' *MGH* edition of Nicholas's letters, p. 614 n. 1. The date given is 18 November in Nicholas's year 4, Louis II's year 11 and the

laying aside all excuses other than serious physical problems which would totally impede you from coming, you are to ensure that you make your way once a year[62] to the apostolic see, unless it happens that you receive permission from the apostolic see to remain behind. Also, we lay down[63] that you may not consecrate the bishops in Emilia unless, after their election by the duke,[64] clergy and people, you receive permission to consecrate them in a letter from the prelate of the apostolic see. And you are never to hinder those bishops from coming to the apostolic see whenever they want. Nor may you at any time exact from them any gift which the canons do not prescribe. **34.** We enjoin also that[65] you may in no way force those bishops to provide or exercise

---

10th indiction (the indiction is repeated twice in the fragment); the first and third formulas give the year 861, though this was Louis's year 12. Then follow six chapters; the LP in c. 33 puts into Nicholas's mouth the first three of these, and in almost identical wording; in c. 34 the LP gives the 'tricesimal custom', and then the 4th canon, again in the same words. The 5th and 6th canons run: 'You are not to attempt in any way to excuse or to claim free men from public jurisdiction, whether they are from Ravenna or from the cities of Pentapolis and Emilia, whether nobles or non-nobles; likewise you are also not to presume in any way to excuse or claim freeborn tenants from public jurisdiction. Seek out carefully the estates which by destroying charters you have transferred from the right of St Peter to the right of St Apollinaris and have conferred on individuals by *emphyteusis* or documents, and when they are found destroy these *emphyteuses* or documents and restore them to the rights of St Peter who had them before and against whom you are never to act in this way again'; then follow the bishops' signatures. For the last article cf. c. 22. Nicholas's letter (*Ep.* 105, pp. 616.14-617.21) explained and expanded the restrictions placed on the archbishop of Ravenna.

[62] Once every two years in the acts.

[63] This (canon 2) was really the most important canon. The council stated that John and his successors at Ravenna should have no more jurisdiction over the bishops of Emilia than the metropolitans of Liguria, Venetia and Istria had over their suffragans. Ravenna's independence of the papacy was destroyed. For the effect on John's later behaviour, cf. Nicholas *Ep.* 152, J2868, undated but after this: Nicholas blamed John for sending without his permission someone to arrange for the replacement of Oleobert the murdered bishop of, perhaps, Gavello, and ordered the election to be postponed; the guilty parties must be found and punished first, a worthy man must be found, agreement must be achieved between the clergy, the people, and the duke who had Nicholas's authority and was one of the same people, then the election could be held, and as had been decided in the synod (of November 861) John must inform the pope and with his permission he might then consecrate the bishop.

[64] The duke is omitted from the text of the canons, but cf. previous note. The LP text may be more reliable than even the better Modena MS of the canons.

[65] This clause is missing from the acts. Evidently John had contrived to have his own place supplied by his suffragans, who came on a monthly rota to preside at religious services in Ravenna. Nicholas's *Ep.* 105 mentioned this as a complaint of the suffragans (p. 616.17ff): 'that he forces you desert your bishoprics and as if you were priests to minister every month in alternating or changing turns, and that beyond these days licence to depart is not granted and you are detained by force 20 or 30 days at Ravenna, and during all these days no cleric of any bishop dare at all to ride on horseback through Ravenna without danger to himself, constrained by the archbishop's order' (from 'turns' to this point the inferior MS substitutes 'and in these days the small children of your

for the church of Ravenna that evil custom some call 'tricesimal', and that you may not attempt in any manner to exact from them any custom contrary to the privileges of bishops. Furthermore we enjoin on you that you may not now occupy, or set an additional claim of your own on, the property of any person soever, whether acquired or long possessed by any device or document soever, until you prove its ownership by judgment according to the due process of law in the apostolic presence or in that of his envoy or *vestiarius* at Ravenna.'[66] **35.** When this had been enjoined and ordered by the blessed pope to be heeded by archbishop John, the holy synod rose and thrice acclaimed: 'We all agree with the supreme pontiff's right judgment, with the shepherd of the whole church's just decision, and with Christ's disciple's salutary teaching. We all say the same; we all know the same; we all judge the same!' Then the archbishop and all the holy synod, refreshed with the food of the sacred word and filled by the blessed prelate with the nectar of sweet savour,[67] received the pontiff's leave and each one went forth home.[68]

* * * * *

36. Then this noteworthy pope - God preserve him! - provided in

---

paroecia die without chrism', apparently a reference to infant confirmation accompanying baptism); 'an end is to be put to this as well as the other things: they may in no way force you to carry out what they call the 'tricesimal'' (i.e. a custom of 'thirty' days). Relevant to the 'tricesimal custom', as Ewald and Perels observed, is an undated fragment of a letter of Nicholas, *Ep.* 136, J2842, in which he told John: 'We never let bishops desert the people entrusted to them on other feasts; so there is no clear reason how a bishop can desert his own church at Easter and minister to another church, especially as the canons give no order to that effect'.

[66] Here and in the text of the council *Ravennae* is to be taken as locative not genitive: otherwise the reference would be either to a *vestiarius* of the Ravenna archbishopric, who would have scarcely been chosen to represent the pope in such cases, or to a papal *vestiarius* of Ravenna, and the only recorded papal *vestiarius* is a Roman official. It is this official who is intended. The meaning is that John must prove his entitlement to property either in Rome before the pope or in Ravenna before the pope's representative or his *vestiarius*, who is evidently competent to be sent from Rome to deal with such cases. The *vestiarius* had in 772 been made judge of all disputes between the abbey of Farfa and Rome (Noble, 158, 237-8; J2395); since then judicial competence may have been extended to similar cases between other parties.

[67] This seems to mean the Eucharist, following the reading of the word (scripture) at mass.

[68] In a further (cf. J2693, *Ep.* 154) fragmentary letter to Ado of Vienne (J2697, *Ep.* 106), dealing with rules about divorce, concubinage, espousals, dowries, and church property, Nicholas told Ado that John had been paternally received by the apostolic see and had purged himself on oath of the error of which he was charged; he had sworn that he and his successors would show due reverence towards the Roman see.

God's mother St Mary's church called *Cosmedin* a fine silver *calpi* weighing 5 lb 2 oz. In Vestina's *titulus* he provided an expressed-figure icon of St Vitalis[69] the martyr, weighing 4½ lb. In Christ's martyr St Anastasius's basilica[70] he provided round the holy altar 4 veils with a fringe of purple. In St Peter the apostle's basilica, in pope St Gregory's oratory, he presented 3 gold-interwoven cloths decorated around with all-silk. **37.** In St Paul the apostle and teacher of the nations' church, this blessed and distinguished pontiff with pure mind presented a gold-worked cloth of wondrous beauty, with jewels round it, jacinths, pearls, prases and also carbuncles; there too he provided and presented 2 veils also gold-worked and with jewels.

As for God's mother the ever-virgin Mary's church originally called Antiqua,[71] but now called Nova, which lord pope Leo IV had constructed from its foundations but had not given it any pictorial adornment, this blessed prelate had it depicted in beautiful and varying colours,[72] increasing its splendour, and with pure heart he decorated it with many species.[73]

* * * * *

38. Now I have explained a little above[74] how a certain schism had grown up in the holy church of Constantinople, in that, deposing the reverend patriarch Ignatius from that church's throne, they had suddenly replaced him as bishop there with the neophyte Photius, one of the laity and the soldiers, who had been given the tonsure, against what is laid down by the reverend canons; and also how Michael the emperor of the Greeks humbly consulted the Roman see through his envoy the *spatharius* Arsabir and with letters in his own hand: he reviled Ignatius patriarch of Constantinople, whom in lord pope Leo IV's time they had raised up with acclamations of praise, he lauded Photius the intruder,

---

[69] This seems to mean that the icon, whether of the whole saint or merely of his face, was in relief, almost three-dimensional.

[70] Probably the church of the monastery of St Anastasius ad Aquas Salvias, since none of the other five churches listed in Hülsen, *Chiese*, as dedicated to Anastasius is known to have existed before the 12th century.

[71] See 106 n. 50. S. Maria Antiqua had been so called long before there was any question of a new building. The LP here 'legally identifies' the new church with that on the old site. The next reference to the church is not until 982.

[72] If this refers to mosaic work, it does not survive. The present apse-mosaic at S. Maria Nova (S. Francesca Romana) is of the 12th century, Oakeshott 1967:250ff.

[73] Or 'types (of adornment)'; elsewhere *species* seems to refer to precious metal.

[74] cc. 18-20. On the action of Nicholas's legates at Constantinople see Anastos 1990.

and he asked this blessed and remarkable pope to send his envoys there to investigate what was being said. **39.** Furthermore, because he wished for the church's strength to remain undefiled, the supreme prelate in no way refused to do this, as he yearned to root up the heaps of tares, in case inactivity should allow a stain somehow to burgeon in God's holy church. Then he sent from his side two bishops, as mentioned above, Radoald of Porto and Zacharias of Anagni, whom he reckoned competent for the task.[75] He commanded and ordered them only to look into the matter of Ignatius's deposition and replacement by Photius, and to report back to him; meanwhile they were to avoid communion with the neophyte Photius, until they returned and carefully gave a sure response about everything.

40. But these went on their journey and, scorning what was in the mandates they had received,[76] not only did they communicate with the neophyte Photius contrary to the formal prohibition laid on them, but they were also bribed with gifts and, in favour of his consecration, they renewed the deposition of patriarch Ignatius in a general synod that was convened: this may easily be discovered in the acts[77] they compiled at Constantinople, and verified as fact both from the envoys, one of whom was the secretary Leo, and from this emperor's letter. When these envoys came home they played up and greatly eulogized what they had done about Photius, and they reviled and kept denouncing what they had wickedly achieved about patriarch Ignatius. **41.** So the ruler and prince of the whole church, the notable and discerning prelate of the apostolic see, considered all this in holy contemplation. But when he was told what had been accomplished against his own arrangement, he refused to believe it until he could investigate it all according to his own wisdom's mystic understanding. For the meantime, he composed letters[78]

---

[75] What follows is related at length in Nicholas's letter in 866 to the eastern bishops (*Ep.* 98, J2821), in wording sometimes like that in the LP: Nicholas describes the bishops, much as here, as 'those who seemed to us competent to perform this great task'; and cf. next note. The compiler may well have had this letter in front of him.

[76] *Ep.* 98 (cf. previous note) has 'but they went, and scorning our admonishments...'.

[77] For the synod at Constantinople in May 861 over which Photius presided with Radoald and Zacharias cf. n. 37. The Greek acts do not survive. Evidently the LP used a Latin translation ('easily discovered'!), presumably one made for Nicholas's use. Deusdedit's canonical collection, which extracted much from no longer extant papal archives, has a slightly shortened Latin text of the synod.

[78] Nicholas's *Ep.* 98 (cf. nn. 75-6) preserves the two letters here mentioned (*Epp.* 85-86, J2692, 2691), and another (*Ep.* 84, J2690) not mentioned in the LP. All three are dated 18 March 862 and were taken to Constantinople by the imperial secretary Leo. They show that Nicholas had held a council, presumably earlier that year, and that in the presence of Michael III's legates he had explained that Radoald and Zacharias had had no authority to give judgment about Ignatius, and that he did not accept his removal. From this point

of his holy authority, which are preserved in the office of this see, both to Michael emperor of the Greeks and to Photius, and he gave them to the same secretary Leo, sending word that he would not consent either to the deposition of patriarch Ignatius or to his replacement by Photius, until the truth was acknowledged in his own presence and the affair was brought to a lawful end.[79] And while some were saying that there was a decision of this prelate on this matter, and others were clamouring that Ignatius had been unjustly deposed, this supreme pontiff unremittingly begged the Judge on High that, through the clemency of him from whom no secrets are hidden,[80] he might show God's church that there had been no consent of his will to such matters.

42. Then, relying on his zeal for God, he summoned a council of bishops[81] at which it was clearly shown that he had refused consent to

---

on Nicholas refused to recognize Photius. In *Ep.* 85 Nicholas wrote to Michael that a few days after his legates had returned, Leo had given him the acts of the synod of Constantinople, from which he learned of the wicked judgment of deposition against Ignatius; he had ordered the case to be investigated, not judged, so he regarded Ignatius as not deposed and Photius as not patriarch 'until the truth shone forth in his own presence'; but he approved what had been decreed about images (cf. c. 19). He complained that his earlier letter (*Ep.* 82) to Michael III had been tampered with; and he urged veneration of the Roman church. In *Ep.* 86 Nicholas wrote to 'the most prudent' Photius about the primacy of the Roman church; he denied that Photius, a layman replacing the living Ignatius, was comparable with the precedents cited (Nectarius, Tarasius and Ambrose), and blamed Photius for his breaking the canons of Sardica and the decretals of the popes. If Photius's claim not to have the latter was true he was guilty of negligence, if false, guilty of rashness. He complained that his own letter had been tampered with and his legates at Constantinople treated unworthily. In *Ep.* 84 Nicholas wrote to all the faithful rulers of the catholic churches of Alexandria, Antioch and Jerusalem and all the eastern metropolitans and bishops, that Ignatius had been deposed in the presence of his legates without his order and replaced by 'the most wicked' Photius; he ordered that Photius be regarded as an intruder and Ignatius as patriarch; he was sending them copies of his letters to Michael and to the church of Constantinople.

[79] The language reflects that of *Ep.* 85 (previous note).

[80] Cf. Ezek. 28.3 (addressed to the Prince of Tyre), Prov. 20.27; the immediate source is the prayer 'God, unto whom every heart is open and every will speaks, and from whom no secret is hidden, purify by the inpouring of the Holy Ghost the thoughts of our hearts, that we may deserve perfectly to love thee and worthily to praise thee'.

[81] Nicholas's letters in 866 (especially *Ep.* 98, and *Ep.* 91 which includes the decrees) give full details of this council of bishops from many western provinces, which began at St Peter's and then moved to the Lateran. The acts do not survive and the exact date is unknown: *pace* Duchesne, who suggested winter 862-3, it is clear from both *AB* 863 Nelson 106 (see n. 83) and Nicholas's *Ep.* 98 that the council was later than that at Metz in mid-June 863; so late summer 863. Zacharias confessed to corruption and was deprived and excommunicated (the only decision mentioned in the LP). Photius was also deposed and excommunicated; an anathema was hurled against Gregory of Syracuse, who had previously been deprived of his bishopric (by Ignatius), if he continued to claim it; Photius's supporters were deprived of offices received from him; Ignatius and his followers were restored; the cult of images was confirmed; and John (VII; 834-843), former patriarch of Constantinople, and his supporters were anathematized. It is clear that

Ignatius's deposition and that the apostolic see's envoys had deviated in such matters. Then this godly prelate issued a decree with the holy synod, depriving the aforesaid bishop Zacharias who was then present from his sacerdotal rank and even from ecclesiastical communion, in that he was found to have trespassed in many matters beyond the apostolic prohibitions on him. This was just what blessed pope Felix [III] had done to bishops Vitalis and Misenus who had been induced to give approval to Peter of Alexandria when he was besmirched with the filth of heresy.[82] The matter of bishop Radoald was left in suspense:[83] but the godly pope with the holy synod later condemned him too,[84] for violating his commands even further than this in the Gauls as well,[84] for infringing an excommunication[85] and for undermining a canonical judgment.

43. This distinguished man, this pontiff of holy endeavour, ordered the reinstatement of one Pepo, a deacon who appealed to the apostolic see that he had been deposed from his office by bishop Landulf[86]

Ignatius's side had the upper hand at Rome. In a fragment of a letter (*Ep.* 87, J2736) sent to an unknown addressee (hardly Michael III; Perels suggested the prince of the Armenians) Nicholas stated that he had confirmed Ignatius as guiltless and as patriarch; he condemned Ignatius's opponents and the defenders of the adulterous Photius as the holy Roman synod had decided; he also condemned Gregory, and all who followed him or had been consecrated by him or by Photius; he was writing to tell the recipient whom to communicate with and whom to shun in his province; he sent him a Latin version of the Tome of Leo, praising it highly; he praised his faith and urged him to convert his subjects from idolatry, promising wholesome teaching through his *apocrisiarii* when they ended their journey; and as a gift he sent the blessing of the Apostles on an image.

[82] Referred to already in c. 20; LP (Felix III) 50:3-4 BP 42; cf. Thiel, *Epistulae Romanorum pontificum genuinae* 1.252ff. Nicholas himself drew the parallel between Radoald and Zacharias and the two earlier bishops three times: *Ep.* 90 p. 491f, *Ep.* 91 p. 518, and (Radoald alone) *Ep.* 98 p. 562.

[83] He was clearly still employable on the mission to France (c. 46), though the LP fails to name him after the present chapter. Compare *AB* 863 Nelson 106: (after the synod of Metz mid-June 863) Nicholas 'wished to condemn Radoald on another similar charge' to that against Gunther and Theutgaud, 'for he had lately been corrupted by greed in Constantinople along with his fellow bishop Zacharias. The pope himself therefore now summoned a synod. Radoald, when he got wind of this, fled by night and disappeared'. Nicholas (*Ep.* 98) also notes that Radoald fled when no one was pursuing him. Radoald avoided condemnation by deliberate failure to attend. He was finally deposed and excommunicated (and anathematized if he communicated with Photius) at a synod in the Lateran basilica in early November 864, and it is to this synod that *AB* 863 Nelson 106 and *AB* 864 Nelson 120 refer. Radoald's successor at Porto was Formosus. Nicholas's own account of these events occupies nearly two quarto pages in Perels' edition (*Ep.* 98 at pp. 561.6-562.22).

[84] The reference is to Radoald's involvement in Lothar II's divorce.

[85] On this, cf. c. 48. Eastern events are resumed in the LP at c. 68.

[86] Landulf was bishop of Capua. The incident is known only from the LP, but Landulf's reputation is known from Erchampert, *Historia Langobardorum Beneventanorum*, esp. cc. 21 and 31, *MGH SSrL* 242, 246. The remark most closely connected with this affair is (c.

without judicial process. As the deacon had been judged deposed without the fixed number of bishops,[87] indeed without proof of the charge and without his own verbal statement, he quashed the entire judicial sentence and brought the affair back to the path of rectitude by his apostolic piety.

* * * * *

While this outstanding prelate governed the apostolic pinnacle, emperor Louis conferred these gifts on St Peter the apostle, to wit...

* * * * *

44. This clement pontiff was so careful about keeping watch over the Lord's flock that when any stumbling block arose in holy church he let his body have no rest and his limbs no sleep until, through his envoys or his letters, peace was restored and the faithful people regained the benefit of calm. Now king Lothar[88] had abandoned his wife Theutberga

---

31, p. 246.30): 'So he, putting church dogmas and episcopal rights behind him, only loved half-men and gave them preferment over all, fulfilling the prophecy of Isaiah (3.4, Vulgate): 'Effeminates shall rule over them''.

[87] This was three (six for deposing priests, twelve for bishops). In *Ep.* 107 (J2708) Nicholas, about 862, insisted that duke Salomon allow the deposed Breton bishops to be judged either by the archbishop of Tours with twelve bishops, or by the pope (on Leo IV's and Benedict III's involvement in this case see pp. 106-7, 165). But there is no trace of this principle in Italy before 848. Landulf's deposition of one of his own deacons was procedurally satisfactory under previous law. Leo IV's principle can be traced back to African sources (the 'fixed number of bishops' is ultimately from the African council under Gratus in 345-8, c. 11, *CChr* 149.8 lines 177-9; cf. Ferrandus, *Breviatio canonum* 55, 128, *CChr* 149.292, 298). Leo IV had also required 72 witnesses to the crimes of a bishop: this is from the Symmachean apocrypha (*Constitutum Silvestri* c. 3; the 'council of Sinuessa', Duchesne I.CXXIIIf). Both African canons and the forged *Constitutum* were now accepted as Roman canon law. Leo IV lists the sources of this (*MGH Ep* 5.593 n. 16, J2599): the canons of the Apostles, those of the councils of Nicaea, Ancyra, Neocaesarea, Gangra, Antioch, those of Carthage and those of Africa, also the decretals of popes Silvester (!), Siricius, Innocentius, Zosimus, Caelestinus, Leo, Gelasius, Hilarius, Symmachus, Simplicius, Hormisdas and Gregory II. When in 861 Photius had 72 witnesses testify against Ignatius in a session at which the Roman envoys Radoald and Zacharias presided (Nicetas, *Vita S. Ignatii*, Mansi 16.237D), he may have been deliberately applying current Roman principles to forestall procedural objections from Nicholas. For the use of twelve judges to judge a bishop the case of Rothad (c. 58) is also relevant; see Devisse 1976:592-4.

[88] On these and related events see p. 163, *AB* (Nelson 77, 84, 91-3, 102-3 with notes), Hincmar, *de divortio* (*PL* 125. 629ff) and Nicholas's letters, especially *Ep.* 53, J2886, of 31 October 867, which relates the 'tragedy' of Theutgaud and Gunther; cf. Dümmler 1887-8:3.1-4; Devisse 1975; Konecny 1976:103-17; Stafford 1983; Bishop 1985:54-84; Kottje 1988:97-103. Lothar II had married Theutberga in 855; he later tried to argue he was already married to Waldrada (Hugh, her son by Lothar II, may have been born as

and taken his concubine Waldrada in marriage, though he had consulted[89] the Roman see and this godly pontiff about it in the flesh,[90] and was caught up in the rottenness of lechery and in carnal wantonness. **45.** When the supreme pontiff was long contemplating within himself how he could expel this evil from God's church in case that king might pollute others with the plague of this sickness, he began to be troubled. Grieving in his inmost heart he mourned mightily over these errors; all the more so when he heard that Theutgaud and Gunther, the archbishops of Trier and Cologne, with Hagano[91] of Bergamo and other bishops, had given the king such authority freely to dismiss

---

early as 855, though perhaps not till c. 860). Waldrada was of noble family, though not from the imperial aristocracy. By 857 *AB* records that Lothar put Theutberga aside and kept concubines (none other than Waldrada is known), and significantly follows this with portents involving the archbishops of Trier and Cologne who would soon, as Lothar's defenders, clash with pope Nicholas. At two councils at Aachen in January and February 860 (*MGH Cap* 2.463-6, 466-8, see Hartmann 1989:275-8; *AB* 860 Nelson 92) Lothar forced Theutberga to confess to sodomy with her brother Hubert, and having had an abortion (her conception of a child by him was attributed to witchcraft), and she was condemned to a convent. In fear of Lothar, Theutberga fled to her brother Hubert (on whom see p. 163). At a further council at Aachen on 29 April 862 (Mansi 15.611 ff) Lothar was given authority to marry Waldrada, cf. *AB* 862 Nelson 102: 'Lothar crowned Waldrada and treated her as his lawful wife and queen while his friends grieved and objected to this'. Clearly Lothar also had supporters, most notably the two archbishops. Meanwhile Charles the Bald's daughter Judith, widow of both Æthelwulf and Æthelbald of Wessex, had eloped with Baldwin count of Flanders, with her brother Louis's consent. Charles held a council; the bishops anathematized Baldwin and Judith, who therefore sought help against Charles from Lothar II, and also from Nicholas (*Epp.* 7-8, of 23 November 862). So Charles broke off relations with Lothar, because of (a) the divorce, (b) the fact that Lothar and Waldrada were in communion with Engeltrude (cf. c. 48), and (c) Baldwin (*AB* 862 Nelson 97, 103).

[89] Nicholas (*Ep.* 53 at pp. 342.33-343.2) later wrote that two counts had brought him the news of the decisions of the councils (two at Aachen in 860) that Lothar could divorce Theutberga and (Aachen, 29 April 862) that he could marry Waldrada: 'King Lothar sent two counts to us, through whom he informed us in writing and orally that the bishops of his kingdom with some others were giving him authority to reject Theutberga and choose Waldrada in marriage, but that he, so that order might be preserved, sought rather from us the authority and judgment for such a matter and awaited advice'. Nicholas here, and the next lines in the LP (probably based on Nicholas's account), seem to conflate the decisions of all three councils. It was bishops Theutgaud and Hatto who reported to Nicholas on the second council; the two counts will be Liutfrid and Walter who brought Nicholas the report of only the first council.

[90] *carnaliter* seems to mean 'on a personal matter', but the compiler is influenced by the context. Lothar did not come to Rome in person.

[91] That Hagano was involved even before the synod of Metz (next chapter) is not otherwise attested but plausible in view of his later role. Nicholas refers (*Ep.* 53) to other bishops than those of Lothar's kingdom at the council(s) of Aachen; the archbishop of Rouen and the bishop of Avignon were at the council of February 860; but the allusion may also be to Hagano's involvement (though he was not at the council of 862). Nelson (*AB* 106 n. 10) notes that Hagano's role suggests the influence of Louis II. Louis would shortly be concerned to get the archbishops reinstated.

Theutberga and lawfully to marry the concubine Waldrada; the blessed prelate had discovered that those who ought to have been his helpers and leaders before the Lord had been, through their giving of this authority, his betrayers to everlasting fire.

46. Then with no delay he straightaway despatched his envoys[92] to France, ordering and advising them that at a synodal meeting convened in the city of Metz they were to inquire why this king was setting aside Theutberga and marrying Waldrada; and after inquiring and finding out, they were to impose a lawful conclusion. On reaching there, the apostolic see's envoys began to investigate[93] the nature of this affair,

---

[92] Radoald and John, bishops of Porto and of Ficuclae (Cervía), who took with them Nicholas's letters (*Epp.* 3-8, J2702, 2701, 2699, 2698, 2703-4) dated 23-24 November 862; Nicholas later described his letters as synodical (*Ep.* 11, J2726, early 863). In *Ep.* 3 he urged the archbishops and bishops at Metz to judge the marriage case canonically, with his own legates, and with no distinction of persons; he ordered the acts to be sent to him for approval or rejection. In *Ep.* 4 he asked Louis II to assist his legates on their way to the synod. In *Ep.* 5 he ordered Charles the Bald to send two bishops to the synod, and said he had sent the same order to his brother Louis the German (presumably there were also letters to Charles of Provence and the bishops of his kingdom and that of Louis). In *Ep.* 6 Nicholas commended to Lothar his legates who were to hold the synod, and ordered that two bishops each from the kingdoms of Louis the German, Charles of Provence, and Charles the Bald were to attend. In *Ep.* 7 Nicholas asked Charles the Bald to restore Baldwin to favour, despite his marriage to Judith, for fear Baldwin might strike an alliance with the Norman enemies of the church. In *Ep.* 8 Nicholas begged Ermentrude (wife of Charles the Bald and Judith's mother) on Baldwin's behalf. At some point (later in 862?) he wrote (J2707, Perels p. 278 n. 1 gives the fragment, as suspect) to the bishops of Gaul about the divorce. Early in 863 Nicholas (*Ep.* 10) ordered all the archbishops and bishops of Gaul and Germany to attend at Metz and give canonical judgment about Lothar, who would be excommunicated if he failed to attend or did not accept penance. To his legates Nicholas wrote (*Ep.* 11, J2726) that if Lothar did not appear they were to take him Nicholas's mandates, then go to Charles the Bald on the matter of Baldwin, and show him in public the synodic letters and the one that Nicholas was now sending them along with its appended statement on the Lothar affair. In a letter (*Ep.* 57, J2723, end of April 863) to the bishops who had attended the council of Soissons in 862 (cf. c. 58 with n. 124), Nicholas urged them to beg Charles on behalf of Baldwin, and wrote about eradicating Lothar's crime. Another letter of the same time (*Ep.* 60, J2722), to Charles the Bald, dealt with the case of Baldwin, who after being anathematized by the bishops of Charles's kingdom had come to Rome, and asked him to let him marry Judith legally. On Radoald and John's successful intervention with Charles about Baldwin (who was restored to favour and allowed to marry Judith) cf. *AB* 863 Nelson 106, 110. In May 863 (*Ep.* 16, J2729) Nicholas replied to a letter from Theutberga's brother, abbot Hubert; he urged him to patience and informed him that he had ordered his legates to deal with his case and that of his sister in synod.

[93] On the synod of Metz in mid-June 863 (date, *AB* 863 Nelson 106) cf. *AF* 863 Reuter 50-51 and *AB* 863 Nelson 106. The acts of the council are lost; but it duly condemned Theutberga, *AB* asserts by bribery (see n. 95); Hartmann 1989:280-282, Devisse 1976:441-2. Note the end of the *AB* account (Nelson 106): 'in order to give the impression that they had achieved something, with the connivance of Hagano, a crafty and very greedy Italian bishop, they ordered Gunther archbishop of Cologne and Theutgaud his fellow-archbishop of Trier to go to Rome with the childish nonsense which the bishops of Lothar's realm had had written out and had subscribed in that synod, so that the case might be settled by

and what they heard Lothar say included: 'Whatever[94] I have done, I have followed these bishops' advice'. Now the distinguished archbishops referred to were there, Theutgaud and Gunther, whom the holy pope had already discovered to be the instigators of the great crime. They were affirming and stating that king Lothar's marriage with the concubine Waldrada was lawful, and undertaking that they could come before the noteworthy lord pope and defend their statement. **47.** When the apostolic see's envoys, albeit led astray[95] in many matters, made their homeward journey back to Rome, they related to the supreme pontiff what they had heard and learnt from the king and from archbishops Theutgaud and Gunther. While the godly prelate waited for the arrival of those archbishops, lo! at the behest of the Clemency on high archbishops Theutgaud and Gunther came to the city of Rome and asked to be presented to this prelate's holy footsteps. They were kindly received by the outstanding prelate[96] and they presented him with a document,[97] saying they had done neither more nor less than was recited in it. When that document was carefully scrutinized, a great deal in it was found to contain a profane baseness of language that many found unprecedented, and which ensnared those archbishops for their frenzied

---

the judgement of the pope'.

[94] The text is close to Nicholas *Ep.* 53 (p. 347.20), which was no doubt citing the lost acts of Metz: Lothar says 'Whatever I have done in this matter, I have followed these holy bishops' advice'. The LP may be using either the acts or Nicholas's letter.

[95] Nicholas's own expression is harsher (*Ep.* 53 p. 343.21): 'with our legates being corrupted, nay even traduced into his favour'. Cf. *Ep.* 36, J2777, a fragment in which Nicholas complains to Lothar of the treatment of his legates; *AB* 863 Nelson 106: 'At this synod, the two legates, corrupted by bribes, concealed the pope's letters and carried out none of the things that had been entrusted to them by sacred authority'; Regino, *Chronicon* 865 (ed. Kurze, 82).

[96] Apart from the LP only Gunther himself, in the *Libellus VII capitulorum* (*AB* 864 c. 2 Nelson 115), suggests that the initial reception of the archbishops at Rome was kind. The pope even said publicly that their report suggested they could be excused and were innocent: 'But we have awaited your reply for three weeks, and you gave us no expression of certainty, no sound teaching, but only admitted publicly one day that we seemed to be excusable and innocent according to the assertion of our own published statement.' Duchesne noted that the two prelates seem hardly to have had a chance to anticipate the blow that suddenly and skilfully brought them down.

[97] Lost, but mentioned in *Ep.* 53 at pp. 343.27-344.4: 'A certain profane document was written about what at the behest of the king was uttered there (at Metz) by wicked throats, and deciding that these things should stay unaltered they signed it with their own hands, and in those signatures just as in the rest of what was done Theutgaud firstly and Gunther were at the fore and like a plague they forced the others to follow them. Then they fully undertook to come to Rome and provide us with an account of what they had done. At last they arrived and before the whole church they were presented to our sight. And when we were inquiring of them how these things had been done, they presented the said document and testified that they had done nothing more or less or otherwise than the presented document contained.' Note the similarity between these last words and the LP.

trespassing beyond their episcopal rank.

48. After this a synod[98] was convened in the Lateran palace beneath the Apostles,[99] and reasons were found for these same archbishops, as has been said, to incur a mark of condemnation, particularly since they claimed to have been the instigators of that great divorce. Nor did they deny they had dissolved the sentence on Boso's wife Engeltrude[100] - she had abandoned her husband Boso[101] for seven years[102] and, even when

---

[98] This council was held at the Lateran; a letter of Nicholas (*Ep.* 17, J2747), inviting to it Vitalis patriarch of Grado, gives the scheduled date as 30 October 863. The acts of the synod are lost, but apart from the version given in the LP and Gunther's version of events (*Libellus VII capitulorum*, c. 3, Nelson *AB* 115) its decrees are inserted in a letter of Nicholas which circulated widely and of which four copies are known (*Epp.* 18-21, J2750, 2749, 2751, 2748; the text of *Ep.* 19 is in *AB* 863 Nelson 107-110; *Ep.* 20, essentially the same text, is in one version of *AF* 863 cf. Reuter 51 n. 15); *Ep.* 18 is the version sent to Ado of Vienne, *Ep.* 19 is a copy sent to Hincmar, to Wenilo bishop of Rouen, and to the other archbishops and bishops in Charles's kingdom, *Ep.* 20 is to the archbishops and bishops in Louis the German's kingdom, and *Ep.* 21 is to the archbishops and bishops in Gaul, Italy and Germany. In brief the decisions were as follows: 1) the acts of the synod of Metz were quashed, just like the robber-synod of Ephesus (in 449, denounced by Leo I); 2) Theutgaud and Gunther were deprived of all sacerdotal office and all episcopal rule, because of Waldrada and because they had violated the sentence which archbishop Tudo of Milan and other bishops had asked Nicholas to pronounce against Engeltrude (on whom see c. 48); 3) the same penalty was applied to their followers unless they confessed their fault through legates and letters; 4) Engeltrude was again anathematized; 5) those who spurned the decrees of the apostolic see were also threatened with an anathema. Cf. *AF* 863 Reuter 51 (which adds: 'If anyone is interested in knowing what was said in the writings of both sides, he can find them in several places in Germany'); and *AB* 863 Nelson 106; Hartmann 1989:282-4.

[99] LP 86:9 (Sergius I) BP 85 mentions a location 'beneath the Apostles' in the Lateran palace outside the basilica of Theodore. Some 40 years later, pope Zacharias restored this part of the palace and made many changes: in particular, he built in front of the basilica of Theodore a *triclinium* adorned with pictures and mosaics (93:18). But this *triclinium* was at the exact spot where at the end of the 12th century Cencius Camerarius mentions images of Peter and Paul; so Zacharias must have left them in their earlier position. Duchesne thought that it was either in Zacharias' *triclinium* or in the nearby basilica of Theodore that the council here mentioned was held. Theodore's basilica was the venue of a council under Zacharias, in October 745.

[100] On Engeltrude, and Benedict III's involvement in this case, cf. pp. 163-4, Wemple 1981:87, Nelson *AB* 103 n. 31, 109 n. 16. Later she even threatened to seek refuge with the Northmen, Hincmar *de divortio PL* 125.754-5. Nicholas had been involved since 860 when he had written *Ep.* 1, J2684, ordering Hincmar and all archbishops and bishops in kingdom of Charles the Bald to excommunicate her if she did not return to Boso (the same order was also sent to king Lothar and his bishops); and *Ep.* 2, J2685, referring to his previous letter and ordering Charles to try to stop Lothar allowing Engeltrude to remain in his kingdom. The case would continue. At Attigny Arsenius read out a letter from Nicholas excommunicating Engeltrude (*AB* 865 Nelson 126). And late in 865 (*Ep.* 41, J2800) Nicholas told Hincmar that Charles the Bald had asked him, Nicholas, for advice on those who communicated with those who communicated with Engeltrude, a woman often condemned; he ordered them to be absolved if they had acted through necessity or ignorance, but not if they had committed the fault deliberately.

[101] This Boso, the brother of Theutberga and Hubert, is generally assumed to be the son

she was excommunicated, bound and anathematized[103] by the godly pope of the supreme see, had shown no concern to return to him; they communicated and treated and even spoke with her; and they falsified the godly pontiff's letter as they wished, as is proved in those acts they evilly compiled, which are deposited in this see's office. **49.** Then by the judgment and decree of the holy prelate with the synod, they were deprived of sacerdotal office and rightly incurred the censure of deposition. In this synod the kind pope immediately quashed the synod of Metz at which those acts had been drawn up contrary to God's will and his own, and he promulgated certain chapters such as the holy church needed.

50. This done, the above-mentioned bishop Hagano was summoned; as some of the bishops wrote to this angelic prelate, he was called Elihu[104] on account of the 'words without knowledge' that resounded in the above-mentioned profane acts that Theutgaud and Gunther presented, for Hagano himself was their chief author and had, with the archbishops, put them together out of inept and mendacious phrases;[105] along with archbishop John, who is dealt with in the text above, and his brother Gregory, who were held liable for many transgressions, forgetful of the oath they had given. These were deposed, as they did not beg for penitential weeping nor did they yet grieve for the great crime they had committed against king Lothar's wife. These same men, that is Hagano, John bishop of Ravenna, and his brother Gregory, had started fraudulently and impudently to carry out - against the Roman see, indeed particularly against the Roman pontiff and the people subject to him and entrusted to him by the lord Jesus Christ through St Peter the apostle, keybearer of the kingdom of heaven - many wicked, many contrary and many sacrilegious acts, acts which trespass openly and secretly against the standard of christendom. In consequence their wickedness pierced through mountains and seas, and opposing heaven with effrontery they cruelly tore the Lord's people asunder and deceived

---

of the count Boso at 104:14, though there is no reason why the earlier reference might not also be to the younger Boso.

[102] The figure is confirmed by c. 4 of Nicholas's letters on the council, *AB* 863 Nelson 109: 'Engeltrude... who abandoned her own husband Boso and, look, has now for about seven years been running about here and there, a vagabond...'.

[103] Duchesne resolved the anacoluthon in the Latin by bracketing *extiterat*; alternatively insert *cum* earlier in the clause. Probably the fault was the writer's.

[104] Job 32.2 etc. Hagano is compared with one of Job's accusers; note particularly Job 38.2 ('words without knowledge'). Theutgaud, Gunther and John of Ravenna were no doubt likened to Job's other three 'friends', and Nicholas to Job himself.

[105] Cf. *AB*, quoted in n. 93.

innocent souls with their viperish faction. And, as past evils were not enough for them, at the devil's persuasion they did not refuse to do other novel and unprecedented acts, worse than the former ones: they even rashly presumed to touch on[106] what had been individually forbidden to each and had been, in accordance with the nature of the crime, prohibited by synod. Alas!, oh! anguish, they spurned God and did the things I now expansively[107] recall.[108]

* * * * *

51. This friend of Christ kept in his possession a record of the names of all the lame, the blind and the totally disabled in the city of Rome, and took care and concern to serve them daily sustenance. For the rest of the poor who could walk or had strength, he wisely invented this kind of method to feed them in turns: he ordered disks to be made engraved with his own name, and bade these be given them, so that it would be easy to know from the mark on the disks how many were to take food on Sunday, Monday, Tuesday or the remaining days of the week. On those disks that were given them, for those who were to be refreshed on Sunday he made on each of the disks two[109] bosses, and so on them all through to Saturday, so that for whichever day of the week it was, there would be that number of bosses on each of the disks, including notches on them where the bosses were made. Thus there

---

[106] The reference is to liturgical celebration by Gunther at Easter 864, despite the ban laid on him at this synod. This was true only of Gunther, not of Theutgaud.

[107] *intentando*; perhaps the compiler was making fun of his own style - in the original the entire chapter is one convoluted sentence of 213 words.

[108] Late in 863 Nicholas wrote to Lothar (*Ep.* 22, J2752): 'You have so consented to yield to the motions of your body, given rein to your passions and cast yourself down into the forbidden 'desolate pit and miry bog' (Ps. 39 (40).2), that you who had been set up to govern the peoples have become the ruin of many. The legal case of the former bishops Theutgaud and Gunther proves it; because they instructed you most incompetently, and moreover tried to conceal your transgression by their arguments, and under a certain mask of justice to obstruct equity with certain falsified subtle inventions, they have been deposed by our apostolic authority and canonically barred from all episcopal rule... Should you not be treated with vengeance unsheathed - you who are known with two wives to have aped the adultery and crime of Lamech? - a crime which the Lord blotted out by his wholesome coming only after 77 generations, though the fratricide of Cain was wiped out by the waters of the flood after seven generations'. In another fragment of the same period (*Ep.* 23, J2753) Nicholas ordered Lothar not to let anyone be elected at Trier or Cologne until a report had been sent to himself. Perhaps he was leaving open the possibility that the bishops might be restored, even if he was not impressed by their legal arguments (Kottje 1968). But subsequent events made such an outcome unlikely: Louis II marched on Rome in support of them. The sequel is omitted by the LP; see p. 193.

[109] The sequence seems to run from two to eight; more logically it will have run from one to seven. The text is likely to be at fault. The purpose of the notches is unclear.

would be no poor person in the city who would not be refreshed by his almsgiving on at least one day during the week.

52. Meanwhile king Charles[110] presented to the holy apostle a cloth constructed of fine gold and jewels, with prases, jacinths and pearls.

The holy and splendid pontiff, grieving that the people were oppressed with so many calamities, invoked God alone with countless prayers and lauded him with unlimited praises, yet he did not abandon his concern for God's churches, but rather increased it fittingly at this time of trouble and trial. For in God's mother Mary's basilica called *Cosmedin*[111] he renewed the *secretarium*, and there he built a *triclinium* of beautiful work, with parlours, for its honour and splendour. Close to that *secretarium* he renewed the portico and constructed and built there an oratory in honour of Christ's martyr[112] St Nicholas; and the bountiful man conferred many gifts there.

53. This kind shepherd also renewed St Felix the martyr and confessor's cemetery on the Via Portuensis. As for the cemetery *Ad ursum pileatum* on the same road, where the bodies of Christ's martyrs[113] SS Abdon and Sennen[114] were at rest, as it was now in ruins, he restored it with beautiful and wondrous splendour. On the Via Appia, at the cemetery of Christ's martyr St Sebastian *in Catacumbas*, where the apostles' bodies lay, as it had collapsed for many years, he renewed it with improved construction; he created[115] a monastery and gathered monks from wherever he could under the rule of an abbot, and enjoined that what was needed for food be provided and that other means be supplied for them.

54. In his time, when the reputation of his holiness was attracting many, some of the race of the English came to Rome, and in the oratory of Christ's confessor pope St Gregory, which was built within the prince

---

[110] Presumably Charles the Bald, rather than Charles king of Provence who died 24 January 863, before the council of 30 October 863 dealt with in cc. 48-50.

[111] The first significant alterations to this church since it was built (97:72 and n.142).

[112] A surprising epithet for St Nicholas, whose legend might have been better known while his namesake was pope.

[113] 'Martyr and confessor' is odd. Perhaps 'confessor' is a slip for pontiff. The cemetery on the Via Portuensis is that known as *Ad insalatos* at about the 3rd mile, still undiscovered. The cult was to SS Felix and Alexander (*Not. eccl.*, *CChr* 175.309. 41-52, has them in a church south of that containing Abdon and Sennen; but *Itin. Malm.*, *CChr* 175.327.95, has them in the same church). Felix, about whom nothing is known, had come to be identified with (anti-)pope Felix II, Amore 1975:234-6.

[114] Also known as the cemetery of Pontian, cf. 97 n. 168, Amore 1975:227-233.

[115] There was already a monastery here, the oldest known in Rome, founded by Xystus III (56:7 BP 37; see *LECP* 178). S. Sebastiano's absence from the 807 list (98:69-81), even as a basilica, suggests it had by then gone out of use, Ferrari, 163-5.

of the apostles' sacred house, they placed 1 silver panel weighing .. lb. In the church of St Peter the apostle, keybearer of the kingdom of heaven, this clement pontiff provided 5 gold-interwoven veils, decorated around with the best all-silk, which are hung for the basilica's splendour aloft on the beams inside this great house's vestibule; he conferred these to gain the palm of life everlasting.

* * * * *

55. In this blessed prelate's time, the teaching of his distinguished doctrine being known clearer than light, so many and such important consultations were sent to the apostolic see from various provinces, as are never at all recorded from times of old to have arrived. This farseeing prelate abundantly refreshed every single one of them with the nurture of the sacred word; giving them precepts and mystic laws, he filled them with beatific injunctions, he taught them and sent them back home well taught and trained. **56.** But when he knew or heard through anyone that anything was being done at all erroneously, he preferred to correct it with his gaze on God alone; with deep laments he devoted himself to countless prayers that almighty God in his clemency might change any such thing, by good and distinguished examples, as if it had never been. For instance, a report came from the island of Sardinia,[116] and he also knew it through those of his household who were of Sardinian race, in which it was reported to him in some such words as these: that the judges who were inhabitants of that island, with the people subject to their government, were contracting incestuous and illicit liaisons with their close ones and those near to them by blood, as they had been wont to do in the time of lord pope Gregory IV.[117] **57.** Then, taught by the Holy Ghost, he composed honey-sweet letters[118] of his preaching which shone throughout the world, but were terrible ones

---

[116] In theory Sardinia was still a dependancy of the Byzantine empire. In the 10th century its chief magistrate was an ἄρχων (Constantine Porphyrogenitus, *de Caerimoniis* 2.48).

[117] This will be from some document no longer extant, perhaps a letter of Nicholas recounting the background. Leo IV's surviving correspondence includes three fragments addressed to the Judge of Sardinia (J2611, 2612, 2648); they do not mention marriage laws. Nicholas *Ep.* 141, J2853, is a fragment of a letter to a bishop Jeremias against consanguineous marriages; Jeremias's see is unknown and there is no reason to suppose it was in Sardinia, though he might be the same Jeremias as the bishop (see also unknown) to whom Leo IV addressed *MGH Ep* 5.586 n. 3 (J2604).

[118] The LP evidently knew of these from the register of Nicholas (cited at the end of this chapter). The letters are lost (though cf. last note), and no source outside the LP refers to the embassy. From its place in the text it should be dated to 864.

to the transgressors, and summoned stalwart envoys, Paul bishop of Populonia[119] and Saxu abbot of SS John and Paul's venerable monastery.[120] He sent them there to recall that Sardinian race from so great an error. They went, and found some of them mightily hostile to the teaching, scorning to accept the warnings. But on the warrant of the supreme prelate's order, they excommunciated and anathematized the deaf listeners, until they should beg the medicines of repentance and flee the evil of incestuous liaisons, as is contained in the letters which these envoys took to Sardinia, and which are inserted in the register of this prelate.

58. Moreover one Hincmar,[121] archbishop of Rheims, deposed Rothad bishop of the city of Soissons while he was appealing to the judgment of the apostolic see, against the rules of the council of Sardica,[122] and ordered him to be kept under close guard. So when the thrice-blessed pope had received documents[123] from the deposed on his innocence, he

---

[119] Here first mentioned in the LP, he was one of the 70 bishops who attended the council of 18 November 861, and would later be one of the missionaries to Bulgaria.

[120] At St Peter's, the only monastery so named known this early; cf. 98 n. 137; 105:93.

[121] On Hincmar see pp. 194-7 and Devisse 1975-6. On the case of Rothad (whom Hincmar, *AB* 862 Nelson 100, calls 'a singularly stupid man') see Nelson 1991, Dümmler 1887-8:3.4. Rothad had acknowledged as his metropolitan Hincmar's predecessor, the deposed archbishop Ebbo, during his short reinstatement by Lothar I in 840-1, and therefore at the council of Soissons in 853 did not support Hincmar's stand against ordinations conducted by Ebbo. Hincmar's letters show that from then on he found Rothad's conduct objectionable. In 861 he told Rothad to restore a cleric whom Rothad had deposed; Rothad refused, and at a synod at Soissons (the acts are lost) Hincmar excommunicated him for disobedience, but did not depose him (*AB* 861 Nelson 96). Rothad appealed to the archbishop of Trier, and also to Rome. To Hincmar this was a personal affront; if Trier judged the appeal this would imply the subordination of Rheims to another metropolis in Gaul, so Hincmar argued that the canons of Sardica (see nn. 122, 137) required Rothad to appeal only, and directly, to the pope, to whom his judges must also refer the case (Nelson *AB* p. 123 n. 8; Fuhrmann 1972-4:1.197-8, Devisse 1976:588-9). At a synod of several provinces (Sens, Rheims, Rouen, Tours, and perhaps Bourges) Rothad agreed to attend a tribunal of twelve bishops (on this procedure see n. 87); in 862 this deposed him and imprisoned him in a monastery (*AB* 862 Nelson 100-101, 865 Nelson 123).

[122] Canons 3 and 7 of Sardica (343; Mansi 3.23, 24) were cited by Nicholas in *Ep.* 57 (J2723, *MGH Ep* 6.358.6-11, 11-20). It was only by considerably stretching their meaning that Nicholas (at 358.26ff) could produce the interpretation that even if a bishop did not appeal to Rome the judges should refer the case there anyway. Hincmar's own interpretation was different (cf. n. 137).

[123] No communication to Rome from Rothad between his appeal and his arrival is mentioned elsewhere: his *libellus proclamationis* was only presented to the pope 6 months after his arrival in Rome, towards the end of 864, whereas the first letters sent from Rome to Hincmar on this affair were early in 863. But the LP does not make it quite clear whether Rothad himself wrote these documents. Nicholas states (*Ep.* 55) that he had been informed 'by the true report of many of the faithful grieving there', and (*Ep.* 57) by 'very many of your (Hincmar's) neighbours'. This links in with Hincmar's statement that the

warned the archbishop in letters[124] and ordered him to send the deposed Rothad to Rome with his own envoys for a hearing. But when he came to this city of Rome[125] in accordance with the pope's mandates, and

---

protest came from the bishops of Louis the German's kingdom and especially from that of Lothar, who was then on bad terms with him.

[124] Surviving relevant letters of Nicholas to Hincmar (and others) down to this point are as follows. Early 863, *Ep.* 55, J2712: Nicholas blamed Hincmar for depriving Rothad while he was appealing to Rome and ordered him within 30 days of receiving this letter either to recall him from exile and restore him or to send him to Rome with his accusers and come with him or send a legate, under pain of abstaining from saying mass. At about the same date, *Ep.* 56, J2713: Nicholas wrote to Charles the Bald to see to it that Rothad, fully restored, comes to Rome, and mentions his letter to Hincmar. About 28 April 863, *Ep.* 57, J2723: replying to their (lost) letter to him, Nicholas wrote to the bishops who had convened at the synod (of Soissons, 862), refusing to confirm their acts, expounding how Roman privileges had been broken in the matter of Rothad, blaming them as supporters of illegality, and ordering them to recall Rothad from exile within thirty days and send him to Rome to have his case reexamined, or they must abstain from celebrating the liturgy. About the same date, *Ep.* 58, J2721: writing to Hincmar, Nicholas attacked what had been done at Soissons and the replacement of Rothad by another; his own judgment should have been awaited, even if Rothad had never appealed; he delayed confirming Hincmar's privileges and again ordered him, with threats, to send Rothad to Rome. At the same time, *Ep.* 60, J2722: writing to Charles the Bald Nicholas mentioned his order to Hincmar and the other bishops about Rothad and urged him to send Rothad to Rome for judgment. On 28 April 863, *Ep.* 61, J2727: Nicholas told Rothad about his letters to Hincmar, the bishops, and the king, and urged him to come to Rome as soon as possible; if he were hindered, he should not stop appealing to Rome; Nicholas would never let him be forgotten. Perhaps connected with Rothad (if so, to be dated later in 863) is a fragmentary letter, *Ep.* 128, J2838, to Hincmar in which the pope insisted on the need for accuser and accused both to be heard at the same time, however one outranked the other. Early in October 863, *Ep.* 62, J2737: Nicholas told Rothad of the various letters about him to and from Gaul, and that Hincmar had reported that Rothad had been released from his monastic prison and entrusted to a bishop; Nicholas had again ordered Charles and Hincmar to send him honourably to Rome, and if he was sure of his case he should hasten to come. At the same time, *Ep.* 63, J2738: Nicholas praised Charles for his ready obedience; he urged him to let Rothad have everything needed for his journey; and in *Ep.* 64, J2739, replying to queen Ermentrude who had asked Nicholas to listen to Charles about Rothad's case, Nicholas wrote that if life were granted him, he would not neglect the case.

[125] *AB* 863 Nelson 110 (after synod of 25 October) reports that Charles sent Rothad to Rome, as Nicholas had ordered him to do, with letters and envoys from himself and from the bishops. *AB* 864 Nelson 117-18 again states that Charles was obeying Nicholas in sending Rothad; with him travelled Robert bishop of Le Mans with letters, and the bishops of Charles's kingdom also sent envoys to Rome with synodical letters on the case; but Louis II blocked their journey (Nelson *AB* 121 n. 18 comments on Louis's concern about any deal between Charles and Nicholas over the Lotharingian succession). The envoys secretly let Nicholas know why they could not come to Rome. Rothad feigned illness and stayed at Besançon; when all the others had gone home he travelled via Chur, with the help of Lothar and Louis the German, to Louis II of Italy, by whose aid he wanted to reach Rome. In May 864 (*Ep.* 66, J2756) Nicholas told Hincmar to see that his letters to Charles were delivered, and expressed surprise that against his orders Rothad had not been restored to his former position, had not been presented to himself 'on the 1st May of this 12th indiction', and had even been hindered after he began the journey; he and Hincmar's envoys were to be sent immediately. Rothad had clearly not yet arrived; he will have done

stayed here for about nine months,[126] no one at all from the side of the accusers was at any time present to contend with Rothad or accuse him before the supreme prelate. **59.** Then on the day of the vigils[127] of our Lord Jesus Christ's Nativity, on which the prelate of this apostolic see had been accustomed, according to ancient tradition, to celebrate the offices of mass with the clergy and people in God's mother's basilica *in Praesepe*, this kind pope came together with them all and at the ambo he made a public speech[128] about Rothad, showing how he had been deposed while appealing to the apostolic see and[129] none of the accusers had appeared in his sight for so many months. **60.** Then with a council of bishops, priests and deacons, and all of them agreeing with him, he decreed that Rothad was worthy to be garbed in sacerdotal vestments, as no one was accusing him for so many months and he was appealing[130] to the judgment of the apostolic see when being deprived of his office. Then Rothad was clothed in an episcopal vestment, and he promised he would respond to his attackers at any time; he waited some days extra, until St Agnes the virgin's feastday which is on 21 January, and not even so was there anyone present to raise any dispute against the now reinstated bishop Rothad. **61.** So the blessed prelate came together with everyone in that virgin's basilica[131] outside the city-walls on the Via Nomentana, and bishop Rothad handed the supreme pontiff a document[132] with his defence and the promise which he had made to

---

so in June (at Christmas his *libellus proclamationis* stated he had been in Rome six months).

[126] Rothad was still in Rome at the end of January 865, and 'about nine months' implies he was there for a further two months; the start of Arsenius's mission to Gaul should be dated accordingly. Arsenius had left Rome before Nicholas penned *Ep.* 38, J2788, about 22 April 865.

[127] Probably Christmas Eve rather than 'vigils' in the old sense, though the mass at Cockcrow (*in galli cantu*, 'Midnight Mass') was, like the stational mass on Christmas Eve, held in S. Maria Maggiore.

[128] This survives, and is printed by Perels with Nicholas's letters (*MGH Ep* 6.379-81) as *Ep.* 66a; in it, and in the letters about Rothad sent soon after, occur the earliest clear traces in papal documents of the influence of the False Decretals, attributed to Isidore of Seville (d. 636); Perels p. 381 n. 8 gives full details of the correspondences. They were forged in France about 850 to protect bishops against provincial synods and metropolitans by exalting the rights of Rome; Duchesne suggested that the Decretals were brought to Rome by Rothad himself. They certainly suited Rothad's case against Hincmar. Whether Nicholas knew they were forgeries is an unresolved question.

[129] From this point the LP text is based on Nicholas's account in *Ep.* 67.

[130] *proclamabat*; the equivalent noun appears in the title of the protestation presented by Rothad on this occasion, the *Libellus proclamationis* (Mansi 15.682-5).

[131] Probably this meeting on 21 January 865 was in the Honorian basilica over St Agnes's tomb, not in Constantine's nearby cemeterial basilica, cf. Frutaz 1992.

[132] Not surviving, unless it was merely a copy of his previous *Libellus proclamationis*.

respond to his accusers at any time. Everyone listened while it was read out in their presence at the noteworthy prelate's bidding. When the form of his restoration[133] was read, and after all had given their agreement, on the decision of this blessed prelate the now reinstated bishop Rothad solemnly celebrated the ceremonies of mass in the church of St Constantia[134] close to that basilica of the holy virgin.

62. Next day,[135] the synod gathered again in the house called Leonine, and Rothad's own defence was made, as it is contained in the documents which were edited[136] by him, and on the two quires inserted, sent and presented at one time or another, and deposited in this see's archive, in case *sacerdotes* and particularly appellants to the apostolic see should in future endure such hazards. He was, as is recorded above, reinstated in his former rank; and he was sent back to his own see with apostolic enactments,[137] that, were an appeal to be made against him, it

---

[133] Duchesne and others identify this with *Ep.* 67, J2782, in which Nicholas formally notified the bishops and priests of the Roman church and the whole commonalty of the Roman people about the restoration of Rothad. If so it will have been composed at Christmas 864 but read and published on this occasion.

[134] The real dedicatee of S. Costanza was named not Constantia but Constantina; she was the daughter of Constantine and the wife of Gallus Caesar, and this was her mausoleum. The reference in LP 34:23 (BP 21) to a 'baptistery' is a confused memory of its foundation. It has survived the cemeterial basilica of St Agnes onto which it was built; Frutaz 1992:106-18; Duchesne I.196 n. 80.

[135] 22 January 865.

[136] This collection of Rothad's documents probably contained more material than now survives. Duchesne noted the precision of the LP's information on both the contents and the material arrangement of the dossier, and commented that it must have comprised at least: 1: the *libelli innocentiae* (c. 58); 2: the *libellus proclamationis* (cf. c. 60); and 3: the *libellus excusationis et promissionis* read on 21 January.

[137] These are letters of Nicholas, taken to Gaul by Arsenius when he accompanied Rothad (he presented him to Charles the Bald in mid-July): *Ep.* 67 (see n. 133). *Ep.* 68, J2781: Nicholas urged the restored Rothad to regather the dispersed property of his church. *Ep.* 69, J2783: Nicholas commended Rothad, whom he had restored, to Charles the Bald, ordered the stolen property of the church to be given back to him, and threatened excommunication against any who hindered Rothad. *Ep.* 70, J2784: Nicholas informed Hincmar of Rothad's restoration and attacked him for his obstructionism throughout; he ordered him either to let him enjoy his former office or, if he wished to prolong the affair, to come to Rome with Rothad, with the latter fully restored to office; otherwise Hincmar would be deposed. *Ep.* 71, J2785 (part translated in Baldwin 1970:158-61): Nicholas blamed the Gallic episcopate for daring to eject Rothad while he was appealing to Rome, against so many great decretals and without consulting him; sentences on bishops are rightly reckoned 'among the *maiora negotia*' (Leo I to Anastasius of Thessalonica) in which the pope should have a say; the decretals and works on church discipline by any pope who persevered in the faith are to be accepted; these are kept by the Roman church from of old, are entrusted to Nicholas also to keep, and are venerated in its own archive; the decretal letters of the popes are to be received even if they are not included in the codex of canons; he announced the restoration of Rothad and commended him. *Ep.* 72, J2786: Nicholas congratulated the clergy and people of Soissons on their restored bishop, and urged them to accept him. For Hincmar's icy reaction to the way events had turned

would be while vested in episcopal insignia that he would in future respond to his accusers before the prelate of the apostolic see. 63. With him the holy prelate - whom God preserve! - immediately despatched bishop Arsenius,[138] this bountiful apostolic see's *apocrisiarius* and envoy, both to reinstate him and to dissolve king Lothar's liaison, and also to maintain peace and concord between the kings of the Gauls, so as to join them together, with peace restored, in the holy church's bosom without resistance, and to disseminate carefully and plentifully in the church of the Gauls some needful matters laid down by apostolic tradition.

64. Furthermore this pope, through his envoys, reinstated Seufred bishop of the see of Piacenza[139] in his own see; he had been expelled from it by the disloyalty of a certain deacon Paul. As for that deacon, who had presumed to intrude into that see when its own ruler was alive, he reproved him and his partisans with a fitting rebuke. With the zeal of holiness, for the utter removal of this deacon's hapless and wicked presumption, and for the peace of God's church, he ordered and enjoined on him never to try again to achieve any such thing, and not

---

out see *AB* 865 Nelson 123-4: Rothad's deposition had followed the canons (for these cf. n. 122); Nicholas had arbitrarily and overbearingly restored him. The canons said that if a bishop deposed by his provincial synod appeals to Rome, the pope should write to the bishops of nearby provinces for them to investigate the case and make their decision; if the deposed bishop appeals again to Rome, the pope must either send his representatives to be judges alongside the bishops, or trust the bishops' competence to conclude the affair. But Nicholas had done neither; he had set aside the judgment of the bishops who had passed sentence and reported the case to Rome, and had restored Rothad on his own authority. He had sent Rothad to Charles with letters (see above) hurling an anathema against anyone who refused Rothad anything to do with his status or belonging to his see. His legate Arsenius had restored Rothad without any inquiry of, or consent from, the bishops who had deposed him.

[138] Bishop of Orte, cf. 106:6-8 and p. 74.

[139] 839-870. In a fragmentary letter from Nicholas to Louis II (*Ep.* 120 § 2, J2791 s. 2, mid 865), after advising him, with the example of Constantine, that if he hears anything about *sacerdotes* which could confuse pious minds he should 'cover a father's shame' (Genesis 9.22-3), Nicholas referred to one stage of this affair (whereas the LP summarizes all that followed and the outcome): 'If Seufred knew he had committed a crime for which he could rightly be deprived of his see, or perhaps felt he was overburdened by an illness that prevented anyone benefiting from his being a prelate, he should have awaited the judgment of his own primate (*sc.* the archbishop of Milan), not that of the bishops of other dioceses. But if any doubt or dispute had perchance arisen about his trial or his abdication of the see, it should by custom have been referred to the apostolic see, and in all these matters everyone should have fully followed our decrees. We grieve that so far this has not been done. I strongly beg you, my glory, dearly-beloved, that the said Seufred who was removed a while ago be restored to his own see, and if he has done anything blameworthy, let it be settled later by correction or fitting punishment'. Evidently Seufred had abdicated without the authority of his primate. Nicholas wanted him to be made to resume his see; there would then be a regular inquiry into any reasons there might be for him to leave it.

to presume to seek again or accept that see of Piacenza, whether bishop
Seufred was alive or dead.[140]

* * * * *

65. This remarkable and distinguished pontiff anticipated everyone's
distress and needs with the duty of a master. In his clemency he
sympathized with everyone and with swift gaze came to the help of the
needy. And he undertook enormous labours in imitation of our Lord
Jesus Christ who came down from high heaven to the depths to redeem
the human race. **66.** Thus, he noticed that the lame and the blind, and
those affected by various pains who lie in St Peter the apostle's portico
at the bank of the river Tiber, were unable to walk[141] so as to move
anywhere else, and he divinely attended to the need of the various races
which from all sides came to the homes of the apostles for their own
sins: never sparing his own body, he ordered the aqueduct, which had
collapsed for a long time and so was not bringing water to St Peter the
apostle's, to be restored with very great effort to a better condition than
previously. As a result it would not only benefit the maimed but also be
a distinguished work for all entering St Peter the prince of the apostles'
church; and just so, to the present day it is splendidly visible and
reckoned to be to the beauty of the Leonine city.

67. Furthermore the city of Ostia, which blessed pope Gregory[142] of
godly memory had constructed for the safety of many in case the
wicked race of the Saracens should capture or kill the Lord's people
around it, was lying in ruins. Touched by inspiration from on high, this
holy prelate ordered it to be rebuilt with stronger and more solid
building, and he restored and improved it, fortifying it also with very
strong gates and towers. In it he stationed men ready for battle, so that
in no way could the incursion of a foreign race in future gain mastery
of it or cause its fellow-citizens losses anyhow, except, forbid the idea,
through idleness.

* * * * *

68. Meanwhile, as the power of the most high God, who daily works
great signs and wonders through his servants, caused this blessed man's

---

[140] In fact Paul succeeded Seufred in 870, after Nicholas's death. Hadrian II either did
not know of, or was powerless to enforce, Nicholas's decision.

[141] *tendere gressum*, from Virgil, *Aeneid* 1.410.

[142] Gregory IV; cf. 103:38-40.

merits to abound truly throughout the world, the king of the Bulgarians[143] acknowledged the teachings of christianity and the holy faith, and deserved to be baptized. In this man's time he that was formerly in thrall to creation and savage in his cruelty submitted his neck and began to live by the full religion, and he employed great piety. Then in August of the 14th indiction [866] he despatched his envoys to this catholic and truly orthodox prelate, and conferred no small gifts[144] both on the holy places and on the supreme pontiff. And so that he might fulfil the sacraments of faith he inquired[145] of his Apostleship

---

[143] Named in the next chapter as Michael, but before his baptism called Boris (Bogoris). On his baptism and the conversion of the Bulgarians see Dümmler 1887-8:3.8; Dvornik 1926:184-95; Vlasto 1970:155-65; Barbouskos 1990; Holmes 1990. The LP gives no material on the conversion before Boris's baptism, fails to mention that Boris was baptized by a Greek, and ignores both Boris's contacts with Louis the German and the involvement of the Moravian Slavs. It was believed (*AF* 863 Reuter 49) that Bulgarians were coming to aid Louis the German against the Slav leader Rastiz. The rumour may have been unfounded, but if such an alliance between the Bulgarians and Louis existed it could explain why Rastiz looked to Constantinople for missionaries in 862/3 while the Bulgarians looked to the west (Sullivan 1955:91, Dvornik 1970:100-1, Vlasto 1970:26-7). If Anastasius is trustworthy (*Praef. concilii oecum. VIII*, Mansi 16.10), '... the king of the Bulgarians with his own race had received Christ's faith through a man of Rome, a certain priest named Paul' (who, from his status, cannot be Paul bishop of Populonia, mentioned in c. 69). Salomon bishop of Constance told Nicholas that Louis intended to meet Boris at Tuln, make an alliance with him, and force Rastiz into obedience; Nicholas prayed for the success of their journey and their safe return; and because Louis hoped that Boris was willing to convert to the faith, which many Bulgarians had already done, Nicholas promised to fast and pray for them (*Ep.* 26, J2758, mid 864, at p. 293.1ff; cf. *Ep.* 99 c. 17). In 864 Louis and his army met Boris 'who had promised he was willing to become a Christian' (*AB* 864 Nelson 118); then, later in 864 or in 865 Boris was baptized, apparently by a Greek priest or bishop, and took the name Michael, as much after the emperor who was so interested in the conversion of Bulgaria, as after the archangel (Vlasto 1970:159). In 866 Boris defeated a pagan rebellion, which gave the Christian party the ascendancy in Bulgaria (*AB* Nelson 136-7). Wanting to establish a balance between eastern and western influence in his kingdom and to show less reliance on Constantinople, Boris requested help from Louis at Regensburg and from Nicholas, both of whom were also interested in converting Bulgaria (Reuter, *AF* 56 n. 11, Nelson, *AB* 137 n. 35, Obolensky 1966:498-9, Vlasto 1970:159-61). His messengers stated that there were already many converts, including Boris, and requested a bishop and priests. Louis sent to his brother Charles for sacred vessels, vestments, and books to help these priests; and Charles received a large sum from his bishops which he sent to Louis to send to Boris (*AB* 866 Nelson 137). To lead the mission Louis chose Ermanrich, bishop of Passau (from 866), a choice revealing the importance he attached to the mission. But Ermanrich was delayed (cf. n. 151), perhaps by the need to gather priests and materials (Reuter, *AF* 56 n. 1). Meanwhile Boris sent to Rome.

[144] *AB* 866 Nelson 137-8 relates how Boris sent his son and many leading men to Rome with gifts for St Peter including the armour he had worn when he put down the pagan rebellion (cf. n. 143). Hearing of the gifts, Louis II told Nicholas to send the weapons and other things on to himself. Nicholas, through his envoy Arsenius, did send some items to Louis who was near Benevento, but sent excuses about others.

[145] *AB* 866 Nelson 137 continues that Boris also sent questions to Nicholas to get his ruling on them, and asked him to send bishops and priests; all these requests were met.

what he ought to do more wholesomely and what should be done for the rest of the Bulgarian people who still lacked holy baptism. **69.** The blessed pope heard this, was filled with great joy, gave full thanks to Christ, rejoiced with the whole church entrusted to him by God, and with devout mind and suppliant voice uttered infinite praises to our God who had worked so great a wonder in these last times. The envoys of Michael, the Bulgarian king already mentioned, were received by the holy pope and he kept them honourably at his own home. Meanwhile he appointed as the apostolic see's envoys Paul of Populonia and Formosus of Porto, bishops of great holiness, instructed them with holy advice and honey-sweet teaching, and decreed that they should go to preach to that race. **70.** This pope had already published throughout the east once and again[146] in apostolic letters all that he had decided about the church of Constantinople. Even so, in order to make it known to that church, since the route by land to Constantinople extends through the Bulgarian kingdom, he sent along with them[147] suitable envoys -

---

There survives the collection of 106 answers to Boris's questions on doctrine and discipline written by Nicholas (in a slightly anti-byzantine tone), the famous *Responsa ad consulta Bulgarorum*; they were taken by the papal envoys when they set out in November 866 (*Ep.* 99, J2812, *MGH Ep* 6.568-600); cf. Sullivan 1955:92-95.

[146] *Epp.* 84-86 of 18 March 862, cf. c. 41 and n. 78; *Ep.* 87 of 863, cf. n. 81; then, in *Ep.* 88, J2796, on 28 September 865 (for the date, Perels in *MGH Ep* 6.454 n. 1 and 487), Nicholas replied at length to a 'blasphemous' letter from Michael III written in 864-5 and sent by the *protospatharius* Michael, in which the emperor objected to the excommunication of Photius. Nicholas accused Michael of falsehood and insolence for writing that he was giving Nicholas orders; earlier emperors had been wont to make requests; as for Michael calling Latin barbarous and Scythian - if he called the language barbarous because he did not understand it he should think how ridiculous it was for him to be called Roman emperor and not know the Roman language, so he should drop the title. Nicholas defended Ignatius who had been condemned on an imperial decision by suspect and hostile judges. He defended the privileges of Rome as given by Christ, not by synods, and therefore immutable. He refused to send back to Constantinople Theognostus and the other monks staying in Rome. He demanded that Ignatius and Photius be sent to Rome with other bishops and provided with their travelling needs. If he obeyed, Michael could enjoy communion with him, but he should not hurl threats at a pope who did not fear them and who would not be forced into obedience by them; and he anathematized any who concealed this letter or part of it from Michael. It seems that the *protospatharius* Michael had not waited to take this reply; Nicholas had to send it on to him to take to Constantinople with a covering letter (*Ep.* 89, J2797) in which Nicholas told the *protospatharius* the gist of its contents, claiming that he, Nicholas, in exchange for the emperor's injuries was returning advice and that he had already done what he had been asked: he had modified the sentence and promised peace and communion to the church and to the emperor. He asked the *protospatharius* to present the letter to the emperor and use a translator who would remove, add or change nothing in it, and he asked that the emperor have it read intact, translated into Greek; he threatened to excommunicate him if he failed to deliver it to the emperor. At least Nicholas was leaving the door ajar for some further discussion, but his tone was scarcely helpful.

[147] Paul and Formosus.

Donatus bishop of Ostia, Leo priest of the holy Roman church,[148] and Marinus deacon of the holy apostolic see[149] - so that the former might convert the people of Bulgaria to the faith, while the latter might announce by every means what and how the apostolic see had deliberated about that church of Constantinople.[150] And this was done in the Lord's name with St Peter's help.

71. The venerable bishops Paul and Formosus stayed in Bulgaria,[151] but when the reverend bishop Donatus, Leo the priest and Marinus the minister[152] of the apostolic see wanted to go to Constantinople, lo! between the borders of Bulgaria and of the Constantinopolitans they came upon one Theodore, who guarded that frontier, and he would let them go no further; instead, he branded them with countless wrongs and so abused the legates of so great a see that he even struck the heads of the horses on which they were mounted, and said: 'Our emperor

---

[148] Leo was cardinal priest of St Laurence *in Damaso* (so Nicholas, *Ep.* 90).

[149] Marinus was envoy to the council of Constantinople in 869-70, and in 882 he became pope. He had attended the Roman councils of 860, cf. n. 32, and 861 (*PL* 106.792) as a subdeacon. His promotion was therefore fairly recent. Cf. n. 165.

[150] They took nine letters (*Epp.* 90-98, J2813, 2819, 2814-8, 2820-1) all dated 13 November 866, but (cc. 71-2) never delivered. In them Nicholas commended his three legates to the recipients and sought support from every possible quarter. In *Ep.* 90 he told Michael that Radoald and Zacharias had been excommunicated for succumbing to his threats and ignoring Nicholas's orders; he explained which parts of his own letters had been tampered with, demanded Ignatius's restoration and Photius's removal, and that they both be sent to Rome; he again attacked the poisonous letter the *protospatharius* had brought him the previous year and ordered the copy to be burnt, or he would convoke a council, anathematize all involved with that letter, and burn it publicly. In *Ep.* 91 he explained the whole schism to the archbishops and bishops subject to Constantinople and to all the clergy of that city, sent them the text of the Roman synod of 863, and ordered them to shun communion with Photius or be excommunicated. In *Ep.* 92 he warned Photius he would be anathematized for ever if he did not renounce the patriarchate. In *Ep.* 93 he urged Caesar Bardas to take up Ignatius's cause. In *Ep.* 94 he wrote to Ignatius how he mourned his fate, telling him what the council had done against Photius, and encouraging him to hope. In *Ep.* 95 he praised the dowager empress Theodora (widow of Theophilus, and effective ruler from 842-856), and explained his own zeal for Ignatius. In *Ep.* 96 he urged the empress Eudocia to have her husband Michael eject Photius and restore Ignatius. In *Ep.* 97 he warned every senator of Constantinople to shun communion with Photius. In *Ep.* 98 he told the patriarchs, metropolitans, bishops, and all the faithful in Asia and Libya what he had done about Ignatius and Photius, and sent them copies of his earlier letters on the matter (*Epp.* 82-86, J2682-3, 2690,2692, 2691), with *Ep.* 88, and the current series. There survives also an undated fragment of a letter of Nicholas in Greek (*Ep.* 98a) to the faithful of Asia, Europe and Lydia on the same matters.

[151] The connexion between the Roman mission and that sent by Louis the German (cf. n. 143) is ignored in the LP. When Ermanrich arrived with priests and deacons to evangelize Bulgaria, Boris received them properly, but the bishops sent by Nicholas had already filled the whole country with preaching and baptisms; so with Boris's leave they went home (*AF* 867 Reuter 56, *AB* 866 Nelson 137). For the date of Ermanrich's mission (any time before May 868, not necessarily early 867) see Reuter, *AF*, 56 n. 1.

[152] i.e. deacon.

certainly has no need of you!'[153] **72.** What is more, the emperor himself is reported to have told the envoys of the king of the Bulgarians: 'If the apostolic see's envoys had not come through Bulgaria, they would not have lived to see either my face or Rome again'.[154] They stayed there for 40 days, and when they knew that the emperor of the Greeks had ordered this to be done they turned their backs and returned perforce to Rome, to report these things.

73. The apostolic envoys were welcomed by the aforementioned king of the Bulgarians [agree]ably[155] and with keen devotion; they began to teach the people with wholesome counsel, and - thanks be to God! - they bathed them from greatest to least in the holy font, and delivered the entire practice of the christian faith to the custom of the Bulgarians, as they had been instructed to do by the holy pope. The glorious king of the Bulgarians, allured by this dutiful father's advice, began to burn with such great steadfastness of faith that he expelled all foreigners from his kingdom, employed only the preaching of these apostolic envoys, decreed indeed that his kingdom needed continuous refreshment in the pastures of eternal life, and petitioned that one of them, bishop Formosus, [handsome][156] in his life and character, be given him as archbishop. **74.** Then he sent his envoys to Rome again; his petition to the blessed pope included that point, and he asked his holiness for priests to instruct his race. The pope, learning such things, rejoiced mightily and, requiting God with countless praises, he tested no small number of priests in his presence; and those he found worthy of the grace of preaching he sent to Bulgaria. With them he despatched

---

[153] The eastern reaction to the Roman embassy was not surprising. Quite apart from the tone of his earlier letters to the east, Nicholas's excommunication of Photius, and the vitriolic letter (*Ep.* 92) the envoys were taking to Photius, the pope was rubbing salt into the wound by linking the embassy so directly to the mission to Bulgaria, itself seen by the Greeks as an infringement of their jurisdiction: the Replies to the Bulgarians (*Ep.* 99) bear the same date as the letters to the east (n. 150). Both Michael III and Photius were indignant. The incident in this chapter is mentioned by Nicholas in his letter of October 867 (*Ep.* 100, J2879, *MGH Ep* 6.603.11) to Hincmar and the other bishops in Charles the Bald's kingdom: 'Not merely did the emperors of the Greeks refuse to receive them (the legates), but they strongly stirred up the minds of the Bulgarians against them, as they allowed them to cross through their land, no doubt hinting precisely that, if they had crossed through regions subject to themselves, they would have given them over to those dangers to which the heretical princes of the said city are recorded to have often given over the apostolic see's legates when they were sent for the sake of the faith or of church discipline'.

[154] The emperor seems to concede that the Roman envoys have diplomatic immunity which would not have applied had they not been in Bulgarian territory; cf. last note.

[155] *grata* was supplied by Duchesne to provide an adjective with *mente*.

[156] Understand *formosus* to be repeated in the sense of 'handsome'.

Dominic[157] bishop of Trevi and Grimuald bishop of Bomarzo, so that, as it was inexpedient for bishop Formosus to relinquish the people entrusted to him,[158] whichever of these priests might be found worthy of the archbishopric might eventually be elected in the Lord's name and sent for consecration to the apostolic see.

75. Meanwhile this blessed pope, the skilful corrector of vices and worshipper of God, laid down that, when these bishops penetrated Bulgaria, bishop Paul of Populonia, whom we mentioned above,[159] and this bishop Grimuald, should bring about in Bulgaria everything that pertained to God's service for that people's instruction, while the venerable bishops the oft-mentioned Formosus and Dominic should set out again on to Constantinople to deal with the schism that had arisen there, about which I have already treated extensively.[160] **76.** While this was happening, by God's judgment a just vengeance overthrew Michael the emperor of the Greeks and destroyed him with an unspeakable death. And once Basil was emperor in Constantinople, since God wanted to complete with a good outcome the unremitting labours that this holy pontiff endured on behalf of the church of Constantinople, as rumour had it, Photius the neophyte and intruder was expelled as an adulterer, and in accordance with the apostolic see's decree patriarch Ignatius was

---

[157] He was one of the 70 bishops who attended the council of 18 November 861.

[158] He already held the see of Porto, and the ancient canons forbade transfer to another bishopric (in fact, of course, he later became pope); Boris's wish for an archbishop is resumed in the next life.

[159] In c. 69.

[160] What Nicholas will never have known, and what the LP fails to mention in this life, is that Photius, who had denounced Roman intervention in Bulgaria to the eastern patriarchs, summoned a council at Constantinople in August-September 867. In retaliation for Nicholas's excommunication and deposition of Photius, the council did the same to Nicholas, Dvornik 1966[a]:453. Nor will Nicholas have known of Michael's death and Ignatius's reinstatement, though the LP does record this in c. 76. Even so, Nicholas was preoccupied with the Greek question as his death approached (cf. n. 167). On 23 October 867 (*Ep.* 100, J2879, cf. *AB* 867 Nelson 141-2, *AF* 868 Reuter 57) he wrote to Hincmar and the bishops of Charles's kingdom about Greek machinations against the Rome; he explained why the emperors Michael and Basil hated the Latin church, including the fact that Boris had asked for teachers and teaching from Rome; he explained what customs the Greeks interpreted as evil in the Latin church (the objections are summarized by Hincmar, *AB* 867 Nelson 141, cf. Nicol 1967, Vlasto 1970:161-2). He ordered each metropolitan to convoke his suffragans to find what was needed to counter the slanders and to transmit their findings to him as a top priority, so that he could send their findings with his own statements against the Greeks' madness. On 24 October (*Ep.* 101, J2882) he wrote to Charles that he had ordered all the bishops of his kingdom to convene, and asked him to assist them; on 30 October (*Ep.* 102, J2883) he wrote the same to Louis the German, mentioning that he had entrusted the holding of the synod to Liutbert archbishop of Mainz. The council was to discuss the schism and the Bulgarian mission and present a united Latin front against the Greeks. Hincmar received *Ep.* 100 on 13 December, and circulated it as Nicholas wanted. But by then Nicholas was dead.

restored to the throne of Constantinople.[161]

77. Now this performer of God's works, this godly and catholic pope, made it his priority to seek not what was his own but what was God's, and with St Peter's help he took care with supreme poise of management to fight the Lord's battles spiritually. Like a father he guided and warned with great foresight each of those in positions of power not to harm their subjects; and he also pastorally decreed that those who were subject to them should be so in accordance with each one's privileges.[162] Anyone who wants to know his holy endeavour will be able to find it clearer than light in his letters, well-balanced ones which he sent through the districts of the world. **78.** He was one who put his life in his hands, who thought on none but heavenly things, who by devoting himself to fasting, watching and praying night and day gave his body no rest and his limbs no sleep. If we mean to insert on paper all the works he did by Christ's grace, full of virtues and the faith of holiness, and all that he taught and fulfilled by his life and character, perhaps the parchment would run out before the words. Yet before we turn our pen to the end of his life, let us return to what he conferred on the holy places.

* * * * *

79. For love of Peter the apostle and prince of the apostles his mentor, this noteworthy pope provided in his basilica .. tapestries, of cross-adorned silk, of gold-interweave and of other beautiful and varying colours; they provide for every one of the great beams all around, that face on to the *presbyterium*; they splendidly augment the decoration and beauty, and they provide full honour with their wondrous size. There too he provided a silver arch weighing .. lb, which no one after the Saracens' looting had striven to do, and he placed it, better than it had once been, on top of the higher beam in the middle in front of the canopy. And underneath it he placed 3 silver images, one of which he engraved with the figure of the Lord Saviour and two with

---

[161] Michael III was assassinated 23 or 24 September 867; Basil, who had been coemperor since 26 May 866, was immediately hallowed as emperor by Photius. Soon after, Photius was deposed, and on 23 November Ignatius resumed the patriarchate. When Nicholas's biographer was completing his text, these events were not yet officially known at Rome, but there was a 'rumour'. The official news arrived only in the spring of 868; so Michael's assassination is dealt with in the next life, 108:22. For the speed at which official news travelled note how on 13 November 866 Nicholas had written *Ep.* 93 (cf. n. 150) to Caesar Bardas, murdered the previous 21 April.

[162] *praelati* is used twice in this sentence, but nowhere else in the LP, in the sense of 'prelates', 'those in positions of power'.

effigies of angels, and he gilded them with 9 lb of gold; one of them weighs 80 lb, another 70 lb, and the third also 70 lb. **80.** There he provided 1 gold cross, adorned with precious jewels, weighing .. lb, and he placed it on the summit of the same arch, and there, for the fullness of its beauty and appearance, he hung 1 gold crown, 2 silver crosses, 2 silver chalices and 2 silver *staupi*. He also presented 2 silver crosses, weighing .. lb, and placed them to right and left on the purple marble which supports the railings in front of St Peter the apostle's body.

81. In the Lateran patriarchate he ordered the building of a beautiful and very fine house;[163] and, constructing there an oratory of God's holy mother, this blessed pontiff presented cloths and fitting adornments, with resplendent vows for love of eternal life.

This God-protected man, encompassed with heavenly grace, renewed many locations of the saints which were at risk of total collapse; he conferred various things on various churches, and splendidly increased what was useful. On the canopy of the Constantinian basilica he hung 4 fine tapestries of *silfori* and of gold-interweave. He also presented an equal number of fine tapestries for the canopy of the kingdom of heaven's keybearer. **82.** He provided the same in the teacher of the nations' church. In God's holy mother's church *ad Praesepe* he provided the same, to gain the prizes of eternal reward. In Christ's martyr St Laurence's church outside the city-walls he also gave 4 fine tapestries for the canopy.

In this blessed prelate's time[164] there was such luxuriance and plentifulness of foodstuffs that this abundance consigned the memory of the famine in his predecessor's days to oblivion.

83. He performed[165] one March ordination, 7 priests, 4 deacons; for various places 65 bishops.

*   *   *   *   *

After he had ruled the apostolic see victoriously, as God's true

---

[163] Evidently the *basilica Nicolaitana* mentioned at 108:14; the location is unknown. Without documentary proof, Duchesne conjectured that it was the building which under Callixtus II (1119-24) became the Chapel of St Nicholas.

[164] The phraseology is based on 90:1 BP 89.

[165] Duchesne pointed out that this single ceremony cannot have been before 862 or after 866. At the council of 18 November 861 there were only three deacons (John the archdeacon, Lunicius, and another John); at this stage Marinus, who was a deacon by 866 (c. 70 and n. 149), was still a subdeacon. The four deacons created at this ordination exactly filled the vacancies among the seven deacons in 861.

athlete,[166] as a catholic and as a prince, he departed from this life to the Lord on 13 November in the 1st indiction [867].[167] And what more can I say, when not only the various races of men that have full use of reason, but even the very elements of the world (inasmuch as the weather was inclement),[168] long wept and remained sad at the death of so great a man?

* * * * *

On his death his body was buried before the doors of St Peter's.[169]

---

[166] Cf. athletic metaphors in 1 Cor. 9.24, 2 Tim. 4.7, etc.

[167] In August 867 Hincmar's legates to Rome found Nicholas (*AB* 867 Nelson 141) 'very ill, and greatly harassed by the dispute he was carrying on against Michael and Basil, the Emperors of the Greeks, and against the eastern bishops'. For Nicholas's concern with the east see n. 160; as a consequence of Michael's assassination (c. 76), the matter of Ignatius and Photius would be resolved in favour of Ignatius, as Nicholas wished, but Nicholas did not live to see it. The date of his death, 13 November, is confirmed by Anastasius's letter to Ado archbishop of Vienne: 'Our pope Nicholas, taken from this wretched life to heavenly bliss on the ides of November' (*PL* 129.741-2, Mansi 15.453-4). *AB* 867 tortuously expressed the same date as 'the ides next preceding the month of December'.

[168] Or, 'the atmosphere was intemperate'. The compiler is saying that it rained.

[169] Cf. n. 2 for the length of the vacancy added here wrongly in MSS C⁴E⁶. Mallius confused Nicholas's tomb with that of Nicholas II; Ado, *Chron. (MGH SS* II.323), states that Nicholas was buried 'in the atrium before the doors of St Peter's not far from the limbs of his predecessor Benedict' (cf. 106 n. 90). Part of the epitaph survives in the grottoes beneath St Peter's (restored text in Duchesne). It praises his virtues, laying stress on his *dogma* and *sophia*, words both occurring in the LP life (cc. 55, 41; cf. *sophistico* c. 7).

108. HADRIAN II (867-872).

The author of this, the last life in the 'continuous' LP, is likely to be identical with the interpolator of the historical passages in life 107. He continues to display familiarity with papal letters (cf. n. 31) and maintains the same partisanship for Anastasius and his family: hence the omission of certain sordid details (see below). But even if, when dealing with the council of Constantinople in 869-70, the LP (c. 42, cf. n. 103) and Anastasius both remark on the risk of the Greeks behaving 'swinishly', our compiler is not Anastasius. The style alone is enough to rule out his authorship; nor does the LP give quite the same version of, or emphasis to, the facts (cf. nn. 107, 115, 131). And would Anastasius, who had been present at that council, have listed the patriarchates as they are given in c. 19 (though see n. 47)?

There is some possibility that the author of 108 was John (Hymmonides) the Deacon, best known as the author in the 870s of the life of Gregory the Great (Arnaldi 1956:49, Bertolini 1960). If so, he is responsible for the self-reference in c. 13, and is there exculpating himself from an accusation made against him, claiming that the charge was a 'shameless calumny'. The content of the first part of 108 is very different from the original version of 107, as it is from life 106. The miracle of Hadrian's multiplication of the denarii (108:2), before his election as pope, is not material in which any previous compiler of the LP would have indulged; but it is to be expected from the hagiographer of Gregory. The references to Job in 107:50 and 108:3 (also 108:27 but in a quotation) are suitable from the author of a life of Gregory. Minor points of contact between John and life 108 may be seen in nn. 25 and 127, and the Glossary, s.v. 'Worthies', but they do not show common authorship. If John was not the author we should look to the eyewitness account of the arrival of the papal envoys to the council of Constantinople (34ff): Donatus, Stephen, Marinus, or someone in their entourage (which did not, incidentally, include Anastasius, *pace AB* 872 Nelson 178).

The life is unfinished. Though the author knew (unless it is an insertion) the length of Hadrian's pontificate (c. 1, n. 1), and of the conspiracy of the Lamberts in August 871 (c. 21), his main text goes no further than December 870. Yet even in the period covered there are serious and significant omissions. After describing events at the time of Hadrian's ordination and his policy in regard to Nicholas, the author from c. 22 to the end is interested only in the east and Bulgaria. This blinkered approach was adopted perhaps deliberately to cover the most striking gap in the story, a sordid incident whose omission cannot be accidental. After c. 22 might have been expected the story of the kidnapping of the pope's daughter by Arsenius's son Eleutherius, and of the assassination by Eleutherius, at the instigation (it was alleged) of Anastasius, both of the pope's daughter and of her mother. While our author, writing during and or even after Hadrian's lifetime, may have failed to finish his work for other reasons, it is likely that he had found no way to resolve the difficulty he would face, as a supporter of Anastasius, in treating that incident. He would have encountered a further difficulty in explaining Hadrian's later abandonment of Anastasius's policy towards Charles the Bald and Hincmar, when Hadrian disavowed letters written in his name by Anastasius. Unfortunately no one else stepped in to complete his task; and the lives of the next three popes were also (as far as we know) unchronicled. The reasons may again have been political. But perhaps the cause now was the very fact that our author, a man of distinction and education, had taken the LP out of the hands of the humble clerks who alone might have been willing to continue it after their fashion. Our author lacked a successor from his own milieu.

The life is one whose compiler, uniquely, failed to fall back on donations and restorations (unless c. 14 be counted) to fill out the text. It is not reasonable therefore to blame him for omissions, but he might have seen fit to include Hadrian's transfer of the relics of St Clement from the Crimea to Rome, an incident perhaps connected with the eastern events which occupy so much of the text.

Nicholas's death produced violence between that pope's supporters and opponents: and the LP makes it clear that the attitude Hadrian would take to Nicholas's actions was to be a major concern (cc. 14-19; see n. 39). Lambert duke of Spoleto was directly involved (this is recorded as an afterthought in c. 20), though it is unclear how far (or until when) he was pursuing his own interests rather than those of Louis II. The LP describes how Hadrian as a compromise candidate was able to acquire unanimous support (cf. Lapôtre 1885:210f). He was a conciliator, and could be seen as vacillating; he was acceptably aristocratic; he was elderly (he had been a candidate for the papacy twice before), and he may have been regarded as a stop-gap. In 855 and 858 he had stood aside, it may be surmised, in favour of the imperial candidates. Louis II's reaction (he was busy fighting Saracens) to the election suggests that he found Hadrian acceptable. Matters began well with Louis graciously consenting to Hadrian's request for the return of exiles (c. 13), and Hadrian would prove conveniently weaker than Nicholas in the face of imperial pressure.

What is not clear is where the different factions among the Roman aristocracy stood in relation to Louis. Nor do we know if Eleutherius's action against Hadrian's family was politically connected. It is unfortunate that the author of this part of *AB*, which provides most of our information on these events, was Hincmar, a man violently opposed to Anastasius and his family (see below; and *AB* 867 Nelson 142 describes Arsenius as a man of great cunning and excessive greed); he recounts the details with evident glee. Hadrian no doubt wished for independence from the powerful family of Arsenius and his sons Eleutherius and Anastasius (on the relationship see 106 n. 9), and was prepared to use Louis's help to defeat Eleutherius. On the other hand Anastasius's influence with the emperor had already been enough to secure his return to favour with Hadrian: on the day of his ordination (c. 10) Hadrian allowed him to take communion among ecclesiastics rather than with the laity, restored him to his priesthood, and made him librarian (cf. *AB* 868 Nelson 145, Lapôtre 1885:11f). But on 10 March 868 Eleutherius raped Hadrian's daughter (who was engaged to a man whose name is unknown) and kidnapped her and her mother Stephania; *AB* states that this was the result of Arsenius's plotting. True or not, Arsenius, and also Anastasius, were inevitably embroiled. Arsenius went to Louis at Benevento, where he died after committing his treasure to Engelberga. Hadrian informed Louis, who sent officials to judge Eleutherius by Roman law. Evidently aware of this, and reputedly on the advice of Anastasius (so it was claimed by one of Anastasius's kinsmen, a priest Ado, *AB* 868 Nelson 148), Eleutherius killed Hadrian's wife and daughter. Louis's envoys then killed Eleutherius.

Hadrian's problem was that he had shown favour to the family by his restoration of Anastasius, and was now confronted not merely with a personal tragedy but with a scandal involving that family. And Anastasius's reputation was such that he was likely to be regarded as the true instigator of his brother's action, quite apart from any information a kinsman laid against him. Hadrian dismissed him from all his official posts and summoned a synod to meet on 12 October 868 at S. Prassede. The decree then passed in Anastasius's presence, together with an account of the facts, survives in *AB* 868 Nelson 145-150; Hincmar records the details as they were rehearsed at this synod of Anastasius's earlier condemnations back to 850 (on which see pp. 104-6). At the synod Hadrian renewed Leo IV's excommunications of 16 December 850, 29 May, 19 June and 8 December 853, related the events of 855 (see life 106 with notes), and then explained how Nicholas had wanted to receive Anastasius back, despite his crimes: he had plundered the patriarchate, stolen the synodal documents about himself, and seized 'from us' the synod's decree reissued with an added anathema. He had blinded and cut out the tongue of a certain Adalgrim who had taken sanctuary in the church (it is not clear at which stage this occurred); and now his kinsman Ado had implicated him as instigator of the murder Eleutherius had committed. So Hadrian treated Anastasius as Leo and Benedict had done; he renewed his excommunication, and if he broke his oath by going more than 40 miles from Rome, the penalty was perpetual anathema.

Hadrian feared conflict with Louis, with whom Anastasius had more influence than he did, and whom he did not want to offend. Even if Louis had accepted Hadrian's election as unanimous, he had been involved in the matter of the papal succession, perhaps through Lambert. It may be a sign of the vacillation with which Hadrian is accused, or a sign of his need for imperial support, that within a year Hadrian reinstated Anastasius to his office: he is described as librarian of Rome when he arrived at Constantinople on the business of Louis II in time to act in the papal interest at the Council of 869-70 (c. 42). All is far from fully explained. Why did the priest Ado implicate his own relative Anastasius? To whom was Hadrian's daughter espoused? She at least can have been no stripling. Hadrian had been a priest since 842 and should have put aside his wife at ordination; if the girl was at least 26, perhaps considerably older, what politics underlie the fact that she was espoused at such an age?

Outside Rome, Hadrian's concerns were with Byzantium (fully covered in the LP), with the Slav princes of the Danubo-Balkan regions (covered where relevant to relations with the east; Bulgaria, and not Moravia), and with the Carolingians (barely alluded to).

The situation at Constantinople had changed with accession of Basil, who restored Ignatius on 23 November 867, and proceeded towards restoring relations with Rome, broken since Photius's council had anathematized Nicholas. Hadrian received the letters Basil sent to Nicholas, and dealt with the question at a council convoked in St Peter's before 10 June 869. This council anathematized Photius (if he repented he could be readmitted but only as a layman), allowed that there might be an amnesty to those who subscribed at Contantinople in 867, threatened those whom he had ordained with deprivation from all church offices, and welcomed Basil's proposal that Rome send envoys to a council at Constantinople designed to put an end to the whole issue. Bishops Donatus and Stephen and the deacon Marinus went with letters for Basil and Ignatius.

The Fourth Council of Constantinople (on its status as the Eighth Ecumenical Council see n. 100) held sessions from 5 October 869 to 28

February 870 (Dvornik 1948:145-158; *AB* under the year 872, Nelson 178-9; Hadrian's letters to the east in 868, *Epp.* 37-38 (nn. 63, 90), and in 869, *Epp.* 39-40 (nn. 64, 79, 81, 85)). Hadrian's request that his legates preside was ignored: Basil appointed the patrician Baanes as president in his own stead. The council proclaimed the validity of all the synodal decisions of Nicholas and Hadrian in favour of Ignatius and against Photius; it also dealt with the question of images (in a way not to Hincmar's liking). Nicholas and Hadrian, it was stated, were speaking as an instrument of the Holy Ghost. But this Roman victory did not last. Basil's reasons for rapprochement with Rome were political: at the same time he was making overtures to Louis by offering him Byzantine forces against the Saracens, as the only means by which he could stop all southern Italy falling into the hands of Louis, the Saracens, or (perhaps) the pope.

As to Bulgaria, we saw in life 107 how in 866 Boris wanted Rome to give him an independent archbishopric under Formosus; Rome objected because of the transfer of see involved. Boris rejected all the other candidates put forward and turned to Constantinople (108:61-3). His embasssy reached there in time for the last session of the council, 28 February 870, and three days later there began, summoned by Basil, a discussion with Ignatius and the Roman legates on the question of jurisdiction over the Bulgarian church. Ignatius, for all that he owed to Rome, turned things to his own advantage by having the representatives of the other patriarchates speak for him: they were naturally favourable to an eastern claim to jurisdiction. The Roman legates vainly protested, appealed to a letter of Hadrian's kept secret until this point but now thrust into Ignatius's hands, and forbade Ignatius to send any of his missionaries to Bulgaria. This Bulgarian debate is given at length in the LP (108:46-60): it is the only occasion that our text adopts the form of dialogue. Some months afterwards Ignatius, in spite of the assurances he then gave of obedience to Rome, consecrated an archbishop and later various bishops to create a Bulgarian church under Byzantine control. Meanwhile the Roman bishops and priests were brutally expelled from Bulgaria, though at the time of writing the author was still not clear exactly what had happened (108:64). These acts throw a further revealing light on the true intentions of the easterners; they had been prepared to use Rome to help in the restoration of Ignatius, but it was Photius, not Nicholas or Hadrian, whose policies for Bulgaria had suited Constantinople, and Ignatius could not toe the Roman line. Hadrian's reaction was inadequate; he complained that Basil had shown such disregard for the Roman envoys that they had fallen into the hands of pirates, he deplored Ignatius's consecration of a bishop in Bulgaria, and he threatened spiritual penalties. But when Basil and Ignatius received his letters, dated 10 November 871, they will have concentrated more on his expression of thanks for the way in which they had conducted the council (*Epp.* 41-2, cf. nn. 90, 125-6, 141).

Bulgaria was lost to the papacy; but Hadrian hoped he could compensate for this in a region where eastern and Germanic influences stood opposed, among the Slavs of central Pannonia and Moravia. Ratislav king of Moravia had begun dealings with Photius on religious matters in 862, and Photius had sent to Moravia the Greek brothers Constantine and Methodius as missionaries. Nicholas and Hadrian drew them into the Roman orbit. After their first successes they were on the way to Constantinople with a group of neophytes to arrange for the organization of their church; in the winter of 866-7 they reached Venice and Nicholas invited them to Rome. When they arrived Nicholas was dead, but Hadrian welcomed them with honour. Constantine was already a priest, but Hadrian ordained as priests Methodius and some of the new converts, while others were made deacons. Hadrian accepted the arguments of the brothers for some use of Slavonic rather than Latin in the liturgy, and this liturgy was even witnessed at Rome. On 14 February 869 Cyril died at Rome and was buried in S. Clemente. Even Kocel, prince of the Slavs around Lake Balaton, turned to the pope and asked for Methodius to be sent as bishop missionary for Pannonia. Hadrian consecrated Methodius bishop with the title of Archibishop of Sirmium and with authority not only over the Moravians but for the former Roman provinces of Pannonia Superior and Inferior, now also inhabited by Slavs (cf. Hadrian *Ep.* 43, J2924, of 868-9, a letter from Hadrian borne by Methodius to Rotislav, Svjatopolc and Kocel, though it may be a forgery based on a letter of John VIII, *Ep.* 255, *MGH Ep* 7.222, J3319, June 880). So Rome regained at least a part of the jurisdiction in Illyricum lost long before to Byzantium. But the cost was a quarrel with Louis the German. Ecclesiastically the lands were regarded as in the sphere of the German archbishopric of Salzburg and the bishopric of Passau. In secular terms Ratislav in 864 had sworn allegiance to Louis the German, and Kocel could not accept the increased power of the neighbouring Moravians. So when Methodius returned to the Moravians in 869-70 to organize the church in the areas Hadrian had entrusted to him, he was imprisoned by Louis's troops, who had invaded Ratislav's kingdom when it came into conflict with Louis; Methodius was charged with exercising illegal jurisdiction in these lands. Such a charge was a grave blow from Louis against Hadrian who had given Methodius his jurisdiction.

The life's last hints about relations with the Carolingians are made in the account of Hadrian's consecration as pope: Theutgaud of Trier was admitted to communion, c. 10 (Gunther of Cologne is not mentioned). This reflected a possible compromise with king Lothar, whose divorce from Theutberga and marriage to Waldrada, with the approval of the two archbishops, had been so firmly opposed by Nicholas; further details of the case, which was terminated by Lothar's death in August 869, are given in n. 25. Readers may judge whether Hadrian's attitude was one of weakness or of sensible compromise. Another ongoing sore in the Carolingian realms, Hincmar's concern over the clerics ordained by his deposed predecessor Ebbo, was one with which Hadrian had no patience: in a letter (*Ep.* 7, J2902, 23 February 868; cf. *AB* 868 Nelson 144) brought from Rome by bishop Actard to Charles the Bald at Senlis, Hadrian thanked the king for restoring the clerics and insisted that the whole question of Ebbo was to be consigned to silence. Actard, who had objected to remaining in his own bishopric of Nantes which was infested by the Northmen, was (to the annoyance of Hincmar, *PL* 126.218-221) to be found a new bishopric, and in recompense for his merits and his exile Hadrian granted him the pallium (*Ep.* 9, J2904, 25 February 868). The questions of Ebbo and Actard were thus laid to rest precisely as Charles the Bald wanted. But Hadrian also wanted good relations with Hincmar, and was careful to write him a letter full of praise (*Ep.* 10, J2905, 8 March 868), urging him to continue in his region, with Hadrian's own authority, Nicholas's policies on the then still ongoing question of Lothar's divorce.

Lothar's death opened the complex matter of the succession in Lotharingia (Lorraine), to which the LP has not a single allusion. Louis II believed his claim was well-grounded, and he relied on Hadrian's support. On 5 September 869 the pope wrote four letters in an attempt to impose this solution (*Epp.* 16-19, J2917-20): the nobles and the bishops of the kingdom of Lothar's nephew, Charles the Bald, and Hincmar, were to stop Charles invading Lothar's kingdom as this now belonged to Louis II; Lothar's nobles were to keep their faith with Louis II as the legitimate heir. But Hadrian's action was preempted by the coronation at Metz on 9 September of Charles as king of Lorraine, long before Hadrian's envoys, bishops Paul of Populonia and Leo of Sabina, could reach Charles. When the addressees of Hadrian's letters, including Hincmar, received them, it seems they could not be bothered to reply (cf. *AB* 869 Nelson 164).

The next year Hadrian tried, with Louis II, to intervene again and more decisively. A series of six letters, dated 27 June 870 (*Epp.* 21-6, J2926-31), instructed Charles to renounce Lorraine, Charles's bishops and Hincmar to see that he did so, and the bishops in Louis the

German's kingdom to encourage Louis to stay at peace with Hadrian's candidate Louis II. But Hadrian had misjudged Louis the German, who was like Charles a nephew of Lothar, and thought a different outcome to the Lotharingian question was preferable. Even if the envoys (Wibod of Parma, the imperial envoy at Rome, and count Bernard of Verona were Louis II's envoys; Hadrian's were John and Peter, bishops of unknown sees, and a priest John) had arrived in time, it is doubtful if Hadrian's letters would have affected the outcome. Some two months before they arrived Charles and Louis the German, by the treaty of Meersen, partitioned Lothar's territory between themselves. At least this time Charles and Hincmar vouchsafed Hadrian a reply. What Charles said is not known, but Hincmar's reply survives: he claimed that the new arrangements accorded with the unanimous wishes of the clergy and nobles from all of France who had gathered with him at Rheims, and in effect told the pope not to meddle in secular matters that were none of his business. On the same occasion, and with as little success, Hadrian had protested at the ordination, when Rome had not been consulted, of Willibert as archbishop of Cologne (cf. *Ep.* 27, J2932, 15 July 870; *AB* 870 Nelson 168-70; *AF* 870 Reuter 64). Charles sent envoys to Rome with gifts for St Peter (*AB* 870 Nelson 171), as peace-offerings to Hadrian perhaps, or as an affirmation that however he disagreed with St Peter's successor all was well between him and St Peter. Hadrian's ineffectual intervention over Lorraine was attributed by the next pope, John VIII, in one of his early letters to Charles (*Ep.* 6, J2961, *MGH Ep* 7.277), to Hadrian's continuous illnesses.

Another cause of strained relations between Charles and Hadrian was the case of the former's son Carloman, a deacon of the diocese of Meaux. Carloman had been excommunicated for his behaviour as the leader of brigands in northwest France and had been imprisoned by his father at Senlis in spring 870. The papal envoys to Charles did at least manage to secure his release (*AB* 870 Nelson 171). Carloman came to Rome, where through the influence of Louis II he gained the support of Hadrian. On 13 July 871 the pope sent three letters (*Epp.* 31-3, J2940-2) to Charles, his nobility, and his archbishops (including those in what had been Lothar's kingdom: the pope had accepted the fait accompli). Charles was accused of behaving savagely against his son, who was to be restored to favour and given back his benefices until his case was dealt with by papal envoys; the nobles were threatened with anathema if they did not do their best to secure peace between Carloman and his father; and the bishops were told not to excommunicate Carloman while he was appealing to Rome.

In that case Hadrian was clearly having as much trouble asserting authority over a cleric (who happened to be royal) as he had had when he attempted to interfere in what was really purely a secular matter, the Lotharingian succession. Another ecclesiastical dispute also brought about conflict. In 868 Hincmar bishop of Laon, and nephew of his namesake at Rheims, who had quarrelled with Charles the Bald and with his own uncle about the extent of royal rights over church property, had sent to Rome (with arguments based on the Forged Decretals) and gained Hadrian's support: the pope wrote to both Charles and Hincmar of Rheims (*Epp.* 14-15, J2911, 2910, cf. *AB* 868 Nelson 152) telling them not to harm his bishopric while he came to Rome. This approach to Rome annoyed Charles, and was seen by Hincmar of Rheims as threatening his own metropolitan authority over his nephew. It is not clear whether Hincmar of Laon did visit Rome at this time; in 869 Hadrian wrote to Hincmar of Rheims (*Ep.* 20) about his treatment of his nephew; but in the spring of 871 he wrote to the nephew (*Ep.* 30, J2938) that he should remember that he was subject to his uncle the archbishop, and should not delay his own promised visit to Rome. Charles's reaction was to summon a council at Douzy in August 871, at which the archbishop deposed the nephew (and Actard was given an archbishopric, that of Tours). On Charles's behalf Hincmar wrote sternly to Hadrian, in effect defying the pope to overrule a council legitimately conducted. Hadrian replied (*Epp.* 34-5, J2945-6, 26 December 871) to Charles and the bishops who had convened at Douzy: he accepted Actard's appointment, but he sharply rejected the deposition of Hincmar of Laon. This bishop and an accuser were to appear before Hadrian who would decide the matter in a full council of the Roman church.

Hincmar of Rheims again replied for Charles, attacking the pope's language against a king whose title came from God, asserting the validity of Douzy and the irrelevance of papal authority in such a question, and proclaiming that, should Louis II allow it, Charles would come in person to Rome as accuser of the bishop of Laon (*PL* 124.881ff). When Actard brought this letter to Rome the sequel was extraordinary. Hadrian announced that he had never heard either of the council of Douzy or of his own letters against which Charles had taken offence. He wrote secretly to Charles, claiming that these letters had either been forged in his name or extorted from him when he was ill. He no longer regarded the bishop of Laon as he had done before. Of course, the bishop had a right of appeal to Rome, but only on procedural grounds, and if he did appeal judges would be chosen from his own province, or instead Hadrian would send his own envoys with power to pronounce on the appeal. This was not how Nicholas would have acted. Hadrian left Hincmar of Laon to whatever fate his uncle and his king had in mind for him. It was no doubt true that Hadrian's letters on this affair, as on the Lotharingian question and on Carloman, were drafted by Anastasius and in phraseology that Charles regarded as impertinent; how far Anastasius had really acted without informing his master is difficult to know. The clue to what may have been, even at the cost of diminishing papal prestige in France and of disowning his own secretary, a volte-face by Hadrian himself lies in the promise he added that when Louis II died (he had no sons) Charles could take the imperial title (*Ep.* 36, J2951).

But Louis II still had some years to live. His concerns in Hadrian's lifetime were the defence of Italy against the Saracens, and, for a time, to see to his daughter's marriage into the eastern imperial family (cf. n. 104). Basil sent Nicetas the patrician to Bari with 400 ships to aid Louis in his siege of the city and to bring back Louis's daughter. But Louis changed his mind on the marriage, Nicetas departed, Louis abandoned the siege and was chased by Saracens who captured 2000 of his horses. Before returning to Bari, they used these to sack the sanctuary of St Michael on Mt Gargano; Louis's failure caused much anxiety to Hadrian and others at Rome (*AB* 869 Nelson 162). Louis eventually stormed Bari on 2 February 871, only to meet with further humiliation when Adalgis led Benevento in revolt (cf. n. 57). The pope gave Louis what support he could: he absolved him from the oath that had been extorted from him never to set foot in Benevento or to wreak vengeance for what he had suffered there; and on 18 May 872 he crowned him at St Peter's, to show his continuing support for the imperial status of one who, it may be supposed, had literally lost his crown along with the rest of his treasure to Adalgis. The Roman nobles held an assembly at which they declared Adalgis a usurper and a public enemy. But Louis may have felt that their support and that of Hadrian could have taken a more practical form.

108. 1. HADRIAN [II; 14 December 867 - *c.* 24 November 872],[1] of Roman origin, son of Talarus who was later a bishop,[2] of the 3rd region,[3] held the see 5 years. He was closely descended from the family of the pontiffs of blessed memory Stephen IV and Sergius the younger [II]. When he was accomplished in wondrous actions, he was allotted the ministry of the subdiaconate by Gregory IV of venerable memory, prelate of the apostolic see. He was taken into his household in the Lateran patriarchate, and as his behaviour was praiseworthy he was ordained priest to rule Christ's confessor and pontiff St Mark's *titulus*;[4] so blamelessly did he live, so manfully did he minister, that everyone reverently regarded him as not merely a new-made priest but a future pontiff. Such great confidence did he have in Christ and his Mother, at whose Manger he devoted himself to continuous prayers, that he did not fail in doing well, nor was he afraid he would incur any loss while he very quietly gave away all he was able to possess. **2.** One day, along with his fellow-priests he received the customary 40 denarii[5] from holy pope Sergius, returned to his house and meant to go indoors, but because of the crowd of pilgrims which had as usual confidently flocked there as to a public granary he was utterly unable to do so. He was moved by pity and remarked to his squire that he wanted nothing to do with such a paltry number of denarii when so many brethren had none. As he reckoned that all the denarii could not be enough for even a third of the poor, he said: 'By the power of Christ who filled 5000 men from

---

[1] Hadrian II was certainly consecrated pope on Sunday 14 December 867 (c. 9); the day of his death is not recorded, but his archdeacon and successor John VIII was consecrated in 872, also on Sunday 14 December (*AB* 872 Nelson 180). Hadrian's last dated document is 13 November 872 (J2952, a privilege to the bishop of Arezzo). Duchesne suggested that John might have succeeded the very day that Hadrian died; this, though not quite impossible, is improbable, and '5 years' in the LP is likely to be a rounded figure (it must have been added afterwards to the text, as the life breaks off unfinished at the very end of 870). For what it is worth, the catalogue in MS Paris 5140 gives Hadrian 4 years 11 months 10 days (i.e. to about 24 November 872); while Vat. 3762 (the MS of Petrus Guglielmus) gives 5 (read 4?) years 11 months 12 days.

[2] Presumably Talarus bishop of Minturnae, known from his attendance at the Roman council of 853; the next conciliar list (for 861) has no bishop from that see.

[3] The 3rd ecclesiastical region contained S. Clemente (97:64), and S. Martino ai monti (34:33, BP 26) which the LP places next to Trajan's baths, in the 3rd civil region according to the fourth-century Regionary Catalogues. The 3rd ecclesiastical region therefore coincided at least in part with the 3rd civil region (Isis et Sarapis).

[4] It was as priest of this *titulus* that Hadrian signed at the council of 853. Since c. 4 states that (in 867) he was in his 25th year as a priest, he was ordained in 842-3.

[5] An example of the distributions called *presbyteria*; cf. 98:2 with n. 6.

five loaves and two fish,[6] I will disburse not one denarius but three to each'. So saying, he went up outside the door and taking them from his squire's hand, he disbursed three denarii each to all the pilgrims as they went out. When the squire marvelled at this abundance, not merely that the denarii did not run out but that some were left over, the generous priest ended by taking what was left over and additionally bestowing three coins apiece to the multitude of his household. But when six were still left over, [he said:] 'You see how bountiful and good is the most almighty Lord, who has distributed the quantity of 40 coins in threes to our brethren and has kept three for you and three for me as a fair share'.

3. He was a man of such great hospitality and bounty that in this he can be compared not unjustly with blessed Job. Kindness grew with him from childhood, came forth with him from his mother's womb. He would not scorn the passer-by for having no clothing but would surely warm him with the fleeces his own sheep provided; nor would he eat his morsel alone when he could eat it with orphans and the needy. He was esteemed as an eye for the blind and a foot for the lame, and, to relate his manifold virtues briefly, he was the father of the poor and the comforter of the widow's heart, he opened his door to travellers, and did not close the gate of his house on those who sought anything from him. The result was that every rank of the clergy and all the unanimous assembly of senate and people would have forced him to take on the supreme pontificate both after the death of pope Leo IV and after the demise of pontiff Benedict III, had he not modestly evaded it with various arguments and shrewd[7] excuses.

4. But when holy pope Nicholas of apostolic memory had departed this human life, and Hadrian was passing his 25th year as a priest, all the city of Rome's citizens and all those from abroad who chanced to be present, poor and rich alike, both the order of the clergy and the whole crowd of the people of every age, occupation and sex, spurning all his excuses, wanted Hadrian and yearned that he be given them as prelate and pastor. No one in the whole wide world was found, unless he wanted the promotion of himself or his own favourite, who did not long in his inmost heart for Hadrian to be promoted to this pinnacle. Though the dignitaries were as usual physically divided into two factions,[8] they burned for him with one mind and equal ardour, for it

---

[6] Matthew 14.13-21, Mark 6.31-44, Luke 9.10-17, John 6.1-13.

[7] Does the author mean, or imply, 'disingenuous'? Hadrian may have wished to avoid blocking the imperially-backed candidates, Anastasius in 855, Nicholas in 858.

[8] The theme occurs in the LP as early as 686 (85:1, BP 81), and 687 (86:2, BP 83, 'as

was only great affection and love for this great man that caused their division: each faction were longing for him to be preferred to themselves, so that, if one faction loved him, the other faction deeply hesitated, nor did one faction have the will to hold the other back, except because it reckoned it was destining its votes for another. **5.** This was all the more so since many of the monks and many of the religious *sacerdotes* and faithful laity, with visions sent down from heaven, had already for a long time not only had no doubt that Hadrian would be pontiff but were even proclaiming him openly. Some among them had seen[9] Hadrian reclining on the apostolic throne with the *pallium* drawn over his shoulders, others had seen him celebrating mass with the apostolic insignia, a number had seen him disbursing gold coins in the Lateran basilicas[10] in the apostolic fashion,[11] and many had beheld him with the pontifical *pallium* mounted on the horse which holy pope Nicholas had ridden for going to St Peter's, returning to the City and entering the patriarchate with the Worthies preceding him and the rest of the crowds in his train. When these signs became clear, both factions displayed their love for this same man, and there was such great unity of minds and bodies for him that they all had a single heart and spirit towards the Lord's same *sacerdos*. As a result he can be called, saving reverence for Jesus Christ our Lord, 'the cornerstone',[12] since by his appearance, and certainly by his advancement, he has 'broken down the hostility' of hearts and has 'made both one'.[13]

6. So when all were gathered, the bishops with the whole clergy and the City's dignitaries with their compliant people, he was seized and taken from God's mother the ever-virgin St Mary's church called *Praesepe*[14] and eagerly brought by the crowd of dignitaries and people

---

usually happens'); for violence see the end of c. 9. It is clear that the attitude Hadrian, once elected, was to take to the critics and supporters of Nicholas's actions was a very delicate one. The LP seems to mean here that each side would support Hadrian if they knew in advance that the other side would do so. But (cc. 14-15) there was a significant faction which, at any rate soon after, saw Hadrian as undesirable.

[9] Such visions are a commonplace in hagiography; Duchesne cited Pseudo-Pionius, *Life of Polycarp*, c. 22. In this, the 5th-century author has a dove hover round the head of Polycarp on the eve of his appointment as bishop of Smyrna (in the Letter of the Smyrnaeans on Polycarp's Martyrdom, c. 16, the dove leaves his body at his death, an incident significantly missing from the text used by Eusebius, *HE* 4.15).

[10] Not the Constantinian basilica of the Saviour (St John Lateran), but basilicas inside the Lateran patriarchate, such as those named after Vigilius, Theodore, etc.

[11] Duchesne thought that the regular *presbyteria* of c. 2 were meant.

[12] Ephesians 2.20.

[13] Ephesians 2.14, 16.

[14] Where he was presumably pursuing his devotions at the Manger (it was Advent).

to the Lateran patriarchate. The prince's envoys[15] heard this and took it ill, indignant not because they did not wish for this great man as pontiff - in fact they wanted him very anxiously - but because, though they were present, the Roman Citizens did not invite them and agree to their involvement in their intended election of the prelate to be. When they heard the reason, that this omission was not done out of despite for the Augustus but entirely with an eye to the future, in case a custom of waiting for the envoys of princes at the election of Roman prelates might be fuelled in this way and take root,[16] they laid to rest all the indignation they felt, and they too humbly approached to hail the one elected.   7. When they were going up and down to the Lateran patriarchate, they were beset with such shouting from all the people clamouring that the man they had long wanted should be given them for consecration, that none of them could hear what was being said by his colleague talking with him. For in regard to the pontiff's consecration[17] [it was clear] to one and all [that they neither] possessed [any other man with such religious humility] or such efficacious love, nor had they seen nor did they reckon they would see one anywhere. Then they were all eagerly striving to seize this man in the presence of those envoys[18] and to drag him and anxiously bring him to be promoted to the supreme height of the pontificate, only they were calmed somewhat by the senators' allurements and advice.

8. The christian emperor Louis heard that they all unanimously desired it, and also learned how they had confirmed the decree for him with their signatures. He rejoiced greatly and yearned in his inmost heart that the Lord's great servant should be prelate for the christian people, as he was desired by and desirable for all races,[19] both Romans and different foreigners. Then he wrote an imperial letter in praise of all the Romans for selecting a prelate worthy of such great office; in it, he let it be known that no promise to pay anything in any way was to be

---

[15] The *princeps* is the emperor Louis II.

[16] The *Constitutio* of 824 gave the emperor and his envoys no role in the actual election. But when the candidate was elected, the proceedings, if they seemed in order, were approved by the emperor's envoys; if these were absent there would be a delay (103 n. 11). But from the viewpoint of 867, at the previous papal election (858) it was not merely the envoys but Louis II himself who had been present, not just at the ordination but (to all intents and purposes) at the election (107:5 and n. 8).

[17] Some words are missing in the text; I translate Dr Cheesman's neat suggestion: *certum se nec alium hominem vel tantam ... (e.g. religionis humilitatem).*

[18] The people clearly thought that the envoys would try to block the election.

[19] The writer has in mind the only occurrence of *desideratus* in the Vulgate ('The Desired of all nations shall come', Haggai 2.8), used in the Advent liturgy (in December).

made to anyone for his consecration, as he ardently desired this to take place not at the prompting of his own men, but rather because he was moved by the unanimity of the Romans; especially since, he said, he was anxious that what had been stolen should be restored, not stolen, from the Roman church, and that nothing should be lost.[20]

9. So when the prayers, vigils and almsgiving had been duly carried out on Saturday, on Sunday as is the custom[21] this venerable holy man was taken by them all to St Peter prince of the apostles' church; and on 14 December in the 1st indiction [867] in the 19th year of the said emperor, he was worthy to receive in the Lord's name the blessing of the supreme pontificate through reverent bishops. These were Peter of Gabii, Leo of Silva Candida, and, in the third[22] place, Donatus of Ostia, because the bishop of Albano[23] had died, while Formosus of Porto had been despatched by blessed pope Nicholas to preach and give instruction to the Bulgarians. It was a comfort for holy church's many sons, who were being driven into various exiles[24] and troubled by different problems through the tyranny of factious men, which was raging more freely than usual between one pontiff's decease and his replacement by another. 10. Indeed, at the celebration of his mass there was such an unbelievable multitude that, while they all eagerly strove to communicate from his hand, Theutgaud archbishop of Trier[25] and

---

[20] The last part of the sentence is obscure. It may mean that the right to free election of a pope had been stolen from the Romans and Louis wanted them to have it back.

[21] This is the first explicit reference in the LP to this being the custom; as far as is known no exception had ever occurred, nor did it do so until the time of Gregory VII, from which time a high feastday was held to be an adequate substitute for a Sunday.

[22] The bishop of Ostia was the principal consecrator. The explanation for 'third place' is that the three bishops each read a prayer in ascending order of dignity and the third place was the place of highest honour. See, e.g., *Liber Diurnus Romanorum Pontificum* (ed. Foerster), 111, 209, 315 (V57 = C56 = A51), which explains that after the litany the bishop of Albano said the first prayer, the bishop of Porto said a prayer, the gospels were brought and held by deacons over the head of the pope-elect, the bishop of Ostia then consecrated him, the archdeacon gave him the pallium, and the pope went to the throne, gave the Peace to all *sacerdotes*, and said the *Gloria*.

[23] Not the disreputable Benedict (104:40ff), brother of Sergius II and therefore a relative of Hadrian (c. 1), but Petronacius (who was bishop by 853; cf. 105:92, 106:16) or a successor of his.

[24] Cf. c. 13 with n. 33, and c. 20 with n. 54.

[25] This is the last reference in the LP to the archbishop of Trier whose support, with that of Gunther of Cologne, for Lothar II's divorce had caused problems in the previous pontificate; both archbishops had been deposed on 30 October 863 (107:49). Both were present now because they had been summoned by Arsenius, 'a man of great cunning and excessive greed' who 'deceived them with false hopes of their restitution, in order to extract money (*xenia*) from them. They stayed in Rome for a long time, and lost nearly all their supporters' (*AB* 867 Nelson 142). While in Rome, Theutgaud stayed in St Gregory's monastery on the Clivus Scauri (John the Deacon, *Vita s. Greg.*, 4.95). At some

Zacharias bishop of Anagni²⁶ who had been stripped by lord Nicholas and had been deprived of communion, and also Anastasius²⁷ who had long been stripped of the priesthood by the pontiffs Leo and Benedict and had been wont to communicate among the laity, received the church's communion under a suitable penance.

11. So he then returned to the Lateran patriarchate, and he outlawed its custom by which, of the various gifts²⁸ that flow in from here and there, only those were kept which would suffice for the needs of tables, while the rest were sold for money. He said: 'It is not godly that we sell for money what we receive for nothing, and that we hold lifeless coins dearer than our living brethren for whom Christ's blood is the ransom; but, I pray, let this shameful trafficking in precious objects be reckoned of less account; let us divide Christ's offerings among his guests and the needy for whom we know God grants them to us, so that what we receive without pay we may also bestow without pay in accordance with the Lord's command'.²⁹

12. His predecessor pope Nicholas of sacred memory had bidden

---

point after Hadrian cancelled his excommunication he died in Rome (*AB* 867). In February 868, at Louis II's request, Hadrian lifted Nicholas's excommunication of Waldrada (*Ep.* 4, J2897). Gunther's case was more serious than that of Theutgaud: he had continued to officiate liturgically despite his sentence. He was not yet readmitted to communion and he nearly died in Rome (*AB*). Lothar, whose divorce the two archbishops had sanctioned, set out for Rome, but finding Nicholas had died he went to Benevento to persuade his brother Louis II to get Hadrian to recognize his marriage to Waldrada, but although *AF* (868, 869 Reuter 58-9) claims that Louis would not cooperate and that Lothar broke off the negotiations for which he had come to Rome and planned to return home, Hadrian had already agreed to have the question of his marriage reopened at a synod, though in the meantime he was to take Theutberga back (*Ep.* 1, J2892). Louis and his wife Engelberga did persuade Hadrian to meet Lothar at Montecassino; there on 1 July 869 Hadrian received Lothar's assurance that he accepted Nicholas's refusal to grant a divorce, and he gave him communion. There too, Gunther swore that he accepted the validity of the sentence against him (and so should not have officiated as a bishop); this put him into the same position that Theutgaud had been in, and Hadrian now readmitted him to lay communion (*AB*). Hadrian went back to Rome; Lothar followed him and again asked about divorce. Aware that he had the support of the Gallic episcopate if he upheld Nicholas's policy, Hadrian again agreed that the matter could be dealt with by a synod of bishops from France, Lorraine and Germany (for further details see *AB* 869 Nelson 154, 156). The entire affair of the divorce was ended when on his way home Lothar and many of his entourage died at Piacenza on 8 August 869 (cf. *AF* 869 Reuter 59).

²⁶ Zacharias had been deposed and excommunicated earlier in 863 (107:42); he had apparently stayed in Rome (cf. 112:1 with n. 4).

²⁷ On Anastasius see 105:92, 106:6-19, and pp. 104-6, 250-2.

²⁸ By a curious coincidence the LP, which has so often mentioned gifts, here alone employs the word *xenia*, used of the gifts that *AB* (n. 25) claims Arsenius wanted to extort at this very time.

²⁹ Matthew 10.8.

bishops Dominic and Grimuald[30] go to the country of the Bulgarians and had sent them off at the very moment of his decease, but in view of the death of so great a father they had delayed leaving. So he forthwith sent them to carry out the same mission, with certain of the letters[31] he had chosen for despatch to show that he had the same intention and enthusiasm, and which he instructed to be titled with his own name; so, as far as the season of stormy weather would allow, as a dutiful heir he fulfilled a dutiful father's prayer.

13. When these were sent away from the city, he straightaway endeavoured to ask from the emperor's gentleness, with many documents and letters,[32] for the exiles Gauderic bishop of Velletri, Stephen bishop of Nepi and John surnamed Hymmonides;[33] by a shameless calumny they had been accused before the serene emperor and had been outlawed from house and homeland. For he said he could not be a good shepherd to God's church unless he had brought back the sheep that an unfaithful man had by his stealth outlawed from the faith of holy church. The emperor, with his christian wife,[34] was gladdened by this religious request, and he not only honourably sent back to the city those on whose behalf the supreme pontiff had written, but he also gave orders that all whom anyone had through private animosity confined in workhouses on charges of treason against the emperor were to be discharged and let go home.

14. After this the supreme pontiff, to fulfil his predecessor's vow, adorned the Nicolaitan basilica[35] with various pictures; holy pope Nicholas had so splendidly raised it from its foundations with three artificial water-channels, that it surpassed all the Lateran basilicas in its beauty. And he followed the precedents of his behaviour so skilfully that holy Nicholas's enemies, since they were trying totally to wreck all he had done, both in writing and in open speech commonly called him

---

[30] Cf. 107:74-5; Nicholas had in fact intended Dominic to go on to Constantinople.

[31] The letters do not survive. Note here again that the author is familiar with details on the writing and despatch of papal letters.

[32] Hadrian's letter to Louis II does not survive.

[33] Hence the references in c. 9 to those who had suffered exile; and cf. 20. Duchesne suggested that these three had been exiled while the see was vacant by Lambert duke of Spoleto (c. 20); if so, either Lambert had not been (at least in this respect) acting as an agent of Louis II, or Louis II was now prepared to make a conciliatory gesture. Stephen of Nepi would play an important role as one of Hadrian's legates to the Fourth Council of Constantinople (cc. 34ff). On the significance of the mention of John Hymmonides (John the Deacon) by name see p. 249.

[34] Engelberga.

[35] Cf. 107:81 with n. 163.

'the Nicolaitan'.[36] **15.** He knew that a number of these enemies were going to pour out the sorrow they had conceived and bring injustice to birth, but as a steward he was keeping them under his own control like tares[37] among the corn until the time of ripening; so, thanks to a rumour that arose to deceive,[38] it was believed he intended to overturn all the acts his predecessor had with God's zeal authorized, but which his enemies were lambasting as much as they pleased. Hence it came about that all the bishops of the western districts, in the solemn and honorific letters[39] they were issuing, continuously impressed on the supreme pontiff that his memory was to be revered as that of a pontiff of orthodox and true philosophy.

16. When certain of God's servants,[40] Greeks and other races, who

---

[36] 'Nicolaitan' is a slur based on the Nicolaitan heretics mentioned in Revelation 2.6,15. The 'enemies of holy Nicholas' were, Duchesne suspected, Arsenius and his faction, the most devoted partisans of imperial authority. Arsenius is evidently intended in the next chapter's references to those in the pope's close company who were secretly nourishing pernicious schemes that the pope knew of but did not wish to fight prematurely. On Louis II's behalf, Arsenius wanted to reach an agreement on the question of Lothar's divorce and the status of the two archbishops (cf. n. 25). The rumour was that he was using his influence to have Hadrian quash Nicholas's acts, an exaggeration which it may have suited Anastasius and his party to spread. But the reality was that Anastasius had been Nicholas's adviser and secretary and cannot have intended a blanket condemnation of that pope's acts: indeed Anastasius wrote to Ado of Vienne, to provoke the campaign mentioned here in favour of Nicholas's acts (*PL* 129.741); cf. Lapôtre 1885:218 f.

[37] Matthew 13.25 etc.

[38] The author avoids saying that Hadrian himself was responsible for a deceptive rumour designed to produce precisely the reponse mentioned in the next sentence!

[39] Not surviving, but one of Hadrian's replies (*Ep.* 13, J2907, 8 May 868; perhaps drafted by Anastasius) reflects the letter he had received from Ado asking him not to alter Nicholas's decrees, and shows how Hadrian grasped an opportunity to emphasize his view of Nicholas: 'So we praise what you encourage about safeguarding intact the Roman church's privileges and the decrees of my predecessor pope Nicholas of apostolic memory, what you urge we acknowledge, what you advise we thoroughly approve. Indeed so far are we from in any way letting that pontiff's acts be annulled, that we regard him as like some new star that appears after great lengths of time amid the clouds of the present life, as one who by the splendour of his life and teaching, with God as author, drives away the darkness of errors, as one who both did and taught not what was to be abolished but what was to be imitated.' With that description of Nicholas cf. Hadrian's speech to the synod of Rome in 869 (Mansi 16.123): '... how in the murky course of this dark age he eventually appeared like a new star'. Hadrian approves of his predecessor's zeal and his own policies will be the same, though in some matters Nicholas's decrees while not being broken may need modification. Cf. Ado, *Chron.*, in *MGH SS* 2.323. Already in *Ep.* 3, J2894, 2 February 868, Hadrian had approved the decisions of synod of Troyes, granted the pallium to Wulfad of Bourges, and ordered Nicholas's decrees to be kept. Cf. *Ep.* 38 in which on 1 August 868 Hadrian assured Ignatius he would always keep to Nicholas's decrees in his favour.

[40] These Greek and oriental monks are adversaries of Photius, supporters of Ignatius and therefore supporters of Nicholas's policies. One of them was Theognostus (c. 35). They are afraid, in view of the rumour in c. 15, that Hadrian will abandon Nicholas's policies.

were staying in Rome at the time privately withdrew[41] for some days from association with this holy pope Hadrian, on Septuagesima Friday[42] this supreme bishop according to custom invited a greater number than usual to take refreshment. In humility he personally poured water over the hands of them all, he set the meal, he served the cups, and, to make them more disposed to take part in the luncheon, he did what he knew no pontiff before himself had done: he reclined with them, joining in with them in praising God with hymns and spiritual chants, [going through] the whole vast company of them there as they kept up a constant chorus [of praise]. **17.** When he had risen from the banquet he prostrated himself before them all, saying: 'I ask you and humbly pray you, fathers, brethren and sons, to pour forth prayers to the Lord for his holy catholic and apostolic church, to pray for our christian son the emperor Louis Augustus that almighty God may make subject to him the race of the Saracens for our everlasting peace,[43] and to pray also for me who am frail and weak that Christ, who entrusted the rule of all he had redeemed to St Peter the apostle, may give me strength to rule the great multitude of his church in holiness and righteousness,[44] so that though I am blinded by the dust of the world's cares and for the most part see spiritual things not very clearly,[45] your unceasing prayer, which is the purer for being further distanced from the world's pollution, may gain me support from God'. **18.** And when they clamoured that it was more appropriate for him, rather than themselves, to pour forth the prayers, as he was held the more acceptable before God the more he alone was fervent in his labour for all, he was moved with kindness within and spoke tearfully: 'Since praying for the truly good, dearly beloved, is an act of thanksgiving to God, I ask that you keep the lord

---

When their demonstration took place, Photius had already been deposed (23 November 867), two months after the death of Michael III and the accession of Basil. But these events were not yet known for certain at Rome (cf. 107:76). Louis II, wanting Michael as an ally in expelling the Saracens from Italy, showed himself favourable to Photius, who welcomed his advances in the hope that Louis could persuade Nicholas to recognize him. The monks now thought that Louis's influence with Hadrian might bring him to recognize Photius, which would leave them high and dry; cf. Lapôtre 1885:215.

[41] In spite of Dvornik 1973:45, *se suspendissent* does not mean that they hanged themselves. Protest suicide is pointless when secret.

[42] Friday after the third Sunday before Lent; 20 February 868. There is no other evidence that such a meeting was normally held on this day. The LP may mean that the pope customarily received monks at the Lateran on any date he found convenient.

[43] The phrasing is from the fourth of the Good Friday Solemn Prayers, for the emperor; but the next clause, for the pope, is not from the second of those prayers.

[44] Luke 1.75. In general Hadrian is here echoing Nicholas's view of papal power.

[45] Or 'less clearly' than the monks do (or, just possibly, than Nicholas did).

my father and predecessor the holy and orthodox pope Nicholas ever present in your prayers and so give thanks to God who took mercy on his church and chose him, and who, to drive out the world's billowing turmoil, armed him with the shield of his protection and strengthened him with the sword of spiritual power'.[46]   **19.** Hearing this, all the Lord's servants, those of Jerusalem, Antioch, Alexandria and Constantinople,[47] some of whom were engaged in the embassies of the world's princes,[48] were for a long time surprised and amazed, and burst out in a clear voice with the words: 'Thanks be to God! Thanks be to God who has arranged that one such as you should be in charge of his church, you who kept before your eyes reverence for your father and predecessor, and knew how to shepherd the Lord's flock with rod and staff,[49] and how not to overthrow but to fulfil the ancestral covenant. Thanks be to God! Thanks be to God who has not set an apostate pope on the throne of his apostle; who has founded his house not on sand but on solid rock;[50] who has made you succeed holy pope Nicholas and not depart from his decrees. Let envy retire, let lying rumour depart! To our lord Hadrian, the supreme pontiff and universal pope decreed by God, long life!' - said three times. When his hand had signified silence, the supreme prelate intoned the words: 'To the most reverent and orthodox lord Nicholas, the supreme pontiff and universal pope decreed by God, everlasting memory!' - said three times. 'To the new Elijah,[51] everlasting life and unfading glory!' - said three times. 'To the new Phinehas,[52] the insignia of everlasting *sacerdotium!*' - said three times.

---

[46] With Hadrian's view of Nicholas here cf. his letter to Ado (n. 39).

[47] At first sight one is struck by the way in which our Roman author manages to list Constantinople last among the patriarchates, and this in spite of the fact that the council of 869-70 (canon 21) was shortly to classify the patriarchates in the eastern order of precedence: Rome, Constantinople, Alexandria, Antioch, Jerusalem; Rome had until now objected to Constantinople being given precedence over Alexandria. On the other hand, the present text presents all four patriarchates in the reverse order of the new official list; perhaps the author is working from least to greatest.

[48] This is obscure. The monks are pro-Ignatius, many of them in Rome for a number of years as exiles from Michael and Photius, and can hardly be Michael's envoys; nor would there yet have been time for an embassy from Basil to have reached Rome.

[49] Ps. 22 (23).1,4.

[50] Cf. Matthew 7.24-26, with a subsidiary allusion, of course, to Matthew 16.18.

[51] Nicholas is called a second Elijah in the Acts of the Council of 869-70 (Mansi 16.309, and Anastasius's version, 16.17, *PL* 129.28); cf. Regino of Prüm, *Chronicon* 868: 'that he may deservedly be believed to be a second Elijah'.

[52] Numbers 25.6-15; Phinehas was the grandson of Aaron; he slew Zimri and Cozbi, an Israelite and his Midianite woman, 'through her body' (other versions of the difficult Hebrew give 'in the belly'; but the Septuagint has μήτρα and the Vulgate *in locis genitalibus*), thus causing God to stay the plague (cf. 1 Macc. 2.26, 54; 1 Cor. 10.8) and

'To his followers, peace and favour!' - said three times.[53]

20. Now[54] at the time of the venerable pontiff's consecration, the duke of Spoleto, Lambert son of Guy, entered the city of Rome like a tyrant as was his custom, and though it was not in rebellion he gave it over as if he had vanquished it to his followers for plundering. He sold the houses of the great for many favours; he spared no monasteries or churches; he even granted the girls of noble family, whether inside the city or without, to his followers indiscriminately for ravishing. That was why, loaded with the complaints of the Romans before the godly emperors, he lost the dukedom, and as one truly judged by the apostolic see he incurred the anger of the princes and the odium of almost all the Gauls. **21.** Then the Roman pontiff, delivered from such great tyranny, deprived them all of ecclesiastical communion, Austald,[55] Walter, Hilpian, Odo[56] and Theopert with all the other ravishers and plunderers, until they returned the women seized and made reparation for themselves in law. Theopert made no difficulty about returning the woman he had seized; while Austald, a man devoted to God and a mighty warrior, turned to the prelate, smiting himself, with all humility, and received his leave to make reparation according to the full pleasure

---

grant Phinehas 'the covenant of a perpetual *sacerdotium*' alluded to in the LP text. The Vulgate has the incident take place in a brothel. The point is that Nicholas had preserved orthodoxy from doctrinal contamination just as Phinehas preserved Israel from racial contamination; the implication that Constantinople was a brothel will have been lost on the Greeks as the Septuagint locates the incident in a warm place (κάμινος; the Hebrew, again, is obscure; RSV 'inner room').

[53] Such acclamations were common at councils, e.g. at that of 869-70 (Mansi 16.319-320) they are made to the emperors and empress, then 'Everlasting memory to pope Nicholas of Rome; many years to Hadrian', then to Ignatius and the eastern patriarchs.

[54] Duchesne noted that Lambert's intervention was connected with the troubles during the vacancy of the see. Lambert was son and successor of Guy (in Latin, Wito) as *marchio* or duke of Spoleto (see notes to 104:17 and 104:47) from c. 860 - c. 879. Since 866 he had headed the Lombard principality of Capua. It is not clear how far his expedition against Rome was in accordance with Louis II's wishes; Louis was then in the south, fighting the Saracens of Bari and Taranto. Lambert's disgrace did not occur very quickly; the LP is wrong to attribute it solely to the Romans' complaints. It actually followed his involvement with Adalgis duke of Benevento (on whom see Erchampert, *Hist. Lang. Ben.* 20, 29-38, *MGH SSrL* 242, 245-9) against Louis II in August 871. On this occasion he had with him another Lambert, count of Camerino, later called by *AB* 873 Nelson 183 Lambert the Bald; hence the LP's allusion just below to the 'conspiracy of the Lamberts' (cf. n. 57). Lambert the Bald may have been a close relative of the Lambert count of Nantes mentioned in *AB* 844 Nelson 58 (with n. 7) and may have come to be embroiled in Italian adventures. Lambert the ex-duke of Spoleto was able to recover his duchy after Louis II's death (875). On these Lamberts and on south Italian politics at this time Nelson, *AB*, 176 n. 15 cites Hlawitschka 1960:59-60, 214 and Wickham 1981:62-3, 153-5.

[55] *Austaldus*, so spelt here in Duchesne's text, but *Aistaldus* four lines lower down.

[56] Possibly Odo, son of count Robert, mentioned (unnamed) in *AB* 868, the future (888-898) king of West Francia.

of the Romans, and he frequently received also the hope of resuming communion. Indeed he would have become able to receive it except that later he was an accomplice in the conspiracy of the Lamberts[57] and he preferred to flee with excommunicates and rebels and make for Benevento.[58] **22.** With matters settled in this way, after Michael the emperor of the Greeks destroyed the Caesar Bardas, a supporter of Photius, who was, so they testify, plotting his death, he adopted Basil as his colleague and made him emperor;[59] and since the new emperor Basil was revered with great enthusiasm by the catholics as one who always favoured them, Michael was done away with[60] by his eunuchs, it being unclear whether this was his son's intention. Then Basil, with power in his hands, immediately satisfied everyone that he had not been, as it was reported, an accomplice in Michael's death. **23.** Then in accordance with what the Roman church laid down, he expelled the intruder Photius and he reinstated[61] the patriarch Ignatius in the patriarchate, which was what the people were striving for;[62] and from each side, that of the patriarch Ignatius and that of Photius the neophyte, he sent envoys to Rome[63]

---

[57] Cf. *AB* 871 Nelson 175-6: Adalgis and other Beneventans conspired against Louis II because Louis, at his wife's instigation (on Engelberga's role, Nelson 176 n. 14 cites Odegaard 1951:79), intended to exile Adalgis permanently (Erchampert, *Hist. Lang. Ben.*, *MGH SSrL* 247, says vaguely that the Beneventans rebelled because 'the Gauls had begun to persecute them'). Adalgis planned a night attack on Louis, but Louis, his wife, and the men with him, occupied a strong tower where they held out for three days. The bishop of Benevento got the Beneventans to agree terms; in return for his giving them solemn oaths they were to let Louis leave. Louis, his wife and daughter, and the men with them, forswore all vengeance or reprisals in person or through agents for what had happened, and Louis was never to take an army to Benevento. So Louis journeyed by way of Spoleto to Ravenna, but sent to Hadrian to meet him en route and absolve him from his oath. The two Lamberts believed they were under Louis's suspicion for what had happened, so they left him and went to the Benevento region, because Adalgis was their associate. Louis sent his wife to Ravenna and pursued the Lamberts; but failing to catch them he began his return to Ravenna.

[58] Before turning irrevocably to eastern affairs the writer might have mentioned the murder of Hadrian's daughter and her mother by Eleutherius; see pp. 250-2.

[59] Bardas was Caesar from 862; his death was 21 April 866 (Theophanes Continuatus 206.13; not in 865 as sometimes given); Basil became coemperor on 26 May 866.

[60] 23/24 September 867, before Hadrian II became pope; see 107:76 with n. 161.

[61] 23 November 867.

[62] Cf. the remark attributed to Michael III (Nicetas, *Vita S. Ignatii*, PG 105.528B): Theophilus (an actor) was his own patriarch, Photius was the patriarch of the Caesar Bardas, and Ignatius the patriarch of the Christians.

[63] Before this embassy, an official letter from Basil, addressed to Nicholas and brought by the *spatharius* Euthymius, had informed Rome of the restoration of Ignatius; this is lost, but Hadrian's reply survives (*Ep.* 37, J2908), evidently written at the same time as his letter to Ignatius (*Ep.* 38, J2909). Hadrian stated that he would keep to Nicholas's policies, praised Basil for restoring Ignatius, urged him also to recall Ignatius's supporters,

through his *spatharius* named Basil, to contend alternately in the supreme bishop's presence and, with the support of justice, either to justify Photius or condemn him for ever. **24.** But by God's judgment the sea swallowed up Photius's fine-talking side yet preserved Ignatius's plain-spoken side safe, with the imperial envoy;[64] none of the neophyte's side escaped apart from a single little monk named Methodius.[65] Later on he accepted neither Photius for whose side he had come, nor Ignatius against whom he had come, nor the rights of the universal church to which he had come; three times he was summoned, three times he was marked out for his perfidy, once he was anathematized and he departed.

25. It had been to Nicholas that Basil, the emperor's envoy, and John, the metropolitan of Caesarea in Cappadocia,[66] had been sent. They

---

and commended Theognostus who had been in exile at Rome for seven years and was now returning with Euthymius; to Ignatius Hadrian expressed gentle surprise that he had not received from him notification of his restoration, and hoped that Ignatius would use Theognostus as his particular representative at Rome. The embassy bringing these letters was slow, hence Hadrian's letters in reply were only dated 1 August 868. Meanwhile Basil on 11 December 867 (Mansi 16.47) wrote again to Nicholas (the embassy mentioned here), taking up his suggestion (107 n. 146) that the Photians and Ignatians should explain their case in Rome; Basil regarded this as a hearing preliminary to the council to be held in Constantinople. The point at issue was now no longer the possession of the see but what was to be done with those whom Photius had ordained or who had subscribed to the council which had excommunicated Nicholas in 867 (Beck 1969:181).

[64] Anastasius in his preface to the Council of 869-70 (Mansi 16.6-7, *PL* 129.15; cf. Leonardi 1987) gives the names of the legates and notes the suitability of shipwreck as the cause of the death of Photius's legate: 'So John metropolitan of Sylaeum, who was also in charge of the church of Perge in Pamphylia, was sent to Rome from the side of Ignatius, while from Photius's side there was Peter metropolitan of Sardis, who with the already-mentioned Gregory' (the bishop of Syracuse deposed by Ignatius) 'had been the initiator of the church schism; moreover the prince sent the royal *spatharius* named Basil, who was to be regarded as intermediary between the two sides before the apostolic see and as the faithful listener and messenger of what that see had decreed. But Peter, though he was travelling on a new ship and one which he had selected for himself, suffered shipwreck and with it a perilous death; and he who had split Christ's ship, that is the church, not inappropriately incurred the splitting of his ship. But the other legates reached Rome...'. In *Ep.* 39 (*MGH Ep* 6 at 753.33) to Ignatius, Hadrian commends John of Sylaeum who on his way to Rome 'endured infinite perils not only at sea but also travelling by land'; and in *Ep.* 40 (at 758.7) to Basil, he commends Ignatius's legate John, and Basil the imperial *spatharius*, who, sent from Constantinople to Nicholas, 'after they set out they endured obstructions, as we have learnt, so that on their journey they escaped hardly any of the perils that Paul lists in his epistles' (2 Cor. 11.26). These adventures explain why, though sent before Nicholas's death was known at Constantinople, they did not leave Rome until after 10 June 869 (the date of Hadrian's next letters to Basil and Ignatius, *Epp.* 39-40), though Hadrian apologized to Basil that they had stayed at Rome *diutissime*.

[65] He and his adventures are nowhere else recorded. Now in a minority of one, he perhaps felt it unwise to defend Photius's case.

[66] False; his see was Sylaeum in Pamphylia: Anastasius (n. 64, stating that he held the see of Perge as well); confirmed by Hadrian, *Ep.* 40 (758.4); Ignatius's *Ep.* in *PL* 129.61; and John's own subscription to the synod, *PL* 129.15: 'John archbishop of Perge in

presented themselves with adequate humility to this holy pope Hadrian
as he sat with the bishops and the dignitaries in the *secretarium* of St
Mary Major, according to the custom of the holy apostolic see, and they
presented gifts and letters.[67] These were accepted, and they rendered
manifold thanks to the holy Roman church by whose pains the church
of Constantinople had risen up, cleansed from schism; and after
countless acclamations of praise they spoke with harmonious voice:
'When your most devoted son the emperor Basil, and the patriarch
Ignatius who has been reinstated by your good offices, ejected the
intruder Photius from the church of Constantinople through your
intervention, they discovered in his archive a book[68] containing
enormous calumnies against the holy Roman church's character and that
of holy pope Nicholas. As something truly infectious they sealed it up
and utterly ejected it from their city, and they sent it to you as the
supreme head to whom Christ has granted the power of binding and
loosing in heaven and on earth.[69] **26.** Take it, we pray, and examine it;
observe exactly the fraudulence - though the Constantinopolitans were
guiltless - which our crafty Photius was able to include, from the fact
that he whetted his bold tongue[70] against this holy Roman church 'which
is without spot or wrinkle or any such thing';[71] and promulgate openly
what God's church must think about this robbery[72] that he has stealthily

---

Pamphylia, *apocrisiarius* of holy Ignatius patriarch of Constantinople'.

[67] No detail of this assembly at St Mary Major's is recorded elsewhere; Jaffé-Ewald date
it vaguely to 868-869, but it was only shortly before (cf. c. 32) the council held in St
Peter's not long before 10 June 869. Nicholas's letters to Gaul had spurred the western
church into presenting a united front against the east, and although this was no longer so
necessary once Basil had removed Photius, the Council of Worms (16 May 868) passed
various canons for the good of the church and gave 'suitable responses to the stupidities
of the Greeks', *AF* 868 Reuter 58. The concern in Rome was now to avenge the synod
of 867 which had excommunicated Nicholas.

[68] The book was that of the Acts of the council of 867 (not now surviving). The LP has
never mentioned that council (see 107 n. 160), and now avoids referring to the book as
conciliar acts; see further the canons cited in n. 81, and Anastasius (Mansi 16.5, *PL*
129.13). Nicetas, *Vita S. Ignatii* (Mansi 16.257-61), gives details about copies of the acts
which were seized after the fall of Photius. One was his own copy, taken from his
servants who were about to hide it underground; it was adorned with pictures of Ignatius
as antichrist, done by Gregory of Syracuse. Another was taken from the two bishops
(Zacharias and Theodore) whom Photius had charged to take it to Louis II in Italy in the
hope that he would carry out the sentence of deposition on Nicholas. One of these may
be the copy taken to Rome and burnt, and the other that which stayed at Constantinople,
to be burnt by the council of 869-70.

[69] Matthew 16.19.

[70] Cf. Ps. 63(64).3.

[71] Ephesians 5.27.

[72] *latrocinium*; the reference is to the 'Robber-council' of Ephesus in 449, so termed by
Leo I, and condemned by the council of Chalcedon in 451. Hadrian (*Ep.* 40, *MGH Ep* 6

fabricated under the name of a synod.'

27. With the pontiff's permission, the assembly of both sides[73] replied: 'Because Photius had no right to bring an action, he could perhaps hurl an opinion against the apostolic see and its pontiff but he could not deliver a judgment;[74] whereas he has been twice judged and twice condemned by the apostolic see. And because he was using his power to climb to higher places and did not fear to prate calumnies against our holy pontiff Nicholas, he assuredly opposed heaven with his effrontery and thrust his tongue out across the earth; so we admit his so-called synod's book for scrutiny, so that its author may be judged a third time, as both a fabricator of lies[75] and an inventor of twisted dogmas'. **28.** The metropolitan[76] came forth, produced the book, hurled it to the ground and addressed imprecations to it: 'You are cursed at Constantinople, be cursed again at Rome! The devil's servant Photius, the new Simon, the compiler of lying, prepared you; Christ's servant Nicholas, the new Peter, the lover of truth, has crushed you!' And the *spatharius* struck the book with his heel and his sword, and also said: 'I know the devil dwells in that work, because he uses the mouth of Photius his accomplice to vomit up what he is unable to say on his own. **29.** As for its containing, after the signature of Michael whom he persuaded at night to sign when he was very drunk, the signature of our emperor Basil, that is a great calumny.[77] His reinstatement of Ignatius has proved that it is not his, and, if you agree, our giving satisfaction on oath will confirm it. For as Basil was always catholic, he could not insert his name in his bestial fabrications other than by forgery, just as by changing the handwriting he was able to write down the names of many absent bishops along with his few accomplices. **30.** The whole number of these bishops no more shared in signing it than they were

---

at 756.29) also calls the council of 867 as detestable as the *latrocinium* of Ephesus and as the council of Rimini in 359. The parallel with the *latrocinium* had also been used by Nicholas (*Ep.* 18 at 285.6) when he condemned the council of Metz.

[73] Perhaps the Romans and the easterners; hardly the Photian and Ignatian sides since Photius was unrepresented (unless Basil, supposedly neutral, is counted).

[74] He had no competence to pass his sentence against Nicholas in summer 867.

[75] Job 13.4 (Vulgate).

[76] John of Sylaeum.

[77] It is alleged that Photius persuaded the drunken Michael to sign, and that Basil's signature was a forgery. Michael III was regularly portrayed under the Macedonian dynasty as a drunken sot (Ostrogorsky 1969:223). All that follows may be a sham designed to secure the destruction of the copy of the acts, so that there would be no record at Rome of the fact that Basil and most eastern bishops had signed in 867: whether or not they were enthusiasts for Photius, they had all regarded Nicholas's involvement in Bulgaria as an attack on the whole eastern church, Dvornik 1973:43.

aware of its contents. Indeed when this so-called council had been gathered none of the Constantinopolitans acknowledged it, because it really was not one. But because the provincials come up to Constantinople, it being the royal city, on the various business of that kind of city, the headstrong Photius rubbed the medicine of truth into his lying, just as he had been taught to do from childhood, when in place of some of the holy bishops[78] he made some of their citizens sign - though they were renegades, so common rumour has it, and were blinded with bribes. **31.** This is why its signatures seem to be in different writing; some of them write with quite a sharp quill, some with a broad one, while a number, to feign old age, write with a broader one and blot the parchment; in consequence there is deception practised by the fraud of those present against the ingenuousness of those absent, and the world at large believes more easily in the genuineness of what forgery has made look different by using different writing. If you open the book you will immediately see the differences between the signatures, though without sending to Constantinople you will never recognize there has been fraud'. **32.** Then the supreme pontiff decreed that the book was to be examined for several days by experts in both languages, and that everything contained in it was to be faithfully made public before the synod.

When it was rigorously examined, the venerable pontiff, with the assent of the whole gathering of senate and people, summoned a holy council at St Peter the apostle's in defence of his church and his predecessor.[79] First of all the truth of the matter was clearly heard from the envoys of Constantinople, and he[80] read over his predecessor's letters

---

[78] Anastasius (*PL* 129.12, Mansi 16.5) accepted the truth of this charade (last note). He too alleges false representatives of the eastern patriarchates, about 1000 false signatures, and only 21 genuine adherents of Photius: 'he gathered a so-called council under the emperor Michael's presidency, he lined up false men as representatives of the easterners, he armed accusers with bribes and heaped them with lies, he adopted as witnesses those whom he also brought forward as accusers' (against Nicholas) '... while all who were present, except for a very few who were promoters of iniquity, cried out that it was not right to deliver a sentence against the supreme and first pontiff, and particularly for it to come from an inferior... he inserted about 1000 false signatures of bishops, though apart from 21 prelates not one of that numerous crowd of bishops consented or joined in writing their names'.

[79] Hadrian, *Epp.* 39-40 of 10 June 869, provides the date when the eastern legates left Rome; it is likely that the council was held not long before this. For the delays cf. n. 64. Mansi 15.882, 886 wrongly conjectured that the council was before August 868, thinking it predated *Epp.* 37-38 of 1 August 868; but these letters do not allude to it, and *Ep.* 13 of 8 May 868 does not suggest that any envoys of Ignatius were likely to arrive in Rome, though John metropolitan of Sylaeum was certainly present at it.

[80] The translation takes Hadrian, rather than the council, as the subject from here to the end of the chapter, since, although the remains of the acts contain a long encomium of

on this matter and cleared his unfavourable reputation. Then with a third anathema he cast down Photius with his assembly and accomplices. Lastly, with the verdicts confirmed by everyone's signatures, he discarded the book of wicked dogma in front of the doors by the steps, to be trampled under everyone's feet.[81] **33.** In fact it was used as kindling for a bonfire, which consumed it with a big stench and a pitch-black colour almost before one could have believed it would be half burnt. When it chanced that there was a deluge of rain which ought naturally to have put the fire out, the flames gained strength as if the raindrops were drops of oil, and amazement at this marvel opened the hearts of both Latins and Greeks in praise of God, of holy pope Nicholas, and of Hadrian the supreme pontiff.

34. After this he despatched[82] Donatus bishop of Ostia and Marinus[83] the deacon to Constantinople with his predecessor's letters, just as he had composed them.[84] To them he added his own letters, headed by his name alone,[85] and a letter of instructions, and also Stephen bishop of Nepi. He ordered them to lay skilfully to rest every stumbling-block in the way of the church of Constantinople; they were to restore to their own churches those consecrated by Methodius[86] and Ignatius under the penance in a document they had taken from the church-office;[87] but as

---

pope Nicholas, it does not seem that his letters were read out. If the council is the subject, *litteras relegens* here would probably be false.

[81] Hadrian's next letters to Ignatius and Basil (*Epp.* 39-40, J2913-14, 10 June 869) supplement the LP's account of this council. A summary of the acts survives through quotation in the acts of the 7th session of the Council of 869-70: Hadrian's speeches were read out by archdeacon John and deacons Marinus and Peter, there were interventions by Gauderic bishop of Velletri and by the notary Benedict, and five canons were agreed: 1) the Council of Constantinople in 867 is condemned, and all copies of its acts consigned to the flames; 2) two conventicles held against Ignatius are cursed; 3) Photius is condemned and anathematized; 4) if those who had signed that council repent they may be restored to communion by the pope, and Basil is assigned a place among catholic and pious emperors; 5) any who retain copies of that council are anathematized. Then come the signatures of Hadrian, John of Sylaeum, 29 bishops and 1 representative of a bishop, 9 priests and 5 deacons (Mansi 16.122-131, 372-80, *PL* 129.105-116). On the council cf. Dümmler 1887-8:1.690.

[82] Donatus and Marinus had been sent (with a priest Leo) to Constantinople in 866 but had failed to get through (107:71). They now had a different companion, Stephen.

[83] The future pope; for his earlier activities see 107:70-72. It has been claimed that Marinus was actually Hadrian II's son, and a brother therefore of the girl killed by Anastasius's brother (Jaffé-Ewald, 704 addenda to n. 2914). But the papal catalogues are likely to be right in stating that he was from Gallese, son of a priest Palumbus.

[84] Cf. n. 87.

[85] *Epp.* 39-40, J2913-2914, to Ignatius and Basil respectively, dated 10 June 869.

[86] Ignatius's predecessor as patriarch of Constantinople (843-7).

[87] Bishops consecrated by Methodius and Ignatius (not by Photius) who had later recognized Photius are to be reinstated. The text of the *libellus* (*Prima salus est...*) which

for the Photians, though they were to communicate with them under this and a more severe penance, they were to prolong the repeated verdict of the apostolic see on *sacerdotes*, holy pope Nicholas's judgment remaining in force.[88]

35. So, betaking themselves round many laborious and tortuous deviations, with Christ as their guide they came[89] at last to Thessalonica, to which the emperor Basil had despatched the white-robed *spatharius* Eustathius to meet the holy Roman church's envoys with the task of giving them his greeting. They led them very honourably along the neighbouring areas of the route and left them at Selymbria, where they were received by Sisinnius the imperial *protospatharius* and Theognostus[90] the patriarchal *hegumenus* (who had been a zealous intermediary before holy pope Nicholas in Rome for Ignatius's reinstatement), with 40 horses from the imperial stable and a complete set of silver tableware,[91] and with officials to serve their every whim. **36.** At Castrum Rotundum,[92] in which there is a church of wondrous

---

they would have to sign is given in the acts of the first session of the council of 869-70 (Mansi 16.27-8 and a shorter version in Greek, 16.316; *PL* 129.35-7). In a note at this point in his translation of that council, Anastasius (Mansi 16.29, *PL* 129.37-8) states that the document had been prepared for the embassy sent by Nicholas in 866, and that the only change in 869 was the name of the pope. But the nucleus of the document was much older: it had been composed by pope Hormisdas as a profession of faith to be taken by repentant Acacian heretics (LP 54.3, 5, 8, BP 47-48), and its use now was to prove heavy-handed and tactless.

[88] These *sacerdotes* are bishops and priests who had been ordained by Photius; their excommunication may be lifted, but they may not officiate as bishops or priests.

[89] The compiler now adopts a vivid historic present tense, maintained (but not in the translation), though not quite consistently, till c. 47.

[90] The MSS of LP spell Theognistus. He is mentioned in a letter of Nicholas (*Ep.* 88, *MGH Ep* 6.477.22, J2796, 28 September 865) as having received from Ignatius 'the task of being exarch over certain provinces'. In 861-2 he had taken refuge in Rome with other Ignatian monks. Michael III vainly demanded that Nicholas send him back (cf. summary of *Ep.* 88 in 107 n. 146); but he returned to Constantinople only in 868 with Euthymius (n. 63; Hadrian, *Epp.* 37-38, J2908-9; *Ep.* 37 at 748.6 states that he had spent seven years in Rome). No doubt he was one of the monks who defied Hadrian early in his pontificate (c. 16). Hadrian's letters (*Ep.* 37 at 748.5, *Ep.* 38 at 749.15) and the acts of the council of 869-70 call him 'exarch', a title often occurring at councils for the head of a group of monasteries (an 'abbot-general'). In view of Nicholas's expression 'over certain provinces', the term 'patriarchal *hegumenus*' may mean he had authority over all monasteries in the patriarchate of Constantinople. Hadrian, *Ep.* 41 at 761.15, calls him 'a most wise and religious man, *hegumenus* and custodian of the sacred vessels', cf. Basil, *Ep.* (*PL* 129.192): 'Theognostus... the God-beloved *hegumenus*... and guardian of the vessels of the great church'; cf. also Ignatius, *Ep.* (*PL* 129.193ff).

[91] This provision by Theognostus might seem appropriate, given his former job (end of previous note); the *custos vasorum* was now Joseph (c. 37).

[92] A place previously mentioned in the LP (54:5, BP 48) in the context of a reception like the present one, that of pope Hormisdas's envoys in 519, for which event the LP is the only account to mention the placename. Comparison of the LP with other accounts of that

size dedicated to the name of St John the Evangelist, by the emperor's favour they took lodgings on Saturday. And on Sunday the 15th of September[93] in the 3rd indiction [869] they each received from the emperor's devotion horses with gold saddles, and were met by all the *scholae*, those of the white-robed *spatharii*, the *strati*, the *mandati* and the other palatine orders, and by all the chasuble-wearing orders of the clergy, and they came to the Golden Gate.[94]   **37.** There they were greeted by Paul the guardian of the books, by Joseph the guardian of the vessels, by Basil the *sacellarius*, and by those clothed in church vestments, on behalf of the patriarch of Constantinople; these went solemnly in front of them, while the whole people followed with candles and lamps; and so they went down to the palace of Irene,[95] and were laudably received in the house called Magnaura[96] by John the *a secretis* and white-robed *spatharius* and by Strategis the white-robed *spatharius*. These had been given the assignment of looking after them; and through them they received imperial notifications, intimating with great devotion - there is no doubt about that - that they should not perchance take it ill that they could not be received the next day, as the

---

event shows that it was the Στρογγύλον φρούριον of Procopius, *De aedificiis* 4.8, some 10 miles from Constantinople; cf. Janin 1964:454.

[93] False (perhaps a gloss or a copyist's error), since 15 September 869 was a Thursday; in view of the mention of Basil's *natalicius* (see n. 97), read 25 September.

[94] The ancient Golden Gate was at the 'Επταπύργιον fortress (Yédi-Koulé).

[95] Duchesne suggested that this might have been the name of some building close to the church of Hagia Irene, north of Hagia Sophia and outside the palace area. But it might be an alternative name for the palace of Eleutherios, built by the empress Irene; cf. Mango 1985:59, who notes that it was in an elegant quarter constructed at this period amid the ruins of ancient buildings.

[96] The MSS spell Magna Aura. This building, in which the emperor (here, his high officials) received ambassadors in solemn audience, lay north of the palace complex, south-east of the Augusteum, immediately south-west of the fourth-century senate (beyond which was Hagia Sophia, immediately north-east of the Forum Augusteum), see Müller-Wiener 1977:229 (and fig. 263, reproduced in Krautheimer 1983:50, plan 42); cf. Labarte 1861:no. 116 on plan (reproduced by Leclercq, *DACL* 2, i (1925), 1410). It may well have been a 4th-century building, no doubt repaired later. Mango speculates that it may even have been the original senate-house. Like other buildings in the area it can only be visualized from literary descriptions, especially the *De caerimoniis*, as the whole palace was abandoned in the 12th century, and by 1422 the traveller Buondelmonte found no traces left. By the early 9th century it was a basilica with central nave and two aisles, about 50 m by 22 m overall, and fronted by an open portico; two rows of six columns supported the ceiling; at the far end, a platform occupied the whole width; on this the imperial throne was placed, approached by steps, and with a half-dome above; columns, two on each side of the half-dome, supported large curtains which decorated this end of the chamber; at first-floor level there were galleries for the ladies of the court. Cf. Mango 1959:57-8 and *ODB* 2.1267-8; Janin 1964:106ff; Guilland 1969:1.141-50; Krautheimer 1983:49.

emperor's *natalicius* was imminent.[97]

38. When this had been happily celebrated, the emperor sent all the palatine orders to meet them. These went ahead of them and they came before the emperor in the Golden *Triclinium*,[98] where he immediately rose to greet them. They presented the apostolic letters to the emperor. The emperor received them personally and kissed them. He systematically inquired about the state of the Roman church, about the health of lord Hadrian the supreme pontiff, and about every order of churchmen and senators. He kissed the envoys amiably, and gave them leave to present the apostolic mandate to Ignatius the patriarch. **39.** It was with him that they came back next day to the emperor, who thus addressed them: 'The holy church of Constantinople was torn by various waves of schismatic men through the ambition of the headstrong Photius. The holy Roman church, mother of all God's churches, has had regard for it through the trusty providence of the holy lord and universal pope Nicholas, as can be clearly understood from his letters, on the authority of which our present father Ignatius, who had been violently expelled by the Photians, has recently with the Lord's help been restored to his own see. We, with all the eastern patriarchs, metropolitans and bishops, have for two years been awaiting the judgment of our holy mother the Roman church; therefore, on God's behalf, we ask that God's business be manfully completed, and that by the authority of your sacred college the really pestilential stumbling-blocks of Photian subterfuge may at long last be cast forth; so may the unity and tranquillity long hoped-for be restored in accordance with holy pope Nicholas's decree'.

40. The envoys of the holy apostolic see replied: 'That is why we also have come, that is why we have been sent. But there is no way that we can ever receive any one of your easterners in our synod unless they present a document to give us satisfaction, the text for which we have

---

[97] Basil cannot have been proclaimed emperor before 23/24 September 867 when Michael III was killed (cf. 107 n. 161); perhaps 26 September was his official accession-anniversary.

[98] This, the *Chrysotriclinos*, was the throne-room, located in the south-eastern part of the palace, and separated from the rest of the palace by the huge gallery called Lausiacos. It was an octagonal building about 30 m across; the octagon itself was roofed by a cupola (with 16 glass windows) supported on pendentives, and with a chandelier suspended in the centre. Each of the eight walls was hollowed to make an apse surmounted by a half-dome, and each apse was closed by a curtain hung on a silver beam. The throne was in the apse at the end, which was closed off by silver-panelled doors. A large cornice with a balustrade went round the room at the base of the cupola above the arch of each of the apses. Mosaics covered the walls and the floor (Labarte 1861:no. 95 on plan; Leclercq, *DACL* 2, i, 1413; Janin 1964:115-117).

taken from the holy apostolic see's church-office'.[99] The emperor and patriarch said: 'Since you assert this new and unheard of thing about presenting a document, we must see what its text contains'. With no delay the text of the document was presented, translated from Latin into Greek, and shown to everyone to look at. Some of them did present a document and sat in the holy synod, but those refusing to present one were left ingloriously outside the synod.[100] But tempered by the fire of the Holy Ghost, they day by day returned to the holy synod's unity, first issuing the satisfaction in a document.[101] **41.** That intruder Photius was brought into this synod[102] to render account of the many crimes he had perpetrated, all the letters of the holy Roman church issued against him were read, and the verdict of deposition and anathema, formerly issued by the apostolic see, was time and again hurled at him by everyone. In his sight the unhallowed tomes of his wicked assembly, in which, muttering in his gullet, he had yelped against holy pope Nicholas, were burnt by fire, and the torch of truth and innocence shone bright. For he had now through the power of reason been reduced to a final silent inactivity and had entered the snare that in his boasting he had once set for another; like a blind man at midday he had turned aside from the door to communion that was open to him, by which, as he was advised, he could be received if he gave satisfaction in a document.

42. Then, with everything wholesomely done which the text of the synod contains in its ten sessions, the holy Roman church's envoys

---

[99] Cf. c. 34 with n. 87.

[100] After its expansive treatment of the reception of the envoys, the text now devotes barely a chapter to the ten sessions of the Fourth Council of Constantinople (*PL* 129.27-496 has Anastasius's translation of the acts, also in Mansi 16.16-208, who gives the shortened Greek acts, 16.308-409). For all its brevity, the LP does record Photius's stubborn silence. The Council came to be reckoned in the west as the Eighth Ecumenical Council (so already 'by those who attended it', according to the acts and to *AB* 872 Nelson 178). As late as the time of Gregory VII (1073-85), Cardinal Deusdedit reckoned only 7 ecumenical councils, but at that time canonists found canon 22 of this council, forbidding lay influence in the election of prelates, useful in the investiture controversy, and reckoned this council as the Eighth Ecumenical, despite the fact that its acts had been cancelled (and the full Greek version destroyed) by the Photian council of 879-80. The status and consequential numbering of medieval western councils as ecumenical was only finalized by Cardinal Robert Bellarmin at the end of the 16th century, mainly to justify the status of the Council of Trent, Dvornik 1948:314ff, 1966[b]:321-6.

[101] The LP is misleading. When the council opened on 5 October 869 only 12 Ignatian bishops attended; even by the ninth session the number had reached only 66, though 103 were at the tenth and last session (28 February 870), Beck 1969:182.

[102] Basil in fact refused to sign the acts of the council if Photius were not given a hearing; he refused to say a word, and a bishop who tried to put his case for him was cut short by the Roman legates, Beck 1969:183.

entrusted the synod's text, in case Greek fickleness should swinishly[103] interpolate anything false, to Anastasius[104] the librarian of the holy apostolic see, so that it could be carefully examined before they signed it. It is believed that it was by God's providence that he had at that time arrived at Constantinople after them on the business of our serene emperor Louis, with Suppo the chief counsellor.[105] It was very zealously scrutinized by him, since he was most fluent in both languages; and they discovered that everything that the holy lord pontiff Hadrian had added in his predecessor's letter, on bishop Arsenius's insistence,[106] in praise of our serene Caesar had been cut out.[107] **43.** So they complained very

---

[103] Note that Anastasius in his Preface to the acts (*PL* 129.24, Mansi 16.13) writes: 'So in case the cunning of the Greeks, or rather their trickery, swinishly does something also about the present synod...'

[104] Anastasius had presumably by now been reinstated as librarian despite the sentence against him on 12 October 868 (see p. 251). The LP's claim that he arrived after the papal envoys is correct in spite of the statement in *AB* 873 Nelson 178 that he travelled with them (Hincmar was not soon aware of these events). He arrived in time for the 10th and last session of the council, whose acts (*PL* 129.147-8, Mansi 16.158, not in the Greek) mention his presence and that of his colleagues: 'Likewise there took their seats on the right-hand side the glorious princes and the *apocrisiarii* of the remarkable Louis, emperor of the Italians and Franks, namely Anastasius the God-beloved librarian of Rome, Suppo the leader of the gonfalonieri and cousin of his wife, and Eurard, the steward of his table'. Anastasius himself relates in his Preface to the acts that he had been sent by Louis II to arrange a marriage between the eastern and western imperial families. At the council he will have heard recited the papal letters which he speaks of as his own work (*PL* 129.17, Mansi 16.8-9, addressing Hadrian): 'So when this venerable synod was being held, it happened that I your servant was present, sent by the pious emperor Louis with two other notable men, and carrying out an embassy ... arranging the marriage which both sides were hoping and preparing for, between the emperor Basil's son and the daughter of the said God-worshipping Augustus (Louis II). For in such a godly business, one which was believed without doubt to relate to the unity of both empires, indeed to the freedom of all Christ's church, your assent as supreme pontiff was particularly sought. So by God's will it happened that I too rejoiced at the conclusion of so great an affair (the council) with the apostolic see's representatives, and that I, coming home with shouts of joy, could bring my sheaves with me (Ps. 125 (126).6).' For some seven years I had worked tirelessly on it, and by writing I had broadcast the seeds of words throughout the world. It was in obedience to the supreme pontiffs, your predecessor (Nicholas) and yourself, that I expounded almost everything that relates to the present affair and that has been issued by the apostolic see in Latin, whether contained in the codex of this synod or in other volumes. After I chanced to be at Constantinople for the reason I have mentioned, I provided many comforts for these representatives of yours, as they too bear witness' (he then claims further credit for making the copy of the acts which actually reached Rome, n. 126). Cf. Leonardi 1987.

[105] Suppo is called by Anastasius (previous note) 'first of the gonfalonieri (standard-bearers)', and cousin of Louis's wife Engelberga. On the death of Louis II in 875, he would support Charles the Bald's claim to Italy, Nelson, *AB*, 189 n. 12.

[106] Arsenius had died in 868 after his son's plot against the pope's daughter. Hadrian was trying to be rid of his family's influence, but he apparently stayed on good terms with Louis, whose envoy at Rome Arsenius was. Cf. 106 n. 9; p. 251; Nelson, *AB*, 145.

[107] As Duchesne noted, it is odd that Anastasius mentions this neither in his preface nor

loudly that the apostolic see's letter had been tampered with and said there was no way they would subscribe to what was done in the synod unless the full text of the whole letter was joined to the synodal acts. That was how the Romans argued, while the Greeks vociferously replied that the business of a synod was to praise God alone and not an emperor - they deeply resent our Caesar's imperial name. Things came to such a pass that they signed the decided verdicts less decisively, inserting a condition about the apostolic will, in these words: 'I, *N.*, representing my lord the holy and universal pope Hadrian, and presiding in this holy synod, have consented to all that is written above as far as it accords with the will of that noteworthy prelate, and I have signed with my own hand'.[108]

44. This done,[109] some of the Greeks came to the emperor, lamenting

---

in his notes on the Council (unless 'I provided many comforts...', n. 104 at end, alludes to it). His Latin version of the Greek acts shows that he did not reinsert any of the passages here claimed to have been suppressed.

[108] The quotation is not verbatim. The signatures at the end of the last session read (*PL* 129.175-6, Mansi 16.189-90, not in the Greek): 'I, Donatus, by the grace of God bishop of the holy church of Ostia, taking the place of my lord the supreme pontiff and universal pope Hadrian, and presiding at this holy and universal synod, have promulgated all things that are written above as far as they accord with the will of that noteworthy prelate, and I have signed with my own hand. I, Stephen, by the grace of God bishop of the holy church of Nepi, taking ... . I, Marinus, deacon of the holy catholic and apostolic Roman church, taking ...' (these two legates otherwise using the same wording as Donatus).

[109] Anastasius also tells the story of the stolen papers in his notes to the first session of the Council; he does not mention the conditional clause in the signatures among the reasons that pushed the Greeks into this exploit, but otherwise his account harmonizes with the LP. He sets the scene very carefully (*PL* 129.38-9, Mansi 16.29): 'But after they had all signed and handed their signatures to witnesses, some of them rose up and approached the holy patriarch Ignatius and the godly emperor Basil, and told them privately that it was something not well done that they had let the church of Constantinople be subdued to the Roman church with such great subjection that they had handed it over like a servant to her mistress. These words disturbed the emperor and he ordered the chief men who had been assigned to the retinue of the apostolic see's representatives that, when the latter went with their people to some church, they were to enter their lodging and remove the signatures surreptitiously, for he utterly refused to scandalize them openly. So when the representatives, bishops Donatus and Stephen and the deacon Marinus, had gone for a discussion with the patriarch, the guardians turned into thieves, got into the house and quietly removed a portion of those numerous signatures. The representatives returned and discovered this, and their speech to the emperor included the comment: 'The loss of the signatures means that we cannot dare return to Rome, yet you will gain no reward at all for the state of godliness which has begun in the church.' But we who have been here to arrange a marriage contract between both emperors have sent him a report in these words: 'It is not fitting for the imperial power to do what has to be undone afterwards or to undo what is not to be undone. So since the signatures were made with your consent, if you were wrong to agree, then repent and undo what you have done, in the open, not in secret. But if you did well to agree that the bishops should make their signatures as a caution for the future to the apostolic see, why is it that you repent of what was good and agree to their being taken away and hidden? But if you say that it was not by your wish that the signatures happened to be

and grumbling that by presenting the documents the church of
Constantinople had been subjected to the power of Rome; they said that,
given the uncertainty of the signatures, everything decreed in the synod
could be overturned, everything could be confounded with recurring
errors, and, so they made out, without getting the documents back they
could not get back their ancient liberty. **45.** Immediately some of the
documents were tinkered with by the guardians, though the holy Roman
church's envoys, foreseeing what would happen, had well hidden the
documents of the more distinguished bishops. At this they[110] were
incredibly alarmed, and they fell back on the ever-reliable help of Suppo
the chief counsellor and of Anastasius the holy apostolic see's most
eloquent librarian. These brought various pressures to bear and, though
the task was fraught with danger and difficulty, they eventually
managed to get the documents back, but they seriously incurred the
emperor's anger for the great rigour of their faith.

46. So[111] three days later, by when the holy synod with its signatures

---

taken away, our reply is: Then it will clearly emerge that it was not at your wish that this
great crime was committed, when you detain the men you provided as guardians for the
representatives, and rightly compel them to return what was taken away. For if the
representatives have lost anything or suffered anything underhand, the only people obliged
to made restoration or amendment are those to whom, with all their men, the imperial
piety gave the task to guard them reverently and preserve them intact'. But hearing this
the emperor sent for the representatives and returned all the signatures to them, so that it
was clear that not a single one was missing; he said: 'It was I who through my legates
approached the apostolic see as a mistress in church affairs and that was why I waited for
you to come here, so that your decision and diligence might cause our church to get the
cure of her sickness and that we might obey your verdict rather than our own impulses.
So, take the signatures which you have wholesomely exacted from our *sacerdotes* and
from all the clergy, and present them to our spiritual father the holy pope; so that if any
of them try to walk as usual along dangerous and vicious paths or along crooked and
depraved tracks, he may with these reins check them somehow, and with such bridles call
them back to the right path of justice'. At this the representatives happily handed the
documents they had received to us to be carefully taken away.' Anastasius's account
continues in n. 126.

[110] The Roman envoys.

[111] Anastasius (Preface to the Council of 869-70, *PL* 129.20-21, Mansi 16.11-12) gives
few details of this debate, to which he implies he was not admitted, but he claims that the
emperor had instructed the eastern arbitrators what verdict they were to reach, and that
advantage was taken of linguistic difficulties between Romans, Bulgarians and Easterners:
'Although the Roman representatives and the envoys of the Bulgarians met with emperor
and patriarch and the representatives of the East, they were all placed in one chamber and
no one from outside had any access unless the emperor or patriarch happened to let him
in. Consequently, neither the representatives of the East nor the Bulgarian envoys
understood anything the Romans stated, and again neither the Roman representatives nor
the Bulgarian envoys understood anything the easterners said; since there was actually no
one present apart from the emperor's lone interpreter who dared to produce the speeches
of the Romans or the eastern representatives otherwise than as the emperor had already
ordered to achieve the subversion of the Bulgarians; except that a certain writing, made

had been fully completed and edited with all neatness in the church of St Sophia, they were cunningly summoned by the emperor to the house where he was residing with the representatives[112] of the patriarchs of Alexandria, Antioch and Jerusalem, and with the patriarch Ignatius and some others. Bidden to take their seats, they were told that the prince of the Bulgarians had, through Peter and others, sent them letters and gifts.[113] **47.** As the emperor was particularly insistent, they received the Bulgarians' embassy; and so, after the greeting Peter, envoy of the Bulgarians,[114] began: 'Lord Michael, the Bulgarian prince, has heard and joyfully welcomed the fact that on apostolic authority you have gathered together from various regions for the needs of God's holy church, and he gives manifold thanks to you who were sent from the apostolic see for having seen fit in your journey to visit him with your letters'. The envoys of the holy Roman church replied: 'It was both our duty and our wish not to pass you by ungreeted, as we know you are the holy Roman church's sons, whom the holy apostolic see certainly embraces as its own members'. **48.** The envoys of the Bulgarians said: 'Till today we were pagans and we have but recently come to the grace of christianity. And so, in case we make any mistake, we want to know from you who represent the supreme patriarchs to which church we must be subject'. The envoys of the holy Roman church replied: 'You do belong and you ought to belong to the holy Roman church; to it, to St Peter prince of the apostles, through you, Peter, your master has given himself with all

---

out in Greek words and letters, was given to the envoys of the Bulgarians, whose contents were that the representatives of the East were, so to speak, to arbitrate between the Roman representatives and the patriarch Ignatius, and were to decide that the land of the Bulgarians in Illyricum was to be subjected to the diocese of Constantinople, though from long ago it is clear that the organization in both Epiruses, Dardania, Dacia, Thessaly, and the other provinces in Illyricum, has always belonged to the apostolic see: various letters of the Roman pontiffs from pope Damasus sent through these provinces testify to this; and the princes of the Greeks, with the support of the prelates of Constantinople, have by force alone, for the precise reason that we mentioned above, subdued these provinces from the apostolic see.'

[112] Joseph, archdeacon of Alexandria, representing his patriarch Michael, arrived in time for only the 9th session of the council on 12 February 870; Thomas, metropolitan of Tyre, represented the vacant patriarchate of Antioch; a priest Helias was sent by Theodorus patriarch of Jerusalem. Thomas, unlike the others, could not speak Greek.

[113] Before embarking on the Bulgarian debate, the reader may find it helpful to read cc. 61-63, which give the background to the arrival of these Bulgarian envoys.

[114] As the legates remind him just below, Peter had led the Bulgarian embassy to Nicholas in 866. Cf. John VIII, *Ep.* 67 (*MGH Ep* 7.60, J3131, 16 October 878), urging Peter, whom John styles a 'count', to continue to work for the Roman church with Boris; *Ep.* 183 (7.147, J3247, May 879), to Peter, Cerbula and Sundica, the *optimates* of the Bulgarians, urging them to return with Boris to the Roman obedience; *Ep.* 192 (7.153, J3261, 8 June 879), urging Boris himself to do this, and reminding him how he had sent his 'kinsman' Peter, along with John and Martin, as envoys to Nicholas.

the kingdom of his people, and from his successor the noteworthy pope Nicholas he has deserved to receive precepts for living, and bishops and priests; and you demonstrate it by this too, that you have received our *sacerdotes* whom you asked for, and you also still keep them with suitable reverence'. **49.** The envoys of the Bulgarians said: 'We grant that it was from the holy Roman church that we asked for, received, and still have *sacerdotes*, and we resolve to obey them in everything. But decide, with these representatives of the patriarchs, whether we ought more reasonably to be subject to the Roman or the Constantinopolitan church'. The envoys of the holy Roman church replied:[115] 'We have with the Lord's help completed those matters for whose decision with the easterners the holy apostolic see had instructed us. But as for determining your cause otherwise than it has been decided, as we have received nothing in our instructions, we decide nothing, and we think nothing should be decided, to the prejudice of the holy Roman church; rather, because your entire country is filled with our *sacerdotes*, we promulgate in a verdict, which is decisive in so far as it is within our competence, that you must belong to no church other than the holy Roman church'. **50.** The representatives of the eastern patriarchs said to the Bulgarians: 'Tell us to whose power that country had been subject, and whether it had Latin or Greek *sacerdotes*, when you captured it'.[116] The envoys of the Bulgarians said: 'We conquered that country by arms from the power of the Greeks, and in it we found *sacerdotes* who were Greek, not Latin'. The representatives of the easterners replied: 'If you found Greek *sacerdotes* there, it is clear that that country was of Constantinople's organization'.[117] **51.** The envoys

---

[115] Anastasius, though absent from the debate, will have heard the details from the Roman envoys afterwards. His account (*PL* 129.20-22, Mansi 16.11-12) is entirely independent of, yet basically in agreement with, the LP. He summarizes and reworks the material, but gives the Roman envoys much the same arguments: the eastern representatives are not competent to arbitrate in a matter in which the envoys themselves (whose mandate was confined to the affair of Photius) have no delegated power. He guarantees that his Latin version of the Council is genuine, whatever the Greeks on past form might do to their copies, then at the end of his Preface (*PL* 129.23, Mansi 16.13) refers again to 'the debate after the synod was finished, which we have mentioned above to have been before the emperor, the representatives, and the Bulgarians, only about the land of the Bulgarians...'. He was evidently concerned that the Greeks might add an account of this debate to the acts of the council (they were liable to act 'swinishly', see n. 103). In fact the Greek acts were not interpolated, but suppressed ten years later by Photius. Cf. Leonardi 1987.

[116] Thanks to the defeat of Constantine IV in 679-80 the Bulgarians had crossed the Danube and occupied the (already slavicized) province of Moesia; their kingdom later expanded from there; Ostrogorsky 1969:125-7.

[117] Note how linguistic difference is taken to identify different churches (Nelson, *AB*, 142 n. 15), though the Roman envoys immediately object to such a principle.

of the holy Roman church replied: 'You must not construct an argument from the *sacerdotes* being Greek, because difference of language does not affect church organization. Thus the apostolic see, though it is Latin, has always appointed and still appoints Greek *sacerdotes* in many places by reason of the country, and it ought not now or in the past to feel that its prerogative suffers damage'. The representatives of the eastern patriarchs said: 'Even if you claim that the organization of Greek priests has been in your jurisdiction, you can never deny that that country used to belong to the kingdom of the Greeks'. **52.** The envoys of the holy Roman church replied: 'Just as we speak no falsehood when we say that the organization of Bulgaria belongs to us on a different basis, so we certainly never deny that this Bulgaria came from the kingdom of the Greeks. But you must observe that the jurisdiction of sees organizes things otherwise than the divisions of kingdoms allow.[118] We are not treating of the division of kingdoms, we are speaking of the jurisdiction of sees'. The representatives of the eastern patriarchs said: 'We want you to make us understand what you are saying, that Bulgaria belongs to you on a different basis'. **53.** The envoys of the holy Roman church replied: 'As you will be able to learn from the decretals of the holy Roman prelates, the apostolic see of old canonically organized, and obtained, both Epirus Nova and Epirus Vetus, and the whole of Thessaly and Dardania, in which the Dardanian city[119] is pointed out even today, and whose country these Bulgarians now call Bulgaria;[120]

---

[118] For this principle, the traditional Roman point of view, cf., e.g., Leo I to Marcian in 452 (*Acta Conciliorum Oecumenicorum* II.4.56 lines 15-17): 'the order of the world's affairs is one thing, and that of God's affairs is another'. In the present instance Anastasius puts it as follows, as background to the debate rather than as part of it (*PL* 129.20, Mansi 16.11): '... there is one juridical organization in worldly affairs, another in those of the church, and although that region had been previously subject to the Greeks, they could not legitimately claim for themselves any jurisdiction in it, as it was lost long ago by force of arms and they had been unable to retake it in war for such a length of time; although it is manifest both that the Romans possessed it before it was subjected to the Greeks and that the Greeks, as is proved above, are not recorded to have held it except when they held power by the sceptres of Rome.'

[119] Or 'city of Dardania'. Duchesne took the curious expression to refer perhaps to Achrida, then the Bulgarian capital, which had succeeded the ancient city of Lychnidus; but it was in the old province of Epirus Nova, not that of Dardania. More probably (Duchesne III) the reference is to the ancient capital of the province of Dardania, Scupi (Zlokučan near Skoplye). As Prima Justiniana this had become the residence of the praetorian prefect of Illyricum; it was also from Justinian's time the see of the papal vicar for the diocese of Dacia (a vicariate created out of the vicariate of Macedonia held by the metropolitan of Thessalonica). The Dacian vicariate was still functioning at the time of the Slav invasions; Gregory I (*Ep.* 11.29) was involved when the emperor Maurice wanted to remove the ailing archbishop John in 601 (which incidentally shows that Roman jusrisdiction in Illyricum was still operative at the start of the 7th century).

[120] Anastasius (quoted in n. 111) lists these provinces in much the same way. Duchesne

and, in this way, it did not, as is now pretended, steal the organization from the church of Constantinople. It had previously lost it through the invasion of the pagan Bulgarians; and it got it back from them when they became christians. Secondly: because the Bulgarians subjugated the country to themselves by the law of nations (look how many years they have kept what they captured!), and specially committed themselves, as we have said above, to the patronage and organization of the apostolic see, it ought not to be unjust for them to be subject to us, whom they chose of their own volition as masters. **54.** Thirdly: because the holy apostolic see brought these Bulgarians over from various errors to the truth of the catholic faith on the order of the former pope lord Nicholas. This was done both through some of us who are now present[121] and have dedicated many churches there and have created *sacerdotes*, also through the venerable bishops[122] Paul, Dominic, Leopardus and Formosus, and also through our fellow-bishop Grimuald whom, as these Bulgarians have admitted in our presence, they still have, with many of our *sacerdotes*.[123] It took much toil, but Christ's grace went before them; and look, the apostolic see has held them more than three years, it holds them, it organizes them and it administers them. And it therefore follows that the Roman church is not to be stripped of those with whom it is at present clearly vested, without the cognizance of the supreme pontiff'. **55.** The representatives of the eastern patriarchs said: 'Tell us which one of these arguments you want to draw on'. The envoys of the holy Roman church replied: 'The holy apostolic see has not chosen you as judges in its own cause, because you are in fact of lower status; nor has it chosen [to be judged] by us, since it alone has the particular right to be the judge of every church; nor has it entrusted it to us to pronounce a verdict on this cause. Therefore we fully reserve for its trial and judgment what it has not given us to do; it is able to produce many things from many books in defence of itself, and it can

---

noted that this part of the legates' reasoning is flawed. True, certain provinces now occupied by the Bulgarians had once belonged to the civil dioceses of Dacia and Macedonia and so fell within the jurisdiction of the now-defunct papal vicariates (last note), and their capital was in this area. But the eastern parts of their kingdom, between Sardica (Sofia) and the Black Sea, were in the former diocese of Thrace, indisputably in the jurisdiction of Constantinople.

[121] Strictly, only Donatus; though he was not one of the missionaries to Bulgaria, he had passed through it in 867 when leading Nicholas's embassy to Michael III (107:71).

[122] On the despatch of these to Bulgaria see 107:68-76, 108:12 and 61-64.

[123] From this it follows that when this debate was held, about 3 March 870, the Roman envoys already knew that bishops Leopardus and Dominic (c. 62) had been sent back to Rome. Perhaps Peter, the Bulgarian envoy to Constantinople, had told them; if so it will be he, mainly, who is meant by 'these Bulgarians'.

overturn your entire verdict with a facility equal to the fickleness with which you pronounce it'. **56.** The representatives of the eastern patriarchs said: 'It really is improper for you, who reject the empire of the Greeks[124] and cling to treaties with the Franks, to keep the jurisdiction of organization in the kingdom of our prince. So we know for certain that the country of the Bulgarians formerly came from the power of the Greeks and that it had Greek *sacerdotes*, and we judge that it should now be restored through christianity to the holy church of Constantinople from which it departed through paganism'. **57.** The envoys of the holy Roman church said loudly: 'The verdict which, whether by fear or favour or whatever, you have just hurled rather than pronounced, though you were not chosen and not allowed to, we totally abrogate by the authority of the Holy Ghost until the holy apostolic see decides, so that in no way may it merit even the name of a verdict. And by the authority of the holy princes of the apostles, before God and his angels and all here present, we arraign you as answerable, patriarch Ignatius, that in accordance with this letter[125] of the holy lord Hadrian the supreme pontiff who reinstated you - here it is, we present it to you - you keep the whole organization of Bulgaria free from your meddling and send none of your men there; in case the holy apostolic see which gave you back what you owned should lose what it owns through you. However, if you think you have a just complaint - and we do not believe it - do not neglect to notify it formally to the holy Roman church your restorer'. **58.** Then the patriarch Ignatius took the apostolic letter, and, though much advised to read it, replied that he was postponing doing so: 'Far be it from me to be implicated in these rash acts against the splendour of the apostolic see. Neither do I act so like a child that I can be taken in, nor am I so old and deranged as to allow myself what I would have to blame in others'. With that this conference ended.

59. But the emperor's agitation increased, though he maintained a façade of hope. He summoned the envoys of the holy Roman church to luncheon and adorned them with excellent gifts; he commended them to Theodosius the *spatharius* for conducting home, without the appropriate degree of concern. He took them as far as Dyrrachium[126]

---

[124] As Duchesne noted pointedly, the speakers (and their patriarchs) were themselves subjects of muslim princes in Bagdad and Cairo, and not of the Greek Emperor.

[125] Not surviving. Ignatius did not obey the letter, and with Basil's support he ordained a bishop for the Bulgarians. Hadrian (*Ep.* 41, 10 November 871) complained to Basil that this utterly destroyed the hope that he, Hadrian, had had in the emperor.

[126] Anastasius's account of this, in his note on the first session of the council, is as follows (*PL* 129.39, Mansi 16.29-30, continuing from n. 109): 'Before they undertook

and negligently made no further provision when he left them. They sailed for some days, were brought among the Slavs and - oh, what anguish! - fell into the hands of Domagoi.[127] They were stripped of all their goods, and of the authentic copy which had contained all the signatures; and they would have been put to death but for fear of the consequences from those of them who had escaped. **60.** At last they were delivered from exile by apostolic[128] and imperial letters; on 22

---

their homeward journey we were separated from them, since from Dyrrachium we came by ship to Sipontum, then overland to Benevento, then to Rome, carrying those documents; whereas the apostolic see's envoys, also embarking at Dyrrachium, were making for Ancona, but encountered pirates of the Sclaveni and totally lost everything they possessed, including the codex of the acts of the present synod. But I, who was in charge of the Roman library, had been careful to bring away with me from Constantinople a codex of this synod, and I brought it and presented it to the supreme pontiff. So it happened that the apostolic see, by God's authorship, received a codex of the synod through us, and possessed those documents, that were got back by us for the envoys, saved by us. The envoys, if they had kept them in their own possession, would undoubtedly have lost them, like the codex of the synod and the other writings.' Cf. Anastasius (*PL* 129.18, Mansi 16.9; continued from n. 104): 'It was also I who considered the various things that can happen to men and decided to transcribe into another codex, and bring back all the way to Rome, the acts of this synod which the apostolic see's representatives had written in one volume for themselves to carry. So it happened that when these representatives fell among robbers and lost the actual codex with all their equipment I was recognized as the one who conveyed to Rome the codex which I had brought away. Your holiness received it with gratitude and handed it to me for translation into Latin, a task for which I denied my competence, though at the moment I try to make some attempt at translating writings from the archive into the Roman language, and am reckoned to have interpreted and published many already for the edification of many men, especially at the urging of your predecessor.' Hadrian II, in the letter (*Ep.* 41, J2943, 10 November 871) he wrote to Basil, complained about what happened to his envoys and blamed Basil for giving them inadequate protection: 'We have at length, though late, received our *apocrisiarii* also, stripped, and after many dangers, depredations and the slaughter of their own men... So everyone grieves to hear this... that your arrangement and organization could turn out without foresight, so that they miserably fell among the swords of barbarians, supported by no aid from your empire.' Louis II alluded to the incident in a letter to Basil (*MGH SS* 3.525): 'It would have befitted your excellency to send more back guarded so that no attack of pirates or other wicked men had occurred.'

[127] Domagoi was prince or duke of the Croatian Slavs from c. 865 to 876 when he was succeeded by Sedesclav. He is mentioned in John the Deacon's *Chronicon Venetum* (*MGH SS* 7.21) and in John VIII's letters, *Ep.* 9 (*MGH Ep* 7.278, J2964, Dec. 872 - May 873, telling him about Greek treachery in Bulgaria), *Ep.* 38 (7.295, J2997, 874 - early 875, telling all the Slavonic faithful that the Venetian priest John is to be restored, despite his escape when Domagoi was trying to take his life), *Ep.* 39 (7.295, J2998, of the same date, telling Domagoi to punish conspirators against him with exile rather than death, and to put down pirates who claimed to be acting in his name). From the 8th century and for long afterwards the coast and islands from Split to Dubrovnik were infested with Slav pirates called Paganiani or Narentani. The area was also under threat from Arabs who besieged Dubrovnik in 867, but were defeated by a Byzantine fleet. Despite this attempt to restore Byzantine control along the eastern coast of the Adriatic, the cities and islands of Dalmatia depended more on the Slavs than on Constantinople; they paid tribute to the Slavs, but only symbolic sums to the Byzantine *strategi*; Ostrogorsky 1969:236.

[128] Not surviving.

December in the 4th indiction [870][129] they arrived back in Rome and related all that we have stated above before the supreme pontiff and the dignitaries. They were able to display none of the writings apart from the book of Ignatius's action,[130] the documents[131] they had recovered from the Slavs, and the other documents they had previously entrusted at Constantinople to Suppo the chief counsellor and to Anastasius the holy apostolic see's wise librarian; it was through his concern and foresight that the Roman church received a copy of the lost synod which he had had written for himself.[132]

61. Earlier on,[133] the venerable bishops Formosus of Porto and Paul of Populonia, who had been despatched with the others to preach on the order of pope Nicholas, came home, and they refreshed the apostolic see about the christianity of the Bulgarians and the absolute subjection in which they had specially submitted their devout necks to the holy Roman church; and they presented the Bulgarian king Michael's envoy, named Peter, to the supreme pontiff. This envoy presented, with royal gifts, a royal letter as well, which earnestly begged the supreme prelate either to send back Marinus, the deacon whom he knew well, as a consecrated archbishop, or to send to the Bulgarians for their choice one of the cardinals, provided he was one of his church and a man worthy in wisdom, person and life: after they approved of him he could go back home again, and he could raise him up to the archiepiscopal ministry. **62.** But as Marinus had been, as we have said, allotted the legateship to

---

[129] As the envoys had left Constantinople in March, they had been about 8 months with the Slavs. Their delay, and Lothar's death, had meant the abandonment of a council which Hadrian had meant to hold in Rome. He had intended this to meet in early March 870 to deliberate on Lothar's divorce, and had hoped that the envoys at Constantinople would be back in time to attend, *AB* 869 Nelson 156.

[130] The Greek text of this survives, Mansi 16.295-301.

[131] Duchesne plausibly suggested that these were the 'documents of the more distinguished bishops' (c. 45): the envoys had hidden these more carefully than the others and they had not been stolen from them at Constantinople. Anastasius had only brought those which had been stolen and then returned to the envoys on his intervention. In his own account (n. 126) Anastasius says nothing of documents saved by the envoys from the Slavs and presents himself as saviour of the whole dossier.

[132] See n. 126.

[133] Formosus and Paul had returned to Rome late in 867, very shortly after Hadrian II's consecration, and two years before the events just narrated; cf. Lapôtre 1880:413. Probably when Formosus was pope (891-6), though possibly earlier, a painting was provided in a small church near the Temple of Claudius, showing Christ in the midst of SS Peter, Paul, Laurence and Hippolytus, with at his feet a barbarian prince (Boris) on one side and Formosus on the other. The painting, found in 1689, was published by De Rossi, *Bull.* 1869:59. Formosus's figure had even then disappeared, but his name was still recognizable: FORMOSVs. Duchesne noted with regret that this interesting piece of evidence had long since become invisible. Cf. Ruysschaert 1992.

Constantinople and devoutly resisted it,[134] the supreme pontiff sent one Silvester, a subdeacon, to the Bulgarians for them to choose; but he received him back very speedily as the Bulgarians sent him back with bishops Leopardus of Ancona and Dominic of Trevi,[135] and a letter very brusquely demanding the despatch of an archbishop or of Formosus bishop of Porto.[136] The reply[137] he wrote them included the statement that the provident pontiff would no doubt bestow as archbishop on the Bulgarians whomsoever the devoted king should express by name.

63. But the king of the Bulgarians was unable to bear waiting and delaying any longer, and ...[138] he sent the same Peter,[139] whom he had lately received from Rome without achieving his desire, with others from his side, to Constantinople to inquire to whom he ought particularly to belong. There they were clearly shown[140] by our legates that they belonged to the Roman jurisdiction; they have subsequently been persuaded with gifts and promises by the easterners and the Constantinopolitans, **64.** and, according to bishop Grimuald, who says he has been repulsed by them, they have accepted Greek *sacerdotes* and thrown ours out. By the same bishop Grimuald, who without the cognizance of the apostolic see has abandoned the task of preaching entrusted to him and has returned to Rome very wealthy, he[141] has

---

[134] The meaning seems to be that Marinus resisted becoming archbishop, falling back on his legateship as an excuse, rather than that he had been appointed legate unwillingly, or that he was devoutly enduring the legateship.

[135] Hadrian must have given Leopardus the task of conducting Silvester to Bulgaria. Dominic had left at the same time as Grimuald, in the first weeks of Hadrian's pontificate (c. 12).

[136] The LP avoids offending Silvester by saying that the Bulgarians did not want him (as a subdeacon he was not a cardinal, cf. c. 61), and merely says that they wanted either (another) archbishop or Formosus.

[137] Not surviving.

[138] In the Latin follows a corrupt and lacunose passage: *quanta esse quam a Grecorum imperatore, quoniam natorum thororum occasione alterna regna sibi alternatim rapere machinabantur abductus.* Duchesne wanted to correct *thororum* into *suorum* and see a reference to the internal difficulties that Boris's sons were causing their father (the sons Vladimir and Symeon succeeded him in turn after his abdication). Perhaps the LP was trying to say that Boris, impatient of so many delays and threatened by family dissension, thought it inappropriate to make an enemy of the Greek emperor by resisting his advances. A reconstruction along the following lines might be suggested: '*(he considered) how much greater (the delays) were than (they would be) from the emperor of the Greeks, (with whom, also, he wanted to be on friendly terms) since, on the occasion of (his) sons' nuptials, they were taking turns to engineer abductions in order to seize kingdoms in turn for themselves, (so)...*'

[139] The Peter mentioned in cc. 46-8 and 61, envoy of the Bulgarian king.

[140] i.e. in the dialogue beginning in c. 46.

[141] Duchesne noted that either this verb should be plural or it should be preceded by another subject (Boris); the writer, hurried along by the flow of his account, did not notice

despatched to the apostolic see, as an excuse for himself, a most voluminous letter, enveloped in frivolous allegations and pretending to be the deliberative verdict of the presidents of a synod. Because the bishop is asserting he has been expelled by the Bulgarians, though the letter is silent about it, and because the priests are all murmuring that it was not Greeks or Bulgarians who expelled them but the bishop who gathered them in and sheltered them for no clear reason, the shape of treachery is somehow suspected in this activity. But the whole truth will not be apparent until Christ, the searcher of minds[142] and hearts, brings it to light when he examines his servants.[143]

---

the anacoluthon. By November 871 when Hadrian wrote to Basil and Ignatius (*Epp.* 41-2, cf. n. 125), he knew that Ignatius had consecrated a bishop for the Bulgarians, which the LP does not mention; while in those letters the pope does not mention the expulsion or return of Grimuald, which he would surely have done if it had just happened. So Grimuald probably left Bulgaria (without resisting Greek encroachments) in 870, while the envoys were still in the hands of the pirates. Duchesne thought that the last page of this life was written at the very end of 870 or very early in 871; written any later, it would not have ended in this way. But note the reference to the conspiracy of the Lamberts (c. 21), not written before August 871.

[142] Duchesne prints *rerum*, but read *renum*; cf. Vulgate Wisdom 1.6, Ps. 7.10, Jer. 17.10, Apoc. 2.23.

[143] Here the life breaks off. The 'third edition' of the LP (Přerovský, 623-639) gives a brief summary of this life to the same point (the view of March 1925:124, that part of it provided an older version of the text than the corresponding parts of LP, 108:2,4-8, is not acceptable); it then adds a single sentence 'This blessed man anointed Charles son of Louis and made him emperor', a note which as it stands should belong to the life of Hadrian's successor John VIII (so Přerovský, 639), who crowned Charles the Bald in St Peter's on 25 December 875, cf. *AB* 875-6 Nelson 187-9, *AF* 875 Reuter 78 (and his son Louis the Stammerer in France on 7 September 878, *AB* 878 Nelson 210). That it has been attached to Hadrian's life may be through an understandable confusion with the first of three imperial coronations in six years, for Hadrian did crown Louis II: *AB* 872 Nelson 179: on the eve of Pentecost Louis came to Rome and was crowned next day (18 May 872) by Hadrian; a solemn procession to the Lateran followed, and Louis left for Benevento.

ADDENDUM: LIFE 108 IN MS PARISINUS 2400

This 11th-century manuscript from St Martial de Limoges contains the abridgment of the LP by Adhémar of Chabannes, c. 1030 (cf. *LECP*, xvii) but concludes with a peculiar version of life 108 and the names of the next four popes. It is translated from the text in Duchesne I clxxxii-clxxxiii. Whatever the value of this material, it is highly unlikely that it comes from a longer version of the main text than now survives.

108. Pope Hadrian held the see 5 years, of Roman origin, son of Julius (*sic*). He abundantly supplied many precious adornments for churches. Like the earlier Hadrian he confirmed the Gregorian antiphonary in many places, and he laid down that a second prologue in hexameter verses was to be sung at the high mass on the first day of our Lord's Advent; this begins like the proemium of the earlier Hadrian, which he had composed very carefully for all masses on the same first Sunday of the Lord's Advent, but it consists of more verses. He laid down that in monasteries at high mass on special solemnities not only were those interpolated hymns that they call 'praises' to be sung in the angelic hymn 'Glory be to God on high', but also in the psalms of David that they call 'introits' there were to be sung the inserted chants which Romans call 'festival praises' and Franks call 'tropes', which means figured adornments in praise of God. He also handed down the melodies for singing before the gospel, those which they call 'sequences' because the gospel 'follows' them. And because these festival chants had been established and composed by lord pope Gregory I and afterwards by Hadrian, together with abbot Alcuin the favourite of emperor Charles the Great (and this Caesar Charles took great delight in them), but they were now being omitted by the neglect of the singers, they were so confirmed to our Lord Jesus Christ's praise and glory by this bounteous prelate of whom we speak, that through the care of scholars the tropiary also should thenceforth be kept in use alongside the antiphonary for honourable chants on solemn days at high mass. He laid down that Roman clerics should instruct our brethren the poor of our Lord Jesus Christ that for three days before holy Easter Sunday, that is on the day of the Lord's Supper, the day of Preparation, and the day of the Lord's being in the tomb, they should beg alms in this city of Rome in no other way than by singing this chant loudly in the streets and in front of monasteries and churches: 'Kyrie eleison, Christe eleison, Lord have pity on us, Christ the Lord became obedient unto death'.[144] He

---

[144] Cf. Philippians 2.8.

performed two ordinations in December and March, 8 priests, 5 deacons; for various places 60 bishops.[145]

109. John held the see 10 years. **110.** Marinus held the see 1 year 4 months. **111.** Hadrian III held the see 1 year 4 months. **112.** Stephen held the see 1 year. Reader, I ask you to seek out the rest of the pontiffs in the archive of the holy Roman church down to your own age, that with them you may deserve to share in the everlasting kingdom of our Lord Jesus Christ, whose honour, glory and rule endure for ever and ever without end. Amen.

---

[145] The ordination statistics are nowhere else recorded; those given may be fictional. None of the versions records the fact that Hadrian II was buried in St Peter's, though this was known to the compiler of the papal catalogue inserted in the *Chronicon Vulturnense* (Duchesne III.111). His tomb was on the right-hand side of the basilica between one of the intercolumniations in the area of the *sacrarium*, according to Pietro Sabino who copied the epitaph (several fragments of which survive in the crypt of St Peter's; De Rossi, *Inscr. christ.*, 2, p. 419). The text mentions his piety and placidity, and his generosity to poor and rich, and praises his virtues in general terms.

112. STEPHEN V (885-891).

Life 108, itself incomplete, might well be regarded as the end of the LP. Of the four MSS which give the full text of that life, C^4 goes no further. When Flodoard of Rheims visited Rome in the time of Leo VII (936-9), with the aim of including verses about all the popes back to Peter in his poem 'On Christ's triumphs in Italy' (*PL* 135), he was able to find much of his material in a copy of the LP which stopped at life 107; but for Hadrian II and all his successors he could do little more than copy and rework the often banal epitaphs on their tombs at St Peter's. In the poem that resulted there is no trace of the use of these epitaphs for earlier popes, and no likelihood that he had biographical sources for later popes. It seems that for all the welcome he was evidently given in Rome, there was no one there who could provide him even with life 108, let alone any later lives. Again, when in the early 12th century the labours of Pietro Guglielmo and Cardinal Pandolfo produced what is now called the 'third edition' of the LP, this was founded on the ancient LP down to life 108 (lives 95 to 108 being very heavily abbreviated), but from that point on nothing more could be done than give a basic list of the names of the popes, their places of birth, their fathers' names, and the lengths of their tenure. From the time of John XII (955-964) short historical notes are sometimes added (and in one MS only this is done for John VIII, 872-888, with a text culled from two of that pope's letters). It was only with Gregory VII (1073-1085) that an attempt was made to write a biography of significant length, based on extracts from the papal registers.

The catalogue of names exists in a number of other forms apart from that included in the third edition; it may be regarded as the regular continuation of the LP. Those MSS which stop at earlier points than life 108 quite normally continue with a list of names down to the time when these MSS or their ancestors were copied, often with even less detail than was available to the compilers of the third edition. One short example has just been presented in the addendum to life 108. Sometimes the list is presented before the text of the biographies, running from Peter down to a point later than the last biography given: so, for example, in C^4, where the initial catalogue, with names and tenures only, goes down to Silvester II (999-1003).

The fact that even the extant life 108 was not available to Flodoard shows that the text was not widely dispersed, and also leaves open a theoretical possibility that the lives of the next popes once existed. If they did, no trace survives of the lives which should bear the serial numbers 109, 110 and 111. Yet of the four MSS which have life 108, three of them (E^1, E^2 and E^6) do give part of another life, presented after 108 without a break. It concerns Stephen V (886-891), though what there is does not seem to get beyond the first year of his pontificate, nor did the text have any influence on the third edition or other later writers. The copyist of E^6, unaware of the three intervening pontificates, did not understand how the fragment could refer to Stephen V having had a predecessor named Marinus; twice in c. 2, and again in cc. 3 and 11, he 'corrects' this name to Nicholas; Hadrian III he probably confused with Hadrian II (though this does not affect the text he presents, even in c. 11 where Hadrian is specifically called *tertius*). The fragment is given below. Because it is so incomplete no attempt is made here to provide a full introduction to Stephen V's pontificate.

The reader must also look elsewhere for fuller details of the eventful pontificates of the three popes whose lives are totally missing. The gap is bridged here by giving no more than a basic catalogue of names and dates (not from any single manuscript). Except for John VIII's ordination (*AB* 872 Nelson 180), precise dates are not on record.

109: John VIII [14 December 872 - .. December 882], of Roman origin, son of Gundus, held the see 10 years 2 days; buried in St Peter's.

110: Marinus [882/3 - May/June 884], from Gallese by origin, son of the priest Palumbus; held the see 1 year 5 months; buried in St Peter's.

111: Hadrian III [May/June 884 - .. September 885], of Roman origin, son of Benedict; held the see 1 year 3 or 4 months; buried at Nonantola (see n. 3 below).

112. 1. STEPHEN [V; 26 September 885 - c. 4 October 891], of Roman origin, son of Hadrian,[1] from the region Via Lata,[2] held the see 4 years 7 months 14 days.[3] This blessed pontiff was born from an ancestry of noble, and Roman, parents; while he grew by God's grace, he was trained in holy teachings by the endeavour and anxiety of his kinsman, holy bishop Zacharias,[4] librarian of the holy see. The pontiff

---

[1] Auxilius (E. Dümmler, 1866, 95) confirms Stephen's paternity, as does the *Invectiva in Romam pro Formoso papa*, PL 129.826 and 832 (quoted in nn. 6 and 12). Hadrian long outlived his son: as late as 916, with other Roman nobles, he signed the alliance between John X and the southern Italian princes: 'Hadrian father of lord pope Stephen' (Duchesne, citing Federici, *Storia dei duchi di Gaeta* 150). This could imply that when elected Stephen V was not 30 (theoretically the canonical age). He had become a subdeacon by 872, and was presumably in his 20s when made priest in 884-5. At Constantinople in 886, Leo VI deposed Photius and, to keep the church under his own control, installed as patriarch his own brother Stephen who was barely 16.

[2] Rome's aristocratic quarter since the 8th century, cf. 97:1 with n. 1 (Hadrian I), 102:1 (Valentine); the homes of Stephen II and his brother Paul were not far distant, and in the 10th century Alberic, prince of the Romans, lived in this area, at the site of the present Palazzo Colonna.

[3] These figures are wild, though (reading the months as *xi* rather than *vii*) they might belong to Hadrian II. The Montecassino catalogue gives Stephen 6 years 8 days, that of S. Maria in Trastevere 5 years 8 days, Pietro Guglielmo (the third edition of the LP) 6 years 14 days, the catalogue in C[4] 6 years, other catalogues 6 years and some (9, 4, 13) days. The date of Stephen's ordination cannot be precisely fixed. The news of Hadrian III's death at Nonantola reached Charles the Fat at Frankfurt (where he issued diplomata between September 6 and September 23, *MGH DD C III* 130-2), and after hearing it he moved by way of Mainz to Worms (where he was by 1 October, *MGH DD C III* 133). Stephen's successor Formosus certainly died on Easter Sunday (4 April) 896 (*AF* 896 Reuter 135) after a pontificate of 4 years 6 months 2 days (Montecassino catalogue; he had certainly succeeded before 13 November 891). If there was a short vacancy after Hadrian III's death, Stephen could have succeeded him in late September 885, i.e. on Sunday 19th or 26th. If the latter is correct there is still room for a number of days over his full 6 years before Formosus's accession, which could be dated to Sunday 6 October 891. The last certain date in Stephen's pontificate is 1 June 891, but he may have died as late as 4 October. Duchesne noted that a diploma published by Fantuzzi (1901-4:I.90) is dated 20 November in indiction 8 (889) and Stephen V year 4; this would mean that Stephen's pontificate began after 20 November 885, but the text may be corrupt (it is rejected by Jaffé-Ewald, 427).

[4] Cf. 107:20 etc. Zacharias became bishop of Anagni between 855 and 860; in 860 he and Radoald bishop of Porto were on the embassy to Constantinople. They both betrayed their trust and were penalized by pope Nicholas: Zacharias was deposed and reduced to lay communion (107:42). But at his accession Hadrian II reinstated him to communion among ecclesiastics (108:10). Louis II favoured him, no doubt because of his family's rank, and in 869 insisted on his fuller rehabilitation (see the speech delivered in the council held then to deal with this matter and with Lothar's marriage (Mansi 15.890; Lapôtre 1880:408f). This was granted: 'but pope Hadrian recalled him to his former status in the church' (*Invectiva in Romam pro Formoso papa*, PL 129.835). He became Librarian under John VIII, probably on Anastasius's death, and is called such in a document of 29 March 879 (J3230; Lapôtre 1885:287). He was probably dead when Stephen V became pope.

Hadrian the younger [II] of godly memory noticed that he was accomplished in good character and ardent in the study of letters, took him from his distinguished above-named father, and by God's favour advanced him to the rank of the subdiaconate, setting him to serve in his household and to carry out church duty in the Lateran patriarchate; and after receiving this honour he led an admirable life. **2.** He was chaste in body, kind in heart, cheerful in appearance, wise in conversation; with his wealth he was generous, in character he was eloquent, he was a consoler of the grieving, he was a mentor to orphans and the needy and, to summarize generally, he was adorned with the blossoms of every virtue. That was why this eminent prelate, as he continued in the holy Roman church's service and devoted himself more and more to spiritual endeavours, became well-known to and loved by the supreme pontiff Marinus[5] of reverend memory and was even more closely attached to the service of his household. When this supreme pope Marinus saw his purity, wisdom and loyalty in every way, because of what his faith and wisdom deserved he assigned him to be his household servant all the days of his life; and recognizing his spiritual behaviour, he consecrated him priest[6] of the SS Quattuor Coronati,[7] and allowed him to be in no way detached from himself while he lived.

3. So pope Hadrian [III] of memorable renown, who had succeeded that blessed pope Marinus, died on the river Scultinna at the villa called Viulzachara;[8] in his time the Roman citizens had suffered many

---

[5] Given Stephen's probable youth there may be no significance in the lack of progress in his career during the 10-year pontificate of John VIII (872-882), which intervened between those of Hadrian II and Marinus.

[6] The *Invectiva in Romam pro Formoso papa* (*PL* 129.832) speaks of Stephen as having been ordained deacon, not priest, by Marinus ('So, if Marinus was not a bishop, then Stephen son of Hadrian, who was later Apostolicus, was not a deacon'). The anonymous writer is clearly wrong in practice, though not technically so, since 9th-century Roman *ordines* regularly assume that priests have been previously ordained deacons. Stephen will have passed on the same day from the subdiaconate through the diaconate to the priesthood, without ever exercising the diaconate.

[7] Conveniently close to the Lateran for a priest whom the pope wanted near at hand.

[8] Since Muratori (*Annali* V, 168) the Scultinna has been identified with the River Panaro, and the villa with S. Cesario sul Panaro, near Modena. The purpose of Hadrian's journey north is given by *AF* 885 Reuter 98-9: 'The emperor held an assembly at Frankfurt and sent envoys to Rome to invite Pope Hadrian to Francia. For he wished, as the rumour went, to depose certain bishops unreasonably and set up Bernard, his son by a concubine, as heir to the kingdom after him, and because he doubted that he could do this himself, he wanted to have it done by the Roman pontiff, as if by apostolic authority. By the judgement of God his deceitful plans were frustrated' (by Hadrian's death en route). Reuter notes that Charles may have revived these plans in early 887: Stephen V (*Ep.* 14, J3428, *MGH Ep* 7.340) had been asked by him to attend an assembly. Hadrian III's body was apparently never taken back to Rome (even though his father was still living) but buried at Nonantola. This and the lack of record of his obituary date suggest that he was

problems both from devastation by locusts and also from the insufficiency of rain and from want and hunger, and they then believed they could be relieved by this venerable man's sanctity. By God's mercy there was a gathering of holy bishops and the whole clerical order and also an assembly of the noble senates and of the illustrious men, and they all cried out, together with the whole people and the multitude of the commons of both sexes: 'The lord priest Stephen is worthy of God, we all want him, we all ask and pray that he be our prelate, since we know without doubt that through his holiness we can be delivered from the dangers that threaten us'. **4.** To look after the city, the pontiff we have named, Hadrian [III], had then left at Rome John, the venerable bishop of Ticinum and envoy of His Excellency the emperor Charles;[9] and all, joined with this imperial envoy, came with one accord to the house where with his father this bountiful Stephen was engaged in holy discourse. When they broke down the doors, they seized and took the God-elected pontiff to that *titulus* of the SS Quattuor Coronati which was entrusted to him, though he greatly resisted, along with his father, and both of them cried out and protested that they were unworthy of so great an office. And there too all the *scholae*[10] of the holy Roman church linked together in joy took this venerable elected man, and with Christ as their leader brought him to the Lateran palace with every honour and reverence that was due. **5.** Before he reached the sacred palace there was such a deluge of rain from heaven that its fruitfulness refreshed the earth which had been dry for a long time back, so that God showed by a clear sign that he was willing to forgive all the people through this great and bounteous man's merits and prayers. While he stayed in that palace the dignitaries of both orders rejoiced and began to parade their due fealty. When the next Sunday came,[11] the whole

---

not popular in Rome; but a local cult developed around his tomb, and his feast came to be celebrated on 8 July.

[9] John bishop of Pavia was the permanent imperial envoy, appointed by Charles the Fat in accordance with the *Constitutio* of 824 (pp. 33ff). This passage confirms the implication of the *Constitutio* that the city of Rome's government was not part of his normal duties, and that it was only delegated to him by the pope (cf. the case of Benedict, brother of Sergius II, 104:41 and pp. 73-4). John was rewarded for his involvement in Stephen's election: soon after his ordination Stephen gave the duchy of Comácchio to him rather than to another (unknown) claimant on whose behalf one Gaudo shortly afterwards petitioned the pope (J3411).

[10] The palatine *scholae*, corporations of the papal court's clerics and officials, analogous to those of the Byzantine court mentioned at 108:36; cf. 98:19 and n. 49.

[11] For the date of this Sunday see n. 3. There was no delay while the consent of the emperor was obtained and the pope swore fidelity to him, presumably because, as assumed by the *Constitutio* of 824, the imperial envoy John of Pavia was in Rome and (for a promised bribe, cf. n. 9) acted in the emperor's stead. But Charles the Fat was not

Roman church honourably led him to the homes of St Peter prince of the apostles, and there too he was consecrated pontiff[12] and celebrated the ceremonies of mass in the usual way. He returned with due honour and honouring to the Lateran palace, and began to adorn his ministry with wondrous works.

6. Then with the venerable bishops, the imperial legate and the honourable senate, he proceeded round all the vestries of the sacred palace, which he found looted[13] to such an extent that of the hallowed vessels with which the pontiffs had been used to hold banquets on feastdays very few were found, and of the rest of the wealth nothing at all. But no wonder he found all the treasures of the vestries taken away, when on investigation he found almost none of the many offerings and decorations of the churches. Even that famous gold cross that Belisarius the patrician[14] had set up in honour of St Peter prince of the apostles, and most of the gold altarcloths with the other precious ornaments, were missing. So this blessed pope had the foresight to investigate these things in front of many witnesses, so that all would know it was not in his time that such misappropriation had taken place. 7. So he was deeply touched with grief because, apart from the vestries being looted, the granaries and cellars were found to be empty, and he had nothing

---

happy: *AF* 885 Reuter 99: 'When the Romans heard of the death of their pontiff, they set up Stephen in his place. The emperor was furious at the fact that they had presumed to ordain anybody without consulting him, and sent Liutward [bishop of Vercelli, archchancellor of the empire] and some [suburbicarian] bishops of the Roman see to depose him. But they were unable to do this. For the said pontiff sent by ambassadors to the emperor the names of more than thirty bishops, and of all the cardinal priests and deacons and persons of lesser rank, and also letters from the leading laymen of the region, who had all unanimously elected him and subscribed his ordination'. Once Charles knew that Stephen had acted in agreement with the imperial envoy he had little choice but to accept the fait accompli, however many clerics and nobles vouched for the unanimity of the election.

[12] Formosus, bishop of Porto, exercised his right to take part in the ceremony; *Invectiva in Romam pro Formoso papa* (*PL* 129.826): 'Also, pope Stephen, son of Hadrian, whom the same Formosus had consecrated...'. Though deposed and replaced under John VIII, Formosus had been reinstated by Marinus.

[13] The pillaging of the Lateran palace on the death of a pope, and of other bishoprics on the death of bishops, had now become a custom, as can be seen by the attempt made by John IX, in a council at St Peter's in 898, to abolish it (Mansi 18.221, c. 11): 'Because a most wicked custom has also grown up that at the death of the pontiff of the see of the holy Roman church the patriarchate itself is wont to be plundered, and such presumption is rampant not only in the holy patriarchate but also throughout the whole city and its suburbs, and also because this has hitherto been left unavenged, with the result that all bishoprics at the death of the pontiff of every single church suffer the same, we totally prohibit this presumption ever occurring again. Let him who presumes to do this be smitten not only with the censure of the church but with the wrath of the emperor.'

[14] LP Vigilius, 61:2 (BP 56), mentions this cross, the engravings on which commemorated Belisarius's victories.

to disburse to the clergy and the *scholae*, and lacked anything to use for ransoming captives[15] or feeding orphans and widows in the serious famine that threatened. What could he do? He turned to his father, and took the wealth that his distinguished parents had owned; with bountiful right-hand he disbursed it to the poor as far as possible, and so by God's mercy it came about that he lightened the need and famine by his endeavour.

So he searched on all sides and gathered such ministers and household-servants for his service who were accomplished in holiness of life, sincerity of faith, wise teaching, eloquence and probity of character. When he sat to a meal, every day he called in orphans whom he nourished like his children; when he invited nobles and fed them with physical foods he used to refresh them with spiritual nourishment. So great was the fear of God which he bore in his mind's eyes and devoted himself to in God's praises, that every day holy reading was recited at his meal. **8.** Every day he celebrated the ceremonies of mass, night and day he devoted himself to prayer, and he never ceased the chanting of the psalms except when he wanted to fulfil the need of the people that called to him, in order to raise up the crushed and help the afflicted.

He observed the people's insolence and blindness of heart as they were devoted in church to chatter, wicked myths and idle gossip,[16] and he heard by common report that some were involved in sorceries and charms, so, while celebrating mass, he addressed this admonition to the people: 'Dearly beloved sons, we admonish you that when you gather in God's holy temple you must endeavour to occupy yourselves diligently with that for which you come. For if you truly believe that it is God's temple in which you gather, there is no doubt that you must do therein what pleases the owner of the temple in which you gather. For while God is everywhere, he ought to be sought especially in his temple, and, as far as he has seen fit to inspire, what pleases him must be sought after therein. Therefore he is a merciful God, yet he so disposes it that everyone must seek after his mercy, that he grants it to those who ask, freely, and he grants it to each one with more bountiful piety the more he is besought by someone with greater groanings and more fervent mind, as he says: 'Her sins, which are many, are forgiven, for she loved much.'[17] For God's temple is a place of prayer, as he says

---

[15] Saracen raids were increasing at this time.
[16] The expressions seem to be calqued from 1 Tim. 5.13.
[17] Luke 7.47.

somewhere: 'My house is a house of prayer for all the nations';[18] and the psalmist: 'Holiness befits thy house, O Lord'.[19] So if it is a house of prayer, one must do therein what it is called, that is, pray, chant psalms, confess sins, wash away transgressions with bitter tears in the eyes and groanings in the mind, and confidently implore pardon for faults committed. God's gaze is there especially; there the orders of angels attend, the choirs of saints, who bear the vows of the faithful and the prayers of the *sacerdos* praying for the people to the ears of the Lord of Sabaoth. By what effrontery, I ask, does someone attend in God's holy temple, when he devotes himself to empty myths and careless words? For if account must be rendered on the day of judgment for every careless word,[20] account will be rendered and punishment exacted most of all for those which are obstinately uttered in the sight of so many saints in a place dedicated to God. By what hope, I ask, does anyone think he will gain pardon for past transgressions, who not only neglects to wash away his sins but rather strives to increase them? Fear him who made a whip of cords and drove those who sold and bought out of the temple.[21] Yet they were engaged in useful trade, which is more tolerable than chattering emptily and carelessly. When you gather in the place of prayer, stand in silence, and with attentive heart pray God to receive the vows and to hear the prayers of the *sacerdos* who prays for you; and keep before your eyes the Lord's admonition when he says: 'Whenever you stand praying, forgive, if you have anything against anyone; so that your Father also who is in heaven may forgive you your trespasses.'[22] Meditate on these things and do them by the inspiration of God's grace, and, imbued with the teachings of the gospel and the Apostle, joyfully enlightened as with lamps by the mercy obtained from almighty God with the fruit of good works, you will be worthy to be presented to Christ and to be crowned with the saints. For the rest, dearly beloved, we wish you to know that the Lord in giving the law to his people, as Moses bears witness, laid down the words: 'You shall not permit a sorcerer to live.'[23] Now in this city - I say it with grief - some are found who, far from assailing sorcerers, even harbour and maintain them, and they do not shrink from using

---

[18] Based on Mark 11.17 (Isaiah 56.7).
[19] Ps. 92 (93).5 (in the text of the Roman Psalter); the first psalm at morning prayer (lauds) on feastdays and Sundays (except from Sexagesima to Palm Sunday).
[20] Matthew 12.36.
[21] John 2.15; Matthew 21.12, Mark 11.15, Luke 19.45.
[22] Mark 11.25.
[23] Exodus 22.18 (where Vulgate has 'sorcerers' and RSV 'a sorceress').

them to consult demons with certain charms, even forgetting God's law and the Apostle's teaching, the words of which resound: 'What fellowship has light with darkness? What accord has Christ with Belial?'[24] For by spurning Christ and consulting demons as the gentiles do, they acknowledge that they are in no way christians. Let everyone consider how terrible it is, and how godless, for a christian to spurn Christ and worship demons, so that he may shrink from committing such a crime. Therefore, whoever henceforth attempts to stain himself with such infection, we adjudge him by the judgment of the Holy Ghost to be estranged from our Lord Jesus Christ's lifegiving body and blood until he repent of such great slackness. But he who spurns such healthy prohibitions, perseveres in plague-ridden obstinacy, and neglects to repent, let him by God the Father and Jesus Christ his son be forever anathema.'

9. Such was this outstanding prelate, and he persevered to the end in what suited God's worship; hence so much grace was granted him from God, that he used whatever he could own for enriching the holy churches and ransoming captives, and he was anxious for everyone's safety. And so, when the fame of his reputation and actions was spread through the regions of both east and west, just about everyone came to him to receive his blessing. **10.** Among other matters, it is a lengthy thing to recount the donations he conferred on various churches.

But, to summarize, when he noticed that in St Peter the prince of the apostle's basilica, where he rests in his holy body, the burning of incense was scarcely offered once at night-time praises, he laid down that it should be burnt at each of the readings and responsories.[25] On that basilica's pergola this reverend pope in his love for St Peter his mentor placed 1 gold incense-boat, with precious pearls and jewels and enamel, with a peg for hanging. Also in St Peter's venerable basilica he presented 1 gold diadem with various pearls, and 1 sword with sheath, of gold and jewels, and sword-belt. **11.** On this basilica he also conferred 1 cloth with gold and pearls; 4 silk veils around the altar; and the 40 homilies of St Gregory.

In this same basilica this holy pope, the mighty extirpator of all vices, discovered there was an evil custom that the priests who daily offered

---

[24] 2 Cor. 6.14-15.

[25] The earlier custom was for one incensation at the night office, carried out while the canticle *Benedictus* was sung at lauds. This was also the later custom, so if this is what Stephen changed he had no success. But in view of the next sentence, the LP may be referring to a special custom at St Peter's of burning incense in fixed censers, rather than to censing with a thurible swung on chains from the bearer's hand.

sacrifice to the Lord there customarily paid one fine[26] every year. His predecessor lord pope Marinus of holy memory had broken this custom but by the stealth of certain men it had sprouted up again in the time of pope Hadrian III, so he ordered with earnest adjuration that no one should ever take either this or any other payment from them, but they should be permitted to fulfil their duty with every honour as befits *sacerdotes*.

When he noticed that the *consuetudinarius* at the night-time vigils in the great church called that of God's highly-exalted mother St Mary *ad Praesepe* lacked lamps, this holy prelate, for his everlasting memory, presented silver bowls with lamps and ordered that they blaze continuously at the vigils. In the same basilica this gentle pontiff provided 4 veils around the high altar, 2 of which are topped with silk, the third of violet, and the fourth with alexandrian, all of them decorated around with all-silk.

12. Then this God-protected holy pope, for the reward of his soul, provided in the church of St Paul the apostle and teacher of the nations, 1 fine gold diadem, with various jewels, pearls, prases and jacinths, and in the middle of the diadem one small hanging gold cross with its chains; one silk cloth for the high altar, with gold and jewels. In the same basilica of the nations' noteworthy teacher he provided 4 portal-veils[27], one of which is gold-worked.

In the Lord Saviour's church called Constantinian this venerable and distinguished pontiff provided one gold-worked cloth for the high altar with various pearls. **13.** This reverent prelate also conferred on this basilica 4 silk portal-veils of byzantine purple around the high altar, two of them with representations of eagles, and two with basilisks,[28] decorated around with all-silk; and for each of the arches of the *presbyterium* 90 silk veils representing lions. For the future cure of his soul he conferred there one gilt *cantrella*, 1 Comes-book, 1 book of the Prophets, and 2 books of acts.[29]

14. As he had anxiety for the condition of God's churches[30] in case those that were set to fall should collapse in his time, he renewed from

---

[26] *witta* (*wita*), a Saxon word.

[27] It appears that the curtains were used to surround the altar, with the spaces between the columns supporting the altar-canopy being thought of as doorways or 'portals'. The veil that is gold-worked is presumably the one facing the nave.

[28] For basilisks see the story of Leo IV, 105:18-19.

[29] Two volumes of martyr-acts, rather than two copies of the Acts of the Apostles.

[30] Cf. 2 Cor. 11.28, where, however, by 'anxiety for all the churches' St Paul is not referring to buildings.

its foundation SS James and Philip the apostles' church, which consumed by great age was close to falling;[31] he adorned it with a chalice and paten that he conferred, gilded and inscribed with his name in Latin and Greek letters; furthermore, for his everlasting salvation he conferred on that basilica of the Apostles 1 linen curtain, and 3 silk portal-veils[32] around the altar. In St Thomas's oratory in St Andrew the apostle's monastery[33] close to the basilica of the Apostles he provided one cloth.

15. As he knew that the basilica of the SS Quattuor Coronati, in which he used to carry out his sacerdotal duty, had little decoration, out of his reverence and love for these saints this noteworthy and wise pope presented in it a gold cross above the altar with jewels and enamel, a *sugulum* to hang from a diadem, and 2 pairs of candlesticks[34] coated in silver. For his great love of them, this kind pope conferred there 1 gilt incense-boat, 1 Solomon,[35] 1 gold diadem with precious jewels, 1 cloth with gold and pearls, 1 book of Sermons, 1 book of acts,[36] and 1 book of the gospels with the epistles. **16.** This distinguished prelate, ever more drawn by God's zeal and moved with love for those saints, provided in their basilica 15 fine silver canisters worked with wondrous beauty, weighing in all 30 lb, and he bestowed 1 codex of St John Chrysostom.

In St Marcellus the martyr and pontiff's *titulus* this bountiful pope provided 1 silver canister weighing 3 lb; 1 gold cross; 26 linen veils;[37] 1 linen curtain; also 1 book of Histories, and 20 homilies of St

---

[31] Nothing now visible at SS Dodici Apostoli on the Via Lata is earlier than 1702-1742, Krautheimer, *Corpus* 1.79. The church was founded by Pelagius I (LP 62:3 BP 59), dedicated by his successor John III (LP 63:1 BP 60), but is traditionally identified with pope Julius's basilica near the Forum (LP 36:2 BP 27), cf. remarks in BP xxvii.

[32] Unless '3' is an error for '4', the fourth side of the altar will either have remained uncurtained or have been draped with the linen curtain just mentioned (though one would expect the most prominent curtain to have been of the more expensive material); cf. a similar arrangement in c. 12, with n. 27.

[33] Cf. 98:77 and n. 147. The monastery of St Andrew *de Biberatica* was attached to the service of the basilica of SS Dodici Apostoli just mentioned.

[34] So, rather than 'a pair of two candlesticks' as Krautheimer, *Corpus* 4.3, takes it.

[35] The various Wisdom Books of the Old Testament and the Apocrypha, attributed to Solomon.

[36] Again, martyr-acts which, with Sermons or Homilies, were read at the night office.

[37] The number 26 may give the only clue to the original nave arcade of this church, built perhaps c. 380-450 to replace the original *titulus*. Its plan is unknown; it was replaced by a new building in 1125-1150, and this in turn was rebuilt in 1519 with reversed orientation (before 1519 it was entered from the east), Krautheimer, *Corpus* 2.206. This is the last literary reference to S. Marcello until 1116.

Gregory.[38]

In God's mother the ever-virgin St Mary's church in Monterano[39] he placed 1 book of Kings and 1 silk altarcloth.

17. In the monastery[40] of Clivus Scauri this gentle pope provided 1 gold cross.

With the anxiety he had for all the churches,[41] this dutiful father conferred on St Silvester's monastery[42] on Mount Soracte 1 silver censer and 1 silver *cantrella*.

Ever more inflamed with God's love he provided in St Pudentiana's *titulus* 1 book of Sermons. In St Anastasia's *titulus*,[43] 1 book of Sermons and Epistles. In the church called Jerusalem at the Sessorian[44] he presented 1 book of Kings and 1 of Solomon. With reverence for his predecessor St Gregory before the eyes of his heart, this supreme pontiff bestowed on St Gregory's hostel[45] in St Peter the apostle's portico, 1 book of holy Sermons; and on the *Schola Cantorum* formerly called the Orphanage,[46] 1 Heptateuch.[47]

18. This elegant prelate and mighty preacher of the true faith sent back to the church of Ravenna for the cure of his soul 12 lb gold and .. lb silver, which had been stolen from there by the stealth of certain men. He also restored to the church of Imola 7 lb gold and .. lb silver which had been stolen. With God before his eyes he also restored 1 silver paten to the church of Bologna.

And for his everlasting reward, in the church of...[48]

---

[38] The last two items are for use at the night office. 'Histories' refers to the collections of readings, and/or the responsories accompanying them, used at the first (or only) nocturn. Gregory's Homilies (though this church was now provided with only half of them) were read as commentaries on the gospel at the third nocturn when appropriate.

[39] For the location of this church, then a cathedral, see n. 67 to 91:23. The bishopric survived into the 10th century: one Florus, bishop of Monterano, was still a priest in 924 and died before 952 (*Registrum Sublacense* nos. 122, 27).

[40] Cf. 103:28, and 96 n. 28.

[41] 2 Cor. 11.28 again.

[42] Cf. 103:12 and n. 25.

[43] The last reference to this church before 1140-43.

[44] The last reference to S. Croce before 1144-45.

[45] Mentioned at 97:66 (cf. n. 131) as near where Hadrian I built St Silvester's deaconry.

[46] *Orphanotrophium*; cf. 104:24 and n. 46.

[47] The first seven books of the Old Testament, Genesis through to Judges (possibly with Ruth as an appendix).

[48] There is a lacuna in the text, at the precise point where MS E[2] happens to end. The text had begun to deal with donations or restorations to some church; when it resumes it is dealing with relics distributed to the *tituli* of cardinal priests and to monasteries: the words 'glitter with many miracles' can only refer to relics.

... he bestowed some to the *tituli* of various cardinals,[49] and others to the various monasteries all around, where they glitter with many miracles, but the greatest part he placed with worthy honouring at the church called the Apostles. As[50] this was consumed by old age and was close to falling, the same holy pope renewed it from the foundations, and he embellished it by the gift of many adornments. Indeed his entire purpose was always to do what was acceptable to God.

19. Now since the disaster of locusts which in his predecessor Hadrian's time[51] had consumed virtually the whole country, with their seed evilly multiplied, had begun to be born and had filled everything, this holy pope had pity on the afflicted people and first of all he announced that anyone who caught a pint of them and brought it to him would receive five or six[52] denarii from him. **20.** The people heard this and began to scurry round in every direction, to catch them and bring them for the merciful father to buy. But when they were unable to wipe them out by this means, he took refuge in the Lord's mercy, came to St Gregory's oratory, where his bed is preserved,[53] close to the prince of the apostles' church, and tearfully gave himself to prayer. When he had prayed at length, he rose up, blessed water with his own hands, and gave this order to the *mansionarii*: 'Take this and give them all a portion; advise them to go round their lands in the Lord's name and sprinkle this water over the crops and vines, and beg for relief from God's support'. **21.** When this was done, such great mercy ensued from almighty God that wherever this water was sprinkled there remained not a single locust. Hearing this, everyone from the neighbourhood all around flooded into the City and begged for help, crying out that the whole land was covered in locusts like dust. The dutiful pope kindly.

---

[49] Amending *diversi cardinales* to *diversorum cardinalium*.

[50] This restoration of SS Dodici Apostoli may duplicate c. 14 above.

[51] Cf. c. 3 above.

[52] Is the variation to allow for pint-pots of different sizes? Or does the expression mean 5½ denarii (though that would be a very odd sum for the pope to decide on).

[53] This oratory (not the one built by Gregory IV, 103:6) was a building separate from the main structure of St Peter's and immediately north of the basilica's entrance-portico. It already existed in the 8th century; cf. the description of St Peter's (*Notitia Ecclesiarum* § 41, *CChr 175*.311.208-210): 'proceed to the portico of Petronilla, and happily go up to the holy father Gregory's bed, on which he gave up the ghost, a worthy gift to God who gave it; and there you have 11 altars'. The '11 altars' suggested to De Rossi (*Inscr.* 2, p. 227), perhaps rightly, that the next building immediately east of the Oratory of Gregory's bed, which was called St Vincent's church by the time of Mallius, was once part of this oratory; LP 105:94 (cf. n. 139) does not show that St Vincent's existed in the 9th century; cf. Duchesne 1902:420. But a further difficulty remains: the *Notitia*'s reference to the portico of Petronilla ought to refer to some structure at the diagonally opposite end of St Peter's.

advised them that they ought to ask help from heaven against the scourge that threatened. Then joyful ...[54]

---

[54] Who or what (feminine singular or neuter plural) was joyful we do not know, since here the life finally breaks off, having hardly got beyond the first year of Stephen V's pontificate (886-887). The fragmentary state of the text makes it likely that more was written, though whether the life was ever completed we do not know; at any rate the damage to the archetype is likely to have been early. Stephen lived until 891 and was buried in St Peter's. His tomb was in the entrance-portico, to the north of that of Benedict III. Mallius (De Rossi, *Inscr.* 2, p. 214) preserved the epitaph: it states that he ruled the people and the city for six years and did what pleased the Lord.

GLOSSARY

This glossary is intended to supplement that in *LECP*. Occurrences in lives 100-112 of terms which are defined and registered there are registered here without definition.

alabandinae (**103**:25), explained by Isidore (*Origines* 16.14.6) as precious stones, named after the city of Alabanda in Asia (Caria), famed for its wealth and luxury; Pliny, *NH* 37.82 describes some carbuncles (*q.v.*) as 'alabandic', and speaks also (*NH* 36.62) of a black alabandic stone which tended to look purple.

albaverae (**103**:16, **106**:31), precious stones, literally 'white-crimsons' (not 'true-whites'), since the second element of the word represents Greek ἀληθινόν, a word which in Latin spelling occurs 13 times in life 98 and 6 times in life 100 and is rendered 'crimson'.

beaker (*bauca*, **105**:104, **106**:34), a goblet (German derivative Pokal); cf. *Chron. Casinensis, MGH SSrL* 473.9-10, where Siconulf's thefts from Montecassino include '1 pair beakers (*vaucae*) in jewels and emeralds, 1 pair spurs (*spora*), 1 silk tunic (*q.v.*; *sarica*, occurring also in the former of these LP passages) of *silfori* (*q.v.*) with gold and jewels'.

bowl (*gabata*); a frequent usage; as is clear from **100**:20 *gabatae* are lighting fixtures; at **100**:11 they were evidently to be hung above the confessio.

buticulae (2 of them, and 3 smaller ones), and (its diminutive) *buticellae* (33 of them; both words at **103**:26 only). The word is the origin of English 'bottle', but this meaning (or 'keg, small barrel') offered by Niermeyer, and by Ducange I.795 citing *buticula* from the LP, does not easily suit the context (Ducange cites *buticella* from a Justinianic charter, evidently also as 'bottle'). The words evidently refer to parts of a necklace, perhaps pendants shaped like thin bottles, whereas the *petinantes* in the same context may have been thinner and straighter.

buttercup (*ran(n)unculus*, **105**:57 only); some kind of decorative object (context of a silver lily and crystal melons). The meanings 'little frog, tadpole', or 'the ligament under the tongue' hardly suit. More plausible is 'a medicinal plant, batrachion, perhaps crowfoot, ranunculus'. The translation uses 'buttercup' (Linnaeus: *ranunculus tuberosus*), 'ranunculo' in Italian.

calpi (**107**:36 only); evidently for *calpar* (Greek κάλπη and κάλπις), 'a vessel for liquids, especially a wine-cask' (see citations in Lewis & Short, but the object in the LP is silver, not *fictilis*, 'earthenware'). The translation retains the Latin, because of its rarity, and to distinguish it from numerous words for similar vessels.

canister (*canistrum*), occurs 22 times in these lives. At **100**:20, **103**:18, **105**:60 and **106**:24, the objects are stated to have six or nine wicks (*exafoti, ennafoti*). This makes the suggestion in *LECP* (based on Leclercq in *DACL*) unlikely; the word may represent κανίσκιον, from the same root, which *ODB* states was an openwork silver lamp. Perhaps its construction was such that the wicks were in multiples of three.

cantrella (**112**:13,17 only). Ducange II.107 (s.v. *cantulla*), suggests it is for *cannula*, but Ducange's editor suggests that *cantulla* may be from Greek κανθήλιον, a type of vessel, and that it may be the boat-shaped container for storing grains of incense. If so, it will be the same as (or a diminutive of) *cantra*, see 'incense-boat' below.

carbuncle (*carbunculus*, **107**:37), perhaps any fiery-red precious stone (probably including the ruby, hyacinth, garnet). At Ezekiel 28.13 the Vulgate uses it where RSV has 'carbuncle' (but at Exodus 28.18 and 39.11 it corresponds to RSV 'emerald').

cercellus (**103**:25), i.e. *circellus*. The objects seem to be too heavy (30 jewels were suspended from them) to be earrings, the meaning given by Niermeyer in 14th-century Italian usage. Ducange II.269, citing the LP, gives French 'cerceau'; perhaps 'circlet' in English.

chevrons (*gammadias*); 33 occurrences in lives **100**, **103-6**). Cf. 98:65 where (n. 118) it is suggested that 'pointed arches' might be meant. Ducange IV.22, citing lives 98 and 103, admitted that the contexts are not enough to elucidate their nature; but, at *gamma* 2, he stated without qualification that *gamma* is the same as *gammadium* and is a decoration shaped like the Greek upper-case letter. This must be right; the decoration is the cross gammadion, or fylfot (swastika) pattern. The LP (83.2, BP 79) also has *gammula*, presumably a diminutive of *gamma*, hence the translation 'chevron'.

clamasterii (**105**:14 only); some kind of pendants. Ducange II.348 (s.v. *clamacterius*) wanted to read *cremasterios*, from Greek κρεμαστῆ ρες, 'bullae, or other adornments hanging from lights of this kind'; Greek κρεμαστῆ ρ is 'suspender', and κρεμαστῆ ριον is 'a drop in a necklace' (cf. Liddell & Scott with citations). Ducange also gave two occurrences in a bull of Benedict IX in 1033: *candelas vero pendentes cum clamasteriis et cicindellas ad sufficientiam ...*, and *... clamateriis*.

cluster (**105**:13,60) *butro*, a lighting fixture of some kind; cf. 98:30 with n. 76.

Comes-book (**112**:13). A 'companion', or lectionary giving the extracts of scripture to be read at mass in full and in order, to save searching for them in full texts of the scriptural books concerned. It often omitted the gospel lessons, which were in a separate book used by the deacon, and merely gave the readings needed by subdeacons or lectors. The oldest reference to a book of this kind is in Valila's charter, published in Duchesne I.CXLVII col. 1 line 49. See 'liturgical books'.

consuetudinarius (**112**:11); this must be 'a book customarily used' (not the person who customarily did the readings). Note also how the compiler has already used *consuetudo* or similar forms three times within this chapter.

cornice (**100**:19); *regularis*; a cross-beam at the iconostasis.

counts: the following are mentioned (see index): Adalbert, Adalgis, Bernard, Boso, John, Maurinus, Vuldo, Wifrid. All except for Adalbert occur together at **104**:14, and are the group of unnamed counts at **104**:8.

dependants (*familiae*) occur at **100**:18 (twice), 22; at **105**:80 in connexion with the Corsican volunteers; at **108**:2 as belonging to Hadrian II (before his election); *familiares* occur at **112**:7.

dextra (**105**:104 only, described as Saxon). Without citing the LP, Ducange defines *dextrum* as a kind of measure, French 'dextre'. This appears to have been a measure of length or area, not one of capacity. The context is insufficient to elucidate the meaning.

The LP elsewhere has Saxon bowls (*gabatae*), but here a bowl (not described as Saxon) occurs almost immediately after.

digitiae (**103**:26 only); evidently finger-shaped pendants on a necklace (cf. Ducange III.116); cf. *buticulae* above.

domucella (diminutive of *domusculta*); Balnearola is mentioned at **105**:97.

dukes; two are mentioned: Gregory, duke of Rome, **106**:10 (note how he is 'sent' on a mission by the pope), and Lambert, duke of Spoleto, **108**:20. The former is the leader of the Roman militia; the latter's status is that of a Lombard ruler, subject (when it suited him) to the emperor. At **107**:33 is a reference to the duke of Ravenna's rights in elections to the archbishopric there.

exagia (**105**:76 only). Apart from the meanings 'weighing' and 'an assay of weights' (the word is the origin of English 'assay' and 'essay'), Niermeyer gives *exagium* as 'a weight apparently smaller than an ounce' and cites *uncias tres et exaja dua* in a document of the year 991. But it is likely to be significantly larger than the English 'grain'.

gemelliones (**103**:32 only). Yet another word for some kind of sacred vessels. Ducange IV.51 cites the LP and *Ordo Romanus* 1 c. 21 (now, Andrieu, 2.73); that chapter, dealing with which officials are in charge of which liturgical items, lists *amae* and *scyphi* along with *gemelliones*, as here in the LP ('from the Saviour's church the chief *mansionarii* take by hand, and the bearers carry, the handbasin, paten for daily use, chalice, *scyphi*, *pugillares* and other gold ones and silver *gemelliones*, silver cullender and gold one and another large silver one, silver *amae*, chant-book and other gold and silver vessels, gold and silver candlesticks'). Ducange cites *gemellarium* from Augustine (in Ps. 80), notes the identity of this with *gemellio*, and records the suggestion that it contained a double measure. Certainly the word must be connected with *geminus*, twin.

hegumenus; in these lives only Theognostus occurs (**108**:35); for his functions see **108**:n.90.

images, designs, representations (possibly three-dimensional is the icon of St Vitalis, **107**:36). The following analytical index of icons, objects and the contents of figurative designs (mainly on textiles), may be of use (see also chevrons, lattice-work, lily):
  God **103**:18; Christ (Saviour, Redeemer), **100**:6,26,35, **103**:14, **104**:26A,30B,34,34B, 35,36A, **105**:21,24,33,34,44,57,75,87-89,95,108, **106**:21, **107**:12,18,79; annunciation, **103**:27, **106**:27; incarnation, **104**:20; birth, **100**:12,33, **103**:10,16,17,20,27,33, **104**:20(?), **105**:59, **106**:24; presentation (*hypapante*), **103**:16, **106**:27; with the teachers, **106**:27; baptism, **100**:33, **103**:10,16; feeding of 5000, **105**:89; Palm Sunday, **100**:34,37; Last Supper, **103**:37; passion, **100**:38,39; resurrection, **100**:23,29,33,38,39, **103**:10,11,16,17,20,33, **104**:35,36A, **105**:14,33,56; ascension, **100**:34; descent of Holy Ghost, **100**:34;
  cross (design): **100**:6,12,13,20,24-28,39, **103**:11,26, **104**:35,36A, **105**:10,24,33,36,37,42-5,63,65-7,87,95,104, **106**:22,33; cross (object), **103**:9, **104**:33, **105**:17,28,31,56,75,83,104, **106**:27,28, **107**:12,13,17,79,80, **112**:6,16,17; crucifix, **105**:46,89,104; cross-adorned (silk) **100**:12,20,21,24,27, **103**:15,20-22,28,29, **107**:11,14;
  archangels, **100**:26, **103**:18; Cherubim, **105**:34; angels (designs), **100**:12,20, **104**:26A, **105**:95, **107**:79; angels (objects), **105**:64;
  StMary, **100**:12,23,25,27,29,32, **103**:25,33, **104**:38A, **105**:10,11,44,108; birth, **100**:35, **104**:20(?); assumption, **100**:34,35, **106**:24;

prophets, **105**:11,45; Daniel, **103**:21,22; John the Baptist, **103**:41;

apostles, **100**:8,26, **103**:18, **104**:26A,30B, **105**:34,44,87,108, **107**:18; evangelists, **105**:44; disciples, **105**:89; Peter, **100**:23,27, **105**:14,24,33,34,44,87, **107**:18; receiving keys, **105**:95; release by angel, **100**:5; miracles, **105**:105; preaching, **105**:55; passion **103**:13, **105**:95; Paul, **100**:27, **103**:30, **105**:33,34,44,87, **107**:18; passion, **103**:13, **105**:95; Andrew, passion **103**:13, **105**:24,33; John the Evangelist, **103**:41; Mark, **103**:18; Stephen, **105**:45; Zacchaeus, **103**:16;

Cosmas & Damian, **100**:25 (with 3 brothers), **103**:12; Gorgonius, Tiburtius, **103**:7; Gregory (= George?), **103**:14; Laurence, **105**:57; Processus and Martinian, **100**:6,23; Quattuor Coronati, **105**:14,22; Claudius, **105**:57; Nicostratus, **105**:57; Sebastian, **103**:7,14; Synzygius, **105**:75; Tiburtius & Valerian, **100**:20; Vitalis, **107**:36;

Silvester, **104**:34B,35,36A; Martin, **104**:34B,35,36A, **105**:21;

virgins, **100**:10, **104**:38A; Agatha, **105**:21; Caecilia **100**:20; Petronilla, **105**:24

saints, **105**:45,88; miracles, **100**:8, **105**:105; men, **103**:11, **105**:9,10,36,37,97

Gregory IV, **103**:18,33; Leo IV, **105**:14,21,22,24,33,56,57,59,75,87,89,95; Lothar, emperor, **105**:33; Louis the Pious, emperor, **103**:27;

basilisks, **112**:13; birds, **105**:9; dolphins (decoration?), **105**:67; ducks **103**:11; eagles, **103**:10,11,17,20-22, **105**:9,15,23,36,37,44,57,63,89,95, **112**:13; feathers, **103**:43; fledglings, **104**:37A; griffins, **103**:10,16,17,21,29,41, **106**:25; horses, **103**:11, **104**:36A; lambs, **105**:67; lions, **103**:11,15,17,26,28,29, **105**:13, **105**:106 (on a lectern), **106**:21, **107**:11,16,17, **112**:13; lioncubs, **103**:26; ostrich-eggs, **105**:104; peacocks, **100**:12, **105**:9,10, **107**:18; pheasants, **103**:43; serpents, **103**:26, **106**:21; unicorns, **103**:10;

almonds, **105**:108, **106**:31; apples (design), **103**:10; leaves, **103**:18; melon, **107**:17; palms (decoration), **105**:66; pine-cone, **103**:26; roses **100**:20, **103**:11, **104**:36A, **106**:33, **107**:11,18; trees, **103**:11,17, **105**:9, **107**:18; vine **105**:97;

Leonine City, **105**:95; gospels (design), **103**:13; keys, **100**:6, **103**:22; lamps, **100**:10; medallions, **100**:20, **105**:34,61; roundels, **105**:104,107,109, **106**:34; shield, **107**:18; swords (design), **103**:10,11; (object), **106**:34, **112**:10; wheels, **103**:11, **105**:9;

unspecified, **100**:5,6,10,19,31,35-7, **101**:3, **103**:5,7,12,14,15, **104**:23,25B,37A, **105**:37.84.97,108, **106**:30,33,34.

imizilum (**100**:35), *imizilo* **100**:35,36, *mizine* **105**:109, *mizinum* **107**:16; the context is always textiles. Ducange, IV 299, records the idea that in these places the word refers either to a soft silk called 'ermesino' in Italian, or to 'byssus'. A possibility is 'ermine', the fur of the stoat, white as symbol of purity, said to derive either from Latin 'mus Armenius' or from Old High German 'harmin' (German 'Hermelin').

incense-boat: *cantra*, **105**:10,58, **106**:22,26,27, all in the context of censers or incense; the meaning 'incense-boat' seems certain. See above on *cantrella*, which does seem to be 'incense-boat'. Note also that in Life 104 *cantara* occurs in the context of a censer and is taken in the translation as equivalent to *cantra*, not as *canthera*, 'chandelier'. But at **112**:10 a *cantra* 'hangs', and the context at **112**:15 is no help. At **112**:10 alone, at first sight, the meaning 'incense-boat' seems awkward; how could it have been of any use on top of a pergola? Perhaps it was fixed on one of the columns of the pergola low enough for the incense to be placed in it or taken from it for burning. Ducange II.104-5 has *canterata*, a type of vessel, or vessel-shaped container for water, Italian 'catero'; and *cantharus*, § *cantrum*, a vessel for wine.

iugulum (**107**:13 only, but cf. *sugulum*, below); Ducange IV 446 cites **107**:13, recording the notion, as far-fetched, that it was a small *iugum*, 'yoke', made of gold, to remind those in the basilica of the text 'My yoke is easy...'.

lattice-work (*cancelli*, 'lattice, bars, balustrade, grating'); at **105**:88 and **106**:33, with roses also mentioned, the word must refer to decoration. But at **105**:94 the context is railings, and though the meaning could be decorative (and the translation so takes it), the word might mean 'chancel-rails'.

lily: *lilium* (but at **105**:57 *gilium* and at **105**:66, twice, *giliis*, with the Italian phonetic change, cf. Ducange IV.68). Usually this refers to the capital of a column (e.g. **105**:61,66) though at **100**:5 it is a decoration. At **105**:57, the meaning 'capital' is hardly plausible; it cannot be suspended; Ducange has a word *gillo*, 'earthenware vessel', scarcely relevant here; nor is it easy to make anything from the military usage recorded for *lilium* in Caesar *BG* 7.73.8, a sort of defence consisting of several rows of pits, in which stakes were planted, rising only 4 inches above ground. Krautheimer, *Corpus* 4.3, paraphrases **105**:57 as a silver crown to be suspended from a pergola standing before the altar; this may be guesswork. In view of the next note, perhaps the 'lily' is the 'fastener' on which the decorative melons are suspended.

lily and hook (*lilio et uncino*, **103**:26, *lilium et uncinu*, **105**:88, in both places of a crown with chains and a dolphin; and *uncinus* alone, also in **103**:26 and connected with chains). *Uncinus* is certainly 'hook': Ducange VIII.367 cites these passages and defines it as *uncus cui inhaerent catenulae*; he cites glossaries giving *repagulum, reticulus*. In these contexts, and perhaps in **105**:57 (see last note), 'lily' seems to mean some kind of fastener; Professor Scott concurs with this; Dr Cheesman suggests that 'lily and hook' might rather refer to a repeated decorative design.

liturgical books mentioned: Scriptural: Comes-book (*q.v.*), **112**:13; epistle-book, **106**:32 (partly Greek), **112**:15,17; gospel-books: **100**:27, **104**:38A, **105**:86,105, **106**:25,29,33 (Greek?), **107**:30, **112**:15; Heptateuch, **112**:17; Histories, **105**:105, **112**:16; King(dom)s, **105**:86, **112**:16,17; Prophets, **112**:13; Psalter, **105**:86,105; Solomon, **105**:105, **112**:15,17. Non-scriptural: Acts (of martyrs), **105**:105, **112**:13,15; Antiphonary, **105**:105; Homilies, **105**:86,105, of Chrysostom, **112**:15, of Gregory, **112**:11,16; (readings and responsories, **112**:10); Sacramentary, **105**:105; Sermons, **112**:17. At Constantinople there was a 'guardian of the books' (Paul, **108**:37).

liturgical days mentioned: Christmas eve, **107**:59, Christmas day, **105**:16, St John the Evangelist, **107**:15, Epiphany **106**:23, St Agnes **107**:60-61, Palm Sunday, **100**:34, Holy Saturday, **106**:32, Easter, **105**:88, Saturday before Pentecost, **106**:32, Assumption of the Virgin **105**:19, Octave of the Assumption **105**:26, St Caecilia **104**:22A.

liturgical texts quoted: collects **105**:51,73.

lora, **103**:27; Ducange V.143 explains *lorum* as the garment of an emperor or consul, citing the Donation of Constantine, and Leo Grammaticus on the emperor Basil (Photius hallows Basil, who is wearing a *loron*); he states that it amounts to the same as a papal *pallium*, Greek ὠμοφόριον. But this cannot be the meaning in this context. A plausible guess for the present passage might be 'thongs, strings, tapes', 5 on each veil, to fasten the veils in some way round the altar (Professor Scott concurs). They may have deserved mention if they were gold filaments.

magister militum, master of the soldiers: the following are named (see index): Christopher, Daniel, Gratian, Gregory, Mercurius, Peter, Sergius; cf. Caesarius.

mandati (**108**:36), so for the plural of *mandator*, a messenger in the Byzantine Empire.

Although they were no mere public-service messengers, they normally performed real functions and were not simply holders of a dignity; their insignia were a red stick; they were headed by the *protomandator*; cf. Bury 1911:113; Oikonomides 1972:90 n. 4, 298; Haldon 1984:108 etc., 285-295.

manor (**103**:42) renders *curtis*; two are named.

masoricae (**105**:96 only): 'three olive *masoricae*... worked in silk and colourfully embroidered' or, if not textiles, 'depicted'; alternatively render 'three *masoric* olives/olive-berries'. Perhaps cf. **105**:64: 'a canopy of olive which hangs round the altar'. Note that Wigbert of Toul, *Vita Leonis IX papae* 2.6, Watterich 1862:157 (also in *AaSS Apr.* 2.648-665; in fact written by Cardinal Humbert) mentions a *scyphus* of precious *mazer*; and a Jumièges charter of 1077 (Vernier 1916:I.85 no. 30) uses the adjective *mazerinus* with a *scyphus*. In these two examples, *mazer* is maplewood or the like. Similarly, for the present passage, Ducange V.295 cited with little approval the notion that 'masoric' is an Arabic word for Egyptian; he preferred to see the word as a spelling of *mazerica*, and the olive not as the product of an olive-tree but as a kind of jewel or a large nodule made out of 'mazer', or from the stone 'murra', and cited the example from Wigbert. If this is right, the alternative translation given above would have to be adopted. But how, then, can the objects (*oleae*), if made of maplewood, have also been worked in silk and colourfully embroidered? This can hardly be said of objects of either maplewood or precious stone. The objects must surely be textiles. The translation printed therefore takes 'olive' as an adjective, and *masoricae* as an unknown noun. The context suggests some kind of curtains hanging round three sides of an altar, not dangling baubles. Pliny, *NH* 37.5.20 §77, has *berylli oleagini* to mean 'olive-coloured beryls' which shows that the notion of 'olive' can refer to colour (and, admittedly, be applied to precious stones).

matroneum (**103**:32): women's area or section in a church, cf. Niermeyer; cf. LP Symmachus (53:8, BP 45); but see **100**: n. 82. Either a women's enclosure, or possibly the site where, across a chancel-screen, the clergy would accept the women's gifts; see Mathews 1962:73ff, Krautheimer, *Corpus* 3.69.

melon (*melum*, **107**:17), must be Greek μῆλον, though the expected Latin *melum* seems elsewhere to be supplanted by *melo/-onis*. At any rate a finial over the canopy consisting of a ball with a cross must surely be intended. Cf. *mela* at **105**:57, again decorative, though in a different context. At **105**:55 *malum* (apple) occurs in the functional sense of bell-clapper.

missa in the singular is used only twice **108**:10, **112**:8, to mean 'mass', which is otherwise always plural *missae*.

mizine (**105**:109); *mizinum* (**107**:16); see *imizilum*.

monocossis (**105**:104 only, as *monocossim*, evidently an accusative form). Ducange V.295, citing this passage, recorded as an empty guess the emendation *mancosus*, and suggested that it was a precious stone of some kind.

necklace; in **103**:26 this renders *morena*. The *murena* is a fish, but Jerome (*Ep.* 24.3) already records the diminutive *murenula* as a colloquial word for necklace, and elsewhere uses it with this meaning. At **103**:37 (as at 98:25) 'necklace' renders *siclo*.

needlework (**105**:10,58) renders *acupictile*, in the one place referring to a veil, in the other

to a panel in a textile. Servius gives *acupictae* as the name of certain kinds of garments; '
cf. Virgil, *Aeneid* 11.777. Isidore, *Orig.* 19.20, states that an *acupicta* garment is one
worked or decorated with a needle, and is also called Phrygian, from the people renowned
for their skill at such embroidery.

net, **106:**31,33; a kind of lighting-fixture.

notch (*nusca*, **107:**51). The word is Germanic in origin (now Nuschel); Niermeyer, and
Ducange V.27, give 'fibula'; but even in its non-anatomical meaning ('clasp, buckle, kind
of bracelet, a woman's ornament') this does not suit the context. Professor Scott concurs
that, despite the absence of this precise meaning for *nusca*, 'notch' seems the sensible
translation.

office (*scrinium*), **107:**23,41,48, **108:**34,40; the only *scriniarius* mentioned is Theodore
106:11.

pallium (**108:**5).

patrician: occurs in these lives for no living individual, only for Belisarius (**112:**6).

petinantes (**103:**26 only); despite the spelling the word must be connected with *pecten*,
'comb'. Ducange VI.296 explained it as referring to spokes inserted into the necklaces
(*q.v.*) mentioned in the section. Perhaps 'radial spokes'; or perhaps, since no number is
given with them, the word is a general one to cover the various elements of necklaces,
buticulae, *buticellae*, and *digitiae* (*qq.v.*), for which the numbers are given.

pint (*sextarius*, **112:**19; cf. pint-pots, *sextaria*, **104:**34). Strictly, the sixth part of a *congius*
(itself an eighth of an *amphora*, or 12 *heminae* or about 206 cubic inches or nearly six
pints English), liquid measure; or the sixteenth part of a *modius* (itself the sixth of a Greek
medimnus), dry measure.

pommel; the word renders *bulla* at **104:**33 (on bowls, cf. n.65), **105:**10 (golden, on
textiles), **105:**14 (gilt, with jewels, on crowns), 59 (with chains, round a thurible), 62
(gold, in a diadem), 88 (with chains and jewels, on crowns).

prases (**105:**10 and frequently), green precious stones, not excluding emeralds though
these appear as *smaragdi*. In **105:**87 and elsewhere the adjective *prasinus* is used with
textiles (the dictionaries want 'leek-green', but 'green is sufficient: the LP nowhere uses
viridis).

Propitiatorium (six times in life **100:** cc. 6,10,11,19,31,38; otherwise only at **105:**109).
It occurs four times in Vulgate Exodus and in Hebrews 9.5, where English versions give
'mercy seat'; ninth-century writers have applied the word, however they understood it, to
something connected with an altar. Ducange VI.533 suggested it was the same as the
canopy (*ciburium*) which covered the confessio and the whole altar, just as (he stated) the
Ark of the Covenant was covered by the Propitiatorium or Oraculum, which is also called
in Exodus the lid or cover of the Ark. But in **100:**11 and 19 it is clearly distinct from the
canopy. Niermeyer has 'plateau on top of the altar'. Duchesne, n. 23 on **100:**19, takes it
to be the facing or revetment of the altar. For **100:**11 Krautheimer has a 'panel' or
'frontale' for the altar; and for **100:**31 he gives 'altar-frontal' (*Corpus* 2.310, 319, 4.3).
This seems at least a plausible interpretation. Note that at **100:**38 and **105:**109 it is
'spanoclist' (*q.v.*), while at **100:**6 silver sheets are added to it.

psilliae (**100**:20 only). There are three possible bases for interpretation. Firstly 'shaggy cloths': *psila* is said to be a covering shaggy on one side (Lewis & Short cite Lucilius), derived from Gk ψιλή. Secondly, Ducange VI.555, citing the LP, commented that Ψίλλον is Greek for a bracelet or armband, but could not see the relevance of this to altarcloths, unless they were sown on as a fringe (could the word have meant 'tassels'?). Thirdly, *Acta Sanctorum* (Maii III.398, the life of Paschal) emended *psillia* to *psyllia*, and took it to mean purple neatly spattered with small spots, the spots taking their name from the shape of fleas (ψύλλα is a 'flea'), but noted that there is also a plant called ψύλλιον (plantago psyllium, flea-wort), and that the ornamentation may have resembled the leaves of this plant.

refined gold (**105**:34) renders *obrizum* (as at **97**:89,90,93 twice, 96, **98**:6,110). Niermeyer has 'of fine gold', citing Benveniste 1953. The Vulgate uses *obrizum* at Isaiah 13.12 where most English versions now give 'gold of Ophir'. The Vulgate uses *Ophir* at 1 Kings 9.28, 10.11, 22.49, 1 Chr. 29.4; LXX Isaiah has ὁ λίθος ἐκ Σουφιρ; and elsewhere Σουφιρ or Σωφηρ. Though clearly a place name originally, it is very unlikely that *obrizum* was seen as a reference to Ophir in the 8th and 9th centuries, so the translation avoids 'gold of Ophir'.

regionary; the only one named is Theodore **107**:1-2 (where see n. 1).

repida (*-i, -ae*?) (**107**:18); the word is a hapax of totally unknown meaning (Ducange VII.130). The context might suggest some kind of handles, or (perhaps more likely) precious stones.

rhodian (**103**:11), *de rodino*, of three veils; Niermeyer cites this passage only, and gives 'rosa dyed material, from Rhodos'. At **106**:28 occurs *diarodina* (without citing the passage, Niermeyer gives 'rosa-dyed'), where the translation accepts that colour is involved and renders 'rhodian red'). Yet in view of the occurrences of forms like tyrian, alexandrian, etc., the reference may be to a material rather than to a dye. Lewis & Short cite *unguentum rhodinum* from Pliny 13.1.2 s. 9 ('rose-salve') and *oleum rhodinum* from Pliny 15.7.7. s. 30 ('oil of roses'); in neither case is a colour involved. If this is true in the LP, translate 'red rhodian' rather than 'rhodian red'.

sacellarius: Basil **108**:37, an official of the church at Constantinople.

secretarium; for **103**:14 Krautheimer renders 'sacristy', as he does for **108**:25, where, at least, it is probably not the meaning, since a formal meeting was held in it. It occurs also at **106**:30 (a portico and baptistery with a *secretarium*) and at **107**:52 (S. Maria in Cosmedin) in conjunction with a *triclinium* and parlours (*caminatae*).

secundicerius: Hadrian **106**:10-11; second in command (after the *primicerius*) of the notaries.

shirt (*camisa*, **106**:34); possibly a liturgical 'alb'.

silfori (**107**:81 only; the MSS have *sifori*); Ducange VII.488 cites this passage and Leo Ostiensis I.29: 'moreover a silk tunic (*q.v.*) *de silfori*'; see above, s.v. 'beaker', for another version of the same story about Siconulf stealing a tunic *de silfori*. Ducange gives (and the *MGH* editor, Waitz, accepts) *silfori* as from σίλφη, referring to the insect *blatta*, and with an added Lombardic termination. The translation renders the relatively common *blatta* as 'purple', but retains *silfori* since the compiler's use of such a rare word may mean that he did not regard it as fully synonymous.

spanish, *spaniscus*; first in the LP at **103**:11, then **105**:9, 67 (twice), 86, 97, 105 (all of *vela* or *vestes*); and **106**:27 when one hangs over an altar. Ducange VII.540 defines as *pannus hispanicus*; but in the last case listed the meaning does not seem to fit, since the object is given a weight, which is never the case for textiles in the LP; perhaps the text there is corrupt - a *spanoclist* object?

spanoclist; as in *LECP* the word is transliterated. In lives 100-112 it is used of a *regnum* (diadem) at **100**:10, **106**:27, and of a *propitiatorium* at **100**:38, **105**:109. Ducange VII.51 (a crown closed on top, ἐπανώ κλειστος) may be right, despite the doubts expressed in *LECP* (98 n. 115). Krautheimer, *Corpus* 3.235, renders 'jewel-incrusted covered gold crown'.

spatharius: *protospatharii* mentioned are Arsabir **107**:18,38, Sisinnius **108**:35; *spatharii* are Basil **108**:23-32, Eustathius **108**:35, John (also a secretary) **108**:37, Strategis **108**:37, Theodosius **108**:59; *spatharii* in general, **108**:36. They are white-robed in **108**:36-7. The kind of sword (*spatha*) from which their name derived occurs at **106**:34 and **112**:10.

squat chandelier (**107**:12), (cantharus) sessilis; Ducange VII.459 (not citing LP) defines *sessilis* from glossaries as 'short in stature' (because a short person might appear to be sitting; cf. Ovid: 'if you are short you should sit, in case if you stand you seem to be sitting'). Perhaps; but had the LP's compiler read these glossaries? If he meant 'small' he had other ways of saying it. The meaning is more likely to be what in English is called a 'standard lamp', a chandelier which 'stands' (or 'sits') on the ground rather than one which hangs from a beam or wherever; cf. LP Vigilius (61:2, BP 56, where Belisarius presented to St Peter's 'two great silver-gilt candlesticks which still stand today before St Peter's body'). The translation avoids 'sessile' which does not have this meaning in English, and 'standard' since the Latin concept is sitting, not standing, and adopts 'squat' which means sitting and also connotes Ducange's meaning.

staupi (**107**:80), cups of some kind; from an old Teutonic root *staupo*-. English 'stoup' in this sense is related.

strati (**108**:36), so for the plural of *strator*, 'groom, squire, equerry'. They were members of a Byzantine palatine *schola* already in the 6th century. The title is attested as a dignity perhaps in the 7th century; but they were functionaries and not merely dignitaries; commissions could be purchased; the insignia were a gold whip adorned with precious stones; at least from the time of Constantine V their *schola* came under the *protostrator*, who gained importance from his frequent contact with the emperor, and by the 11th century had become one of the greatest state officials; see Bury 1911:113; Oikonomides 1972:90 n. 6, 298-9, 337-8; Haldon 1984:108 etc.

sugulum (**112**:15 only). Duchesne cites no variants (there are only two MSS anyway). The old editions printed *sagulum*, with which spelling Ducange cited the word from LP, but offered no suggestion as to its meaning, presumably because he took it in its classical sense as a diminutive of *sagum*; Lewis & Short give 'small military cloak, usually the purple-coloured one of the general', citing Cicero, Livy, Tacitus, Suetonius, Virgil etc. (Niermeyer offers 'blanket'). Perhaps therefore 'cloak', even 'purple cloak'. But this does not seem a suitable object to hang from a diadem. Krautheimer, *Corpus* 4.3, paraphrases this passage: 'a jewelled and enamelled gold cross to hang from a crown above the altar', but this does not solve the problem of *sugulum*. Is there a connexion with the mysterious *iugulum* (see above) at **107**:13?

superista: only Gratian is named, **105**:110-112, **106**:11.

tribunal (**103**:32 only); the word refers to a high-level (elevated) sanctuary (so Niermeyer, Krautheimer), the meaning being derived from *tribunal* in the sense of 'gallery, platform'. Cf. *Ordo Romanus* 6.21 (Andrieu, II.244): 'the pontiff should come to the *tribunal* and bow his head opposite the altar'.

triclinium: Gregory IV's at the Lateran, **103**:15; one at S. Maria in Cosmedin, **107**:52; and the Golden Triclinium (*in chrisotriclinio*) at Constantinople, **108**:38.

tunic (*saraca*, **106**:34); Niermeyer, s.v. *sarica* 1, 'tunic (primitively a silken, later a fine linen or woollen one)'. See note on beaker.

vestiarium, a bureau at the Lateran, occurs at **104**:25A (it contains an oratory of St Caesarius), and in the plural at **112**:6-7. None of its chief officials are named in these lives, though there is a general reference to the competence of the *vestiarius* to act at Ravenna, **107**:34 (where see n. 66).

Worthies (*axiomatici*, **108**:5 only); Ducange I.502 defines as magistrates, magnates, chief men, citing glossaries, the present passage in LP, Anastasius, *Hist. Eccl.*, John the Deacon, *Vita S. Greg.* 1.25, and the *Liber Diurnus*.

BIBLIOGRAPHY

H. Adelson and R. Baker, 'The Oath of Purgation of Pope Leo III in 800', *Traditio* 8 (1952), 35-80.

C. M. Aherne, 'Sergius II', *New Catholic Encyclopedia* (New York, 1967), 13, 112.

S. S. Alexander, 'Studies in Constantinian Church Architecture', *Rivista di archeologia cristiana* 47 (1970), 281ff.

A. Amore, *I martiri di Roma* (Rome, 1975).

M. V. Anastos, 'The Papal Legates at the Council of 861 and their Compliance with the wishes of the Emperor Michael III', *Armos* (Thessalonica, 1990), I.185-200.

M. Andrieu, 'Les ordres mineurs dans l'ancien rit romain', *Revue des sciences réligieuses* 5 (1923), 235-274.

M. Andrieu, *Les Ordines Romani du haut moyen age*, Spicilegium Sacrae Lovaniense, études et documents, fascicules 11, 23-4, 28-9 (5 volumes, Leuven, 1931-61).

M. Andrieu, 'La chapelle de S. Grégoire dans l'ancienne basilique vaticane', *Rivista di archeologia cristiana* 13 (1936), 61-101.

M. Armellini (ed. 3 by C. Cecchelli), *Le Chiese di Roma dal secolo IV al XIX*, 2 volumes (Rome, 1942).

G. Arnaldi, 'Giovanni Immonide e la cultura a Roma al tempo di Giovanni VIII', *Bollettino dell'Istituto Storico Italiano per il medioevo* 68 (1956), 33-89.

G. Arnaldi, 'Anastasio', *Dizionario Biografico degli Italiani* 3 (1961), 25-37.

F. Baix, 'Benoit III', *Dictionnaire d'histoire et de géographie ecclésiastique* 8 (1935), 14-27.

J. Baldwin, *Christianity through the thirteenth century* (New York, 1970).

K. A. Barbouskos, 'Ρώμη καὶ Κωνσταντινού πολις εἰς τὰ βουλγαρικὰ πράγματα', *Armos* (Thessalonica, 1990), I.277-280.

H. G. Beck, 'Nicholas I', *New Catholic Encyclopedia* 10 (New York, 1967), 441.

H. G. Beck, 'The Byzantine Church in the Age of Photius' in F. Kempf et al. ed., *The Church in the Age of Feudalism*, Handbook of Church History, ed. H. Jedin and J. Dolan, volume 3 (New York and London, 1969), 174-193.

E. Benveniste, 'Le terme obryza et la métallurgie de l'or', *Revue de philologie*, 27 (1953), 122-6.

C. Bertelli, *La Madonna di Santa Maria in Trastevere, storia, iconografia, stile di un dipinto romano dell'ottavo secolo* (Rome, 1961).

J. J. Berthier, *L'église de Sainte-Sabine à Rome* (Rome, 1910).

O. Bertolini, 'Osservazioni sulla Constitutio Romana e sullo Sacramentum cleri et populi Romani dell' 824', *Studi medievali in onore di A[ntonino] de Stefano* (Palermo, 1956).

O. Bertolini, 'Adriano II', *Dizionario Biografico degli Italiani* 1 (1960), 323-329.

O. Bertolini, 'Benedetto III', *Dizionario Biografico degli Italiani* 8 (1966), 330-7.

O. Bertolini, 'Il 'Liber Pontificalis'' in *La storiografia altomedievale* (Spoleto, 1970), 387-455.

J. Bishop, 'Bishops as marital advisors in the ninth century' in J. Kirshner and S. Wemple eds., *Women of the Medieval World* (Oxford, 1985), 54-84.

U. Broccoli, 'Ostia Antica, S. Aurea, Gregoriopoli: spigolature sulle vicende di Ostia dalla tarda antichità all'alto medio evo', *Lunario Romano XII: Il Lazio nell'antichità romana*, ed. R. Lefevre (Rome, 1982).

J. B. Bury, *The Imperial Administrative System in the ninth century* (London, British Academy Supplementary Papers, I, 1911).

C. Calisse, *Storia di Civitavecchia* (Florence, 1908).

Y. Congar, 'S. Nicolas Ier: ses positions ecclésiologiques', *Rivista di storia della chiesa in Italia* 21 (1967), 393-410.

F. Curschmann, *Die älteren Papsturkunden des Erzbistums Hamburg, eine diplomatische*

Untersuchung (Hamburg and Leipzig, 1909).

F. Darsy, *Santa Sabina* (Le chiese di Roma illustrate 63-4) (Rome, 1961).

F. W. Deichmann and A. Tschira, 'Das Mausoleum des Kaiserin Helena und die Basilika der Heiligen Marcellinus und Petrus an der Via Labicana vor Rom', *JDAI* 72 (1957), 44-110.

H. Delehaye, *Étude sur le légendier romain. Les saints de novembre et de décembre* (Brussels, 1936).

P. Delogu, 'Strutture politiche e ideologia nel regno di Ludovico II', *Bollettino dell'Istituto Storico Italiano per il medioevo* 80 (1968), 137-189.

G. B. de Rossi, *Roma sotterranea cristiana*, 3 volumes (Rome, 1864-77).

J. Devisse, *Hincmar, archevêque de Reims, 845-882*, 3 volumes (Geneva, 1975-6).

P. Devos, 'Anastase le Bibliothécaire: sa contribution à la correspondance pontificale; la date de sa mort', *Byzantion* 32 (1962), 97-115.

L. Duchesne, 'Notes sur la topographie de Rome au moyen-âge III, Sainte-Anastase *Mélanges de l'école française de Rome* 7 (1887), 386-413 (= *Scripta Minora*, 1973, 45-71).

L. Duchesne, 'S. Maria Antiqua, Notes sur la topographie de Rome au moyen-âge VIII', *Mélanges de l'école française de Rome* 17 (1897) 13-37 (= *Scripta Minora*, 1973, 141-165).

L. Duchesne, 'Saint-Denis in Via Lata, Notes sur la topographie de Rome au moyen-âge IX', *Mélanges de l'école française de Rome* 20 (1900), 317-330 (= *Scripta Minora*, 1973, 167-180).

L. Duchesne, 'Vaticana: notes sur la topographie de Rome au moyen-âge XI', *Mélanges de l'école française de Rome* 22 (1902), 385-428 (= *Scripta Minora*, 1973, 201-44).

L. Duchesne, 'Les monastères desservants de S. M. Majeure', *Mélanges de l'école française de Rome* 27 (1907), 479-494 (= *Scripta Minora*, 1973, 329-44).

L. Duchesne, *The Beginnings of the Temporal Sovereignty of the Popes, A.D. 754-1073* (translation by A. H. Mathew of *Les premiers temps de l'État pontifical (754-1073)*, London, 1908).

L. Duchesne, 'Le culte romain des Quatre-Couronnés (Santi Quattro)', *Mélanges de l'école française de Rome* 31 (1911), 231-246 (= *Scripta Minora*, 345-60).

L. Duchesne, *Scripta Minora, études de topographie romaine et de géographie ecclésiastique* (Rome, École française de Rome, 1973).

E. Dümmler, *Geschichte des ostfränkischen Reiches*, 3 volumes (Leipzig, 1887-8).

J. Duhr, 'Humble vestige d'un grand espoir deçu: épisode de la vie de Formose', *Revue de sciences réligieuses* 42 (1954), 361-87.

F. Dvornik, *Les Slaves, Byzance et Rome au IXe siècle* (Paris, 1926).

F. Dvornik, *The Photian Schism: history and legend* (Cambridge, 1948).

F. Dvornik 'Constantinople and Rome', *Cambridge Medieval History*, volume IV (1966[a]), 431-472.

F. Dvornik, 'Which councils are ecumenical?', *Journal of Ecumenical Studies* 3 (1966[b]), 321-6 (= *Photian and Byzantine ecclesiastical studies*, Variorum, 1974, c. XX).

F. Dvornik, 'Patriarch Ignatius and Caesar Bardas', *Byzantinoslavica* 27.i (1966[c]), 7-22 (= *Photian and Byzantine ecclesiastical studies*, Variorum, 1974, c. XIX).

F. Dvornik, *Byzantine missions among the Slavs. SS. Constantine-Cyril and Methodius* (New Brunswick, NJ, 1970).

F. Dvornik, 'Photius, Nicholas I and Hadrian II, *Byzantinoslavica* 34.i (1973), 33-50 (= *Photian and Byzantine ecclesiastical studies*, Variorum, 1974, c. IX).

P. Egidi, *I monasteri di Subiaco, notizie storiche* (Rome, 1904).

E. Ewig, 'Climax and turning point of the Carolingian Age, 814-849' in F. Kempf et al. ed., *The Church in the Age of Feudalism* (Handbook of Church History, ed. H. Jedin and J. Dolan, volume 3, New York and London, 1969), 103-125.

E. Ewig, 'The Western Church from the Death of Louis the Pious to the End of the Carolingian Period', *ibidem*, 126-173.

G. Fantuzzi, *Monumenti Ravennati de' secoli di mezzo per la maggior parte inediti*, 6 volumes (Venice, 1901-4).

G. Ferrari, *Early Roman Monasteries. Notes for the history of the monasteries and convents at Rome from the V through the X century*, Studi di antichità cristiana XXIII (Vatican, 1957).

R. J. Forbes, *Studies in Ancient Technology²*, (6 volumes, Leiden, 1964-6).

P. Franchi de' Cavalieri, 'Note agiografiche', *Studi e Testi* 24 (1912).

J. Fried, 'Ludwig der Fromme, das Papsttum und die fränkische Kirche' in P. Godman and R. Collins eds., *Charlemagne's Heir* (Oxford, 1990), 231-273.

A. P. Frutaz, *Il complesso monumentale di Sant'Agnese*, ed. 5 (Rome, 1992).

H. Fuhrmann, 'Eine im Original erhaltene Propagandaschrift des Erzbischofs Gunthar von Köln (865)', *Archiv für Diplomatik, Schriftsgeschichte, Siegel- und Wappenkunde* 4 (1958), 1-51.

H. Fuhrmann, *Einfluss und Verbreitung der pseudoisidorischen Fälschungen* (Schriften der MGH 24), 3 volumes (Munich, 1972-4).

D. Ganz, *Corbie in the Carolingian Renaissance* (Sigmaringen, 1990).

H. Geertman, *More veterum, il Liber Pontificalis e gli edifici ecclesiastici di Roma nella tarda antichità e nell'alto medioevo* (Archaeologia Traiectina 10, Groningen, 1975, also published in Dutch).

S. Gibson and B. Ward-Perkins, 'The Surviving Remains of the Leonine Wall', *Papers of the British School at Rome* 47 (1979), 30-57 with plates III-VI, and 51 (1983), 222-239 with plates XI-XII.

G. Giovannoni, 'La chiesa vaticana di San Stefano Maggiore', *Atti Pont. Accademia romana di archeologia, memorie* 4, i (1934), 1-28.

W. J. Glanvell, *Die Kanonessammlung des Kardinal Deusdedit* (Paderborn, 1905).

H. Grégoire, 'The Amorians and Macedonians', *Cambridge Medieval History*, volume IV (1966), 105-152.

P. Grierson, 'Carolingian Europe and the Arabs: the myth of the mancus', *RPBH* 32 (1954), 1059-1074.

H. Grisar, *Analecta Romana, dissertazioni, testi, monumenti dell'arte* I (Rome, 1899).

H. Grisar, 'Le testi dei SS Apostoli', *La Civiltà Cattolica* 58, 3 (1907), 457.

H. Grotz, *Erbe wider Willen, Hadrian II (867-872) und seine Zeit* (Vienna-Cologne-Graz, 1970).

R. Guilland, *Études de topographie de Constantinople byzantine*, 2 volumes in 1 (Amsterdam, 1969).

A. Guglielmotti, *Storia della marina pontificia* (10 volumes, Rome, 1886-93).

F. Haldon, *Byzantine Praetorians* (Bonn, 1984).

L. Halphen, *Charlemagne et l'empire carolingien* (Paris, 1947).

W. Hartmann, *Die Synoden der Karolingerzeit im Frankreich und in Italien* (Paderborn, 1989).

K. Herbers, 'Der Konflikt Papst Nikolaus' I mit Erzbischof Johannes VII von Ravenna (861)', in P. J. Heinig (ed.), *Diplomatische und chronologische Studien aus der Arbeit am den Regesta Imperii* (Cologne, 1991), 166ff.

L. Hertling, 'Kanoniker, Augustinerregel und Augustinerorden', *Zeitschrift für katholische Theologie* 54 (1930), 335-59.

E. Hlawitschka, *Franken, Alemannen, Bayern und Bergunder in Oberitalien 774-962* (Freiburg, 1960).

P. A. Holmes, 'Nicholas I's Reply to the Bulgarians Revisited', *Ecclesia Orans* 7 (1990), 131-143.

C. Hülsen, *Le Chiese di Roma nel medio evo* (Florence, 1927).

J. Hyam, 'Ermentrude and Richildis', in M. T. Gibson and J. L. Nelson edd., *Charles the Bald* (Aldershot, 1990), 154-168.

R. Janin, *Constantinople byzantine* (2nd ed., Paris, 1964).

E. H. Kantorowicz, *Laudes Regiae, a study in liturgical acclamation and mediaeval ruler worship* (California, 1946).

P. F. Kehr, *Italia Pontificia, I Roma* (Berlin, 1906), *II Latium* (Berlin, 1907).

J. N. D. Kelly, *The Oxford Dictionary of the Popes* (1986).

S. Keynes & M. Lapidge, *Alfred the Great: Asser's Life of Alfred and other contemporary sources* (Harmondsworth, 1983).

J. P. Kirsch, *Die römischen Titelkirchen im Altertum*, Studien zur Geschichte und Kultur des Altertums 9 (Paderborn, 1918).

E. Kirschbaum, *The Tombs of St Peter and St Paul* (London, 1959).

S. Konecny, *Die Frauen des Karolingischen Königshauses* (Vienna, 1976).

R. Kottje, 'Kirchliches Recht und päpstlicher Autoritätanspruch. Zu den Auseinandersetzungen über die Ehe Lothars II', in H. Mordek, ed., *Aus Kirche und Reich: Studien zu Theologie, Politik und Recht im Mittelalter. Festschrift für F. Kempf* (Sigmaringen, 1988), 97-103.

R. Krautheimer, S. Corbett, W. Frankl, *Corpus Basilicarum Christianarum Romae. The Early Christian Basilicas of Rome (IV-IX Centuries)*, 5 volumes (Vatican, 1937-77).

R. Krautheimer, *Rome: profile of a city, 312-1308* (Princeton, 1980).

R. Krautheimer, *Three Christian Capitals* (California, 1983).

S. Kuttner, 'Cardinalis: the history of a canonical concept', *Traditio* 3 (1945), 129-214.

J. Labarte, *Le palais impériale de Constantinople* (Paris, 1861).

F. Lanzoni, *Le diocesi d'Italia dalle origini al principio del secolo VII (an. 604)*, Studi e Testi 35 (Faenza, 1927).

A. Lapôtre, *De Anastasio Bibliothecario sedis apostolicae* (Paris, 1885).

A. Lapôtre, 'Adrien II et les fausses décrétales', *Revue des questions historiques* 27 (1880), 377-431.

P. Lauer, 'Le poème de la destruction de Rome', *Mélanges de l'école française de Rome* 19 (1899), 307.

P. Lauer, 'La cité carolingienne de Cencelle (Léopoli)', *Mélanges de l'école française de Rome* 20 (1900), 147ff and plan.

P. Lauer, *Le palais de Latran: étude historique et archéologique* (Paris, 1911).

H. Leclercq, 'Schola', *Dictionnaire d'archéologie chrétienne et de liturgie* 15 (1950), 1008-1013.

H. Leclercq, 'Byzantium', *Dictionnaire d'archéologie chrétienne et de liturgie* 2.i (1925), 1363-1454.

C. Leonardi, *Studi Medievali³* 8 (1967), 59-192.

C. Leonardi, *Anastasio Bibliotecario e l'ottavo concilio ecumenico*, Centro italiano di studi sull'alto medioevo (Spoleto, 1987).

P. Liebaert, 'Le reliquaire du chef de saint Sébastien', *Mélanges de l'école française de Rome* 34 (1913), 479f.

P. Llewellyn, *Rome in the Dark Ages* (London, 1971).

R. J. Loenertz, 'Un prétendu sanctuaire romain de S. Denys de Paris', *Analecta Bollandiana* 66 (1948), 118 f.

R. S. Lopez, 'Silk industry in the Byzantine Empire', *Speculum* 20 (1945), 1-42.

M. McCormick, *Eternal Victory: triumphal rulership in Late Antiquity, Byzantium and the Early Medieval West* (Cambridge, 1966).

G. Mackie, 'The Zeno Chapel - a prayer for salvation', *Papers of the British School at Rome* 57 (1989), 172-199 with plates XXXI-XXXVII.

R. McKitterick, *The Frankish Kingdoms 751-987* (London, 1983).

C. A. Mango, *The Brazen House: a study of the vestibule of the imperial palace of*

Constantinople (Copenhagen, 1959).

C. A. Mango, *Le développement urbain de Constantinople (IVᵉ - VIIᵉ siècles)* (Paris, 1985; reprint with addenda, 1990).

T. F. Mathews, 'An early Roman chancel arrangement and its liturgical uses', *Rivista di archeologia cristiana* 38 (1962), 71-95.

M. B. Mauck, 'The Mosaic of the Triumphal Arch of S. Prassede: a liturgical interpretation', *Speculum* 62 (1987), 813-828.

R. Meiggs, *Roman Ostia* (Oxford, 1960).

G. Morin, 'Les monastères bénédictines de Rome au moyen âge (suite et fin)', *Revue Bénédictine* 4 (1887), 351-6.

W. Müller-Wiener, *Bildlexikon zur Topographie Istanbuls* (Tübingen, 1977).

A. Muthesius, 'A practical approach to the history of Byzantine Silk weaving, *J.Ö.B.* 34 (1984), 235-254.

J. L. Nelson, 'Not bishops' bailiffs but lords of the earth', in D. Wood ed., *The Church and Sovereignty. Essays in Honour of Michael Wilks* (Oxford, 1991).

J. L. Nelson, *Charles the Bald* (London, 1992).

D. M. Nicol, 'The Byzantine view of Western Europe,' *Greek, Roman and Byzantine Studies* 8 (1967), 315-339.

T. F. X. Noble, *The Republic of St Peter: the birth of the papal state 680-825*, (Philadelphia, 1984).

T. F. X. Noble, 'A new look at the Liber Pontificalis', *Archivum Historiae Pontificiae* 23 (1985), 347-358.

F. A. Norwood, 'The Political Pretensions of Pope Nicholas I', *Church History* 15 (1946), 271-85.

W. Oakeshott, *The Mosaics of Rome* (London, 1967).

D. Obolensky, 'The Empire and its Northern Neighbours', *Cambridge Medieval History* volume IV (1966), 473-518.

C. Odegaard, 'The Empress Engelberge', *Speculum* 26 (1951), 77-103.

R. M. Ogilvie, *A Commentary on Livy Books 1-5* (Oxford, 1965).

N. Oikonomides, 'Silk Trade and Production in Byzantium from the sixth to the ninth century: the seals of Kommerkiaroi', *Dumbarton Oaks Papers* 40 (1986), 33-53.

N. Oikonomides, *Les listes de préséance byzantine des IXᵉ et Xᵉ siècles* (Paris, 1972).

G. Ostrogorsky, *History of the Byzantine State* (New Brunswick, NJ, 1969).

M. Pagano and J. Rougetet, 'Il Battistero della basilica costantiniana di Capua (cosidetto *Catabulum)*, *Mélanges de l'école française de Rome* 96 (1984), 987-1016.

P. Partner, *The Lands of St Peter, the papal state in the middle ages and the early Renaissance* (London, 1972).

E. Perels, *Papst Nikolaus I und Anastasius Bibliothecarius. Ein Beitrag zur Geschichte des Papsttums im IX. Jahrhundert* (Berlin, 1920).

A. Petrucci, 'Arsenio', *Dizionario Biografico degli Italiani* 4 (1962), 339.

A. M. Piazzoni, 'Biografie dei papi del secolo X nelle continuazioni del Liber Pontificalis', *Mittellateinische Jahrbuch* 24-25 (1989-1990), 369-382.

S. B. Platner and T. Ashby, *A Topographical Dictionary of Ancient Rome* (Oxford, 1929).

M. Reinhold, *History of Purple as a status symbol in antiquity* (Brussels, 1970).

G. Rohault de Fleury, *Le Latran au moyen âge* (Paris, 1877).

G. McN. Rushforth, 'S. Maria Antiqua', *Papers of the British School at Rome* I (1902), 1-123.

J. Ruysschaert, 'L'oratoire romain de Formose (fin du IXᵉ siècle), son site et son plan d'après les relations Ciampini et Schelstrate de 1689', *Memoriam sanctorum venerantes, Miscellanea in onore di Monsignor Victor Saxer*, Studi di antichità cristiana 48 (Vatican, 1992), 725-734.

St Scholastica's Abbey (tourist guide, ed. Lozzi, Rome, 1971).

L. Schiaparelli, 'Le carte antiche dell'Archivo capitulare di S. Pietro', *ASR* 24 (1901).

R. Schieffer, 'Arsenius', *Lexikon des Mittelalters* 1 (1980), 1054-5.

W. Schlesinger, 'Die Auflösung des Karlsreiches', in H. Beumann ed., *Karl der Grosse, Lebenswerk und Nachleben*, volume 1 (Düsseldorf, 1965), 792-857.

A. Silvagni, 'La basilica di S. Martino ai monti', *ASR* 35 (1913), 329-88.

P. Stafford, 'Charles, the Bald, Judith and England', in M.T. Gibson and J.L. Nelson edd., *Charles the Bald, Court and Kingdom* (Aldershot, 1990), 139-153.

P. Stafford, *Queens, Concubines and Dowagers* (Atlanta and London, 1983).

N. Staubach, *Das Herrscherbild Karls des Kahlen. Formen und Funktionen monarchischer Repräsentation im früheren Mittelalter* (Münster, 1982).

P. Styger, *Römische Märtyrergrüfte*, 2 volumes (Berlin, 1935).

R. E. Sullivan, 'The papacy and missionary activity in the early middle ages', *Medieval Studies* 17 (1955), 46-106.

R. E. Sullivan, 'Paschal I', *New Catholic Encyclopedia* 11 (New York, 1967), 1048-9.

R. E. Sullivan, 'Leo IV', *New Catholic Encyclopedia* 8 (New York, 1967), 640-1.

G. Tomassetti, 'Campana Romana', in *Archivio romano di storia patria* 19 (1896), 111.

P. Toubert, *Les structures du Latium médiévale*, 2 volumes (Paris, 1973).

J. M. C. Toynbee and J. Ward Perkins, *The Shrine of St Peter and the Vatican Excavations* (London and New York, 1956).

W. Ullmann, *The Growth of Papal Government in the Middle Ages* (2nd ed., London 1962).

W. Ullmann, *A short history of the papacy in the middle ages* (London, 1972).

J.-J. Vernier, *Chartes de l'abbaye de Jumièges (825-1024) conservées aux archives de la Seine inférieure*, 2 volumes (Rouen, Société de l'histoire de Normandie, 1916).

R. Vielliard, *Les origines du titre de Saint-Martin-aux-Monts à Rome* (Studi di antichità cristiana 4, Vatican, 1931).

A. P. Vlasto, *The entry of the Slavs into Christendom* (Cambridge, 1970).

W. F. Volbach, *Early Decorative Textiles* (London, 1969).

J. M. Watterich, *Pontificum romanorum qui fuerunt inde ab exeunte saeculo IX usque ad finem saeculi XIII ab aequalibus conscriptae*, 2 volumes (Leipzig, 1862).

S. F. Wemple, *Women in Frankish Society* (Philadelphia, 1981).

K. F. Werner, 'Die Nachkommen Karls des Grossen', in W. Braunfels and P. E. Schramm edd., *Karl der Grosse, Lebenswerk und Nachleben*, volume IV (Düsseldorf, 1967), 403-79.

C. Wickham, *Early Medieval Italy* (London, 1981).

R. Wisskirchen, 'Zur Zenokapelle in S. Prassede', *Frühmittelalterliche Studien* 25 (1991), 96-108.

H. Zielinski, 'Ein unbeachter Italienzug Kaiser Lothars I im Jahre 847', *Quellen und Forschung aus italienischen Archiven und Bibliotheken* 70 (1990), 1-22.

H. Zielinski, 'Reisengeschwindigkeit und Nachrichtenübermittlung als Problem der Regestenarbeit am Beispiel eines undatieren Kapitulars Lothars I. von 847 Frühjahr (846 Herbst?)' in P.-J. Heinig ed., *Diplomatische und chronologische Studien aus der Arbeit an den Regesta Imperii* (Cologne, 1991), 37-49.

H. Zimmermann, 'Imperatores Italiae,' in H. Beumann ed., *Historische Forschungen für Walter Schlesinger* (Cologne, 1974), 379-399.

A. Zucchi, *Roma Domenicana, note storiche* (Florence, 1938).

INDEX
(see also the Glossary, especially under 'images')

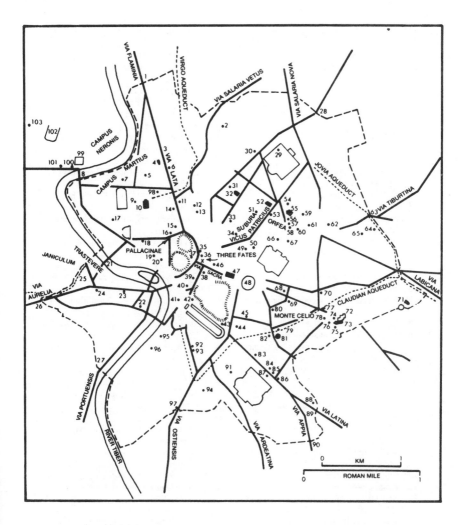

1	Flaminian Gate
2	St Felix in pincis basilica
3	Three Sickles arch
4	St Laurence's titulus in Lucina
5	St Gregory's oratory in Campus Martius
6	St Silvester's (pope Paul's) monastery
7	St Apollinaris' basilica/church (inside Rome)
8	St Peter's Gate
9	St Eustace's deaconry (xenodochium in Platana)
10	St Mary's church ad martyres
11	St Marcellus' titulus
12	Apostles' basilica
13	St Andrew's monastery by Apostles' basilica
14	St Mary's deaconry on Via Lata
15	St Mark's titulus
16	St Laurence's monastery in Pallacinis
17	St Laurence's titulus in Damaso
18	St Mary's (Julia's) monastery

19 St Mary's (Ambrose's) monastery
20 Archangel's deaconry with St Abbacyrus' altar
21 Antoninus, bridge of
22 St Caecilia's titulus
23 St Chrysogonus' titulus and monastery
24 St Mary's (Callistus') titulus in Trastevere
25 Sabbatina Aqueduct
26 St Pancras' Gate
27 Portuensis Gate
28 Nomentan Gate
29 St Cyriac's titulus
30 St Susanna's titulus
31 St Agatha's deaconry
32 St Vitalis' titulus
33 St Agatha's monastery/basilica over Subura
34 SS Sergius and Bacchus' oratory in Callinicum
35 St Martina's altar/basilica
36 St Hadrian's deaconry
37 SS Sergius and Bacchus' deaconry inside Rome
38 St Mary's deaconry Antiqua
39 St Theodore's deaconry
40 St George's deaconry at the Velabrum
41 St Mary's deaconry in Cosmedin
42 St Anastasia's titulus
43 St Lucy's deaconry in Septem Vias
44 St Andrew's monastery in Clivus Scauri
45 SS John and Paul's (Pammachius') titulus
46 SS Cosmas and Damian's deaconry on Via Sacra
47 Temple of Rome
48 Colosseum
49 St Agapitus' monastery ad vincula
50 St Peter's ad vincula (Apostles', Eudoxia's) titulus
51 St Laurence ad Formonsum church
52 St Pudentiana's (Pudens) titulus
53 St Euphemia's (and Archangel's) basilica/monastery
54 SS Cosmas and Damian's monastery by praesepe
55 St Mary's basilica ad praesepe
56 St Hadrian's (and St Laurence's) monastery
57 Dua Furna monastery with 'St Agnes' oratory
58 St Praxedes' titulus
59 St Andrew's church by the praesepe
60 St Andrew's monastery Massa Juliana (cata Barbara patricia)
61 St Vitus' deaconry
62 St Eusebius' basilica
63 St Laurence's Gate
64 St Isidore's monastery
65 St Bibiana's monastery
66 St Lucy's deaconry in Orfea
67 St Silvester's (and/or St Martin's) titulus/deaconry
68 St Clement's titulus
69 SS Quattuor Coronati (Aemiliana's) titulus
70 SS Marcellinus and Peter's by the Lateran
71 Jerusalem basilica at the Sessorian
72 Lateran patriarchate
73 Saviour's/Constantinian basilica
74 St Stephen's monastery by Lateran
75 St Pancras' monastery by Lateran
76 Constantinian baptistery
77 St Sergius' monastery
78 SS Andrew and Bartholomew's (pope Honorius') monastery
79 St Erasmus' monastery in Monte Celio
80 St Agatha's monastery in Caput Africae
81 St Stephen's basilica on Monte Celio
82 St Mary's deaconry Dominica
83 Tempulus' monastery with St Agatha's oratory
84 St Xystus' titulus
85 Monastery de Corsas with St Caesarius' oratory
86 St Symmetrius' monastery
87 SS Nereus and Achilleus' deaconry
88 St John's church at the Latin Gate
89 Latin Gate
90 Appian Gate
91 St Balbina's titulus
92 St Donatus' monastery
93 St Prisca's titulus
94 St Saba's (Cella Nova) monastery
95 St Sabina's titulus
96 St Boniface's deaconry
97 St Paul's Gate
98 St Mary's deaconry in Aquiro
99 Hadrianium
100 St Mary's deaconry at Hadrianium
101 St Mary's Deaconry outside St Peter's Gate
102 Naumachia
103 St Peregrinus' in Lord's Hospital